The Barbara Johnson Reader

A John Hope Franklin Center Book

The Barbara Johnson Reader
The Surprise of Otherness

Barbara Johnson

EDITED BY

MELISSA FEUERSTEIN

BILL JOHNSON GONZÁLEZ

LILI PORTEN

KEJA VALENS

With an Introduction by
JUDITH BUTLER
and an Afterword by
SHOSHANA FELMAN

Duke University Press
Durham and London
2014

© 2014 Duke University Press
Afterword © 2014 Shoshana Felman
All rights reserved
Printed in the United States of America on acid-free paper ∞
Designed by April Leidig
Typeset in Minion Pro by Westchester Publishing Services

Library of Congress Cataloging-in-Publication Data

The Barbara Johnson reader : the surprise of otherness / edited by Melissa Feuerstein,
Bill Johnson Gonzalez, Lili Porten, and Keja Valens, with an introduction by Judith
Butler and an afterword by Shoshana Felman.
pages   cm
"A John Hope Franklin Center Book."
Includes bibliographical references and index.
ISBN 978-0-8223-5419-2 (pbk : alk. paper)
ISBN 978-0-8223-5403-1 (cloth : alk. paper)
1. Johnson, Barbara, 1947–2009.   2. Feminist literary criticism.   I. Feuerstein,
Melissa.   II. Johnson Gonzalez, Bill, 1970–   III. Porten, Lili.   IV. Valens, Keja,
1972–
PN98.w64B37 2014
801.'95092—dc23
                                                            2013045003

Contents

Acknowledgments

"BARBARA JOHNSON"
BY BARBARA JOHNSON
"Barbara Johnson Biography," from
*Norton Anthology of Theory and
Criticism*, edited by Vincent B.
Leitch et al. Copyright © 2010, 2001
by W. W. Norton & Company, Inc.
Used by permission of W. W. Norton
& Company, Inc.

CHAPTER 1
"The Critical Difference." *Diacritics*
8, no. 2 (1978): 2–9. Reprinted with
permission of The Johns Hopkins
University Press.

CHAPTER 2
From Jacques Derrida,
Dissemination. Barbara Johnson,
trans. (1981), vii–xvii. Excerpts
from "Translator's Introduction"
are reprinted by permission of
the publisher © The University of
Chicago 1981.

CHAPTER 3
"Poetry and Syntax: What
the Gypsy Knew." From *The
Critical Difference: Essays in the
Contemporary Rhetoric of Reading*,
67–75. © 1980 The Johns Hopkins
University Press. Reprinted with
permission of The Johns Hopkins
University Press.

CHAPTER 4
"A Hound, a Bay Horse, and a Turtle
Dove: Obscurity in *Walden*." From
A World of Difference, 49–56. ©
1987 The Johns Hopkins University
Press. Reprinted with permission
of The Johns Hopkins University
Press.

CHAPTER 5
"Strange Fits: Poe and Wordsworth
on the Nature of Poetic Language."
From *A World of Difference*,
89–99. © 1987 The Johns Hopkins
University Press. Reprinted with

permission of The Johns Hopkins
University Press.

CHAPTER 6
"The Frame of Reference: Poe,
Lacan, Derrida." *Yale French Studies*
55/56 (1978): 457–505. Reprinted by
permission of *Yale French Studies*.

CHAPTER 7
"Euphemism, Understatement, and
the Passive Voice: A Genealogy
of Afro-American Poetry." From
Reading Black, Reading Feminist,
Henry Louis Gates Jr., ed. © 1990
by Henry Louis Gates Jr. Used
by permission of Dutton Signet,
a division of Penguin Group
(USA) Inc.

CHAPTER 8
"Metaphor, Metonymy, and Voice
in *Their Eyes Were Watching God*."
From *Black Literature and Literary
Theory*, Henry Louis Gates Jr.,
ed. (New York: Routledge, 1984).
Reproduced with permission of
Taylor & Francis Group LLC.
Permissions conveyed through
Copyright Clearance Center.

CHAPTER 9
"Moses and Intertexuality: Sigmund
Freud, Zora Neale Hurston, and the
Bible." From *Poetics of the Americas:
Race, Founding, and Textuality*,
Bainard Cowan and Jefferson
Humphries, eds. © 1997 Louisiana
State University Press. Reprinted
by permission.

CHAPTER 10
"Lesbian Spectacles: Reading *Sula*,
Passing, Thelma and Louise, and *The
Accused*." From *Media Spectacles*,
Marjorie Garber, Jann Matlock,
and Rebecca Walkowitz, eds. (New
York: Routledge, 1993). Reproduced
with permission of Taylor & Francis
Group LLC. Permissions conveyed
through Copyright Clearance
Center.

CHAPTER 11
"Bringing Out D. A. Miller."
Narrative 10, no. 1 (January 2002):
3–8. © 2002 The Ohio State
University Press. Reproduced with
permission.

CHAPTER 12
"Correctional Facilities," reprinted
by permission of the publisher from
Barbara Johnson, *Mother Tongues:
Sexuality, Trials, Motherhood*,
1–25 (Cambridge, MA: Harvard
University Press), © 2003 by the
President and Fellows of Harvard
College.

CHAPTER 13
"My Monster/My Self." *Diacritics*
12, no. 2 (1982): 2–10. © 1982
The Johns Hopkins University
Press. Reprinted with permission
of The Johns Hopkins University
Press.

CHAPTER 14
Introduction to *Freedom and
Interpretation: Oxford Amnesty*

Lectures of 1992 (abridged). Copyright © 1993 Barbara Johnson. Reprinted by permission of Basic Books Press, a member of the Perseus Books Group.

CHAPTER 15
"Muteness Envy." From *Human, All Too Human*, Diana Fuss, ed. (New York: Routledge, 1995). Reproduced with permission of Taylor & Francis Group LLC. Permissions conveyed through Copyright Clearance Center.

CHAPTER 16
"Apostrophe, Animation, and Abortion." *Diacritics* 16, no. 1 (1986): 29–39. © 1986 The Johns Hopkins University Press. Reprinted with permission of The Johns Hopkins University Press.

CHAPTER 17
"Anthropomorphism in Lyric and Law." Reprinted by permission of the *Yale Journal of Law & the Humanities* 10, no. 2 (1998): 549–74.

CHAPTER 18
"Using People: Kant with Winnicott." From *The Turn to Ethics*, Marjorie Garber, Beatrice Hanssen, and Rebecca Walkowitz, eds. (New York: Routledge, 2000). Reproduced with permission of Taylor & Francis Group LLC. Permissions conveyed through Copyright Clearance Center.

CHAPTER 19
"Ego Sum Game," reprinted by permission of the publisher from Barbara Johnson, *Persons and Things*, 47–60 (Cambridge, MA: Harvard University Press). © 2003 by the President and Fellows of Harvard College.

CHAPTER 20
"Melville's Fist: The Execution of *Billy Budd*." *Studies in Romanticism* 18, no. 4 (1979): 567–99. Reprinted with permission.

CHAPTER 21
"Nothing Fails Like Success." *SCE Reports* 8 (fall 1980). Reprinted with permission of the University of Houston-Victoria.

CHAPTER 22
"Bad Writing." From Jonathan Culler and Kevin Lamb, *Just Being Difficult? Academic Writing in the Public Arena*. © 2003 by the Board of Trustees of the Leland Stanford Jr. University. All rights reserved. Used with permission of Stanford University Press, www.sup.org.

CHAPTER 23
"Teaching Destructively." From *Writing and Reading Differently: Deconstruction and the Teaching of Composition and Literature*, G. Douglas Atkins and Michael L. Johnson, eds. (1985), 140–48. Reprinted with permission of the University Press of Kansas.

CHAPTER 24
"Poison or Remedy? Paul de Man as Pharmakon." *Colloquium Helveticum* 11/12 (1990): 7–20.

CHAPTER 25
Reprinted from "Taking Fidelity Philosophically," from *Difference in Translation*, Joseph F. Graham, ed. © 1985 by Cornell University. Used by permission of the publisher, Cornell University Press.

CHAPTER 26
"The Task of the Translator," reprinted by permission of the publisher from Barbara Johnson, *Mother Tongues: Sexuality, Trials, Motherhood*, 40–64 (Cambridge, MA: Harvard University Press), © 2003 by the President and Fellows of Harvard College.

CHAPTER 27
"Teaching Ignorance." *Yale French Studies* 63 (1982): 165–82. Reprinted by permission of *Yale French Studies*.

AFTERWORD
Copyright © 2014 Shoshana Felman.

Editors' Preface

Melissa Feuerstein, Bill Johnson González,
Lili Porten, and Keja Valens

> The surprise of otherness is that moment when a new form
> of ignorance is suddenly activated as an imperative.
> —Barbara Johnson, "Nothing Fails Like Success"

To encounter and propagate "the surprise of otherness"—the otherness of another gender, race, culture, or language, the irreducible otherness of another person, the contradictions within the self—this is the "impossible but necessary task" and guiding imperative of the work of Barbara Johnson, one of the most original and influential literary critics of her generation.[1] Why seek the surprise of otherness? Because such an encounter, Johnson explains, can alert us to an ignorance we never knew we had. And ignorance is an abiding preoccupation of Johnson's work. We should reevaluate our purely negative view of ignorance as a simple gap that additional knowledge can fill, she proposes, and recognize the transformative power of truly experiencing our doubt, which can change the nature of what we thought we knew. In studies that intrepidly cross cultural traditions, historical periods, and academic disciplines, Johnson investigates the role of what we do not know—the "power of ignorance, blindness, uncertainty, or misreading"—in shaping meanings and lives.[2] In particular, "through the careful teasing out of warring forces of signification," Johnson's work explores the consequences of uncertainties that attend language.[3]

Johnson began her career during a period in which otherness was emerging as a key issue for intellectual scrutiny in American literary studies. In particular, critical approaches associated with the Yale School and poststructuralist theory were foregrounding the traces of otherness (other voices, other meanings, other intentions) traversing and subverting apparently unified identities and texts. At the same time, somewhat differently framed questions of otherness, exclusion, and authority were being raised in emergent fields such as feminist criticism, African American studies, postcolonial studies, and queer theory, which focused on historically marginalized authors and on literary representations of African Americans, women, homosexuals, and others. Johnson played a crucial role in articulating the continuity between and mutual importance of what initially seemed incongruous approaches to otherness: the rhetorical analysis of linguistic otherness, or repressed "difference within," and the political analysis of oppressed otherness in the world, or social "differences between."

Johnson's earliest essays provided exemplary models of deconstructive reading strategies, quickly establishing her as one of the preeminent exponents of poststructuralist literary analysis. Before long, however, she came to critique the insularity of early poststructuralist work, including her own, because of its preoccupation with the study of otherness *within* the white male literary canon. Responding to issues raised by feminist criticism and African American studies, she undertook to extend deconstructive analysis to texts by historically marginalized authors and to challenge the boundaries of the traditional literary canon, with "its sexual and racial exclusions and effacements."[4] Over the course of her career, she critiqued and amplified the scope of not only deconstructive analysis, feminist criticism, and African American studies but also translation studies, psychoanalytic criticism, cultural studies, law and literature studies, and ethics. In these cross-disciplinary interventions, Johnson remained committed to opening up these fields not only to new insights but also to new voices and new perspectives, committed to attending to the ethical stakes in literature, investigating the complexities of language, and pursuing the impossible task of accounting for the role of language in human experience.

Although the tremendous range of topics and disciplines across which her incisive contributions reach is striking, no less significant, perhaps, are the many instances in which Johnson revisits authors (Baudelaire, Mallarmé, Barthes) and issues (translation, motherhood, apostrophe) to find in them anew "the surprise of otherness." Indeed, the combination of transit and return, breadth of vision and depth of focus, that describes the trajectory of

Johnson's career also characterizes her individual essays. Following the intersecting paths of texts and exploring questions both expansive and tightly focused, her essays can read like detours that turn out to be shortcuts from and to the heart of a literary text or issue, offering readers the very surprise of otherness that she investigates. In some essays, this surprise emerges through improbably illuminating juxtapositions of texts, as in "Bad Writing," which brings together Anne Sexton and Charles Baudelaire, a 1995 report on *Comparative Literature in the Age of Multiculturalism* and the film *Clueless* (1995), W. E. B. Du Bois and *Life's Little Deconstruction Book*. In other essays the surprise is enacted through Johnson's playful yet resonant wordplay, as in "The Frame of Reference," with its multilingual punning *"pli* ['fold'] for understanding." In almost every essay, the encounter with otherness is precipitated by close readings of particular portions of text and by keen attention to the uncanny whims and wisdom of language.

Johnson's attention to language is a key feature not only of her close readings but also of her writing. Although her own prose is known for its incomparable clarity—especially striking as she participates in a theoretical practice famous for its opacity—it performs the same destabilization of "binary notions of 'clarity'" and "obscurity" she discovers in literary texts.[5] Thus she frequently begins her essays with accessible questions that draw readers in but also set them up to be surprised (as in "Apostrophe, Animation, and Abortion" and "Ego Sum Game"), yet she just as frequently ends her essays with rhetorical sleights of hand (such as the closing chiasmus of "Gender and Poetry" and the recasting of Keats's chiastic "Beauty is truth, truth beauty" as "the truth behind the beauty" in "Muteness Envy") that manage at once to clarify and confound, and thereby to bring together experiences of understanding and ignorance.

THE BARBARA JOHNSON READER brings together Johnson's most important contributions to literary and cultural studies, including essays from all phases of her career selected to represent the range of her investigations and the development of her thought. The selections are grouped into four parts. The first, "Reading Theory as Literature, Literature as Theory," includes some of the seminal essays that very early in her career earned Johnson recognition as a pioneering and exemplary practitioner of deconstruction. These essays engage in readings that proceed by "identifying and dismantling differences," binary oppositions that structure and complicate texts by lending an illusion of unequivocal meaning that the text itself can be shown to subvert.[6] The essays in Part II, "Race, Sexuality, Gender," represent Johnson's engagement with the challenge of multiculturalism and her effort to extend the practice of deconstruction by "transfer[ing] the analysis of difference . . . out of the realm of linguistic universality . . . and into contexts in which difference is very much at issue in the 'real world.'"[7] These essays illustrate her participation in the "canon wars," the project of critiquing the boundaries of the literary canon with its "sexual and racial exclusions and effacements."[8] They also exemplify her role in articulating the conditions and challenges of emergent theoretical approaches involving identity politics and the construction of gender, race, and sexuality.

Whereas the first two parts roughly correspond to the early and middle phases of Johnson's career, the last two bring together essays from throughout her career that represent her enduring concern with fundamental questions concerning language, teaching, and ethics. Part III, "Language, Personhood, Ethics," includes essays that explore connections between language and personhood and relations between figurative and literal violence, showing how the analysis of nonreferential aspects of language may illuminate ethical problems yet at the same time pose challenges to commonsense assumptions about human rights and human relations. The essays in Part IV, "Pedagogy and Translation," reflect on dilemmas of pedagogy and the lessons of translation. Revealing overlaps between the tasks of teaching and translation, these essays illuminate Johnson's characterization of herself as "a translator in various senses of the word" and show that, for her, teaching and translation are about cultivating rather than resolving encounters with complexity, unfamiliarity, and otherness.

Having had the good fortune to be mentored by Johnson as graduate students at Harvard, the editors of this volume can attest that her investment in teaching was not only theoretical but also practical. In the classroom, her generally understated lectures could take unexpected performative turns that variously discomfited, disrupted, and delighted the audience whose intellectual enterprise she "surprised." On one memorable occasion, she concluded a discussion of Carolyn Forché's poem "The Colonel," whose eponymous character empties a sack of severed ears that the speaker compares to dried peach halves, by silently overturning a jar of dried fruit and slowly eating a piece. What was the meaning of this performance? Was Johnson simply trying to defuse the classroom tension, which was focused on the grotesque and violent image of severed human ears, by reminding us that, after all, dried fruit is sometimes just delicious dried fruit? Was she pointing to a distinction, or a coexistence, of the figurative and the literal? Or might she, by reenacting the colonel's gesture in the poem, also have been calling attention to the unwanted and troubling sense of complicity that we share with the speaker of the poem, and thus pointing out the poem's traumatic structure, which incites us to relive and reenact the experience it relates, without being able to walk away from it with a sense of comfort? Her enigmatic teaching moments forced her students to think about teaching as performance—a performance that raised questions that did not always resolve themselves into clear answers.

Although Johnson sometimes taught by inciting discomfort to provoke thought, she also had a knack for inspiring students to learn by experimenting. Indeed, perhaps the best characterization of her pedagogy comes from her evocation, at the end of her essay "Using People," of "a space of play and risk that does not depend on maintaining intactness and separation." This space of play and risk also aptly describes the learning environment that she created for students through her prodigious intellectual generosity.

Like literature, teaching, for Johnson, raised fundamental questions of self and other, with those terms representing both "differences *between*" and "differences *within*" people.[9] Thus, she remarked in an email, "Teaching is teaching people to think as themselves. Which means the teacher has to try to think as herself. Really hard, but also what else is as valuable?"[10] As demonstrated in the essays collected here, one of the ways that Johnson teaches us to think as ourselves is by showing us how she herself thinks. Indeed, making her thought process palpable and accessible as she asks and thinks her way through questions to which she has no easy answers is one way that she, in these essays, exemplifies what it means to think as oneself. Johnson's work is so pedagogically useful in part because it offers a mode of inquiry that inspires imitation yet defies it, for it demands of its readers that we think for and as ourselves, and at the same time—another turn of the screw—asks us continuously to embrace the impossible task of seeking out the surprise of otherness within ourselves.

NOTES

1. Barbara Johnson, "Nothing Fails Like Success," in *A World of Difference* (Baltimore: Johns Hopkins University Press, 1987), 15–16.
2. Barbara Johnson, "Opening Remarks," in *The Critical Difference* (Baltimore: Johns Hopkins University Press, 1987), xii.
3. Barbara Johnson, "Translator's Introduction," in Jacques Derrida, *Dissemination*, trans. Barbara Johnson (Chicago: University of Chicago Press, 1981), xv.

4. Barbara Johnson, "Introduction," in *A World of Difference* (Baltimore: Johns Hopkins University Press, 1987), 4.
5. Johnson, "Nothing Fails like Success," 13.
6. Johnson, "Opening Remarks," x.
7. Johnson, "Introduction," 2.
8. Johnson, "Introduction," 4.
9. Johnson, "Opening Remarks," 10.
10. Barbara Johnson, personal communication, August 31, 2002.

Personhood and Other Objects
The Figural Dispute with Philosophy

Judith Butler

Barbara Johnson's singular contribution to literary theory can hardly be summarized by a quick set of formulations. One writes sentences like the previous one because one has to begin somewhere, and one knows in advance that any "account" will be partial and, in that sense, fail. This volume has a complex task because, on the one hand, we are treating "Barbara Johnson" as the author and, on the other hand, Barbara Johnson as a teacher. So how, then, do we formulate our guiding questions? Are we asking who she was, who she was to us, to others (questions that could involve engaging in a contextualization of her formation and ours, the way she taught us, and perhaps the way she teaches us still)? Or are we asking some questions about the texts she wrote that brought her an unparalleled form of recognition as a literary critic and theorist? If we are asking about the texts, then it would seem we are putting the person aside. Yet oddly and felicitously, we find that Barbara Johnson's texts, including many that appear in this volume, are centrally concerned with the theoretical question of what a person is. Thus, as we try to find our way between the person of the author and the texts by the author, Johnson herself proves to be something of a useful guide. The questions she posed are ones that we struggle with today as we try to think about how to understand her pedagogy and her writing. In Johnson's various readings of Winnicott, Kohut, Lacan, de Man, Plath, and Baudelaire, and again in her engagement with legal cases, she made a strong set of claims: persons are not thinkable without objects; personification and anthropomorphism are discursive figures that enter the way we think persons and objects; the self is less an origin of action than a content of thought, always to some extent imaginary; another self only becomes real on the occasion that it survives its destruction.

It would appear that the question, what is a person?, is a quintessentially philosophical query. It is true that Johnson trafficked with philosophical texts and their modes of argumentation and interrogation. Yet as we follow her arguments, we see how a literary theorist can and must engage a philosophical question in a distinctive way. In the first place, she pursues the question through a reading of a particular text, and that text may be literary, legal, philosophical, or drawn from popular discourse. In the second place, or perhaps simultaneously, she tracks how the question itself is formulated in the terms of the text, not only how certain figures are presupposed but how the figures presuppose certain philosophical claims. What makes this work "theory" would be difficult to summarize, but it seems possible to say minimally that philosophical questions are pursued precisely in light of the terms in which they are formulated. The philosophical proposition never quite stands alone, because to declare a philosophical truth is still to deploy the declarative mode of speech and so, already, to engage the history and techniques of rhetoric and, more specifically, modes of address. To whom is the philosopher speaking when he or she makes such a claim? Is there not implicitly a problem of audience and address even in the simplest of propositional claims? What shadow of the other haunts every true proposition? To what legacy of figures do its referents belong?

Although Johnson asks about the status of the person and the object in a nearly philosophical mode, she does so to subject certain moral formulations of both to a serious challenge. This challenge takes place partly through mobilizing a reading of texts that show how the person and the object are not thinkable outside of the moments in which their separate status is questioned. Primary among the philosophical positions she challenges is the Kantian precept that humans should only be treated as ends, never as means.[1] This maxim implies that no human should instrumentalize or "use" another human for his or her own ends and that in general, humans ought never to be treated as instruments, understood as objects. The result of such instrumentalization is dehumanization. Kant's moral precept then depends on a stable human/object distinction; indeed, our moral charge is precisely to maintain the distinction such that humans only use instruments but are themselves never instrumentalized. But what if humanization—that is, the process of becoming human—requires personified objects and the instrumentalization of humans?

In "Using People" (chapter 18) Johnson turns to the child psychology of D. W. Winnicott to interrogate those dimensions of a self's emergence that require the animation of objects with human qualities (the transitional object) and must "use" humans as objects to test the limits of the child's own destructive powers. In the first instance, objects take on human qualities precisely because they mediate the uncertain space between child and mother. Johnson writes, "Transitional objects . . . are the first 'not-me' possessions, objects that are neither 'internal' to the baby (that is, hallucinatory, like, at first, the mother's breast) nor 'external,' like reality, of which at first the baby has no knowledge, but something in between." Prior to any question of what we, as humans, ought to do is the question of how, if at all, we got to be humans to begin with. Thus Johnson's turn to psychoanalytic theory is an effort to establish how humans are formed, and it turns out that no human can be formed, no human can become individuated, without establishing a space that is neither inside nor outside. The object famously mediates the absence of the mother for the child, and it becomes both precious (like the mother's presence) and the target of heightened aggression (against the mother for going away). Strictly speaking, at this developmental level, there is no clear distinction between object and child, and no clear distinction between object and mother; it is the scene in which the child entertains the fantasy of the mother's full accessibility and adaptability to the child's needs only to come up against the reality of the mother's imperfection. Johnson writes, "The most valuable property of the transitional object is probably its lack of perfection, its in relevance to the question of perfection." Through aggressive fantasy and play, the child mutilates its object, seeking to assert its omnipotence over those human-objects that have a way of always going away. How precisely this destructive action is handled has significant implications for the formation of the child into an adult. First, the child's destructiveness has to be encountered and "met" for the fantasy of omnipotence to come up against the effect of reality. Indeed, the object must somehow survive this mutilation, but so, too, must the mother or parent who is not fully distinguishable from that object. In Johnson's words, "the object becomes real because it survives, because it is outside the subject's area of omnipotent control." This is one reason that parents and analysts alike must not only make themselves available for mutilation but survive it. The human figure, then, is differentiated from the transitional object only on the condition that the human figure survives the mutilation that the object does not. For the child to emerge without the psychic conviction that he or she is a murderer, the adult, understood ambiguously as human and object, must submit to its instrumentalization and survive. If philosophers are, as Winnicott presumes, those who must have distinctions to continue to do what they do, they will, as Johnson points out, have trouble with this "intermediate" zone in which objects and humans cannot be rigorously distinguished. Winnicott imagines that the philosopher must leave his armchair and sit on the floor with the child, losing his upright posture to understand this zone of psychic meaning that eludes philosophical concepts. Johnson follows suit: "Something about that intermediate position is enacted by this passage from metaphor to literality. The intermediate position is not in space but in what it is possible to say." The intermediate position is prior to the world of established persons and objects, and we cannot understand how they are established without this zone—an understanding that shows how metaphors themselves become literalized. If they do not, the child suffers from an endless sense of destructive power and fails to encounter the reality of others. The other becomes real on the occasion of survival, a "check" that alone can check the fantasmatic life of the child with an encounter with reality.

In her reading of both Winnicott and Kohut[2] ("Ego Sum Game," chapter 19), Johnson suggests that nothing less than the locatability of the self is in question. In this essay that considers the implications of the myth of Narcissus for a rereading of Descartes, Johnson makes clear again that whatever is called "the self" is not a given of experience or the presumed source of all agency but is a "content of the mental apparatus," in Kohut's terms. So ideation is already in operation as the idea of the self is developed. Narcissus provides the allegory here because he seems to know that the reflection of himself in the water is a delusion, but he is not seeking the truth. Descartes will want to know how, if at all, one might distinguish the certain sense of the self from a delusional appearance, but Narcissus only "regrets . . . not being able to merge with what he already is." Is there a substantial self and a shadow self? These are the questions with which the philosopher begins, but in this essay Johnson points out that the only way for a self to know itself is precisely by becoming an object, and thus not as a subject. In other words, like Narcissus, every subject encounters a noncoincidence among what he or she takes him- or herself to be, what can be seen or known, and some other operation that troubles the sphere of appearance or seems to challenge its sufficiency. Descartes's worries are recast by Lacan, for whom it is a question of "whether I am the same as that of which I speak," or whether a certain self-division persists as long as "I" do. The self is cast outside itself, as content, image, or form (Gestalt), and this establishes the imaginary conditions under which the ego first assumes a shape. The "me" who I am is thus anticipated within the field of the imaginary, which means precisely that this self, or ego, is not the ground of my experience, but its future coordinate articulated in what Lacan called "a fictional direction." For Johnson, there is no escape from Narcissus, even though there are various checks on narcissism. She writes, "the subject must drink from the waters of reflection in order to tie together libidinal and aesthetic fascination—in order to desire an image." We might on the basis of her reading continue the argument this way: "and to desire at all, the subject must desire an image." The image is the condition and shadowy substance of that very self that Descartes seeks to separate definitively from the self. Thus those figures and shadows against which Descartes seeks to ground his own certainty of himself as man and as a philosopher turn out to be preconditions for any self at all. Through Johnson, Narcissus teaches Descartes a lesson or two.

If it is the Kantian moral precept that prohibits the instrumentalization of persons that is undone in "Using People," it is now the Cartesian presumption that the cogito is a sufficient starting point for philosophical reflection on the self that is introduced into crisis in "Ego Sum Game." Although we could follow this procedure in any number of essays, I think it is important to turn to "Apostrophe, Animation, and Abortion" (chapter 16) to make clear the legal and political salience of Johnson's reading practice. In this essay, she foregrounds the ethical stakes of her inquiry: "Is there any *inherent* connection between figurative language and questions of life and death, of who will wield and who will receive violence in a given human society?" Directly after this probing and open question, she turns to an analysis of the rhetorical figure of apostrophe (the act of addressing someone who is absent or dead or inanimate) and then to a masterful reading of the use of apostrophe in Baudelaire's "Morsta et Errabunda." Where we might expect apostrophe to install a human form at the site of its absence, it follows a countertrajectory in Baudelaire, undoing the human figure. Johnson accumulates examples, including this one: "Does your heart sometimes take flight"—an animation of the "heart" that takes the place of the human form, even rendering it dispensable. Johnson writes, "Instead of conferring a human shape, this question starts to undo one." Her point is not only to distinguish anthropomorphism (the conferral of human form on nonhuman things) and personification (the attribution of human qualities to human parts or nonhuman things) but to show how within some of Baudelaire's poems (especially "Moesta et Errabunda"), "the inanimate has entirely taken over . . . the poem is as if emptying itself of all its human characters and voices. It seems to be acting out a *loss* of animation." In Shelley's "Ode to the West Wind," it turns out the poet "gives animation, gives the capacity of responsiveness, to the wind," but that same wind circulates "dead thoughts" and, in Johnson's reading, is a "giver of death." The poem ends with a rhetorical question, according to Johnson: "does death necessarily entail rebirth?" The question stands in a condition of suspended animation, so we do not know whether the question animates or deanimates. Indeed, the question form seems to stall or still the distinction itself.

What precisely are we meant to track about these figures that animate and deanimate, making and undoing human forms? How are they related to the question of whether figurative language is inherently linked to questions of life and death? As Johnson reads poems and stories from various centuries and languages, she poses this question anew, and her reading begins to crystallize around the question of whether we can know whether someone has been lost. This question proves central to debates on abortion that focus on the question of whether a fetus is a person. Can such a question be definitively answered, or is the status of the fetus animated within some discourses and deanimated within others? Is there any way beyond or outside this unknowingness about whether the fetus should be considered a living person?

Johnson moves us toward this consideration slowly, and it is pedagogically important that we understand the various ways that apostrophe and animation can work (and fail to work), the distinction between personification and anthropomorphism, to be prepared to encounter this most important question. In the poem "The Mother" by Gwendolyn Brooks, apostrophe takes the form of an address to children lost before they were born and, of course, it is animated by a doubt over whether that was the loss of children at all. If conventional forms of apostrophe assume the distinctness between the I who utters the address and the you to whom the address is uttered, that distinction breaks down when the "you" turns out to be of one's own flesh and blood. It is not that the two figures effectively merge, but that "the you" is at once an externalized version of the "I" and an ambiguous part of the "I." The apostrophic utterance thus enacts the unknowingness about the animated status of the addressee; it animates and deanimates, and remains caught precisely in a state of suspended animation that recalls the end of Shelley's poem. But this time the question is not whether the poem can reanimate the life, or whether it already treats the life as unambiguously animated, but whether the life that is mourned, the "you," is finally separable from the "I" at all. In this way, the poem articulates precisely that state of suspended animation ("living person" or not?), indeed, of undecidability that governs debates on the life or personhood of the fetus. "What is the debate over abortion about," Johnson asks, "if not the question of when, precisely, a being assumes a human form?"

Johnson is clear that the poem cannot answer the question of whether abortion is legitimate or whether the embryo has the right to life. In fact, she argues very clearly that even if the right to abortion is justified through argumentative means, that does not take away a woman's "right to mourn." Indeed, there may well be a sense of loss for the woman who undergoes an abortion regardless of how we define the legal status of the embryo or fetus. But what proves most important for Johnson's reading of these poems is that they bring to the linguistic surface "the fundamental difficulty of defining personhood in general." One might say that it is well and good that poems can remind us of such a difficulty, but isn't the realm of law precisely where undecidability has to be set aside in favor of decisions and judgments? Johnson's rejoinder to this kind of question is to show that "undecidability" characterizes these debates within law and politics from the start. In fact, if there were no undecidability, there would be no open-ended debate, and no field of the political. In Johnson's words, "there is politics precisely because there is undecidability." She makes this abundantly clear in "Anthropomorphism in Lyric and Law" (chapter 17), where she makes her strongest arguments about how figural language becomes literalized as legal language. Those entities or persons who are effectively figured within the legal institution of "personhood" alone have the status to make certain claims and exercise certain rights. There is no legal act that legitimates the claims of persons, whether corporate or civic, that does not rely on personification to establish legal personhood. Thus, there is no way to eliminate personification from law just as there is no way to eliminate apostrophe from debates on life and death. Moreover, there is no single concept of the person that might serve as a criterion by which to distinguish true from false descriptions. If one wants to argue that a specific claim that someone is or should be a person should show that the "person" in question resembles the idea of persons or established versions of personhood, then it would seem that there is no way to identify persons without the problem of resemblance entering the picture. This is another way typology and distinction, legal and philosophical, cannot escape figural language.

In the abortion poems that Johnson considers, she is clear that figuration does not simply humanize. The direct address to the "you" who is the aborted fetus does not presume that the "you" is human. Apostrophe can animate or deanimate or be caught in the bind of doing both at once without resolution. It can presume the separability of the I and the you only to problematize that distinction in the course of its articulation. When apostrophe becomes maternal, new complications come into play. Is the mother who "speaks" or writes presumed to be in the position of giving life or, indeed, taking it away? Johnson ends her essay with the provocative suggestion that motherhood is itself induced through apostrophe, one that establishes the mother less as a person than as "a personification of presence or absence." One might be reminded of the problem of the fantasy of omnipotence attributed to the child by Winnicott. Here, it seems, the maternal itself is invested with the ultimate power over life and death, a personification that effectively takes the place of the person. When Johnson makes this suggestion, her referent is no longer Winnicott, but Lacan, though she subtly brings Winnicott back into the reading. The child demands presence or absence, and this is the meaning of the fort-da game: "go away" and "come back" as I wish! For Johnson, distancing herself from Lacan's claim that this happens at a level that has nothing to do with "real dependence," "there is precisely a link between demand and animation, between apostrophe and life-and-death dependency." In other words, the question of survival reemerges in the cry "mama!" The poems written about abortion find themselves in another predicament, the one in which that cry is precisely the one that is never heard; the one that does take form as lyric is precisely the apostrophe to the tissue that did not yet assume human form or perhaps to the dead child, a cry that cannot answer even that question and does not know precisely what has been lost.

For Johnson, lyric poetry is "summed up in the figure of apostrophe," which means that it engages the questions of what lives and what dies, what is animated and what is not. But instead of giving us fine and fast distinctions between life and death, it articulates another intermediate zone, one in which the sure distinction between the two cannot hold. Like Winnicott, who counseled that with the transitional object, it is not possible to pose the question, did it originate from the outside or from the inside? In fact, Johnson reminds us, he remarks that "the question is not to be formulated." Winnicott's counsel is not to prohibit questions but to underscore that that question brings with it a set of assumptions about the distinctions among child, object, and adult that will keep us from understanding the intermediate status of the object and the ambiguity of those relations. In the questions posed by lyric, there is similarly no one answer. The question instates itself as such, opening up the field of the undecidable without resolution.

This question seems nowhere more pertinent than in the question of mourning, a topic that Johnson pursues in relation to Paul de Man's reading of Baudelaire's "Obsession" in "Anthropomorphism in Lyric and Law." Who can be mourned and who cannot are clearly political questions as well and depend on how the "grievable life" is figured. De Man remarks that the most true mourning can do is "allow for non-comprehension." His comment leads Johnson to query further: "Is mourning—or, rather, 'true mourning'"—human or inhuman? Or is it what makes it impossible to close the gap between 'man' and rhetoric?" Do we personify mourning when we call it true, and is the process then extracted from the persons who mourn? If we do not have a sure way to define those persons, but are always engaged in modes of personification, apostrophe, and anthropomorphism when we seek to settle that question, then there is no question of the human that is not also a question of lyric. For Johnson, lyric insists on our unknowingness about what precisely in or of the human can be defined. If our definitions falter, we are left precisely with what cannot be presupposed. We are not precisely stopped or paralyzed there, but we do continue with an understanding, not a certainty, that unknowingness defines the human, which is to say, there is no sure definition. So even when we ask what we have lost (or who), we are left with a question, open-ended and suspended, that does not mitigate our mourning.

NOTES

1. Immanuel Kant, *The Moral Law: Kant's Groundwork of the Metaphysic of Morals*, trans. H. J. Paton (London: Hutchinson, 1948), 74–77.
2. Heinz Kohut, *The Analysis of the Self* (New York: International Universities Press, 1983), xv.

Barbara Johnson

Barbara Johnson | *b. 1947–d. 2009*

Barbara Johnson is known as a translator in various senses of the word. She is the celebrated translator of Jacques Derrida's *Dissemination* (1972; trans. 1981), and she is also one of the earliest and most interesting translators of structuralist and poststructuralist theory into literary insights. Often praised for her "lucidity" and "clarity," she has nevertheless emphasized, again and again, the unavoidability and necessity of linguistic complexity and difficulty in formulating intractable problems. For her, language cannot be extricated from what is problematic; language is not simply *about* problems, it *participates in* them.

Born in 1947 near Boston, she was the first of four children. Her father was a school principal and her mother a librarian. She attended Oberlin College (1965–69), majoring in French, and completed a Ph.D. in French at Yale University in 1977. Her studies at Yale took place at a complicated intersection of politics and criticism: while the effects of the 1969 student strike against the Vietnam War and the trial of Black Panther Bobby Seale in New Haven lingered, the "Yale School" of academic literary theory was developing, and, around 1968, there had exploded onto the scene "French Theory"—a shorthand designation for structuralism and poststructuralism in many fields. The "Yale School" was the label by which the academic and popular press referred to a group of male literary critics (Paul de Man, Harold Bloom, Geoffrey Hartman, J. Hillis Miller) who were all interested in Romanticism and who often incorporated structuralist and poststructuralist perspectives in their work. At the same time, the works of Derrida, Jacques Lacan, and other French theorists were gaining recognition, but because most had not yet been translated into English, French departments provided one of the first points of entry into the American academy for their revolutionary ideas. The challenge of translating between one context and another thus itself became part of the theoretical enterprise.

Johnson's work has been profoundly engaged with and by the work of a number of teachers and colleagues, both at Yale, where she taught French and comparative literature from 1977 to 1983, and at Harvard University, where she has taught French, comparative literature, and English since 1983: in particular, Paul de Man (her thesis director at Yale) and colleagues Shoshana Felman (at Yale), Henry Louis Gates Jr. (at both Yale and Harvard), and Marjorie Garber (at Harvard). Her first book, published in France in 1979, examined the prose poems of the nineteenth-century French writers Charles Baudelaire and Stéphane Mallarmé. Titled *Défigurations du langage poétique: la seconde révolution baudelairienne* (*Disfigurations of Poetic Language: The Second Baudelairean Revolution*), it analyzed the significance of Baudelaire's turn to prose after the publication of his one book of lyric verse, *Les Fleurs du mal* (*Flowers of Evil*). Johnson's second book, *The Critical Difference: Essays in the Contemporary Rhetoric of Reading* (1980), which ranged more widely over theory, quickly followed. The word *difference* in the title is meant to name two different conceptions of difference and the tension between them: binary difference in its traditional sense (prose and poetry, male and female, etc.), and Derridean *différance*, a nonidentity within each term that is concealed or repressed in the process of establishing opposition. Johnson named these "the difference between" and "the difference within," terms that have entered the critical lexicon.

The Critical Difference collected what might be called Johnson's first "allegories of theory": the essays focused on the process of finding in literary texts preoccupations that have become newly readable through new theoretical perspectives. Rather than viewing theory as something applied to the text, she contends that theoretical questions already inhabit the text. The theory can draw them out, and, perhaps, provide the means of analyzing the text's resistances to the very theory that illuminates it. Theory thus becomes a subset of literature: a process of formulating a knowledge the literary text is presumed to store. The key words of the theory are themselves *words*; they are therefore subject to the same play, seriousness, and instability that literary texts can give to all words. What constitutes "literature," however, is not fixed but constantly changing, a function of the kinds of questions asked of it: what is "stored" in the text both is and isn't in it. As the text and the theory interact, the two constantly shift ground. Johnson's reading of Herman Melville's *Billy Budd* sees Melville's short novel as deeply preoccupied by the same issues about language that occupied Ferdinand de Saussure (1857–1913) and J. L. Austin (1911–60). *Billy Budd* is a particularly good example of a text fissured by conflicting assumptions about words: the final revision was never finished by Melville, and competing versions of it have been published posthumously. Another well-known essay from *The Critical Difference*, "The Frame of Reference," examines the influential analyses, by Lacan and Derrida, of Edgar Allan Poe's story "The Purloined Letter" (1844) and meditates explicitly on the structure of mutual framing between text and theory.

In 1981 Johnson published her translation of Derrida's *Dissemination*, with a much-cited introduction. In 1982 she edited an issue of *Yale French Studies* titled *The Pedagogical Imperative: Teaching as a Literary Genre*. In this collection of essays, such authors as Derrida, de Man, Felman, Jane Gallop, and Jean-François Lyotard explored not how to teach literary texts but how literature depicts teaching, and how "the literary" and "the pedagogical" are linked.

In 1980 a student introduced Johnson to the work of Zora Neale Hurston (1891–1960); aided by a series of conversations with Henry Louis Gates Jr., Johnson became one of the first scholars to apply French literary theory to African American texts. Hurston was a particularly productive novelist for this enterprise, since her rhetorical virtuosity and folkloric imagination were at odds with the kinds of realist texts that dominated the canon of African American literature. Feminists, prompted by the writer Alice Walker's essays of the mid-1970s about Hurston's importance to the literary tradition of black women, were beginning to rethink both the canon and canonical aesthetics through Hurston's novels and folktales. The resultant boom in Hurston studies contributed to a change in African American studies itself, epitomized by Gates's *The Signifying Monkey: A Theory of Afro-American Literary Criticism* (1988). Johnson's two essays on Hurston appear in her collection *A World of Difference* (1987), a book in which she attempts to think deconstructively about a wide set of questions. For example, the often-reprinted essay "Apostrophe, Animation, and Abortion," which ends the book, brings together in striking ways literature (lyric poetry) and law (the abortion debates).

In 1991 Johnson coedited a volume titled *Consequences of Theory*, whose contributors attempted to refute the notorious assertion, made by Stanley

Fish in his *Doing What Comes Naturally: Change, Rhetoric, and the Practice of Theory in Literary and Legal Studies* (1989), that theory has no consequences. There followed in 1993 *Freedom and Interpretation*, Johnson's edited volume of the Oxford Amnesty Lectures of 1992, part of a project designed to raise money for Amnesty International. The lecturers invited to Oxford that year had been asked by the organizers to address what happens to the idea of "human rights" in an age of the "deconstruction of the subject." Johnson's introduction attempts to analyze what is at stake in the question, especially when its two elements are viewed as not simply opposed. This volume belongs to the larger investigation of the relations between deconstruction and politics, a topic hotly debated at the time.

Johnson's own lectures on literary theory given at Bucknell University yielded *The Wake of Deconstruction* (1994), in which she discusses the questions deconstruction had both awakened and left in its wake, especially after the double "death" of Paul de Man (his literal death in 1983, followed by the revelation in 1987 of his collaborationist journalism). The two lectures, "Double Mourning and the Public Sphere" and "Women and Allegory," analyze the conflation of deconstruction, political correctness, and identity politics, which had all become strangely and wrongly linked in the public mind.

In the late 1990s, a series of attacks on feminism and on women's studies programs led Johnson to write about the status of ambivalence within oppositional movements. She argues in the introduction to *The Feminist Difference* (1998) that the trap of unanimity, even when called forth by a common target, is ultimately impoverishing except on specific and strategic occasions. The debates within feminism—among black and white feminists, among lesbians and heterosexuals, among women from different classes or different countries—had revealed that the strength of the feminist movement lay not in unity but in the ability to face differences and conflicts and still go on, and that it was the continued functioning of the powers being contested (even *within* feminists themselves) that made going on so difficult. The essays in *The Feminist Difference* take up the issues raised in the book's subtitle— *Literature, Psychoanalysis, Race, and Gender*—and are loosely structured around paired texts.

In describing the processes by which forces of uncertainty are institutionalized as certainties—and thus, as theories—Johnson once lamented that "nothing fails like success" (*A World of Difference*). The "linguistic turn" in the human sciences during the twentieth century has in some ways been superseded and critiqued, but Johnson remains unconvinced that the project of accounting for the role of language can ever really become outmoded. We need to find, she implies, not something "beyond the linguistic turn" but a way to keep being surprised by it.

At Harvard University, Johnson has been named the Fredric Wertham Professor of Law and Psychiatry in Society, a title reflective of her ongoing interdisciplinary work. Like Samuel Taylor Coleridge's Ancient Mariner, whom she cites as a model teacher, she seems determined to repeat the story of the importance of language in widely differing contexts. But the lesson she derives from the Mariner about pedagogy is not simple: "Teaching," she writes in her introduction to *The Pedagogical Imperative*, "is a compulsion to repeat what one has not yet understood."

NOTES

"Barbara Johnson Biography," from *Norton Anthology of Theory and Criticism*, edited by Vincent B. Leitch et al. Copyright © 2001 by W. W. Norton & Company, Inc. Used by permission of W. W. Norton & Company, Inc.

This biographical account, which originally appeared as the headnote accompanying Johnson's entry in the *Norton Anthology of Theory and Criticism*, was written by Johnson in collaboration with the other editors of that anthology.

PART I

Reading Theory as Literature, Literature as Theory

CHAPTER 1

The Critical Difference

BartheS/BalZac

Literary criticism as such can perhaps be called the art of rereading. I would therefore like to begin by quoting the remarks about rereading made by Roland Barthes in *S/Z*:

> Rereading, an operation contrary to the commercial and ideological habits of our society, which would have us "throw away" the story once it has been consumed ("devoured"), so that we can then move on to another story, buy another book, and which is tolerated only in certain marginal categories of readers (children, old people, and professors), rereading is here suggested at the outset, for it alone saves the text from repetition (*those who fail to reread are obliged to read the same story everywhere*).[1] (emphasis mine)

What does this paradoxical statement imply? First, it implies that a single reading is composed of the already-read, that what we can see in a text the first time is already in us, not in it; in us insofar as we ourselves are a stereotype, an already-read text; and in the text only to the extent that the already-read is that aspect of a text that it must have in common with its reader in order for it to be readable at all. When we read a text once, in other words, we can see in it only what we have already learned to see before.

Secondly, the statement that those who do not reread must read the same story everywhere involves a reversal of the usual properties of the words *same* and *different*. Here, it is the consuming of different stories that is equated with the repetition of the same, while it is the rereading of the same that engenders what Barthes calls the "text's difference." This critical concept of difference, which has been valorized both by Saussurian linguistics and by the Nietzschean tradition in philosophy—particularly the work of Jacques Derrida—is crucial to the practice of what is called deconstructive criticism. I would therefore like to examine here some of its implications and functions.

In a sense, it could be said that to make a critical difference is the object of all criticism as such. The very word *criticism* comes from the Greek verb *krinein*, "to separate or choose," that is, to differentiate. The critic not only seeks to establish standards for evaluating the differences between texts but also tries to perceive something uniquely different within each text he reads and in so doing to establish his own individual difference from other critics. But this is not quite what Barthes means when he speaks of the text's difference. On the first page of *S/Z*, he writes:

> This difference is not, obviously, some complete, irreducible quality (according to a mythic view of literary creation), it is not what designates the individuality of each text, what names, signs, finishes off each work with a flourish; on the contrary, it is a difference which does not stop and which is articulated upon the infinity of texts, of languages, of systems: a difference of which each text is the return. (3)

In other words, a text's difference is not its uniqueness, its special identity. It is the text's way of differing from itself. And this difference is perceived only in the act of rereading. It is the way in which the text's signifying energy becomes unbound, to use Freud's term, through the process of repetition, which is the return not of sameness but of difference. Difference, in other words, is not what distinguishes one identity from another. It is not a difference between (or at least not between independent units), but a difference within. Far from constituting the text's unique identity, it is that which subverts the very idea of identity, infinitely deferring the possibility of adding up the sum of a text's parts or meanings and reaching a totalized, integrated whole.

Let me illustrate this idea further by turning for a moment to Rousseau's *Confessions*. Rousseau's opening statement about himself is precisely an affirmation of difference: "I am unlike anyone I have ever met; I will even venture to say that I am like no one in the whole world. I may be no better, but at least I am different."[2] Now, this can be read as an unequivocal assertion of uniqueness, of difference between Rousseau and the whole rest of the world. This is the boast on which the book is based. But in what does the uniqueness of this self consist? It is not long before we find out: "There are times when I am so unlike myself that I might be taken for someone else of an entirely opposite character" (126). "In me are united two almost irreconcilable characteristics, though in what way I cannot imagine" (112). In other words, this story of the self's difference from others inevitably becomes the story of its own unbridgeable difference from itself. Difference is not engendered in the space between identities; it is what makes all totalization of the identity of a self or the meaning of a text impossible.

It is this type of textual difference that informs the process of deconstructive criticism. *Deconstruction* is not synonymous with *destruction*, however. It is in fact much closer to the original meaning of the word *analysis*, which etymologically means "to undo"—a virtual synonym for "to de-construct." The de-construction of a text does not proceed by random doubt or arbitrary subversion, but by the careful teasing out of warring forces of signification within the text itself. If anything is destroyed in a deconstructive reading, it is not the text, but the claim to unequivocal domination of one mode of signifying over another. A deconstructive reading is a reading that analyzes the specificity of a text's critical difference from itself.

I have chosen to approach this question of critical difference by way of Barthes's *S/Z* for three reasons:

1. Barthes sets up a critical value system explicitly based on the paradigm of difference, and in the process works out one of the earliest, most influential, and most lucid and forceful syntheses of contemporary French theoretical thought;
2. The Balzac story that Barthes chooses to analyze in *S/Z* is itself in a way a study of difference—a subversive and unsettling formulation of the question of sexual difference;
3. The confrontation between Barthes and Balzac may have something to say about the critical differences between theory and practice, on the one hand, and between literature and criticism, on the other.

I shall begin by recalling the manner in which Barthes outlines his value system:

Our evaluation can be linked only to a practice, and this practice is that of writing. On the one hand, there is what it is possible to write, and on the other, what it is no longer possible to write. . . . What evaluation finds is precisely this value: what can be written (rewritten) today: the *writerly* [*le scriptible*]. Why is the writerly our value? Because the goal of literary work (of literature as work) is to make the reader no longer a consumer, but a producer of the text. . . . Opposite the writerly text is its countervalue, its negative, reactive value: what can be read, but not written: the *readerly* [*le lisible*]. We call any readerly text a classic text. (4)

Here, then, is the major polarity that Barthes sets up as a tool for evaluating texts: the readerly versus the writerly. The readerly is defined as a product consumed by the reader; the writerly is a process of production in which the reader becomes a producer: it is "ourselves writing." The readerly is constrained by considerations of representation: it is irreversible, "natural," decidable, continuous, totalizable, and unified into a coherent whole based on the signified. The writerly is infinitely plural and open to the free play of signifiers and of difference, unconstrained by representative considerations, and transgressive of any desire for decidable, unified, totalized meaning.

With this value system, one would naturally expect to find Barthes going on to extol the play of infinite plurality in some Joycean or Mallarméan piece of writerly obscurity, but no; he turns to Balzac, one of the most readerly of readerly writers, as Barthes himself insists. Why then does Barthes choose to talk about Balzac? Barthes skillfully avoids confronting this question. But perhaps it is precisely the way in which Barthes's choice of Balzac does not follow logically from his value system—that is, the way in which Barthes somehow differs from himself—which opens up the critical difference we must analyze here.

Although Balzac's text apparently represents for Barthes the negative, readerly end of the hierarchy, Barthes's treatment of it does seem to illustrate all the characteristics of the positive, writerly end. In the first place, one cannot help but be struck by the plurality of Barthes's text, with its numerous sizes of print, its "systematic use of digression," and its successive superposable versions of the same but different story, from the initial reproduction of Girodet's *Endymion* to the four appendixes, which repeat the book's contents in different forms. The reading technique proper also obeys the demand for fragmentation and pluralization, and consists of "manhandling" the text:

What we seek is to sketch the stereographic space of writing (which will here be a classic, readerly writing). The commentary, based on the affirmation of the plural, cannot work with "respect" to the text; the tutor text will ceaselessly be broken, interrupted without any regard for its natural divisions . . . the work of the commentary, once it is separated from any ideology of totality, consists precisely in *manhandling* the text, *interrupting* it [*lui couper la parole*]. What is thereby denied is not the *quality* of the text (here incomparable) but its "naturalness." (15)

Barthes goes on to divide the story diachronically into 561 fragments called *lexias* and synchronically into five so-called voices or codes, thus transforming the text into a "complex network" with "multiple entrances and exits."

The purposes of these cuts and codes is to pluralize the reader's intake, to effect a resistance to the reader's desire to restructure the text into large, ordered masses of meaning: "If we want to remain attentive to the plural of a text . . . we must renounce structuring this text in large masses, as was done by classical rhetoric and by secondary-school explication: no construction of the text" (11–12). In leaving the text as heterogeneous and discontinuous as possible, in attempting to avoid the repressiveness of the attempt to dominate the message and force the text into a single ultimate meaning, Barthes thus works a maximum of disintegrative violence and a minimum of integrative violence. The question to ask is whether this "anti-constructionist" (as opposed to "de-constructionist") fidelity to the fragmented signifier succeeds in laying bare the functional plurality of Balzac's text, or whether in the final analysis a certain systematic level of textual difference is not also lost and flattened by Barthes's refusal to reorder or reconstruct the text.

Let us now turn to Balzac's *Sarrasine* itself. The story is divided into two parts: the story of the telling and the telling of the story. In the first part, the narrator attempts to seduce a beautiful Marquise by telling her the second part; that is, he wants to exchange narrative knowledge for carnal knowledge. The lady wants to know the secret of the mysterious old man at the party, and the narrator wants to know the lady. Story-telling, as Barthes points out, is thus not an innocent, neutral activity, but rather part of a bargain, an act of seduction. But here the bargain is not kept; the deal backfires. The knowledge the lady has acquired, far from bringing about her surrender, prevents it. In fact, the last thing she says is: "No one will have *known* me."

It is obvious that the key to this failure of the bargain lies in the content of the story used to fulfill it. That story is about the passion of the sculptor Sarrasine for the opera singer La Zambinella, and is based not on knowledge but on ignorance: the sculptor's ignorance of the Italian custom of using castrated men instead of women to play the soprano parts on the operatic stage. The sculptor, who had seen in La Zambinella the perfect female body for the first time realized in one person, a veritable Pygmalion's statue come to life, finds out that this image of feminine perfection literally has been carved by a knife, not in stone but in the flesh itself. He who had proclaimed his willingness to die for his love ends up doing just that, killed by La Zambinella's protector.

How is it that the telling of this sordid little tale ends up subverting the very bargain it was intended to fulfill? Barthes's answer to this is clear: "castration is contagious"—"contaminated by the castration she has just been told about, [the Marquise] impels the narrator into it" (36).

What is interesting about this story of seduction and castration is the way in which it unexpectedly reflects upon Barthes's own critical value system. For in announcing that "the tutor text will ceaselessly be broken, interrupted without any regard for its natural divisions," is Barthes not implicitly privileging something like castration over what he calls the "ideology of totality"? "If the text is subject to some form," he writes, "this form is not unitary . . . , finite; it is the fragment, the slice, the cut up or erased network" (20; translation modified). Indeed, might it not be possible to read Balzac's opposition between the ideal woman and the castrato as metaphorically assimilable to Barthes's opposition between the readerly and the writerly? Like the readerly text, Sarrasine's deluded image of La Zambinella is a glorification of perfect unity and wholeness:

> At that instant he marveled at the ideal beauty he had hitherto sought in life, seeking in one often unworthy model the roundness of a perfect leg; in another, the curve of a breast; in another, white shoulders; finally taking some girl's neck, some woman's hands, and some child's smooth knees, without ever having encountered under the cold Parisian sky the rich, sweet creations of ancient Greece. La Zambinella displayed to him, *united*, living, and delicate, those exquisite female forms he so ardently desired. (237–38; emphasis mine)

But like the writerly text, Zambinella is actually fragmented, unnatural, and sexually undecidable. Like the readerly, the soprano is a product to be "devoured" ("With his eyes, Sarrasine devoured Pygmalion's statue, come down from its pedestal" [238]), while, like the writerly, castration is a process of production, an active and violent indetermination. The soprano's appearance seems to embody the very essence of "woman" as a *signified* ("This was woman herself" [248]), while the castrato's reality, like the writerly text, is a mere play of signifiers, emptied of any ultimate signified, robbed of what the text calls a "heart": "I have no heart," says Zambinella, "the stage where you saw me . . . is my life, I have no other" (247).

Here, then, is the first answer to the question of why Barthes might have chosen this text; it explicitly thematizes the opposition between unity and fragmentation, between the idealized signified and the discontinuous empty play of signifiers, which underlies his opposition between the readerly and the writerly. The traditional value system that Barthes is attempting to reverse is thus already mapped out within the text he analyzes. Three questions, however, immediately present themselves: (1) Does Balzac's story really uphold the unambiguousness of the readerly values to which Barthes relegates it? (2) Does Balzac simply regard ideal beauty as a lost paradise and castration as a horrible tragedy? (3) If Barthes is really attempting to demystify the ideology of totality, and if his critical strategy implicitly gives a positive value to castration, why does his analysis of Balzac's text still seem to take castration at face value as an unmitigated and catastrophic horror?

In order to answer these questions, let us take another look at Balzac's story. To regard castration as the ultimate narrative revelation and as the unequivocal cause of Sarrasine's tragedy, as Barthes repeatedly does, is to read the story more or less from Sarrasine's point of view. It is in fact Barthes's very attempt to pluralize the text which thus restricts his perspective; however "disrespectfully" he may cut up or manhandle the story, his reading remains to a large extent dependent on the linearity of the signifier and thus on the successive unfoldings of the truth of castration to Sarrasine and to the reader. Sarrasine's ignorance, however, is not only a simple lack of knowledge but also a blindness to the injustice that is being done to him and that he is also potentially doing to the other. This does not mean that Balzac's story is a plea for the prevention of cruelty to castrati, but that the failure of the couple to unite can perhaps not simply be attributed to the literal fact of castration. Let us therefore examine the nature of Sarrasine's passion more closely.

Upon seeing La Zambinella for the first time, Sarrasine exclaims: "To be loved by her, or to die!" (238). This alternative places all of the energy of the passion not on the object, La Zambinella, but on the subject, Sarrasine. To be loved, or to die; to exist as the desired object, or not to exist at all. What is at stake is not the union between two people, but the narcissistic awakening of one. Seeing La Zambinella is Sarrasine's first experience of *himself* as an object of love. By means of the image of sculpturesque perfection, Sarrasine thus falls in love with none other than himself. Balzac's fictional narrator makes explicit the narcissistic character of Sarrasine's passion and at the same time nostalgically identifies with it himself when he calls it "this golden age of love, during which we are happy almost by ourselves" (240). Sarrasine contents himself with La Zambinella as the product of his own sculptor's imagination ("This was more than a woman, this was a masterpiece!" [238]) and does not seek to find out who she is in reality ("As he began to realize that he would soon have to act . . . to ponder, in short, on ways to see her, speak to her, these great, ambitious thoughts made his heart swell so painfully that he put them off until later, deriving as much satisfaction from his physical suffering as he did from his intellectual pleasures" [240]). When the sculptor is finally forced into the presence of his beloved, he reads in her only the proof of his own masculinity—she is the ideal woman, therefore he is the ideal man. When Sarrasine sees La Zambinella shudder at the pop of a cork, he is charmed by her weakness and says, "My strength [*puissance*] is your shield" (244). La Zambinella's weakness is thus the inverted mirror image of Sarrasine's potency. In this narcissistic system, the difference between the sexes is based on symmetry, and it is precisely the castrato that Sarrasine does indeed love—the image of the lack of what he thereby thinks he himself possesses. When Sarrasine says that he would not be able to love a strong woman, he is saying in effect that he would be unable to love anyone who was not his symmetrical opposite and the proof of his masculinity. This is to say that even if La Zambinella *had* been a real woman, Sarrasine's love would be a refusal to deal with her as a real other. This type of narcissism is in fact just as contagious in the story as castration: the Marquise sees the narcissistic delusion inherent in the narrator's own passion, and, banteringly foreshadowing one of the reasons for her ultimate refusal, protests: "Oh, you fashion me to your own taste. What tyranny! You don't want me for myself!" (233).

Sarrasine cannot listen to the other as other. Even when Zambinella suggests the truth by means of a series of equivocal remarks culminating in the question (directed toward Sarrasine's offers to sacrifice everything for love)—"And if I were not a woman?"—Sarrasine cries: "What a joke! Do you think you can deceive an artist's eye?" (247). Sarrasine's strength is thus a shield *against* La Zambinella, not *for* her. He creates her as his own symmetrical opposite and through her loves only himself. This is why the revelation of the truth is fatal. The castrato is simultaneously outside the difference between the sexes as well as representing the literalization of its illusory symmetry. He subverts the desire for symmetrical, binary difference by fulfilling it. He destroys Sarrasine's reassuring masculinity by revealing that it is based on castration. But Sarrasine's realization that he himself is thereby castrated, that he is looking at his true mirror image, is still blind to the fact that he had never been capable of loving in the first place. His love was from the beginning the cancellation and castration of the other.

What Sarrasine dies of, then, is precisely a failure to *reread* in the exact sense with which we began this chapter. What he devours so eagerly in La Zambinella is actually located within himself: a collection of sculpturesque clichés about feminine beauty and his own narcissism. In thinking that he knows where difference is located—between the sexes—he is blind to a difference that cannot be situated between, but only within. In Balzac's story, castration thus stands as the literalization of the "difference within" which prevents any subject from coinciding with itself. In Derrida's terms, Sarrasine reads the opera singer as pure voice ("his passion for La Zambinella's voice" [241]), as an illusion of imaginary immediacy ("The distance between himself and La Zambinella had ceased to exist, he possessed her" [239]), as a perfectly readable, motivated sign ("Do you think you can deceive an artist's eye?"), as full and transparent Logos, whereas she is the very image of the empty and arbitrary sign, of writing inhabited by its own irreducible difference from itself. And it can be seen that the failure to reread is hardly a trivial matter: for Sarrasine, it is fatal.

Balzac's text thus itself demystifies the logocentric blindness inherent in Sarrasine's reading of the Zambinellian text. But if Sarrasine's view of La Zambinella as an image of perfect wholeness and unequivocal femininity is analogous to the classic, readerly conception of literature according to Barthes's definition, then Balzac's text has already worked out the same type of deconstruction of the readerly ideal as that which Barthes is trying to accomplish as if it stood in opposition to the classic text. In other words, Balzac's text already "knows" the limits and blindnesses of the readerly, which it personifies in Sarrasine. Balzac has already in a sense done Barthes's work for him. The readerly text is itself nothing other than a deconstruction of the readerly text.

But at the same time, Balzac's text does not operate a simple reversal of the readerly hierarchy; Balzac does not proclaim castration as the truth behind the readerly's blindness in as unequivocal a way as Barthes's own unequivocality would lead one to believe. For every time Balzac's text is about to use the word *castration*, it leaves a blank instead. "Ah, you are a woman," cries Sarrasine in despair; "for even a . . ." He breaks off. "No," he continues, "he would not be so cowardly" (251). Balzac repeatedly castrates his text of the word *castration*. Far from being the unequivocal answer to the text's enigma, castration is the way in which the enigma's answer is withheld.

Castration is what the story must, and cannot, say. But what Barthes does in his reading is to label these textual blanks "taboo on the word castrato" (75, 177, 195, 210). He fills in the textual gaps with a name. He erects castration into *the* meaning of the text, its ultimate signified. In so doing, however, he makes the idea of castration itself into a readerly fetish, the supposed answer to all the text's questions, the final revelation in the "hermeneutic" code. Balzac indeed shows that the answer cannot be this simple, not only by eliminating the word *castration* from his text but also by suppressing the name of its opposite. When Sarrasine first feels sexual pleasure, Balzac says that this pleasure is located in "what we call the heart, for lack of any other word" (238). Later Zambinella says, "I have no heart" (247). Barthes immediately calls "heart" a euphemism for the sexual organ, but Balzac's text, in stating that what the heart represents cannot be named, that the word is lacking, leaves the question of sexuality open, as a rhetorical problem which the simple naming of parts cannot solve. Balzac's text thus does not simply reverse the hierarchy between readerly and writerly by substituting the truth of castration for the delusion of wholeness; it deconstructs the very possibility of naming the difference.

On the basis of this confrontation between a literary and a critical text, we could perhaps conclude that while both involve a study of difference, the literary text conveys a difference from itself which it "knows" but cannot say, while the critical text, in attempting to say the difference, reduces it to identity. But in the final analysis, Barthes's text, too, displays a strange ambivalence. For although every metaphorical dimension in Barthes's text proclaims castration as the desirable essence of the writerly—the writerly about which "there may be nothing to say" (4) just as the castrato is one "about whom there is nothing to say" (214)—the literal concept of castration is loudly disavowed by Barthes as belonging to the injustices of the readerly: "To reduce the text to the unity of meaning, by a deceptively univocal reading, is . . . to sketch the castrating gesture" (160). By means of this split, Barthes's own text reveals that it, like Balzac's, cannot with impunity set up any unequivocal value in opposition to the value of unequivocality. Just as Balzac's text, in its demystification of idealized beauty, reveals a difference not between the readerly and the writerly, but within the very ideals of the readerly, Barthes's text, in its ambivalence toward castration, reveals that the other of the readerly cannot but be subject to its own difference from itself. Difference as such cannot ever be affirmed as an ultimate value because it is that which subverts the very foundations of any affirmation of value. Castration can neither be assumed nor denied, but only enacted in the return of unsituable difference in every text. And the difference between literature and criticism consists perhaps only in the fact that criticism is more likely to be blind to the way in which its own critical difference from itself makes it, in the final analysis, literary.

NOTES

"The Critical Difference." *Diacritics* 8, no. 2 (1978): 2–9. Reprinted with permission of The Johns Hopkins University Press.

1. Roland Barthes, *S/Z*, trans. Richard Miller (New York: Hill and Wang, 1974), 15–16.
2. Jean-Jacques Rousseau, *Confessions* (New York: Penguin, 1954), 17.

CHAPTER 2

Translator's Introduction to *Dissemination* (abridged)

All translation is only a somewhat provisional way of coming to terms with the foreignness of languages.
—Walter Benjamin, "The Task of the Translator"

Jacques Derrida, born in Algiers in 1930, teaches philosophy at the Ecole Normale Supérieure in Paris. His tremendous impact on contemporary theoretical thought began in 1967 with the simultaneous publication of three major philosophical works: *La Voix et le phénomène* (an introduction to the problem of the *sign* in Husserl's phenomenology),[1] *L'écriture et la différence* (a collection of essays on the problematics of writing in literature, philosophy, psychoanalysis, and anthropology),[2] and *De la grammatologie* (a sustained analysis of the repression of writing in Western theories of language and culture and a methodological and theoretical outline of a new "science" of writing).[3]

Five years later, in 1972, came another tripartite Derridean biblioblitz: *Positions* (a collection of interviews),[4] *Marges: de la philosophie* (a collection of essays in/on the "margins" of philosophy, linguistics, and literature),[5] and *La Dissémination*.

Since 1972, Derrida's work has continued to proliferate and diversify. *Glas* (a giant montage of textual grafts and hardworking wordplays in which Hegel and Genet are shuffled into each other from juxtaposed columns of print) appeared in 1974, followed, among numerous articles and short works, by a collection of critical essays on painting, *La Vérité en peinture* (1978), and, in

1980, by *La Carte Postale: de Socrate à Freud et au-delà*, an intriguing collection of essays that treat the psychoanalytical writings of Freud and Jacques Lacan, preceded by a pseudo-fictional, pseudo-autobiographical epistolary preface that hinges on a postcard depicting Plato dictating behind the back of a writing Socrates.

A Critique of Western Metaphysics

Best known in this country for having forged the term *deconstruction*, Jacques Derrida follows Nietzsche and Heidegger in elaborating a critique of "Western metaphysics," by which he means not only the Western philosophical tradition but "everyday" thought and language as well. Western thought, says Derrida, has always been structured in terms of dichotomies or polarities: good versus evil, being versus nothingness, presence versus absence, truth versus error, identity versus difference, mind versus matter, man versus woman, soul versus body, life versus death, nature versus culture, speech versus writing. These polar opposites do not, however, stand as independent and equal entities. The second term in each pair is considered the negative, corrupt, undesirable version of the first, a fall away from it. Hence, absence is the lack of presence, evil is the fall from good, error is a distortion of truth, etc. In other words, the two terms are not simply opposed in their meanings, but are arranged in a hierarchical order which gives the first term *priority*, in both the temporal and the qualitative sense of the word. In general, what these hierarchical oppositions do is to privilege unity, identity, immediacy, and temporal and spatial *presentness* over distance, difference, dissimulation, and deferment. In its search for the answer to the question of Being, Western philosophy has indeed always determined Being as *presence*.

Derrida's critique of Western metaphysics focuses on its privileging of the spoken word over the written word. The spoken word is given a higher value because the speaker and listener are both present to the utterance simultaneously. There is no temporal or spatial distance between speaker, speech, and listener, since the speaker hears himself speak at the same moment the listener does. This immediacy seems to guarantee the notion that in the spoken word we know what we mean, mean what we say, say what we mean, and know what we have said. Whether or not perfect understanding always occurs *in fact*, this image of perfectly self-present meaning is, according to Derrida, the underlying ideal of Western culture. Derrida has termed this belief in the self-presentation of meaning "Logocentrism," from the Greek word *Logos* (meaning speech, logic, reason, the Word of God). Writing, on the other hand, is considered by the logocentric system to be only a *representation* of speech, a secondary substitute designed for use only when speaking is impossible. Writing is thus a second-rate activity that tries to overcome distance by making use of it: the writer puts his thought on paper, distancing it from himself, transforming it into something that can be read by someone far away, even after the writer's death. This inclusion of death, distance, and difference is thought to be a corruption of the self-presence of meaning, to open meaning up to all forms of adulteration which immediacy would have prevented.

In the course of his critique, Derrida does not simply reverse this value system and say that writing is better than speech. Rather, he attempts to show that the very possibility of opposing the two terms on the basis of presence versus absence or immediacy versus representation is an illusion, since speech is *already* structured by difference and distance as much as writing is. The very fact that a word is divided into a phonic *signifier* and a mental *signified*, and that, as Saussure pointed out, language is a system of differences rather than a collection of independently meaningful units, indicates that language as such is already constituted by the very distances and differences it seeks to overcome. To mean, in other words, is automatically *not* to be. As soon as there is meaning, there is difference. Derrida's word for this lag inherent in any signifying act is *différance*, from the French verb *différer*, which means both "to differ" and "to defer." What Derrida attempts to demonstrate is that this *différance* inhabits the very core of what appears to be immediate and present. Even in the seemingly nonlinguistic areas of the structures of consciousness and the unconscious, Derrida analyzes the underlying necessity that induces Freud to compare the psychic apparatus to a structure of scriptural *différance*, a "mystic writing-pad."[6] The illusion of the self-presence of meaning or of consciousness is thus produced by the repression of the differential structures from which they spring.

Derrida's project in his early writings is to elaborate a science of writing called *grammatology*: a science that would study the effects of this *différance* which Western metaphysics has systematically repressed in its search for self-present Truth. But, as Derrida himself admits, the very notion of a perfectly adequate *science* or *-logy* belongs to the logocentric discourse which the science of writing would try, precisely, to put in question. Derrida thus finds himself in the uncomfortable position of attempting to account for an error by means of tools derived from that very error. For it is not possible to show that the belief in truth is an error without implicitly believing in the notion of Truth. By the same token, to show that the binary oppositions of metaphysics are illusions is *also*, and perhaps most importantly, to show that such illusions cannot simply in turn *be opposed* without repeating the very same illusion. The task of undoing the history of logocentrism in order to disinter *différance* would thus appear to be a doubly impossible one: on the one hand, it can only be conducted by means of notions of revelation, representation, and rectification, which are *the* logocentric notions par excellence, and, on the other hand, it can only dig up something that is really nothing—a difference, a gap, an interval, a trace. How, then, can such a task be undertaken?

Supplementary Reading

Any attempt to disentangle the weave of *différance* from the logocentric blanket can obviously not long remain on the level of abstraction and generality of the preceding remarks. Derrida's writing, indeed, is always explicitly inscribed in the margins of some preexisting text. Derrida is, first and foremost, a *reader*, a reader who constantly reflects on and transforms the very nature of the act of reading. It would therefore perhaps be helpful to examine some of the specific reading strategies he has worked out. I begin with a chapter from *Of Grammatology* entitled "That Dangerous Supplement," in which Derrida elaborates not only a particularly striking reading of Rousseau's *Confessions* but also a concise reflection on his own methodology.

Derrida's starting point is the rhetoric of Rousseau's discussions of writing, on the one hand, and masturbation, on the other. Both activities are called *supplements* to natural intercourse, in the sense both of conversation and of copulation. What Derrida finds in Rousseau's account is a curious bifurcation within the values of writing and masturbation with respect to the desire for presence.

Let us take writing first. On the one hand, Rousseau condemns writing for being only a representation of direct speech and therefore less desirable because less immediate. Rousseau, in this context, privileges speech as the more direct expression of the self. But on the other hand, in the actual experience of living speech, Rousseau finds that he expresses himself much less successfully in person than he does in his writing. Because of his shyness, he tends to blurt out things that represent him as the opposite of what he thinks he is:

I would love society like others, if I were not sure of showing myself not only at a disadvantage, but as completely different from what I am. The part that I have taken of *writing and hiding myself* is precisely the one that suits me. If I were present, one would never know what I was worth.[7]

It is thus absence that assures the presentation of truth, and presence that entails its distortion. Derrida's summation of this contradictory stance is as follows:

> Straining toward the reconstruction of presence, [Rousseau] valorizes and disqualifies writing at the same time.... Rousseau condemns writing as destruction of presence and as disease of speech. He rehabilitates it to the extent that it promises the reappropriation of that of which speech allowed itself to be dispossessed. But by what, if not already a writing older than speech and already installed in that place? (141–42)

In other words, the loss of presence has always already begun. Speech itself springs out of an alienation or *différance* that has the very structure of writing.

It would seem, though, that it is precisely through this assumption of the necessity of absence that Rousseau ultimately succeeds in reappropriating the lost presence. In sacrificing himself, he recuperates himself. This notion that self-sacrifice is the road to self-redemption is a classical structure in Western metaphysics. Yet it can be shown that this project of reappropriation is inherently self-subverting because its very starting point is not presence itself but the *desire* for presence, that is, the *lack* of presence. It is not possible to desire that with which one coincides. The starting point is thus not a *point* but a différance:

> Without the possibility of différance, the desire of presence as such would not find its breathing-space. That means by the same token that this desire carries in itself the destiny of its nonsatisfaction. Différance produces what it forbids, making possible the very thing that it makes impossible. (143)

The same paradoxical account of the desire for presence occurs in Rousseau's discussions of sexuality. On the one hand, masturbation is condemned as a means of "cheating Nature" and substituting a mere image (absence) for the presence of a sexual partner. On the other hand:

> This vice, which shame and timidity find so convenient, has a particular attraction for lively imaginations. It allows them to dispose, so to speak, of the whole female sex at their will, and to make any beauty who tempts

them serve their pleasure without the need of first obtaining her consent. (151 [109])

It is thus the woman's absence that gives immediacy to her imaginary possession, while to deal with the woman's presence would inevitably be to confront differance. Masturbation is both a symbolic form of ideal union, since in it the subject and object are truly one, and a radical alienation of the self from any contact with an other. The union that would perfectly fulfill desire would also perfectly exclude the space of its very possibility.

Just as speech was shown to be structured by the same differance as writing, so, too, the desire to possess a "real" woman is grounded in distance, both because the prohibition of incest requires that one's love-object always be a substitute for the original object, and because of the fundamental structure of desire itself. Rousseau's autobiography offers us a particularly striking example of the essential role of differance in desire. Faced with the possibility of a quasi-incestuous relation with the woman he called "Mama"—incest being the very model of the elimination of differance—Rousseau finds that his desire manifests itself in inverse proportion to Mama's physical proximity: "I only felt the full strength of my attachment to her when she was out of my sight" (152 [107]). Not only does the enjoyment of presence appear to Rousseau to be impossible; it also could be fatal: "If I had ever in my life tasted the delights of love even once in their plenitude," he writes, "I do not imagine that my frail existence would have been sufficient for them. I would have been dead in the act" (155).

Presence, then, is an ambiguous, even dangerous, ideal. Direct speech is self-violation; perfect heteroeroticism is death. Recourse to writing and autoeroticism is necessary to recapture a presence whose lack has not been preceded by any fullness. Yet these two compensatory activities are themselves condemned as unnecessary, even dangerous, supplements.

In French, the word *supplément* has two meanings: it means both "an addition" and "a substitute." Rousseau uses this word to describe both writing and masturbation. Thus, writing and masturbation may *add to* something that is already present, in which case they are *superfluous*, AND/OR they may *replace* something that is *not* present, in which case they are *necessary*. Superfluous and necessary, dangerous and redemptive, the supplement moves through Rousseau's text according to a very strange logic.

What Derrida's reading of Rousseau sketches out is indeed nothing less than a revolution in the very logic of meaning. The logic of the supplement wrenches apart the neatness of the metaphysical binary oppositions. Instead of "A is opposed to B" we have "B is both added to A and replaces A." A and B are no longer opposed, nor are they equivalent. Indeed, they are no longer even equivalent to themselves. They are their own differance from themselves. "Writing," for example, no longer means simply "words on a page," but rather any differential trace structure, a structure that *also* inhabits speech. "Writing" and "speech" can therefore no longer be simply opposed, but neither have they become identical. Rather, the very notion of their "identities" is put in question.

In addition to this supplementary logic in the text's *signified*, the inseparability of the two senses of the word *supplément* renders any affirmation that contains it problematic. While Rousseau's explicit intentions are to keep the two senses rigorously distinct—to know when he means "substitute" and when he means "addition"—the shadow presence of the other meaning is always there to undermine the distinction. On the level both of the signified and of the signifier, therefore, it is not possible to pin down the dividing lines between excess and lack, compensation and corruption. The doubleness of the word *supplément* carries the text's signifying possibilities beyond what could reasonably be attributed to Rousseau's conscious intentions. Derrida's reading shows how Rousseau's text functions *against* its own explicit (metaphysical) assertions, not just by creating ambiguity, but by inscribing a *systematic* "other message" behind or through what is being said.

Deconstruction

Let us now examine more closely the strategies and assumptions involved in this type of critical reading. It is clear that Derrida is not seeking the "meaning" of Rousseau's text in any traditional sense. He neither adds the text up into a final set of themes or affirmations nor looks for the reality of Rousseau's life outside the text. Indeed, says Derrida, there *is* no outside of the text:

> There is nothing outside of the text [*il n'y a pas de hors-texte*]. And that
> is neither because Jean-Jacques' life, or the existence of Mama or Thérèse
> *themselves*, is not of prime interest to us, nor because we have access to
> their so-called "real" existence only in the text and we have neither any
> means of altering this, nor any right to neglect this limitation. All rea-
> sons of this type would already be sufficient, to be sure, but there are
> more radical reasons. What we have tried to show by following the guid-
> ing line of the "dangerous supplement," is that in what one calls the
> real life of these existences "of flesh and bone," beyond and behind

what one believes can be circumscribed as Rousseau's text, there has never been anything but writing; there have never been anything but supplements, substitutive significations which could only come forth in a chain of differential references, the "real" supervening, and being added only while taking on meaning from a trace and from an invocation of the supplement, etc. And thus to infinity, for we have read, *in the text*, that the absolute present, Nature, that which words like "real mother" name, have always already escaped, have never existed; that what opens meaning and language is writing as the disappearance of natural presence. (158–59; emphasis in original)

Far from being a simple warning against the biographical or referential fallacy, "il n'y a pas de hors-texte" is a statement derived from Rousseau's autobiography itself. For what Rousseau's text tells us is that our very relation to "reality" already functions like a text. Rousseau's account of his life is not only itself a text, but it is a text that speaks only about the textuality of life. Rousseau's life does not *become* a text through his writing: it always already *was* one. Nothing, indeed, can be said to be *not* a text.

Derrida's reading of Rousseau's autobiography thus proposes a "deconstruction" of its logocentric claims and metaphysical assumptions. Deconstruction is not a form of textual vandalism designed to prove that meaning is impossible. In fact, the word *de-construction* is closely related not to the word *destruction* but to the word *analysis*, which etymologically means "to undo"—a virtual synonym for "to de-construct." The deconstruction of a text does not proceed by random doubt or generalized skepticism, but by the careful teasing out of warring forces of signification *within the text itself*. If anything is destroyed in a deconstructive reading, it is not meaning but the claim to unequivocal domination of one mode of signifying over another. This, of course, implies that a text signifies in more than one way, and to varying degrees of explicitness. Sometimes the discrepancy is produced, as here, by a double-edged word, which serves as a hinge that both articulates and breaks open the explicit statement being made. Sometimes it is engendered when the figurative level of a statement is at odds with the literal level. And sometimes it occurs when the so-called starting point of an argument is based on presuppositions that render its conclusions problematic or circular.

Derrida defines his reading strategy as follows:

The reading must always aim at a certain relationship, unperceived by the writer, between what he commands and what he does not command of the patterns of the language that he uses. This relationship is not a certain quantitative distribution of shadow and light, of weakness or of force, but a signifying structure that the critical reading should *produce*. (158; emphasis in original)

In other words, the deconstructive reading does not point out the flaws or weaknesses or stupidities of an author, but the *necessity* with which what he *does* see is systematically related to what he does *not* see.

It can thus be seen that deconstruction is a form of what has long been called a *critique*. A critique of any theoretical system is not an examination of its flaws or imperfections. It is not a set of criticisms designed to make the system better. It is an analysis that focuses on the grounds of that system's possibility. The critique reads backwards from what seems natural, obvious, self-evident, or universal, in order to show that these things have their history, their reasons for being the way they are, their effects on what follows from them, and that the starting point is not a (natural) given but a (cultural) construct, usually blind to itself. For example, Copernicus can be said to have written a critique of the Ptolemaic conception of the universe. But the idea that the Earth goes around the sun is not an *improvement* of the idea that the sun goes around the Earth. It is a shift in perspective which literally makes the ground move. It is a deconstruction of the validity of the commonsense perception of the obvious. In the same way, Marx's critique of political economy is not an improvement in it but a demonstration that the theory which starts with the commodity as the basic unit of economy is blind to what *produces* the commodity—namely, labor. Every theory starts somewhere; every critique exposes what that starting point conceals, and thereby displaces all the ideas that follow from it. The critique does not ask "what does this statement *mean*?" but "where is it being made from? What does it presuppose? Are its presuppositions compatible with, independent of, and anterior to the statement that seems to follow from them, or do they already follow from it, contradict it, or stand in a relation of mutual dependence such that neither can exist without positing that the other is prior to it?"

In its elaboration of a critique of the metaphysical forces that structure and smother differance in every text, a deconstructive reading thus assumes:

1. That the rhetoric of an assertion is not necessarily compatible with its explicit meaning.
2. That this incompatibility can be read as systematic and significant *as such*.

3. That an inquiry that attempts to study an object by means of that very object is open to certain analyzable aberrations (this pertains to virtually all important investigations: the self analyzing itself, man studying man, thought thinking about thought, language speaking about language, etc.).
4. That certain levels of any rigorous text will engender a systematic double mark of the insistent but invisible contradiction or differance (the repression of) which is necessary for and in the text's very elaboration.

But if the traditional logic of meaning as an unequivocal structure of mastery *is* Western metaphysics, the deconstruction of metaphysics cannot simply combat logocentric meaning by opposing some other meaning to it. Differance is not a "concept" or "idea" that is "truer" than presence. It can only be a process of textual *work*, a strategy of *writing*.

Derrida's Styles

Early in "The Double Session," in the course of a discussion of the possible Hegelian or Platonic overtones of the word *Idea* in Mallarmé's writing, we read the following warning:

> But a reading here should no longer be carried out as a simple table of concepts or words, as a static or statistical sort of punctuation. One must reconstitute a chain in motion, the effects of a network and the play of a syntax. (194)

This warning applies equally well to Derrida's own writing, in which it is all too tempting to focus on certain "key" terms and to compile them into a static lexicon: *supplément, différance, pharmakon, hymen*, etc. Because Derrida's text is constructed as a moving chain or network, it constantly frustrates the desire to "get to the point" (see the remarks on the dancer's "points" in "The Double Session"). In accordance with its deconstruction of summary meaning, Derrida's writing mimes the *movement* of desire rather than its fulfillment, refusing to stop and totalize itself, or doing so only by feint. Some of the mechanisms of this signifying frustration include:

1. *Syntax.* Derrida's grammar is often "unspeakable"—that is, it conforms to the laws of writing but not necessarily to the cadences of speech. Ambiguity is rampant. Parentheses go on for pages.

A sentence beginning on p. 319 does not end until p. 323, having embraced two pages of *Un Coup de dés* and a long quotation from Robert Greer Cohn. Punctuation arrests without necessarily clarifying.

2. *Allusions.* The pluralization of writing's references and voices often entails the mobilization of unnamed sources and addressees. All references to castration, lack, talking truth, and letters not reaching their destination, for example, are part of Derrida's ongoing critique of the writings of Jacques Lacan.

3. *Fading in and out.* The beginnings and endings of these essays are often the most mystifying parts. Sometimes, as in the description of Plato working after hours in his pharmacy, they are also cryptically literary, almost lyrical. It is as though the borderlines of the text had to be made to bear the mark of the silence—and the pathos—that lie beyond its fringes, as if the text had first and last to more actively disconnect itself from the logos toward which it still aspires.

4. *Multiple coherences.* The unit of coherence here is not necessarily the sentence, the word, the paragraph, or even the essay. Different threads of *Dissemination* are woven together through the bindings of grammar (the future perfect), "theme" (stones, columns, folds, caves, beds, textiles, seeds, etc.), letters (*or, d, i*), anagrammatical plays (graft/graph, semen/semantics, *lit/lire*), etc.

5. *Nonbinary logic.* In its deconstruction of the either/or logic of noncontradiction that underlies Western metaphysics, Derrida's writing attempts to elaborate an "other" logic. As he puts it in *Positions*:

> It has been necessary to analyze, to set to work, *within* the text of the history of philosophy, as well as *within* the so-called literary text . . . certain marks . . . that *by analogy* . . . I have called undecidables, that is, unities of simulacrum, "false" verbal properties (nominal or semantic) that can no longer be included within philosophical (binary) opposition, resisting and disorganizing it, *without ever* constituting a third term, without ever leaving room for a solution in the form of speculative dialectics (the *pharmakon* is neither remedy nor poison, neither good nor evil, neither the inside nor the outside, neither speech nor writing; the *supplement* is neither a plus nor a minus, neither an outside nor the complement of an inside, neither accident nor essence,

etc.; the *hymen* is neither confusion nor distinction, neither identity nor difference, neither consummation nor virginity, neither the veil nor the unveiling, neither the inside nor the outside, etc. . . . Neither/nor, that is, *simultaneously* either/or . . .)[8]

Because Derrida's writing functions according to this type of "other" logic, it is not surprising that it does not entirely conform to traditional binary notions of "clarity."

NOTES

From Jacques Derrida, *Dissemination*. Barbara Johnson, trans. (1981), vii–xvii. Excerpts from "Translator's Introduction" are reprinted by permission of the publisher © The University of Chicago 1981.

1. Translated by David Allison as *Speech and Phenomena* (Evanston, IL: Northwestern University Press, 1973).
2. Translated by Alan Bass as *Writing and Difference* (Chicago: University of Chicago Press, 1978).
3. Translated by Gayatri Chakravorty Spivak as *Of Grammatology* (Baltimore: Johns Hopkins University Press, 1974).
4. Translated by Alan Bass as *Positions* (Chicago: University of Chicago Press, 1981).
5. Translated by Alan Bass as *Margins of Philosophy* (Chicago: University of Chicago Press, 1982).
6. See "Freud and the Scene of Writing," in *Writing and Difference*, 196–231.
7. Quoted in *Of Grammatology*, 142. Page numbers in brackets following references to *Of Grammatology* refer to J. M. Cohen's translation of Rousseau's *Confessions* (New York: Penguin, 1954), which I have sometimes substituted for the translation used by Spivak.
8. *Positions*, 42–43.

CHAPTER 3

Poetry and Syntax

What the Gypsy Knew

Pivotal Intelligibility

Syntax is somehow not an inherently exciting subject. But without it, no subject would ever be capable of exciting us. Ever present but often taken for granted, like skin—which, as everyone knows, is a thing that when you have it outside, it helps keep your insides in—syntax is a thing that when you have it in your surface structure, it helps keep your deep structure deep. But what happens when you examine syntax as such? What can be said about this necessary but insufficient condition for saying anything at all?

Faced with this question, I did what any modern student of poetics would do: I went to see what Mallarmé said about it. In his essay on the uses of obscurity, *Le Mystère dans les lettres* (*The Mystery in Letters*), Mallarmé writes:

> Quel pivot, j'entends, dans ces contrastes, à l'intelligibilité? il faut une garantie—
> La Syntaxe—[1]

> [What pivot, I understand, in these contrasts, for intelligibility? / A guarantee is needed—/ Syntax—]

It should be noted that Mallarmé does not say that syntax guarantees intelligibility. He says it guarantees the *pivoting* of intelligibility. Intelligibility, indeed, is not an entirely positive value in Mallarmé's essay. It plays a role analogous to that of the word *entertainment* in today's discussions of art or pedagogy: it is a bone thrown to those who will never understand and a necessary evil or necessary tease for those who will. Mallarmé contrasts ordinary writers with the manipulator of obscurity by saying that the former "puisent à quelque encrier sans Nuit la vaine couche suffisante d'intelligibilité que lui s'oblige, aussi, à observer, mais pas seule" ("draw from some Nightless inkwell the vain sufficient layer of intelligibility that he, too, obliges himself to observe, but not exclusively") (383). Using an almost Chomskyan distinction between depth and surface, he explains:

> Tout écrit, extérieurement à son trésor, doit, par égard envers ceux dont il emprunte, après tout, pour un objet autre, le langage, présenter, avec les mots, un sens même indifférent: on gagne de détourner l'oisif, charmé que rien ne l'y concerne, à première vue.
>
> Salut, exact, de part et d'autre—
>
> Si, tout de même, n'inquiétait je ne sais quel *miroitement, en dessous,* peu séparable de la *surface* concédée à la rétine—il attire le soupçon: les malins, entre le public, réclamant de couper court, opinent, avec sérieux, que, juste, la teneur est inintelligible. (382; emphasis mine here and passim)

> [Any piece of writing, outside of its treasures, ought, in deference to those from whom it borrows, after all, for a different purpose, language, to present, with words, a meaning however indifferent: one profits from thus turning away the idlers, charmed that nothing concerns them in it, at first sight.
>
> Greetings and just deserts on both sides—
>
> If, nevertheless, there were not I don't know what glimmering from underneath, hardly separable from the surface conceded to the retina— which awakens suspicion: the wise guys in the public, demanding that it be cut short, pronounce their seriously considered opinion that, precisely, the tenor is unintelligible.]

It is thus an obscure perception of the hidden possibility of obscurity that attracts the suspicions of the sly, casual reader, who would otherwise have been satisfied with whatever intelligibility the surface of the writing might present. Obscurity, in other words, is not encountered on the way to intelligibility, like an obstacle, but rather lies beyond it, as what prevents the reader from being satisfied with his own reading. Obscurity is an excess, not a deficiency, of meaning.

The poet does not seek to be unintelligible; his writing enacts the impossibility of a transparent, neutral style through its plays of depth and surface, darkness and light:

> Je partis d'intentions, comme on demande du style—neutre l'imagine-t-on—que son expression ne se fonce par le plongeon ni ne ruisselle d'éclaboussures jaillies: fermé à l'alternative qui est la loi. (385)

> [I began with intentions as one demands of style—neutral style, one imagines—that its expression not plunge down into darkness nor surge up with a stream of splashes: closed to the alternative that is the law.]

The opposition between *plonger* (plunge) and *jaillir* (surge up) here merges with the opposition between darkness and light through the use of the verb *se foncer*, which means both "to become darker" and "to dive deeper." In going on to say, after speaking of "the alternative that is the law," that syntax acts as a pivot "in these contrasts," Mallarmé is making the very *fact of alternation* into the fundamental law of writing. Writing becomes an alternation between obscurity and clarity rather than a pursuit of either, a rhythm of intelligibility and mystery, just as time is a rhythm of days and nights:

> Ce procédé, jumeau, intellectuel, notable dans les symphonies, qui le trouvèrent au répertoire de la nature et du ciel. (385)

> [This procedure, twin and intellectual, notable in symphonies, which found it in the repertory of nature and the sky.]

It should not be forgotten that day and night, *jour* and *nuit*, are in themselves examples of the law of simultaneous contradictory alternatives, since Mallarmé complains elsewhere that their sounds and their meanings are directly opposed:

> A côté d'*ombre*, opaque, *ténèbres* se fonce peu; quelle déception, devant la perversité conférant à *jour* comme à *nuit*, contradictoirement, des timbres obscur ici, là clair. Le souhait d'un terme de splendeur brillant, ou qu'il s'éteigne, inverse; quant à des alternatives lumineuses simples— *Seulement*, sachons *n'existerait pas le vers*: lui, philosophiquement rémunère le défaut des langues, complément supérieur. (364; emphasis in original)

[Alongside *ombre* [shade], which is opaque, *ténèbres* [shadows] is not particularly dark; what a disappointment to face the perversity that gives to *jour* [day] and *nuit* [night], contradictorily, a dark timbre here and a light one there. The hope of finding a term of splendor glowing, or else, inversely, being extinguished; as far as simple luminous alternatives are concerned—*Only*, let us note that *verse would not exist*: it is verse that philosophically compensates for the faults of languages, a superior complement.]

Verse, then, in its rhythms and rhymes, is a practice of pivoting, as its etymology (*versus*) indicates. It is an enactment of the alternative as law and of law as alternative, necessitated precisely by the perverse way language has of disappointing the search for simple alternatives. It is because language does *not* function as a perfect light meter, does not correspond to any "simple luminous alternatives," that constant alternation between clarity and obscurity becomes its law.

While pursuing this concept of syntax as a pivot for the turnings of darkness and light, I was startled to discover that the word *syntaxis* occurs in the title of a treatise by the second-century Greek astronomer, Ptolemy,[2] whose geocentric view of the relations among the bodies in the solar system also deals with the question of what in the world turns around what. Could Ptolemy's outmoded *Syntaxis* tell us anything about syntax and modern poetry? Is there a relation between grammar and gravitation? Could the relations between clarity and obscurity really be as simple—or as complex—as night and day?

The question Ptolemy's work mis-answers is, of course, the question of a center. Ptolemy saw the universe revolving around the Earth; Copernicus saw the Earth revolving around the sun in a universe in which the sun turns out to be merely one of many stars. The displacement of the center from Earth to sun is also a movement away from the centrality of man himself; the human observer is no longer the pivot of the universe but only a parasite on a satellite. Freud, another revolutionizer of the status of man, compared his discovery of the unconscious precisely to a Copernican revolution. As Lacan puts it:

It was in fact the so-called Copernican revolution to which Freud himself compared his discovery, emphasizing that it was once again a question of the place man assigns to himself at the centre of a universe. . . . It is not a question of knowing whether I speak of myself in a way that conforms to what I am, but rather of knowing whether I am the same person as the one I am speaking of. . . . Is the place that I occupy as the subject of a signifier concentric or ex-centric, in relation to the place I occupy as subject of the signified?—That is the question.[3]

For Lacan, this psychoanalytical Copernican revolution takes place as a rewriting of the Cartesian *cogito*. Instead of "I think, therefore I am," we have: "I think where I am not, therefore I am where I do not think. . . . I am not wherever I am the plaything of my thought; I think of what I am where I do not think to think" (166).

This mention of Descartes brings us back to the question of syntax, not only because Lacan has syntactically strung out the *cogito* but also because the modern theorist of the concept of syntax, Chomsky, is a self-proclaimed Cartesian. After contrasting the rationalist view of knowledge proposed by Descartes and Leibniz with the empiricist views proposed by Hume and the modern behaviorists, Chomsky writes of his own project: "A general linguistic theory of the sort described earlier . . . must . . . be regarded as a specific hypothesis, of an essentially rationalist cast, as to the nature of mental structures and processes."[4] But who is the syntaxer that will play Lacan to Chomsky's Descartes? Who is it that will revolutionize ratiocentric syntax?

The syntactical Copernicus we are seeking is, of course, none other than Mallarmé, who describes himself as "profondément et scrupuleusement syntaxier"[5] ("profoundly and scrupulously a syntaxer"), and whose *cogito* could be not "I think, therefore I am," but "I write, therefore I disappear." Mallarmé, although he is historically prior to Chomsky, does indeed displace the verb-centered structures of Chomskyan grammars, putting a definitive crick in the syntax of what was once known as "la clarté française." In Mallarmé's syntax, there is often no central verb, or no verb at all, or a series of seemingly subordinate verbs with no main one. The sentences that conform to "le génie de la langue" are either semantically ambiguous or skeletons draped with conflicting interruptions. Mallarmé's syntax is never confused; it is, as he says, profound and scrupulous, as decentered as possible without being cut loose from the gravitational pull of incompatible grammatical possibilities.

Thus we can say that Mallarmé is to Chomsky as Copernicus is to Ptolemy as Freud is to Descartes, in that the former in each case works out a strategically rigorous decentering of the structure described by the latter, not by abandoning that structure but by multiplying the forces at work in the field of which that structure is a part. It is not by chance that Lacan, who makes much of Freud's discovery as a Copernican revolution, should also stylistically be one of the most important of Mallarmé's syntactic descendants. No one indeed in twentieth-century French literature is more "profondément et scrupuleusement syntaxier" than Lacan.

The Syntax of Assertion

If you do know that *here is one hand*, we'll grant you all the rest.
—Ludwig Wittgenstein, *On Certainty*

In order to analyze further the implications of the Mallarméan revolution in syntax,[6] let us first consider two facets of Mallarmé's syntactic practices. While traditional syntax is what makes meaning decidable—what makes it impossible, for example, for "John kills Paul" to mean "Paul kills John"— Mallarmé's syntax, as has often been noted, is precisely what makes the meaning of his poetry undecidable. In giving equal legitimacy to two contradictory syntactic arrangements in the same assertion,[7] Mallarmé renders the very nature of assertion problematic.

In Mallarmé's critical prose, where his syntactical revolution is carried out with equal precision, a second type of problematization of the status of assertion is often manifest. To take just one example, consider the following remarks about "literary art":

> Son sortilège, à lui, si ce n'est libérer, hors d'une poignée de poussière ou réalité sans l'enclore, au livre, même comme texte, la dispersion volatile soit l'esprit, qui n'a que faire de rien outre la musicalité de tout. (645)

> [Its spellbinding power, if it is not the liberation, out of a handful of dust or reality without enclosing it, in the book, even as a text, of the volatile dispersal, that is, the mind—which has to do with nothing outside the musicality of all.]

In violation of one of the most fundamental rules of syntax, there is no main verb in this passage. Where we might expect "son sortilège est," we find "son sortilège, si ce n'est." The verb *to be* has become hypothetical, negative, and subordinate. The syntax of the description of the relations between literature and the world withdraws it from the possibility of affirmation. In other words, what at first looks like a statement that literature disperses rather than states is *itself* dispersed, not stated. Instead of affirming that literature does not state, Mallarmé's syntax *enacts* the very incapacity to state which it is incapable of stating.

It is not by chance that the verb *to be* should be the verb Mallarmé most often skips or conjugates otherwise. What Mallarmé's syntactical revolution amounts to is a decentering of the epistemological or ontological functioning of language. The syntax of polyvalent, decentered, or failed assertion reveals the unreliability of language as a conveyer of anything other than the functioning of its own structure, which is perhaps what Mallarmé is here calling "la musicalité de tout." This does not mean that language speaks only about itself, but that it is incapable of *saying* exactly what it is *doing*.

In the wake of Mallarmé, twentieth-century poetry has questioned the nature and possibility of assertion in a number of other ways. In surrealistic or automatic writing, effects of strangeness are often achieved by replacing normal semantic associations with bizarre incompatibilities within a syntax that remains relatively intact. "The Earth is blue like an orange," for example, can only achieve its flash of impossibility through the tranquil assertiveness of its structure. Another modern phenomenon, pictorial or concrete poetry, suspends the syntax of assertion by transferring the reader's attention from the content of the signified to the typographical syntax of the signifier. It is through these and other poetic procedures that modern poetry makes explicit the problematizations enacted in Mallarmé's syntax. But must an assertion be—syntactically or semantically—manhandled in order to be problematic? Is there not something intrinsically enigmatic about the act of asserting as such?

All discourses, including poetry, make assertions. Assertions create referential effects. To assert is to appear to know, even if it is a knowledge of doubt. It would seem that the structure of knowledge and the syntax of assertion are inseparable. But it also seems necessary to cling to the belief that it makes a difference which comes first; the ground of everything seems to shift if we consider knowledge as an effect of language instead of language as an effect of knowledge.

The Swiss psychologist Jean Piaget, whose views of the development of operational thought in many ways parallel Chomskyan linguistics, concludes on the basis of certain tests that syntax acquisition in children can only occur when cognitive development is ready for it. He writes that "language serves to translate what is already understood. . . . The level of understanding seems to modify the language used rather than vice versa."[8] While experimental science here seems to believe that syntax follows and translates prior understanding, I would like now to analyze how literature can be seen to say neither this nor the opposite, but to dramatize something quite different about the relations between syntax and knowledge. I shall turn to a poem by Apollinaire, "La Tzigane," in which obvious syntactic signals of the problematization of assertion are conspicuously absent:

La Tzigane

La tzigane savait d'avance
Nos deux vies barrées par les nuits
Nous lui dîmes adieu et puis
De ce puits sortit l'Espérance

L'amour lourd comme un ours privé
Dansa debout quand nous voulûmes
Et l'oiseau bleu perdit ses plumes
Et les mendiants leurs *Ave*

On sait bien que l'on se damne
Mais l'espoir d'aimer en chemin
Nous fait penser main dans la main
A ce qu'a prédit la tzigane[9]

[*The Gypsy*. The gypsy knew in advance / Our two lives crossed by nights / We told her farewell and then / Out of that well sprang hope // Love as heavy as a private bear / Danced upright whenever we wanted / And the blue bird lost its feathers / And the beggars their *Ave*'s // Everyone knows that we are damned / But the hope of loving along the way / Makes us think, hand in hand, / Of what the gypsy once foretold.]

The assertiveness of this poem is reinforced by the repetition of the verb *savoir* (to know): the poem begins with "La tzigane savait d'avance" and ends with "on sait bien." But what is the content of this knowledge? What is the poem affirming? In the first sentence—"La tzigane savait d'avance / Nos deux vies barrées par les nuits"—what the gypsy knew is not immediately intelligible. "Nos deux vies barrées par les nuits" could mean "our lives crisscrossed by nights of love," "our lives crossed out by darknesses," "our lives fettered by intimations of mortality," or "our lives ruined by our love." The prophecy would seem to be readable both positively and negatively, both as a prediction of love and as a prediction of loss. In the last stanza, the sentence "On sait bien que l'on se damne" reinforces the negative reading, yet in pivoting on a *mais*—"Mais l'espoir d'aimer en chemïn / Nous fait penser main dans la main / A ce qu'a prédit la tzigane"—the poem returns to the gypsy's prediction in *opposition* to damnation. What then did the gypsy actually know? The answer seems both indicated and refused by the ambiguous word *barrées*. *Barrer*, which means both "to mark" and "to block," has thus itself marked out and blocked our very attempt to interpret the poem. The word *barré*, in other words, is enacting its meaning in its very refusal to mean. It is as though Apollinaire had made our interpretation turn on a crossed-out word instead of a word meaning "crossed out."

But this effectively displaces the poem's center of gravity. Instead of re-counting the *content* of a prediction, the poem is recounting the *effects* of a prediction the content of which is never clear. The reader, like the consulters of the gypsy, is fooled into thinking he has been told something that can then turn out to be true or false. The syntax of affirmation causes him to forget that he has not really been told anything at all. If the gypsy's predic-tion is derived from a reading of the lines of the hand—which is also per-haps suggested by *barré*—then the final image of thinking of the gypsy while walking hand in hand, which casts the lines of the hand into total darkness, indicates that the message has become dark precisely because it has been embraced.

The fact of the gypsy's prediction, therefore, acts as the syntactical over-determination of an unintelligible meaning that produces the same effects as knowledge. Life, love, death, happiness, deprivation, and damnation here revolve around the *syntax* of knowledge, not around knowledge itself. The same assertiveness that preserves outmoded knowledge in Ptolemy's writing produces anticipatory knowledge not in the gypsy but in her readers. Here, reading is believing that something has been predicted, as the poem's third and fourth lines suggest:

Nous lui dîmes adieu et puis
De ce puits sortit l'Espérance.

It is out of the well (*puits*) of anticipation (*puis*) that the hope of under-standing arises. The juxtaposition of the homonyms *puits* and *puis* can be read as a figure for the relations between the syntactical and the seman-tic functions in the poem. The well is a traditional image for the locus of truth, for depth of meaning, while the linear, temporal seriality of syntax can be represented by the expression "and then." If the well of meaning is here bottomless, however, it is precisely because of its syntactical overde-termination: the *puits* of sense is both produced and emptied by the *puis* of syntax.

Thus, it is not the gypsy that knows in advance, but the syntax of assertion that is always in advance of knowledge. Knowledge is nothing other than an effect of syntax, not merely because any affirmation creates an illusion of knowledge, but precisely because syntax is what makes it possible for us to treat as *known* anything that we do not *know* we do not know. And this, in one form or another, is what poetry has always known.

NOTES

"Poetry and Syntax: What the Gypsy Knew." From *The Critical Difference: Essays in the Contemporary Rhetoric of Reading*, 3–12, 67–75. © 1980 The Johns Hopkins University Press. Reprinted with permission of The Johns Hopkins University Press.

1. Stéphane Mallarmé, *Oeuvres complètes* (Paris: Pléiade, 1945), 385. All translations from Mallarmé are my own.
2. ΜΑΘΗΜΑΤΙΚΗΣΥΝΤΑΞΙΣ.
3. Jacques Lacan, *Ecrits*, trans. Alan Sheridan (London: Tavistock, 1977), 165 (translation slightly modified).
4. Noam Chomsky, *Aspects of the Theory of Syntax* (Cambridge, MA: MIT Press, 1965), 53.
5. Letter to Maurice Guillemot, quoted by Jacques Scherer, *L'Expression littéraire dans l'oeuvre de Mallarmé* (Paris: Droz, 1947), 79.
6. See also Julia Kristeva, *La Révolution du langage poétique* (Paris: Seuil, 1974).
7. One example among hundreds: In his "Cantique de Saint Jean," Mallarmé uses the instant of decapitation in order to discuss the relation between head and body in terms of the opposition between up and down. The syntax of the poem is such that we are never able to determine whether the head is rising or falling. This indeterminacy is produced by numerous ambiguities. Depending, for example, on whether the word *que* in the phrase "qu'elle s'opiniâtre à suivre" introduces a subjunctive command or a relative clause, the poem is saying either "que la tête s'opiniâtre à suivre son pur regard là-haut" or "la tête refoule ou tranche les anciens désaccords avec le corps qu'elle s'opiniâtre à suivre." It is equally plausible, therefore, to see the head rising up after its *pur regard*, or falling down in reconciliation with the body. For a more detailed analysis of the effects of such ambiguities, see Barbara Johnson, "Poetry and Performative Language: Mallarmé and Austin," in *The Critical Difference: Essays in the Contemporary Rhetoric of Reading*, 52–65 (Baltimore: Johns Hopkins University Press, 1980).
8. Jean Piaget, quoted in Ruth Tremaine, *Syntax and Piagetian Operational Thought* (Washington, DC: Georgetown University Press, 1975), 7.
9. Guillaume Apollinaire, *Alcools* (Paris: Gallimard, 1920), 78. Translation is my own.

CHAPTER 4

A Hound, a Bay Horse, and a Turtle Dove
Obscurity in *Walden*

The experience of reading Thoreau's *Walden* is often a disconcerting one. The very discrepancy between the laconic, concrete chapter titles and the long, convoluted sentences of the text alerts the reader to a process of level-shifting that delights and baffles—indeed, that delights because it baffles. Consider, for example, the following passage:

> I sometimes despair of getting anything quite simple and honest done in this world by the help of men. They would have to be passed through a powerful press first, to squeeze their old notions out of them, so that they would not soon get upon their legs again; and then there would be some one in the company with a maggot in his head, hatched from an egg deposited there nobody knows when, for not even fire kills these things, and you would have lost your labor. Nevertheless, we will not forget that some Egyptian wheat was handed down to us by a mummy.[1]

It is difficult to read this passage without doing a double take. The logical seriousness of the style of "Nevertheless, we will not forget . . ." in no way prepares the reader for the sudden appearance of wheat in a mummy. The passage shifts with unruffled rapidity from abstract generalization to dead figure ("squeeze their old notions out of them") to a soon-to-reawaken figure hidden in a cliché ("maggot in the head") to mini-narrative ("deposited there nobody knows when") to folk wisdom ("Not even fire kills these things") to counterclaim ("Nevertheless, we will not forget . . ."). By the time one reaches the mummy, one no longer knows what the figure stands for, whether it, like the mummy, is dead or alive, or even where the boundaries of the analogy (if it *is* an analogy) lie.

It is paradoxical that a writer who constantly exhorts us to "Simplify, simplify" should also be the author of some of the most complex and difficult paragraphs in the English language. What is it about this seemingly simple account of life in the woods that so often bewilders the reader, making him, in Emerson's words, "nervous and wretched to read it"?

In an article entitled "*Walden*'s False Bottoms," Walter Benn Michaels amply demonstrates the book's capacity to engender nervousness as he details the long history of readers' attempts to cope with *Walden*'s obscurity, first by attributing it to Thoreau's alleged "want of continuity of mind" (James Russell Lowell), then by subsuming it under the larger patterns of *Walden*'s literary unity (Matthiessen, Anderson), then by considering it as a challenge to the reader's ability to read figuratively (Cavell, Buell). Michaels ends his own account of the undecidability of *Walden*'s contradictions by saying, "It's heads I win, tails you lose. No wonder the game makes us nervous."[2]

The passage through which I would like to gain access to one of the principal difficulties of *Walden*'s game is precisely a passage about losing. It is one of the most often-discussed passages in the book, a fact that is in itself interesting and instructive. The passage stands as an isolated paragraph, seemingly unrelated to what precedes or follows:

> I long ago lost a hound, a bay horse, and a turtle dove, and am still on their trail. Many are the travellers I have spoken concerning them, describing their tracks and what calls they answered to. I have met one or two who had heard the hound, and the tramp of the horse, and even seen the dove disappear behind a cloud, and they seemed as anxious to recover them as if they had lost them themselves. (16)

It should come as no surprise that the hound, the bay horse, and the turtle dove are almost universally seen as symbols by Thoreau's readers. The questions asked of this passage are generally, What do the three animals symbolize? and Where did the symbols come from? The answers to these questions are many and varied: for T. M. Raysor, the animals represent the "gentle boy" Edmund Sewall, Thoreau's dead brother John, and the woman to whom he unsuccessfully proposed marriage, Ellen Sewall; for Francis H. Allen, the symbols represent "the vague desires and aspirations of man's spiritual nature"; for John Burroughs, they stand for the "fine effluence" that for Thoreau constitutes "the ultimate expression of fruit of any created thing." Others have seen in the symbols "a mythical record of [Thoreau's] disappointments" (Emerson), a "quest . . . for an absolutely satisfactory condition of friendship" (Mark Van Doren), the "wildness that keeps man in touch with nature, intellectual stimulus, and purification of spirit" (Frank Davidson), and a "lost Eden" (Alfred Kazin). Sources for Thoreau's symbols are said to be found in such diverse texts as Voltaire's *Zadig* (Edith Peairs), the "Chinese Four Books" that Thoreau edited for *The Dial*, an old English ballad, an Irish folk tale, and a poem by Emerson.[3]

The sense shared by all readers that the hound, the bay horse, and the turtle dove *are* symbols, but that what they symbolize is unclear, is made explicit in the following remarks by Stanley Cavell:

> I have no new proposal to offer about the literary or biographical sources of those symbols. But the very obviousness of the fact that they are symbols, and function within a little myth, seems to me to tell us what we need to know. The writer comes to us from a sense of loss; the myth does not contain more than symbols because it is no set of desired things he has lost, but a connection with things, the track of desire itself.[4]

The notion that what is at stake here is not any set of lost *things* but rather the very fact of *loss* seems to find confirmation in the replies that Thoreau himself gave on two different occasions to the question of the passage's meaning. In a letter to B. B. Wiley, dated April 26, 1857, he writes:

> How shall we account for our pursuits if they are original? We get the language with which to describe our various lives out of a common mint. If others have their losses, which they are busy repairing, so have I *mine*, & their hound & horse may *perhaps* be the symbols of some of them. But also I have lost, or am in danger of losing, a far finer & more etherial treasure, which commonly no loss of which they are conscious will symbolize—this I answer hastily & with some hesitation, according as I now understand my own words. (*Annotated Walden*, 157–58)

And on another occasion, as the *Variorum* tells it:

> Miss Ellen Watson, in "Thoreau Visits Plymouth" . . . , reports that when Thoreau visited Plymouth, Mass., a year or two after the publication of *Walden*, he met there "Uncle Ed" Watson who asked him what he meant when he said he lost "a hound, a horse, and a dove." Thoreau replied,

"Well, Sir, I suppose we have all our losses." "That's a pretty way to answer a fellow," replied Uncle Ed. (270)

Most readers have shared Uncle Ed's disappointment at this answer that seems no answer at all. The editors of the *Annotated* and *Variorum Waldens* both conclude their surveys of the literature on the subject in a similar way:

> In conclusion, however, it should be pointed out that there is no unanimity on interpretation of these symbols and the individual critic is left free to interpret as he wishes. (*Variorum*, 272)

> Since there is no clear explanation, each reader will have to supply his own. (*Annotated Walden*, 158)

In attempting to fill these enigmatic symbols with interpretive content, most readers have assumed that the hound, the bay horse, and the turtle dove were figurative containers or concrete vehicles into which some deeper, higher, or more abstract meanings could be made to fit. This is what the business of interpreting symbols is all about. In cases like the present, where there exists no unanimity or clarity about the symbols' meanings, readers tend to believe *not* that there is something inadequate about the way they are asking the question, but that each individual becomes "free" to settle on an answer for himself.

Before going back to attempt a different type of analysis of this passage, I would like first to quote in its entirety the paragraph that immediately precedes the hound-horse-dove passage in the text:

> In any weather, at any hour of the day or night, I have been anxious to improve the nick of time, and notch it on my stick too; to stand on the meeting of two eternities, the past and the future, which is precisely the present moment; to toe that line. You will pardon some obscurities, for there are more secrets in my trade than in most men's, and yet not voluntarily kept, but inseparable from its very nature. I would gladly tell all that I know about it, and never paint "No Admittance" on my gate.
>
> I long ago lost a hound, a bay horse, and a turtle dove, and am still on their trail. Many are the travellers I have spoken concerning them, describing their tracks and what calls they answered to. I have met one or two who had heard the hound, and the tramp of the horse, and even seen the dove disappear behind a cloud, and they seemed as anxious to recover them as if they had lost them themselves. (16)

There appears at first sight to be no relation between these two paragraphs. Yet the very abruptness of the transition, the very discrepancy of rhetorical modes, may perhaps indicate that the first paragraph consists of a set of instructions about how to read the second. It is surely no accident that one of the most enigmatic passages in *Walden* should be placed immediately after the sentence "You will pardon some obscurities." If the secret identities of the hound, the horse, and the dove are never to be revealed, it is not, says Thoreau, that they are being *voluntarily* withheld. Such secrets are simply inseparable from the nature of my trade—that is, writing. "I would gladly tell all that I know about it, and never paint 'No Admittance' on my gate." But all I *know* about it is not all there *is* about it. You are not being forcibly or gently kept away from a knowledge I possess. The gate is wide open, and that is why the path is so obscure. The sign "obscurity" is pointing directly at the symbols, making the sentence read, "I long ago lost an X, a Y, and a Z," and you are supposed to recognize them not as obscure symbols but as symbols standing for the obscure, the lost, the irretrievable.

But yet, we insist, your x, y, and z are so *particular*—so hound-like, so horselike, so birdlike. If they merely symbolize the lost object as such, why do we hear the baying of the hound and the tramp of the horse? Why do those fellow travellers give us such precise reports?

Ah, but you see, Thoreau might answer, the symbols *are* symbols, after all. What is lost is always intensely particular. Yet it is known only in that it is lost—lost in one of the two eternities between which we clumsily try to toe the line.

To follow the trail of what is lost is possible only, it seems, if the loss is maintained in a state of transference from traveler to traveler, so that each takes up the pursuit as if the loss were his own. Loss, then, ultimately belongs to an other; the losses we treat as our own are perhaps losses of which we never had conscious knowledge ourselves. "If others have their losses, which they are busy repairing, so have I *mine*, & their hound & horse may *perhaps* be the symbols of some of them. But also I have lost, or am in danger of losing, a far finer & more etherial treasure, which commonly no loss *of which they are conscious* will symbolize."

Walden's great achievement is to wake us up to our own lost losses, to make us participate in the transindividual movement of loss in its infinite particularity, urging us passionately to follow the tracks of we know not quite what, as if we had lost it, or were in danger of losing it, ourselves.

In order to communicate the irreducibly particular yet ultimately unreadable nature of loss, Thoreau has chosen to use three symbols that clearly *are* symbols but that do not really symbolize anything outside themselves. They are figures for which no literal, proper term can be substituted. They are, in other words, catachreses—"figures of abuse," figurative substitutes for a literal term that does not exist. Like the "legs" and "arms" of our favorite recliner, Thoreau's hound, horse, and dove belong to a world of homely figurative richness, yet the impersonal literality they seem to presuppose is nowhere to be found. The structure of catachretic symbolism is thus the very structure of transference and loss. Through it Thoreau makes us see that every lost object is always, in a sense, a catachresis, a figurative substitute for nothing that ever could be literal.

It could be said that Nature itself is for Thoreau a catachretic symbol that enables him to displace his discourse without filling in its symbolic tenor. But in order to analyze a more particular aspect of the way in which Thoreau's catachretic rhetoric creates obscurity in *Walden*, let us first look at a more traditional and semantically "full" use of nature imagery: the *analogies* drawn between natural objects and human predicaments.

I begin with a somewhat atypically explicit analogy:

One day . . . I saw a striped snake run into the water, and he lay on the bottom, apparently without inconvenience, as long as I staid there, or more than a quarter of an hour; perhaps because he had not yet fairly come out of the torpid state. It appears to me that for a like reason men remain in their present low and primitive condition; but if they should feel the influence of the spring of springs arousing them, they would of necessity rise to a higher and more ethereal life. (33)

No rhetorical strategy could be more classical than this weaving of analogy between the natural and the human worlds. It is the mark of the moralist, the evangelist, the satirist, and the lyric poet, all of which Thoreau indeed is. From the New Testament to Aesop and Swedenborg, the natural world has been a source of figures of the preoccupations and foibles of man. As Emerson puts it in his own essay on Nature:

The memorable words of history and the proverbs of nations consist usually of a natural fact, selected as a picture or parable of a moral truth. Thus; A rolling stone gathers no moss; A bird in hand is worth two in the bush; A cripple in the right way will beat a racer in the wrong; Make hay while the sun shines; 'Tis hard to carry a full cup even; Vinegar is the son of wine; The last ounce broke the camel's back; Long-lived trees make roots first;—and the like. In their primary sense these are trivial facts, but we repeat them for the value of their analogical import. What is true of proverbs, is true of all fables, parables, and allegories.[5]

Yet although Thoreau draws on many centuries of analogical writing, there is a subtle difference in his rhetorical use of nature, and it is the specificity of that difference that I would like to attempt to identify in conclusion. The difference begins to become perceptible in the following examples:

> Why has man rooted himself thus firmly in the earth, but that he may rise in the same proportion into the heavens above?—for the nobler plants are valued for the fruit they bear at last in the air and light, far from the ground, and are not treated like the humbler esculents, which, though they may be biennials, are cultivated only till they have perfected their root, and often cut down at top for this purpose, so that most would not know them in their flowering season. (5)

> We don garment after garment, as if we grew like exogenous plants by addition without. Our outside and often thin and fanciful clothes are our epidermis or false skin, which partakes not of our life, and may be stripped off here and there without fatal injury; our thicker garments, constantly worn, are our cellular integument, or cortex; but our shirts are our liber or true bark, which cannot be removed without girdling and so destroying the man. (21)

In both these examples, what begins as a fairly routine analogy tends, in the course of its elaboration, to get wildly out of hand. The fascination with the vehicle as an object of attention in its own right totally eclipses the original anthropomorphic tenor. Words like *esculents*, *biennials*, *cortex*, and *liber* pull away from their subordinate, figurative status and begin giving information about themselves, sidetracking the reader away from the original thrust of the analogy. In the first example, what begins as an opposition between nobler and humbler men and plants collapses as it is revealed that the humbler plants are humble only because they are never *allowed* to flower. In the second example, the hierarchy of integuments ends by privileging not the skin but the shirt as that part of a man that cannot be removed without destroying him. In an effort to show that man is confused about where his inside ends and his outside begins, Thoreau resorts to a logic of tree growth which entirely takes over as the exogenous striptease procedes.

It is perhaps in the "Bean-field" chapter that the rhetorical rivalries between the literal and the figurative, the tenor and the vehicle, become most explicit. On the one hand, Thoreau writes, "I was determined to know beans," and goes on to detail the hours of hoeing and harvesting, listing the names of weeds and predators, and accounting for outgo and income down to the last half penny. And on the other, he admits that "some must work in fields if only for the sake of tropes and expression, to serve a parable-maker one day." He speaks of sowing the seeds of sincerity, truth, simplicity, faith, and innocence, asking, "Why concern ourselves so much about our beans for seed, and not be concerned at all about a new generation of men?"

The perverse complexity of *Walden*'s rhetoric is intimately related to the fact that it is never possible to be sure what the rhetorical status of any given image is. And this is because what Thoreau has done in moving to Walden Pond is to move *himself*, literally, into the world of his own figurative language. The literal woods, pond, and bean field still assume the same classical rhetorical guises in which they have always appeared, but they are suddenly readable in addition as the nonfigurative ground of a naturalist's account of life in the woods. The ground has shifted, but the figures are still figures. When is it that we decide that Thoreau never lost that hound, that horse, and that dove? It is because we can never be absolutely sure that we find ourselves forever on their trail.

Walden is obscure, therefore, to the extent that Thoreau has *literally* crossed over into the very parable he is writing, where *reality itself* has become a catachresis, both ground and figure at once, and where, he tells us, "if you stand right fronting and face to face with a fact, you will see the sun glimmer on both its surfaces, as if it were a cimeter, and feel its sweet edge dividing you through the heart and marrow."

NOTES

"A Hound, a Bay Horse, and a Turtle Dove: Obscurity in *Walden*." From *A World of Difference*, 49–56. © 1987 The Johns Hopkins University Press. Reprinted with permission of The Johns Hopkins University Press.

1. Henry David Thoreau, *Walden; or, Life in the Woods* (New York: Signet, 1960), 22. All page references to *Walden* are to this edition.
2. Walter Benn Michaels, "*Walden*'s False Bottoms," *Glyph: Johns Hopkins Textual Studies* 1 (1977): 132–49.
3. For detailed bibliographical information on these and other readings of the passage, see *The Annotated Walden*, ed. Philip Van Doren Stern (New York: Clarkson N. Potter, 1970), 157–58, and *The Variorum Walden*, ed. Walter Harding (New York: Twayne, 1962), 270–72.
4. Stanley Cavell, *The Senses of Walden* (San Francisco: North Point, 1981), 51.
5. Ralph Waldo Emerson, *Selected Prose and Poetry* (New York: Holt, Rinehart, and Winston, 1964), 20.

CHAPTER 5

Strange Fits

Poe and Wordsworth on the Nature of
Poetic Language

No two discussions of poetry could at first sight appear more different than Wordsworth's "Preface to the *Lyrical Ballads*" and Poe's "Philosophy of Composition."[1] The first has been read as an important Romantic manifesto, sometimes inconsistent, sometimes dated, but always to be taken seriously. The second has been read as a theoretical spoof which, because it cannot be taken at face value, cannot be taken seriously at all. Both, however, can be read as complex texts in their own right—as texts whose very complexities tell us a great deal about the nature of poetic language. I would like to suggest here some directions for such a reading, first by examining the rhetorical slipperiness of each theoretical text, then by invoking for each a poem—Wordsworth's "Strange Fits of Passion" and Poe's "The Raven"—that both exemplifies and undermines the neatness of the explicit theory.

Despite their differences, Poe and Wordsworth do in fact agree on one thing, that the object of poetry is to produce pleasure:

Wordsworth: The first Volume of these Poems has already been submitted to general perusal. It was published, as an experiment, which, I hoped, might be of some use to ascertain, how far, by fitting to metrical arrangement a selection of the real language of men in a state of vivid sensation, that sort of pleasure and that quantity of pleasure may be imparted, which a Poet may rationally endeavor to impart. (69)

Poe: Beauty is the sole legitimate province of the poem. . . . That pleasure which is at once the most intense, the most elevating, and the most pure, is, I believe, found in the contemplation of the beautiful. (1082)

The nature of the pleasure in question, however, is, in both cases, pushed to the edge of trauma: dead women, mad mothers, idiot boys, lugubrious birds—the poems are populated with images that are clearly situated beyond any simple notion of a pleasure principle. Poe indeed goes so far as to make his poem aim for the utmost "luxury of sorrow" to be obtained by "the human thirst for self-torture" (1088). What is at stake in both cases would seem to have something to do with the beyond of pleasure, which for Freud was associated with two highly problematic and highly interesting notions: the repetition compulsion and the death instinct. Questions of repetition and death will indeed be central to our discussion both of Wordsworth and of Poe.

I will begin by outlining, somewhat reductively, the broadest possible differences between the two theoretical texts. Many of the differences are, of course, historical, and can be derived from the type of fashionable poetry each poet is writing *against*. Poe designs his poetics in opposition to the American tradition of long, sentimental, or didactic poetry associated with such figures as Longfellow or Bryant. Wordsworth is writing against the eighteenth-century British tradition of witty, polished, mock-heroic or rhetorically ornate verse associated with such names as Johnson, Pope, and Gray. But the poetic boundary lines each poet attempts to draw are perhaps of broader applicability, and their attempts can be read as exemplary versions of tensions inherent in the modern Western poetic project as such.

What, then, are the salient differences between these two theories of poetic language? In a well-known passage from the Preface, Wordsworth states that "Poetry is the spontaneous overflow of powerful feelings: it takes its origin from emotion recollected in tranquillity" (85). Poe, on the other hand, writes of his method of composing "The Raven" that it was written backwards, beginning with a consideration of the desired *effect*. "It is my design to render it manifest that no one point in its composition is referrible either to accident or intuition—that the work proceeded, step by step, to its completion with the precise and rigid consequence of a mathematical problem" (1081). Poe's poetic calculus leads him to choose an optimal length of about one hundred lines; then, after consideration of the desired effect and tone (beauty and sadness), he decides that the poem should be structured around a refrain ending in the most sonorous of letters, *o* and *r*. The syllable *-or* is thus the first element of the text of the poem to be written. "The sound of the refrain being thus determined," Poe goes on, "it became necessary to select a word embodying this sound, and at the same time in the fullest possible keeping with that melancholy which I had predetermined as the tone of the poem. In such a search it would have been absolutely impossible to overlook the word 'Nevermore.' In fact it was the very first which presented itself" (1083–84).

Spontaneous overflow versus calculation, emotion versus rigid consequence, feelings versus letters of the alphabet: a first comparison would lead us to see Wordsworth's poetry as granting primacy to the *signified* while Poe's grants primacy to the *signifier*. This distinction is borne out by the fact that while Wordsworth claims that the language of poetry should be indistinguishable from that of good prose, Poe aims to maximize the difference between prose and poetry, excluding for that reason the long poem from the canon of true poetry. But neither text presents its case as simply as it might appear.

For all his emphasis on emotion, Wordsworth is of course acutely conscious of the centrality of form to the poetic project. He describes the use of verse as a kind of contract made between form and expectation. Form itself constitutes a promise which Wordsworth then claims to have broken:

> It is supposed, that by the act of writing in verse an Author makes a formal engagement that he will gratify certain known habits of association; that he not only apprizes the Reader that certain classes of ideas and expressions will be found in his book, but that others will be carefully excluded. I will not take upon me to determine the exact import of the promise which by the act of writing in verse an Author, in the present day, makes to his reader; but I am certain, it will appear to many persons that I have not fulfilled the terms of an engagement thus voluntarily contracted. (70)

Verse, then, is a contract made by form, a formal promise to include and to exclude certain classes of ideas. Wordsworth's violation of that contract comprises both inclusions and exclusions. He warns the reader that these shifts in boundary lines may produce "feelings of strangeness and awkwardness." Feelings of strangeness are, of course, often the subjects of the poems, as is the case with the poem to which we will later turn, "Strange Fits of Passion." That poem may well tell us something about the nature of strangeness of Wordsworth's poetics, but strangeness is not the only metapoetic expression glossed by the poem. For Wordsworth's first description of his experiment, in the opening paragraph of the Preface, speaks of the poems as "*fitting* to metrical arrangement a selection of the real language of men in a state of vivid sensation." The word *fit*, which occurs several times in the Preface,[2] thus in the poem takes on the double meaning of both uncontrolled overflow and formal containment. Interestingly, the word *fytt* is also a term for a medieval stanza form. As I will try to show, Wordsworth's entire Preface can be read as an attempt to fit all the senses of the word *fit* together.

What does Wordsworth mean by "the real language of men"? In the 1798 "Advertisement to the *Lyrical Ballads*," Wordsworth had spoken of "the language of conversation in the middle and lower classes of society." These, then, are the "classes of ideas" that poetry had previously excluded. But Wordsworth includes them only to again exclude them; the substitution of the expression "the real language of men" for "the conversation of the middle and lower classes" acts out an erasure of "class," a gesture of dehistoricization and universalization. Poetic inclusions and exclusions clearly operate on more than one level at a time. Others are more qualified than I am to comment on Wordsworth's tendency to pastoralize away the historical reality of the rural along with the urban and the industrial, grounding "*human nature*" instead in a state of congruence with "the beautiful and permanent forms" of *external* Nature. Let it suffice here to suggest that, in the discussion that follows, the complex fate of the word *mechanical* may not be unconnected to a set of attitudes toward the Industrial Revolution.

There is one type of exclusion about which Wordsworth's preface is very clear—or at least it tries to be. The crucial exclusion for Wordsworth would seem to be the exclusion of personification.

> The reader will find that personifications of abstract ideas rarely occur in these volumes; and, I hope, are utterly rejected as an ordinary device to elevate the style, and raise it above prose. I have proposed to myself to imitate, and, as far as possible, to adopt the very language of men; and assuredly such personifications do not make any natural or regular part of that language. They are, indeed, a figure of speech occasionally prompted by passion, and I have made use of them as such; but I have endeavored utterly to reject them as a mechanical device of style. (74)

The operative opposition here is the opposition between the "natural" and the "mechanical." Personifications, says Wordsworth, are not "natural," but rather "a mechanical device of style." But already there is an exception: they are sometimes naturally prompted by passion. If poetry is located at a point of vivid sensation, if it is defined as always being in some sense a strange fit of passion, then where does Wordsworth draw the line? Are personifications natural or mechanical? How natural is the natural language of passion?

Let us look further at Wordsworth's attempts to distinguish between the natural and the mechanical. Since his whole sense of value and originality seems to depend on his making that distinction clear, we would expect him to clarify it in the essay. One of the ways in which Wordsworth works the distinction over is by telling it as a story. He tells it twice, once as a story of degradation, and once as a story of recollection. The first is a history of abuse; the second, a history of recovery. What we will do is look closely at the rhetorical terms in which the two stories are told. They are both, of course, stories *of* rhetoric, but what we will analyze will be the rhetoric of the stories.

First, from the "Appendix on Poetic Diction," the history of abuse:

> The earliest Poets of all nations generally wrote from passion excited by real events; they wrote *naturally*, and as men: feeling powerfully as they did, their language was daring, and figurative. In succeeding times, Poets, and men ambitious of the fame of Poets, perceiving the influence of such language, and desirous of producing the same effect, without having the same animating passion, set themselves to a *mechanical* adoption of those figures of speech, and made use of them, sometimes with propriety, but much more frequently applied them to feelings and ideas with which they had *no natural connection* whatsoever. A language was thus insensibly produced, differing materially from the real language of men in *any situation* [original emphasis]. The Reader or Hearer of this *distorted language* found himself in a perturbed and unusual state of mind: when affected by the genuine language of passion he had been in a perturbed and unusual state of mind also: in both cases he was willing that his common judgment and understanding should be laid asleep, and he had no instinctive and infallible perception of the true to make him reject the false. . . . This *distorted language* was received with admiration; and Poets, it is probable, who had before contented themselves for the most part with *misapplying* only expressions which at first had been dictated by real passion, *carried the abuse still further*, and introduced phrases composed apparently in the spirit of the original figurative language of passion, yet altogether of their own invention, and distinguished by various degrees of *wanton deviation* from good sense and *nature*. . . . In process of time metre became a symbol or promise of this unusual language, and whoever took upon

him to write in metre, according as he possessed more or less of true poetic genius, introduced less or more of this *adulterated phraseology* into his compositions, and the true and false became so inseparably interwoven that the taste of men was gradually *perverted;* and this language was received as a *natural* language; and at length, by the influence of books upon men, did to a certain degree really become so. (90–91; emphasis mine unless otherwise indicated)

In this history of abuse, the natural and the mechanical, the true and the false, become utterly indistinguishable. It becomes all the more necessary—but all the more difficult—to restore the boundary line. Each time Wordsworth attempts to do so, however, the distinction breaks down. The natural becomes unnatural, life imitates art, and mechanical inventions are mistaken for the natural language of passion.

Wordsworth's other developmental narrative is one that leads not to degradation but to amelioration. This time the story takes place in a temporality of the self, the temporality expressed by the juxtaposition of the two clauses: "Poetry is the spontaneous overflow of powerful feelings," and "it takes its origin from emotion recollected in tranquillity." For Wordsworth, in other words, the poet is a man who attempts to write in obedience to the classic example of the double bind: "be spontaneous." In an early paragraph in the Preface, Wordsworth makes the double bind into a developmental narrative, in which the acrobatics of grammar—the sustained avoidance of any grammatical break—mimes the desire for seamless continuity. If the whole story can be told in one breath, Wordsworth implies, then nothing will be lost, the recuperation of the spontaneous will be complete.

For all good poetry is the spontaneous overflow of powerful feelings: but though this be true, Poems to which any value can be attached, were never produced on any variety of subjects but by a man, who being possessed of more than usual organic sensibility, had also thought long and deeply. For our continued influxes of feeling are modified and directed by our thoughts, which are indeed the representatives of all our past feelings; and, as by contemplating the relation of these general representatives to each other we discover what is really important to men, so, by the repetition and continuance of this act, our feelings will be connected with important subjects, till at length, if we be originally possessed of much sensibility, such habits of mind will be produced, that, by obeying blindly and mechanically the impulses of those habits, we shall describe objects, and utter sentiments, of such a nature and in such connection with each other, that the understanding of the being to whom we address ourselves, if he be in a healthful state of association, must necessarily be in some degree enlightened, and his affections ameliorated. (72)

The astonishing thing about this story is that it uses the word *mechanical*—which has been the name of a negative value everywhere else in the Preface—as the height of poeticity. "Obeying blindly and mechanically the impulses of habits" was exactly what produced abuse and corruption in the other story, but here it produces health, enlightenment, and amelioration. What can be said about the relation between the two stories?

Both stories are designed to define and judge the relation between an original moment of feeling and utterance and its later repetition. Wordsworth's task is to distinguish between good repetition and degraded, hollow repetition. In describing his own creative process, he speaks of the art of developing habits that will lead to a "blind, mechanical" reproduction of the original emotion. In describing the poetic degradations he wants to condemn, he again speaks of a "mechanical" adoption of figures of speech. For Wordsworth's theory to stand, it is urgent for him to be able to distinguish between good and bad repetition. Yet the good and the bad are narrated in almost the same terms. Wordsworth again and again repeats the story of repetition, but is never able to draw a reliable dividing line. He can *affirm* good repetition, but he can't tell a story that will sufficiently distinguish it from bad. What Wordsworth's essay shows is that talking about poetry involves one in an urgent and impossible search for that distinction, for a recipe for reliable blindness. This is not an inability to get it right, but rather the acting out of an insight into the nature of poetry and the poetic process. For what, indeed, is the problem in any modern theory of poetic language, if not the problem of articulating authenticity with conventionality, originality and continuity, freshness with what is recognizably "fit" to be called poetic?

While Wordsworth is thus attempting to instate the naturalness of "genuine" repetition, Poe would seem to be doing just the opposite: mechanical repetition is clearly in some sense what "The Raven" is all about. In turning to Poe, we can therefore expect some sort of inversely symmetrical plea for the poeticity of the mechanical, the empty, and the hollow. It is as though a talking bird were the perfect figure for the poetic parroting of personification that Wordsworth would like to leave behind. But before moving on to Poe, let us look at Wordsworth's "Strange Fits of Passion" as another inscription of the theories expounded by the Preface.

It has already become clear in our discussion that the phrase "Strange Fit of passion" can be read in at least two ways as a summary of Wordsworth's poetic project: poetry is a fit, an outburst, an overflow, of feeling;[3] and poetry is an attempt to fit, to arrange, feeling into form. The poem would seem to be about an example of an experience fit to be made into poetry:

Strange fits of passion have I known:
And I will dare to tell,
But in the Lover's ear alone,
What once to me befell.

When she I loved looked every day
Fresh as a rose in June,
I to her cottage bent my way,
Beneath an evening-moon.

Upon the moon I fixed my eye,
All over the wide lea;
With quickening pace my horse drew nigh
Those paths so dear to me.

And now we reached the orchard-plot;
And, as we climbed the hill,
The sinking moon to Lucy's cot
Came near, and nearer still.

In one of those sweet dreams I slept,
Kind Nature's gentlest boon!
And all the while my eyes I kept
On the descending moon.

My horse moved on; hoof after hoof
He raised, and never stopped:
When down behind the cottage roof,
At once, the bright moon dropped.

What fond and wayward thoughts will slide
Into a lover's head!
"O mercy!" to myself I cried,
"If Lucy should be dead!"

The lover's alarm at his wayward thought indicates that he does not know what put it into his head, that he sees no connection between that thought and any part of his waking or dreaming life. The obvious connection the poem invites us to make is between the moon dropping and Lucy dying. But in the poem, that connection is elided, replaced by a mere discontinuity. That connection can in fact be made only in a world that admits the possibility of personification. The moon must be seeable as a correlative, a personification of Lucy.[4] And the hiatus marks the spot where that possibility is denied. The strange fit depicted in the poem can in some sense be read, therefore, as the revenge of personification, the return of a poetic principle that Wordsworth had attempted to exclude. The strangeness of the passion arises from the poem's uncanny encounter with what the theory that produced it had repressed.[5] Indeed, this is perhaps why the *Lyrical Ballads* are so full of ghosts and haunting presences. It is as though poetry could not do without the figures of half-aliveness that the use of personification provides. Or perhaps it is the other way around: that personification gives us conventionalized access to the boundary between life and death which Wordsworth, by repressing explicit personification, uncovers in a more disquieting way.[6]

It is doubtless no accident that a by-product of this fit is the death of a woman. In speaking to the lover's ear alone, Wordsworth is profoundly, as he says in the Preface, "a man speaking to men." Even when Wordsworth speaks of or as a woman, the woman tends to be abused, mad, or dead. If Wordsworth's aim in these poems is to undo the abuse of dead poetic figures and recover a more natural language, he seems to have transferred the abuse from personifications to persons.

Poe makes the connection between poetry and dead women even more explicit when he writes, "The death of a beautiful woman is, unquestionably, the most poetic topic in the world—and equally is it beyond doubt that the lips best suited for such topic are those of a bereaved lover" (1084). The work of poetry may well be the work of mourning, or of murder—the mourning and murder necessitated by language's hovering on the threshold between life and death, between pleasure and its beyond, between restorative and abusive repetition. But why, in Poe's case, does the male mourner require a talking bird to make his grief into a poem?

The raven, as Poe explains it in "The Philosophy of Composition," is chosen as a plausible vehicle for the repetition of the refrain—the word *nevermore*. The bird is thus a figure for mechanical poetic repetition. The purveyor of the burden has to be a bird: the intentional relation to a signified is denied through the nonhuman repetition of a pure signifier. The word *nevermore*, offered here as the most poetical of words, in fact crops up uncannily in Wordsworth's essay too as a distinguishing poetic mark. In differentiating between admirable and contemptible uses of "real language," Wordsworth juxtaposes two short stanzas, one by Dr. Johnson, the other from "Babes in the Wood." Johnson's contemptible stanza goes:

> I put my hat upon my head,
> And walked into the Strand,
> And there I met another man
> Whose hat was in his hand.

The admirable stanza reads:

> These pretty Babes with hand in hand
> Went wandering up and down;
> But never more they saw the Man
> Approaching from the Town.

It is hard to see what Wordsworth considers the key distinction between the two if it is *not* the expression "never more." In choosing to have the raven repeat the single word *nevermore*, Poe may well have put his finger on something fundamental about the poetic function as a correlative, precisely, of loss.

If the word *nevermore* stands in Poe as a figure for poetic language as such, a number of theoretical implications can be drawn. Since the bird is not human, the word is proffered as a pure signifier, empty of human intentionality, a pure poetic cliché. The empty repetition of the word therefore dramatizes the theoretical priority of the signifier over the signified which Poe claimed when he said that he began the text of the poem with the letters *o* and *r*. The plot of "The Raven" can be read as the story of what happens when the signifier encounters a reader. For the narrator of the poem first introduces himself as a reader, not a lover—a reader of "quaint and curious forgotten lore." Poe's claim, in "The Philosophy of Composition," that the poem was written backwards (commencing with its *effect*) applies both to the poem and to the essay about it: both are depictions not of the writing but of the *reading* of "The Raven."

The poem's status as mechanical repetition is signified in another way as well. It would be hard to find a poem (except perhaps "Strange Fits of Passion") which is packed with more clichés than "The Raven": ember, remember, December, midnight, darkness, marble busts—all the bric-a-brac of poetic language is set out in jangling, alliterative trochees to hammer out a kind of ur-background of the gothic encounter. And the conversation begins in pure politeness: "Tell me what thy lordly name is," asks the speaker of the bird, and the bird says, "Nevermore."

The poem within the poem—the single word *nevermore*—has at this point finally been spoken and the reader sets out to interpret it. He begins by finding it obscure:

> Much I marveled this ungainly fowl to hear discourse so plainly,
> Though its answer little meaning—little relevancy bore.

Then he tries a little biographical criticism:

> "Doubtless," said I, "what it utters is its only stock and store
> Caught from some unhappy master whom unmerciful Disaster
> Followed fast and followed faster. . . .

Sinking onto a velvet couch, the reader then turns to free association—"linking fancy unto fancy"—until the air grows denser and the reader sees the bird as a messenger of forgetfulness (psychoanalytic criticism), to which the Raven's "nevermore" comes as a contradiction. It is at this point that the reader begins to ask questions to which the expected "nevermore" comes as a ferociously desired and feared answer. The reader cannot leave the signifier alone. Reader-response criticism has set in. In this way, he writes his *own* story around the signifier, letting it seal the letter of his fate until, finally, it utterly incorporates him:

> And my soul from out that shadow that lies floating on the floor
> Shall be lifted—nevermore.

Sense has been made through the absorption of the subject by the signifier. The poem has sealed, without healing, the trauma of loss. What began as a signifier empty of subjectivity has become a container for the whole of the reader's soul. A poetry of the pure signifier is just as impossible to maintain as a poetry of the pure signified. Repetition engenders its own compulsion-to-sense. Poetry works *because* the signifier cannot remain empty—because, not in spite, of the mechanical nature of its artifice.

Paradoxically, then, Poe is writing a highly artificial poem that describes the signifier as an artifice that somehow captures the genuine. Yet generations of American readers have responded to it backwards: rejecting it for the artifice its own genuineness is demystifying. It cannot communicate its insight about how poems work if it does not work as a poem. Yet if the poem worked better, it would not carry the insight it carries.

Wordsworth and Poe are thus telling symmetrically inverse stories about the nature of poetic language. Wordsworth attempts to prevent the poetic figure from losing its natural passion, from repeating itself as an empty, mechanical device of style. But the formula for recollection in tranquillity involves just such a blind, mechanical repetition of the lost language. Poe writes a poem packed with clichés in order to show that those clichés cannot succeed in remaining empty, that there is also a natural passion involved in repetition, that the mechanical is of a piece with the profoundest pain. Yet the poem's very success in embodying its message entails its failure to make it true. If it were possible to differentiate clearly between the mechanical and the passionate, between the empty and the full, between the fit and the fit, between "real" language and "adulterated phraseology," there would probably be no need for extensive treatises on the nature of poetic language. But there would also, no doubt, be no need for poetry.

NOTES

"Strange Fits: Poe and Wordsworth on the Nature of Poetic Language." From *A World of Difference*, 89–99. © 1987 The Johns Hopkins University Press. Reprinted with permission of The Johns Hopkins University Press.

1. I shall refer to the 1805 version of the Preface, as printed in *Wordsworth's Literary Criticism*, ed. W. J. B. Owen (London: Routledge and Kegan Paul, 1974). The "Philosophy of Composition" appears in *The Unabridged Edgar Allan Poe* (Philadelphia: Running Press, 1983).

2. For example, "I hope that there is in these Poems little falsehood of description, and that my ideas are expressed in language *fitted* to their respective importance" (75); "If the Poet's subject be judiciously chosen, it will naturally, and upon *fit* occasion, lead him to passions the language of which, if selected truly and judiciously, must necessarily be dignified and variegated, and live with metaphors and figures" (77); "As it is impossible for the Poet to produce upon all occasions language as exquisitely *fitted for the passion* as that which the real passion suggests, it is proper that he should consider himself as in the situation of a translator" (79). The question then becomes, Is every fit that fits fit?

3. In addition to its meaning of "outburst," *fit* can also refer to an arrest, a stroke, a hiatus. Silas Marner's strange fits, for example, freeze him in stop-action stillness while the rest of life continues around him. That the notion of "fits" carries with it a suggestion of the supernatural or the mysterious is indicated by George Eliot's report of folk belief: "Some said that Marner must have been in a 'fit,' a word which seemed to explain things otherwise incredible." *Silas Marner* (Hammondsworth, UK: Penguin, 1967), 55.

4. See Geoffrey Hartman: "To take the moon's drop as the direct cause of the thought assumes that the lover has identified his beloved with the moon." *Wordsworth's Poetry* (New Haven, CT: Yale University Press, 1964), 23. The imputation of a suppressed personification here implies that Lucy herself is a person.

But is she? The long-standing and unresolved debate over the identity of Wordsworth's Lucy would suggest that Lucy is already in fact not a person but a personification. For a fascinating conceptualization of the question of rhetorically mediate, "naturalized" personifications (that is, those that are made to seem real, "found" rather than allegorically made) and their relation to eighteenth-century allegory, see Steven Knapp, *Personification and the Sublime* (Cambridge, MA: Harvard University Press, 1985). At one point Knapp essentially uses the notion of a "strange fit" to refer to the Wordsworthian sublime: "Sometimes—and most strikingly in episodes of naturalized personification—the gap between two moments is replaced by a *curious lack of fit* between two ways of perceiving a single object" (108).

5. It might be objected that this is not the type of personification Wordsworth had in mind, that what he wished to avoid was personifications of abstract ideas, not celestial bodies. Yet the example of bad personification Wordsworth cites in the Preface *does* in fact involve celestial bodies, not abstract ideas. In the sonnet by Gray in which Wordsworth italicizes only the parts he considers valuable, it is the personification of the sun and of the natural world ("reddening Phoebus lifts his golden fire," etc.) that Wordsworth does *not* italicize.

6. A very suggestive gloss on what is unsettling in Wordsworth's rejection of personification is given by Frances Ferguson: "The insistence of the cottage girl in 'We are Seven' that she and her dead siblings are not separated from one another by death involves a kind of personification, but it is personification pushed to such an extreme that it becomes a virtual anti-type to personification. This girl personifies *persons*, and the radically disquieting element in her remarks is the growing consciousness in the poem that persons should need to be personified, should need to be reclaimed from death by the imagination. Her version of personification revolves around death as the essential abstract idea behind personification. Persons and personifications become united members in the community of the living and the dead." Frances Ferguson, *Wordsworth: Language as Counter-Spirit* (New Haven, CT: Yale University Press, 1977), 26–27.

CHAPTER 6

The Frame of Reference
Poe, Lacan, Derrida

The Purloined Preface

A literary text that both analyzes itself and shows that it actually has neither a self nor any neutral metalanguage with which to do the analyzing, calls out irresistibly for analysis. When that call is answered by two eminent French thinkers whose readings emit their own equally paradoxical call-to-analysis, the resulting triptych, in the context of the question of the act-of-reading (-literature), places its would-be reader in a vertiginously insecure position.

The three texts in question are Edgar Allan Poe's short story "The Purloined Letter," Jacques Lacan's "Seminar on The Purloined Letter" and Jacques Derrida's reading of Lacan's reading of Poe, "The Purveyor of Truth" ("Le Facteur de la Vérité").[1] In all three texts, it is the *act of analysis* which seems to occupy the center of the discursive stage, and the *act of analysis of the act of analysis* which in some way disrupts that centrality. In the resulting asymmetrical, abyssal structure, no analysis—including this one—can intervene without transforming and repeating other elements in the sequence, which is thus not a stable sequence, but which nevertheless produces certain regular effects. It is the functioning of this regularity, and the structure of these effects, which will provide the basis for the present study.

The subversion of any possibility of a position of analytical mastery occurs in many ways. Here, the very fact that we are dealing with *three* texts is in no way certain. Poe's story not only fits into a triptych of its own, but is riddled with a constant, peculiar kind of intertextuality (the epigraph from Seneca which is not from Seneca, the lines from Crébillon's *Atrée* which serve as Dupin's signature, etc.). Lacan's text not only presents itself backwards (its introduction *following* its conclusion), but it never finishes presenting itself (*"Ouverture de ce recueil," "Présentation de la suite," "Presentation"* to the *Points* edition). And Derrida's text is not only preceded by several years of annunciatory marginalia and footnotes but is itself structured by its own deferment, its *différance* (see the repetition of such expressions as "mais nous n'en sommes pas encore là" ["but we are getting ahead of ourselves"], etc.). In addition, an unusually high degree of apparent digressiveness characterizes these texts, to the point of making the reader wonder whether there is really any true subject matter there at all. It is as though any attempt to follow the path of the purloined letter is automatically purloined from itself. Which is, as we shall see, just what the letter has always already been saying.

Any attempt to do "justice" to three such complex texts is obviously out of the question. But in each of these readings of the act of analysis the very question being asked is, What is the nature of such "justice"? It can hardly be an accident that the debate proliferates around a *crime* story—a robbery and its undoing. Somewhere in each of these texts, the economy of justice cannot be avoided. For in spite of the absence of mastery, there is no lack of effects of power.

As the reader goes on with this series of prefatory remarks, he may begin to see how contagious the deferment of the subject of the purloined letter can be. But the problem of how to present these three texts is all the more redoubtable since each of them both presents itself and the others and clearly shows the fallacies inherent in any type of "presentation" of a text. It is small comfort that such fallacies are not only inevitable but also *constitutive* of any act of reading—also demonstrated by each of the texts—since the resulting injustices, however unavoidable in general, always appear corrigible in detail. Which is why the sequence continues.

The question of how to present to the reader a text too extensive to quote in its entirety has long been one of the underlying problems of literary criticism. Since a shorter version of the text must somehow be produced, two solutions constantly recur: paraphrase and quotation. Although these tactics are seldom if ever used in isolation, the specific configuration of their combinations and permutations determines to a large extent the "plot" of the critical narrative to which they give rise. The first act of our own narrative, then, will consist of an analysis of the strategic effects of the use of paraphrase versus quotation in each of the three texts in question.

Round Robbin'

Round robin: 1) A tournament in which each contestant is matched against every other contestant. 2) A petition or protest on which the signatures are arranged in the form of a circle in order to conceal the order of signing. 3) A letter sent among members of a group, often with comments added by each person in turn. 4) An extended sequence.
—*American Heritage Dictionary*

In 1845, Edgar Allan Poe published the third of his three detective stories, "The Purloined Letter," in a collective volume entitled—ironically, considering all the robberies in the story—*The Gift: A Christmas, New Year, and Birthday Present.* "The Purloined Letter" is a first-person narration of two scenes in which dialogues occur among the narrator, his friend C. Auguste Dupin, and, initially, the Prefect of the Parisian police. The two scenes are separated by an indication of the passage of a month's time. In each of the two dialogues, reported to us verbatim by the narrator, one of the other two characters tells the story of a robbery. In the first scene, it is the Prefect of Police who repeats the Queen's eyewitness account of the Minister's theft of a letter addressed to her; in the second scene, it is Dupin who narrates his own theft of the same letter from the Minister, who had meanwhile readdressed it to himself. In a paragraph placed between these two "crime" stories, the narrator himself narrates a wordless scene in which the letter changes hands again before his eyes, passing from Dupin—not without the latter's having addressed not the letter but a check to himself—to the Prefect (who will pocket the remainder of the reward) and thence, presumably, back to the Queen.

By appearing to repeat to us faithfully every word in both dialogues, the narrator would seem to have resorted exclusively to direct quotation in presenting his story. Even when paraphrase could have been expected—in the description of the exact procedures employed by the police in searching unsuccessfully for the letter, for example—we are spared none of the details. Thus it is all the more surprising to find that there *is* one little point at which direct quotation of the Prefect's words gives way to paraphrase. This point, however brief, is of no small importance, as we shall see. It occurs in the concluding paragraph of the first scene:

"I have no better advice to give you," said Dupin. "You have, of course, an accurate description of the letter?"

"Oh, yes!"—And here the Prefect, producing a memorandum-book, proceeded to read aloud a minute account of the internal, and especially of the external, appearance of the missing document. Soon after finishing the perusal of this description, he took his departure, more entirely depressed in spirits than I had ever known the good gentleman before. (Poe, 206–7)

What is paraphrased is thus the description of the letter the story is about. And, whereas it is generally supposed that the function of paraphrase is to strip off the form of a speech in order to give us only its contents, here the use of paraphrase does the very opposite: it withholds the contents of the Prefect's remarks, giving us only their form. And what is swallowed up in this ellipsis is nothing less than the contents of the letter itself. The fact that the letter's message is never revealed, which will serve as the basis for Lacan's reading of the story, is thus negatively made explicit by the functioning of Poe's text itself, through what Derrida might have called a repression of the written word (a suppression of what is written in the memorandum-book— and in the letter). And the question of the strategic use of paraphrase versus quotation begins to invade the literary text as well as the critical narrative.

Lacan's presentation of Poe's text involves the paraphrase, or plot summary, of the two thefts as they are told to the narrator by the Prefect and by Dupin. Since Derrida, in his critique of Lacan, chooses to quote Lacan's paraphrase, we can combine all the tactics involved by, in our turn, quoting Derrida's quotation of Lacan's paraphrase of Poe's quoted narrations.[2]

There are two scenes, the first of which we shall straightway designate the primal scene, and by no means inadvertently, since the second may be considered its repetition in the very sense we are considering today.

The primal scene is thus performed, we are told [by neither Poe, nor the scriptor, nor the narrator, but by G, the Prefect of Police who is *mis en scène* by all those involved in the dialogues—J.D.[3]] in the royal *boudoir*, so that we suspect that the person of the highest rank, called the "exalted personage," who is alone there when she receives a letter, is the Queen. This feeling is confirmed by the embarrassment into which she is plunged by the entry of the other exalted personage, of whom we have already been told [again by G—J.D.] prior to this account that the knowledge he might have of the letter in question would jeopardize for the lady nothing less than her honor and safety. Any doubt that he is in fact the King is promptly dissipated in the course of the scene which begins with the entry of Minister D. . . . At that moment, in fact, the Queen can do no better than to play on the King's inattentiveness by leaving the letter on the table "face down, address uppermost." It does not, however, escape the Minister's lynx eye, nor does he fail to notice the Queen's distress and thus to fathom her secret. From then on everything transpires like clockwork. After dealing in his customary manner with the business of the day, the Minister draws from his pocket a letter similar in appearance to the one in his view, and having pretended to read it, places it next to the other. A bit more conversation to amuse the royal company, whereupon, without flinching once, he seizes the embarrassing letter, making off with it, as the Queen, on whom none of his maneuver has been lost, remains unable to intervene for fear of attracting the attention of her royal spouse, close at her side at that very moment.

Everything might then have transpired unseen by a hypothetical spectator of an operation in which nobody falters, and whose *quotient* is that the Minister has filched from the Queen her letter and that—an even more important result than the first—the Queen knows that he now has it, and by no means innocently.

A *remainder* that no analyst will neglect, trained as he is to retain whatever is significant, without always knowing what to do with it: the letter, abandoned by the Minister, and which the Queen's hand is now free to roll into a ball.

Second scene: in the Minister's office. It is in his hotel, and we know—from the account the Prefect of Police has given Dupin, whose specific genius for solving enigmas Poe introduces here for the second time—that the police, returning there as soon as the Minister's habitual nightly absences allow them to, have searched the hotel and its surroundings from top to bottom for the last eighteen months. In vain,—although everyone can deduce from the situation that the Minister keeps the letter within reach.

Dupin calls on the Minister. The latter receives him with studied nonchalance, affecting in his conversation romantic *ennui*. Meanwhile Dupin, whom this pretense does not deceive, his eyes protected by green glasses, proceeds to inspect the premises. When his glance catches a rather crumbled piece of paper—apparently thrust carelessly in a division of an ugly pasteboard card-rack, hanging gaudily from the middle of the mantelpiece—he already knows that he's found what he's looking for. His conviction is reinforced by the very details which seem to contradict the description he has of the stolen letter, with the exception of the format, which remains the same.

Whereupon he has but to withdraw, after "forgetting" his snuff-box on the table, in order to return the following day to reclaim it—armed with a facsimile of the letter in its present state. As an incident in the street, prepared for the proper moment, draws the Minister to the window, Dupin in turn seizes the opportunity to seize the letter while substituting the imitation, and has only to maintain the appearances of a normal exit.

Here as well all has transpired, if not without noise, at least without all commotion. The quotient of the operation is that the Minister no longer has the letter, but, far from suspecting that Dupin is the culprit who has ravished it from him, knows nothing of it. Moreover, what he is left with is far from insignificant for what follows. We shall return to what brought Dupin to inscribe a message on his counterfeit letter. Whatever the case, the Minister, when he tries to make use of it, will be able to read these words, written so that he may recognize Dupin's hand: ". . . Un dessein si funeste/S'il n'est digne d'Atrée est digne de Thyeste,"[4] whose source, Dupin tells us, is Crébillon's *Atrée*.

Need we emphasize the similarity of these two sequences? Yes, for the resemblance we have in mind is not a simple collection of traits chosen only in order to delete their difference. And it would not be enough to retain those common traits at the expense of the others for the slightest truth to result. It is rather the intersubjectivity in which the two actions are motivated that we wish to bring into relief, as well as the three terms through which it structures them.

The special status of these terms results from their corresponding simultaneously to the three logical moments through which the decision is precipitated and the three places it assigns to the subjects among whom it constitutes a choice.

That decision is reached in a glance's time. For the maneuvers which follow, however stealthily they prolong it, add nothing to that glance, nor does the deferring of the deed in the second scene break the unity of that moment.

This glance presupposes two others, which it embraces in its vision of the breach left in their fallacious complementarity, anticipating in it the occasion for larceny afforded by that exposure. Thus three moments, structuring three glances, borne by three subjects, incarnated each time by different characters.

The first is a glance that sees nothing: the King and the police.

The second, a glance which sees that the first sees nothing and deludes itself as to the secrecy of what it hides: the Queen, then the Minister.

The third sees that the first two glances leave what should be hidden exposed to whoever would seize it: the Minister and finally Dupin.

In order to grasp in its unity the intersubjective complex thus described, we would willingly seek a model in the technique legendarily attributed to the ostrich attempting to shield itself from danger; for that technique might ultimately be qualified as political, divided as it here is among three partners: the second believing itself invisible because the first has its head stuck in the ground, and all the while letting the third calmly pluck its rear; we need only enrich its proverbial denomination by a letter, producing *la politique de l'autruiche*,[5] for the ostrich itself to take on forever a new meaning.

Given the intersubjective modulus of the repetitive action, it remains to recognize in it a *repetition automatism* in the sense that interests us in Freud's text. (SPL, 41–44; PT, 54–57)

Thus, it is neither the character of the individual subjects, nor the contents of the letter, but the position of the letter within the group which decides what each person will do next. Because the letter does not function as a unit of meaning (a *signified*) but as that which produces certain effects (a *signifier*), Lacan reads the story as an illustration of "the truth which may be drawn from that moment in Freud's thought under study—namely, that it is the symbolic order which is constitutive for the subject—by demonstrating . . . the decisive orientation which the subject receives from the itinerary of a signifier" (SPL, 40). The letter acts like a signifier to the extent that its function in the story does not require that its meaning be revealed: "the letter was able to produce its effects *within* the story: on the actors in the tale, including the narrator, as well as *outside* the story: on us, the readers, and also on its author, without anyone's ever bothering to worry about what it *meant*" (not translated in SPL; *Ecrits*, 57, translation and emphasis mine). "The Purloined Letter" thus becomes for Lacan a kind of *allegory of the signifier*.

Derrida's critique of Lacan's reading does not dispute the validity of the allegorical interpretation on its own terms, but questions its implicit presuppositions and its modus operandi. Derrida aims his objections at two kinds of target: (1) what Lacan puts into the letter and (2) what Lacan leaves out of the text.

1. *What Lacan puts into the letter.* While asserting that the letter's meaning is lacking, Lacan, according to Derrida, makes this lack into *the* meaning of the letter. But Derrida does not stop there. He goes on to assert that what Lacan means by that lack is the truth of lack-as-castration-as-truth: "The truth of the purloined letter is the truth itself. . . . What is veiled/unveiled in this case is a hole, a non-being [non-étant] ; the truth of being [l'être], as non-being. Truth is 'woman' as veiled/unveiled castration" (PT, 60–61). Lacan himself, however, never uses the word *castration* in the text of the original "Seminar." That it is suggested is indisputable, but Derrida, by filling in what *Lacan* left blank, is repeating the same gesture of blank-filling for which he criticizes Lacan.

2. *What Lacan leaves out of the text.* This objection is itself double: on the one hand, Derrida criticizes Lacan for neglecting to consider "The Purloined Letter" in connection with the other two stories in what Derrida calls Poe's "Dupin Trilogy." And on the other hand, according to Derrida, at the very moment Lacan is reading the story as an allegory of the signifier, he is being blind to the disseminating power of the signifier in the *text* of the allegory, in what Derrida calls the "scene of writing." To cut out part of a text's frame of reference as though it did not exist and to reduce a complex textual functioning to a single meaning are serious blots indeed in the annals of literary criticism. Therefore it is all the more noticeable that Derrida's own reading of Lacan's text repeats the crimes of which he accuses it: on the one hand, Derrida makes no mention of Lacan's long development on the relation between symbolic determination and random series. And on the other hand, Derrida dismisses Lacan's "style" as a mere ornament, veiling, for a time, an unequivocal message: "Lacan's 'style,' moreover, was such that for a long time it would hinder and delay all access to a *unique* content or a single unequivocal meaning determinable beyond the writing itself" (PT, 40). Derrida's repetition of the very gestures he is criticizing does not in itself invalidate his criticism of their effects, but it does problematize his statement condemning their existence.

What kind of logic is it that thus seems to turn one-upmanship into inevitable one-downmanship?

It is the very logic of the purloined letter.

Odd Couples

Je tiens la reine!

    O sûr châtiment . . .
—Mallarmé, "L'après-midi d'un faune"

L'ascendant que le ministre tire de la situation ne tient don pas à la lettre,
mais, qu'il le sache ou non, au personnage qu'elle lui constitue.
—Lacan, SPL

We have just seen how Derrida, in his effort to right (write) Lacan's wrongs, can, on a certain level, only repeat them, and how the rectification of a previous injustice somehow irresistibly dictates the filling in of a blank which then becomes the new injustice. In fact, the act of clinching one's triumph by filling in a blank is already prescribed in all its details within Poe's story, in Dupin's unwillingness to "leave the interior blank" (Poe, 219) in the facsimile he has left for the Minister, in place of the purloined letter he, Dupin, has just repossessed by means of a precise repetition of the act of robbery he is undoing. What is written in the blank is a quotation-as-signature, which curiously resembles Derrida's initialed interventions in the passages he quotes from Lacan, a resemblance on which Derrida is undoubtedly playing. And the text of the quotation transcribed by Dupin describes the structure of rectification-as-repetition-of-the-crime which has led to its being transcribed in the first place:

> —Un dessein si funeste,
>   S'il n'est digne d'Atrée, est digne de Thyeste.

Atreus, whose wife had long ago been seduced by Thyestes, is about to make Thyestes eat (literally) the fruit of that illicit union, his son Plisthenes. The avenger's plot may not be worthy of him, says Atreus, but his brother Thyestes deserves it. What the addressee of the violence is going to get is simply his own message backwards. It is this vengeful anger that, as both Lacan and Derrida show, places Dupin as one of the "ostriches" in the "triad." Not content simply to return the letter to its "rightful" destination, Dupin jumps into the fray as the wronged victim himself, by recalling an "evil turn" the minister once did him in Vienna and for which he is now, personally, taking his revenge.

    Correction must thus posit a previous pretextual, pre-textual crime that will justify its excesses. Any degree of violence is permissible in the act of getting even ("To be *even* with him," says Dupin, "I complained of my weak eyes" [Poe, 216, emphasis mine]). And Dupin's backward revision of the story repeats itself in his readers as well. The existence of the same kind of prior aggression on Lacan's part is posited by Derrida in a long footnote in his book *Positions*, in which he outlines what will later develop into *Le Facteur de la Vérité*: "In the texts I have published up to now, the absence of reference to Lacan is indeed almost total. That is *justified* not only by the *acts of aggression* in the form of, or with the intention of, reappropriation which, ever since *De la grammatologie* appeared in *Critique* (1965) (and even earlier, I am told) Lacan has multiplied . . ." (emphasis mine). The priority of aggression is doubled by the aggressiveness of priority: "At the time of my first publications, Lacan's *Ecrits* had not yet been collected and published."[6] And Lacan, in turn, mentions in his *Presentation* to the "Points" edition of his *Ecrits*: "what I properly call the instance of the letter *before any grammatology*"[7] (emphasis mine). The rivalry over something neither man will credit the other with possessing, the retrospective revision of the origins of both their resemblances and their differences, thus spirals backward and forward in an indeterminable pattern of cancellation and duplication. If it thus becomes impossible to determine "who started it" (or even whether "it" was started by either one of them), it is also impossible to know who is ahead or even whose "turn" it is—which is what makes the business of getting even so *odd*.

This type of oscillation between two terms, considered as totalities in binary opposition, is studied by Lacan in connection with Poe's story of the eight-year-old prodigy who succeeded in winning, far beyond his due, at the game of even and odd. The game consists of guessing whether the number of marbles an opponent is holding is even or odd. The schoolboy explains his success by his identification with the physical characteristics of his opponent, from which he deduces the opponent's degree of intelligence and its corresponding line of reasoning. What Lacan shows, in the part of his seminar which Derrida neglects, is that the mere identification with the opponent as an image of totality is not sufficient to insure success—and in no way explains Dupin's actual strategy—since, from the moment the opponent becomes aware of it, he can then play on his own appearance and dissociate it from the reasoning that is presumed to go with it. (This is, indeed, what occurs in the encounter between Dupin and the Minister: the Minister's feigned nonchalance is a true vigilance but a blinded vision, whereas Dupin's feigned blindness ["weak eyes"] is a vigilant act of lucidity, later to succumb to its own form of blindness.) From then on, says Lacan, the reasoning "can only repeat itself in an indefinite oscillation" (*Ecrits*, 58, translation mine). And Lacan reports that, in his own classroom tests of the schoolboy's technique, it was almost inevitable that each player begin to feel he was losing his marbles.[8]

But if the complexities of these texts could be reduced to a mere combat between ostriches, a mere game of heads and tails played out in order to determine a "winner," they would have very little theoretical interest. It is, on the contrary, the way in which each mastermind avoids simply becoming the butt of his own joke that displaces the opposition in unpredictable ways and transforms the textual encounter into a source of insight. For if the very possibility of meeting the opponent on a common ground, without which no contact is possible, implies a certain symmetry, a sameness, a repetition of the error that the encounter is designed to correct, any true avoidance of that error entails a nonmeeting or incompatibility between the two forces. If to hit the target is in a way to become the target, then to miss the target is perhaps to hit it elsewhere. It is not how Lacan and Derrida meet each other but how they miss each other that opens up a space for interpretation.

Clearly, what is at stake here has something to do with the status of the number 2. If the face-off between two opponents or polar opposites always simultaneously backfires and misfires, it can only be because 2 is an extremely "odd" number. On the one hand, as a specular illusion of symmetry or metaphor, it can be either narcissistically reassuring (the image of the other as a reinforcement of my identity) or absolutely devastating (the other whose existence can totally cancel me out). This is what Lacan calls the "*imaginary duality.*" It is characterized by its absoluteness, its independence from any accident or contingency that might subvert the unity of the terms in question, whether in their opposition or in their fusion. To this, Lacan opposes the *symbolic*, which is the entrance of difference or otherness or temporality into the idea of identity—it is not something that befalls the imaginary duality, but something that has always already inhabited it, something that subverts not the symmetry of the imaginary couple, but the possibility of the independent unity of any one term whatsoever. It is the impossibility not of the number 2 but of the number *1*—which, paradoxically enough, turns out to lead to the number 3.

If 3 is what makes 2 into the impossibility of *1*, is there any inherent increase in lucidity in passing from a couple to a triangle? Is a triangle in any way more "true" than a couple?

It is Derrida's contention that, for psychoanalysis, the answer to that question is yes. The triangle becomes the magical, Oedipal figure that explains the functioning of human desire. The child's original imaginary dual unity with the mother is subverted by the law of the father as that which prohibits incest under threat of castration. The child has "simply" to "assume castration" as the necessity of substitution in the object of his desire (the object of desire becoming the locus of substitution and the focus of repetition), after which the child's desire becomes "normalized." Derrida's criticism of the "triangles" or "triads" in Lacan's reading of Poe is based on the assumption that Lacan's use of triangularity stems from this psychoanalytical myth.

Derrida's criticism takes two routes, both of them numerical:

1. The structure of "The Purloined Letter" cannot be reduced to a triangle unless the narrator is eliminated. The elimination of the narrator is a blatant and highly revealing result of the way "psychoanalysis" does violence to literature in order to find its own schemes. What psychoanalysis sees as a triangle is therefore really a quadrangle, and that fourth side is the point from which literature problematizes the very possibility of a triangle. Therefore: $3 = 4$.
2. Duality as such cannot be dismissed or simply absorbed into a triangular structure. "The Purloined Letter" is traversed by an uncanny capacity for doubling and subdividing. The narrator and Dupin are doubles of each other, and Dupin himself is first introduced as a "Bi-Part Soul" (Poe, 107), a sort of Dupin Duplex, "the creative and the resolvent." The Minister, D——, has a brother for whom it is possible to mistake him, and from whom he is to be distinguished because of his doubleness (poet and mathematician). Thus the Minister and Dupin become doubles of each other through the fact of their both being already double, in addition to their other points of resemblance, including their names. "The 'Seminar,'" writes Derrida,

> mercilessly forecloses this problematic of the double and of *Unheimlichkeit*—no doubt considering that it is confined to the imaginary, to the dual relationship which must be kept rigorously separate from the symbolic and the triangular. . . . All the "uncanny" relations of duplicity, limitlessly deployed in a dual structure, find themselves omitted or marginalized [in the "Seminar"]. . . . What is thus kept under surveillance and control is the Uncanny itself, and the frantic anxiety which can be provoked, with no hope of reappropriation, enclosure, or truth,

by the infinite play from simulacrum to simulacrum, from double to double. (omitted in PT; FV, 124, translation mine)

Thus the triangle's angles are always already bisected, and 3 = (a factor of) 2.

In the game of odd versus even, then, it would seem that Derrida is playing evens (4 or 2) against Lacan's odds (3). But somehow the numbers 2 and 4 have become uncannily odd, while the number 3 has been evened off into a reassuring symmetry. How did this happen, and what are the consequences for an interpretation of "The Purloined Letter"?

Before any answer to this question can be envisaged, several remarks should be made here to problematize the terms of Derrida's critique:

1. If the narrator and Dupin are a strictly dual pair whose relationship is in no way mediated by a third term in any Oedipal sense, how is one to explain the fact that their original meeting was brought about by their potential rivalry over the same object: "the accident of our both being in search of the *same* very rare and very remarkable volume" (emphasis mine). Whether or not they ever found it, or can share it, is this not a triangular relationship?

2. Although Lacan's reading of "The Purloined Letter" divides the story into triadic structures, his model for (inter-)subjectivity, the so-called schema L, which is developed in that part of the "Seminar's" introduction glossed over by Derrida, is indisputably quadrangular. In order to read Lacan's repeating triads as a triangular, Oedipal model of the subject instead of as a mere structure of repetition, Derrida must therefore lop off one corner of the schema L in the same way as he accuses Lacan of lopping off a corner of Poe's text—and Derrida does this by lopping off that corner of Lacan's text in which the quadrangular schema L is developed.

But can what is at stake here really be reduced to a mere numbers game? Let us approach the problem from another angle, by asking two more questions:

1. What is the relation between a divided unity and a duality? Are the two 2's synonymous? Is a "Bi-Part Soul," for example, actually composed of two wholes? Or is it possible to conceive of a division which would not lead to two separate parts, but only to a problematization of the idea of unity? This would class what Derrida

calls "duality" not in Lacan's "imaginary," but in Lacan's "symbolic."

2. If the doubles are forever redividing or multiplying, does the number 2 really apply? If $1 = 2$, how can $2 = 1 + 1$? If what is uncanny about the doubles is that they never stop doubling up, would the number 2 still be uncanny if it did stop at a truly dual symmetry? Is it not the very limitlessness of the process of the dissemination of unity, rather than the existence of any one duality, which Derrida is talking about here?

Clearly, in these questions, the very notion of a number becomes problematic, and the argument on the basis of numbers can no longer be read literally. If Derrida opposes doubled quadrangles to Lacan's triangles, it is not because he wants to turn Oedipus into an octopus.

To what, then, does the critique of triangularity apply?

The problem with psychoanalytical triangularity, in Derrida's eyes, is not that it contains the wrong number of terms, but that it presupposes the possibility of a successful dialectical mediation and harmonious normalization, or *Aufhebung*, of desire. The three terms in the Oedipal triad enter into an opposition whose resolution resembles the synthetic moment of a Hegelian dialectic. The process centers on the phallus as the locus of the question of sexual difference; when the observation of the mother's lack of a penis is joined with the father's threat of castration as the punishment for incest, the child passes from the alternative (thesis versus antithesis; presence versus absence of penis) to the synthesis (the phallus as a sign of the fact that the child can only enter into the circuit of desire by assuming castration as the phallus's simultaneous presence and absence; that is, by assuming the fact that both the subject and the object of desire will always be substitutes for something that was never really present). In Lacan's article "La signification du phallus," which Derrida quotes, this process is evoked in specifically Hegelian terms:

All these remarks still do nothing but veil the fact that it [the phallus] cannot play its role except veiled, that is to say as itself sign of the latency with which anything signifiable is stricken as soon as it is raised (*aufgehoben*) to the function of signifier.

The phallus is the signifier of this *Aufhebung* itself which it inaugurates (initiates) by its disappearance. (*Ecrits*, 692; PT, 98)

"It would appear," comments Derrida, "that the Hegelian movement of *Aufhebung* is here reversed since the latter sublates [relève] the sensory signifier in the ideal signified" (PT, 98). But then, according to Derrida, Lacan's privileging of the spoken over the written word annuls this reversal, reappropriates all possibility of uncontainable otherness, and brings the whole thing back within the bounds of the type of "logocentrism" that has been the focus of Derrida's entire deconstructive enterprise.

The question of whether or not Lacan's privileging of the voice is strictly logocentric in Derrida's sense is an extremely complex one with which we cannot hope to deal adequately here.[9] But what does all this have to do with "The Purloined Letter"?

In an attempt to answer this question, let us examine how Derrida deduces from Lacan's text that, for Lacan, the letter is a symbol of the (mother's) phallus. Since Lacan never uses the word *phallus* in the "Seminar," this is already an interpretation on Derrida's part, and quite an astute one at that, with which Lacan, as a later reader of his own "Seminar," implicitly agrees by placing the word *castrated*—which had not been used in the original text—in his "Points" *Presentation*. The disagreement between Derrida and Lacan thus arises not over the *validity* of the equation "letter = phallus," but over its *meaning*.

How, then, does Derrida derive this equation from Lacan's text? The deduction follows four basic lines of reasoning, all of which will be dealt with in greater detail later in the present essay:

1. The letter "belongs" to the Queen as a substitute for the phallus she does not have. It feminizes (castrates) each of its successive holders and is eventually returned to her as its rightful owner.
2. Poe's description of the position of the letter in the Minister's apartment, expanded upon by the figurative dimensions of Lacan's text, suggests an analogy between the shape of the fireplace from the center of whose mantelpiece the letter is found hanging and that point on a woman's anatomy from which the phallus is missing.
3. The letter, says Lacan, cannot be divided: "But if it is first of all on the materiality of the signifier that we have insisted, that materiality is *odd* [singulière] in many ways, the first of which is not to admit partition" (SPL, 53). This indivisibility, says Derrida, is odd indeed, but becomes comprehensible if it is seen as an *idealization* of the phallus, whose integrity is necessary for the edification of the

entire psychoanalytical system. With the phallus safely idealized and located in the voice, the so-called signifier acquires the "unique, living, non-mutilable integrity" of the self-present spoken word, unequivocally pinned down to and by the *signified*. "Had the phallus been per(mal)chance divisible or reduced to the status of a partial object, the whole edification would have crumbled down, and this is what has to be avoided at all cost" (PT, 96–97).

4. And finally, if Poe's story "illustrates" the "truth," the last words of the "Seminar" proper seem to reaffirm that truth in no uncertain terms: "Thus it is that what the 'purloined letter,' nay the 'letter in sufferance' means is that *a letter always arrives at its destination*" (SPL, 72, emphasis mine). Now, since it is unlikely that Lacan is talking about the efficiency of the postal service, he must, according to Derrida, be affirming the possibility of unequivocal meaning, the eventual reappropriation of the message, its total equivalence with itself. And since the "truth" Poe's story illustrates is, in Derrida's eyes, the truth of veiled/unveiled castration and of the transcendental identity of the phallus as the lack that makes the system work, this final sentence in Lacan's "Seminar" seems to affirm both the absolute truth of psychoanalytical theories and the absolute decipherability of the literary text. Poe's message will have been totally, unequivocally understood and explained by the psychoanalytical myth. "The hermeneutic discovery of meaning (truth), the deciphering (that of Dupin and that of the 'Seminar'), arrives itself at its destination" (PT, 66).

Thus, the law of the phallus seems to imply a reappropriating return to the place of true ownership, an indivisible identity functioning beyond the possibility of disintegration or unrecoverable loss, and a totally self-present, unequivocal meaning or truth.

The problem with this type of system, counters Derrida, is that it cannot account for the possibility of sheer accident, irreversible loss, unreappropriable residues, and infinite divisibility, which are necessary and inevitable in the system's very elaboration. In order for the circuit of the letter to end up confirming the law of the phallus, it must begin by transgressing it; the letter is a sign of high treason. Phallogocentrism mercilessly represses the uncontrollable multiplicity of ambiguities, the disseminating play of *writing*, which irreducibly transgresses any unequivocal meaning. "Not that the letter never arrives at its destination, but part of its structure is that it is always capable of not arriving there. . . . Here dissemination threatens the law of the signi-fier and of castration as a contract of truth. Dissemination mutilates the unity of the signifier, that is, of the phallus" (PT, 66).

In contrast to Lacan's "Seminar," then, Derrida's text would seem to be setting itself up as a "Disseminar."

From the foregoing remarks, it can easily be seen that the disseminal criticism of Lacan's apparent reduction of the literary text to an unequivocal message depends for its force upon the presupposition of unambiguousness in Lacan's text. And indeed, the statement that a letter always reaches its destination seems straightforward enough. But when the statement is rein-serted into its context, things become palpably less certain:

> Is that all, and shall we believe we have deciphered Dupin's real strategy above and beyond the imaginary tricks upon which he was obliged to deceive us? No doubt, yes, for if "any point requiring reflection," as Dupin states at the start, is "examined to best purpose in the dark," we may now easily read its solution in broad daylight. It was already im-plicit and easy to derive from the title of our tale, according to the very formula we have long submitted to your discretion: in which the sender, we tell you, receives from the receiver his own message in reverse form. Thus it is that what the "purloined letter," nay, the "letter in sufferance" means is that a letter always arrives at its destination. (SPL, 72)

The meaning of this last sentence is problematized not so much by its own ambiguity as by a series of reversals in the preceding sentences. If the "best" examination takes place in darkness, what does "reading in broad daylight" imply? Could it not be taken as an affirmation not of actual lucid-ity but of delusions of lucidity? Could it not then move the "yes, no doubt" as an answer, not to the question, "Have we deciphered?" but to the ques-tion, "Shall we *believe* we have deciphered?" And if this is possible, does it not empty the final affirmation of all unequivocality, leaving it to stand with the *force* of an assertion, without any definite content? And if the sender re-ceives from the receiver his own message backward, who is the sender here, who the receiver, and what is the message? It is not even clear what the ex-pression "the purloined letter" refers to: Poe's text? the letter it talks about? or simply the expression "the purloined letter"?

We will take another look at this passage later, but for the moment its am-biguities seem sufficient to problematize, if not subvert, the presupposition of univocality that is the very foundation on which Derrida has edified his interpretation.

But surely such an oversimplification on Derrida's part does not result from mere blindness, oversight, or error. As Paul de Man says of Derrida's similar treatment of Rousseau, "the pattern is too interesting not to be deliberate."[10] Derrida being the sharp-eyed reader that he is, his consistent forcing of Lacan's statements into systems and patterns from which they are actually trying to escape must correspond to some strategic necessity different from the attentiveness to the letter of the text which characterizes Derrida's way of reading Poe. And in fact, the more one works with Derrida's analysis, the more convinced one becomes that although the critique of what Derrida calls psychoanalysis is entirely justified, it does not quite apply to what Lacan's text is actually saying. Derrida argues, in effect, not against Lacan's *text* but against Lacan's *power*—or rather, against "Lacan" as the apparent cause of certain effects of power in French discourse today. Whatever Lacan's text may *say*, it functions, according to Derrida, as if it said what *he* says it says. The statement that a letter always reaches its destination may be totally undecipherable, but its assertive force is taken all the more seriously as a sign that Lacan himself has everything all figured out. Such an assertion, in fact, gives him an appearance of mastery like that of the Minister in the eyes of the letterless Queen. "The ascendancy which the Minister derives from the situation," explains Lacan, "is attached not to the letter but to the character it makes him into."

Thus Derrida's seemingly "blind" reading, whose vagaries we shall be following here, is not a mistake but the positioning of what can be called the "average reading" of Lacan's text—the true object of Derrida's deconstruction. Since Lacan's text is read as if it said what Derrida says it says, its actual textual functioning is irrelevant to the agonistic arena in which Derrida's analysis takes place and which is suggested by the very first word of the epigraph: *ils* (they):

> They thank him for the grand truths he has just proclaimed,—for they have discovered (o verifier of what cannot be verified) that everything he said was absolutely true; even though, at first, these honest souls admit, they might have suspected that it could have been a simple fiction . . . (PT, 31, translation mine)

The fact that this quotation from Baudelaire refers to Poe and not Lacan does not completely erase the impression that the unidentified "him" in its first sentence is the "Purveyor of Truth" of the title. The evils of Lacan's analysis of Poe are thus located less in the letter of the text than in the gullible readers, the "braves gens" who are taken in by it. Lacan's ills are really *ils*.

If Derrida's reading of Lacan's reading of Poe is actually the deconstruction of a reading whose status is difficult to determine, does this mean that Lacan's text is completely innocent of the misdemeanors of which it is accused? If Lacan can be shown to be opposed to the same kind of logocentric error that Derrida opposes, does that mean that they are both really saying the same thing? These are questions that must be left, at least for the moment, hanging.

But the structure of Derrida's transference of guilt from a certain reading of Lacan onto Lacan's text is not indifferent in itself, in the context of what, after all, started out as a relatively simple crime story. For what it amounts to is nothing less than a *frame*.

The Frame of Reference

Elle, défunte *nue* en le miroir, encor
Que, *dans l'oubli fermé par le cadre*, se fixe
De scintillations sitôt le septuor.
—Mallarmé, "Sonnet en X"

If Derrida is thus framing Lacan for an interpretative malpractice of which he himself is, at least in part, the author, what can this frame teach us about the nature of the act of reading, in the context of the question of literature and psychoanalysis?

Interestingly enough, one of the major crimes for which Derrida frames Lacan is the psychoanalytical reading's elimination of the literary text's *frame*. That frame here consists not only of the two stories that precede "The Purloined Letter" but also of the stratum of narration through which the stories are told, and, "beyond" it, of the text's entire functioning as *écriture*:

> Without breathing a word about it, Lacan excludes the textual fiction within which he isolates the so-called "general narration." Such an operation is facilitated, too obviously facilitated, by the fact that the narration covers the entire surface of the fiction entitled "The Purloined Letter." But *that* is the fiction. There is an invisible but structurally irreducible frame around the narration. Where does it begin? With the first letter of the title? With the epigraph from Seneca? With the words, "At Paris, just after dark . . ."? It is more complicated than that and will require reconsideration. Such complication suffices to point out everything that is misunderstood about the structure of the text once the frame is ignored. Within this invisible or neutralized frame, Lacan takes

the borderless narration and makes another subdivision, once again leaving aside the frame. He cuts out two dialogues from within the frame of the narration itself, which form the narrated history, i.e. the content of a representation, the internal meaning of a story, the all-enframed which demands our complete attention, mobilizes all the psychoanalytical schemes—Oedipal, as it happens—and draws all the effort of decipherment towards its center. What is missing here is an elaboration of the problem of the frame, the signature and the *parergon*. This lack allows us to reconstruct the scene of the signifier as a signified (an ever inevitable process in the logic of the sign), writing as the written, the text as discourse or more precisely as an "intersubjective" dialogue (there is nothing fortuitous in the fact that the Seminar discusses only the two *dialogues* in "The Purloined Letter"). (PT, 52–53, translation modified)

It is well known that "The Purloined Letter" belongs to what Baudelaire called a "kind of trilogy," along with "The Murders in the Rue Morgue" and "The Mystery of Marie Rogêt." About this Dupin trilogy, the Seminar does not breathe a word; not only does Lacan lift out the narrated triangles (the "real drama") in order to center the narration around them and make them carry the weight of the interpretation (the letter's destination), but he also lifts one third of the Dupin cycle out of an ensemble discarded as if it were a natural, invisible frame. (Not translated in PT; FV, 123; translation mine)

In framing with such violence, in cutting a fourth side out of the narrated figure itself in order to see only triangles, a certain complication, perhaps a complication of the Oedipal structure, is eluded, a complication which makes itself felt in the scene of writing. (PT, 54; translation entirely modified)

It would seem, then, that Lacan is guilty of several sins of omission: the omission of the narrator, the nondialogue parts of the story, the other stories in the trilogy. But does this criticism amount to a mere plea for the inclusion of what has been excluded? No; the problem is not simply quantitative. What has been excluded is not homogeneous to what has been included. Lacan, says Derrida, misses the specifically literary dimension of Poe's text by treating it as a "real drama," a story like the stories a psychoanalyst hears every day from his patients. What has been left out is literature itself.

Does this mean that the frame is what makes a text literary? In an issue of *New Literary History* devoted to the question "What is literature?" (and totally unrelated to the debate concerning the purloined letter) one of the contributors comes to this very conclusion: "Literature is language . . . but it is language around which we have drawn a *frame*, a frame that indicates a decision to regard with a particular self-consciousness the resources language has always possessed"[11] (emphasis mine).

Such a view of literature, however, implies that a text is literary because it remains inside certain definite borders; it is a many-faceted object, perhaps, but still, it is an object. That this is not quite what Derrida has in mind becomes clear from the following remarks:

> By overlooking the narrator's position, the narrator's involvement in the content of what he seems to be recounting, one omits from the scene of writing anything going beyond the two triangular scenes.
>
> And first of all one omits that what is in question—with no possible access route or border—is a scene of writing whose boundaries crumble off into an abyss. From the simulacrum of an overture, of a "first word," the narrator, in narrating himself, advances a few propositions which carry the unity of the "tale" into an endless drifting-off course: a textual drifting not at all taken into account in the Seminar. (PT, 100–101; translation modified)

> These reminders, of which countless other examples could be given, alert us to the effects of the frame, and of the paradoxes in the parergonal logic. Our purpose is not to prove that "The Purloined Letter" functions within a frame (omitted by the Seminar, which can thus be assured of its triangular interior by an active, surreptitious limitation starting from a metalinguistic overview), but to prove that the structure of the framing effects is such that no totalization of the border is even possible. Frames are always framed: thus, by part of their content. Pieces without a whole, "divisions" without a totality—this is what thwarts the dream of a letter without division, allergic to division. (PT, 99; translation slightly modified)

Here the argument seems to reverse the previous objection; Lacan has eliminated not the frame but the unframability of the literary text. But what Derrida calls "parergonal logic" is paradoxical precisely because both of these incompatible (but not totally contradictory) arguments are equally valid. The total inclusion of the frame is both mandatory and impossible. The frame thus becomes not the borderline between the inside and the outside, but precisely what subverts the applicability of the inside/outside polarity to the act of interpretation.

The frame is, in fact, one of a series of paradoxical "borderline cases"—along with the tympanum and the hymen—through which Derrida has recently been studying the limits of spatial logic as it relates to intelligibility. Lacan, too, has been seeking to displace the Euclidean model of understanding (comprehension, for example, means spatial inclusion) by inventing a "new geometry" by means of the logic of knots. The relation between these two attempts to break out of spatial logic has yet to be articulated, but some measure of the difficulties involved may be derived from the fact that *to break out of* is still a spatial metaphor. The urgency of these undertakings cannot, however, be overestimated, since the logic of metaphysics, of politics, of belief, and of knowledge itself is based on the imposition of definable objective frontiers and outlines whose possibility and/or justifiability are here being put in question. If "comprehension" is the framing of something whose limits are undeterminable, how can we know what we are comprehending? The play on the spatial and the criminal senses of the word *frame* with which we began this section may thus not be as gratuitous as it seemed. And indeed, the question of the fallacies inherent in a Euclidean model of intelligibility, far from being a tangential theoretical consideration here, is central to the very plot of "The Purloined Letter" itself. For it is precisely the notion of space as finite and homogeneous that underlies the Prefect's method of investigation: "I presume you know," he explains, "that, to a properly trained police-agent, such a thing as a 'secret' drawer is impossible. Any man is a dolt who permits a 'secret' drawer to escape him in a search of this kind. The thing is *so* plain. There is a certain amount of bulk—of space—to be accounted for in every cabinet. Then we have accurate rules. The fiftieth part of a line could not escape us" (Poe, 204). The assumption that what is not seen must be hidden—an assumption Lacan calls the "realist's imbecillity"—is based on a falsely objective notion of the act of *seeing.* The polarity "hidden/exposed" cannot alone account for the police's *not* finding the letter—which was entirely exposed, inside out—let alone for Dupin's finding it. A "subjective" element must be added, which subverts the geometrical model of understanding through the interference of the polarity "blindness/sight" with the polarity "hidden/exposed." The same problematic is raised by the story of "The Emperor's New Clothes," which Derrida cites as an example of psychoanalysis's failure to go beyond the polarity "hidden/exposed" (in Freud's account). We will return to the letter's "place" later on in this essay, but it is already clear that the "range" of any investigation is located not in geometrical space, but in its implicit notion of what "seeing" is.

What enables Derrida to problematize the literary text's frame is, as we have seen, what he calls "the scene of writing." By this he means two things.

1. *The textual signifier's resistance to being totally transformed into a signified.* In spite of Lacan's attentiveness to the path of the letter in Poe's story as an illustration of the functioning of a signifier, says Derrida, the psychoanalytical reading is still blind to the functioning of the signifier in the narration itself. In reading "The Purloined Letter" as an allegory of the signifier, Lacan, according to Derrida, has made the "signifier" into the story's truth: "The displacement of the signifier is analyzed as a signified, as the recounted object in a short story" (PT, 48). Whereas, counters Derrida, it is precisely the textual signifier that resists being thus totalized into meaning, leaving an irreducible residue: "The rest, the remnant, would be 'The Purloined Letter,' the text that bears this title, and whose place, like the once more invisible large letters on the map, is not where one was expecting to find it, in the enclosed content of the 'real drama' or in the hidden and sealed interior of Poe's story, but in and as the open letter, the very open letter which fiction is" (PT, 64).

2. *The actual writings*—the books, libraries, quotations, and previous tales that surround "The Purloined Letter" with a frame of (literary) references. The story begins in "a little back library, or book-closet" (Poe, 199), where the narrator is mulling over a previous conversation on the subject of the two previous instances of Dupin's detective work as told in Poe's two previous tales, the first of which recounted the original meeting between Dupin and the narrator—in a library, of course, where both were in search of the same rare book. The story's beginning is thus an infinitely regressing reference to previous writings. And therefore, says Derrida, "nothing begins. Simply a drifting or a disorientation from which one never moves away" (PT, 101). Dupin, himself, is in fact a walking library; books are his "sole luxuries," and the narrator is "astonished" at "the vast extent of his reading" (Poe, 106). Even Dupin's last, most seemingly personal words—the venomous lines he leaves in his substitute letter to the Minister—are a quotation, whose transcription and proper authorship are the last things the story tells us. "But," concludes Derrida, "beyond the quotation marks that surround the

entire story, Dupin is obliged to quote this last word in quotation marks, to recount his signature: that is what I wrote to him and how I signed it. What is a signature within quotation marks? Then, within these quotation marks, the seal itself is a quotation within quotation marks. This remnant is still literature" (PT, 112–13).

It is by means of these two extra dimensions that Derrida intends to show the crumbling, abyssal, nontotalizable edges of the story's frame. Both of these objections, however, are in themselves more problematic and double-edged than they appear. Let us begin with the second. "Literature" in Derrida's demonstration is indeed clearly the beginning, middle, and end—and even the interior—of the purloined letter. But how was this conclusion reached? To a large extent, by listing the books, libraries, and other writings recounted in the story. That is, by following the theme—and not the functioning—of "writing" within "the content of a representation." But if Dupin's signing with a quotation, for example, is for Derrida a sign that "this remnant is still literature," does this not indicate that "literature" has become not the signifier but the signified in the story? If the play of the signifier is really to be followed, does it not play beyond the range of the *seme* "writing"? And if Derrida criticizes Lacan for making the "signifier" into the story's signified, is Derrida not here transforming "writing" into "the written" in much the same way? What Derrida calls "the reconstruction of the scene of the signifier as a signified" seems indeed to be "an inevitable process" in the logic of reading the purloined letter.

Derrida, of course, implicitly counters this objection by protesting—twice—that the textual drifting for which Lacan does not account should not be considered "the *real subject* of the tale," but rather the "remarkable ellipsis" of any subject (PT, 102). But the question of the seemingly inevitable slipping from the signifier to the signified still remains, and not as an objection to the logic of the frame, but as its fundamental question. For if the "paradoxes of parergonal logic" are such that the frame is always being framed by part of its contents, it is this very slippage between signifier and signified, *acted out* by both Derrida and Lacan against their intentions, which best illustrates those paradoxes. Derrida's justification of his framing of the "Lacan" he is reading as neither being limited to the "Seminar" nor as including Lacan's later work, itself obeys the contradictory logic of the frame. On the one hand, Derrida will study that part of Lacan's work which seems to embody a system of truth even though other writings might put that system in question, and on the other hand this same part of Lacan's work, says Derrida, will probably some day be called the work of the "young Lacan" by "academics eager to divide up *what cannot be divided*" (PT, 82, translation modified). Whatever Derrida actually thinks he is doing here, his contradictory way of explaining it obeys the paradoxes of parergonal logic so perfectly that this self-subversion may have even been deliberate.

If the question of the frame thus problematizes the object of any interpretation by setting it at an angle or fold (*pli*) with itself, then Derrida's analysis errs not in opposing this paradoxical functioning to Lacan's allegorical reading but in not following the consequences of its own insight far enough. For example, if it is the frame that makes it impossible for us to know where to begin and when to stop, why does Derrida stop within the limits of the Dupin trilogy? And if the purpose of studying "writing" is to sow an uncanny uncertainty about our position in the abyss, is not the disseminal library Derrida describes still in a way just a bit too comfortable?

"The Purloined Letter," says Derrida, is signed "literature." What does this mean, if not that the letter's contents—the only ones we are allowed to see—are in another text? That the locus of the letter's meaning is not in the letter, but somewhere else? That the context of that meaning is the way in which its context is lacking, both through the explicit designation of a proper origin (Crébillon's *Atrée*) *outside* the text and through a substitutive structure from letter to letter, from text to text, and from brother to brother, *within* the text, such that the expressions *outside* and *within* have ceased to be clearly definable? But until we have actually opened that other text, we cannot know the modality of the precise otherness of the abyss to itself, the way in which the story's edges do not simply crumble away.

In order to escape the reduction of the "library" to its thematic presence as a *sign* of writing, let us therefore pull some of the books off the shelves and see what they contain. This is a track neither Lacan nor Derrida has taken, but we will soon see how it in some way enfolds them both.

First of all, the name *Dupin* itself, according to Poe scholars, comes out of Poe's interior library: from the pages of a volume called *Sketches of Conspicuous Living Characters of France* (Philadelphia: Lea & Blanchard, 1841), which Poe reviewed for *Graham's Magazine* during the same month his first Dupin story appeared. André-Marie-Jean-Jacques Dupin, a minor French statesman, is there described as himself a walking library: "To judge from his writings, Dupin must be a perfect living encyclopedia. From Homer to Rousseau, from the Bible to the civil code, from the laws of the twelve tables to the Koran, he has read every thing, retained every thing" (224). Detective Dupin's "origin" is thus multiply bookish. He is a reader whose writer read his name in a book describing a writer as a reader—a reader whose nature can only be described in writing, in fact, as irreducibly double: "He is the personage for whom the painters of political portraits, make the most enormous consumption of antithesis. In the same picture, he will be drawn as both great and little, courageous and timid, trivial and dignified, disinterested and mercenary, restive and pliable, obstinate and fickle, white and black; there is no understanding it" (210). And the writing that serves as the vehicle of this description of written descriptions of double Dupin is itself double: a translation, by a Mr. Walsh, of a series of articles by a Frenchman whose name is not even known to the translator but who is said to call himself "an *homme de rien*, a nobody" (2). "Nobody" thus becomes the proper name of the original author in the series.[12]

But the author of the last word in "The Purloined Letter" is clearly *not* nobody. It is not even Poe; it is Crébillon. When read as the context from which Dupin's letter to the Minister has been purloined, Crébillon's *Atrée* is remarkable not simply because it tells the story of revenge as a symmetrical repetition of the original crime, but because it does so precisely by means of a purloined letter. A *letter* informs King Atreus of the extent of his betrayal and serves as an instrument of his revenge; the King himself has purloined the letter—written by the Queen to her lover, Thyestes, just before her death. The letter reveals that Plisthenes, whom everyone believes to be Atreus's son, is really the son of his brother Thyestes. Having kept the letter and its message secret for twenty years, Atreus plans to force Plisthenes, unaware of his true parentage, to commit patricide. Thwarted in this plan by Plisthenes's refusal to kill the father of his beloved, Theodamia, who is, unknown to him, his sister, Atreus is forced to produce the letter, reunite the illicit family, and transfer his revenge from Plisthenes's patricide to Thyestes's infantophagy. A Queen betraying a King, a letter representing that betrayal being purloined for purposes of power, an eventual return of that letter to its addressee, accompanied by an act of revenge which duplicates the original crime—"The Purloined Letter" as a story of repetition is itself a repetition of the story from which it purloins its last words. The Freudian "truth" of the repetition compulsion is not simply illustrated *in* the story; it is illustrated *by* the story. The story obeys the very law it conveys; it is framed by its own content. And thus "The Purloined Letter" no longer simply repeats its own "primal scene": what it repeats is nothing less than a previous story of repetition. The "last word" names the place where the "nonfirstness" of the "first word" repeats itself.

This is not the only instance of the folding-in of the frame of references upon the purloined letter's interior. Another allusion, somewhat more hidden, is contained in the description of the Minister as someone "who dares all things, those unbecoming as well as those becoming a man" (Poe, 201). These words echo Macbeth's protestation to his ambitious wife: "I dare do all that may become a man. / Who dares do more is none" (1, 7). The reference to *Macbeth* substantiates Lacan's reading of the description of the Minister as pointing toward femininity; it is indeed Lady Macbeth who dares to do what is unbecoming a man. And what is Lady Macbeth doing when we first catch sight of her? She is reading a letter. Not a purloined letter, perhaps, but one that contains the ambiguous letter of destiny, committing Macbeth to the murder of the King, whose place Macbeth will take and whose fate he will inevitably share. Kings seem to be unable to remain unscathed in the face of a letter—Atreus betrayed by his wife's letter to his brother; Duncan betrayed by Macbeth's letter to Lady Macbeth; Macbeth himself betrayed by his own confidence in his ability to read the letter of his Fate; and of course, the King in "The Purloined Letter," whose power is betrayed by his not even knowing about the existence of the letter that betrays him.

The questions raised by all these texts together are legion. What is a man? Who is the child's father? What is the relation between incest, murder, and the death of a child? What is a king? How can we read the letter of our destiny? What is seeing? The crossroads where these stories come together seems to point to the story of what occurred at another crossroads: the tragedy of Oedipus the King. We seem to have returned to our starting point, then, except for one thing: it is no longer "The Purloined Letter" that repeats the story of Oedipus, but the story of Oedipus that repeats all the letters purloined from "The Purloined Letter" 's abyssal interior.

But the letter does not stop there. For the very Oedipal reading that Derrida attributes to Lacan is itself, according to Derrida, a purloined letter— purloined by Lacan from Marie Bonaparte's psychobiographical study of the life and works of Edgar Allan Poe: "At the moment when the Seminar, like Dupin, finds the letter where it is to be found, between the legs of the woman, the deciphering of the enigma is anchored in truth. . . . Why then does it find, at the same time that it finds truth, the same meaning and the same topos as Bonaparte when, leaping over the text, she proposes a psycho-biographical analysis of 'The Purloined Letter'?" (PT, 66). In that analysis, Bonaparte sees Dupin's restitution of the letter to the Queen as the return of the missing maternal penis to the mother. The letter's hiding place in the Minister's apartment, moreover, is "almost an anatomical chart" of the female body— which leads Bonaparte to note that Baudelaire's translation of "hung from a little brass knob just beneath the middle of the mantelpiece" as "suspendu à

un petit bouton de cuivre—au dessus du manteau de la cheminée" ("*above
the mantelpiece*") is "completely wrong" (quoted in PT, 68). Bonaparte's frame
of reference—the female body—cannot tolerate this error of translation.

A note that Lacan drops on the subject of the letter's position enables Derrida to frame Lacan for neglecting to mention his references: "The question
of deciding," says Lacan, "whether he [Dupin] seizes it [the letter] above the
mantelpiece as Baudelaire translates, or beneath it, as in the original text,
may be abandoned without harm to the inferences of those whose profession is grilling [aux inférences de la cuisine]." Lacan's note: "And even to the
cook herself" (SPL, 66–67). In this cavalier treatment of Bonaparte as the
"cook," Lacan thus "makes clear" to Derrida "that Lacan had read Bonaparte,
although the Seminar never alludes to her. As an author so careful about
debts and priorities, he could have acknowledged an irruption that orients
his entire interpretation, namely, the process of rephallization as the proper
course of the letter, the 'return of the letter' restored to its 'destination' after
having been found between the legs of the mantelpiece" (PT, 68). The interpretation of the letter (as the phallus that must be returned to the mother)
must itself be returned to the "mother" from whom it has been purloined—
Marie Bonaparte. Derrida thus follows precisely the logic he objects to in
Lacan, the logic of rectification and correction: "to return the letter to its
proper course, supposing that its trajectory is a line, is to correct a deviation,
to rectify a divergence, to recall a direction, an authentic line" (PT, 65). But the
mere fact that Derrida's critique repeats the same logic he denounces is in
itself less interesting than the fact that this rectification presupposes another,
which puts its very foundations in question. For when Lacan says that the
question of the exact position of the letter "may be abandoned without harm"
to the grillers, Derrida protests, "Without harm? On the contrary, the harm
would be decisive, within the Seminar itself: *on* the mantelpiece, the letter
could not have been 'between the cheeks of the fireplace,' 'between the legs of
the fireplace'" (PT, 69). Derrida must thus correct Lacan's text, eliminate its
apparent contradiction, in order to return the letter of interpretation to its
rightful owner. And all this in order to criticize Lacan's enterprise as one of
rectification and circular return. If "rectification" as such is to be criticized, it
is difficult to determine where it begins and where it ends. In rectifying Lacan's
text in order to make it fit into the logic of rectification, Derrida thus problematizes the very status of the object of his criticism.

But if the correction of Lacan's text is itself a mutilation that requires correction, how *are* we to interpret the contradiction between Lacan's description of the Minister's apartment as "an immense female body" (SPL, 66) and

his statement that the letter's exact location does not matter? This, it seems to me, is the crux of the divergence between Derrida's and Lacan's interpretation of what the equation "letter = phallus" means.

For Bonaparte, it was precisely the analogy between the fireplace and the female body which led to the letter's phallic function. The phallus was considered as a real, anatomical referent serving as the model for a figurative representation. Bonaparte's frame of reference was thus *reference* itself.

For Derrida, on the other hand, the phallus's frame of reference is "psychoanalytical theory"'s way of preserving the phallus's referential status in the act of negating it. In commenting on Lacan's discussion of "The Meaning of the Phallus," Derrida writes:

> Phallogocentrism is one thing. And what is called man and what is called woman might be subject to it. The more so, we are reminded, since the phallus is neither a phantasy ("imaginary effect") nor an object ("partial, internal, good, bad"), even less the organ, penis or clitoris, which it symbolizes [*Ecrits*, 690]. Androcentrism ought therefore to be something else.
>
> Yet what is going on? The entire phallogocentrism is articulated from the starting-point of a determinate *situation* (let us give this word its full impact) in which the phallus *is* the mother's desire inasmuch as she does not have it. An (individual, perceptual, local, cultural, historical, etc.) situation on the basis of which is developed something called a "sexual theory": in it the phallus is not the organ, penis or clitoris, which it symbolizes; but it does to a larger extent and in the first place symbolize the penis. . . . This consequence had to be traced in order to recognize the meaning [the direction, *sens*] of the purloined letter in the "course *which is proper to it*." (PT, 98–99)

Thus, says Derrida, the very nonreferentiality of the phallus, in the final analysis, insures that the penis is its referent.

Before trying to determine the applicability of this summary to Lacan's actual statements in "The Meaning of the Phallus"—not to mention in the "Seminar"—let us follow its consequences further in Derrida's critique. From the very first words of "The Purveyor of Truth," psychoanalysis is implicitly being criticized for being capable of finding only itself wherever it looks: "Psychoanalysis, supposing, finds itself" (PT, 31, translation mine). In whatever it turns its attention to, psychoanalysis seems to recognize nothing but its own (Oedipal) schemes. Dupin finds the letter because "he knows that the letter finally *finds itself* where it must *be found* in order to return circularly and adequately to its proper place. This proper place, known to Dupin and to the psychoanalyst who intermittently takes his place, is the place of castration" (PT, 60, translation modified). The psychoanalyst's act, then, is one of mere *recognition* of the expected, a recognition that Derrida finds explicitly stated as such by Lacan in the underlined words he quotes from the "Seminar": "Just so does the purloined letter, like an immense female body, stretch out across the Minister's office when Dupin enters. But just so does he already *expect to find it* [emphasis mine—J.D.] and has only, with his eyes veiled by green lenses, to undress that huge body" (PT, 61–62, emphasis and brackets in original).

But if recognition is a form of blindness, a form of violence to the otherness of the object, it would seem that, by eliminating Lacan's suggestion of a possible complication of the phallic scheme, and by lying in wait between the brackets of the fireplace to catch the psychoanalyst at his own game, Derrida, too, is "recognizing" rather than reading. He recognizes, as he himself says, a certain classical conception of psychoanalysis: "From the beginning," writes Derrida early in his study, "*we recognize* the classical landscape of applied psychoanalysis" (PT, 45, emphasis mine). It would seem that the theoretical frame of reference which governs recognition is a constitutive element in the blindness of any interpretative insight. That frame of reference allows the analyst to frame the author of the text he is reading for practices whose locus is simultaneously beyond the letter of the text and behind the vision of its reader. The reader is framed by his own frame, but he is not even in possession of his own guilt, since it is that which prevents his vision from coinciding with itself. Just as the author of a criminal frame transfers guilt from himself to another by leaving *signs* that he hopes will be read as insufficiently erased traces or referents left by the other, the author of any critique is himself framed by his own frame of the other, no matter how guilty or innocent the other may be.

What is at stake here is therefore the question of the relation between referentiality and interpretation. And here we find an interesting twist: while criticizing Lacan's notion of the phallus as being too referential, Derrida goes on to use referential logic against it. This comes up in connection with the letter's famous "materiality," which Derrida finds so odd. "It would be hard to exaggerate here the scope of this proposition on the indivisibility of the letter, or rather on its identity to itself inaccessible to dismemberment . . . as well as on the so-called materiality of the signifier (the letter) intolerant to partition. But where does this idea come from? A torn-up letter may be purely and simply destroyed, it happens . . ." (PT, 86–87, translation modified). The so-called materiality of the signifier, says Derrida, is nothing but an *idealization*.

But what if the signifier were precisely what put the polarity "materiality/ ideality" in question? Has it not become obvious that neither Lacan's description ("Tear a letter into little pieces, it remains the letter that it is") nor Derrida's description ("A torn-up letter may be purely and simply destroyed, it happens") can be read literally? Somehow, a rhetorical fold (*pli*) in the text is there to trip us up whichever way we turn. Especially since the expression "it happens" (*ça arrive*) uses the very word on which the controversy over the letter's *arrival* at its destination turns.

Our study of the readings of "The Purloined Letter" has thus brought us to the point where the word *letter* no longer has any literality.

But what is a letter that has no literality?

A "Pli" for Understanding

I pull in resolution, and begin
To doubt the equivocation of the fiend
That lies like truth.
—Macbeth

Why do you lie to me saying you're going to Cracow so I should believe
you're going to Lemberg, when in reality you *are* going to Cracow?
—Joke quoted by Lacan after Freud

The letter, then, poses the question of its own rhetorical status. It moves rhetorically through the two long, minute studies in which it is presumed to be the literal object of analysis, without having any literality. Instead of simply being explained by those analyses, the rhetoric of the letter problematizes the very rhetorical mode of analytical discourse. And if *literal* means "to the letter," the literal becomes the most problematically figurative mode of all.

As the locus of rhetorical displacement, the letter made its very entrance into Poe's story by "traumatizing" the Prefect's discourse about it. After a series of paradoxes and pleas for absolute secrecy, the Prefect describes the problem created by the letter with a proliferation of *periphrases* which the narrator dubs "the cant of diplomacy":

"Well, then; I have received personal information, from a very high quarter, that a certain document of the last importance has been purloined from the royal apartments. The individual who purloined it is known; this beyond a doubt; he was seen to take it. It is known, also, that it still remains in his possession."

"How is this known?" asked Dupin.

"It is clearly inferred," replied the Prefect, "from the nature of the document, and from the non-appearance of certain results which would at once arise from its passing *out* of the robber's possession— that is to say, from his employing it as he must design in the end to employ it."

"Be a little more explicit," I said.

"Well, I may venture so far as to say that the paper gives its holder a certain power in a certain quarter where such power is immensely valuable." The Prefect was fond of the cant of diplomacy. (Poe, 200)

The letter thus enters the discourse of Poe's story as a rhetorical fold that actually hides nothing, since, although *we* never find out what was written in the letter, presumably the Queen, the Minister, Dupin, the Prefect—who all held the letter in their hands—and even the narrator, who heard what the Prefect read from his memorandum-book, *did.* The way in which the letter dictates a series of circumlocutions, then, resembles the way in which the path of the letter dictates the characters' circumvolutions—not that the letter's contents *must* remain hidden, but that the question of whether or not they are revealed is immaterial to the displacement the letter governs. The character and actions of each of the letter's holders are determined by the rhetorical spot it puts them in *whether or not* that spot can be read by the subjects it displaces.

The letter, then, acts as a signifier *not* because its contents are lacking, but because its function is not dependent on the knowledge or nonknowledge of those contents. Therefore, by saying that the letter cannot be divided Lacan does not mean that the phallus must remain intact, but that the phallus, the letter, and the signifier *are not substances.* The letter cannot be divided because it only functions *as* a division. It is not something with "an *identity* to itself inaccessible to dismemberment" (PT, 86–87, emphasis mine) as Derrida interprets it; it is a *difference.* It is known only in its effects. The signifier is an articulation in a chain, not an identifiable unit. It cannot be known in itself because it is capable of "sustaining itself *only* in a displacement" (SPL, 59, emphasis mine). It is localized, but only as the nongeneralizable locus of a differential relationship. Derrida, in fact, enacts this law of the signifier in the very act of opposing it:

Perhaps only one letter need be changed, maybe even less than a letter in the expression: "missing from its place [*manque à sa place*]. Perhaps we need only introduce a written "a," i.e. without accent, in order to bring out that if the lack *has* its place [*le manque a sa place*] in this atomistic topology of the signifier, that is, if it occupies therein a specific place of definite contours, the order would remain undisturbed. (PT, 45)

While thus criticizing the hypostasis of a lack—the letter as the substance of an absence (which is not what Lacan is saying)—Derrida is illustrating what Lacan *is* saying about both the materiality and the localizability of the signifier as the mark of difference by operating on the letter as a material locus of differentiation: by removing the little signifier " , " an accent mark which has no meaning in itself.[13]

The question of the nature of the "lack," however, brings us back to the complexities of the meaning and place of the "phallus." For while it is quite easy to show the signifier as a "difference" rather than a "lack," the question becomes much trickier in relation to the phallus. There would seem to be no ambiguity in Lacan's statement that "clinical observation shows us that this test through the desire of the Other is not decisive insofar as the subject thereby learns whether or not he himself has a real phallus, but insofar as he learns *that the mother does not*" (*Ecrits*, 693, translation and emphasis mine). The theory seems to imply that at some point in human sexuality, a referential moment is unbypassable: the observation that the mother does not have a penis is necessary. And therefore it would seem that the "lack" is localizable as the substance of an absence or a hole. To borrow a joke from Geoffrey Hartman's discussion of certain solutionless detective stories, if the purloined letter is the mother's phallus, "instead of a whodunit we get a whodonut, a story with a hole in it."[14]

But even on this referential level, is the object of observation really a lack? Is it not instead an interpretation—an interpretation ("castration") not of a lack but of a *difference*? If what is observed is irreducibly anatomical, what is anatomy here but the irreducibility of difference? Even on the most elementary level, the phallus is a sign of sexuality as difference, and not as the presence or absence of this or that organ.

But Lacan defines the phallus in a much more complicated way. For if the woman is defined as "giving in a love-relation that which she does not have," the definition of what the woman does not have is not limited to the penis. At another point in the discussion, Lacan refers to "the gift of what one does not have" as "love" (*Ecrits*, 691). Is "love" here a mere synonym for the phallus? Perhaps; but only if we modify the definition of the phallus. Love, in Lacan's terminology, is what is in question in the "request for love" ("demande d'amour"), which is "unconditional," the "demand for a presence or an absence" (*Ecrits*, 691). This "demande" is not only a reference to "what the Other doesn't have," however. It is also language. And language is what alienates human desire such that "it is from the place of the Other that the subject's message is emitted" (*Ecrits*, 690). The "demande" is thus a request for the unconditional presence or absence not of an organ but of the Other in answer to the question asked by the subject from the place of the Other. But this "demande" is not yet the definition of "desire." Desire is what is left of the "demande" when all possible satisfaction of "real" needs has been subtracted from it. "Desire is neither the appetite for satisfaction, nor the demand for love, but the difference which results from the subtraction of the first from the second, the very phenomenon of their split [*Spaltung*]" (*Ecrits*, 691). And if the phallus as a signifier, according to Lacan, "gives the *ratio* of desire," the definition of the phallus can no longer bear a simple relation either to the body or to language, because it is that which prevents both the body and language from being simple: "The phallus is the privileged signifier of that mark where logos is joined together with the advent of desire" (*Ecrits*, 692; all translations in this paragraph mine).

The important word in this definition is *joined*. For if language (alienation of needs through the place of the Other) and desire (the remainder that is left after the subtraction of the satisfaction of real needs from absolute demand) are neither totally separable from each other nor related in the same way to their own division, the phallus is the signifier of the articulation between two very problematic chains. But what is a signifier in this context? "A signifier," says Lacan, "is what represents a subject for another signifier." A signifier represents, then, and what it represents is a subject. But it only does so for another signifier. What does the expression "for another signifier" mean, if not that the distinction between subject and signifier posed in the first part of the definition is being subverted in the second? "Subject" and "signifier" are coimplicated in a definition that is unable either to separate them totally or to fuse them completely. There are three positions in the definition, two of which are occupied by the same word, but that word is differentiated from itself in the course of the definition—because it begins to take the place of the *other* word. The signifier for which the other signifier represents a subject thus acts like a subject because it is the place where the representation is "understood." The signifier, then, situates the place of something like a reader.

And the reader becomes the place where representation would be understood if there were any such thing as a place beyond representation; the place where representation is inscribed as an infinite chain of substitutions whether or not there is any place from which it can be understood.

The letter as a signifier is thus not a thing or the absence of a thing, not a word or the absence of a word, not an organ or the absence of an organ, but a *knot* in a structure where words, things, and organs can neither be definably separated nor compatibly combined. This is why the exact representational position of the letter in the Minister's apartment both matters and does not matter. It matters to the extent that sexual anatomical difference creates an irreducible dissymmetry to be accounted for in every human subject. But it does not matter to the extent that the letter is not hidden in geometrical space, where the police are looking for it, or in anatomical space, where a literal understanding of psychoanalysis might look for it. It is located "in" a *symbolic* structure, a structure that can only be perceived in its effects, and whose effects are perceived as repetition. Dupin finds the letter "in" the symbolic order not because he knows where to look, but because he knows *what to repeat*. Dupin's "analysis" is the repetition of the scene that led to the necessity of analysis. It is not an interpretation or an insight, but an act—an act of untying the knot in the structure by the repetition of the act of tying it. The word *analyze*, in fact, etymologically means "untie," a meaning on which Poe plays in his prefatory remarks on the nature of analysis as "that moral activity which disentangles" (Poe, 102). The analyst does not intervene by giving meaning, but by effecting a *dénouement*.

But if the act of (psycho-)analysis has no identity apart from its status as a repetition of the structure it seeks to analyze (to untie), then Derrida's remarks against psychoanalysis as being always already *mise en abyme* in the text it studies and as being only capable of finding *itself*, are not objections to psychoanalysis but a profound insight into its very essence. Psychoanalysis is, in fact, itself the primal scene it seeks: it is the first occurrence of what has been repeating itself in the patient without ever having occurred. Psychoanalysis is not the interpretation of repetition; it is the repetition of a *trauma of interpretation*—called "castration" or "parental coitus" or "the Oedipus complex" or even "sexuality"—the traumatic deferred interpretation not *of* an event but *as* an event that never took place as such. The "primal scene" is not a scene but an interpretative infelicity whose result was to situate the interpreter in an intolerable position. And psychoanalysis is the reconstruction of that interpretative infelicity not as its interpretation, but as its first and last act. Psychoanalysis has content only insofar as it repeats the dis-content of what never took place.

But, as Dupin reminds us, "there is such a thing as being too profound. Truth is not always in a well. In fact, as regards the more important knowledge, I do believe that she is invariably superficial" (Poe, 119). Have we not here been looking beyond Lacan's signifier instead of *at* it? When Lacan insists on the "materiality of the signifier" that does not "admit partition," what is *his* way of explaining it? Simply that the word *letter* is never used with a partitive article: you can have "some mail" but not "some letter."

> Language delivers its judgment to whoever knows how to hear it: through the usage of the article as partitive particle. It is there that the spirit—if spirit be living meaning—appears, no less oddly, as more available for quantification than the letter. To begin with meaning itself, which bears our saying: a speech rich with meaning ["plein *de* signification"], just as we recognize a measure of intention ["*de* l'intention"] in an act, or deplore that there is no more love ["plus *d'amour*"]; or store up hatred ["*de la* haine"] and expend devotion ["*du* dévouement"], and so much infatuation ["tant *d'*infatuation"] is easily reconciled to the fact that there will always be ass ["*de la* cuisse"] for sale and brawling ["*du* rififi"] among men.
>
> But as for the letter—be it taken as typographical character, epistle, or what makes a man of letters—we will say that what is said is to be understood *to the letter* [*à la lettre*], that *a letter* [*une lettre*] awaits you at the post office, or even that you are acquainted with *letters* [*que vous avez des lettres*]—never that there is *letter* [*de la lettre*] anywhere, whatever the context, even to designate overdue mail. (SPL, 53–54)

If this passage is particularly resistant to translation, that is because its message is in the "superficial" play of the signifier. Like the large letters on the map which are so obvious as to be invisible, Lacan's textual signifier has gone unnoticed in the search for the signified, "signifier."

But the question of translation in connection with a message so obvious that it goes unseen is not an accident here. For in his discussion of Dupin's statement that " 'analysis' conveys 'algebra' about as much as, in Latin, '*ambitus*' implies 'ambition,' '*religio*,' religion, or '*homines honesti*' a set of '*honorable* men' " (Poe, 212), Lacan asks:

> Might not this parade of erudition be destined to reveal to us the key words of our drama?[15] Is not the magician repeating his trick before

our eyes, without deceiving us this time about divulging his secret, but pressing his wager to the point of really explaining it to us without us seeing a thing. *That* would be the summit of the illusionist's art: through one of his fictive creations to *truly delude us.* (SPL, 50–51)

But the trick does not end here. For has Lacan himself not slipped into the paragraph on the quantification of the letter a parade of "key words" for his reading of the situation? "Full of meaning," "intention," "hatred," "love," "infatuation," "devotion," "ass for sale," and "brawling among men"—all of these words occur as the possible "signifieds" of "The Purloined Letter" in the "Seminar." But if the key words of a reading of the story thus occur only in the mode of a play of the signifier, the *difference* between "signifier" and "signified" in Lacan's text, as well as in Poe's, has been effectively subverted. What the reader finally reads when he deciphers the signifying surface of the map of his misreading is: "You have been fooled." And in this discussion of "being fooled" Lacan, far from excluding the narrator, situates him in the dynamic functioning of the text, as a reader *en abyme* duped by Dupin's trick explanations of his technique; a reader who, however, unconscious of the nonsequiturs he is repeating, is so much in awe of his subject that his admiration blinds *us* to the tricky functioning of what he so faithfully transmits.

To be fooled by a text implies that the text is not constative but performative, and that the reader is in fact one of its effects. The text's "truth" puts the status of the reader in question, "performs" him as its "address." Thus "truth" is not what the fiction reveals as a nudity behind a veil. When Derrida calls Lacan's statement that "truth inhabits fiction" an unequivocal expression or revelation of the truth of truth (PT, 46), he is simply not seeing the performative perversity of the rest of the sentence in which that "statement" occurs: "It is up to the reader to give the letter . . . what he will find as its last word: its destination. That is, Poe's message deciphered and coming back from him, the reader, from the fact that, in reading it, he is able to say of himself that he is not more feigned than truth when it inhabits fiction" (*Ecrits*, 10, translation mine). The play between truth and fiction, reader and text, message and feint, has become impossible to unravel into an "unequivocal" meaning.

We have thus come back to the question of the letter's destination and of the meaning of the enigmatic "last words" of Lacan's "Seminar." "The sender," writes Lacan, "receives from the receiver his own message in reverse form. Thus it is that what the 'purloined letter,' nay, the 'letter in sufferance' means is that a letter always arrives at its destination" (SPL, 72). The reversibility of the direction of the letter's movement between sender and receiver has now come to stand for the fact, underlined by Derrida as if it were an *objection* to Lacan, that there is no position from which the letter's message can be read as an object: "no neutralization is possible, no general point of view" (PT, 106). This is the same "discovery" that psychoanalysis makes—that the analyst is involved (through transference) in the very "object" of his analysis.

Everyone who has held the letter—or even beheld it—including the narrator, has ended up having the letter addressed to him as its destination. The reader is comprehended by the letter; there is no place from which he can stand back and observe it. Not that the letter's meaning is subjective rather than objective, but that the letter is precisely that which subverts the polarity "subjective/objective," that which makes subjectivity into something whose position in a structure is situated by an object's passage through it. The letter's destination is thus *wherever it is read*: the place it assigns to its reader as his own partiality. Its destination is not a place, decided a priori by the sender, because the receiver is the sender, and the receiver is whoever receives the letter, including nobody. When Derrida says that a letter can miss its destination and be disseminated, he reads "destination" as a place that preexists the letter's movement. But if, as Lacan shows, the letter's destination is not its literal addressee, nor even whoever possesses it, but whoever is possessed by it, then the very disagreement over the meaning of "reaching the destination" is an *illustration* of the nonobjective nature of that "destination." The rhetoric of Derrida's differentiation of his own point of view from Lacan's enacts that law:

> Thanks to castration, the phallus always stays in its place in the transcendental topology we spoke of earlier. It is indivisible and indestructible there, like the letter which takes its place. And that is why the *interested* presupposition, never proved, of the letter's materiality as indivisibility was indispensable to this restricted economy, this circulation of property.
>
> The difference I am *interested* in here is that, a formula to be read however one wishes, the lack has no place of its own in dissemination. (PT, 63, translation modified, emphasis mine)

The play of "interest" in this expression of difference is too interesting not to be deliberate. The opposition between the "phallus" and "dissemination" is not between two theoretical objects but between two interested positions. And if sender and receiver are merely the two poles of a reversible message, then Lacan's very substitution of *destin* for *dessein* in the Crébillon quotation—a misquotation that Derrida finds revealing enough to end his analysis upon—*is*, in fact, the quotation's message. The sender (dessein) and the receiver (destin) of the violence which passes between Atreus and Thyestes are equally subject to the violence the letter *is*.

The reflexivity between receiver and sender is, however, not an expression of symmetry in itself, but only an evocation of the interdependence of the two terms, of the *question* of symmetry as a *problem* in the transferential structure of all reading. As soon as accident or exteriority or time or repetition enters into that reflexivity—that is to say, from the beginning—"Otherness" becomes in a way the letter's sender. The message I am reading may be either my own (narcissistic) message backward or the way in which that message is always traversed by its own otherness to itself or by the narcissistic message of the other. In any case, the letter is in a way the materialization of my death. And once these various possibilities are granted, none of them can function in isolation. The question of the letter's origin and destination can no longer be asked as such. And whether this is because it involves two, three, or four terms must remain undecidable.

The sentence "a letter always arrives at its destination" can thus either be simply pleonastic or variously paradoxical; it can mean "the only message I can read is the one I send," "wherever the letter is, is its destination," "when a letter is read, it reads the reader," "the repressed always returns," "I exist only as a reader of the other," "the letter has no destination," and "we all die." It is not any one of these readings, but all of them and others in their incompatibility, which repeat the letter in its way of reading the act of reading. Far from giving us the "Seminar"'s final truth, these last words enact the impossibility of any ultimate analytical metalanguage.

If it at first seemed possible to say that Derrida was opposing the unsystematizable to the systematized, "chance" to psychoanalytical "determinism," or the "undecidable" to the "destination," the positions of these oppositions seem now to be reversed; Lacan's apparently unequivocal ending says only its own dissemination, while "dissemination" has erected itself into a kind of "last word." But these oppositions are themselves misreadings of the dynamic functioning of what is at stake here. For if the letter is what dictates the rhetorical indetermination of any theoretical discourse about it, then the oscillation between unequivocal statements of undecidability and ambiguous assertions of decidability is one of the letter's inevitable effects. For example, the "indestructibility of desire," which could be considered a psychoanalytical belief in the return of the *same*, turns out to name repetition as the repetition not of sameness but of *otherness*, resulting in the dissemination of the subject. And "symbolic determination" is not opposed to "chance": it is what emerges as the *syntax* of chance.[16] But "chance," out of which springs that which repeats, cannot in any way be "known," since "knowing" is one of its effects. We can therefore never be sure whether or not "chance" itself exists at all. "Undecidability" can no more be used as a last word than "destination." "Car," said Mallarmé, "il y a et il n'y a pas de hasard." The "undeterminable" is not opposed to the determinable; "dissemination" is not opposed to repetition. If we could be sure of the difference between the determinable and the undeterminable, the undeterminable would be comprehended within the determinable. What is undecidable is whether a thing is decidable or not.

AS A FINAL FOLD in the letter's performance of its reader, it should perhaps be noted that, in this discussion of the letter as what prevents me from knowing whether Lacan and Derrida are really saying the same thing or only enacting their own differences from themselves, my own theoretical "frame of reference" is precisely, to a very large extent, the writings of Lacan and Derrida. The frame is thus framed again by part of its content; the sender again receives his own message backward from the receiver. And the true otherness of the purloined letter of literature has perhaps still in no way been accounted for.

NOTES

"The Frame of Reference: Poe, Lacan, Derrida." *Yale French Studies* 55/56 (1978): 457–505. Reprinted by permission of *Yale French Studies*.

1. Edgar Allan Poe, *Great Tales and Poems of Edgar Allan Poe* (New York: Pocket Library, 1951); hereafter designated as "Poe." Jacques Lacan, *Ecrits* (Paris: Seuil, 1966); quotations in English are taken, unless otherwise indicated, from the partial translation in *Yale French Studies* 48 (*French Freud*) (1973); hereafter designated as "SPL." Jacques Derrida, published in French in *Poétique* 21 (1975) and, somewhat reduced in *Yale French Studies* 52 (*Graphesis*) (1975); unless otherwise indicated, references are to the English version, hereafter designated as "PT."

2. Such a concatenation could jokingly be called, after the nursery rhyme, "This is the text that Jacques built." But in fact, it is precisely this kind of sequence or chain that is in question here.

3. We will speak about this bracketed signature later; for the time being, it stands as a sign that Derrida's signature has indeed been added to our round robin.

4. "So infamous a scheme / If not worthy of Atreus, is worthy of Thyestes."

5. *La politique de l'autruiche* combines the policy of the ostrich (*autruche*), others (*autrui*), and Austria (*Autriche*).

6. Jacques Derrida, *Positions* (Paris: Minuit, 1972), 112–13; my translation; Derrida, *Positions*, 113.

7. Jacques Lacan, *Ecrits* (Paris: Seuil ["Points"], 1966), 11; my translation.

8. See Lacan's description in *Ecrits*, 60, of the "effect of disorientation, or even of great anxiety," provoked by these exercises.

9. Some idea of the possibilities for misunderstanding inherent in this question can be gathered from the following: in order to show that psychoanalysis *represses* "writing" in a logocentric way, Derrida quotes Lacan's statement against tape recorders: "But precisely because it comes to him through an alienated form, even a retransmission of his own recorded discourse, be it from the mouth of his own doctor, cannot have the same effects as psychoanalytical interlocution." This Derrida regards as a *condemnation* of the "simulacrum," a "disqualification of recording or of repetition in the name of the living and present word." But what does Lacan actually *say*? Simply that a tape recording *does not have the same effects* as psychoanalytical interlocution. Does the fact that psychoanalysis is a technique based on verbal interlocution automatically reduce it to a logocentric error? Is it not equally possible to regard what Lacan calls "full speech" as being *full* of precisely what Derrida calls *"writing"*?

10. Paul de Man, *Blindness and Insight* (London: Oxford University Press, 1971), 140.

11. Stanley E. Fish, "How Ordinary Is Ordinary Language?," *New Literary History* 5, no. 1 (1973): 52, emphasis mine.

12. In a final twist to this *mise en abyme* of writing, the words "by L. L. de Loménie" have been penciled into the Yale library's copy of this book under the title in a meticulous nineteenth-century hand, as the book's *"supplément d'origine."*

13. It is perhaps not by chance that the question here arises of whether or not to put the accent on the letter *a*. The letter *a* is perhaps the purloined letter par excellence in the writings of all three authors: Lacan's "objet *a*," Derrida's "différance," and Edgar Poe's middle initial, *A*, taken from his foster father, John Allan.

14. Geoffrey Hartman, "Literature High and Low: The Case of the Mystery Story," in *The Fate of Reading* (Chicago: University of Chicago Press, 1975), 206.

15. *Ambitus* means "detour"; *religio*, "sacred bond"; *homines honesti*, "decent men." Lacan expands upon these words as the "key words" of the story by saying: "All of this . . . does not imply that because the letter's secrecy is indefensible, the betrayal of that secret would in any sense be honorable. The *honesti homines*, decent people, will not get off so easily. There is more than one *religio*, and it is

not slated for tomorrow that sacred ties shall cease to rend us in two. As for *ambitus*: a detour, we see, is not always inspired by ambition" (SPL, 58).

16. This is what the mathematical model in the "Introduction" of the "Seminar" clearly shows; beginning with a totally arbitrary binary series, a syntax of regularity emerges from the simple application of a law of combination to the series. When it is objected that that syntax *is not*, unless the subject *remembers* the series, Lacan responds in *Ecrits*, 43: "That is just what is in question here: it is less out of anything real . . . than precisely out of *what never was*, that what repeats itself springs" (translation mine). Memory could thus be considered not as *condition* of repetition, but as one of its syntactic effects. What we call a random series is, in fact, already an *interpretation*, not a given; it is not a materialization of chance itself, but only of something which obeys our conception of the laws of probability.

PART II

Race, Sexuality, Gender

CHAPTER 7

Euphemism, Understatement, and the Passive Voice
A Genealogy of Afro-American Poetry

In his well-known essay of 1937, "Blueprint for Negro Writing," Richard Wright expresses an ambivalence toward his precursors that has been shared by many subsequent Afro-American writers. "Generally speaking," he writes:

> Negro writing in the past has been confined to humble novels, poems, and plays, prim and decorous ambassadors who went a-begging to white America. They entered the Court of American Public Opinion dressed in the knee-pants of servility, curtsying to show that the Negro was not inferior, that he was human, and that he had a life comparable to that of other people. For the most part these artistic ambassadors were received as though they were French poodles who do clever tricks.[1]

In this essay I would like to examine some of the more covert strategies of protest implicit in the writings of some of the ambassadors Wright might have had in mind: James Weldon Johnson, Countee Cullen, and, most particularly, Phillis Wheatley, whose 1773 volume was the first book of poems published by a black American. While decorousness may in some ways have been disabling, I will try to show that these writers nevertheless set up conditions of utterance in which the French poodle could sometimes function as a Trojan horse.

In 1921, at the start of what has come to be known as the Harlem Renaissance, James Weldon Johnson edited what he hoped would be a major anthology of Afro-American poetry. The collection was designed to remedy what he called a "lack of information" on the part of "the public." Nothing could be less inflammatory than the desire to supply information that is lacking. Through a carefully calculated use of the passive voice, an avoidance of black/white binary oppositions, and the elaboration of a seemingly syllogistic logic, Johnson attempts nothing less than to convince the world to acknowledge the greatness of the Negro people:

> There is, perhaps, a better excuse for giving an Anthology of American Negro Poetry to the public than can be offered for many of the anthologies that have recently been issued. The public, generally speaking, does not know that there are American Negro poets—to supply this lack of information is, alone, a work worthy of somebody's effort.
>
> Moreover, the matter of Negro poets, and the production of literature by the colored people in this country involves more than supplying information that is lacking. It is a matter which has a direct bearing on the most vital of American problems.
>
> A people may become great through many means, but there is only one measure by which its greatness is recognized and acknowledged. The final measure of the greatness of all peoples is the amount and standard of the literature and art they have produced. The world does not know that a people is great until that people produces great literature and art. No people that has produced great literature and art has ever been looked upon by the world as distinctly inferior.
>
> The status of the Negro in the United States is more a question of national mental attitude toward the race than of actual conditions. And nothing will do more to change that mental attitude and raise his status than a demonstration of intellectual parity by the Negro through the production of literature and art.[2]

Johnson goes on to assert that the Negro has already contributed to American culture the only artistic productions "the world" (that is, Europe) acknowledges as distinctively American: Uncle Remus stories, spirituals, the cakewalk, and ragtime. Again, Johnson uses the passive voice as a cover for unspecified (here, all-conquering) agency:

> As for Ragtime, I go straight to the statement that it is the one artistic production by which America is known the world over. It has been all-conquering. Everywhere it is hailed as "American music." (11)

Through his use of ellipsis, understatement, unspecified agency, and non-binarity, Johnson is thus attempting to bring about a change in the status of the Negro without explicitly acknowledging or processing conflict and dispossession. When such rhetorical strategies are used by a dominant discourse, the reason for the avoidance of conflict is the avoidance of change. But when acknowledging the conflict may mean granting it a legitimacy it does not deserve, when processing difference might seem to involve accepting the premises of racial inequality, then the bootstrap operation of passivity and euphemism may well begin to set the stage for an unimpeded and newly empowered affirmation.

Moving from music to poetry, Johnson continues to employ euphemism and the passive voice to describe the previous history of the Afro-American lyric. The list, he writes, begins with Phillis Wheatley. It soon becomes clear, however, that Johnson's own history, therefore, begins with ambivalence. The passive voice he uses in speaking about Wheatley expresses both an avoidance of conflict and an avoidance of change—that is, both an opposition to and an identification with dominant discourse:

> Phillis Wheatley has never been given her rightful place in American literature. By some sort of conspiracy she is kept out of most of the books, especially the text-books on literature used in the schools. Of course, she is not a *great* American poet—and in her day there were no great American poets—but she is an important American poet. Her importance, if for no other reason, rests on the fact that, save one, she is the first in order of time of all the women poets of America. And she is among the first of all American poets to issue a volume. (23)

Johnson, too, does not grant Phillis Wheatley her rightful place at the head of the list, but rather confines her to the space of his preface, the place of prehistory. She is the ancestor half acknowledged, half obscured. Johnson wishes to combat the injustice of her exclusion, yet cannot quite bring himself to place her first. Is this mere misogyny? Mere identification with male hegemony? Perhaps. Indeed, Wright's scorn for the curtsying ambassadors is also a resistance to the feminine as ancestor. But what Johnson holds against Wheatley is her avoidance of passionate personal utterance: "One looks in vain for some outburst or even some complaint against the bondage of her people, for some agonising cry about her native land. . . . In the poem addressed to the Earl of Dartmouth, she speaks of freedom and makes a reference to the parents from whom she was taken as child, a reference which cannot but strike the reader as rather unimpassioned" (28, 29). In other words, what

Johnson holds against Wheatley is precisely the stylistic avoidance of conflict and outcry that characterizes his own writing in this preface. Could one not, for instance, characterize as "unimpassioned" Johnson's own use of words like *curious* and *strange*, as in the following sentence:

> It seems *strange* that the books generally give space to a mention of Urian Oakes, President of Harvard College, and to quotations from the crude and lengthy elegy which he published in 1667 . . . and yet deny a place to Phillis Wheatley. (23)

Johnson's use of *strange* here echoes Countee Cullen's use of *curious* in what Johnson himself calls "the two most poignant lines in American literature":

> Yet do I marvel at this curious thing—
> To make a poet black and bid him sing. (231)

Johnson's sense of the poignancy of these lines may well stem from his own knowledge of all that a word like *curious* can conceal. Euphemism may be a way of avoiding conflict, but it also functions as an X marking a spot where later, perhaps, a poet will be able to say more: Protest may not yet be voiced, but at least the spot has been marked.

Countee Cullen himself is a master of the marked spot. In his poem "Heritage," he manages to keep the question "What is Africa to me?" in perfect suspension between a rhetorical and a real question. The question itself, like the poem's speaker, "plays a double part," as does the repeated phrase "so I lie," which carries the ambiguity the poem enacts between language and the body, between legend and unconscious desire. Africa may be only a book, says the poem, but nevertheless what is repressed can return. Another of the poem's ploys is its strategic use of the bad rhyme:

> Quaint, outlandish heathen gods
> Black men fashion out of rods,
> Clay, and brittle bits of stone,
> In a likeness like their own,
> My conversion came high-priced;
> I belong to Jesus Christ,
> Preacher of humility;
> Heathen gods are naught to me. (224)

The wince produced by rhyming *Christ* with *priced* soon gives way, I think, to a recognition of its rightness, of all that is condensed behind that rhyme. The Christianization of Africans was indeed accomplished through their transformation into human commodities. Why should a conversion brought about by enslavement produce a *good* rhyme? The seemingly innocuous forcing of the rhyme euphemistically marks the barbarity of the historical process itself.

The art of forcing a rhyme between conversion and enslavement has its origins in the 1773 volume of poetry written by Phillis Wheatley. The eighteen-year-old slave girl from Boston stands indeed as the inventor of a whole tradition of protest through excessive compliance.

Wheatley's poetry repeatedly describes several analogous processes of transformation: death, conversion, and the American struggle for independence. These are usually described in terms of travel from one location to another. In her numerous elegies, Wheatley describes the dead as winging their way to a happier place:

> Ere yet the morn its lovely blushes spread,
> See Sewell numbered with the happy dead.
> Hail, holy man, arriv'd th' immortal shore,
> Though we shall hear thy warning voice no more.
> Come, let us all behold with wistful eyes
> The saint ascending to his native skies.[3]

In her poem "On being brought from Africa to America," she writes:

> 'Twas mercy brought me from my Pagan land,
> Taught my benighted soul to understand
> That there's a God, that there's a Saviour too:
> Once I redemption neither sought nor knew. (53)

(This, as June Jordan remarks, is also a way of saying: "Once I existed on other than your terms.")[4] And finally, in her pro-revolutionary poem to the Earl of Dartmouth, she writes:

> No more, America, in mournful strain
> Of wrongs, and grievance unredress'd complain,
> No longer shalt thou dread the iron chain,
> Which wanton Tyranny with lawless hand
> Had made, and with it meant t' enslave the land. (83)

Then she goes on:

> Should you, my lord, while you peruse my song,
> Wonder from whence my love of Freedom sprung,

Whence flow these wishes for the common good,
By feeling hearts alone best understood,
I, young in life, by seeming cruel fate
Was snatched from Afric's fancy'd happy seat:
What pangs excruciating must molest,
What sorrows labour in my parent's breast?
Steel'd was that soul and by no misery mov'd
That from a father seiz'd his babe belov'd:
Such, such my case. And can I then but pray
Others may never feel tyrannic sway? (83)

By simply repeating the ideology she has learned, Wheatley exposes a glaring contradiction. She presents us with something like the schoolbook exercise: "What's wrong with this picture?" While the voyage from life to death, from paganism to Christianity, and from English rule to American rule might be seen to involve a passage from bondage to freedom, the voyage from Africa to America has clearly gone the other way. Under Wheatley's pen, the lessons she has learned so well self-deconstruct. That she knew exactly what she was doing is evident from a letter she wrote to the Indian minister Samson Occom, which she published a number of times in 1774, several months after she obtained her freedom:

> In every human Breast, God has implanted a Principle, which we call Love of Freedom; it is impatient of oppression, and pants for Deliverance; and by the Leave of our modern Egyptians I will assert that the same Principle lives in us. God grant Deliverance in his own Way and Time, and get him honour upon all those whose Avarice impels them to countenance and help forward the Calamities of their fellow Creatures. This I desire not for their Hurt, but to convince them of the *strange* [emphasis added] Absurdity of their conduct whose Words and Actions are so diametrically opposite. How well the Cry for Liberty, and the reverse Disposition for the exercise of oppressive Power over others agree,—I humbly think it does not require the Penetration of a Philosopher to determine. (204)

By making explicit her history and her status, Wheatley in a sense wrote her way to freedom simply by letting the contradictions in her master's position speak for themselves.

In the preface to her volume of poems, Wheatley speaks of her own enslavement in the following terms:

As to the Disadvantages she has labored under, with Regard to Learning, nothing needs to be offered, as her Master's Letter in the following Page will sufficiently show the Difficulties in this Respect she had to encounter. (46)

There follows a letter from "the author's master" detailing Wheatley's prodigious accomplishments as a slave in his household. The *fact* of that letter speaks for itself. Wheatley has placed in her master's hand the boomerang of her compliance. While the Wheatleys send her book into the world as an ambassador of their own benevolence, it comes back with the response from English readers it was meant to impress: "Why is she still a slave?" John and Susannah Wheatley, caught in the trap of their own self-image, grant Phillis her freedom upon her return from England. And Phillis Wheatley thus becomes the first in a long line of successful manipulators and demystifiers of the narcissism inherent in white liberalism.

NOTES

"Euphemism, Understatement, and the Passive Voice: A Genealogy of Afro-American Poetry." From *Reading Black, Reading Feminist*, Henry Louis Gates Jr., ed. © 1990 by Henry Louis Gates Jr. Used by permission of Dutton Signet, a division of Penguin Group (USA) Inc.

1. Reprinted in *The Richard Wright Reader*, ed. Ellen Wright and Michel Fabre (New York: Harper and Row, 1978), 37.
2. James Weldon Johnson, *The Book of American Negro Poetry* (New York: Harcourt Brace Jovanovich, 1969), 9.
3. Julian D. Mason Jr., ed., *The Poems of Phillis Wheatley* (1773; Chapel Hill: University of North Carolina Press, 1989), 54.
4. June Jordan, "The Difficult Miracle of Black Poetry in America or Something Like a Sonnet for Phillis Wheatley," in *On Call* (Boston: South End Press, 1985), 91.

CHAPTER 8

Metaphor, Metonymy, and Voice in
Their Eyes Were Watching God

Not so very long ago, metaphor and metonymy burst into prominence as the salt and pepper, the Laurel and Hardy, the yin and yang, and often the Scylla and Charybdis of literary theory. Then, just as quickly, this cosmic couple passed out of fashion again. How did it happen that such an arcane rhetorical opposition was able to acquire the brief but powerful privilege of dividing and naming the whole of human reality, from Mommy and Daddy or Symptom and Desire all the way to God and Country or Beautiful Lie and Sober Lucidity?[1]

The contemporary sense of the opposition between metaphor and metonymy was first formulated by Roman Jakobson in an article entitled "Two Aspects of Language and Two Types of Aphasic Disturbances."[2] That article, first published in English in 1956, derives much of its celebrity from the central place accorded by the French structuralists to the 1963 translation of a selection of Jakobson's work entitled *Essais de linguistique générale*, which included the aphasia study. The words *metaphor* and *metonymy* are not, of course, twentieth-century coinages: they are classical tropes traditionally defined as the substitution of a figurative expression for a literal or proper one. In metaphor, the substitution is based on resemblance or analogy; in metonymy, it is based on a relation or association other than that of similarity (cause and effect, container and contained, proper name and qualities or works associated with it, place and event or institution, instrument and user, etc.). The use of the name "Camelot" to refer to King Arthur's world is a metonymy (of place), while the same word applied to John Kennedy's Washington is a metaphor, since it implies an analogy between Kennedy's world and King Arthur's.

Jakobson's use of the two terms is an extension and polarization of their classical definitions. Jakobson found that patterns of aphasia (speech dysfunction) fell into two main categories: similarity disorders and contiguity disorders. In the former, grammatical contexture and lateral associations remain while synonymity drops out; in the latter, heaps of word substitutes are kept while grammar and connectedness vanish. Jakobson concludes:

> The development of a discourse may take place along two different semantic lines: one topic may lead to another either through their similarity or through their contiguity. The metaphoric way would be the most appropriate term for the first case and the metonymic way for the second, since they find their most condensed expression in metaphor and metonymy respectively. In aphasia one or the other of these two processes is restricted or totally blocked—an effect which makes the study of aphasia particularly illuminating for the linguist. In normal verbal behavior both processes are continually operative, but careful observation will reveal that under the influence of a cultural pattern, personality, and verbal style, preference is given to one of the two processes over the other.

> In a well-known psychological test, children are confronted with some noun and told to utter the first verbal response that comes into their heads. In this experiment two opposite linguistic predilections are invariably exhibited: the response is intended either as a substitute for, or as a complement to the stimulus. In the latter case the stimulus and the response together form a proper syntactic construction, most usually a sentence. These two types of reaction have been labeled substitutive and predicative.

> To the stimulus *hut* one response was *burnt out*; another, *is a poor little house*. Both reactions are predicative; but the first creates a purely narrative context, while in the second there is a double connection with the subject *hut*: on the one hand, a positional (namely, syntactic) contiguity, and on the other a semantic similarity.

> The same stimulus produced the following substitutive reactions: the tautology *hut*; the synonyms *cabin* and *hovel*; the autonym *palace*; and the metaphors *den* and *burrow*. The capacity of two words to replace

one another is an instance of positional similarity, and, in addition, all these responses are linked to the stimulus by semantic similarity (or contrast). Metonymical responses to the same stimulus, such as *thatch*, *litter*, or *poverty*, combine and contrast the positional similarity with semantic contiguity.

In manipulating these two kinds of connection (similarity and contiguity) in both their aspects (positional and semantic)—selecting, combining, and ranking them—an individual exhibits his personal style, his verbal predilections and preferences. (76–77)

Two problems immediately arise that render the opposition between metaphor and metonymy at once more interesting and more problematic than at first appears. The first is that there are not two poles here, but four: similarity, contiguity, semantic connection, and syntactic connection. A more adequate representation of these oppositions can be schematized (see figure 8.1). Jakobson's contention that poetry is a syntactic extension of metaphor ("The poetic function projects the principle of equivalence from the axis of selection into the axis of combination"),[3] while realist narrative is an extension of metonymy, can be added to the graph (see figure 8.2).

The second problem that arises in any attempt to apply the metaphor/metonymy distinction is that it is often very hard to tell the two apart. In Ronsard's poem "Mignonne, allons voir si la rose," the speaker invites the lady to go for a walk with him (the walk being an example of contiguity) to see a rose which, once beautiful (like the lady), is now withered (as the lady will eventually be): the day must therefore be seized. The metonymic proximity to the flower is designed solely to reveal the metaphoric point of the poem: enjoy life while you still bloom. The tendency of contiguity to become overlaid by similarity, and vice versa, may be summed up in the proverb "Birds of a feather flock together"—"qui se ressemble s'assemble." One has only to think of the applicability of this proverb to the composition of neighborhoods in America to realize that the question of the separability of similarity from contiguity may have considerable political implications. The controversy surrounding the expression "Legionnaires' disease" provides a more comical example: while the name of the disease derives solely from the contingent fact that its first victims were at an American Legion Convention, and is thus a metonymy, the fear that it will take on a metaphoric color—that a belief in some natural connection or similarity may thereby be propagated between Legionnaires and the disease—has led spokesmen for the Legionnaires to attempt to have the malady renamed. And finally, in the sentence

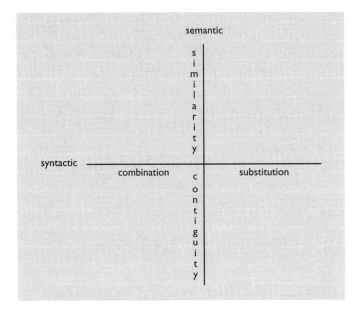

FIG. 8.1

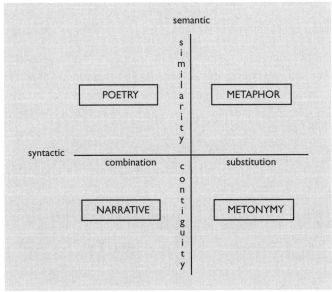

FIG. 8.2

"the White House denied the charges," one might ask whether the place name is a purely contiguous metonymy for the presidency, or whether the whiteness of the house isn't somehow metaphorically connected to the whiteness of its inhabitant.

One final prefatory remark about the metaphor/metonymy distinction: far from being a neutral opposition between equals, these two tropes have always stood in hierarchical relation to each other. From Aristotle to George Lakoff, metaphor has always, in the Western tradition, had the privilege of revealing unexpected truth.[4] As Aristotle puts it, "Midway between the unintelligible and the commonplace, it is a metaphor which most produces knowledge" (*Rhetoric* 3.1410). Paul de Man summarizes the preference for metaphor over metonymy by aligning analogy with necessity and contiguity with chance: "The inference of identity and totality that is constitutive of metaphor is lacking in the purely relational metonymic contact: an element of truth is involved in taking Achilles for a lion but none in taking Mr. Ford for a motor car."[5] De Man then goes on to reveal this "element of truth" as the product of a purely rhetorical—and ultimately metonymical—sleight of hand, thus overturning the traditional hierarchy and deconstructing the very basis for the seductiveness and privilege of metaphor.

I WOULD LIKE now to turn to the work of an author acutely conscious of, and superbly skilled in, the seductiveness and complexity of metaphor as privileged trope and trope of privilege. Zora Neale Hurston—novelist, folklorist, essayist, anthropologist, and Harlem Renaissance personality—cut her teeth on figurative language during the tale-telling, or "lying," sessions that took place on a store porch in the all-black town of Eatonville, Florida, where she was born around 1901.[6] She devoted her life to the task of recording, preserving, novelizing, and analyzing the patterns of speech and thought of the rural black South and related cultures. At the same time, she deplored the appropriation, dilution, and commodification of black culture (through spirituals, jazz, etc.) by the pre-Depression white world, and she constantly tried to explain the difference between a reified "art" and a living culture in which the distinctions between spectator and spectacle, rehearsal and performance, experience and representation, are not fixed. "Folklore," she wrote, "is the arts of the people before they find out that there is such a thing as art."

> Folklore does not belong to any special area, time, nor people. It is a world and an ageless thing, so let us look at it from that viewpoint. It is the boiled down juice of human living and when one phase of it passes another begins which shall in turn give way before a successor.
>
> Culture is a forced march on the near and the obvious. . . . The intelligent mind uses up a great part of its lifespan trying to awaken its consciousness sufficiently to comprehend that which is plainly there

before it. Every generation or so some individual with extra keen perception grasps something of the obvious about us and hitches the human race forward slightly by a new "law." Millions of things had been falling on men for thousands of years before the falling apple hit Newton on the head and he saw the law of gravity.[7]

Through this strategic description of the folkloric heart of scientific law, Hurston dramatizes the predicament not only of the anthropologist but also of the novelist: both are caught between the (metaphorical) urge to universalize or totalize and the knowledge that it is precisely "the near and the obvious" that will never be grasped once and for all, but only (metonymically) named and renamed as different things successively strike different heads. I will return to this problem of universality at the end of this essay, but first I would like to take a close look at some of the figurative operations at work in Hurston's best-known novel, *Their Eyes Were Watching God*.[8]

The novel presents, in a combination of first- and third-person narration, the story of Janie Crawford and her three successive husbands. The first, Logan Killicks, is chosen by Janie's grandmother for his sixty acres and as a socially secure harbor for Janie's awakening sexuality. When Janie realizes that love does not automatically follow upon marriage and that Killicks completely lacks imagination, she decides to run off with ambitious, smart-talking, stylishly dressed Joe Starks, who is headed for a new all-black town, where he hopes to become what he calls a "big voice." Later, as store owner and mayor of the town, he proudly raises Janie to a pedestal of property and propriety. Because this involves her submission to his idea of what a mayor's wife should be, Janie soon finds her pedestal to be a straitjacket, particularly when it involves her exclusion—both as speaker and as listener—from the tale-telling sessions on the store porch and at the mock funeral of a mule. Little by little, Janie begins to talk back to Joe, finally insulting him so profoundly that, in a sense, he dies of it. Sometime later, into Janie's life walks Tea Cake Woods, whose first act is to teach Janie how to play checkers. "Somebody wanted her to play," says the text in free indirect discourse; "Somebody thought it natural for her to play" (146). Thus begins a joyous liberation from the rigidities of status, image, and property—one of the most beautiful and convincing love stories in any literature. In a series of courtship dances, appearances, and disappearances, Tea Cake succeeds in fulfilling Janie's dream of "a bee for her blossom" (161). Tea Cake, unlike Joe and Logan, regards money and work as worth only the amount of play and enjoyment they make possible. He gains and loses money unpredictably until he and Janie begin working side by side picking beans on "the muck" in the Florida everglades. This idyll of pleasure, work, and equality ends dramatically with a hurricane, during which Tea Cake, while saving Janie's life, is bitten by a rabid dog. When Tea Cake's subsequent hydrophobia transforms him into a wild and violent animal, Janie is forced to shoot him in self-defense. Acquitted of murder by an all-white jury, Janie returns to Eatonville, where she tells her story to her friend Phoeby Watson.

The passage on which I would like to concentrate both describes and dramatizes, in its figurative structure, a crucial turning point in Janie's relation to Joe and to herself. The passage follows an argument over what Janie has done with a bill of lading, during which Janie shouts, "You sho loves to tell me whut to do, but Ah can't tell you nothin' Ah see!"

> "Dat's 'cause you need tellin,'" he rejoined hotly. "It would be pitiful if Ah didn't. Somebody got to think for women and chillun and chickens and cows. I god, they sho don't think none theirselves."
>
> "Ah knows uh few things, and womenfolks thinks sometimes too!"
>
> "Aw naw they don't. They just think they's thinkin.' When Ah see one thing Ah understands ten. You see ten things and don't understand one."

Times and scenes like that put Janie to thinking about the inside state of her marriage. Time came when she fought back with her tongue as best she could, but it didn't do her any good. It just made Joe do more. He wanted her submission and he'd keep on fighting until he felt he had it.

So gradually, she pressed her teeth together and learned how to hush. The spirit of the marriage left the bedroom and took to living in the parlor. It was there to shake hands whenever company came to visit, but it never went back inside the bedroom again. So she put something in there to represent the spirit like a Virgin Mary image in a church. The bed was no longer a daisy-field for her and Joe to play in. It was a place where she went and laid down when she was sleepy and tired.

She wasn't petal-open anymore with him. She was twenty-four and seven years married when she knew. She found that out one day when he slapped her face in the kitchen. It happened over one of those dinners that chasten all women sometimes. They plan and they fix and they do, and then some kitchen-dwelling fiend slips a scrochy, soggy, tasteless mess into their pots and pans. Janie was a good cook, and Joe had looked forward to his dinner as a refuge from other things. So when the bread didn't rise and the fish wasn't quite done at the bone, and the rice was scorched, he slapped Janie until she had a ringing sound in her ears and told her about her brains before he stalked on back to the store.

Janie stood where he left her for unmeasured time and thought. She stood there until something fell off the shelf inside her. Then she went inside there to see what it was. It was her image of Jody tumbled down and shattered. But looking at it she saw that it never was the flesh and blood figure of her dreams. Just something she had grabbed up to drape her dreams over. In a way she turned her back upon the image where it lay and looked further. She had no more blossomy openings dusting pollen over her man, neither any glistening young fruit where the petals used to be. She found that she had a host of thoughts she had never expressed to him, and numerous emotions she had never let Jody know about. Things packed up and put away in parts of her heart where he could never find them. She was saving up feelings for some man she had never seen. She had an inside and an outside now and suddenly she knew how not to mix them. (110–13)

This opposition between an inside and an outside is a standard way of describing the nature of a rhetorical figure. The vehicle, or surface meaning, is seen as enclosing an inner tenor, or figurative meaning. This relation can be pictured somewhat facetiously as a gilded carriage—the vehicle—containing Luciano Pavarotti, the tenor. Within the passage cited from *Their Eyes Were Watching God*, I would like to concentrate on the two paragraphs that begin, respectively, "So gradually . . ." and "Janie stood where he left her . . ." In these two paragraphs Hurston plays a number of interesting variations on the inside/outside opposition.

In both paragraphs, a relation is set up between an inner "image" and outward, domestic space. The parlor, bedroom, and store full of shelves already exist in the narrative space of the novel: they are figures drawn metonymically from the familiar contiguous surroundings. Each of these paragraphs recounts a little narrative of, and within, its own figurative terms. In the first, the inner spirit of the marriage moves outward from the bedroom to the parlor, cutting itself off from its proper place, and replacing itself with an image of virginity, the antithesis of marriage. Although Joe is constantly exclaiming, "I god, Janie," he will not be as successful as his namesake in uniting with the Virgin Mary. Indeed, it is his godlike self-image that forces Janie to retreat to virginity. The entire paragraph is an externalization of Janie's feelings onto the outer surroundings in the form of a narrative of movement from private to public space. While the whole of the figure relates metaphorically, analogically, to the marital situation it is designed to express, it reveals the marriage space to be metonymical, a movement through a series of contiguous rooms. It is a narrative not of union but of separation, centered on an image not of conjugality but of virginity.

In the second passage, just after the slap, Janie is standing, thinking, until something "fell off the shelf inside her." Janie's "inside" is here represented as a store that she then goes in to inspect. While the former paragraph was an externalization of the inner, here we find an internalization of the outer: Janie's inner self resembles a store. The material for this metaphor is drawn from the narrative world of contiguity: the store is the place where Joe has set himself up as lord, master, and proprietor. But here, Jody's image is broken and reveals itself never to have been a metaphor, but only a metonymy, of Janie's dream: "Looking at it she saw that it never was the flesh and blood figure of her dreams. Just something she had grabbed up to drape her dreams over."

What we find in juxtaposing these two figural mininarratives is a kind of chiasmus, or crossover, in which the first paragraph presents an externalization of the inner, a metaphorically grounded metonymy, while the second paragraph presents an internalization of the outer, or a metonymically grounded metaphor. In both cases, the quotient of the operation is the revelation of a false or discordant "image." Janie's image, as Virgin Mary, acquires a new intactness, while Joe's lies shattered on the floor. The reversals operated by the chiasmus map out a reversal of the power relations between Janie and Joe. Henceforth, Janie will grow in power and resistance, while Joe deteriorates both in his body and in his public image.

The moral of these two figural tales is rich with implications: "She had an inside and an outside now and suddenly she knew how not to mix them." On the one hand, this means that she knew how to keep the inside and the outside separate without trying to blend or merge them into one unified identity. On the other hand it means that she has stepped irrevocably into the necessity of figurative language, where inside and outside are never the same. It is from this point on in the novel that Janie, paradoxically, begins to speak. And it is by means of a devastating figure—"You look like the change of life"—that she wounds Jody to the quick. Janie's acquisition of the power of voice thus grows not out of her identity but out of her division into inside and outside. Knowing how not to mix them is knowing that articulate language requires the co-presence of two distinct poles, not their collapse into oneness.

This, of course, is what Jakobson concludes in his discussion of metaphor and metonymy. For it must be remembered that what is at stake in the maintenance of both sides—metaphor and metonymy, inside and outside—is the very possibility of speaking at all. The reduction of a discourse to oneness, identity—in Janie's case, the reduction of woman to mayor's wife—has as its necessary consequence aphasia, silence, the loss of the ability to speak: "She pressed her teeth together and learned to hush."

What has gone unnoticed in theoretical discussions of Jakobson's article is that behind the metaphor/metonymy distinction lies the much more serious distinction between speech and aphasia, between silence and the capacity to articulate one's own voice. To privilege either metaphor or metonymy is thus to run the risk of producing an increasingly aphasic *critical* discourse. If both, or all four, poles must be operative in order for speech to function fully, then the very notion of an "authentic voice" must be redefined. Far from being an expression of Janie's new wholeness or identity as a character, Janie's increasing ability to speak grows out of her ability not to mix inside with outside, not to pretend that there is no difference but to assume and articulate the incompatible forces involved in her own division. The sign of an authentic voice is thus not self-identity but self-difference.

The search for wholeness, oneness, universality, and totalization can nevertheless never be put to rest. However rich, healthy, or lucid fragmentation and division may be, narrative seems to have trouble resting content with it, as though a story could not recognize its own end as anything other than a moment of totalization—even when what is totalized is loss. The ending of *Their Eyes Were Watching God* is no exception:

> Of course [Tea Cake] wasn't dead. He could never be dead until she herself had finished feeling and thinking. The kiss of his memory made pictures of love and light against the wall. Here was peace. She pulled in her horizon like a great fish-net. Pulled it from around the waist of the world and draped it over her shoulder. So much of life in its meshes! She called in her soul to come and see.

The horizon, with all of life caught in its meshes, is here pulled into the self as a gesture of total recuperation and peace. It is as though self-division could be healed over at last, but only at the cost of a radical loss of the other.

This hope for some ultimate unity and peace seems to structure the very sense of an ending as such, whether that of a novel or that of a work of literary criticism. At the opposite end of the "canonical" scale, one finds it, for example, in the last chapter of Erich Auerbach's *Mimesis*, perhaps the greatest of modern monuments to the European literary canon. That final chapter, entitled "The Brown Stocking" after the stocking that Virginia Woolf's Mrs. Ramsay is knitting in *To the Lighthouse*, is a description of certain narrative tendencies in the modern novel: "multipersonal representation of consciousness, time strata, disintegration of the continuity of exterior events, shifting of narrative viewpoint," and so on.[9] "Let us begin with a tendency which is particularly striking in our text from Virginia Woolf. She holds to minor, unimpressive, random events: measuring the stocking, a fragment of a conversation with the maid, a telephone call. Great changes, exterior turning points, let alone catastrophes, do not occur" (483). Auerbach concludes his discussion of the modernists' preoccupation with the minor, the trivial, and the marginal by saying:

> It is precisely the random moment which is comparatively indepen-
> dent of the controversial and unstable orders over which men fight and
> despair. . . . The more numerous, varied, and simple the people are who
> appear as subjects of such random moments, the more effectively must
> what they have in common shine forth. . . . So the complicated process
> of dissolution which led to fragmentation of the exterior action, to reflec-
> tion of consciousness, and to stratification of time seems to be tending
> toward a very simple solution. Perhaps it will be too simple to please
> those who, despite all its dangers and catastrophes, admire and love
> our epoch for the sake of its abundance of life and the incomparable
> historical vantage point which it affords. But they are few in number, and
> probably they will not live to see much more than the first forewarnings
> of the approaching unification and simplification. (488)

Never has the desire to transform fragmentation into unity been expressed so succinctly and authoritatively—indeed, almost prophetically. One cannot help but wonder, though, whether the force of this desire has not been pro-voked by the fact that the primary text it wishes to unify and simplify was written by a woman. What Auerbach calls "minor, unimpressive, random events"—measuring a stocking, conversing with the maid, answering the phone—can all be identified as conventional *women*'s activities. "Great changes, exterior turning points," and "catastrophes" have been the stuff of heroic *male* literature. Even plot itself—up until *Madame Bovary*, at least—has been conceived as the doings of those who do *not* stay at home, in other words, men. Auerbach's urge to unify and simplify is an urge to resubsume female difference under the category of the universal, which has always been un-avowedly male. The random, the trivial, and the marginal will simply be added to the list of things all *men* have in common.

If "unification and simplification" is the privilege and province of the male, it is also, in America, the privilege and province of the white. If the woman's voice, to be authentic, must incorporate and articulate division and self-difference, so, too, has Afro-American literature always had to assume its double-voicedness. As Henry Louis Gates Jr. puts it in "Criticism in the Jungle":

> In the instance of the writer of African descent, her or his texts occupy spaces in at least two traditions—the individual's European or American literary tradition, and one of the three related but distinct black traditions. The "heritage" of each black text written in a Western language, then, is a double heritage, two-toned, as it were. . . . Each utterance, then, is double-voiced.[10]

This is a reformulation of W. E. B. Du Bois's famous image of the "veil" that divides the black American in two:

> The Negro is a sort of seventh son, born with a veil, and gifted with second sight in this American world,—a world which yields him no true self-consciousness, but only lets him see himself through the revelation of the other world. It is a peculiar sensation, this double-consciousness, this sense of always looking at one's self through the eyes of others, of measuring one's soul by the tape of a world that looks on in amused contempt and pity. One ever feels his twoness—an American, a Negro; two souls, two thoughts, two unreconciled strivings; two warring ideals in one dark body, whose dogged strength alone keeps it from being torn asunder.
>
> The history of the American Negro is the history of this strife,—this longing to attain self-conscious manhood, to merge his double self into a better and truer self.[11]

James Weldon Johnson, in his *Autobiography of an Ex-Colored Man*, puts it this way:

> This is the dwarfing, warping, distorting influence which operates upon each and every colored man in the United States. He is forced to take his outlook on all things, not from the view-point of a citizen, or a man, or even a human being, but from the view-point of a *colored* man. . . . This gives to every colored man, in proportion to his intellectuality, a sort of dual personality.[12]

What is striking about the above two quotations is that they both assume without question that the black subject is male. The black woman is totally invisible in these descriptions of the black dilemma. Richard Wright, in his review of *Their Eyes Were Watching God*, makes it plain that for him, too, the black female experience is nonexistent. The novel, says Wright, lacks "a basic idea or theme that lends itself to significant interpretation. . . . [Hurston's] dialogue manages to catch the psychological movements of the Negro folk-mind in their pure simplicity, but that's as far as it goes. . . . The sensory sweep of her novel carries no theme, no message, no thought."[13]

No message, no theme, no thought: the full range of questions and experiences of Janie's life are as invisible to a mind steeped in maleness as Ellison's Invisible Man is to minds steeped in whiteness. If the black *man's* soul is divided in two, what can be said of the black woman's? Here again, what is constantly seen exclusively in terms of a binary opposition—black versus white, man versus woman—must be redrawn at least as a tetrapolar structure (see figure 8.3). What happens in the case of a black woman is that the four quadrants are constantly being collapsed into two. Hurston's work is often called nonpolitical simply because readers of Afro-American literature tend to look for confrontational *racial* politics, not sexual politics. If the black woman voices opposition to male domination, she is often seen as a traitor to the cause of racial justice. But if she sides with black men against white oppression, she often winds up having to accept her position within the Black Power movement as, in Stokely Carmichael's words, "prone." This impossible position between two oppositions is what I think Hurston intends when, at the end of the novel, she represents Janie as acquitted of the murder of Tea Cake by an all-white jury but condemned by her fellow blacks. This is not out of a "lack of bitterness toward whites," as one reader would have it,[14] but rather out of a knowledge of the standards of male dominance that pervade both the black and the white worlds. The black crowd at the trial murmurs: "Tea Cake was a good boy. He had been good to that woman. No nigger woman ain't never been treated no better" (276). As Janie's grandmother puts it early in the novel:

> "Honey, de white man is de ruler of everything as fur as Ah been able tuh find out. Maybe it's some place way off in de ocean where de black man is in power, but we don't know nothin' but what we see. So de white man throw down de load and tell de nigger man tuh pick it up. He pick it up because he have to, but he don't tote it. He hand it to his women-folks. De nigger woman is de mule uh de world so fur as Ah can see." (29)

In a very persuasive book on black women and feminism entitled *Ain't I a Woman*, bell hooks (Gloria Watkins) discusses the ways in which black

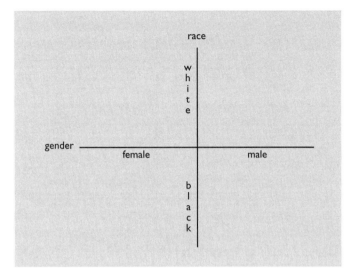

FIG. 8.3

women suffer from both sexism and racism within the very movements whose ostensible purpose is to set them free. hooks argues that "black woman" has never been considered a separate, distinct category with a history and complexity of its own. When a president appoints a black woman to a Cabinet post, for example, he does not feel he is appointing a person belonging to the category "black woman"; he is appointing a person who belongs *both* to the category "black" *and* to the category "woman," and is thus killing two birds with one stone. hooks says of the analogy often drawn—particularly by white feminists—between blacks and women:

> Since analogies derive their power, their appeal, and their very reason for being from the sense of two disparate phenomena having been brought closer together, for white women to acknowledge the overlap between the terms "blacks" and "women" (that is, the existence of black women) would render this analogy unnecessary. By continuously making this analogy, they unwittingly suggest that to them the term "women" is synonymous with "white women" and the term "blacks" synonymous with "black men."[15]

The very existence of black women thus disappears from an analogical discourse designed to express the types of oppression from which black women have the most to suffer.

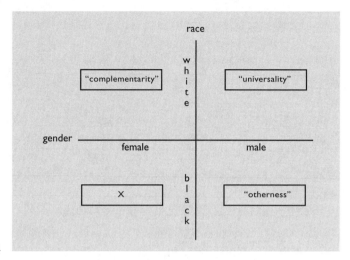

FIG. 8.4

In the current hierarchical view of things, this tetrapolar graph can be filled in as in figure 8.4. The black woman is both invisible and ubiquitous: never seen in her own right but forever appropriated by the others for their own ends.

Ultimately, though, this mapping of tetrapolar differences is itself a fantasy of universality. Are all the members of each quadrant the same? Where are the nations, the regions, the religions, the classes, the professions? Where are the other races, the interracial subdivisions? How can the human world be totalized, even as a field of divisions? In the following quotation from Hurston's autobiography, we see that even the same black woman can express self-division in two completely different ways:

> Work was to be all of me, so I said. . . . I had finished that phase of research and was considering writing my first book, when I met the man who was really to lay me by the heels. . . .
>
> He was tall, dark brown, magnificently built, with a beautifully modeled back head. His profile was strong and good. The nose and lips were especially good front and side. But his looks only drew my eyes in the beginning. I did not fall in love with him just for that. He had a fine mind and that intrigued me. When a man keeps beating me to the draw mentally, he begins to get glamorous. . . . His intellect got me first for I am the kind of woman that likes to move on mentally from point to point, and I like for my man to be there way ahead of me. . . .
>
> His great desire was to do for me. *Please* let him be a *man!* . . .

That very manliness, sweet as it was, made us both suffer. My career balked the completeness of his ideal. I really wanted to conform, but it was impossible. To me there was no conflict. My work was one thing, and he was all the rest. But I could not make him see that. Nothing must be in my life but himself. . . . We could not leave each other alone, and we could not shield each other from hurt. . . . In the midst of this, I received my Guggenheim Fellowship. This was my chance to release him, and fight myself free from my obsession. He would get over me in a few months and go on to be a very big man. So I sailed off to Jamaica [and] pitched in to work hard on my research to smother my feelings. But the thing would not down. The plot was far from the circumstances, but I tried to embalm all the tenderness of my passion for him in *Their Eyes Were Watching God*.[16]

The plot is indeed far from the circumstances, and, what is even more striking, it is lived by what seems to be a completely different woman. While Janie struggles to attain equal respect *within* a relation to a man, Zora readily submits to the pleasures of submission yet struggles to establish the legitimacy of a professional life *outside* the love relation. The female voice may be universally described as divided, but it must be recognized as divided in a multitude of ways.

There is no point of view from which the universal characteristics of the human, or of the woman, or of the black woman, or even of Zora Neale Hurston, can be selected and totalized. Unification and simplification are fantasies of domination, not understanding.

The task of the writer, then, would seem to be to narrate both the appeal and the injustice of universalization, in a voice that assumes and articulates its own, ever-differing self-difference. In the opening pages of *Their Eyes Were Watching God* we find, indeed, a brilliant and subtle transition from the seduction of a universal language through a progressive de-universalization that ends in the exclusion of the very protagonist herself. The book begins:

Ships at a distance have every man's wish on board. For some they come in with the tide. For others they sail forever on the horizon, never out of sight, never landing until the Watcher turns his eyes away in resignation, his dreams mocked to death by Time. That is the life of men.

Now, women forget all those things they don't want to remember, and remember everything they don't want to forget. The dream is the truth. Then they act and do things accordingly.

So the beginning of this was a woman, and she had come back from burying the dead. Not the dead of sick and ailing with friends at the pillow and the feet. She had come back from the sodden and the bloated; the sudden dead, their eyes flung wide open in judgment.

The people all saw her come because it was sundown. (9)

At this point Janie crosses center stage and goes out, while the people, the "bander log," pass judgment on her. The viewpoint has moved from "every man" to "men" to "women" to "a woman" to an absence commented on by "words without masters," the gossip of the front porch. When Janie begins to speak, even the universalizing category of standard English gives way to the careful representation of dialect. The narrative voice in this novel expresses its own self-division by shifts between first and third person, standard English and dialect. This self-division culminates in the frequent use of free indirect discourse, in which, as Gates points out, the inside/outside boundaries between narrator and character, between standard and individual, are both transgressed and preserved, making it impossible to identify and totalize either the subject or the nature of discourses.[17]

Narrative, it seems, is an endless fishing expedition with the horizon as both the net and the fish, the big one that always gets away. The meshes continually enclose and let escape, tear open and mend up again. Mrs. Ramsay never finishes the brown stocking.[18] A woman's work is never done. Penelope's weaving is nightly re-unraveled. The porch never stops passing the world through its mouth. The process of de-universalization can never, universally, be completed.

NOTES

"Metaphor, Metonymy, and Voice in *Their Eyes Were Watching God.*" From *Black Literature and Literary Theory,* Henry Louis Gates Jr., ed. (New York: Routledge, 1984). Reproduced with permission of Taylor & Francis Group LLC. Permissions conveyed through Copyright Clearance Center.

1. For an excellent discussion of the importance of the metaphor/metonymy distinction, see Maria Ruegg, "Metaphor and Metonymy: The Logic of Structuralist Rhetoric," in *Glyph 6: Johns Hopkins Textual Studies* (Baltimore: Johns Hopkins University Press, 1979).
2. Roman Jakobson, "Two Aspects of Language and Two Types of Aphasic Disturbances," in Roman Jakobson and Morris Halle, *Fundamentals of Language* (The Hague: Mouton, 1956).
3. Roman Jakobson, "Linguistics and Poetics," in *The Structuralists from Marx to Lévi-Strauss* (Garden City, NY: Doubleday Anchor, 1972), 95.

4. See George Lakoff and Mark Johnson, *Metaphors We Live By* (Chicago: University of Chicago Press, 1980).

5. Paul de Man, *Allegories of Reading* (New Haven, CT: Yale University Press, 1979), 14.

6. It now appears, according to new evidence uncovered by Cheryl Wall of Rutgers University, that Hurston was born as much as ten years earlier than she claimed. See Robert Hemenway's introduction to the re-edition of *Dust Tracks on a Road* (Urbana: University of Illinois Press, 1984), x–xi.

7. "Folklore Field Notes from Nora Neale Hurston," introduced by Robert Hemenway, *The Black Scholar* 7, no. 7 (1976): 41–42.

8. Zora Neale Hurston, *Their Eyes Were Watching God* (1937), Illini book edition (Urbana: University of Illinois Press, 1978).

9. Erich Auerbach, *Mimesis* (New York: Doubleday Anchor, 1957), 482–83.

10. Henry Louis Gates Jr., "Criticism in the Jungle," introduction to *Black Literature and Literary Theory* (New York: Methuen, 1984), 4, 8.

11. W. E. B. Du Bois, *The Souls of Black Folk*, in *Three Negro Classics* (New York: Avon, 1965), 214–15.

12. James Weldon Johnson, *The Autobiography of an Ex-Colored Man*, in *Three Negro Classics*, 403.

13. Richard Wright, "Between Laughter and Tears," *New Masses*, October 5, 1937, 25–26.

14. Arthur P. Davis, *From the Dark Tower* (Washington, DC: Howard University Press, 1974), 116.

15. bell hooks, *Ain't I a Woman* (Boston: South End Press, 1981), 8.

16. Zora Neale Hurston, *Dust Tracks on a Road* (Philadelphia: Lippincott, 1942), 252–60.

17. See Gates's discussion of *Their Eyes Were Watching God* as what he calls (à la Barthes) a "speakerly text," in *The Signifying Monkey: A Theory of African-American Literary Criticism* (New York: Oxford University Press, 1988).

18. I wish to thank Patti Joplin of Stanford University for calling this fact to my attention.

CHAPTER 9

Moses and Intertextuality
Sigmund Freud, Zora Neale Hurston, and the Bible

Within the Judeo-Christian tradition, the name of Moses is synonymous not with intertextuality but with the very origins of textuality. The first five books of the Bible are known as the five books of Moses. And it was into Moses's hands that God first delivered the law in written form—or rather, in rewritten form, because Moses destroyed the first version before it could reach its unworthy readers. According to Exodus, the first version was written with the finger of God; the second, with the hand of Moses.[1] Perhaps Moses is the father of intertextuality after all.

My subject concerns two twentieth-century rewritings of the Moses story, one by Sigmund Freud, the other by Zora Neale Hurston. Freud published parts of his version, *Moses and Monotheism*, in 1937; Hurston published hers, *Moses, Man of the Mountain*, two years later, the same year Freud's *Moses* first appeared in English.[2] It seems uncanny that two such different writers—one an Austrian Jew, the other an African American; one a man, the other a woman—should set out to rewrite the story of Moses at the very moment that, in Europe, a fanatical theorist of race and nationhood was attempting to put a definitive end to the history of the Jews that Moses began. But it is even more uncanny to find both Freud and Hurston choosing to suggest that Moses was *not* in fact a Hebrew but an Egyptian. How is this to be understood? Why would either Freud or Hurston *want* Moses to be an Egyptian? If Moses is the object of a cultural idealizing transference both for Jews and for blacks, what is the significance of this separation between the idealized leader and the people he liberates?

Let us look first at the means by which Moses's Egyptianness is in each case established. Freud's analysis begins with the fact that the name Moses has long been recognized as being of Egyptian, rather than Hebrew, origin, despite the folk etymology offered in Exodus 2:10 ("because I drew him out of the water" says Pharaoh's daughter). "It is nonsensical to credit an Egyptian princess with a knowledge of Hebrew etymology" scoffs Freud (4). The name Mose is simply the Egyptian word for child and is found as a combining form in the names of pharaohs (Ah-mose, Thut-mose [Thotmes], Ra-mose [Ramses], etc.).

A second indication of Egyptian birth is Freud's interpretation of the "exposure" myth. This is where Freud makes explicit his project of taking insights derived from the psychoanalysis of individuals and applying them to larger cultural phenomena. *Moses and Monotheism* is indeed in part designed to demonstrate the usefulness of this analogy between individual ontogeny and cultural phylogeny. In his attempt to equate psychoanalytic paradigms with national legends, Freud compares various myths concerning the birth of heroes (in which the hero, found and raised by peasants, turns out to be the son of a king) with his concept of the Family Romance (in which a child, disappointed by his parents, dreams that they are not his true parents but that he is really the child of nobler beings). Freud concludes, by emphasizing the structure rather than the content of such tales, that it is in each case the *second* (adoptive) family that is the real one, and hence that in the Moses story, despite the reversal of the humble/noble relation, it is from noble Egyptians that Moses springs. In response to the objection that the religion of the Egyptians was polytheistic and very different from the one bequeathed by Moses, Freud responds by describing a moment in the history of Egyptian religion that is very close to the Mosaic legacy. In Freud's reconstruction of the story, Moses is an Egyptian priest or prince imbued with the radical new religion of the pharaoh Ikhnaton, a religion that includes many features that are later central to Judaism: monotheism, circumcision, the prohibition of images, and a stringent ethical system. Rather than renounce his beliefs at the death of Ikhnaton, this noble Egyptian Moses seeks to confer the now outlawed religion upon a new people, and he chooses for this the oppressed Hebrews.

Hurston's account, which remains closer to the narrative form of the Bible, is slightly less clear about its depiction of Moses as an Egyptian. Her book begins with the labor pains of Hebrew women subject to the cruel Pharaoh's latest decree: "This is law. Hebrew boys shall not be born. All offenders against this law shall suffer death by drowning" (11). A boy is nevertheless born to Amram and Jochebed. To preserve him from Pharaoh's secret police (so named in the text),[3] they set the baby afloat on the Nile and leave the baby's sister Miriam to watch over him. Miriam, however, falls asleep, and when she wakes up, the child and the basket are gone. It is to cover her guilt that she tells her parents the story of Pharaoh's daughter finding the basket and taking the baby home. It is true that Miriam has seen the princess, but she has not seen the princess find the baby. She has seen the princess's attendants retrieve a "dark, oval object" (42) from the water, which at the time she excitedly interprets as a casket containing the princess's toiletries. Hurston has here calculated a maximum of narrative ambiguity: although every scene that takes place in the royal palace presumes that Moses is the legitimate son of the princess and an Assyrian prince, the dark, oval object, misinterpreted by Miriam, stands as what might be called a floating signifier, a warning against certainty about the Egyptian birth that the rest of the novel takes for granted. But whatever the case, the biblical account as we know it would be derived from a little girl's lie.

The reception of both *Moses and Monotheism* and *Moses, Man of the Mountain* has always been intensely ambivalent. Alain Locke called Hurston's book "caricature rather than portraiture," while Ralph Ellison wrote that it suffered from "the blight of calculated burlesque": "This work sets out to do for Moses what *The Green Pastures* did for Jehovah; for Negro fiction it did nothing." Robert Hemenway, Hurston's biographer, calls it "a noble failure" "one of the more interesting minor works in American literary history."[4]

About *Moses and Monotheism*, Daniel Jeremy Silver reports, "Modern Jews were agitated by Sigmund Freud's Egyptianization of Moses . . . less on the quite defensible grounds that the psychoanalyst's venture into Biblical scholarship is unscholarly and unsubstantiated than out of a visceral feeling that Judaism's worth is brought into question by a description of its founder as one who brings foreign ideas and values." Susan Handelman, in her remarkable book *The Slayers of Moses*, concurs: "It is [Freud's] least respected and accepted book, often held up to point to the absurdities of psychoanalysis— psychoanalysis, indeed, as delusion." Even the authors themselves expressed doubts about their books, Freud by obsessively pointing out his lack of certainty in the course of the text, ending chapter 2 by saying, "I hardly trust my powers any further" (65), and Hurston by admitting to a friend, "I thought that in this book I would achieve my ideal, but it seems that I have not yet reached it."[5]

What is the nature of the promised land that neither Freud nor Hurston seem certain of having reached? It is clear that both writers consciously identified with Moses. Freud wrote to Jung, "If I am Moses, then you are Joshua and will take possession of the promised land of psychiatry, which I shall only be able to glimpse from afar."[6] And in a letter to the Guggenheim Foundation, which had just renewed her fellowship for anthropological fieldwork in Haiti, Hurston wrote that the desire to write a definitive study of voodoo was like a "burning bush" flaming inside her.[7] Voodoo and psychoanalysis. We seem to have come a long way from the bulrushes of Exodus.

To get a better sense of the many agendas of these complex works, it might be useful to back up and examine the contexts out of which the two writers first conceived their projects. In a letter of 1934 to Arnold Zweig, Freud writes: "Faced with the new persecutions, one asks oneself again how the Jews have come to be what they are and why they have attracted this undying hatred. I soon discovered the formula: Moses created the Jews. So I gave my work the title: *The Man Moses, a Historical Novel*."[8] The work on Moses, then, was designed to explore the nature of Jewishness and the origins of anti-Semitism. But how does Freud's formula, "Moses created the Jews," serve as an answer? What kind of formula is this?

Before we attempt an answer, let us look at the origins of Hurston's project. While Freud's finished work bears no resemblance to a historical novel, Zora Neale Hurston's does. But *her* project grows out of anthropology. During her research trip in Haiti, Hurston encountered a major voodoo deity named Damballah Ouedo, whose symbol was the serpent and whom the Haitians identified as Moses. In her book on Haitian voodoo, *Tell My Horse*, Hurston writes: "This worship of Moses recalls the hard-to-explain fact that wherever the Negro is found, there are traditional tales of Moses and his supernatural powers that are not in the Bible, nor can they be found in any written life of Moses."[9] What intrigues Hurston about Moses, then, is the fact of undocumented storytelling tradition. "Africa has her mouth on Moses," she writes in her introduction to *Moses, Man of the Mountain*. And Moses, in the novel, is the consummate conjure man.

On a first level, then, we could say that Freud's Moses is a response to the question "How is *hatred* transmitted?" Hurston's Moses is a response to the question "How is *culture* transmitted?" In both cases, it is a matter of *undocumented* transmission, an *unrecognized* tradition, something that might perhaps be called a process of *unconscious intertextuality*. What becomes clear in both writers is that the question of hatred and the question of culture are, at bottom, the same question.

How then does Freud's formula, "Moses created the Jews," explain anti-Semitism? Freud's answer has to do with chosenness. The Egyptian Moses *chose* the Jews, who thus became the *chosen* people. By seeing themselves as chosen by God, the Jews took up an attitude of superiority that prompted the jealousy and hatred of other peoples. Freud thus dignifies anti-Semitism with an explanation based on sibling rivalry. But a more important strand of the story originates not in fratricide but in patricide. For Freud's reconstruction of the Moses story culminates in the murder of Moses by the very people he has just liberated. As in the golden calf episode in the Bible, but with deadly results, the people rebel against the strictness and austerity of Moses's law. The murder as well as the murdered man's religion are then repressed, and a second Moses, a Midianite worshipper of the volcano god Jahve, takes over. (This is a way of explaining the internal intertextuality often studied by biblical scholars: the imperfect fit between the J and E writers, etc.) The memory of the first Moses is all but erased. But in time, like all repressed things, the dead father returns in the form of a higher spirituality, a more abstract God. It is because the Jews originally carried out the murder of the primal father (which all men desire to carry out), says Freud, that they are hated. But they are hated most especially because they will not admit their guilt. Christians, on the other hand, freely admit that their religion is founded on a primal murder—which they often blame on the Jews.

Freud thus equates Moses with the most abstract form of the father, the dead father, or, in Lacan's terms, the name-of-the-father. It is from the dead father that the Law emanates. Freud often sees abstraction itself as an admirable cultural achievement, but there is some irony in the fact that this theorist of monotheism and abstraction wrote out his theories in a room, and at a desk, where he could be surrounded by a huge crowd of polytheistic figures whose dynamic bodies and almost animate eyes exerted upon him a fascination he himself called an addiction. Surely the antiquities themselves mark a return of something the theory is repressing.

It might be said, then, that whereas Freud's Egyptian Moses ultimately represents the psychoanalytic dead father, or even the unconscious—indeed, hieroglyphics often serve as figures for unconscious processes for Freud—Hurston's Egyptian Moses stands for the cultural dead father or mother: Africa, the source of the repressed traditions carried to the Americas by the slaves.

But were the Egyptians black? There seems in fact to be considerable debate about the ethnic makeup of the ancient Egyptians. Recent works by Martin Bernal, St. Clair Drake, and Cheikh Anta Diop have questioned the way in which nineteenth-century cultural historians, interested in denying the importance of black African civilizations, "whitened" the ancient Egyptians despite the evidence of Egyptian art and comments by Herodotus that they had "dark skin and woolly hair." (The Negroid appearance of Ikhnaton in particular has been discussed at length by St. Clair Drake.)[10] In Hurston's novel, Moses's Egyptianness—especially considering that his father is an Assyrian—does not place him in any simple racial type. Rather, it identifies him with the point of acutest ideological polemics about race. But the ethnic nonsimplicity of Hurston's Moses goes further than that. For his Egyptianness introduces a wrinkle into the long-standing African American tradition of equating the biblical Hebrews with the American slaves. Harriet Tubman, a conductor on the Underground Railroad who led many fugitive slaves to freedom, was known by many as "Moses." Marcus Garvey, the leader of the first mass back-to-Africa movement, was called the "Black Moses." Hurston was not even the first African American woman to rewrite the Moses legend: in 1869 Frances E. W. Harper, author of *Iola Leroy*, published a long dramatic poem in blank verse entitled "Moses: A Story of the Nile." And, of course, spirituals abound depicting Moses as the liberator going down to Egypt to tell old Pharaoh to "let my people go." My people? What does it mean, if Moses is not of the same people as the slaves he liberates? Hurston has in fact encoded blackness into her story on *three* incompatible levels: geography, condition, and skin color. Moses the Egyptian is from Africa, the Hebrews are enslaved, and Moses's Midianite wife, Zipporah, is reviled by the Hebrews as "a dark-complected woman." The body of racism has been dismembered, and its parts are distributed on different levels of the allegory. What does this do to the allegory's readability? It indicates, I think, that Hurston is *not*, as many readers have asserted, simply appropriating Moses for the African American tradition but that she is putting into play and into crisis the very notions of race and ethnicity. At a time when Hitler had cornered the market on blood-and-soil nationalism, it is not surprising to find Hurston questioning the grounding of nationhood on racial identity.

"My people." This is perhaps the most highly charged expression that exists both for Freud and for Hurston. Indeed, their rewritings of Moses seem at times to read more like *examples* than like refutations of anti-Semitism or racism. Freud, in a gesture that itself resembles an Oedipal murder, replaces the primal Jewish father with a non-Jew. And Hurston depicts the oppressed Hebrews as small-minded blacks unwilling to face the responsibilities of freedom. The ambivalence that their versions of Moses both express and provoke seems in some sense to be derived from the intensity and complexity of the question of belonging to an oppressed people. The weight of the question can be felt in the very first sentence of Freud's *Moses and Monotheism*: "To deny a people the man whom it praises as the greatest of its sons is not a deed to be undertaken lightheartedly—especially by one belonging to that people" (3). And especially, one might add, in Austria in 1937.

Freud's definition of what it meant for him to belong to that people can perhaps be gleaned from the following passage from his preface to the Hebrew translation of *Totem and Taboo*:

> No reader of [the Hebrew version of] this book will find it easy to put himself in the emotional position of an author who is ignorant of the language of Holy Writ, who is completely estranged from the religion of his fathers—as well as from every other religion—and who cannot take a share in nationalist ideals, but who has yet never repudiated his people, who feels that he is in his essential nature a Jew, and who has no desire to alter that nature. If the question were put to him: "Since you have abandoned all these common characteristics of your country-men, what is there left to you that is Jewish?" He would reply: "A very great deal, and probably its very essence."[11]

For Freud, then, the nature of his Jewishness was to be *sous rature*, under erasure. And yet that erasure was somehow *itself* the very essence of Jewishness.

In Hurston's writing, the phrase "My people! My people!" is always an expression both of belonging and of detachment. In her autobiography, *Dust Track on a Road*, she gives a catalog of uses and an extended gloss to the phrase. Here she is writing less as an autobiographer than as an ethnographer:

> "My people! My people!" From the earliest rocking of my cradle days, I have heard its cry go up from Negro lips. It is forced outward by pity, scorn, and hopeless resignation. It is called forth by the observations of one class of Negro on the doings of another branch of the brother in black. For instance, well-mannered Negroes groan out like that when they board a train or a bus and find other Negroes on there with their shoes off, stuffing themselves with fried fish, bananas and peanuts, and throwing the garbage on the floor. Maybe they are not only eating and drinking. The offenders may be "loud-talking" the place, and holding back nothing of their private lives, in a voice that embraces the entire

coach. The well-dressed Negro shrinks back in his seat at that, shakes his head and sighs, "My people! my people!"[12]

The phrase is not a gesture of rejection but a gesture of ambivalent solidarity. Hurston continues her discussion of this scene by operating a power reversal between these two classes of Negroes, which turns on a reversal of the literal and figurative senses of the notion of literacy:

> So the quiet-spoken Negro man or woman who finds himself in the midst of one of these "broadcasts" as on the train, cannot go over and say, "Don't act like that, brother. You're giving us all a black eye." He or she would know better than to try that. The performance would not only go on, it would get better with the "dickty" Negro as the butt of all the quips. The educated Negro may know all about differential calculus and the theory of evolution, but he is fighting entirely out of his class when he tries to quip with the underprivileged. The bookless may have difficulty in reading a paragraph in a newspaper, but when they get down to "playing the dozens" they have no equal in America. . . . Starting off in the first by calling you a seven-sided son-of-a-bitch, and pausing to name the sides, they proceed to "specify" until the tip-top branch of your family tree has been "given a reading." No profit in that to the upper-class Negro, so he minds his own business and groans, "My people! my people!" (216–17)

Hurston's amusement and pride in the rhetoric of the "Negro lowest down" led to her lifelong efforts both as a novelist and as an anthropologist to record and dramatize a culture of oral performance she feared would some day be lost to the world. But her love for the specificity of African American folk culture was countered by her deep suspicion of the notions of racial purity and of "race pride." About racial separatism, she writes:

> I have been told that God meant for all the so-called races of the world to stay just as they are, and the people who say that may be right. But it is a well-known fact that no matter where two sets of people come together, there are bound to be some in-betweens. . . . There will have to be something harder to get across than an ocean to keep East and West from meeting. But maybe Old Maker will have a remedy. Maybe even He has given up. Perhaps in a moment of discouragement He turned the job over to Adolf Hitler and went on about His business of making more beetles. (236)

And about race pride she writes:

Race pride is a luxury I cannot afford. . . . Instead of Race Pride being a virtue, it is a sapping vice. It has caused more suffering in the world than religious opinion, and that is saying a lot. . . . What the world is crying and dying for at this moment is less race consciousness. The human race would blot itself out entirely if it had any more. (325–26)

It is important to note that Hurston writes these last comments in 1940–41. They are part of a chapter of *Dust Tracks* entitled "Seeing the World as It Is," which was suppressed by Hurston's editors in the 1942 publication because of her harsh critique of American imperialism. The chapter was considered too anti-American to be published after Pearl Harbor.

Neither Freud nor Hurston proclaims that the phrase "my people" has no meaning or that difference does not exist. On the contrary, they both are acutely aware of differences, but they refuse to confine the notion of difference within a logic of identity. "There is no *The Negro* here," asserts Hurston. Both Freud and Hurston describe participation in a people as an experience of *self-difference*. The difference between dominant groups and oppressed groups lies in the fact that the dominant group projects its own self-difference outward onto groups it defines as other. At times, rage against self-difference can be pushed to the point of extermination of other peoples. There are no "pure" races, no unmixed origins, and this may be another reason for the choice both Freud and Hurston make to turn Moses into an Egyptian. By introducing a difference between Moses and the people he liberates, they place difference at the root of a foundational story. And in both versions, Moses's difference is also a self-difference. In Hurston, this is represented by the ambiguity of Moses's origins, whereas in Freud, this is accomplished by choosing an *anomalous* Egyptian, a priest who precisely belongs to a persecuted minority religion. At the origin is difference. Hurston's Moses indeed undergoes a crucial self-differentiation when he leaves Egypt for the first time: it is not until he has killed the overseer, identified with the oppressed, doubted his parentage, and fled his country that he is ready to step into the sandals of leadership. In a highly rhetoricized passage, Hurston writes:

Moses had crossed over. He was not in Egypt. He had crossed over. The short sword at his thigh had a jewelled hilt but he had crossed over and so it was no longer the sign of high birth and power. He had crossed over, so he sat down on a rock near the seashore to rest himself. He had crossed over so he was not of the house of Pharaoh. . . . He had crossed over. He was subject to no law except the laws of tooth and talon. He had crossed over. The sun who was his friend and ancestor in Egypt was arrogant and bitter in Asia. He had crossed over. He felt as empty as a post hole for he was none of the things he once had been. He was a man sitting on a rock. He had crossed over. (103–4)

To achieve the status not of a sign but of a signifier, Moses undergoes the cancellation of all he signifies. The crossing over is also a crossing out. He has become as empty as a hole.

Hurston describes Moses's accession to the solitude and self-difference of leadership as a crossing over, whereas Freud himself literally crosses over during the writing of *Moses and Monotheism*. He wrote the first part of the book in Vienna, but parts of it were not published for fear of losing the protection of the Catholic Church and bringing about Nazi sanctions against psychoanalysis. Here psychoanalysis meets history not as its interpreter but as its victim. With the German invasion of Austria in March 1938, psychoanalysis was forbidden, and Freud himself fled to England, where he succumbed to the temptation of publishing *Moses and Monotheism* as a whole, but was unable to rewrite it in such a way as to eliminate its repetitions. In his preface to the final section, he offers the following apology:

I have not been able to efface the traces of the unusual way in which this book came to be written. [Elsewhere in the book, Freud associates the erasure of traces with the covering up of murder: "The distortion of a text is not unlike a murder. The difficulty lies not in the execution of the deed but in the doing away with the traces." (52)] In truth it has been written twice over. . . . [But] a conclusion should not be emphasized by the sly device of dishing up the same subject twice in the same book. By doing so one proves oneself a clumsy writer and has to bear the blame for it. However, the creative power of an author does not, alas, always follow his goodwill. A work grows as it will and sometimes confronts its author as an independent, even an alien creation. (131, 133)

The uncanny alienation of the crossing over has affected even the writing process itself. It is strange to note how many ways these two books concern themselves with writing and rewriting. Is there perhaps a connection between the twice-written Moses of Freud and the twice-written tables of Moses? Hurston, too, has Moses write twice, not only in the traditional tables scene (to which she devotes very little attention) but also in a strange supplementary scene that occupies a central place in the novel. Moses receives his earliest education from a stableman, Mentu—clearly a version of

Homer's Mentor and of the legendary Egyptian priest Manetho—who, though illiterate himself, describes the book of all knowledge lying in the middle of a river at Koptos, enclosed in many boxes and protected by a deathless snake. The book was written by the god Thoth, the same Egyptian figure who appears in Plato's *Phaedrus* as the inventor of writing. Moses journeys to Koptos, reads the book, copies it over, dissolves the copy in beer, and drinks it. (The perfect fusion of orality and literacy.) The wisdom of the Egyptians is now inside him. Hurston has here placed Egypt—that is, Africa—at the heart of the Western tradition—as in fact did Plato, though much has occurred to erase the connections. But we seem to have returned to our starting point, the primal replication of writing, or writing as originary intertextuality.

Moses returns, then, not as the origin but as the primal self-difference of origins. For both Freud and Hurston are chafing under, as well as rethinking, the mark of difference within a logic of identity. They know that their clear-sightedness, their ways of "seeing the world as it is" in ways that are threatening, to the dominant discourses, derive from the independence of *not* belonging to the "compact majority" as Freud put it. Yet as imaginations shaped for the discourse of universality and for the rhetoric of general persuasion (to use a phrase from Ellen Rooney's critique of pluralism), they cannot find a logic other than that of alienation, self-difference, and displacement to express the necessity and unavailability of nonuniversal paradigms for human subjects. The very notion of the "human" makes the rhetoric of universality inevitable. Yet it also functions to cover up important differences and potential conflicts.

The problematic nature of the rhetoric of universality is made particularly visible if one looks at the question of gender. What one sees is not a difference but an astonishing *similarity* between Freud and Hurston. Both histories of monotheism are stories of male homo-social bonding. In Hurston, this bonding takes the form of the mentoring of Moses by Mentu and then by Jethro. These male–male relationships are far deeper and more formative than any male–female relationships in the novel (as for female–female relationships, they are consistently catty and competitive). In Freud, this bonding is first the loyalty of the priest to Pharaoh and later the loyalty of the sons to each other after the murder of the primal father. The father is prominently displayed as murdered and the sons as patricidal, but however dead or guilty, the males take up all the space of the analysis. In *Totem and Taboo*, which precedes and underlies *Moses and Monotheism*, Freud had elaborately developed his homicidally homosocial world, but he had left behind traces of a question he did not know what to do with: the question of the mother. The mother and matrilineal descent are several times mentioned in parentheses as being earlier than these paternal structures, but this fact is thrown out without any link with the others. At one point Freud writes, "I cannot suggest at what point in this process of development a place is to be found for the great mother-goddesses, who may perhaps in general have preceded the father-gods."[13] He then goes on to describe the passage to paternity. His inability to locate the mother is of no interest to him. The story goes on without her. The father may be prominently dead, but the mother is completely invisible. The equation Freud makes between paternity and speculative abstraction and maternity and material certainty nevertheless suggests one way in which the erased mother returns. That crowd of very concrete polytheistic figures to which Freud was addicted may very well embody the place of the abjected mother. One should, however, guard against simply reversing Freud's hierarchy between father and mother, abstraction and embodiment, as some critics have lately seemed to do. For the form anti-Semitism took in Nazi Germany was precisely a privileging of the soil and the body over what was reviled as Jewish life-denying dryness and abstraction.

Hurston, interestingly enough, *begins* with the silencing of the mother. The book opens with a description of Hebrew women stifling their cries so as not to alert Pharaoh to the birth of Hebrew babies. While Freud simply silences the mother, Hurston displays the mother as silenced. She goes on, however, to describe the women characters in blatantly misogynistic terms. The two main women characters, the Hebrew Miriam and the Midianite Zipporah, Moses's wife, are two different but equally ambivalent stereotypes. Zipporah is sensual and beautiful, but she lusts after finery and fancy titles. She has spent her life "looking for a throne to sit on." In many ways the Moses–Zipporah relation resembles and reverses the Janie–Joe Starks relation from *Their Eyes Were Watching God*. Miriam, too, lusts after power and position, but the novel ends up granting her a certain authority even as it scorns her for being a woman unloved by a man. Moses, in the end, recognizes that she has been necessary to the unfolding of the story. And it was she, after all, who told the lie that has become the biblical version of Moses's birth. But nowhere, it seems, does one find a nonphallocentric perspective in Hurston's novel. Indeed, the novel seems completely organized around Moses's rod: "So all across Africa, America, the West Indies, there are tales of the powers of Moses and great worship of him and his powers. But it does not flow from the Ten Commandments. It is his rod of power, the terror he showed before all Israel and to Pharaoh, and THAT MIGHTY HAND" (xxii).

It is as though, through some sort of irresistible narrative over-determination, an inquiry into the origins of political authority *had* to repress the question of sexual difference. There is nevertheless perhaps a way of reading in the text a covert awareness that there is a perspective missing. At one point, Hurston writes of Moses, "Long ago, before he was twenty, he had found out that he was two beings. In short, he was everybody boiled down to a drop. Everybody is two beings: one lives and flourishes in the daylight and stands guard. The other being walks and howls at night" (82). It could be said that Hurston is placing self-difference in the space where sexual difference might have been.

This might even be a way of understanding the Freudian split between consciousness and the unconscious. It is as though the human story has to have a split subject—as though the difference between the sexes makes it impossible for the human subject to be *one*, even when that splitness gets reappropriated as the property of the self-divided male.

Perhaps, then, Moses had to be an Egyptian—with all the ambiguity that entails—for both Freud and Hurston because *neither* universality *nor* particularity *works* as a way of accounting for their respective subject positions of belonging to a people and a gender while at the same time lusting after theory. If theory is the authority to erase the particularity of one's own subject position, then both Freud and Hurston are attempting to invent a new basis for the authority of theory. The problem with theory is that it is appropriated by dominant groups to underwrite their particularity as if it stood for universality. Dominant discourse both establishes theory as the discourse of universality—a *fiction*—and distributes and assigns differences as forms of nonparticipation in universality. As a man, Freud "fits" the mold that takes itself as universal, but as a Jew, he is in his own eyes a *marked* man, a circumcised man, in some sense a castrated man. If normative maleness is defined as that which is not marked or self-divided, then Freud's insights into maleness as a locus of denied self-difference (which he calls the castration complex) were very much enabled by his ethnicity, through which he could see that masculinity was *never* something that could simply be taken for granted. It has often been remarked that Freud took maleness as normative, but in fact his originality was to open that normativity itself up to question.

Universalization—whether it be in the discourse of humanism or in various other forms of theory—is the creation of an empty set, the fiction of an unmarked subject, a pure subject, a blank subject with no particularity or position, a transparent eyeball or pure mind. That is perhaps the definition the Bible gives of God—I am who I am—a being without qualities. The question arises of whether it is language itself that describes a space (which Lacan calls the Symbolic dimension, or the place of the Other) which makes such an abstract fiction of the God's eye view of human affairs unerasable. Since no human being is *in fact* transparent, unmarked, or unpositioned, and since language itself nevertheless seems to offer that position as a discursive temptation, Freud and Hurston are here dramatizing a predicament that may in fact *be* universal: the double bind of particularity identifying with universality, the subjectivity-constructing transference onto the empty set. This dramatization occurs through the radical defamiliarizing of a foundational legend and through the rewriting of leadership as alterity and erasure. In this way they provide insight into both the appeal and the cost of employing a discourse of universality, and they begin the task of reconceiving the nature of theoretical, as well as historical and political, authority.

NOTES

"Moses and Intertexuality: Sigmund Freud, Zora Neale Hurston, and the Bible." From *Poetics of the Americas: Race, Founding, and Textuality*, Bainard Cowan and Jefferson Humphries, eds. © 1997 Louisiana State University Press. Reprinted by permission.

1. Actually, there may be some ambiguity about who wrote the second version. According to Arthur J. Jacobson, the "he wrote" in Exodus 34:28 could be either God or Moses, even though it is God who has just commanded Moses to do the writing. But the earlier passage leaves no doubt: "And he gave unto Moses, when he had made an end of communing with him upon mount Sinai, two tables of testimony, tables of stone, written with the finger of God" (Exodus 31:18). Arthur J. Jacobson, "The Idolatry of Rules: Writing Law according to Moses, with Reference to Other Jurisprudences," *Cardozo Law Review*, July–August 1990, vol. 11 (5–6), 1079–1132.

2. Parenthetical page references are to Sigmund Freud, *Moses and Monotheism* (New York: Vintage, 1967), and to Zora Neale Hurston, *Moses, Man of the Mountain* (Urbana, University of Illinois Press, 1984).

3. This is not the only point at which Hurston seems to be thinking of Hitler. At another point, during a discussion by several Hebrew elders of rumors of the infant Moses's entry into the palace, one elder says, "The higher-ups who got Hebrew blood in 'em is always the ones to persecute us. I got it from somebody that ought to know, that the grandmother of Pharaoh was a Hebrew woman" (50).

4. Alain Locke, "Dry Fields and Green Pastures," *Opportunity* 18 (1940): 7; Ralph Ellison, "Recent Negro Fiction," *New Masses*, August 5, 1941, 24;

Robert E. Hemenway, *Zora Neale Hurston* (Urbana: University of Illinois Press, 1977), 270, 260.

5. Daniel Jeremy Silver, *Images of Moses* (New York: Basic Books, 1982), 63; Susan A. Handelman, *The Slayers of Moses* (Albany: State University of New York Press, 1982), 145; Hemenway, *Zora Neale Hurston*, 273.

6. Letter of January 17, 1909, in *The Freud-Jung Letters*, ed. William McGuire (Princeton, NJ: Princeton University Press, 1974), 196–97.

7. Hemenway, *Zora Neale Hurston*, 246.

8. Letter of September 30, 1934, in *The Letters of Sigmund Freud and Arnold Zweig*, ed. Ernst L. Freud (New York: Harcourt, 1970), 91.

9. Zora Neale Hurston, *Tell My Horse* (Berkeley, CA: Turtle Island Books, 1981), 139.

10. See Martin Bernal, *Black Athena: The Afroasiatic Roots of Classical Civilization* (New Brunswick, NJ; Rutgers University Press, 1987); St. Clair Drake, *Black Folk Here and There* (Los Angeles: Center for Afro-American Studies, University of California, 1987); and Cheikh Anta Diop, *The Cultural Unity of Black Africa* (Chicago: Third World Press, 1978).

11. Sigmund Freud, *Totem and Taboo* (New York: W. W. Norton, 1950), xi.

12. Zora Neale Hurston, *Dust Tracks on a Road* (Philadelphia: Lippincott, 1942; rpt. Urbana: University of Illinois Press, 1984), 214. Parenthetical page references follow extracts hereafter.

13. Freud, *Totem and Taboo*, 149.

CHAPTER 10

Lesbian Spectacles

Reading *Sula, Passing, Thelma and Louise,*
and *The Accused*

When I proposed this topic for a paper, my intention was to push myself to try something I have never done before: to read explicitly as a lesbian, to take account of my particular desire structure in reading rather than try to make generalizations about desire as such, even lesbian desire "as such." Much has been said about the theoretical and political issues involved in what Nancy Miller calls "reading *as a*."[1] On the one hand, to the extent that dominant discourses have used the fiction of universality to ground their authority and to silence other voices, it is important for the voices thus silenced to speak for and as themselves. But on the other hand, just because something has been silenced doesn't mean it possesses "an" identity, knowable and stable. Speaking "as a" plunges the speaker into new questions of reliable representativity and identity, as Nancy Miller suggests. If I tried to "speak as a lesbian," wouldn't I be processing my understanding of myself through media-induced images of what a lesbian is or through my own idealizations of what a lesbian *should* be? Wouldn't I be treating as *known* the very predicate I was trying to discover? I needed a way of catching myself in the act of reading as a lesbian without having intended to.

To accomplish this, I decided to look at novels or films that did *not* present themselves explicitly as "lesbian," but that could, through interpretation, be said to have a crypto-lesbian plot. I took my inspiration for such a textual category from two readings of literary texts: Barbara Smith's reading of Toni Morrison's *Sula* and Deborah McDowell's reading of Nella Larsen's novel *Passing*. I cite these critics not because they offer me examples of the act of "reading as a lesbian" (Smith does; McDowell does not) but because of the nature of the texts they read. "Despite the apparent heterosexuality of the female characters," Smith writes of *Sula*, "I discovered in rereading *Sula* that it works as a lesbian novel not only because of the passionate friendship between Sula and Nel but because of Morrison's consistently critical stance toward the heterosexual institutions of male-female relationships, marriage, and the family."[2] She grounds her reading of *Sula* in the text's description of the shared fantasies of the friends, the erotic nature of some of their games, and the ways in which the text describes them as two halves of one whole.

Deborah McDowell, who had criticized Smith's reading of *Sula* for pressing the novel into the service of a sexual persuasion, soon made her own foray into lesbian criticism, writing not as a lesbian but as a decoder of lesbian structures of desire in the text, in her reading of *Passing*.[3] After detailing the overwhelming evidence of the fact that the security-seeking, ostensibly black-identified Irene Redfield is consumed with an intense, repressed, erotic fascination with the transgressive Clare, who is passing for white even within her own marriage, McDowell concludes that the plot of racial passing is a cover for an exploration of the more dangerous question of female–female eroticism, that the sexual plot is itself "passing" as a racial plot.

In both *Passing* and *Sula*, the intensity of the relation between two women is broken by a fall into triangulation. In *Passing*, Irene imagines that her husband, Brian, is having an affair with the beautiful Clare. The idea comes to Irene as she looks at her husband in a mirror in which she can also see herself. That is, she projects onto Brian her own fascination with Clare. The novel ends when Clare falls, jumps, or is pushed by Irene to her death.

In contrast with *Passing*, in which there is never any proof of the affair between husband and best friend, Nel, in *Sula*, happens upon Jude and Sula in the act. She tries to howl in grief and rage but cannot until, seventy pages later, after Sula's death, she realizes that she mourns the loss of Sula, not Jude.

FOR ME, despite Barbara Smith's excellent use of textual evidence, *Sula* does not work as a lesbian novel, while *Passing* does. My first task, then, was to explain to myself why I felt that way. Sula and Nel are certainly central to each other's lives. They achieve genuine intimacy and recognize each other's value, and the novel ends by showing how the veil of compulsory hetero-sexuality blinds women to the possibility of seeing each other as anything other than sexual rivals. In *Passing*, the two women remain intensely ambivalent about each other, perhaps even murderously so. Why, then, does my inner lesbo-meter find *Passing* more erotic than *Sula*?

I think it has to do with two things: the description of the long stare between Clare and Irene when they first meet after many years of separation, and the way in which the text is structured by Irene's constantly vowing never to see Clare again, and repeatedly going back on that vow. It is erotic to me that Irene's "no" constantly becomes a yes. The relationship is therefore overinvested and underexplained. This is what creates the effect of irresistible magnetism that is precisely *not* grounded in friendship or esteem. In *Sula*, on the other hand, while the relationship is certainly overinvested, it is also abundantly explained. My identifying signs of a lesbian structure, then, involved protracted and intense eye contact and involuntary re-encounters ungrounded in conscious positive feelings.

To test these categories on another pair of texts, I turned to movies. I remembered my first reactions to two films, one of which has sometimes been discussed as a candidate for lesbianism, the other, to my knowledge, not. The two films are *Thelma and Louise* (Ridley Scott, 1991) and *The Accused* (Jonathan Kaplan, 1988). While *Sula* and *Passing* describe the female–female bond as existing *before* the fall into the triangulation through adultery, *Thelma and Louise* and *The Accused* both build their female–female intimacy around the consequences of rape. Because the image of the rapists is so vivid in both films, many viewers and reviewers of the films could see nothing in the films beyond a negative image of men. While I do not think that the films' critiques of male sexual violence and of patriarchal institutions are irrelevant to my attempt to view them through lesbian spectacles, I do think that to focus on what the films are saying about men is to focus on men, and thus (for me) to view the films heterosexually. Indeed, to see the films as being about the viability of heterosexuality is to make invisible the question of what is or is not happening between the women.

Thinking back to my initial reactions to the films, I remembered my very strong sense that I experienced *The Accused* as a lesbian plot while *Thelma and Louise* promised one but, for me, failed to deliver. My first justifications for these reactions might run as follows: Thelma (Geena Davis) and Louise (Susan Sarandon) hardly ever stop to look at each other—they are either looking straight down the road or Thelma's eyes are wandering toward sexually interesting men and Louise is attempting to keep Thelma's sexual appetite contained. Their intense exchange of looks and a kiss at the end comes too late to count—it is the adrenaline of death, not of desire. Their friendship is a given at the beginning, therefore there is no structure of involuntary return. My first impulse was therefore to say that their relationship was neither overinvested nor underexplained. But actually, it *is* underexplained. What are these two women doing hitting the road together? Why are they friends? What do they have in common? The point of departure of the road trip seemed to me psychologically incomprehensible, but not for that reason erotic.

In *The Accused*, on the other hand, from the moment deputy district attorney Kathryn Murphy (Kelly McGillis) picks up rape victim Sarah Tobias (Jodie Foster) in her car (and there is a lot of what Marge Garber calls "autoeroticism" in *both* films), the two women are intrigued by their differences and cannot leave each other alone. The image of each woman bursting into the house of the other uninvited feels like an echo of the sexual violence around which the film is structured. That Murphy is centrally accused by Tobias of having silenced the victim she was supposed to be defending places her in a male role she has to spend the remainder of the film redeeming herself from. The long looks between the two women are looks across class, education, profession, and size. They fill each other's screen as objects of fascination, ambivalence, and transformation.

After I had finished the first draft of this essay, I looked through the literature to see whether there had not, in fact, been other lesbian interpretations of *The Accused*. The essay that sounded most promising, entitled "Up against the Looking Glass! Heterosexual Rape as Homosexual Epiphany in *The Accused*,"[4] turned out to be a reading of the film as an indictment of heterosexuality and a confrontation for the *male* spectator with the homosexual nature of *male* spectatorship in the film. But I also found out more than I bargained for, and I'm not sure what to do with it. It seems there were rumors of an alleged affair between Kelly McGillis and Jodie Foster during the filming of *The Accused*. Was this what I was seeing in the electricity between the two actresses? Or was their alleged affair itself an *interpretation* of what was happening on the screen? In a film that from the beginning blurred the relation between art and life—McGillis herself had been raped, and Foster pursued by a psychotic literalizer of one of her previous films—it is hard to pin down the origins of a reading effect.

However these overdeterminations may be factored in, what does it mean to say that for me *The Accused* "works" better as a lesbian film than *Thelma and Louise*? On some level, this reading does not make sense. For while Thelma and Louise eventually really get beyond any return to legal patriarchal heterosexual pseudoprotections, *The Accused* ends up validating the legal system, and Murphy and Tobias separate at the end, presumably never to meet again, each returning to a life of presumptive heterosexuality. What is lesbian about this? Isn't Murphy in the place of the one good cop in *Thelma and Louise*, the tragic consciousness that sees the limitations of an institution to which in the end he nevertheless remains loyal? Certainly the relationship between Thelma and Louise is progressively more real than any relationship that is set up between Murphy and Tobias. If I do nevertheless feel that *The Accused* presents me with a plot that corresponds to my own fantasies, I have to acknowledge the role of the patriarchal institution not in impeding those fantasies but in enabling them. Murphy is attractive to me because she is a powerful woman turning her full attention toward another woman precisely *within* the patriarchal institution. It is transference onto the phallic mother, the woman whose appeal arises from her position in a power structure, that infuses my reading of the film, simple as that.

SO MUCH FOR READING with the unconscious.

I THUS HAVE to conclude that the project of making my own erotic unconscious participate in my reading process, far from guaranteeing some sort of radical or liberating breakthrough, brings me face to face with the political incorrectness of my own fantasy life. In a post-Foucauldian world it is perhaps more embarrassing to admit to the attraction of power than it is to confess to the appeal of violence in the era of Kitty MacKinnon. Any attempt to go on from this reading to theorize (my) lesbian desire would therefore have to confront the possibility of a real disjunction between my political ideals and my libidinal investments. But if the unconscious is structured by repetition and the political by the desire for change, there is nothing surprising about this. The question, still, would remain one of knowing what the unconscious changes, and what politics repeats.

NOTES

"Lesbian Spectacles: Reading *Sula*, *Passing*, *Thelma and Louise*, and *The Accused*." From *Media Spectacles*, Marjorie Garber, Jann Matlock, and Rebecca Walkowitz, eds. (New York: Routledge, 1993). Reproduced with permission of Taylor & Francis Group LLC. Permissions conveyed through Copyright Clearance Center.

1. See Nancy K. Miller, *Getting Personal* (New York: Routledge, 1991).
2. Barbara Smith, "Toward a Black Feminist Criticism," in *All the Women Are White, All the Blacks Are Men, But Some of Us Are Brave*, ed. Gloria T. Hull, Patricia Bell Scott, and Barbara Smith (Old Westbury, NY: Feminist Press, 1982), 165.
3. Deborah E. McDowell, introduction to Nella Larsen, *Quicksand and Passing* (New Brunswick, NJ: Rutgers University Press, 1986).
4. By Larry W. Riggs and Paula Willoquet, *Film Quarterly* 4 (1989).

CHAPTER 11

Bringing Out D. A. Miller

My title sounds like the equivalent of "Barging through an Open Door." But "bringing out" is not exactly the same as "outing." One can "bring out one's latest book" (publication), or "bring out the turkey dinner" (serving a meal), or "bring out the best in our students" (education)—or combine the last two, as in the mayonnaise ad, "Bring out the Hellmann's, and bring out the best." In fact, if "outing" means revealing what was previously concealed, "bringing out" cannot be such a simple (logically, anyway) one-shot process. One can never be sure something has been sufficiently "brought out." In other words, it has everything to do with style.

I'll begin with two quotations that use the expression "to bring out" in illuminating ways. The first is from Nathaniel Hawthorne's *The Marble Faun*, in a passage in which the narrator describes the paintings of the dark lady of the novel, Miriam Schaefer: "There was one observable point, indeed, betokening that the artist relinquished, for her personal self, the happiness she could so profoundly appreciate for others. In all those sketches of common life, and the affections that spiritualize it, a figure was pourtrayed apart. . . . Always, it was the same figure, and always depicted with an expression of deep sadness; and in every instance, slightly as they were *brought out*, the face and form had the traits of Miriam's own."[1] There is thus a connection between bringing out and an artist's autobiography, but by no means a direct one. The figure being brought out is present everywhere, in every representation, but it is always supplementary and ghostly, not the painting's subject but its mourner. The lineaments of face and form are dimly recognizable in the figure, whose very superfluity in pictorial reality is a clue to its function in autobiography.

The second quotation is from *Bringing Out Roland Barthes*, by D. A. Miller: "In a culture that without ever ceasing to proliferate homosexual meaning knows how to confine it to a kind of false unconscious, as well in collectivities as in individuals, there is hardly a procedure for bringing out this meaning that doesn't itself look or feel just like more police entrapment. (Unless such, perhaps, were a *folie à deux*—where 'two' stands for the possibility of community—that would bring it out in as subtle and flattering a fashion as, say, the color of a garment is said to bring out a complexion.)"[2] In this quotation, Miller articulates his title twice. "Bringing out" may be a form of torture or police entrapment, and "autobiography" would be, as it often is taken to be, a form of confession (there is also perhaps a reference to the forms of surveillance and social categorization that Miller studied in his earlier book, *The Novel and the Police*). But Barthes's relation to the novel may make possible the second meaning of "bringing out"—the man who wrote about "the fashion system" and the sexiness of gaps in garments allows the reader to think "fashion," not "fascism." Even if, in this sentence, the word *fashion* is used only as a synonym for *manner*—or even, shall we say, for *style*—the word itself deserves to be "brought out." But in which sense?

We can perhaps get some sense of the complexity and at the same time the in-your-faceness of the process of "bringing out" from the first sentence of D. A. Miller's little book on Barthes. I'll spend a certain amount of time talking about this sentence: "Twenty years ago in Paris, long before I, how you say, *knew myself*, a fellow student told me he had seen Roland Barthes late one evening at the Saint Germain Drugstore" (3). The sentence begins in typical New Historicist fashion—he was, after all, at Berkeley—with the form and promise of a dated and located anecdote. But there are two odd things about this anecdote: it antedates something it emphasizes (*knew myself* is in italics) and it consists of a narrative, not an event ("a fellow student told me"). Roland Barthes comes into the sentence as a grammatical object ("he had seen Roland Barthes"). Someone else had seen Barthes. Someone *told me* he had seen Barthes. Twenty years ago, someone told me he had seen Barthes. Late at night. He had seen Barthes late one evening at the Saint Germain Drugstore. "What? That awful, embarrassing, mistranslated, vulgar place?" the "I" says to himself. He goes on: "Not the Americanized mini-mall where I would now and then swallow much disgust . . . and eat a hamburger?" It couldn't be—but on second thought, what a good place to study "the status of the sign in consumer society"! So the "I" swallows his disgust and his disavowed taste for burgers and tries repeatedly to encounter for himself, late at night, the person, Roland Barthes. And not just the good reader of signs, his retrospective narrative suggests. He never does, though. His book is about a missed encounter with Barthes. But in some ways it is also about the structuring role of the changing desire for one.

Let me quote that first sentence again: "Twenty years ago in Paris, long before I, how you say, *knew myself*, a fellow student told me he had seen Roland Barthes late one evening at the Saint Germain Drugstore" (3). The Saint Germain Drugstore doesn't sell aspirin. It is a place to eat American food—at least, the Parisian idea of American food twenty years ago. The name is a bad translation. But is there not another bad translation in the sentence? Why does the "I" say "how you say"? This would be something a French person would say when unsure of the English expression. An English speaker would say, "How *do* you say?" So the narrator is pretending to lack the perfect English phrase. That is why *knew myself* is in italics. It is an expression that may not be exact. But it is also very emphatic. It is emphatic about an expression that may not be exact. The speaker is pretending to lack English, but *in a French way*. He is miming the same bad French English that is present in Le Drugstore. Barthes, the elusive object, has to be pursued in the vicinity of bad translation.

But the role of "how you say" may not be that of a fake French lack of mastery of English, but rather, a convention adopted by English speakers to put an expression in quotation marks that wink toward a knowing interpreter. "Long before I, how you say, *knew myself*" would thus both reveal and conceal something. The "how you say" would indicate that a linguistic question was passing as a code word. If you speak this language, it implies, you know what it means. But why is *knew myself* functioning as a shibboleth?

The command to "Know thyself," propounded by the Delphic Oracle, is the motor for both philosophy and tragedy in ancient Greece. Socrates has it pinned up over his desk (okay, it's Plato's desk). In Sophocles's *Oedipus Rex*, the tragic catastrophe comes about when the criminal that Oedipus is seeking as the Other is discovered to be the self. In the story of Narcissus, the same Tiresias who foresees Oedipus's downfall predicts that the youth will have a long life if he never knows himself. Unfortunately, and too late, he does. He realizes that the other he has fallen in love with is his own image. By "knowing himself," he dooms himself.

In his essay *The Use and Abuse of History*, Nietzsche refers to the Delphic command as "hard." He writes: "The Delphian god cries his oracle to you at the beginning of your wanderings: 'Know thyself.' It is a hard saying, for that god 'tells nothing and conceals nothing but merely points the way,' as Heraclitus said."[3] The Delphic Oracle, in other words, doesn't ask, doesn't tell, and doesn't pursue.

So what is the irresistible and irrefutable knowledge being claimed in D. A. Miller's "*knew myself*"? What did he know and when did he know it? Twenty years ago, he didn't. Now he does. This is a conversion narrative, like all classic coming out stories. I once was fake, but now I'm real—was bound, but now I'm free. . . . Yet not exactly. Nothing except the structure of before and after—then versus now—or rather "long before" and . . . what? The only thing asserted is that knowing oneself has a before. Long before I knew myself. Long before I, how you say, *knew myself*. The word *know* has accrued a subtle sexual connotation from its many occurrences as "know (in the biblical sense)." This is a clumsy translation of a Hebrew word that has both meanings. Would *know* not be sexual in English, then, but only in the Bible?

I *knew myself*. Is this then a disguised form of masturbation? "I knew (in the biblical sense) myself." But as a narrative feature ("long before I knew myself"), the knowledge doesn't behave like a sexual act, but a change of narrative condition. The before and after plot of conversion *is* the narrative. Which takes us to the Balzac story Barthes studies in his book *S/Z. Sarrasine* is a conversion narrative disguised as a heterosexual romance. There is a before and an after, and a long after. In the "before," Sarrasine falls in love with an Italian diva, in the "after," his eyes are opened to what he loves (a castrato), but he never recognizes himself (how he has been duped by his belief in what heterosexuality is). Long after, there is only wealth and repetition. The narrator attempts to make a conversion narrative into a new seduction narrative (that is, he attempts to seduce the Marquise by telling the story of the conversion), but instead, he merely repeats the blindness of the failure. The Marquise exits, murmuring "No one will have *known* me."[4] The seduction fails *because* it fails once again to recognize that it should have been a conversion, and the conditions are set for another seduction. The failed conversion is not a failure to become gay, but a failure to know how heterosexuality has produced itself.

But that is only half the story. Miller writes:

In the days when the structural analysis of narrative obsessed criticism, Barthes produced the only narratology to transcend its overall grim technicity, the only one with a discernable animus. Even at its most laden with formal apparatus (which it yet earned so lightly, almost swishily), this narratology never rested content with assembling a cata-logue raisonné of narrative units, functions, and modes, like its now unreadable rivals; or rather, in doing so, it took malicious aim at the whole ethos of the Novel established on the presumed naturalness of its narrative notations and stabilized by their presumed coherence. (46–47)

Almost swishily? The sexual register of this adverbial phrase (who is speak-ing here? to whom?) stands out in the ostentatiously technical vocabulary that surrounds it. The one with the "discernable animus" hardly needs to be brought out against the "grim technicity" of the vast narratological waste-lands. Life ("animus") will out (itself?) in a context of death ("grim technic-ity"). The shadowy figure in the painting suddenly changes places with its subject. The false naturalness of those "sketches of modern life" are now the shadows; the "marriage plot" that structures both novels and narratologies becomes one of its "grim technicities," relieved only by the "swishy" excess of its analysis here.

The crossing of meanings between "life" and "death" underpins the most influential essay Barthes ever wrote, the essay called "The Death of the Au-thor." Whereas traditional French protocols of criticism derived from Sainte-Beuve and Lanson foregrounded the *life* of the person who wrote the work, Barthes (following Mallarmé and Proust, among others) foregrounded the *death* of the author as origin, intender, and coherence giver. The *text* was no respecter of persons. The reader could find his desire in a text even when the author hadn't put it there. The influence Barthes's essay exerted as a seminal text of structuralism and poststructuralism was not related to sex-uality—in fact, it was seen as a denial of the importance of sexuality, which would have been seen as part of the author's *life*, not his *death*. The false neutrality conferred by the concept of death seemed to militate against con-sidering the gender, race, or geographical origins of the author as part of the text. But the essay begins with a quotation from *Sarrasine* that is very much about the question of sexual difference:

In his story *Sarrasine* Balzac, describing a castrato disguised as a woman, writes the following sentence: "*This was woman herself, with her sudden fears, her irrational whims, her instinctive worries, her impetuous bold-ness, her fussings, and her delicious sensibility.*" Who is speaking thus? Is it the hero of the story bent on remaining ignorant of the castrato hidden beneath the woman? Is it Balzac the individual, furnished by his personal experience with a philosophy of Woman? Is it Balzac the author professing "literary" ideas on femininity? Is it universal wisdom? Romantic psychology? (142)

The death of the author is somehow based on the dissociation of the forces that construct the "naturalness" of femininity. To ask "who is speaking?" is to see sexual difference as constructed, not given; a discourse learned, not a person perceived. Giving voice to a sigh about femininity, Balzac the author falls apart. If all those sighs that emanate from our deepest feelings are just echoes of sentences we have learned somewhere, though, then we ourselves fall apart in the same way. This was the reason the court that prosecuted Flaubert for the immorality of *Madame Bovary* was most worried about free indirect discourse, not adultery. Who is speaking? Who *does* speak? Where does the authority in the novel come from? What kind of *knowledge* is contained in a sentence that is designed to play on the reader's inattention and make the reader fall for the masquerade of femininity the author and the narrator *know* is a trap? These *are* the assumptions of culture and literature, though—how could *they* be a trap? How can this sentence about femininity be both a lie and a truth?

Barthes continues the paragraph: "We shall never know [who is speaking], for the good reason that writing is the destruction of every voice, of every point of origin. Writing is that neutral, composite, oblique space where our subject slips away, the negative where all identity is lost, starting with the very identity of the body writing."[5] This at first seems like a homophobic Aufhebung of the question. Especially since, at bottom, Balzac's story is about castration. That is probably why the essay itself was so influential—it opened the closet door a crack, and then allowed what could be seen from there to become generalized in such a way as to slam it shut. The neuter, or neutral, space of writing can be understood that way, and Miller's book is partly a response to that reading. The later Barthes, it is said, acknowledged gay desire more and more. Miller writes to bring out the gayness of even the early Barthes. And he does so irrefutably. But even there, might Barthes not also be talking about the *sexiness* of writing in a different sense? What if "the negative where all identity is lost, starting with the very identity of the body writing," far from being a denial of the body, is actually the body's own denial of the category of identity? What if sexuality were not a type of identity but a type of loss of identity? After all, it is the traditional criticism Barthes is opposing that speaks of Baudelaire's failure, Van Gogh's madness, Tchaikovsky's vice. The civil status conferred by identity—each must go to his native land and enroll himself—is precisely what Barthes is arguing *against*. But when writing makes you *not* know yourself, he implies, something sexy is happening.

There seems, therefore, to be a contradiction between this theory of writing and Miller's opening sentence. Barthes would seem to equate the sexiness of writing with infinite openness, while Miller would insist that sexuality can only be situated in the pleasures and sacrifices of a choice. But in a way, these sentences are only contradictory if what they presuppose is equally valid, and therefore, if they both stand, constituting a double bind. If either one dominates the other, neither is right. Gold's Gym notwithstanding, the fact that Miller never encountered Barthes—and at the same time kept discovering him in the very haunts Miller thought were original—means that, for Miller, too, there is just nothing sexier than writing. But this remains true only to the extent that he *fails* to say so, and does so *from the gay side*. That is why it is impossible to know whether one is bringing out the person or the writings. And *that* is what Barthes means by "the death of the author."

So we come back to Miller's first sentence. "Long before I, how you say, *knew myself*." Making us believe in the reality of the voice of the living person may be Miller's canniest rhetorical trick. But the rhetoric of this "sujet supposé savoir"—the subject presumed to know *now*—works perfectly in two ways, neither of which is straight. It implies that the proof of the knowledge attained now is in the wandering, the loitering, the acting on fantasy before understanding it—the real as opposed to false unconscious—that the subject experienced *then*. A conversion requires a "before." But it doesn't require that the "after" be permanent or even definite. In fact, the vitality and continued strength of it—or indeed, the sacrifices it might require and the renunciations it might entail—might keep raising the price of the rightness it promises. It might turn out to be interminable but not, for that reason, reversible. One can never be unconscious in the same way again. Perhaps that is what Adam and Eve discovered. The brilliance of Miller's first sentence lies in its way of requiring that every reader stand and unfold himself; even if the reader doesn't want to, the not wanting to is not neutral, and indeed, it gives the lie to neutrality or universality. Wishing this partisan, desiring voice away is a desire. And yet, the self-knowledge that positions all readers right away is only posited, not predicated. Speak *from* your desire, it says, not *of* it. "Know thyself," commands the Oracle. "Long before I knew myself" is the narrative of that imperative. But the imperative remains, in the effects of the telling. And in that imperative, who do we assume *is* speaking?

"Bringing Out D. A. Miller." *Narrative* 10, no. 1 (January 2002): 3–8. © 2002 The Ohio State University Press. Reproduced with permission.

1. Nathaniel Hawthorne, *The Marble Faun* (New York: Penguin, 1990), 46.
2. D. A. Miller, *Bringing Out Roland Barthes* (Berkeley: University of California Press, 1992), 18.
3. Friedrich Nietzsche, *The Use and Abuse of History*, trans. Adrian Collins (Indianapolis: Library of Liberal Arts, 1957), 72.
4. Roland Barthes, *S/Z* (New York: Hill and Wang, 1974), 254.
5. Roland Barthes, "The Death of the Author," in *Image, Music, Text*, trans. Stephen Heath (New York: Hill and Wang, 1977), 142.

CHAPTER 12

Correctional Facilities

I. Trials

The police have blundered. They thought they were attacking a run-of-
the-mill novel and some ordinary little scribbler; whereas now (in part
thanks to the prosecution) my novel is looked on as a masterpiece.
—Gustave Flaubert, letter of January 20, 1857

The two most famous French literary works published in 1857, Flaubert's
Madame Bovary and Baudelaire's *Les Fleurs du Mal*, were both indicted for
outraging public morality and religion. With the advantage of historical hindsight, one can easily feel superior to those officers of the court who wanted
to silence or cut up two great works of art. Or perhaps one can admire them
for recognizing, even negatively, the revolutionary nature of their targets.
The stance of superiority and hindsight is a little more difficult to maintain
when the officer of the court is Plato, and when the expulsion of poetry from
the Republic is an indictment of imitative arts in general. Surely this is going
too far. Plato must be referring to popular or unrefined things like *bad* poetry, romance novels, television—the kind of thing a susceptible person like
Emma Bovary would be affected by.[1] Corruption by images may be widespread, the argument would go, but it *can* be contained and corrected.

Nevertheless, our uncertainty increases if we remember that Socrates will
be—indeed *has been*, by the time Plato is writing—condemned to death for
something like the same things he held against poetry: seducing, leading

astray, creating belief in false images. How can we save Socrates and condemn Athens without casting doubt upon what that same Socrates said in *The Republic*? At least in Benjamin Jowett's translation.[2] Or at least what Plato alleged, in writing, that Socrates said. The same Plato who wrote, however, in Hugh Tredennick's translation of *Phaedo*, that Socrates spent his final days composing poetry.[3] So even if Athens is a bad example of the public sphere and Socrates a bad example of poetry, which side is he on? If the culmination of Socratic irony lies in the invention of *that very difference*, does Socrates have to die in order for this statement to be true? What can be said about this validation of a truth that is necessarily other than life? Is death a good thing? Is Socrates's death his last and best teaching? Of course, there is a whole religion around that kind of paradox. Public executions seem to be useful in creating cultural authority. But even if Socrates and Christ have a lot in common (or at least *come to have* a lot in common in the construction of neo-Platonism), would the Apostles have written *The Republic*? What can be said about a polis that cares enough about poetry to expel it? Or if we want to save poetry, should we applaud those officers of the Second Empire court, finally, for discerning the greatness of works they single out for prosecution?

The more one studies the trials of Flaubert and Baudelaire, the more one can't help noticing that the prosecutor (the same in both cases, Ernest Pinard) is a better reader than the defense lawyers. His reasoning is simple: representation gives existence. No amount of condemnation can substitute for an image's nonexistence. Therefore even if the work in question evokes something in order to prove how bad it is (which was the reasoning of the defense, whether or not Baudelaire or Flaubert would have agreed), condemnation leaves a memory of the thing condemned, and that memory has an independent life. This is always the problem with pointing out something for censure. The representation works upon its reader despite or perhaps even because of the judgment pronounced against it. This is the basis of Catherine MacKinnon's argument against the sex-differentiated, educative function of pornography. It is also Michel Foucault's reading of the Victorian "repressive hypothesis." In Freud's terms, the image unrepresses something that the secondary revision cannot completely erase or control. In both the Freudian and the legal context, the force behind the secondary revision is called *censorship*.

In our present moment, the one thing all critics seem to agree about is the danger and political retrogradeness of Art for Art's Sake—literature detached from any connection with a referent. If a representation is censored, it is presumably referential. That is, what is not wanted is something *in the world* that representation makes real. Political and historical criticism have become very sophisticated; the nonreferential dimension of literature can be historically subversive and disconcerting to such simple mimetic models. Thus, Dominick LaCapra can brilliantly analyze why Flaubert's *style indirect libre* was more upsetting to bourgeois models of realism than any immorality. But he nevertheless draws a line he will not cross:

> The danger of semiotics is the confinement of critical inquiry to meta-criticism that politically and socially neutralizes itself by placing the analyst in a deceptive position above the conflict of interpretations.[4]

The consensus about the dangers of detachment from conflict and of political neutralization is, therefore, still the danger of behaving a certain way *in the world*. The danger is that the attention paid to the operation of the signifier will have necessary referential consequences. While you are parsing a sentence, analyzing a metaphor, or smiling over a meaning entirely produced by the magic of rhyme, you are not paying attention to what is going on in the world. The question I would like to ask is whether *not* paying attention to the signifier *automatically* keeps you there. The Marxist suspicion of formalism does not make a person suspicious of formalism into a Marxist. A Marxist is suspicious of formalism because the temptation to reify forms might arrest an analysis designed to lead to revolutionary action. Merely being suspicious of forms is itself a reification if it is not *for* something. Instead of formalism for its own sake, we would have an even more empty antiformalism for its own sake, not even capable of taking form itself seriously, and certainly not intent on intervening in the world.

Why is the fear of forgetting reality so great? It is a grandiose fantasy of omnipotence to fear that by forgetting reality, a person might damage reality. The fact that the fear of damaging reality cannot be averted should make us more humble, not more in search of mastery, about the consequences of our actions. Even though we know now that the Holocaust really happened—and happened in large part through an accumulation of small actions of many people seen now as people who could have done something to stop it—we have drawn the wrong conclusions, I think. It is not that now we see that the Holocaust happened because of the actions of individuals, but that it happened because those individuals did not see that they were part of a pattern. No individual could have produced or stopped it on his or her own, even though it was through the risky and sacrificial actions of individuals that it could be resisted at all.

Why is the taboo against focusing on rhetorical structures without grounding their effects in the world so strong? It has grown all the stronger with the aversive effects of Paul de Man's wartime journalism.[5] But it was when I realized that the Nazis were just as opposed to the play of forms for their own sake as contemporary critics are—including myself—that I began to wonder why I had bought into the universal disparagement of Art for Art's Sake. Surely the collaborationist journalism of Paul de Man argues at least as strongly against the dangers of politicized criticism as against the dangers of detachment. Why is it that his late work—directed as it is against the temptations he himself had succumbed to—has been taken as a pathway to the same dangers he was resisting? Is his resistance too absolute? Is there something about turning so absolutely against a former temptation that repeats it in a different form? I have no answers to these questions, but they are part of what led me to take the particular intellectual paths I have taken here.

Getting back to what may be just as outrageous as a defense of Art for Art's Sake and is somehow related to it, it will be my contention here that what is censored in the Western tradition derived from Plato is always the fact of sexual difference.

Of course, I realize that sexual difference is not a fact but an interpretation, and it may be an interpretation of something that has nothing to do with sexual difference. Nevertheless, I would say that what is censored is a fact. It becomes an interpretation in the act of getting past the censor.

Surprisingly, female specificity is represented in one of two ways to reduce the threat it poses: it is seen as either motherhood or lesbianism. These two images appear to have little in common, and, in fact, that is the point. The first allows for male and female to be complementary; the second allows for them to be equivalent. Everything else falls into the category of "attractive nuisance." These two images are either central to patriarchy or indifferent to it. Thus, motherhood can be held up as the standard a woman hasn't met ("She may be a CEO, but she's *childless*") or lesbianism an accusation so monstrous it provokes denial if at all possible ("We know what her problem is: she *doesn't like men*"). Of course, the number of women who have negative feelings about men are hardly confined to lesbians—in fact, lesbians should be rather impervious to those feelings. But the trace of bad conscience—sweeping something that can't be incorporated under the rug—remains.

Sexual difference is not censored simply by virtue of the fact that Plato lived in a world of men, but rather the opposite: a certain censorship of sexual difference—one that confined women to the duties of reproduction—permitted the birth of philosophy.

In Plato's warnings against poetry in Book X of *The Republic*, particular attention is paid to representations of overflowing feelings. Witnessing the spectacle of lamentation or terror, Socrates says, "Few persons ever reflect, as I should imagine, that the contagion must pass from others to themselves. For the pity which has been nourished and strengthened in the misfortunes of others is with difficulty repressed in our own."[6] In other words, poetry unrepresses the real through the habit of the simulacrum. Sympathy is an admirable thing, but the wise man recognizes the slippery slope. He prides himself on his lack of reaction when the sorrow happens to him: "This is considered the manly part, and the other which delighted us in the recitation is now deemed to be the part of a woman" (Adams, 36).

The poetry that is expelled from the city, then, is equated with femininity. It is perhaps not an accident that one of the greatest lyric poets at that time was Sappho, whom Plato mentions in the *Phaedrus* ("I'm sure I have heard something better [than Lysias's speech] from the fair Sappho maybe").[7] Expelling poets is expelling femininity; expelling femininity is expelling women. And yet, in the *Phaedrus*, as Page du Bois has pointed out, Socrates seems to borrow from Sappho the rhetoric of inflamed desire. "Plato echoes and appropriates the female position, and then uses the occasion to deny the body and to sublimate erotic desire into philosophy."[8] When Socrates's wife, Xanthippe, visits him in his prison cell on the day he is to die, he sends her away for crying hysterically. Women would seem to represent all that is weak and bodily, all that is not philosophy. Yet what is Xanthippe lamenting as she is dragged away? "Oh, Socrates," she says, "this is the last time that you and your friends will be able to talk together!"[9] It is when she says *that* that Socrates asks that she be taken home. She gives voice not to the body's grief but to philosophy's, not to her own lamentations but to the sadness of the scene of her exclusion. To feel sympathy for the loss felt by those who share something that excludes you, *that* is the role of women. She is taken out not for bringing into the cell the other of philosophy, but for seeing and saying that the other of philosophy is already there.

The condemnation of poetry in Baudelaire's case originally involved two kinds of outrage: as outlined by Jean Pommier, four poems were initially condemned for "atteinte à la morale religieuse" and ten for "atteinte à la morale publique."[10] ("Religious" and "public" make as strange an opposition as "self" and "full" in gas stations!) When the trial was over, the accusation of outrage to religion was dropped, and Baudelaire was required to remove six poems and pay a fine. Given that he was always in debt and that there were exactly one hundred carefully placed poems in the 1857 edition, both parts of the penalty were experienced as harsh.

In the courtroom, the prosecutor Pinard argues that his role is not that of arbiter of literary quality (to which he has just shown himself to be sensitive) but that of a sentinel guarding the bounds of public decency. He says:

> Le juge n'est point un critique littéraire, appelé à prononcer sur des modes opposés d'apprécier l'art et de le rendre. Il n'est point le juge des écoles, mais le législateur l'a investi d'une mission définie: le législateur a in-scrit dans nos codes le délit d'offense à la morale publique, il a punie ce délit de certaines peines, il a donné au pouvoir judiciaire une autorité discrétionnaire pour reconnaître si cette morale est offensée, si la limite a été franchie. Le juge est une sentinelle qui ne doit pas laisser passer la frontière.[11]

(A judge is no literary critic, called upon to pronounce on the opposite modes of appreciating art and making it. He is also not here to judge schools, but rather the legislature has given him a precise mission: the legislator has inscribed among our laws the crime of offending public decency, he has decided on the punishment to mete out for this crime, and he has given discretionary authority to the judiciary to recognize whether such decency has indeed been offended, whether the limit has been crossed. The judge is a border guard who must prevent illicit passages.)

The judge is thus a sentinel preventing illicit "passages." It is perhaps those same "passages" that both Baudelaire and Benjamin will associate with the nineteenth century's modernity. In Benjamin's long, unfinished *Passagen-Werk*, glass and iron arcades are the link between inside and outside, commerce and art, street and store. And in the poems Baudelaire would later add to his "mutilated" masterwork, that same "passage" becomes the very substance of the erotic. As he writes in "A une passante" to the woman who ignites his desire as she suddenly appears through the medium of the city crowd, "Ô toi que j'eusse aimée, ô toi qui le savais!" (O you I would have loved, O you who knew that!)

Pinard cites the dangers of textual promiscuity in the age of the feuilleton. He warns against what will happen to public decency with the mass circula-tion of cheap journals, an argument better suited to Flaubert than to Baudelaire (whose poetry was not cheap). The very existence of the argument, however, implies the presence of an expanding and commercialized readership that Baudelaire could not control. Not all readers would be able to withstand the temptations offered by representations in the service of the moral lesson that is to be derived from them. Taking a page out of Plato's book, Pinard argues:

> Mais la vérité, la voici: l'homme est toujours plus ou moins infirme, plus ou moins faible, plus ou moins malade, portant d'autant plus le poids de sa chute originelle, qu'il veut en douter ou la nier. Si telle est sa nature intime tant qu'elle n'est pas relevée par de mâles efforts et une forte discipline, qui ne sait combien il prendra facilement le goût des frivolités lascives, sans se préoccuper de l'enseignement que l'auteur veut y placer.[12]

> (But here is the painful truth: man is always more or less wavering, more or less weak, more or less sick, carrying the burden of original sin the more he would like to doubt or negate it. If such is his intimate nature so long as it is not strengthened by male efforts and strong discipline, who knows how easily he will get a taste for lascivious frivolities and not give a damn for the lesson that the author means to place there.)

The senses will be awakened by the poems, and can thereafter never be securely contained. Clearly Pinard, as a representative of Second Empire bourgeois decency, is more afraid of being aroused than of being difficult to arouse, which was rather the danger Baudelaire was afraid of ("Je suis comme le roi d'un pays pluvieux. . . . Rien ne peut l'égayer" [I am like the king of a rainy country. . . . Nothing can arouse him]). I am taking *égayer* as a synonym for "arouse." That *égayer* should mean "arouse" to Pinard, too, is suggested by the condemnation of the poem "A celle qui est trop gaie." "To the woman who is too aroused"? As that poem suggests, it is *female* arousal that Pinard is most worried about. For him, arousal itself, as implicitly female, must be combated by the "male efforts" that the upright man expends. But, given the expanding market of *female* readers, what is to prevent these poems from falling into the hands of *women*? What if our daughters are even seduced by what Pinard learnedly calls "les plus intimes moeurs des tribades" (the most intimate customs of Tribades)? Pinard uses an archaic but explicit word meaning "female homosexual" (which Claude Pichois, in the notes to his edition of the works of Baudelaire, finds used in this sense in two dictionaries of the period). In fact, the attempt to understand whether or not the initial title of *Les Fleurs du Mal—Les Lesbiennes*—did or did not have what Pichois refers to as "the modern sense" pushes him into veritable feats of philology. Poetry? Or homosexuality? Geography? Or homosexuality? These same questions arise around the name Sappho. Was she or wasn't she? As Joan de Jean notes in her *Fictions of Sappho*:

> If I learned anything while working on this study, something for which I was totally unprepared, it is quite simply that Sappho makes a great many people nervous.[13]

(While I was working on the first version of this paper on an airplane, surrounded by two translations and two studies of Sappho, I certainly felt as if I were exposing something that I normally hide!)

> One phenomenon I explain in this way is the recurrent, stubborn refusal to mention female homosexuality under any name. (Commentators thus find themselves in the delicate position of attempting to disprove Sappho's homosexuality without actually naming that which they claim she was not.) (de Jean, 2)

This is the logical extension of the logic of censorship: you treat the thing you are condemning as if it could not be represented without creating the harm you are trying to prevent. The resistance to naming is a good example of the attempt to deny existence to the thing to which one is attempting to deny existence. Which doesn't mean that the thing repressed can't be resistant to naming in another sense. But we are getting ahead of ourselves.

In any case, Pinard *does* name female homosexuality as a dangerous moral corruption that might really occur in the world of female readers. But nothing could be further from Baudelaire's mind. The idea that lesbians might be recruited out of the ranks of good bourgeois reading daughters never occurs to him. Several times in his attempts to draft a post-condemnation preface to his *Fleurs du Mal*, he repeats:

> Ce n'est pas pour mes femmes, mes filles ou mes soeurs que ce livre a été écrit; non plus pour les femmes, les filles ou les soeurs de mon voisin.[14]

> (It is not for my wives, my daughters, or my sisters that this book was written, nor for the wives, daughters, and sisters of my neighbor.)

Since Baudelaire never married, had no children, and had no sisters, this is clearly a generic warning. Instead of coveting his neighbor's wife, he is merely preventing her from reading.

So paradoxically it is Pinard, not Baudelaire, who takes lesbianism seriously *in the world*. Pinard's distaste for it does not exclude a certain sensitivity to its charms, which merely increases his desire to prosecute it. In fact, *Les Fleurs du Mal* was prosecuted for "realism." As the court put it, in rendering its final decision to condemn six poems and to fine the author, the editor, and the printer of *Les Fleurs du Mal*:

> Attendu que l'erreur du poète, dans le but qu'il voulait atteindre et dans la route qu'il a suivie, quelque effort de style qu'il ait pu faire, quel que soit le blâme qui précède ou qui suit ses peintures, ne saurait détruire l'effet funeste des tableaux qu'il présente au lecteur, et qui, dans les pièces incriminées, conduisent nécessairement à l'excitation des sens par un réalisme grossier et offensant pour la pudeur. . . . [15]

> (Given that the poet's error, in the goal he envisaged and in the pathway he followed, whatever stylistic efforts he made, whatever blame precedes or follows his images, cannot destroy the deleterious effect of the tableaux he puts before the eyes of the reader, which, in the condemned poems, necessarily excite the senses through a gross realism offensive to modesty. . . .)

This condemnation for realism was a misunderstanding proudly corrected by a 1949 court. The 1857 court should never have taken those poems literally.

> Attendu que les poèmes faisant l'objet de la prévention ne renfermant aucun terme obscène ou même grossier et ne dépassant pas, en leur forme expressive, les libertés permises à l'artiste; que si certaines peintures ont pu, par leur originalité, alarmer quelques esprits à l'époque de la première publication des *Fleurs du Mal* et apparaître aux premiers juges comme offensant les bonnes moeurs, une telle appréciation ne s'attachant qu'à l'interprétation réaliste de ces poèmes et négligeant leur sens symbolique, s'est révélé de caractère arbitraire; qu'elle n'a été ratifiée ni par l'opinion publique, ni par le jugement des lettrés.[16]

> (Given that the condemned poems do not include a single obscene or even crude word and by no means go beyond, in their expressive form, what is permitted as poetic license; that if certain images could, in their very originality, have alarmed some readers at the time of the first publication of *The Flowers of Evil* and appeared to the initial judges as an offense to public decency, such a reading applies only to a realist interpretation of those poems and ignores their symbolic sense, appearing

arbitrary in character—such an interpretation has been ratified neither by public opinion nor by the judgment of literary people.)

The judgment of people of taste was precisely what would not count as evidence in a later obscenity trial where it was again a question of lesbianism: the trial of Radclyffe Hall for *The Well of Loneliness.* That court had become aware that obscenity did not inhere in words, nor could it be protected by literary merit. But note the two senses of "judgment" here: it applies to the legal system, but also to the aesthetic system. Kant's *Critique of Judgment* was not an indictment of the legal system but an investigation of taste. The aesthetic domain is generally seen as that which *escapes* determination by the legal system. Nevertheless, both courts and readers are called upon to make judgments. Perhaps the legal and the aesthetic systems have more in common than we customarily think. The condemnation and rehabilitation of *Les Fleurs du Mal,* for example, depend entirely on the distinction between realism and symbolism.

So in 1949, Baudelaire was rehabilitated. But lesbianism was thereby doubly condemned. If it was real, it was awful; if it was symbolic, it wasn't real. "Realism" was reality unidealized; its realness was proven by its undesirableness. If any reality were desirable, why would we need realism to see it? It wouldn't have been repressed in the first place. If lesbianism connotes "realism," then, it must be because of an inability to repress completely what is undesirable. The possibility that real lesbianism could be idealized would have to wait another twenty years. And when it did become thinkable, it would not take Baudelaire with it.

If real, then condemned; if symbolic, then not real. What is rendered impossible is the idea that lesbians, like philosophers, could be both at once. Or neither.

II. Translation

Thanks to you and your invention, your pupils will be widely read
without benefit of a teacher's instruction; in consequence, they'll
entertain the delusion that they have wide knowledge, while they are, in
fact, for the most part incapable of real judgment.
—The King to the Inventor of Writing in Plato's *Phaedrus*

This is where Sappho comes back in. In Sappho's case, as Page du Bois puts it, "There is no there there."[17] Her poems are preserved in fragments in other people's quotations, in Egyptian garbage dumps, in allusions. "Who is Sappho?" writes Dudley Fitts in his preface to the Mary Barnard translation. "A lyricist unparalleled, a great beauty, no great beauty, a rumor, a writer of cultist hymns, a scandal, a fame, a bitchy sister to a silly brother, a headmistress, a mystic, a mistress of the poet Alkaios, a pervert, a suicide for love of a ferryman, an androgyne, a bluestocking, a pretty mother of a prettier daughter, an avatar of Yellow Book neodiabolism, a Greek."[18] The question of Sappho's real identity gives rise to the very insatiability that lesbians are made to stand for in Baudelaire. Translators have sometimes responded to her incompleteness by filling out Sappho's fragments and thus making a couple with her. Willis Barnstone writes:

Now a Cambridge don, Mr. Edmonds, had come to her rescue and filled in the lost lines with his own conjectured Greek verse. His inventions, often half or whole lines, were bracketed. He bequeathed us a co-authored Greek text by Sappho and Edmonds.[19]

Barnstone decides to treat Sappho's "badly mutilated" texts more respectfully, leaving them fragmentary wherever "reasonable guesses" are impossible. But his description of Sappho is no less flirtatious: the rhetoric of the amorous chase is everywhere.

One day in the late autumn of 1959, I spent an unexpected evening with Sappho. . . . After meeting Sappho, I decided on the spot to know her better and chose a way. . . . She appears in her naked Greek and to read her abroad she requires an attractive outfit in English. . . . When I left Sappho—and at the time I knew her lines by heart—I strayed into koine Greek of the Septuagint and Gospels. Then here in California, thirty-five years after the first evening with her, I was happily visited by a similar *coup de foudre*. (Barnstone, 11, 12, 13, 14)

The plot of this retrospectively narrated tale is self-consciously that of an intense love affair with a somewhat elusive woman. But flirting with Sappho may not be as reassuring as this story makes it out to be. The naturalness of the assumption that Sappho would welcome such advances—on which the charm of Barnstone's writing relies—is unquestioned. Just raising the question attributes an independent will to her, whatever the answer turns out to be. And one begins to suspect that translation's difficulties with "fidelity" might turn out to have something to do with it. It is not a matter of retrieving the lost Sappho, but rather of conceptualizing poetry written from a nonorigin.

In Jacques Derrida's analysis of Plato's *Phaedrus*, reference is repeatedly made to a scene called "the trial of writing." Since we are here in the process of studying the trial of Baudelaire (and, by extension, Flaubert), it seems useful to look closely at a judgment pronounced about writing itself. The inventor of writing, Theuth, presents writing to the King for his judgment. Theuth says that writing is a good remedy for forgetfulness. (Let us not forget that one of Baudelaire's condemned poems was called "Le Léthé.") Writing is not a remedy for forgetfulness, says the King; it's a *recipe* for it. The division between remedy and recipe has to exist in order to make sense of this trial, but the Greek word is in both cases the same: *pharmakon*. The decision to translate the *word* according to "reasonable guesses" about the meaning of the context gives rise to "remedy" and "recipe," "poison" or "antidote." That decision *has to be made* by the translator, but then the translated text performs a judgment that the original suspends. In one of the most illuminating passages I know about translation, Derrida writes:

> It will [also] be seen to what extent the malleable unity of this concept, or rather its rules and the strange logic that links it with its signifier, has been dispersed, masked, obliterated, and rendered almost unreadable not only by the imprudence or empiricism of the translators, but first and foremost by the redoubtable, irreducible difficulty of translation. It is a difficulty inherent in its very principle, situated less in the passage from one language to another, from one philosophical language to another, than already, as we shall see, in the tradition between Greek and Greek; a violent difficulty in the transference of a nonphilosopheme into a philosopheme. With this problem of translation we will thus be dealing with nothing less than the problem of the very passage into philosophy.[20]

And what does that passage consist of? Of dividing the undivided. In the original language, it is as though the *pharmakon* is the medium that exists prior to division. Only the translators have to decide between "poison" and "remedy." Philosophy in its original state is not the union of opposites but that which engenders opposition in the first place. "All translations into languages that are the heirs and depositaries of Western metaphysics thus produce on the *pharmakon* an *effect of analysis* that violently destroys it," writes Derrida (99).

Derrida's reading of Plato's text recaptures the lack of division between the antithetical senses of the word *pharmakon*. But the King would still have pronounced judgment upon Theuth's invention, which Theuth would have presented to him for that purpose. That the separation between positive and negative judgments should be incomplete and ambiguous in Plato's text around the King's judgment does not imply that philosophy exists prior to that separation. After all, whether it was good or bad for philosophy that Socrates died by drinking his own *pharmakon* cannot be decided *within* philosophy. And that Socrates should be the victim of distinctions he himself instituted should not be surprising. Derrida's brilliant reading of Plato's *text* as opposed to its intentions makes visible the fact that philosophy's founding trick is to make us *believe* that it constitutes the prior medium in which translators and, after them, readers, will carve decision. It thus appears that all the founding polarities of the Western metaphysical tradition—good versus evil, health versus sickness, life versus death, and so on—are somehow oversimplifications of an originating ambiguity. But an originating ambiguity is not necessarily the same as a prior medium. Philosophy has thus instituted by back-formation the original unity from which it has fallen and to which it tries to return. But to have ambiguity or undecidability, there has to already have been polarity. Derrida's "correction" of the deformations necessarily produced by translators is itself inevitably a metaphysical look. The text becomes uncanny to the extent that everything in it could point to its opposite. It is simply impossible to fix that uncanniness in an unambiguous way. In the beginning was undecidability?

Genesis says that the world was created by division. By separating the waters from the waters. The whole question is what was there before. It is easy to say "undifferentiation," but is undifferentiation unity? Much later comes the act of separating philosophy from sophistry, of enacting the founding *krinein*, of pronouncing the founding judgment. Philosophy will henceforth separate the serious from the frivolous, truth from falsehood, literal from figurative. Also life from death. Yet somehow philosophy is also the first discourse that does not assume automatically that life is better than death. Philosophy's founding separation may thus be counterintuitive: life is separated from death, but death might henceforth not be entirely negative. After all, philosophy starts out not from biological life but from language.

Even if there had been no trial of writing in Plato's text, there would still have been translation. The one thing we know for sure about translation is that it comes after—and is dependent on—an original. Or do we?

I was at this point in my thinking about trials of and in literary texts when I suddenly thought it might be time to take a look at Franz Kafka's *The Trial*. Since my German is too rudimentary for reading, I turned to the old translation by Willa and Edwin Muir that I happened to have on hand, and began.

"Someone must have traduced Joseph K., for without having done anything wrong he was arrested one fine morning."[21]

"Traduced"? This is an English word I see only in lame attempts to translate the Italian *traduttore, traditore* or the French *traduire, trahir*. To translate is to traduce—the betrayal of the original in the process of transmitting it is inherent in translation. In other words, "traduce" is a bad translation of a pun on the inevitable badness of translations. Joseph K. had been betrayed in exactly the same way. I looked at the first sentence in a more recent edition in which the Muirs' translation had been revised by E. M. Butler: "Someone must have *been telling lies about* Joseph K., for without having done anything wrong he was arrested one fine morning."[22] In German the sentence reads: "Jemand musste Josef K. verleumdet haben, denn ohne dass er etwas Böses getan hätte, wurde er eines Morgens verhaftet."[23] One can see why the translator wanted to replace a somewhat archaic word with a more colloquial expression. My German–English dictionary translates *verleumden* as "calumniate, slander, defame, traduce, accuse wrongfully." But by writing "someone must have been telling lies," the translator has set up an opposition between truth and falsehood that, while it is called for by the context, cannot be stated without destroying the senselessness of the arrest. If someone had been telling lies about Joseph K., it makes perfect sense that he should be (falsely) arrested. The translation "traduce" is thus even better than the original in *not* performing on the ambiguous word a violent "effect of analysis." By making more sense of the arrest, the translator destroys its senselessness. *Only translation can betray* without necessarily instating the polarity from which it deviates. In fact the act of arresting Joseph K. cannot be better figured than by translation. The risk in translating Sappho is expressed in exactly this way by Willis Barnstone: "If a very fragmentary work is to be rendered into English it must function not only as a gloss for reading the original but come through with the dignity and excitement of an original text. *Anything less is to traduce Sappho*" (Barnstone, 12).

To introduce his German translation of "Tableaux Parisiens"—the section Baudelaire added to the original edition of *Les Fleurs du Mal* to make up for the loss of the condemned poems the court had forced him to remove— Walter Benjamin added a preface on the theory of translation. We shall have occasion to revisit this text at length later, but here, let me just quote one of Benjamin's key pronouncements. Translation, he writes, is "a somewhat provisional way of coming to grips with the foreignness of languages."[24] Only through translation does an original *become* an original. In saying this I think that Benjamin does not—or not only—mean to say that the original acquires some new authority from the process, but that the idea of the original is a back-formation from the difficulties of translation. Until one sees that from which something deviates, one does not think of that thing as a starting point. The trajectory from original to translation mimes the process of departing from an origin and thus enhances the belief that there *is* an origin. What translation allows us to see is also a fantasy language uniting the two works, as if all translations were falls away from some original language that fleetingly becomes visible. But nothing proves that this is not another back-formation from the difficulties of translation. We are so used to the model of wholeness falling into multiplicity that we read the effect of the effect as if it were a cause. A review of *The Power of Babel* in the *Financial Times* typifies our commitment to this belief: "Obviously, at the very beginning of human history there was just one language."[25] Obviously? To whom could such a thing be obvious?

It is not, as the myth of Babel would have it, that there was one original language that fell into multiplicity. Rather, the idea of that one original language might be a mere projection out of the process of translation. The inevitability of betrayal is the only evidence we actually have that there is something to betray.

III. Difference

And the rib, which the Lord God had taken from man, made he a
woman, and brought her unto the man. And Adam said, This is now
bone of my bones, and flesh of my flesh: she shall be called Woman,
because she was taken out of Man.—Genesis 2:22–23, King James Bible

And, finally, need I add that I who speak here am bone of the bone and
flesh of the flesh of them that live within the Veil? —W. E. B. Du Bois, *The
Souls of Black Folk*

What work does sexual difference do for us intellectually? For Western metaphysics, "male" and "female" fit neatly into the pattern of polarities like "good" and "evil" or "life" and "death." Indeed, some theorists have considered that pattern to be *derived* from the heterosexual couple:

Where is she?
Activity/Passivity
Sun/Moon

Culture/Nature
Day/Night

Father/Mother
Head/Heart
Intelligible/Palpable
Logos/Pathos.
Form, convex, step, advance, semen, progress.

Matter, concave, ground—where steps are taken, holding—and
dumping—ground.
Man
_____
Woman
   Always the same metaphor: we follow it, it carries us, beneath all
its figures, wherever discourse is organized. If we read or speak, the
same thread or double braid is leading us throughout literature,
philosophy, criticism, centuries of representation and reflection.
Thought has always worked through opposition,
Speaking/Writing
Parole/Ecriture
High/Low
Through dual, hierarchical oppositions.
   Superior/Inferior. Myths, legends, books. Philosophical systems.
Everywhere (where) ordering intervenes, where a law organizes
what is thinkable by oppositions (dual, irreconcilable; or sublatable,
dialectical). And all these pairs of oppositions are *couples*.[26]

Sexual difference considered as the difference between male and female
has helped to organize—or been organized—by all other pairs of difference.
In some languages, sexual difference is tantamount to difference itself ("Vive
la différence!"). But although the "facts of life" have presumably not changed
much over time, the historical conception of those facts has changed a great
deal.[27] In Aristotle's theory of reproduction, for example, woman was only
the formless receptacle, entirely shaped by the generativity of the man. For
Socrates, men and women could coexist because they were not competing
for the same space. He wouldn't have dreamed of the possibility of falling in
love with a woman—men were for that. Romantic love for a woman—courtly
love—was a breakthrough. Women's value was raised enough that men could
fall in love with them (though both Girard's theory of mimetic desire and

Sedgwick's reading of heterosexuality "between men" reveal how the older model shows through). But at first women simply didn't have enough value to worry about. Helen as the origin of the Trojan war was like Eve as the origin of sin: somebody had to do it, and if everything bad could be blamed on women, men would look even better. It is not for nothing that the counterfactual exercise most popular among the sophists to show their rhetorical skills was the praise of Helen. The "bad" woman was the woman who could start a war, while the "good" woman (Penelope) waited faithfully at home. When seen as different from men, women's *only* function is to represent everything men don't want to attribute to themselves. For purposes of inheriting and owning both property and family names, men stood alone. Indeed, the equation between landed property and family names meant that aristocracy was the same as patriarchy.

Shakespeare offers an interesting twist on the metaphor of artistic creation: his sonnets are often seen these days as exemplifying bisexuality, but it seems to me they stick rather closely to the "men = eroticism, women = procreation" thesis in the beginning, but then the moment art and life begin to compete for the fair young man's posterity, the door is open for art to allow women back in as an aesthetic focus, not merely a biological function. The "one thing to my purpose nothing" initially reserves biological reproduction for heterosexuality and frees the subject to desire, love, write about men. But making texts and making babies do not equivalently produce "copies": the need for women's genes means the son will never be merely created in the image of the father. The question of "copies" that made Socrates nervous is bound to wreak havoc in reproduction as well, although patriarchy functions as if it were possible to forget it. Shakespeare's rhetoric sometimes encompasses the difficulty, but pre-Mendelian biological reproduction did not theorize the role of the mother.

> Mark how one string, sweet husband to another,
> Strikes each in each by mutual ordering;
> Resembling sire, and child, and happy mother,
> Who all in one, one pleasing note do sing;
> Whose speechless song, being many, seeming one,
> Sings this to thee: "Thou single wilt prove none."
> (Sonnet 8)

With the idea that difference is complementary, many become parts of a whole. Biological reproduction restores unity and succession. Homosexuality is just a supplement. But if it is damned as sterile and as not admitting difference,

then whenever there is a lack of unity in the couple—that is to say, *all the time*—
the unity it is supposed to preserve breaks down. Two ceases to be equal to
one. And the very fact that there are two people in a couple becomes a critique
of the unity they are supposed to preserve. In homosexuality, because you do
have two people, in fact, without the excuse of complementarity, the impossibility of making two perfectly equal one is fundamental. Homosexuality
just makes the falseness of that ideal more inescapable.

Turning back to Shakespeare's sonnets, we see art starting to win over
life when the question of how to ensure immortality starts to ally with
representation. The depiction of mortality, which both men and women
share, seems to be a new form of unity, but the play of the English language
that expresses that unity cannot be easily duplicated in another language.
Thus the unity is re-produced (universality) in language, but the multiplicity of languages makes that universality in fact not shareable. Baudelaire
expresses this relentless fact about temporality when, in his poem "L'Horloge,"
he says:

> Horloge! dieu sinistre, effrayant, impassible,
> Dont le doigt nous menace et nous dit: "*Souviens-toi!*
> Les vibrantes Douleurs dans ton coeur plein d'effroi
> Se planteront bientôt comme dans une cible;

> "Le Plaisir vaporeux fuira vers l'horizon
> Ainsi qu'une sylphide au fond de la coulisse;
> Chaque instant te dévore un morceau du délice
> A chaque homme accordé pour toute sa saison.

> "Trois mille six cents fois par heure, la Seconde
> Chuchote: *Souviens-toi!*—Rapide, avec sa voix
> D'insecte, Maintenant dit: Je suis Autrefois,
> Et j'ai pompé ta vie avec ma trompe immonde!

> "Remember! Souviens-toi, prodigue! Esto memor!
> (Mon gosier de métal parle toutes les langues.) . . ."

> (Timepiece frightful, sinister, impassive god,
> Who points at us threateningly and says: "*Remember!*
> The quivering Sorrows will embed themselves
> In your fearful heart as if it were a target;

> "Vanishing Pleasure flees toward the horizon
> Like a sylphide disappearing in the wings;

Every instant devours a part of the delight
Accorded to a man to last for his entire season.

"Three thousand six hundred times an hour, the Seconds
Whisper: *Remember!*—Swiftly, with its insect voice,
Each Now says: I am Yesteryear,
And I've sucked your life dry with my filthy trunk!

"Souviens-toi! Remember, prodigal! Esto memor!
[My metal throat speaks every language.) . . ."]

Mortality may speak every language, but it finds a way to do so very differently in each. Here, for example, are some of the puns Shakespeare makes to separate biological mortality from art:

my remains—this remains
thou art—my art
few leaves—must leave
lean penury—that pen
use—usury
still (dead)—still (ongoingly)
stay (stop)—stay (remain)
remains (corpse)—remains (stays)
lie (tell an untruth)—lie (recline, rest)
keep (retain)—keep (prevent)
issue (posterity)—issue (publish)
wear (be dressed in)—wear (be used up)
touch (detail)—touch (feel with hand)
line (wrinkle)—line (verse)
prick (embroider)—prick (penis)
true (faithful)—true (truthful)
rite—write
tongue—tongue

"Tongue" means "language" only for certain expressions in English (like "mother tongue"), but for ordinary use there is another word: "language." In French (and Hebrew), the relation is much closer: *langue* (the same word for "language" and "tongue") and *sapha* (the same word for "language" and "lip") are the literal words for "language." In German, again, we have *Zunge* and *Sprache*. Thus, the French or Hebrew translations might find *more* wordplay, not less, on this point than the original. One of the hardest things to translate is the link between language and the body that the original has made, in part through the linguistic resources of the original. In translation, the body is never in exactly the same place.

The father of modern linguistics, Ferdinand de Saussure, considered language as a system in which every speaker was potentially created equal. But Jacques Lacan took Saussure's diagram of the building block of language—the sign—split Saussure's one into two, and changed the sign's referential function. Saussure had represented the sign as shown in figure 12.1.

Lacan draws two identical doors and makes them signs of "men" and "women" in figure 12.2.

Thus the signs no longer paint an image of the real but serve to discipline the reader into sexual difference. Henceforth, the reader is not told what is real; he or she is told where to "go." There are two doors, and every subject has to pick one.

This cultural "translation" of sexual difference means that in all languages that are structured by grammatical gender, gender both is and is not referential. Female entities tend to be feminine and male masculine, but the form of a noun often plays a greater role in its gender than a referential concept of sex. Thus, if abstract nouns are feminine in Latin and the Romance languages derived from it, allegories are female. There are three genders in German, not two; this makes referential sense, but the gender of inanimate objects is masculine or feminine in French. The moon is feminine in French and masculine in German; the sun is masculine in French and feminine in German. Does this have anything to do with French rationalism and German romanticism? In Hebrew, "I love you" has to reveal the genders of the speaker and addressee—no coy hijacking of discourses, therefore, is possible for uses for which they were not intended. Gender is thus somewhat arbitrary in all languages (who would have thought that "girls" were neuter in German?), but that arbitrariness may nevertheless have an unconsciously internalized referential effect.[28]

The concept of sexual difference is fundamental to two of the theories that came out of the late nineteenth century and still have currency today: Marxism and Freudianism. In the post-Mendelian era, when the woman's contribution to biological reproduction could no longer be denied, male dominance had to come up with a new justification for its existence, and it came up with the notion of "separate spheres." The potential competition between the sexes was to be minimized by assigning the woman to the home and the man to the world.

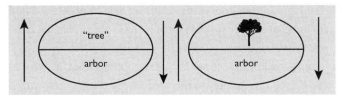

FIG. 12.1

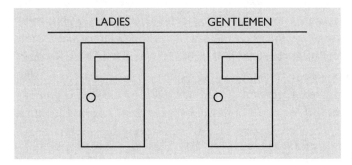

FIG. 12.2

Marx and Freud had to use sexual difference to overcome a different obstacle. The bourgeois revolutions had for the first time theorized equality—political equality for citizens, the absence of inherited privilege, universality, the universal equivalent. "All men are created equal," proclaimed the Declaration of Independence. Coexisting with chattel slavery, such an idea could very well be untrue *in fact*, but its untruth didn't at first inhere in the fact that "all men" didn't stand for "all people." The political problem was NOT inequality—which could go on IN FACT without disrupting the theory, but sexual difference, which was *within* every category of inequality. In France, at least the revolutionaries paid attention to what they were saying and briefly freed slaves, women, Jews—but Napoleon quickly reversed all of that. So if theorists of repression are to represent it as universal—class conflict, civilization as such—they have to find a place for sexual difference that will allow them to get on with it. Marx solved the problem by starting with the sexual division of labor and situating the origin of slavery in the household, but he still acknowledged women's work (women's *labor*) as primarily reproductive. In the workplace, men and women were equivalent. Freud solved the problem by making castration necessary for both sexes—and the concept of castration results directly from the discovery of sexual difference; women thenceforth have to assume it, so that men don't have to.

The placement of sexual difference within a theory of equality is therefore designed to solve a theoretical problem. Then the universality can reappear and remedy something *for everyone*. It was not that sexual difference had not always existed, but that suddenly it became a theoretical *problem*. Given the notions of equality and universality (prerequisites for theory today), where could one put sexual difference? It was a problem that Marx and Freud had to solve before they could go on. One of the things they taught us, in fact, was how to forget sexual difference when they were not thinking about it. Marx forgot quite quickly (and Marxists even more so), but Freud never entirely forgot its effects on the psyche, although those effects could often be described as the same for both sexes. So sexual difference is a problem that must be solved if equality is to work, but because it leaves a residue, it has to be legislated. Marx will see law as preserving bourgeois property and Freud phallic privilege, but both will consider those laws as the source of the damage. Since then, women have won greater and greater legal equality, so that almost all the differences that were maintained by the law have disappeared. At a certain point, sexual difference has stopped mattering legally, which is why gay marriage and sex changes have come to deserve equal rights, and why the Defense of Marriage Act has to reinstitute a legal constraint so that heterosexuality is relegislated. There is no longer a real argument for restricting marriage to one man and one woman, but the defenders of traditional marriage have attempted to invoke God or biology. However, as the example of cloning suggests, science seems to have as its always possible outcome an escaping of sexual difference, not a reinforcement of it, so that what seems like a biological invariant can be gotten around. That, in fact, is one of the aims of science, and perhaps also what makes science seem like a not entirely benign force (Frankenstein: "I thought that I held the corpse of my dead mother in my arms").

What I hope to argue here is that the plurality of languages and the plurality of sexes are alike in that they both make the "one" impossible. Two and two thousand are less different than one and two. Rhetorically, though, a certain eloquence depends on one's not thinking about difference. "What does man want?" depends on universality for a rhetorical effect that any qualification curtails ("What does a woman want?" [Freud]; "What does a black man want?" [Fanon]). But at what price do we maintain a rhetoric of universality—with all the appeal that it entails?

NOTES

"Correctional Facilities," reprinted by permission of the publisher from Barbara Johnson, *Mother Tongues: Sexuality, Trials, Motherhood*, 1–25 (Cambridge, MA: Harvard University Press), © 2003 by the President and Fellows of Harvard College.

1. This is the argument Alexander Nehamas makes in "Plato and the Mass Media" (in *Virtues of Authenticity* [Princeton, NJ: Princeton University Press, 1999]), but he himself does not rest content with it (see his "Eristic, Antilogic, Sophistic, Dialectic: Plato's Demarcation of Philosophy from Sophistry" in the same volume).

2. Hazard Adams, ed., *Critical Theory since Plato* (New York: Harcourt Brace, 1992).

3. Edith Hamilton and Huntington Cairns, eds., *Plato: The Collected Dialogues* (Princeton, NJ: Princeton University Press, 1961).

4. Dominick LaCapra, *"Madame Bovary" on Trial* (Ithaca, NY: Cornell University Press, 1982), 9.

5. See Paul de Man, *Wartime Journalism, 1939–1943*, ed. Werner Hamacher, Neil Hertz, and Thomas Keenan (Lincoln: University of Nebraska Press, 1988).

6. Quoted from Adams, ed., *Critical Theory since Plato*, 37.

7. Hamilton and Cairns, eds., *Plato*, 483.

8. "Sappho in the Text of Plato," in Page du Bois, *Sappho Is Burning* (Chicago: University of Chicago Press, 1995), 87.

9. Hamilton and Cairns, eds., *Plato*, 43.

10. See "Dossier des Fleurs du Mal," in Baudelaire, *Oeuvres complètes*, ed. Claude Pichois (Paris: Gallimard, 1961), 1:1178; henceforth cited as "Dossier."

11. "Dossier," 1206.

12. "Dossier," 1208.

13. Joan de Jean, *Fictions of Sappho, 1546–1937* (Chicago: University of Chicago Press, 1989), 2.

14. Baudelaire, *Oeuvres complètes*, 1:181.

15. "Dossier," 1181–82.

16. Jacques Hamelin, *La Réhabilitation judiciaire de Baudelaire* (Paris: Dalloz, 1952), 73.

17. Du Bois, *Sappho Is Burning*, 82.

18. *Sappho: A New Translation*, trans. Mary Barnard (Berkeley: University of California Press, 1958), vii.

19. Willis Barnstone, *Sappho* (Los Angeles: Sun and Moon Press, 1998), 11.

20. Jacques Derrida, *Dissemination*, trans. Barbara Johnson (Chicago: University of Chicago Press, 1981), 71–72.

21. Franz Kafka, *The Trial*, trans. Willa Muir and Edwin Muir (New York: Modern Library, 1956).

22. Franz Kafka, *The Trial*, trans. Willa Muir and Edwin Muir; rev. and trans. E. M. Butler (New York: Schocken, 1968).

23. Franz Kafka, *Der Prozess* (Frankfurt: Fisher, 1992).

24. Walter Benjamin, *Selected Writings* (Cambridge, MA: Harvard University Press, 1996), 257.

25. A. C. Grayling, *Financial Times,* February 17, 2002, v, in his review of John McWhorter, *The Power of Babel* (New York: Times Books/Henry Holt, 2001),

a book that studies not the appearance but the disappearance of languages, which are becoming extinct as fast as endangered species in the rain forests.

26. Hélène Cixous and Catherine Clément, *The Newly Born Woman*, trans. Betsy Wing (Minneapolis: University of Minnesota Press, 1986), 63–64.

27. For a study of the historicity of theories of reproduction, see the unpublished dissertation of Lilian Porten, "The *Mâle du Siècle:* Creation and Procreation in French Literature" (Cambridge, MA: Harvard University, 1999), especially the discussion of the assumption of natural stability as vehicle in the section "An Equation with Two Unknowns," talking about the metaphor of the author as parent.

28. For a brilliant study of the relations between sexual difference, foreign languages, and the unconscious, based on a reading of the large number of parapraxes involving foreign languages in Freud's *The Psychopathology of Everyday Life*, see Mary Gossy, *Freudian Slips: Woman, Writing, the Foreign Tongue* (Ann Arbor: University of Michigan Press, 1995).

CHAPTER 13

My Monster/My Self

To judge from recent trends in scholarly as well as popular literature, three crucial questions can be seen to stand at the forefront of today's preoccupations: the question of mothering, the question of the woman writer, and the question of autobiography. Although these questions and current discussions of them often appear unrelated to each other, it is my intention here to explore some ways in which the three questions *are* profoundly interrelated. To attempt to shed some new light on each by approaching it via the others, I shall base my remarks upon two twentieth-century theoretical studies—Nancy Friday's *My Mother/My Self* and Dorothy Dinnerstein's *The Mermaid and the Minotaur*—and one nineteenth-century gothic novel, *Frankenstein; or, The Modern Prometheus*, written by Mary Shelley, whose importance for literary history has until quite recently been considered to arise not from her own writings but from the fact that she was the second wife of poet Percy Bysshe Shelley and the daughter of the political philosopher William Godwin and the pioneering feminist Mary Wollstonecraft.[1]

All three of these books, in strikingly diverse ways, offer a critique of the institution of parenthood. *The Mermaid and the Minotaur* is an analysis of the damaging effects of the fact that human infants are cared for almost exclusively by women. "What the book's title as a whole is meant to connote," writes Dinnerstein, "is both (*a*) our longstanding general awareness of our uneasy, ambiguous position in the animal kingdom, and (*b*) a more specific awareness: that until we grow strong enough to renounce the pernicious forms of collaboration between the sexes, both man and woman will remain semi-human, monstrous" (5). Even as Dinnerstein describes convincingly the types of imbalance and injustice the prevailing asymmetry in gender relations produces, she also analyzes the reasons for our refusal to abandon the very modes of monstrousness from which we suffer most. Nancy Friday's book, which is subtitled "A Daughter's Search for Identity," argues that the mother's repression of herself necessitated by the myth of maternal love creates a heritage of self-rejection, anger, and duplicity that makes it difficult for the daughter to seek any emotional satisfaction other than the state of idealized symbiosis that both mother and daughter continue to punish themselves for never having been able to achieve. Mary Shelley's *Frankenstein* is an even more elaborate and unsettling formulation of the relation between parenthood and monstrousness. It is the story of two antithetical modes of parenting that give rise to two increasingly parallel lives—the life of Victor Frankenstein, who is the beloved child of two doting parents, and the life of the monster he single-handedly creates but immediately spurns and abandons. The fact that in the end both characters reach an equal degree of alienation and self-torture and, indeed, become indistinguishable as they pursue each other across the frozen polar wastes indicates that the novel is, among other things, a study of the impossibility of finding an adequate model for what a parent should be.

All three books agree, then, that in the existing state of things there is something inherently monstrous about the prevailing parental arrangements. While Friday and Dinnerstein, whose analyses directly address the problem of sexual difference, suggest that this monstrousness is curable, Mary Shelley, who does not explicitly locate the self's monstrousness in its gender arrangements, appears to dramatize divisions within the human being that are so much a part of being human that no escape from monstrousness seems possible.

What I will try to do here is to read these three books not as mere studies of the monstrousness of selfhood, not as mere accounts of human monsterdom in general, but as autobiographies in their own right, as textual dramatizations of the very problems with which they deal. None of the three books, of course, presents itself explicitly as autobiography. Yet each includes clear instances of the autobiographical—not the purely authorial—first-person pronoun. In each case the autobiographical reflex is triggered by the resistance and ambivalence involved in the act of writing the book. What I shall argue here is that what is specifically feminist in each book is directly related to this struggle for female authorship.

The notion that *Frankenstein* can somehow be read as the autobiography of a woman would certainly appear at first sight to be ludicrous. The novel, indeed, presents not one but three autobiographies of men. Robert Walton, an arctic explorer on his way to the North Pole, writes home to his sister of his encounter with Victor Frankenstein, who tells Walton the story of his painstaking creation and unexplained abandonment of a nameless monster who suffers excruciating and fiendish loneliness, and who tells Frankenstein *his* life story in the middle pages of the book. The three male autobiographies motivate themselves as follows:

[Walton, to his sister:] "You will rejoice to hear that no disaster has accompanied the commencement of an enterprise which you have regarded with such evil forebodings. I arrived here yesterday, and my first task is to assure my dear sister of my welfare." (15)

[Frankenstein, with his hands covering his face, to Walton, who has been speaking of his scientific ambition:] "Unhappy man! Do you share my madness? Have you drunk also of the intoxicating draught? Hear me; let me reveal my tale, and you will dash the cup from your lips!" (26)

[Monster, to Frankenstein:] "I entreat you to hear me before you give vent to your hatred on my devoted head." [Frankenstein:] "Begone! I will not hear you. There can be no community between you and me." [Monster places his hands before Frankenstein's eyes:] "Thus I take from thee a sight which you abhor. Still thou canst listen to me and grant me thy compassion. . . . God, in pity, made man beautiful and alluring, after his own image; but my form is a filthy type of yours, more horrid even from the very resemblance." (95, 96, 97, 125)

All three autobiographies here are clearly attempts at persuasion rather than simple accounts of facts. They all depend on a presupposition of resemblance between teller and addressee: Walton assures his sister that he has not really left the path she would wish for him, that he still resembles *her*. Frankenstein recognizes in Walton an image of himself and rejects in the monster a resemblance he does not wish to acknowledge. The teller is in each case speaking into a mirror of his own transgression. The tale is designed to reinforce the resemblance between teller and listener so that somehow transgression can be eliminated. Yet the desire for resemblance, the desire to create a being like oneself—which is the autobiographical desire par excellence—is also the central transgression in Mary Shelley's novel. What is at stake in

Frankenstein's workshop of filthy creation is precisely the possibility of shaping a life in one's own image: Frankenstein's monster can thus be seen as a figure for autobiography as such. Victor Frankenstein, then, has twice obeyed the impulse to construct an image of himself: on the first occasion he creates a monster, and on the second he tries to explain to Walton the causes and consequences of the first. *Frankenstein* can be read as the story of autobiography as the attempt to neutralize the monstrosity of autobiography. Simultaneously a revelation and a cover-up, autobiography would appear to constitute itself as in some way a repression of autobiography.

These three fictive male autobiographies are embedded within a thin introductory frame, added in 1831, in which Mary Shelley herself makes the repression of her own autobiographical impulse explicit:

> The publishers of the standard novels, in selecting *Frankenstein* for one of their series, expressed a wish that I should furnish them with some account of the origin of the story. . . . It is true that I am very averse to bringing myself forward in print, but as my account will only appear as an appendage to a former production, and as it will be confined to such topics as have connection with my authorship alone, I can scarcely accuse myself of a personal intrusion. (vii)

Mary Shelley, here, rather than speaking into a mirror, is speaking as an appendage to a text. It might perhaps be instructive to ask whether this change of status has anything to do with the problem of specifically feminine autobiography. In a humanistic tradition in which *man* is the measure of all things, how does an appendage go about telling the story of her life?

Before pursuing this question further, I would like to turn to a more explicit version of surreptitious feminine autobiography. Of the three books under discussion, Nancy Friday's account of the mother–daughter relationship relies the most heavily on the facts of the author's life in order to demonstrate its thesis. Since the author grew up without a father, she shares with Frankenstein's monster some of the problems of coming from a single-parent household. The book begins with a chapter entitled "Mother Love," of which the first two sentences are "I have always lied to my mother. And she to me" (19). Interestingly, the book carries the following dedication: "When I stopped seeing my mother with the eyes of a child, I saw the woman who helped me give birth to myself. This book is for Jane Colbert Friday Scott." How, then, can we be sure that this huge book is not itself another lie to the mother it is dedicated to? Is autobiography somehow always in the process of symbolically killing the mother off by telling her the lie that we have given birth to ourselves? On page 460, Nancy Friday is still not sure what kind of lie she has told. She writes: "I am suddenly afraid that the mother I have depicted throughout this book is false." Whose life is this, anyway? This question cannot be resolved by a book that sees the "daughter's search for identity" as the necessity of choosing *between* symbiosis and separation, *between* the mother and the autonomous self. As long as this polarity remains unquestioned, the autobiography of Nancy Friday becomes the drawing and redrawing of the portrait of Jane Colbert Friday Scott. The most truly autobiographical moments occur not in expressions of triumphant separation but in descriptions of the way the book itself attempts to resist its own writing. At the end of the chapter on loss of virginity, Nancy Friday writes:

> It took me twenty-one years to give up my virginity. In some similar manner I am unable to let go of this chapter. . . .
>
> It is no accident that wrestling with ideas of loss of virginity immediately bring me to a dream of losing my mother. This chapter has revealed a split in me. Intellectually, I think of myself as a sexual person, just as I had intellectually been able to put my ideas for this chapter down on paper. Subjectively, I don't want to face what I have written: that the declaration of full sexual independence is the declaration of separation from my mother. As long as I don't finish this chapter, as long as I don't let myself understand the implication of what I've written, I can maintain the illusion, at least, that I can be sexual and have my mother's love and approval too. (331–33)

As long as sexual identity and mother's judgment are linked as antithetical and exclusive poles of the daughter's problem, the "split" she describes will prevent her from ever completing her declaration of sexual independence. "Full sexual independence" is shown by the book's own resistance to be as illusory and as mystifying an ideal as the notion of "mother love" that Friday so lucidly rejects.

Dinnerstein's autobiographical remarks are more muted, although her way of letting the reader know that the book was written partly in mourning for her husband subtly underlies its persuasive seriousness. In her gesture of rejecting more traditional forms of scholarship, she pleads not for the validity but for the urgency of her message:

> Right now, what I think is that the kind of work of which this is an example is centrally necessary work. Whether our understanding makes a difference or not, we must try to understand what is threatening to

kill us off as fully and clearly as we can. . . . What [this book] is, then, is not a scholarly book: it makes no effort to survey the relevant literature. Not only would that task be (for me) unmanageably huge. It would also be against my principles. I *believe* in reading unsystematically and taking notes erratically. Any effort to form a rational policy about what to take in, out of the inhuman flood of printed human utterance that pours over us daily, feels to me like a self-deluded exercise in pseudomastery. (viii–ix)

The typographical form of this book bears out this belief in renouncing the appearance of mastery: there are two kinds of notes, some at the foot of the page and some at the back of the book; there are sections between chapters with unaligned right-hand margins which are called "Notes toward the next chapter." And there are boldface inserts which carry on a dialogue with the controversial points in the main exposition. Clearly, great pains have been taken to let as many seams as possible show in the fabric of the argument. The preface goes on:

I mention these limitations in a spirit not of apology but of warning. To the extent that it succeeds in communicating its point at all, this book will necessarily enrage the reader. What it says is emotionally threatening. (*Part of why it has taken me so long to finish it is that I am threatened by it myself.*) (ix; emphasis mine)

My book is roughly sutured, says Dinnerstein, and it is threatening. This description sounds uncannily like a description of Victor Frankenstein's monster. Indeed, Dinnerstein goes on to warn the reader not to be tempted to avoid the threatening message by pointing to superficial flaws in its physical makeup. The reader of *Frankenstein*, too, would be well advised to look beyond the monster's physical deformity, both for his fearsome power and for his beauty. There are indeed numerous ways in which *The Mermaid and the Minotaur* can be seen as a modern rewriting of *Frankenstein*.

Dinnerstein's book situates its plea for two-sex parenting firmly in an apparently twentieth-century double bind: the realization that the very technological advances that make it possible to change the structure of parenthood also threaten to extinguish earthly life altogether. But it is startling to note that this seemingly contemporary pairing of the question of parenthood with a love-hate relation to technology is already at work in Mary Shelley's novel, where the spectacular scientific discovery of the secrets of animation produces a terrifyingly vengeful creature who attributes his evil impulses to his inability to find or to become a parent. Subtitled "The Modern Prometheus," *Frankenstein* itself indeed refers back to a myth that already links scientific ambivalence with the origin of mankind. Prometheus, the fire bringer, the giver of both creation and destruction, is also said by some accounts to be the father of the human race. Ambivalence toward technology can thus be seen as a displaced version of the love-hate relation we have toward our own children.

It is only recently that critics have begun to see Victor Frankenstein's disgust at the sight of his creation as a study of postpartum depression, as a representation of maternal rejection of a newborn infant, and to relate the entire novel to Mary Shelley's mixed feelings about motherhood.[2] Having lived through an unwanted pregnancy from a man married to someone else only to see that baby die, followed by a second baby named William—which is the name of the monster's first murder victim—Mary Shelley, at the age of only eighteen, must have had excruciatingly divided emotions. Her own mother, indeed, had died upon giving birth to her. The idea that a mother can loathe, fear, and reject her baby has until recently been one of the most repressed of psychoanalytical insights, although it is of course already implicit in the story of Oedipus, whose parents cast him out as an infant to die. What is threatening about each of these books is the way in which its critique of the *role* of the mother touches on primitive terrors of the mother's rejection of the child. Each of these women writers does in her way reject the child as part of her coming to grips with the untenable nature of mother love: Nancy Friday decides not to have children, Dorothy Dinnerstein argues that men as well as women should do the mothering, and Mary Shelley describes a parent who flees in disgust from the repulsive being to whom he has just given birth.

Yet it is not merely in its depiction of the ambivalence of motherhood that Mary Shelley's novel can be read as autobiographical. In the introductory note added in 1831, she writes:

> The publishers of the standard novels, in selecting *Frankenstein* for one of their series, expressed a wish that I should furnish them with some account of the origin of the story. I am the more willing to comply because I shall thus give a general answer to the question so very frequently asked me—how I, then a young girl, came to think of and to *dilate* upon so very hideous an idea. (vii; emphasis mine)

As this passage makes clear, readers of Mary Shelley's novel had frequently expressed the feeling that a young girl's fascination with the idea of monstrousness was somehow monstrous in itself. When Mary ends her introduction to the reedition of her novel with the words, "And now, once again, I bid my hideous progeny go forth and prosper," the reader begins to suspect that there may perhaps be meaningful parallels between Victor's creation of his monster and Mary's creation of her book.

Such parallels are indeed unexpectedly pervasive. The impulse to write the book and the desire to search for the secret of animation both arise under the same seemingly trivial circumstances: the necessity of finding something to read on a rainy day. During inclement weather on a family vacation, Victor Frankenstein happens upon the writings of Cornelius Agrippa and is immediately fired with the longing to penetrate the secrets of life and death. Similarly, it was during a wet, ungenial summer in Switzerland that Mary, Shelley, Byron, and several others picked up a volume of ghost stories and decided to write a collection of spine-tingling tales of their own. Moreover, Mary's discovery of the subject she would write about is described in almost exactly the same words as Frankenstein's discovery of the principle of life: "Swift as light and as cheering was the idea that broke in upon me" (xi), writes Mary in her introduction, while Frankenstein says: "From the midst of this darkness a sudden light broke in upon me" (51). In both cases the sudden flash of inspiration must be supported by the meticulous gathering of heterogeneous, ready-made materials: Frankenstein collects bones and organs; Mary records overheard discussions of scientific questions that lead her to the sudden vision of monstrous creation. "Invention," she writes of the process of writing, but her words apply equally well to Frankenstein's labors, "Invention . . . does not consist in creating out of the void, but out of chaos; the materials must, in the first place, be afforded: it can give form to dark, shapeless substances but cannot bring into being the substance itself" (x). Perhaps the most revealing indication of Mary's identification of Frankenstein's activity with her own is to be found in her use of the word *artist* on two different occasions to qualify the "pale student of unhallowed arts": "His success would terrify the artist" (xi), she writes of the catastrophic moment of creation, while Frankenstein confesses to Walton: "I appeared rather like one doomed by slavery to toil in the mines, or any other unwholesome trade than an artist occupied by his favorite employment" (55).

Frankenstein, in other words, can be read as the story of the experience of writing *Frankenstein*. What is at stake in Mary's introduction as well as in the novel is the description of a primal scene of creation. *Frankenstein* combines a monstrous answer to two of the most fundamental questions one can ask: Where do babies come from? and Where do stories come from? In both cases, the scene of creation is described, but the answer to these questions is still withheld.

But what can Victor Frankenstein's workshop of filthy creation teach us about the specificity of *female* authorship? At first sight, it would seem that *Frankenstein* is much more striking for its avoidance of the question of femininity than for its insight into it. All the interesting, complex characters in the book are male, and their deepest attachments are to other males. The females, on the other hand, are beautiful, gentle, selfless, boring nurturers and victims who never experience inner conflict or true desire. Monstrousness is so incompatible with femininity that Frankenstein cannot even complete the female companion that his creature so eagerly awaits.

On the other hand, the story of Frankenstein is, after all, the story of a man who usurps the female role by physically giving birth to a child. It would be tempting, therefore, to conclude that Mary Shelley, surrounded as she then was by the male poets Byron and Shelley, and mortified for days by her inability to think of a story to contribute to their ghost-story contest, should have fictively transposed her own frustrated female pen envy into a tale of catastrophic male womb envy. In this perspective, Mary's book would suggest that a woman's desire to write and a man's desire to give birth would both be capable only of producing monsters.

Yet clearly things cannot be so simple. As the daughter of a famous feminist whose *Vindication of the Rights of Women* she was in the process of rereading during the time she was writing *Frankenstein*, Mary Shelley would have no conscious reason to believe that writing was not proper for a woman. Indeed, as she says in her introduction, Mary was practically born with ink flowing through her veins. "It is not singular that, as the daughter of two persons of distinguished literary celebrity, I should very early in life have thought of writing. . . . My husband . . . was from the first very anxious that I should prove myself worthy of my parentage and enroll myself on the page of fame" (vii–viii). In order to prove herself worthy of her parentage, Mary, paradoxically enough, must thus usurp the parental role and succeed in giving birth to *herself* on paper. Her declaration of existence as a writer must therefore figuratively repeat the matricide that her physical birth all too literally entailed. The connection between literary creation and the death of a parent is in fact suggested in the novel by the fact that, immediately after the monster's animation, Victor Frankenstein dreams that he holds the corpse of his dead mother in his arms. It is also suggested by the juxtaposition of two seemingly unrelated uses of italics in the novel: Mary's statement that she had "*thought of a story*" (which she inexplicably italicizes twice) and the monster's promise to Frankenstein, "*I will be with you on your wedding night*," which is repeatedly italicized. Both are eliminations of the mother, since the story Mary writes is a tale of motherless birth, and the wedding night marks the death of Frankenstein's bride, Elizabeth. Indeed, Mary herself was in fact the unwitting murderous intruder present on her own parents' wedding night: their decision to marry was due to the fact that Mary Wollstonecraft was already carrying the child that was to kill her. When Mary, describing her waking vision of catastrophic creation, affirms that "his success would terrify the artist," she is not giving vent to any ordinary fear-of-success syndrome. Rather, what her book suggests is that what is at stake behind what is currently being banalized under the name of female fear of success is nothing less than the fear of somehow effecting the death of one's own parents.

It is not, however, the necessary murderousness of any declaration of female subjectivity that Mary Shelley's novel is proposing as its most troubling message of monsterdom. For, in a strikingly contemporary sort of predicament, Mary had not one but *two* mothers, each of whom consisted in the knowledge of the unviability of the other. After the death of Mary Wollstonecraft, Mary's father, William Godwin, married a woman as opposite in character and outlook as possible, a staunch, housewifely mother of two who clearly preferred her own children to Godwin's. Between the courageous, passionate, intelligent, and suicidal mother Mary knew only through her writings and the vulgar, repressive "pustule of vanity" whose dislike she resented and returned, Mary must have known at first hand a whole gamut of feminine contradictions, impasses, and options. For the complexities of the demands, desires, and sufferings of Mary's life as a woman were staggering. Her father, who had once been a vehement opponent of the institution of marriage, nearly disowned his daughter for running away with Shelley, an already married disciple of Godwin's own former views. Shelley himself, who believed in multiple love objects, amicably fostered an erotic correspondence between Mary and his friend Thomas Jefferson Hogg, among others. For years, Mary and Shelley were accompanied everywhere by Mary's stepsister Claire, whom Mary did not particularly like, who had a child by Byron, and who maintained an ambiguous relation with Shelley. During the writing of *Frankenstein*, Mary learned of the suicide of her half-sister Fanny Imlay, her mother's illegitimate child by an American lover, and the suicide of Shelley's wife Harriet, who was pregnant by a man other than Shelley. By the time she and Shelley married, Mary had had two children; she would have two more by the time of Shelley's death and watch as all but one of the children died in infancy. Widowed at age twenty-four, she never remarried. It is thus indeed perhaps the very hiddenness of the question of femininity in *Frankenstein* that somehow proclaims the painful message not of female monstrousness but of female contradictions. For it is the fact of self-contradiction that is so vigorously repressed in women. While the story of a man who is haunted by his own contradictions is representable as an allegory of monstrous doubles, how indeed would it have been possible for Mary to represent feminine contradiction *from the point of view of its repression* otherwise than precisely in the *gap* between angels of domesticity and an uncompleted monsteress, between the murdered Elizabeth and the dismembered Eve?

It is perhaps because the novel does succeed in conveying the unresolvable contradictions inherent in being female that Percy Shelley himself felt compelled to write a prefatory disclaimer in Mary's name before he could let loose his wife's hideous progeny upon the world. In a series of denials jarringly at odds with the daring negativity of the novel, Shelley places the following words in Mary's mouth:

> I am by no means indifferent to the manner in which whatever moral tendencies exist in the sentiments or characters it contains shall affect the reader; yet my chief concern in this respect has been limited to . . . the exhibition of the amiableness of domestic affection, and the excellence of universal virtue. The opinions which naturally spring from the character and situation of the hero are by no means to be conceived as existing always in my own conviction; nor is any inference justly to be drawn from the following pages as prejudicing any philosophical doctrine of whatever kind. (xiii–xiv)

How is this to be read except as a gesture of repression of the very specificity of the power of feminine contradiction, a gesture reminiscent of Frankenstein's destruction of his nearly completed female monster? What is being repressed here is the possibility that a woman can write anything that would *not* exhibit "the amiableness of domestic affection," the possibility that for women as well as for men the home can be the very site of the *unheimlich*.

It can thus be seen in all three of the books we have discussed that the monstrousness of selfhood is intimately embedded within the question of female autobiography. Yet how could it be otherwise, since the very notion of a self, the very shape of human life stories, has always, from Saint Augustine to Freud, been modeled on the man? Rousseau's—or any man's—autobiography consists in the story of the difficulty of conforming to the standard of what a *man* should be. The problem for the female autobiographer is, on the one hand, to resist the pressure of masculine autobiography as the only literary genre available for her enterprise, and, on the other, to describe a difficulty in conforming to a female ideal which is largely a fantasy of the masculine, not the feminine, imagination. The fact that these three books deploy a *theory* of autobiography as monstrosity within the framework of a less overtly avowed struggle with the raw materials of the authors' own lives and writing is perhaps, in the final analysis, what is most autobiographically fertile and *telling* about them.

NOTES

"My Monster/My Self." *Diacritics* 12, no. 2 (1982): 2–10. © 1982 The Johns Hopkins University Press. Reprinted with permission of The Johns Hopkins University Press.

1. Nancy Friday, *My Mother/My Self* (New York: Dell, 1977); Dorothy Dinnerstein, *The Mermaid and the Minotaur* (New York: Harper Colophon, 1976); Mary Shelley, *Frankenstein; or, The Modern Prometheus* (New York: Signet, 1965).
2. See Ellen Moers, "Female Gothic," and U. C. Knoepflmacher, "Thoughts on the Aggression of Daughters," in *The Endurance of Frankenstein*, ed. George Levine and U. C. Knoepflmacher (Berkeley: University of California Press, 1979). Other related and helpful studies include S. M. Gilbert and S. Gubar, "Horror's Twin," in *The Madwoman in the Attic* (New Haven, CT: Yale University Press, 1979), and Mary Poovey, "My Hideous Progeny: Mary Shelley and the Feminization of Romanticism," PMLA 95 (May 1980): 332–47.

PART III

Language, Personhood, Ethics

CHAPTER 14

Introduction to *Freedom and Interpretation* (abridged)

Our lecturers are being asked to consider the consequences of the deconstruction
of the self for the liberal tradition. Does the self as construed by the liberal
tradition still exist? If not, whose human rights are we defending?
—From the letter of invitation by Oxford Amnesty Lectures

In the course of preparing to write the present introduction, I found myself
on a plane, reading a book entitled *Who Comes After the Subject?*[1] ("the most
comprehensive overview to date of contemporary French thinking on the
question of the 'subject'") while seated beside a young man in a baseball cap
who was reading a novel, *Needful Things*, by Stephen King. As I eyed the
pages he held spread before him, wondering what *Needful Things* was about,
I suddenly thought with a start that my seatmate, too, might be wondering
what *Who Comes After the Subject?* could possibly be about. Detection? Es-
pionage? Grammar? "It's about the self," I imagined myself telling him; but
then what would come next? (And was this question the same as the one
posed in the book's title?) What would the notion of "the deconstruction of
the self" mean to the person I imagined him to be? Perhaps I could start from
his text, explaining, "The self has often been seen as a rational and autonomous locus of will and intention, a *res cogitans*, whereas it is, in truth, but a
needful thing . . ."

My task in presenting the Oxford Amnesty Lectures is only slightly less daunting than my imaginary conversation with my seatmate, but the questions asked by the organizing committee to the seven theorists collected in our volume may very well require a consideration of the possibility, or meaningfulness, of such a conversation. While the title of the collection of essays, *Freedom and Interpretation*, should not sound opaque or foreign to an American ear, the issues raised by those questions, quoted as my epigraph, may require some explanation.

What is "the deconstruction of the self"?

While the Anglo-American ("liberal") tradition tends to speak about the "self," the French tradition tends to speak about the "subject." Since the lecturers invited to speak in the first series of Oxford Amnesty Lectures came from both sides of the Channel and both sides of the Atlantic, a word might be said about this difference in "translation." The concept of "self" is closely tied to the notion of property. I speak of "my" self. In the English tradition, the notions of "self" and "property" are inseparable from the notion of "rights": "Though the Earth, and all inferior Creatures be common to all Men, yet every Man has a *Property* in his own *Person*. This no Body has any Right to but himself" (John Locke, *The Second Treatise of Government*). The French tradition, derived most importantly from Descartes's "I think, therefore I am," centers on the importance of reason or thought as the foundation of (human) being. Where the "self," as property, resembles a thing, the "subject," as reason, resembles a grammatical function. The "subject" of a sentence is contrasted with the "object." The "subject" is that to which the predicate applies. In the sentence "I am," what is predicated is that the subject has being, as though "being" were something additional, something not redundant to what is already implicit in the use of the word *I*. And in the sentence "I think, *therefore* I am," what is posited is that it is *thinking* that gives the subject being.

Several late nineteenth-century thinkers began to question these postulates of property and rationality in the self, not in order to eliminate them but in order to recontextualize them within a larger frame of reference. Marx questioned the system of distribution of property and political power, seeing the bourgeois "autonomous self" as an illusion that denies the ways in which the bourgeois subject is dependent on the labor of others and the structure of the material world. Freud questioned the rational ego's control over the self, showing the ego to be a defense mechanism mediating between the surges of inner psychic forces and the requirements of the physical, familial, and societal world. Nietzsche analyzed the ways in which language and cultural forms concealed the role of force and the will to power.

More recently, French thinkers have pursued these critiques in several directions. Jacques Lacan has elaborated Freud's "Copernican revolution" (the displacement of the centrality of the ego, just as Copernicus displaced the centrality of the Earth) by translating the Cartesian *cogito* in the following terms: "I think where I am not, therefore I am where I do not think. . . . I am not wherever I am the plaything of my thought; I think of what I am where I do not think to think."[2] That is, while Descartes saw a *coincidence* of human thinking with human being, Lacan sees a *disjunction*: "I" is a complex place where my thinking—my consciousness—far from being the controlling center of my being, is at odds with, but inseparable from, the unrecognized or rejected parts of me it cannot know or refuses to admit. In Lacan's theory, a founding moment of the formation of the "I," the "mirror stage," occurs when a baby first recognizes his image in the mirror and comes to believe that his "self" has unity, stability, and coherence in the manner of a thing (the image, which presents itself to him as an object of the gaze). This illusion of the stable self motivates a lifelong attempt to "catch up" to the image, to attain the self-mastery and completeness it promises.

What distinguishes Lacan from Freud is his particular focus, informed by structural linguistics, on the inescapably constitutive role of language (and other representational or signifying systems) in the construction of the human subject. Jacques Derrida, with whom the term *deconstruction* is most closely associated, has carried out a rigorous rereading of the constitutive function of language in Western philosophy through the sustained analysis of major texts (Plato, Aristotle, Descartes, Kant, Rousseau, Hegel, Freud, Nietzsche, Husserl, Heidegger, and so on), in an effort to detect, within the texts themselves, the ways in which the postulates of reason, presence, properness, immediacy, and identity are based on the active repression of their binary opposites (madness, absence, impropriety, distance, and difference), and thus are not self-evident and freestanding. If the history of philosophy is the history of an effort to reach the truth in its immediacy, and if that history can only exist as the history of the writings in which that search has been carried out, there is a lag, distance, or difference (what Derrida calls a *différance*) between the object promised by the search (truth) and the means or experience or process of the search (language as *in the way*, in both senses of the phrase). It is not that there is a truth out there (the world, the self) that is or is not properly expressed; it is that the promise of the "out there" is as much a function of the structure of language as its endless deferral and metamorphosis.

In the context of Amnesty International, Michel Foucault is, in many ways, the most relevant of the French rethinkers of the "subject." By studying the ways in which knowledge systems are coordinated with structures of societal control, Foucault sees the human being as subject to a "disciplinary" process designed to produce "proper" members of a given society. He studies the shaping of such "subjects" through constraints imposed by institutions: the family, schools, the medical professions, prisons, the police, factories, and so on. The ideally "disciplined" subject is one who has fully internalized the discourses and constraints of his society. Thus, while Amnesty International operates under the assumption that the arbitrary imprisonment of individuals by governments for reasons of conscience is a transgression of human rights, Foucault, in a sense, sees the evil of such imprisonment as a matter of degree rather than kind, since on some level the very definition of the "human" at any given time is produced by the workings of a complex system of "imprisonments." Far from being an autonomous, rational entity who thinks in isolation, the human "subject" is a function of what a given society defines as thinkable.

Sometime during my work with the Oxford Amnesty Lectures committee, I received a fax with the following unforgettable message: "As the All Souls fax machine is presently out of order, could you please respond to the Corpus Christi fax?" This charming conjunction of modern technology with the medieval Christian origins of the names of Oxford colleges struck me as resonant and relevant to my enterprise as editor. I thought of calling this Introduction "Just the Fax, Ma'am," in order to suggest, through the pun between "fax" and "facts," that what we know as "facts" are always themselves constructed, always already in some way a "facsimile," a "version" of something in whose real presence we come to believe only through the ways in which its absence is pointed to. Like the Corpus Christi but without the authority of a transcendental referent, the modern miracle of transubstantiation—the fax—goes from one material inscription to another.

Does the "deconstruction of the subject" mean that to speak about human rights has as anachronistic a ring to it as the phrase "Corpus Christi fax"? Many people seem to think so. To give just one example, I quote from Tzvetan Todorov's *Literature and Its Theorists*: "I am simply saying that it is not possible, without inconsistency, to defend human rights with one hand and deconstruct the idea of humanity with the other."[3] Many of the essays in *Freedom and Interpretation* address themselves to the question of this "inconsistency," some to claim that human rights can *only* be meaningfully defended if such a deconstruction is taken into consideration, and others to explore the various forms such an "inconsistency" might take.

It should be noted that the deconstruction of the foundational ideals of Western civilization has developed in tandem with—and perhaps as a response to—various race, class, nation, and gender liberation movements that have arisen around the world to eradicate the effects of the discrepancy between the humanist concepts of freedom, justice, rationality, and equality that the West has promoted and the actual forms of oppression and domination (slavery, anti-Semitism, colonialism, labor exploitation, sexual inequality, racism, and so on) in which the West has engaged. Considerable debate exists today around the question of whether it is more urgent for those who have been deprived of rights to fight to acquire such rights or to work to deconstruct them. On the one hand, it is argued that rights, based as they are on problematic models of property and identity, carry with them unhealth in the form of excessive fixity, binarity, and formality that will only reintroduce the problems the acquisition of rights is designed to correct. The Second Amendment to the U.S. Constitution, for example, conceived the "right to bear arms" as a part of national defense, but, times and weapons having changed, the fixed nature of that right does not allow for the flexibility of adaptation to new conditions. Because rights are categorical, they often come in contradictory pairs: the right to life versus the right to reproductive choice, for instance. Nothing in the *concept* of rights can negotiate the conflict that arises out of such binary opposites. Since rights involve recourse to an abstract, impersonal (rather than contextual and interpersonal) domain of *form*, they are context-distant and rigid. But on the other hand, that very rigidity can come to the aid of the powerless against the powerful if the adjudication of disputes in a more negotiated or experience-near manner would always favor those with the greatest resources. Thus, many argue that, despite their flaws, rights may be the only leverage the powerless possess to begin the process of leveling the playing field.

It is not necessarily that the promises of Western humanism were not good, or that some other system would be better; it is that those promises were not kept, and that the very writings in which they were formulated failed to prevent—indeed, somehow covered over—the injustices and oppressions that occurred. The history of amendments to the U.S. Constitution has been a long struggle to instate the civil rights of women and African Americans, the denial of whose rights was never explicitly acknowledged by the original Declaration of Independence in its illusorily "universal" language ("all men are created equal"). If the eighteenth-century French and American revolutions represent the moment of codification of the ideology of human rights, and if the very language through which they were conducted succeeded in concealing the inequities they instated, then a rigorous rereading of that language would be inseparable from the attempt to bring about social change, even—or especially—when that change is conceptualized in terms of that very same language.

If the "deconstruction of humanity" is an *interpretation* of what humanist writings already make available to be read, if the "contemporary" critique of the subject is a rereading of the texts in which that subject has been formulated, it is not that there was once something that is now being taken away, but that a new way of encountering the challenges that those texts were written to meet (or to avoid) should be undertaken. Could it not be that governments imprison dissidents for the same reasons that the rational, controlling ego attempts to banish unwanted impulses from itself? That is, could it not be that the rigidity involved in the casting out or denial of anxiety-inducing otherness both from the polis and from the self would arise out of a similar attempt to become selfsame, unified, without internal difference? In that case, a study of the ways in which the ego attempts to achieve mastery by projection and repression might be of the greatest interest for defenders of prisoners of conscience. And could it not be that the invocation of the "reasonable man" standard in law resembles the way in which the bourgeois white male subject is taken as the "norm" for the human being, and that various oppressions based on race, class, or gender are tied to the ways in which the "human" has been restrictively defined? It should not be forgotten that it is always against *humans* that human rights need to be defended.

The best way to test the viability of as important a concept as that of the "human" is ceaselessly to return to it, critique it, ask it new questions, hold it up to new contexts. As John Stuart Mill wrote in *On Liberty*:

> There is the greatest difference between presuming an opinion to be true because, with every opportunity for contesting it, it has not been refuted, and assuming its truth for the purpose of not permitting its refutation. Complete liberty of contradicting and disproving our opinion is the very condition which justifies us in assuming its truth for purposes of action; and on no other terms can a being with human faculties have any rational assurance of being right.[4]

Mill's dictum deserves to be carried out, even to the point of critiquing the well-foundedness of every word in its formulation. On no other terms can freedom of interpretation truly exist.

NOTES

Introduction to *Freedom and Interpretation: Oxford Amnesty Lectures of 1992* (abridged). Copyright © 1993 Barbara Johnson. Reprinted by permission of Basic Books Press, a member of the Perseus Books Group.

1. Eduardo Cadava, Peter Connor, and Jean-Luc Nancy, eds., *Who Comes After the Subject?* (New York: Routledge, 1991).
2. Jacques Lacan, "The Agency of the Letter in the Unconscious or Reason since Freud," in *Écrits: A Selection,* trans. Alan Sheridan (New York: W. W. Norton, 1977), 166.
3. Tzvetan Todorov, *Literature and Its Theorists,* trans. Catherine Porter (Ithaca, NY: Cornell University Press, 1987), 190.
4. J. S. Mill, *On Liberty* (Harmondsworth, UK: Penguin, 1974), 79.

CHAPTER 15

Muteness Envy

A slumber did my spirit seal;
I had no human fears:
She seemed a thing . . .
—William Wordsworth

In one of the best-known poems in the English language, John Keats proclaims the superiority of silence over poetry by addressing a Grecian urn in
the following terms:

Thou still unravished bride of quietness,
Thou foster child of silence and slow time,
Sylvan historian, who canst thus express
A flowery tale more sweetly than our rhyme . . .
Heard melodies are sweet, but those unheard
Are sweeter . . .

The ego ideal of the poetic voice would seem, then, to reside in the muteness
of things.

Why does Keats choose to write about an urn? Why not, for example, a
Grecian frieze? Is an urn somehow overdetermined as an example of a thing?
When Martin Heidegger had to choose something as an example of a thing
in his essay "The Thing," he chose a jug. And when Wallace Stevens placed
an exemplary object in Tennessee, it was a jar. What is it that might make an

urn impose itself? Why does Cleanth Brooks entitle his New Critical treatise on poetry *The Well-Wrought Urn*?

Urns are containers. They can contain the ashes of the dead. They can also contain water, wine, nourishment. As containers or vehicles, they lend themselves as metaphors for form itself, or language itself, as in Francis Ponge's poem about a jug, which ends, "Couldn't everything I have just said about the jug be said equally well of *words*?" Urns can be metaphors for the relation between form and content, but also between body and soul, expression and intention. Like the most general description of a human being, they have an inside and an outside. Whether we speak of eating or of thinking, we see the human being as a thing with interiority, an outside with something happening inside. Thus, urns are not so much anthropomorphic as humans are urnomorphic. The thing, the human, the poem, and indeed language itself all become metaphors for each other through the urn.

But Keats's urn wears its contents on its *outside*. Does this have anything to do with its idealization of muteness?

Of course, Keats is not the only poet to have made muteness into a poetic ideal. Mallarmé oriented his theory of poetic language toward "le poème tu, aux blancs." And in what is perhaps the most explicit expression of the idealization of muteness as a prerogative of things, Archibald MacLeish proclaims in his "Ars Poetica":

A poem should be palpable and mute
As a globed fruit,

Dumb
As old medallions to the thumb,

Silent as the sleeve-worn stone
Of casement ledges where the moss has grown—

A poem should be wordless
As the flight of birds.

Yet these poems do not seem to be able to maintain the privilege of muteness to the end. No sooner does Keats convince us of the superiority of the Grecian urn's aphonia, than it speaks. "Beauty is truth, truth beauty," it says; "That is all ye know on earth and all ye need to know." MacLeish's poem, too, is unable to leave well enough alone. It concludes, "A poem should not mean / But be," a sentence which disobeys its own prescription, since, in saying what a poem *should* do, it is "meaning" rather than "being." "Ars Poetica" can be read as a more explicit version of the Grecian urn's final violation of its own apparent rules. Is muteness not really a value, then, or is it simply that language cannot, by definition, say so? Or is it that the utterance "Beauty is truth, truth beauty" *is* a form of silence? What is behind the poem's incomplete commitment to its own muteness envy?

In choosing the expression "muteness envy" to name a recurrent poetic condition, I am consciously echoing Freud's expression "penis envy," which for him marked the nature of sexual difference from the woman's point of view. Since muteness envy seems to be a feature of canonical poetry written by men, could it somehow play into the question of sexual difference? Does the muteness that men envy tend to be feminine? Certainly Keats's urn is feminized, a "still unravished bride of quietness." Doubly feminized, indeed, if the container-like shape of the urn is denied as anthropomorphic and affirmed instead as gynomorphic. In an essay published in 1954, Charles Patterson offers a "comprehensive and virile interpretation" of the ode, comparing the urn's shape to "the outlines of the feminine body": "the urn is a receptacle, just as is the body of woman—the receptacle from which life springs."[1]

For Mallarmé, too, the blanks and the "white page" that are the material inscription of silence are also the analogues of the female body. And numerous are the Parnassian poems addressed to silent female statues, marble Venuses and granite Sphinxes whose unresponsiveness stands as the mark of their aesthetic value, and whose whiteness underscores the normative whiteness of canonical representations of women. Baudelaire parodies this conceit by making Beauty *speak* her own unresponsiveness and gloat over the muteness of the poets' love for her, while Stevens parodies it by refusing either to feminize or to idealize his jar as it takes deadpan control over the slovenly wilderness. The parodic edge to these poems seems only to confirm the normative image of a beautiful, silent woman addressed by the idealizing rhetoric of a male poet for whom she "seems a thing." There is, of course, nothing new in saying that, in Western poetry, women are often idealized, objectified, and silent. Feminist criticism has been pointing this out for at least thirty years. But why is female muteness a repository of aesthetic value? And what does that muteness signify?

Interestingly enough, the silence of women seems to be a sine qua non of sexual difference for Jacques Lacan, too, in his translation of Freud's story of anatomical destiny into a story of discursive destiny:

There is woman only as excluded by the nature of things which is the nature of words, and it has to be said that if there is one thing they themselves are complaining about enough at the moment, it is well and truly that—only they don't know what they are saying, which is all the difference between them and me.

It none the less remains that if she is excluded by the nature of things, it is precisely that in being not all, she has, in relation to what the phallic function designates of *jouissance*, a supplementary *jouissance*.

Note that I said *supplementary*. Had I said *complementary*, where would we be! We'd fall right back into the all.[2]

In contrast to Freud, whose geometry of castration implies a complementarity between presence (penis) and absence (vagina), Lacan theorizes feminine *jouissance* as something other than what would fit into that schema of complementarity. In sexual complementarity, everything is a function of only one of the terms: the phallus. In sexual supplementarity, woman is that which exceeds or escapes. Which does not mean that she speaks.

There is a *jouissance* which is proper to her, to this "her" which does not exist and which signifies nothing. There is a *jouissance* proper to her and of which she herself may know nothing, except that she experiences it—that much she does know. She knows it of course when it happens. It does not happen to all of them . . . What gives some likelihood to what I am arguing, that is, that the woman knows nothing of this *jouissance*, is that ever since we've been begging them . . . —begging them on our knees to tell us about it, well, not a word! (145–46)

In his efforts to collect reliable testimony from women about their pleasure, Lacan finally turns, astonishingly, to a statue, thus writing his own Parnassian poem: "You have only to go and look at Bernini's statue [of Saint Theresa] in Rome to understand immediately that she's coming, there is no doubt about it" (147). As Stephen Heath, Luce Irigaray, and Barbara Freeman have remarked,[3] this is a very odd way to listen to women. But it fits in perfectly with the idealization of female muteness already in place in the aesthetic tradition.

Returning now to Keats's urn, we find that the question of feminine *jouissance* (or lack of it) is very much at issue. By calling the urn a "still unravished bride," Keats implies that the urn's destiny is to become a *ravished* bride. The word *ravished* can mean either "raped" or "sent into ecstasy." Both possibilities are readable in the scenes depicted on the urn:

What men or gods are these? What maidens loth?
What mad pursuit? What struggle to escape?
What pipes and timbrels? What wild ecstasy?

The privileged aesthetic moment is a freeze frame just prior to ravishment.[4] But how does pressing the pause button here make us sublate the scene of male sexual violence into a scene of general ecstasy? How does the maidens' struggle to escape congeal into an aesthetic triumph?

If we turn now to one of the primal scenes of Western literature, Apollo's pursuit of the nymph Daphne and her transformation into a laurel tree, we will find that the same questions apply. Whether because of Cupid's mischief or out of her own resistance, Daphne struggles to escape the god's embrace, becoming a tree—a thing—in a last desperate attempt to avoid rape. But Apollo not only does not lose; he enters a whole new dimension of symbolization, plucking off a laurel branch and using it as a sign of artistic achievement. "Instead of becoming the object of a sexual conquest," writes Peter Sacks in his book *The English Elegy*,

> Daphne is thus eventually transformed into something very much like a consolation prize—a prize that becomes *the* prize and sign of poethood. What Apollo or the poet pursues turns into a sign not only of his lost love but also of his very pursuit—a consoling sign that carries in itself the reminder of the loss on which it has been founded . . . If there is a necessary distance between the wreath and what it signifies, that distance is the measure of Apollo's loss. Daphne's "turning" into a tree matches Apollo's "turning" from the object of his love to a sign of her. It is this substitutive turn or act of troping that any mourner must perform.[5]

Thus, "any mourner" must identify with Apollo, not Daphne, and the fact that Apollo does not carry out the intended rape is coded as "loss"—a loss that becomes a model for the aesthetic as such. The rapist is bought off with the aesthetic. And the aesthetic is inextricably tied to a silence in the place of rape.

As Christine Froula and Patricia Joplin have argued, that silence has been so inextricably tied to the aesthetics of the literary canon that even the most subtle and insightful of readers have, as we have just seen, tended to perpetuate it. Joplin analyzes the "elision of gender" and the "mystification of violence" in Geoffrey Hartman's celebration of the phrase "the voice of the shuttle" as a beautifully condensed trope for Philomela's tapestry (which testifies to her rape and mutilation after her tongue has been cut out).

> When Geoffrey Hartman asks of Sophocles' metaphor "the voice of the shuttle": "what gives these words the power to speak to us even without the play?," he celebrates Language and not the violated woman's emer-

gence from silence . . . When Hartman ends his essay by noting that "There is always *something* that violates us, deprives our voice, and compels art toward an aesthetics of silence," the specific nature of the woman's double violation disappears behind the apparently genderless (but actually male) language of "us," the "I" and the "you" who agree to attest to that which violates, deprives, silences only as a mysterious, unnamed "something."[6]

Once again, an "aesthetics of silence" turns out to involve a male appropriation of female muteness as aesthetic trophy accompanied by an elision of sexual violence.

There seem, then, to be two things women are silent about: their pleasure and their violation. The work performed by the idealization of this silence is that *it helps culture not to be able to tell the difference between the two.*

What happens when women attempt to break that silence? Sometimes their speech is simply discounted, as when Lacan claims that feminists get it right about silence but don't know what they are saying, "which is all the difference between them and me." Even in the case of the Grecian urn, penalties apply. Summarizing a history of reservations critics have expressed about the wisdom of allowing the urn to speak at the end of Keats's poem (T. S. Eliot called the final lines "a serious blemish on a beautiful poem"), Cleanth Brooks notes that "Some critics have felt that the unravished bride of quietness protests too much."[7] His reference to Hamlet's mother's reading of women's guilty speech implies that, to many readers, the urn would have been better off keeping still. Overdetermined by the aesthetic tradition of women's silence, any speech at all appears as guilty speech. It is as though women were constantly subject to the Miranda warning: "You have the right to remain silent. If you waive that right anything you say can and will be used against you." No wonder Shakespeare's Miranda can only exclaim as she notes the completion of the patriarchal set, "Oh brave new world, that has such people in it!"

Two recent feminist approaches to the speech of girls corroborates these functions of silence. Carol Gilligan's study of adolescent girls' development suggests that when culture teaches girls that their sexual feelings are unseemly or irrelevant or secondary to the needs and initiatives of men, they learn to say "I don't know" about their desire.[8] (Interestingly, this is Maria Torok's interpretation of the nature of penis envy: girls who have learned to repress knowledge of their own sexuality project their sexual feelings as the unobtainable experience of the other sex.)[9] And recent work on child abuse and father–daughter incest, reinforced by Jeffrey Masson's *The Assault on Truth*, his account of Freud's abandonment of the "seduction" theory of hysteria,[10] suggests that girls learn silence not only about sexual pleasure but also about sexual abuse.

Christine Froula, in an essay entitled "The Daughter's Seduction: Sexual Violence and Literary History," makes an analogy between Homer's silencing of Helen and Freud's discrediting of his hysterical patients. "As the *Iliad* tells the story of a woman's abduction as a male war story, so Freud turned the hysterics' stories of sexual abuse into a tale to soothe a father's ear . . . Freud undertook not to believe the hysterics not because the weight of scientific evidence was on the father's side but because so much was at stake in maintaining the father's credit: the 'innocence' not only of particular fathers— Freud's, Freud himself, the hysterics'—but also of the cultural structure that credits male authority at the expense of female authority."[11] In switching from an alliance with the daughters to an alliance with the fathers, Freud had to translate the "truth" of abuse into the "beauty" of psychoanalysis. At this point we might conclude after Molière, "Et voilà pourquoi votre fille est muette."

But perhaps she is mute because she knows that neither of these accounts is quite right. While it is true that Freud's paradigmatic model of incest seems to switch from the father's desire for the daughter to the son's desire for the mother (thus letting the father off the hook and granting the son the privilege of perversity), it is also true that by crediting the inside/outside, guilt/innocence opposition, critics of psychoanalysis have lost sight of Freud's understanding of the daughter's desire. Why does the father's guilt have to be tied to the daughter's innocence? Can't the daughter's capacity for perverse desire coexist with the fact of abuse?

Now I would like to explore all these issues as they play themselves out in a film and in a series of responses to it. The film, written and directed by Jane Campion, is called *The Piano*. The heroine, Ada McGrath, played by Holly Hunter, is mute. Her "voice" is a piano. It could be said that the piano in the film plays, with respect to Ada, the role traditionally assigned to the Muse with respect to the poet: it is her significant other, herself, and her missing piece. Ada has a daughter, Flora, played by Anna Paquin. Ada has been sent by her father from Scotland to New Zealand to be married to a man she has never met. When she is deposited by sailors on a deserted beach with her daughter, her piano, and a large number of other boxes, she is met by two European men—her husband-to-be, Alisdair Stewart, played by Sam Neill, and another man named George Baines, played by Harvey Keitel—and fourteen Maori men and women. Stewart decides that there are too few people to carry all the boxes plus the piano, and the piano is left on the beach while the party, with Baines translating Stewart's orders to the Maoris, makes its way through the dense, muddy New Zealand bush. Ada communicates by writing on a pad hanging around her neck and by signing to her daughter, who translates. She is enraged at the abandonment of her piano.

Shortly after a marriage which seems to take place as a photographic sitting, Stewart leaves to buy some Maori land, and Ada and Flora attempt to persuade a reluctant Baines to retrieve the piano. The three of them visit the piano on the beach, where Baines is fascinated by the emotional abandon of Ada's playing, so different from her normal resistant demeanor. Soon Baines has brought the piano to his own hut and has traded some of his land to Stewart for ownership of the piano, claiming a desire to learn to play. When Stewart tells Ada of the deal, and indicates that she is to give Baines lessons, she is outraged, writing, "NO, NO, THE PIANO IS MINE!" on her note pad. Stewart disregards her, saying everyone in the family must make sacrifices. Baines then persuades Ada that she can win back her piano, key by key, in exchange for sexual contact, which begins while she plays, but eventually, for a larger number of keys, takes place in his bedroom. His approach is gradual; her response is resistant, then hesitant. Flora is generally left resentfully outside Baines's hut during these sessions. Then Baines abruptly abandons the bargain, saying, "I am giving the piano back to you. I've had enough. The arrangement is making you a whore and me wretched. I want you to care for me, but you can't." Once the piano is installed in Stewart's hut, Ada is confused about her relation to it, and runs back into Baines's arms. Stewart follows her and peers at their lovemaking through the cracks in the hut walls. That night Stewart seems to make no response to what he has seen, but the following day he intercepts Ada as she tries to return to Baines. Stewart wrestles her to the ground and tries to kiss and touch her. Then he locks her into his hut. She plays the piano furiously, then, at night, enters Stewart's room and begins to stroke his body, not allowing him to touch hers. This is the first sexual contact of the marriage. When later Ada learns that Baines is leaving the area, she removes a key from the piano, writes on it "Dear George, you have my heart, Ada McGrath," and asks Flora to take it to him. Instead, Flora takes it to Stewart, who is working with his axe on his boundary fence. In a paroxysm of rage, Stewart returns to Ada and chops off one of her fingers, telling Flora to take it to Baines. That night Stewart hovers over Ada's feverish sleep, apologizing and then on the point of taking sexual advantage of the seemingly unconscious woman when he notices her full attention on him and stops. He then goes to Baines and tells Baines he has heard Ada's voice saying, "Let Baines take me away." Soon Ada, Flora, Baines, and the piano are loaded by Maori oarsmen onto a canoe. As the canoe leaves the shore, Ada asks that the piano be tossed overboard. When the others obey, she puts her foot in a loop of the piano rope and is pulled into the sea after the piano. Yet she does not drown but kicks herself free and returns to the canoe, to Baines, and ultimately to life in Nelson, New Zealand, as a wife and piano teacher. While Ada escapes into banal colonial wifehood, the film ends by seeming to want to display its allegiance to the English poetic tradition of aestheticizing silence: the last lines uttered are a quotation from a sonnet by Thomas Hood called "Silence."

How are we to read Ada's muteness in the movie? First of all, like the urn's, Ada's muteness is not absolute. Not only does she both sign and write, but at the beginning and end of the film there is a voice-over that purports to be the voice of Ada's mind. Similarly, Keats's apostrophe to the urn ensures that it never exists outside the realm of the anthropomorphic, and even then, it has to talk back in the end. Like the urn, Ada reassures the spectator that she is not really other, never absolutely beyond the reach of communication. But also like the urn, she does not directly answer the questions the spectator might ask. The speaker in Keats's poem asks the urn for names, narratives, legends; the urn answers with chiasmus, tautology, abstraction. The speaker asks for history; the urn resists with theory. Inversely, the men in the film attempt to establish an I–Thou relation with Ada, but her voice-over only links the events of the movie to the past and to the future, and does not offer interpretive guidance through the period—the time actually dramatized in the film—between the initial landing and the final departure from the deserted beach.

The voice opens the movie by saying: "I have not spoken since I was six years old. No one knows why, not even me. My father says it is a dark talent and the day I take it into my head to stop breathing will be my last." First interpretation, then: Ada's muteness is a talent, a talent as strong as life itself.

Stewart, the husband-to-be, is said not to mind the muteness before he sees her, considering that it makes her like a dumb animal, but when he meets her, he begins to wonder whether it is a sign of mental deficiency. This is not because he wants to listen to her—he disregards every explicit expression of her wishes concerning the piano—but because he worries that the merchandise he has bought might be defective. Yet it is he who ends up recognizing Ada's muteness as voice, as will, as resistance. As he reports it to Baines, Ada has in the end said to him, "I have to go, let me go, let Baines take me away, let him try and save me. I am frightened of my will, of what it might do, it is so strange and strong." Of course, Stewart, having just chopped off his wife's finger, may well be frightened of what his *own* will might do. But at least he recognizes Ada as a center of will and desire.

That Ada's muteness is a manifestation of will is confirmed when the voice-over returns at the moment Ada frees herself from the piano rope that is dragging her under the sea: "What a death! What a chance! What a surprise! My will has chosen life!?"

But the final voice-over of the movie suggests that Ada, now married to Baines and fitted with a prosthetic finger, is beginning to pronounce syllables aloud. While the voice-over, like the urn's voice, may be read as a projection, a narrative fiction, perhaps even a prosopopoeia, Ada, at the end of the movie, is beginning to fade into the sound of common voice.

Thus, although Ada is passed from father to husband as a piece of merchandise, her muteness is not a form of passivity or object-hood. It is a form of resistance and subjecthood. But does the resistance and subjecthood of Ada's *character* outweigh the object-hood thrust upon her by the male bargains and decisions that structure the *framework* of her life? What is the movie *saying* about the muteness that articulates and confuses women's oppression and women's desire?

Reactions to this movie have been remarkably varied. "Jane Campion Stirs Romance with Mystery," wrote Vincent Canby when the film won the Palme d'Or at the Cannes Film Festival. "Wuthering Heights, Move Over," wrote Jay Carr in one of two long pieces he published in the *Boston Globe*. Yet some viewers of my acquaintance found its pace intolerably slow and its characters and setting repulsive. Some found it fascinatingly romantic and emotionally gripping. Some consider it pretentious; others marvel at its subtlety. Before I saw it, I was told by one friend that it was a hauntingly beautiful love story, and by another that she experienced it as a narrative of rape. How can we determine whether it is about sexual awakening or sexual violence?

Here I am going to quote two representative readings of the film, both written by women. The first is a quotation from the filmmaker, Jane Campion:

> I have enjoyed writing characters who don't have a twentieth-century sensibility about sex. They have nothing to prepare themselves for its strength and power . . . The husband Stewart had probably never had sex at all. So for him to experience sex or feelings of sexual jealousy would have been personality-transforming . . . Ada actually uses her husband Stewart as a sexual object—this is the outrageous morality of

the film—which seems very innocent but in fact has its power to be very surprising. I think many women have had the experience of feeling like a sexual object, and that's exactly what happens to Stewart.[12]

For Campion, then, the film is about sex and power and sexual power reversals. It is also, quite explicitly in the published stage directions, about the appeal of fetishistic displacement as sexual surprise: Baines is surprised into excitement while watching Ada play the piano; Ada is surprised into excitement while watching Baines fondle her clothing; Stewart is surprised into sexual jealousy while watching Ada make love to Baines. In these scenarios, there are only displacements and substitutions—*all* sexuality, not just female sexuality, is supplementarity and excess rather than complementarity. It is interesting, however, that Campion describes the film's depiction of sexual awakening in terms of Stewart rather than Ada. It is he, not Ada, who is the virgin in the story.

Now I would like to quote from another reading of the film, this one a long essay by Margaret Morganroth Gullette published in the *Boston Globe.* Gullette writes:

> I felt sullied by "The Piano," muted, mutilated, threatened by rape, pulled underwater and shrouded. Yes, I identified with the heroine . . . I knew I was supposed to identify as a woman with her Victorian fragility and silencing and her redirected expressiveness . . . Holly Hunter, one of the tiniest stars in American movies, is used for her anorexic vulnerability . . . She has the female body type that can be brutalized by men . . . Serious movies can still get away with torturing women in the audience by portraying them as vulnerable heroines and forcing them through a soft porn experience . . . What is staggering is how we're asked to relinquish instantly the resentment and obstinacy we've felt on [Ada's] behalf. She may fall in love right on time, by [Baines's] emotional time table, but why should we? At this point my vicarious anger turned into disbelief.[13]

Gullette's review continues in a more autobiographical vein, narrating the feeling she had that the movie, which she saw with her husband of twenty-five years, had gendered and sundered its male and female spectators, that while she was seeing women's entrapment in men's bargains and men's timetables, her husband was seeing the revelation of men's vulnerability and awakening.

The response to Gullette's review from the *Boston Globe*'s readers was astonishing. The *Globe* printed two long rebuttals and seven letters to the editor. One rebuttal protested the projection of twentieth-century feminist ideals upon a nineteenth-century woman (even though it is, of course, a twentieth-century film). Written by someone who calls herself "a feminist and a diminutive woman," the first rebuttal also protested Gullette's use of the phrase "anorexic vulnerability." The writer argues that Ada is strong, bold, vital, and in control every moment. The rebuttal ends: "*The Piano*'s subject is the empowerment of women despite difficult circumstances, and, as an extension of that, the voices women developed when silenced by a history of submission. I am curious about the time and space [the *Globe*] devoted to condemning a film like *The Piano* . . . Gullette's article would rather make Ada a victim, and it took a lot of words and, at times, twentieth-century cliches, to do an inadequate job."[14]

The second rebuttal, also written by a woman, also takes the *Globe* to task for giving so much space to Gullette's review. The writer rejects Gullette's reading of the body-for-piano-key bargain as rape, writing, "Rape is out-of-control violence: Here, in contrast, is a lover's painstaking delight in the sight, touch, texture of the beloved."[15] And the writer concludes with a portrait of Baines as sensitive and empathic, able to communicate well not only with Ada but also with the Maoris. The seven letters published in the *Globe* expressed, in less nuanced terms, their contempt for Gullette's feminism, their sympathy for her husband, and their outrage that the *Globe* had given so much space to her review.

I think these reactions are highly significant. The genius of the movie lies in the fact that it can provoke such diametrically opposed readings. Like the aesthetic tradition on which it implicitly comments, *The Piano* would seem to be about telling, or not telling, the difference between women's violation and women's pleasure. Yet the readings are not *simply* symmetrical. Those who view it as a love story and as a reversal of sexual power roles concentrate on the *characters*: Ada is strong, willful, and in control; Baines is sensitive, restrained, and in love; Stewart is surprised by emotion and made physically vulnerable. But Gullette's reading was not based on the individual characters but on their allegorical resonance, the framework within which they operated, and on the way the *movie*, not the characters, spoke. What message does it convey? she asked. It says that women can find the way of their desire within a structure in which they are traded between men like land, ebony, and ivory. It also says that "no" means "yes." Women may be angry, but as soon as men show any restraint, sensitivity, or need, women will abandon their anger, fall in love, and adapt happily to society as it is. Nothing, therefore, needs to be changed in the social *structure*. But in that *structure*, Ada does *not* have power. Stewart and Baines may both be responding to a *sexual* power that Ada does have over them (and there is nothing new in seeing women's power as sexual), but Baines, not Ada, can decide to go away, and Stewart has the power to either mutilate her body or give her to another man. By focusing on the contrast between Stewart and Baines, rather than on the relation of domination between both men and Ada, or, for that matter, between the Europeans and the Maori, the film encourages us to value the better of the two men rather than to question the whole structure. As bell hooks has noted,[16] the film reveals an analogy among sexual violence, patriarchal power, colonialism, capitalism, and violence against the Earth. By romanticizing the borderline between coercion and pleasure in the sexual domain, the film implicitly romanticizes the rest of the chain as well.

While readers of the *Boston Globe* are eager to idealize Ada's muteness—to prove that Ada is *not* a victim, that her muteness is *not* silence—they are intent on producing a silenced woman elsewhere: Margaret Gullette. Calling her "hysterical" and "strident," they castigate the *Globe* for allowing her so much space. It is as though the taboo on women's speech has simply moved to a new place. Now it is possible for Ada to say both her anger and her pleasure, but not for another woman to object to the message Ada's story might convey. The *Boston Globe* has become the new, respectable father who ought to have known how to keep his daughter mute. This recourse to *institutional* power to keep a woman from speaking is precisely what Margaret Gullette was protesting against.

Interestingly, after a period of otherwise almost unanimous critical enchantment with the film, a different kind of disgruntlement began to surface after its nine Oscar nominations. *Newsweek* quoted one "well-known producer" as saying about the pre-Oscar hype, "I think it's pretentious . . . 'Aren't we artsy? We're the fancy movie.'"[17] In the same week, *New York* magazine published "Seven Reasons Not to Like *The Piano*" ("Little Girl Vomits on Beach, Too Much Mud, Too Much Ironic Symbolism, Too Much Harvey, Cruelty to Pianos, Revoke that Poetic License! and Impending Appendage Trend ['Hunter receives a très chic replacement for her severed finger. If *The Piano* wins Best Picture, won't Tiffany's want to sell authorized movie-tie-in versions? And won't they be too expensive for the people who really need them?'"]).[18] Somehow, Steven Spielberg's multiple nominations can translate into greatness, but Jane Campion's make her look like just another spoiled woman with expensive and artsy tastes.

Women with expensive and artsy tastes *can*, of course, be idealized, but probably only if they project an image of graceful muteness. One has only to think of the outpouring of feeling around the death of Jacqueline Kennedy Onassis to realize the genius of her adoption of the role of silent image from the moment of the assassination onward. Prior to that time, the woman with a taste for French cooking, redecoration, and Oscar Wilde was a far less idealized figure in the American press. And the contrast between Jackie O's muteness and Hillary Clinton's outspokenness only served to give cultural reinforcement to the notion that grace, dignity, and class could only be embodied by a woman who remained silent.

But the claiming of silence around the film *The Piano* turns out not to be confined to women. The *International Herald Tribune*, reporting on what it called "the backlash" against the film, speculated:

> One theory holds that the initial critical blast that launched the film into the stratosphere simply stunned any doubters into silence.
>
> Slowly, timidly, the naysayers are gathering courage to speak. Most of them appear to be men. "I defy you to tell me what that film is about," said one hyper-male Hollywood producer . . . Kurt Anderson, the editor of *New York* magazine, said, "I have discovered, to my happiness, that there are significant numbers of people like me who think it has been highly overpraised." The reluctance to carp, he speculated, may have been political: "It arrives with this feminist baggage, or presumed feminist message, that probably shuts people up."[19]

So the whole thing becomes a political game of "muteness, muteness, who's got the muteness," and feminism, having been accused of privileging silence and victimhood, now becomes so powerful that it is a cause of silencing in others.

One of the political successes of feminism, indeed, seems to reside in its understanding of the power of reclaimed silence, a power that is not unrelated to the idealization of muteness found in the aesthetic tradition. It is no accident that every actress who has been nominated for playing the part of a mute woman—Jane Wyman, Patty Duke, Marlee Matlin, and Holly Hunter—has won an Oscar. Indeed, it might be said that the recent hysteria about protecting free speech against political correctness, in implicitly claiming that white heterosexual men were being silenced, was enacting its own form of muteness envy.

Feminism seems to have become reduced, in the public mind, to complaints about sexual victimization. Recent publications exemplifying this trend, many of them written by women, include Katie Roiphe's *The Morning After: Sex, Fear, and Feminism on Campus*. I would like to look for a moment at the ways in which this book intersects with what I have been saying about culture's investment in not being able to tell the difference between female victimization and female pleasure. By calling her book "the morning after," Roiphe implicitly ties that undecidability not to a silence that does cultural work but to the question of retrospective individual interpretation ("one person's rape is another person's bad night"). Much of her irritation is directed at the rituals that have grown up around "Take Back the Night" marches on college campuses, in which women who have been raped or abused testify to their experience. What particularly disturbs her is the way in which the speeches on those occasions have tended to constitute a literary genre:

> As I listen to the refrains, "I have been silent," "I was silenced," "I am finally breaking the silence," the speakers begin to blur together in my mind . . . As the vocabulary shared across campuses reveals, there is an archetype, a model, for the victim's tale. "Take Back the Night" speak-outs follow conventions as strict as any sonnet sequence or villanelle. As intimate details are squeezed into formulaic standards, they seem to be wrought with an emotion more generic than heartfelt.[20]

Perhaps inevitably, the complaint about genre leads to a complaint about false rape accusations. The power of the literary form to engender fictions becomes the danger of feminism out of control.

Yet as we have seen, control over the undecidability between female pleasure and female violation has always already been at the heart of the literary canon. Is the "Ode on a Grecian Urn," then, a meditation on date rape? Roiphe claims that contemporary campus feminism resurrects from the Victorian era an image of women as passive sexual victims, an image that her mother's generation of feminists worked so hard to overturn. "Proclaiming victimhood," she writes, "doesn't help project strength."[21] But doesn't it? Why are so many white men so eager to claim a share in the victimhood sweepstakes? Why did Petrarch, the father of the love sonnet, insist that it was he, not Laura, who was wounded, burned, enslaved, and penetrated by love? Even if this is "just rhetoric," why has it achieved such authority? Is it just the sexual equivalent of Christianity?

To speak about female victimization is to imply that there is such a thing as a model of male power and authority that is other than victimization. But what *The Piano* so convincingly demonstrates is that that is only partly true. Yes, for every sensitive man there is a man who chops off women's fingers. But *both* men are actually depicted in the movie as in some sense powerless. Jane Campion and actor Sam Neill both describe the husband Stewart as "vulnerable."[22] And the movie pivots on George Baines's wretchedness. "I am unhappy because I want you," he tells Ada in true Petrarchan style. "My mind has seized on you and thinks of nothing else. This is how I suffer. I am sick with longing. I don't eat, I don't sleep. If you do not want me, if you have come with no feeling for me, then go!" It is in this male two-step—the axe wielder plus the manipulative sufferer, *both* of whom see themselves as powerless—that patriarchal power lies.

Far from being the opposite of authority, victimhood would seem to be the most effective *model* for authority, particularly literary and cultural authority. It is not that the victim always gets to speak—far from it—but that the most highly valued speaker gets to claim victimhood. This is what leads readers of Apollo and Daphne to see Apollo's failed rape as "loss," or readers of "the voice of the shuttle" to say that there is always *something* that violates "us." If feminism is so hotly resisted, it is perhaps less because it substitutes women's speech for women's silence than because, in doing so, it interferes with the official structures of self-pity that keep patriarchal power in place, and, in the process, tells the truth behind the beauty of muteness envy.

NOTES

"Muteness Envy." From *Human, All Too Human*, Diana Fuss, ed. (New York: Routledge, 1995). Reproduced with permission of Taylor & Francis Group LLC. Permissions conveyed through Copyright Clearance Center.

1. Charles I. Patterson, "Passion and Permanence in Keats's *Ode on a Grecian Urn*," reprinted in *Twentieth Century Interpretations of Keats's Odes*, ed. Jack Stillinger (Englewood Cliffs, NJ: Prentice Hall, 1968), 50.

2. Jacques Lacan, *Feminine Sexuality*, ed. J. Mitchell and J. Rose (New York: W. W. Norton, 1982), 144.

3. Stephen Heath, "Difference," *Screen* 19, no. 3 (1978); Luce Irigaray, "Cosi Fan Tutti," in *This Sex Which Is Not One*, trans. Catherine Porter (Ithaca, NY: Cornell University Press, 1985); Barbara Claire Freeman, "A Union Forever Deferred: Sexual Politics after Lacan," *Qui Parle* 4, no. 2 (spring 1991).

4. For a brilliant analysis of the relation between aesthetics and sexual violence in Keats's urn, see Froma I. Zeitlin, "On Ravishing Urns: Keats in His Tradition," in *Rape and Representation*, ed. Lynn A. Higgins and Brenda R. Silver (New York: Columbia University Press, 1991). The aesthetic displacement of sexual violence by both Keats and his interpreters has also been analyzed by Deborah Pope in "The Dark Side of the Urn: A Re-evaluation of the Speaker in 'Ode on a Grecian Urn,'" *Essays in Literature* 10, no. 1 (spring 1983). Pope reads the poem as the speaker's increasingly egocentric response to the *urn*'s maidenly refusal

to answer his questions, nevertheless culminating in his self-effacement before her oracular, perfectly balanced, final pronouncement.

5. Peter Sacks, *The English Elegy* (Baltimore: Johns Hopkins University Press, 1985).

6. P. Joplin, "The Voice of the Shuttle Is Ours," *Stanford Literature Review* 1, no. 1 (1984): 26, 30.

7. C. Brooks, *The Well-Wrought Urn* (New York: Harcourt Brace, 1947), 152.

8. See C. Gilligan, A. Rogers, and D. Tolman, *Women, Girls, and Psychotherapy* (New York: Harrington Park Press, 1991).

9. Maria Torok, "The Meaning of 'Penis Envy' in Women," *differences* 4 (1992): 1.

10. See J. Herman, *Father-Daughter Incest* (Cambridge, MA: Harvard University Press, 1981), and J. Masson, *The Assault on Truth* (New York: Penguin, 1984).

11. C. Froula, "The Daughter's Seduction: Sexual Violence and Literary History," *Signs* 11, no. 4 (1986): 626, 631.

12. Jane Campion, *The Piano* (New York: Miramax Books, 1993), 135, 138, 139.

13. M. M. Gullette, "'The Piano': Imperfect Pitch," *Boston Globe,* December 3, 1993, 51, 59.

14. Jane Savoca, *The Boston Globe,* December 17, 1993, 93, 102.

15. Ellie Mamber, *The Boston Globe,* December 17, 1993, 93.

16. bell hooks, "Sexism and Misogyny: Who Takes the Rap?," *Z Magazine* 7, no. 2 (February 1994).

17. *Newsweek,* March 14, 1994, 8.

18. *New York,* March 14, 1994, 28.

19. *International Herald Tribune,* March 12–13, 1994.

20. Katie Roiphe, *The Morning After* (Boston: Little, Brown, 1993), 36.

21. Roiphe, *The Morning After,* 44.

22. Campion, *The Piano,* 139, 147.

CHAPTER 16

Apostrophe, Animation, and Abortion

The abortion issue is as alive and controversial in the
body politic as it is in the academy and the courtroom.
—Jay L. Garfield, *Abortion: Moral and Legal Perspectives*

Although rhetoric can be defined as something politicians often accuse each
other of, the political dimensions of the scholarly study of rhetoric have
gone largely unexplored by literary critics. What, indeed, could seem more
dry and apolitical than a rhetorical treatise? What could seem farther away
from budgets and guerrilla warfare than a discussion of anaphora, antithesis, prolepsis, and preterition? Yet the notorious CIA manual on psychological operations in guerrilla warfare ends with just such a rhetorical treatise:
an appendix on techniques of oratory which lists definitions and examples
for these and many other rhetorical figures.[1] The manual is designed to set
up a Machiavellian campaign of propaganda, indoctrination, and infiltra-
tion in Nicaragua, underwritten by the visible display and selective use of
weapons. Shoot softly, it implies, and carry a big schtick. If rhetoric is defined
as language that says one thing and means another, then the manual is in
effect attempting to maximize the collusion between deviousness in language
and accuracy in violence, again and again implying that targets are most
effectively hit when most indirectly aimed at. Rhetoric, clearly, has everything to do with covert operations. But are the politics of violence already
encoded in rhetorical figures as such? In other words, can the very essence
of a political issue—an issue like, say, abortion—hinge on the structure of a

figure? Is there any *inherent* connection between figurative language and questions of life and death, of who will wield and who will receive violence in a given human society?

As a way of approaching this question, I will begin in a much more traditional way by discussing a rhetorical device that has come to seem almost synonymous with the lyric voice: the figure of apostrophe. In an essay in *The Pursuit of Signs*, Jonathan Culler indeed sees apostrophe as an embarrassingly explicit emblem of procedures inherent, but usually better hidden, in lyric poetry as such.[2] Apostrophe in the sense in which I will be using it involves the direct address of an absent, dead, or inanimate being by a first-person speaker: "O wild West Wind, thou breath of Autumn's being." Apostrophe is thus both direct and indirect: based etymologically on the notion of turning aside, of digressing from straight speech, it manipulates the I/thou structure of direct address in an indirect, fictionalized way. The absent, dead, or inanimate entity addressed is thereby made present, animate, and anthropomorphic. Apostrophe is a form of ventriloquism through which the speaker throws voice, life, and human form into the addressee, turning its silence into mute responsiveness.

Baudelaire's poem "Moesta et Errabunda,"[3] whose Latin title means "sad and vagabond," raises questions of rhetorical animation through several different grades of apostrophe. Inanimate objects like trains and ships or abstract entities like perfumed paradises find themselves called upon to attend to the needs of a plaintive and restless lyric speaker. Even the poem's title poses questions of life and death in linguistic terms: the fact that Baudelaire here temporarily resuscitates a dead language prefigures the poem's attempts to function as a finder of lost loves. But in the opening lines of the poem, the direct-address structure seems straightforwardly *un*figurative: "Tell me, Agatha." This could be called a minimally fictionalized apostrophe, although that is of course its fiction. Nothing at first indicates that Agatha is any more dead, absent, or inanimate than the poet himself.

The poem's opening makes explicit the relation between direct address and the desire for the *other*'s voice: "Tell me: *you* talk." But something strange soon happens to the face-to-face humanness of this conversation. What Agatha is supposed to talk about starts a process of dismemberment that might have something to do with a kind of reverse anthropomorphism: "Does your heart sometimes take flight?" Instead of conferring a human shape, this question starts to undo one. Then, too, why the name Agatha? Baudelaire scholars have searched in vain for a biographical referent, never identifying one, but always presuming that one exists. In the Pléiade edition of Baudelaire's complete works, a footnote sends the reader to the only other place in Baudelaire's oeuvre where the name Agathe appears—a page in his *Carnets* where he is listing debts and appointments. This would seem to indicate that Agathe was indeed a real person. What do we know about her? A footnote to the *Carnets* tells us she was probably a prostitute. Why? See the poem "Moesta et Errabunda." This is a particularly stark example of the inevitable circularity of biographical criticism.

If Agathe is finally only a proper name written on two different pages in Baudelaire, then the name itself must have a function *as* a name. The name is a homonym for the word *agate*, a semiprecious stone. Is Agathe really a stone? Does the poem express the Orphic hope of getting a stone to talk?

In a poem about wandering, taking flight, getting away from "here," it is surprising to find that, structurally, each stanza acts out, not a departure, but a return to its starting point, a repetition of its first line. The poem's structure is at odds with its apparent theme. But we soon see that the object of the voyage is precisely to return—to return to a prior state, planted in the first stanza as virginity, in the second as motherhood (through the image of the nurse and the pun on *mer/mère*), and finally as childhood love and furtive pleasure. The voyage outward in space is a figure for the voyage backward in time. The poem's structure of address backs up, too, most explicitly in the third stanza. The cry apostrophizing train and ship to carry the speaker off leads to a seeming reprise of the opening line, but by this point the inanimate has entirely taken over: instead of addressing Agatha directly, the poem asks whether Agatha's heart ever speaks the line the poet himself has spoken four lines earlier. Agatha is replaced by one of her parts, which itself replaces the speaker. Agatha herself now drops out of the poem, and direct address is temporarily lost too in the grammar of the sentence ("Est-il vrai que . . ."). The poem is as if emptying itself of all its human characters and voices. It seems to be acting out a *loss* of animation—which is in fact its subject: the loss of childhood aliveness brought about by the passage of time. The poem thus enacts in its own temporality the loss of animation it situates in the temporality of the speaker's life.

At this point it launches into a new apostrophe, a new direct address to an abstract, lost state: "Comme vous êtes loin, paradis parfumé." The poem reanimates, addresses an image of fullness and wholeness and perfect correspondence ("Où tout ce que l'on aime est digne d'être aimé"). This height of liveliness, however, culminates strangely in an image of death. The heart that formerly kept trying to fly away now drowns in the moment of reaching its destination ("Où dans la volupté pure le coeur se noie!"). There may be something to gain, therefore, by deferring arrival, as the poem next seems to do by interrupting itself before grammatically completing the fifth stanza. The poem again ceases to employ direct address and ends by asking two drawn-out, self-interrupting questions. Is that paradise now farther away than India or China? Can one call it back and animate it with a silvery voice? This last question—"Peut-on le rappeler avec des cris plaintifs / Et l'animer encore d'une voix argentine?"—is a perfect description of apostrophe itself: a trope which, by means of the silvery voice of rhetoric, calls up and animates the absent, the lost, and the dead. Apostrophe itself, then, has become not just the poem's mode but also the poem's theme. In other words, what the poem ends up wanting to know is not how far away childhood is, but whether its own rhetorical strategies can be effective. The final question becomes: Can this gap be bridged? Can this loss be healed, through language alone?

Shelley's "Ode to the West Wind," which is perhaps the ultimate apostrophaic poem, makes even more explicit the relation between apostrophe and animation. Shelley spends the first three sections demonstrating that the west wind is a figure for the power to animate: it is described as the breath of being, moving everywhere, blowing movement and energy through the world, waking it from its summer dream, parting the waters of the Atlantic, uncontrollable. Yet the wind animates by bringing death, winter, destruction. How do the rhetorical strategies of the poem carry out this program of animation through the giving of death?

The apostrophe structure is immediately foregrounded by the interjections, four times spelled "O" and four times spelled "oh." One of the bridges this poem attempts to build is the bridge between the "O" of the pure vocative, Jakobson's conative function, or the pure presencing of the second person, and the "oh" of pure subjectivity, Jakobson's emotive function, or the pure presencing of the first person.

The first three sections are grammatical amplifications of the sentence "O thou, hear, oh, hear!" All the vivid imagery, all the picture painting, comes in clauses subordinate to this obsessive direct address. But the poet addresses, gives animation, gives the capacity of responsiveness, to the wind, not in order to make it speak but in order to make it listen to him—in order to make it listen to him doing nothing but address *it*. It takes him three long sections to break out of this intense near-tautology. As the fourth section begins, the "I" starts to inscribe itself grammatically (but not thematically) where the "thou" has been. A power struggle starts up for control over the poem's grammar, a struggle which mirrors the rivalry named in such lines as "If even / I were as in my boyhood . . . / . . . I would ne'er have *striven* / *As thus with thee* in prayer in my sore need." This rivalry is expressed as a comparison: "less free than thou," but then, "one *too like* thee." What does it mean to be "too like"? Time has created a loss of similarity, a loss of animation that has made the sense of similarity even more hyperbolic. In other words, the poet, in becoming less than, less like the wind, somehow becomes more like the wind in his rebellion against the loss of likeness.

In the final section the speaker both inscribes and reverses the structure of apostrophe. In saying "be thou me," he is attempting to restore metaphorical exchange and equality. If apostrophe is the giving of voice, the throwing of voice, the giving of animation, then a poet using it is always in a sense saying to the addressee, "Be thou me." But this implies that a poet has animation to give. And *that* is what this poem is saying is not, or no longer, the case. Shelley's speaker's own sense of animation is precisely what is in doubt, so that he is in effect saying to the wind, "I will animate you so that you will animate, or reanimate, me." "Make me thy lyre . . ."

Yet the wind, which is to give animation, is also the giver of death. The opposition between life and death has to undergo another reversal, another transvaluation. If death could somehow become a positive force for animation, then the poet would thereby create hope for his own "dead thoughts." The animator that will blow his words around the world will also instate the power of their deadness, their deadness *as* power, the place of maximum potential for renewal. This is the burden of the final rhetorical question. Does death necessarily entail rebirth? If winter comes, can spring be far behind? The poem is attempting to appropriate the authority of natural logic—in which spring always does follow winter—in order to claim the authority of cyclic reversibility for its own prophetic powers. Yet because this clincher is expressed in the form of a rhetorical question, it expresses natural certainty by means of a linguistic device that mimics no natural structure and has no stable one-to-one correspondence with a meaning. The rhetorical question, in a sense, leaves the poem in a state of suspended animation. But that, according to the poem, is the state of maximum potential.

Both the Baudelaire and the Shelley, then, end with a rhetorical question that both raises and begs the question of rhetoric. It is as though the apostrophe is ultimately directed toward the reader, to whom the poem is addressing Mayor Koch's question: "How'm I doing?" What is at stake in both poems is, as we have seen, the fate of a lost child—the speaker's own former self—and the possibility of a new birth or reanimation. In the poems that I will discuss next, these structures of apostrophe, animation, and lost life will take on a very different cast through the foregrounding of the question of motherhood and the premise that the life that is lost may be someone else's.

In Gwendolyn Brooks's poem "The Mother," the structures of address are shifting and complex. In the first line ("Abortions will not let you forget"), there is a "you" but there is no "I." Instead, the subject of the sentence is the word *abortions*, which thus assumes a position of grammatical control over the poem. As entities that disallow forgetting, the abortions are not only controlling but animate and anthropomorphic, capable of treating persons as objects. While Baudelaire and Shelley addressed the anthropomorphized other in order to repossess their lost selves, Brooks is representing the self as eternally addressed and possessed by the lost, anthropomorphized other. Yet the self that is possessed here is itself already a "you," not an "I." The "you" in the opening lines can be seen as an "I" that has become alienated, distanced from itself, and combined with a generalized other, which includes and feminizes the reader of the poem. The grammatical I/thou starting point of traditional apostrophe has been replaced by a structure in which the speaker is simultaneously eclipsed, alienated, and confused with the addressee. It is already clear that something has happened to the possibility of establishing a clear-cut distinction in this poem between subject and object, agent and victim.

The second section of the poem opens with a change in the structure of address. "I" takes up the positional place of "abortions," and there is temporarily no second person. The first sentence narrates: "I have heard in the voices of the wind the voices of my dim killed children." What is interesting about this line is that the speaker situates the children's voices firmly in a traditional romantic locus of lyric apostrophe—the voices of the wind, Shelley's west wind, say, or Wordsworth's "gentle breeze."[4] Gwendolyn Brooks, in other words, is here rewriting the male lyric tradition, textually placing aborted children in the spot formerly occupied by all the dead, inanimate, or absent entities previously addressed by the lyric. And the question of animation and anthropomorphism is thereby given a new and disturbing twist. For if apostrophe is said to involve language's capacity to give life and human form to something dead or inanimate, what happens when those questions are literalized? What happens when the lyric speaker assumes responsibility for producing the death in the first place, but without being sure of the precise degree of human animation that existed in the entity killed? What is the debate over abortion about, indeed, if not the question of when, precisely, a being assumes a human form?

It is not until line 14 that Brooks's speaker actually addresses the dim killed children. And she does so not directly, but in the form of a self-quotation: "I have said, Sweets, if I sinned . . ." This embedding of the apostrophe appears to serve two functions here, just as it did in Baudelaire: a self-distancing function, and a foregrounding of the question of the adequacy of language. But whereas in Baudelaire the distance between the speaker and the lost childhood is what is being lamented, and a restoration of vividness and contact is what is desired, in Brooks the vividness of the contact is precisely the source of the pain. While Baudelaire suffers from the dimming of memory, Brooks suffers from an inability to forget. And while Baudelaire's speaker actively seeks a fusion between present self and lost child, Brooks's speaker is attempting to fight her way out of a state of confusion between self and other. This confusion is indicated by the shifts in the poem's structures of address. It is never clear whether the speaker sees herself as an "I" or a "you," an addressor or an addressee. The voices in the wind are not created *by* the lyric apostrophe; they rather initiate the need for one. The initiative of speech seems always to lie in the other. The poem continues to struggle to clarify the relation between "I" and "you," but in the end it succeeds only in expressing the inability of its language to do so. By not closing the quotation in its final line, the poem, which began by confusing the reader with the aborter, ends by implicitly including the reader among those aborted—and loved. The poem can no more distinguish between "I" and "you" than it can come up with a proper definition of life.

In line 28, the poem explicitly asks, "Oh, what shall I say, how is the truth to be said?" Surrounding this question are attempts to make impossible distinctions: got/did not get, deliberate/not deliberate, dead/never made. The uncertainty of the speaker's control as a subject mirrors the uncertainty of the children's status as an object. It is interesting that the status of the human subject here hinges on the word *deliberate*. The association of deliberateness with human agency has a long (and very American) history. It is deliberateness, for instance, that underlies that epic of separation and self-reliant autonomy, Thoreau's *Walden*. "I went to the woods," writes Thoreau, "because I wished to live deliberately, to front only the essential facts of life."[5] Clearly, for Thoreau, pregnancy was not an essential fact of life. Yet for him as well as for every human being that has yet existed, someone else's pregnancy is the very *first* fact of life. How might the plot of human subjectivity be reconceived (so to speak) if pregnancy rather than autonomy is what raises the question of deliberateness?

Much recent feminist work has been devoted to the task of rethinking the relations between subjectivity, autonomy, interconnectedness, responsibility, and gender. Carol Gilligan's book *In a Different Voice* (and this focus on "voice" is not irrelevant here) studies gender differences in patterns of ethical thinking. The central ethical question analyzed by Gilligan is precisely the decision whether to have, or not to have, an abortion. The first time I read the book, this struck me as strange. Why, I wondered, would an investigation of gender *differences* focus on one of the questions about which an even-handed comparison of the male and the female points of view is impossible? Yet this, clearly, turns out to be the point: there is difference *because* it is not always possible to make symmetrical oppositions. As long as there is symmetry, one is not dealing with difference but rather with versions of the same. Gilligan's difference arises out of the impossibility of maintaining a rigorously logical binary model for ethical choices. Female logic, as she defines it, is a way of rethinking the logic of choice in a situation in which none of the choices are good. "Believe that even in my deliberateness I was not deliberate": believe that the agent is not entirely autonomous, believe that I can be subject and object of violence at the same time, believe that I have not chosen the conditions under which I must choose. As Gilligan writes of the abortion decision, "The occurrence of the dilemma itself precludes non-violent resolution."[6] The choice is not between violence and nonviolence, but between simple violence to a fetus and complex, less determinate violence to an involuntary mother and/or an unwanted child.

Readers of Brooks's poem have often read it as an argument against abortion. And it is certainly clear that the poem is not saying that abortion is a good thing. But to see it as making a simple case for the embryo's right to life is to assume that a woman who has chosen abortion does not have the right to mourn. It is to assume that no case *for* abortion can take the woman's feelings of guilt and loss into consideration, that to take those feelings into account is to deny the right to choose the act that produced them. Yet the poem makes no such claim: it attempts the impossible task of humanizing both the mother and the aborted children while presenting the inadequacy of language to resolve the dilemma without violence.

What I would like to emphasize is the way in which the poem suggests that the arguments for and against abortion are structured through and through by the rhetorical limits and possibilities of something akin to apostrophe. The fact that apostrophe allows one to animate the inanimate, the dead, or the absent implies that whenever a being is apostrophized, it is thereby automatically animated, anthropomorphized, "person-ified." (By the same token, the rhetoric of calling makes it difficult to tell the difference between the animate and the inanimate, as anyone with a telephone answering machine can attest.) Because of the ineradicable tendency of language to animate whatever it addresses, rhetoric itself can always have already answered "yes" to the question of whether a fetus is a human being. It is no accident that the antiabortion film most often shown in the United States should be entitled *The Silent Scream*. By activating the imagination to believe in the anthropomorphized embryo's mute responsiveness in exactly the same way that apostrophe does, the film (which is of course itself a highly rhetorical entity) is playing on rhetorical possibilities that are inherent in all linguistically based modes of representation.

Yet the function of apostrophe in the Brooks poem is far from simple. If the fact that the speaker addresses the children at all makes them human, then she must pronounce herself guilty of murder—but only if she discontinues her apostrophe. As long as she addresses the children, she can keep them alive, can keep from finishing with the act of killing them. The speaker's attempt to absolve herself of guilt depends on never forgetting, never breaking the ventriloquism of an apostrophe through which she cannot define her identity otherwise than as the mother eaten alive by the children she has never fed. Who, in the final analysis, exists by addressing whom? The children are a rhetorical extension of the mother, but she, as the poem's title indicates, has no existence apart from her relation to them. It begins to be clear that the speaker has written herself into a poem that she cannot get out of without violence. The violence she commits in the end is to her own language: as the poem ends, the vocabulary shrinks away, words are repeated, nothing but "all" rhymes with "all." The speaker has written herself into silence. Yet hers is not the only silence in the poem: earlier she has said, "You will never . . . silence or buy with a sweet." If sweets are for silencing, then by beginning her apostrophe, "Sweets, if I sinned . . . ," the speaker is already saying that the poem, which exists to memorialize those whose lack of life makes them eternally alive, is also attempting to silence once and for all the voices of the children in the wind. It becomes impossible to tell whether language is what gives life or what kills.

Women have said again and again "This is *my* body!" and they have
reason to feel angry, reason to feel that it has been like shouting into
the wind.—Judith Jarvis Thompson, "A Defense of Abortion"

It is interesting to note the ways in which legal and moral discussions of abortion tend to employ the same terms as those we have been using to describe the figure of apostrophe. Thus, Justice Blackmun, in *Roe v. Wade*: "These disciplines [philosophy, theology, and civil and canon law] variously approached the question in terms of the point at which the embryo or fetus became 'formed' or recognizably human, or in terms of when a 'person' came into being, that is, infused with a 'soul' or 'animated.'"[7] The issue of "fetal personhood"[8] is of course a way of bringing to a state of explicit uncertainty the fundamental difficulty of defining personhood in general.[9] Even if the question of defining the nature of "persons" is restricted to the question of understanding what is meant by the word "person" in the U.S. Constitution (since the Bill of Rights guarantees the rights only of "persons"), there is not at present, and probably will never be, a stable legal definition. Existing discussions of the legality and morality of abortion almost invariably confront, leave unresolved, and detour around the question of the nature and boundaries of human life. As Justice Blackmun puts it in *Roe v. Wade*: "We need not resolve the difficult question of when life begins. When those trained in the respective disciplines of medicine, philosophy, and theology are unable to arrive at any consensus, the judiciary, at this point in the development of man's knowledge, is not in a position to speculate as to the answer."[10]

In the case of *Roe v. Wade*, the legality of abortion is derived from the right to privacy—an argument which, as Catherine MacKinnon argues in *"Roe vs. Wade: A Study in Male Ideology,"*[11] is itself problematic for women, since by protecting "privacy" the courts also protect the injustices of patriarchal sexual arrangements. When the issue is an unwanted pregnancy, some sort of privacy has already, in a sense, been invaded. In order for the personal to avoid being reduced once again to the nonpolitical, privacy, like deliberateness, needs to be rethought in terms of sexual politics. Yet even the attempt to re-gender the issues surrounding abortion is not simple. As Kristin Luker convincingly demonstrates, the debate turns around the claims not only of woman versus fetus or woman versus patriarchal state, but also of woman versus woman:

> Pro-choice and pro-life activists live in different worlds, and the scope of their lives, as both adults and children, fortifies them in their belief that their views on abortion are the more correct, more moral and more reasonable. When added to this is the fact that should "the other side" win, one group of women will see the very real devaluation of their lives and life resources, it is not surprising that the abortion debate has generated so much heat and so little light. . . .
>
> Are pro-life activists, as they claim, actually reaching their cherished goal of "educating the public to the humanity of the unborn child"? As

we begin to seek an answer, we should recall that motherhood is a topic about which people have very complicated feelings, and because abortion has become the battleground for different definitions of motherhood, neither the pro-life nor the pro-choice movement has ever been "representative" of how most Americans feel about abortion. More to the point, all our data suggest that *neither of these groups will ever be able to be representative.*[12]

It is often said, in literary-theoretical circles, that to focus on undecidability is to be apolitical. Everything I have read about the abortion controversy in its present form in the United States leads me to suspect that, on the contrary, the undecidable *is* the political. There is politics precisely because there is undecidability.

And there is also poetry. There are striking and suggestive parallels between the "different voices" involved in the abortion debate and the shifting address-structures of poems like Gwendolyn Brooks's "The Mother." A glance at several other poems suggests that there tends indeed to be an overdetermined relation between the theme of abortion and the problematization of structures of address. In Anne Sexton's "The Abortion," six three-line stanzas narrate, in the first person, a trip to Pennsylvania where the "I" has obtained an abortion. Three times the poem is interrupted by the italicized lines:

> *Somebody who should have been born*
> *is gone.*

Like a voice-over narrator taking superegoistic control of the moral bottom line, this refrain (or "burden," to use the archaic term for both "refrain" and "child in the womb") puts the first-person narrator's authority in question without necessarily constituting the voice of a separate entity. Then, in the seventh and final stanza, the poem extends and intensifies this split:

> Yes, woman, such logic will lead
> to loss without death. Or say what you meant,
> you coward . . . this baby that I bleed.

Self-accusing, self-interrupting, the narrating "I" turns on herself (or is it someone else?) as "you," as "woman." The poem's speaker becomes as split as the two senses of the word *bleed*. Once again, "saying what one means" can be done only by ellipsis, violence, illogic, transgression, silence. The question of who is addressing whom is once again unresolved.

As we have seen, the question of "when life begins" is complicated partly because of the way in which language blurs the boundary between life and death. In "Menstruation at Forty," Sexton sees menstruation itself as the loss of a child ("two days gone in blood")—a child that exists *because* it can be called:

> I was thinking of a son . . .
> You! . . .
> Will you be the David or the Susan?
> . . .
> my carrot, my cabbage,
> I would have possessed you before all women,
> calling your name,
> calling you mine.

The political consequences and complexities of addressing—of "calling"— are made even more explicit in a poem by Lucille Clifton entitled "The Lost Baby Poem." By choosing the word *dropped* ("i dropped your almost body down"), Clifton renders it unclear whether the child has been lost through abortion or through miscarriage. What is clear, however, is that that loss is both mourned and rationalized. The rationalization occurs through the description of a life of hardship, flight, and loss: the image of a child born into winter, slipping like ice into the hands of strangers in Canada, con-flates the scene of Eliza's escape in *Uncle Tom's Cabin* with the exile of draft resisters during the Vietnam War. The guilt and mourning occur in the form of an imperative in which the notion of "stranger" returns in the following lines:

> if i am ever less than a mountain
> for your definite brothers and sisters. . . .
> . . . let black men call me stranger
> always   for your never named sake.

The act of "calling" here correlates a lack of name with a loss of membership. For the sake of the one that cannot be called, the speaker invites an apostrophe that would expel *her* into otherness. The consequences of the death of a child ramify beyond the mother–child dyad to encompass the fate of an entire community. The world that has created conditions under which the loss of a baby becomes desirable must be resisted, not joined. For a black woman, the loss of a baby can always be perceived as a complicity with genocide. The black mother sees her own choice as one of being either a stranger or a rock. The humanization of the lost baby addressed by the poem is thus carried out at the cost of dehumanizing, even rendering inanimate, the calling mother.

Yet each of these poems exists, finally, *because* a child does not.[13] In Adrienne Rich's poem "To a Poet," the rivalry between poems and children is made quite explicit. The "you" in the poem is again aborted, but here it is the mother herself who could be called "dim and killed" by the fact not of abortion but of the institution of motherhood. And again, the structures of address are complex and unstable. The deadness of the "you" cannot be named: not suicide, not murder. The question of the life or death of the addressee is raised in an interesting way through Rich's rewriting of Keats's sonnet on his mortality. While Keats writes, "When I have fears that *I* will cease to be," Rich writes, "and I have fears that *you* will cease to be." If poetry is at stake in both intimations of mortality, what is the significance of this shift from "I" to "you"? On the one hand, the very existence of the Keats poem indicates that the pen *has* succeeded in gleaning something before the brain has ceased to be. No such grammatical guarantee exists for the "you." Death in the Keats poem is as much a source as it is a threat to writing. Hence death, for Keats, could be called the mother of poetry, while motherhood, for Rich, is precisely the death of poetry. The Western myth of the conjunction of word and flesh implied by the word *incarnate* is undone by images of language floating and vanishing in the bowl of the toilet of real fleshly needs. The word is not made flesh; rather, flesh unmakes the mother-poet's word. The difficulty of retrieving the "you" as poet is enacted by the structures of address in the following lines:

> I write this   not for you
> who fight to write your own
> words fighting up the falls
> but for another woman   dumb

In saying "I write this not for you," Rich seems almost to be excluding as addressee anyone who could conceivably be reading this poem. The poem is setting aside both the I and the you—the pronouns Benveniste associates with personhood—and reaches instead toward a "she," which belongs in the category of "nonperson." The poem is thus attempting the impossible task of directly addressing not a second person but a third person—a person who, if she is reading the poem, cannot be the reader the poem has in mind. The poem is trying to include what is by its own grammar excluded from it, to animate through language the nonperson, the "other woman." This poem, too, therefore, is bursting the limits of its own language, inscribing a logic that it itself reveals to be impossible—but necessary. Even the divorce between writing and childbearing is less absolute than it appears: in comparing the writing of words to the spawning of fish, Rich's poem reveals itself to be trapped between the inability to combine and the inability to separate the woman's various roles.

In each of these poems, then, a kind of competition is implicitly instated between the bearing of children and the writing of poems. Something unsettling has happened to the analogy often drawn by male poets between artistic creation and procreation. For it is not true that literature contains no examples of male pregnancy. Sir Philip Sidney, in the first sonnet from *Astrophel and Stella*, describes himself as "great with child to speak," but the poem is ultimately produced at the expense of no literalized child. Sidney's labor pains are smoothed away by a mid wifely apostrophe ("'Fool,' said my Muse to me, 'look in thy heart, and write!'"), and by a sort of poetic cesarean section, out springs the poem we have, in fact, already finished reading.[14] Mallarmé, in "Don du poème," describes himself as an enemy father seeking nourishment for his monstrous poetic child from the woman within apostrophe-shot who is busy nursing a literalized daughter.[15] But since the woman presumably has two breasts, there seems to be enough to go around. As Shakespeare assures the fair young man, "But were some child of yours alive that time, / You should live twice in it and in my rhyme" (sonnet 17). Apollinaire, in his play *Les Mamelles de Tirésias*, depicts woman as a de-maternalized neo-Malthusian leaving the task of childbearing to a surrealistically fertile husband. But again, nothing more disturbing than Tiresian cross-dressing seems to occur. Children are alive and well, and far more numerous than ever. Indeed, in one of the dedicatory poems, Apollinaire indicates that his drama represents a return to health from the literary reign of the *poète maudit*:

> La féconde raison a jailli de ma fable,
> Plus de femme stérile et non plus d'avortons . . . [16]

> [Fertile reason springs out of my fable,
> No more sterile women, no aborted children]

This dig at Baudelaire, among others, reminds us that in the opening poem to *Les Fleurs du mal* ("Bénédiction"), Baudelaire represents the poet himself as an abortion *manqué*, cursed by the poisonous words of a rejecting mother. The question of the unnatural seems more closely allied with the bad mother than with the pregnant father.

Even in the seemingly more obvious parallel provided by poems written to dead children by male poets, it is not really surprising to find that the substitution of poem for child lacks the sinister undertones and disturbed address exhibited by the abortion poems we have been discussing. Jonson, in "On my First Son," calls his dead child "his best piece of poetry," while Mallarmé, in an only semiguilty *Aufhebung*, transfuses the dead Anatole to the level of an idea. More recently, Jon Silkin has written movingly of the death of a handicapped child ("something like a person") as a change of silence, not a splitting of voice. And Michael Harper, in "Nightmare Begins Responsibility," stresses the powerlessness and distrust of a black father leaving his dying son to the care of a "white-doctor-who-breathed-for-him-all-night."[17] But again, whatever the complexity of the voices in that poem, the speaker does not split self-accusingly or infra-symbiotically in the ways we have noted in the abortion/motherhood poems. While one could undoubtedly find counterexamples on both sides, it is not surprising that the substitution of art for children should not be inherently transgressive for the male poet. Men have in a sense always had no choice but to substitute something for the literal process of birth. That, at least, is the belief that has long been encoded into male poetic conventions. It is as though male writing were by nature procreative, while female writing is somehow by nature infanticidal.

It is, of course, as problematic as it is tempting to draw general conclusions about differences between male and female writing on the basis of these somewhat random examples. Yet it is clear that a great many poetic effects may be colored according to *expectations* articulated through the gender of the poetic speaker. Whether or not men and women would "naturally" write differently about dead children, there is something about the connection between motherhood and death that refuses to remain comfortably and conventionally figurative. When a woman speaks about the death of children in any sense other than that of pure loss, a powerful taboo is being violated. The indistinguishability of miscarriage and abortion in the Clifton poem indeed points to the notion that *any* death of a child is perceived as a crime committed by the mother, something a mother ought by definition to be able to prevent. That these questions should be inextricably connected to the figure of apostrophe, however, deserves further comment. For there may be a deeper link between motherhood and apostrophe than we have hitherto suspected.

The verbal development of the infant, according to Lacan, begins as a demand addressed to the mother, out of which the entire verbal universe is spun. Yet the mother addressed is somehow a personification, not a person— a personification of presence or absence, of Otherness itself.

Demand in itself bears on something other than the satisfactions it calls for. It is demand of a presence or of an absence—which is what is manifested in the primordial relation to the mother, pregnant with that Other to be situated *within* the needs that it can satisfy. . . . Insofar as [man's] needs are subjected to demand, they return to him alienated. This is not the effect of his real dependence . . . , but rather the turning into signifying form as such, from the fact that it is from the locus of the Other that its message is emitted.[18]

If demand is the originary vocative, which assures life even as it inaugurates alienation, then it is not surprising that questions of animation inhere in the rhetorical figure of apostrophe. The reversal of apostrophe we noted in the Shelley poem ("animate me") would be no reversal at all, but a reinstatement of the primal apostrophe in which, despite Lacan's disclaimer, there is precisely a link between demand and animation, between apostrophe and life-and-death dependency.[19] If apostrophe is structured like demand, and if demand articulates the primal relation to the mother as a relation to the Other, then lyric poetry itself—summed up in the figure of apostrophe—comes to look like the fantastically intricate history of endless elaborations and displacements of the single cry, "Mama!" The question these poems are asking, then, is what happens when the poet is speaking *as* a mother, a mother whose cry arises out of—and is addressed to—a dead child?

It is no wonder that the distinction between addressor and addressee should become so problematic in poems about abortion. It is also no wonder that the debate about abortion should refuse to settle into a single voice. Whether or not one has ever been a mother, everyone participating in the debate has once been a child. Psychoanalysis, too, is a theory of development from the child's point of view. Rhetorical, psychoanalytical, and political structures are profoundly implicated in one another. The difficulty in all three would seem to reside in the attempt to achieve a full elaboration of any discursive position other than that of child.

NOTES

"Apostrophe, Animation, and Abortion." *Diacritics* 16, no. 1 (1986): 29–39. © The Johns Hopkins University Press. Reprinted with permission of The Johns Hopkins University Press.

1. I would like to thank Tom Keenan of Yale University for bringing this text to my attention. The present essay has in fact benefited greatly from the suggestions of others, among whom I would like particularly to thank Marge Garber,

Rachel Jacoff, Carolyn Williams, Helen Vendler, Steven Melville, Ted Morris, Stamos Metzidakis, Steven Ungar, and Richard Yarborough.

2. Jonathan Culler, "Apostrophe," in *The Pursuit of Signs* (Ithaca, NY: Cornell University Press, 1981), 135–54. See also Paul de Man: "Now it is certainly beyond question that the figure of address is recurrent in lyric poetry, to the point of constituting the generic definition of, at the very least, the ode (which can, in turn, be seen as paradigmatic for poetry in general." Paul de Man, "Lyrical Voice in Contemporary Theory," in *Lyric Poetry: Beyond New Criticism*, ed. Chaviva Hosek and Patricia Parker (Ithaca, NY: Cornell University Press, 1985).

3. The texts cited are taken from the following sources: Charles Baudelaire, *Oeuvres complètes* (Paris: Pléiade, 1976); *The Norton Anthology of Poetry* (New York: W. W. Norton, 1975), for Shelley; Anne Sexton, *The Complete Poems* (Boston: Houghton Mifflin, 1981); Lucille Clifton, *Good News about the Earth* (New York: Random House, 1972); and Adrienne Rich, *The Dream of a Common Language* (New York: W. W. Norton, 1978). The translation of Baudelaire's "Moesta et Errabunda" is my own. Gwendolyn Brooks refused permission to reprint "The Mother," which can be found in Gwendolyn Brooks, *Selected Poems* (New York: Harper and Row, 1963), in *The Norton Anthology of Literature by Women* (New York: W. W. Norton, 1985), or in *The Black Poets* (New York: Bantam, 1971).

4. It is interesting to note that the "gentle breeze," apostrophized as "Messenger" and "Friend" in the 1805–6 *Prelude* (book 1, line 5), is significantly *not* directly addressed in the 1850 version. One might ask whether this change stands as a sign of the much-discussed waning of Wordsworth's poetic inspiration, or whether it is, rather, one of a number of strictly rhetorical shifts that *give the impression* of a wane.

5. Henry David Thoreau, *Walden* (New York: Signet, 1960), 66.

6. Carol Gilligan, *In a Different Voice* (Cambridge, MA: Harvard University Press, 1982), 94.

7. Quoted in Jay L. Garfield and Patricia Hennessey, eds., *Abortion: Moral and Legal Perspectives* (Amherst: University of Massachusetts Press, 1984), 15.

8. Patricia King, "Personhood." In Garfield and Hennessey, *Abortion: Moral and Legal Perspectives*, 55–57.

9. See Kristin Luker, *Abortion and the Politics of Motherhood* (Berkeley: University of California Press, 1984), 6.

10. Garfield and Hennessey, eds., *Abortion: Moral and Legal Perspectives*, 27.

11. In Garfield and Hennessey, eds., *Abortion: Moral and Legal Perspectives*, 45–54.

12. Luker, *Abortion and the Politics of Motherhood*, 215, 224.

13. For additional poems dealing with the loss of babies, see the anthology *The Limits of Miracles*, collected by Marion Deutsche Cohen (South Hadley, MA: Bergin and Garvey, 1985). Sharon Dunn, editor of the *Agni Review*, told me

recently that she has in fact noticed that such poems have begun to form almost a new genre.

14. Poems cited here and on the following pages from Sidney, Jonson, and Silkin may be found in *The Norton Anthology of Poetry* (New York: W. W. Norton, 1975).

15. Mallarmé, *Oeuvres complètes* (Paris: Pléiade, 1945), 40.

16. Guillaume Apollinaire, *Les Mamelles de Tirésias*, in *L'Enchanteur pourrissant* (Paris: Gallimard, 1972), 101.

17. Michael Harper, title poem in *Nightmare Begins Responsibility* (Urbana: University of Illinois Press, 1975).

18. Jacques Lacan, *Ecrits*, trans. Alan Sheridan (New York: W. W. Norton, 1977), 286.

19. An interesting example of a poem in which an apostrophe confers upon the totally Other the authority to animate the self is Randall Jarrell's "A Sick Child," which ends: "All that I've never thought of—think of me!" In *The Voice That Is Great within Us*, ed. Hayden Carruth (New York: Bantam, 1970), 402.

CHAPTER 17

Anthropomorphism in Lyric and Law

Anthropomorphism. n. The attribution of human motivation, characteristics, or behavior to inanimate objects, animals, or natural phenomena.—*American Heritage Dictionary*

Through a singular ambiguity, through a kind of transposition or intellectual quid pro quo, you will feel yourself evaporating, and you will attribute to your . . . tobacco, the strange ability to *smoke you.*—Baudelaire, *Artificial Paradises*

Recent discussions of the relations between law and literature have tended to focus on prose—novels, short stories, autobiographies, even plays—rather than on lyric poetry.[1] Literature has been seen as a locus of plots and situations that parallel legal cases or problems, either to shed light on complexities not always acknowledged by the ordinary practice of legal discourse or to shed light on cultural crises and debates that historically underlie and inform literary texts. But in a sense, this focus on prose is surprising, since lyric poetry has, at least historically, been the more law-abiding or rule-bound of the genres. Indeed, the sonnet form has been compared to a prison (Wordsworth[2]) or at least to a bound woman (Keats[3]), and Baudelaire's portraits of lyric depression ("Spleen"[4]) are often written as if from behind bars. What are the relations between the laws of genre[5] and the laws of the state? The present essay might be seen as asking this question through the juxtaposition, as it happens, of two sonnets and a prisoners' association.

More profoundly, though, lyric and law might be seen as two very different ways of instating what a "person" is. There appears to be the greatest possible discrepancy between a lyric "person"—emotive, subjective, individual—and a legal "person"—rational, rights-bearing, institutional. In this essay I will try to show, through the question of anthropomorphism, how these two "persons" can illuminate each other.

My argument develops out of the juxtaposition of two texts: Paul de Man's essay, "Anthropomorphism and Trope in the Lyric,"[6] in which I try to understand why for de Man the question of anthropomorphism is at the heart of the lyric, and the text of a Supreme Court opinion from 1993, *Rowland v. California Men's Colony* (506 U.S. 194 [1993]). This case has not become a household name like *Roe v. Wade* (1973) or *Brown v. Board of Education* (1954), and probably with good reason. What is at stake in it appears trivial—at bottom, it is about an association of prisoners suing for the right to have "free cigarette" privileges restored. But the Supreme Court's task is not to decide whether the prisoners have the right to smoke (an increasingly contested right, as it happens, in the United States today). The case has come before the court to resolve the question of whether their council can be counted as a juridical "person" under the law. What is at stake, then, in both the legal and the lyric texts is the question: What is a person?

I

I will begin by discussing the article by Paul de Man, which is one of the most difficult, even outrageous, of his essays. Both hyperbolic and elliptical, it makes a number of very strong claims about literary history, lyric pedagogy, and the materiality of "historical modes of language power."[7] Toward the end of his text, de Man somewhat unexpectedly reveals that the essay originated in an invitation to speak on the nature of lyric. But it begins with some general remarks about the relation between epistemology and rhetoric (which can stand as a common contemporary way of framing the relations between law and literature). The transition between the question of the lyric and the question of epistemology and rhetoric is made through the Keatsian chiasmus, "Beauty is truth, truth beauty,"[8] which de Man quotes on his way to Nietzsche's short and "better known than understood"[9] essay, "Truth and Falsity in an Ultramoral Sense."[10] "What is truth?" Nietzsche asks in that essay's most often-quoted moment: "a mobile army of metaphors, metonymies, and anthropomorphisms."[11] Thus it would seem that Nietzsche has answered, "Truth is trope, trope truth" or "epistemology is rhetoric, rhetoric epistemology." But de Man wants to show in what ways Nietzsche is *not* saying simply this. First, the list of tropes is, he says, "odd."[12] While metaphor and metonymy are the names of tropes that designate a pure structure of relation (metaphor is a relation of similarity between two entities, while metonymy is a relation of contiguity), de Man claims that anthropomorphism, while structured similarly, is not a trope. It is not the name of a pure rhetorical structure, but the name of a comparison, one of whose terms is treated as a given (as epistemologically resolved). To use an anthropomorphism is to treat as *known* what the properties of the human are.

> "Anthropomorphism" is not just a trope but an identification on the level of substance. It takes one entity for another and thus implies the constitution of specific entities prior to their confusion, the *taking* of something for something else that can then be assumed to be *given*. Anthropomorphism freezes the infinite chain of tropological transformations and propositions into one single assertion or essence which, as such, excludes all others. It is no longer a proposition but a proper name.[13]

Why does he call this a proper name? Shouldn't the essence that is taken as given be a concept? If "man" is what is assumed as a given, why call it a proper name? (This question is particularly vexed when the theorist's proper name is "de Man.") The answer, I think, is that "man" as concept would imply the possibility of a proposition. "Man" would be subject to definition, and thus transformation or trope. But proper names are not subjects of definition: They are what they are. If "man" is taken as a given, then, it can only be because it is out of the loop of qualification. It is presupposed, not defined.

Yet the examples of proper names de Man gives are surprising: Narcissus and Daphne.[14] Nietzsche's triumvirate of metaphor, metonymy, and anthropomorphism then functions like the plot of an Ovidian metamorphosis: from a mythological world in which man and nature appear to be in metaphorical and metonymic harmony, there occurs a crisis wherein, by a process of seamless transformation, a break nevertheless occurs in the system of correspondences, leaving a residue that escapes and remains—the proper name. De Man's discussion of Baudelaire's sonnets will in fact be haunted by Ovidian presences: Echo is lurking behind every mention of Narcissus, while one of the recurring cruxes is whether there is a human substance in a tree. It is perhaps not an accident that the figures that occupy the margins of de Man's discussion are female. If de Man's enduring question is whether linguistic structures and epistemological claims can be presumed to be compatible, the question of gender cannot be located exclusively either in language (where the gender of pronouns, and often of nouns, is inherent in each language) or in the world. By extension, the present discussion of the nature of "man" cannot fail to be haunted by the question of gender.

The term *anthropomorphism* in Nietzsche's list thus indicates that a *given* is being forced into what otherwise would function as a pure structure of relation. In addition, Nietzsche calls truth an *army* of tropes, thus introducing more explicitly the notion of power, force, or violence. This is not a notion that can fit into the oppositions between epistemology and rhetoric, but rather disrupts the system. In the text of the Supreme Court decision that I will discuss in a moment, such a disruption is introduced when the opposition on which the case is based, the opposition between natural person and artificial entity, opens out onto the question of policy. There, too, the question is one of truth and power, of the separation of the constative—what does the law say?—from the performative—what does it do?

The bulk of de Man's essay is devoted to a reading of two sonnets by Baudelaire: "Correspondances" and "Obsession," reproduced here.[15]

Correspondances

La Nature est un temple où de vivants piliers
Laissent parfois sortir de confuses paroles;
L'homme y passe à travers des forêts de symboles
Qui l'observent avec des regards familiers.
Comme de longs échos qui de loin se confondent
Dans une ténébreuse et profonde unité,
Vaste comme la nuit et comme la clarté,
Les parfums, les couleurs et les sons se répondent.
Il est des parfums frais comme des chairs d'enfants,
Doux comme les hautbois, verts comme les prairies,
—Et d'autres, corrompus, riches et triomphants,
Ayant l'expansion des choses infinies,
Comme l'ambre, le muse, le benjoin et l'encens,
Qui chantent les transports de l'esprit et des sens.[16]

Correspondences

Nature is a temple, where the living pillars
Sometimes utter indistinguishable words;
Man passes through these forests of symbols
Which regard him with familiar looks.
Like long echoes that blend in the distance

Into a unity obscure and profound,
Vast as the night and as the light,
The perfumes, colors, and sounds correspond.
There are some perfumes fresh as a baby's skin,
Mellow as oboes, verdant as prairies,
—And others, corrupt, rich, and triumphant,
With all the expansiveness of infinite things,
Like ambergris, musk, benjamin, incense,
That sing the transports of spirit and sense.

Obsession

Grands bois, vous m'effrayez comme des cathédrales;
Vous hurlez comme l'orgue; et dans nos coeurs maudits,
Chambres d'éternel deuil où vibrent de vieux râles,
Répondent les échos de vos *De Profundis*.
Je te hais, Océan! tes bonds et tes tumultes,
Mon esprit les retrouve en lui; ce rire amer
De l'homme vaincu, plein de sanglots et d'insultes,
Je l'entends dans le rire énorme de la mer.
Comme tu me plairais, ô nuit! sans ces étoiles
Dont la lumière parle un langage connu!
Car je cherche le vide, et le noir, et le nu!
Mais les ténèbres sont elles-mêmes des toiles
Où vivent, jaillissant de mon oeil par milliers,
Des êtres disparus aux regards familiers.[17]

Obsession

You terrify me, forests, like cathedrals;
You roar like organs; and in our cursed hearts,
Chambers of mourning that quiver with our dying,
Your *De Profundis* echoes in response.
How I hate you, Ocean! your tumultuous tide
Is flowing in my spirit; this bitter laughter
Of vanquished man, strangled with sobs and insults,
I hear it in the heaving laughter of the sea.
O night, how I would love you without stars,
Whose light can only speak the words I know!
For I seek the void, and the black, and the bare!
But the shadows are themselves a screen

That gathers from my eyes the ones I've lost,
A thousand living things with their familiar looks.

Both poems end up raising "man" as a question—"Correspondances" looks upon "man" as if from a great distance, as if from the outside; "Obsession" says "I," but then identifies with "vanquished man" whose laugh is echoed in the sea.

"Correspondances" is probably the most canonical of Baudelaire's poems in that it has justified the greatest number of general statements about Baudelaire's place in literary history. The possibility of literary history ends up, in some ways, being the real topic of de Man's essay. De Man will claim that the use of this sonnet to anchor the history of "the symbolist movement" is based on a reading that ignores a crucial element in the poem, an element that, if taken seriously, will not allow for the edifice of literary history to be built upon it.

"Correspondances" sets up a series of analogies between nature, man, symbols, and metaphysical unity, and among manifestations of the different physical senses, all through the word *comme* ("like"). A traditional reading of the poem would say that the lateral analogies among the senses (perfumes fresh as a baby's skin, mellow as oboes, green as prairies) are signs that there exists an analogy between man and nature and between man and the spiritual realm.

De Man focuses on this analogy-making word, *comme*, and notes an anomaly in the final instance. Whereas the first uses of *comme* in the poem equate different things into likeness, the last one just introduces a list of examples— there are perfumes that are rich and corrupt, like musk, ambergris, and frankincense. This is thus a tautology—there are perfumes like . . . perfumes. De Man calls this a stutter. He writes, "Comme then means as much as 'such as, for example.' "[18] "Ce Comme n'est pas un comme comme les autres,"[19] writes de Man in a sudden access of French. His sentence performs the stutter he attributes to the enumeration of the perfumes. Listing examples would seem to be quite different from proposing analogies. If the burden of the analogies in *Correspondances* is to convince us that the metaphorical similarities among the senses point to a higher spiritual unity, then sheer enumeration would disrupt that claim.

There is another, more debatable suggestion in de Man's reading that attempts to disrupt the anthropomorphism of the forest of symbols. De Man suggests that the trees are a mere metaphor for a city crowd in the first stanza. If the living pillars with their familiar glances are metaphorically a city crowd, then the anthropomorphism of nature is lost. Man is surrounded by tree-like men, not man-like trees. It is not "man" whose attributes are taken on by all of nature, but merely a crowd of men being compared to trees and pillars. De Man notes that everyone resists this reading—as do I—but the intensity with which it is rejected does make visible the seduction of the system that puts nature, god, and man into a perfect unity through the symbol, which is what has made the poem so important for literary history. Similarly, if the last *comme* is sheer enumeration rather than similarity, then the transports in the last line of the poem would not get us into a transcendent realm, but would be like getting stuck on the French transportation system (which, as de Man points out, uses the word *Correspondance* for changes of station within the system). All these tropes would not carry us away into the spiritual realm, but would be an infinite series of substitutions. The echoes would remain echoes and not merge into a profound unity.

If "Correspondances" is said to place man in the center of a universe that reflects him in harmony with all of nature, the poem "Obsession" places all of nature and the universe inside the psychology of man. Even the senses are projections. "Obsession" is the reading of "Correspondances" as hallucination. While "Correspondances" was entirely declarative, "Obsession" is almost entirely vocative. (Interestingly, de Man does not comment on another anomaly in the meaning of the word *comme*—the *comme* in "Obsession" that means "How!"—which is surprising, since it enacts precisely what he calls "the tropological transformation of analogy into apostrophe."[20]) Nature is addressed as a structure haunted by the subject's obsessions. Everywhere he looks, his own thoughts look back. For psychoanalytically inclined readers, and indeed for de Man himself in an earlier essay,[21] "Obsession" demystifies "Correspondances." There is no profound unity in the world, but only, as Lacan would say, paranoid knowledge.[22] But de Man sees the psychological gloss as another mystification, another anthropomorphism—the very anthropomorphic mystification that it is the duty of lyric, and of lyric pedagogy, to promote. "The lyric is not a genre, but one name among several to designate the defensive motion of understanding."[23] De Man concludes provocatively: "The resulting couple or pair of texts indeed becomes a model for the uneasy combination of funereal monumentality with paranoid fear that characterizes the hermeneutics and the pedagogy of lyric poetry."[24] What comes to be at stake, then, is lyric poetry itself as a poetry of the subject. By juxtaposing lyric and law in this essay, I am implicitly asking whether there is a relation between the "first person" (the grammatical "I") and the "constitutional person" (the subject of rights).

"Only a subject can understand a meaning," claims Lacan.[25] "Conversely, every phenomenon of meaning implies a subject."[26] What de Man seems to be arguing for here is the existence of a residue of language or rhetoric that exists neither inside nor outside the "phenomenon of meaning." Does lyric poetry try to give a psychological gloss to disruptions that are purely grammatical? Are the periodizations in literary history like "Parnassian" and "Romantic" merely names for rhetorical structures that are not historical? For de Man, "Obsession" loses the radical disruption of "Correspondances" by making enumeration into a symptom, which is more reassuring than endless repetition. It is as though de Man were saying that "Obsession," despite, or rather because, it is so psychologically bleak, falls back within the pleasure principle—that is, the psychological, the human—whereas "Correspondances," which seems so sunny, contains a disruption that goes beyond the pleasure principle. When de Man says that we can get "Obsession" from "Correspondances" but not the other way around, this is a way of repeating Freud's experience of the disruption of the pleasure principle in *Beyond the Pleasure Principle*, a study in which Freud grappled with the very limits of psychoanalysis.[27] Freud noticed that there were experiences or facts that seemed to contradict his notion of the primacy of the pleasure principle in human life (negative pleasures, the repetition compulsion, the death instinct). As Derrida has shown, Freud kept bringing the "beyond" back within explainability, but the "beyond" of Freud's theory kept popping up elsewhere.[28] He could, in effect, get the pleasure principle to explain its beyond, but not anticipate it. The beyond of the pleasure principle could only exist as a disruption.

De Man makes the surprising claim that "Correspondances" is *not* a lyric, but contains the entire possibility of lyric: " 'Obsession,' a text of recollection and elegiac mourning, *adds* remembrance to the flat surface of time in 'Correspondances'—produces at once a hermeneutic, fallacious, lyrical reading of the unintelligible."[29] The act of making intelligible, whether in the lyric or in the terminology of literary history, is for de Man at the end of the essay always an act of "resistance and nostalgia, at the furthest remove from the materiality of actual history."[30] This would mean that "actual history" is what escapes and resists intelligibility. Notice how de Man ends the essay:

> If mourning is called a "chambre d'éternel deuil où vibrent de vieux râles," then this pathos of terror states in fact the desired consciousness of eternity and of temporal harmony as voice and as song. True "mourn-

ing" is less deluded. The most *it* can do is to allow for non-comprehension and enumerate non-anthropomorphic, non-elegiac, non-celebratory, non-lyrical, non-poetic, that is to say, prosaic, or, better, *historical* modes of language power.[31]

Earlier in the essay, de Man had said of Nietzsche's general analysis of truth that "truth is always at the very least dialectical, the negative knowledge of error."[32] In another essay, de Man speaks of "literature as the place where this negative knowledge about the reliability of linguistic utterance is made available."[33] Negativity, then, is not an assertion of the negative, but a non-positivity within the possibility of assertion. The final sentence of "Anthropomorphism and Trope in the Lyric" is clearly a version of stating negative knowledge. But it is also a personification. "True 'mourning'" is said to be "less deluded."[34] Underlining the word *it* as the agent, he writes, "the most *it* can do is to allow for non-comprehension."[35] "True mourning" becomes the subject of this negative knowledge. The subjectivizations performed by lyric upon the unintelligible are here rejected, but by a personification of mourning. Is mourning—or rather, "true 'mourning'"—human or inhuman? Or is it what makes it impossible to close the gap between "man" and rhetoric? In other words, does this type of personification presuppose knowledge of human essence, or does it merely confer a kind of rhetorical agency? Is it anthropomorphic? Is there a difference between personification and anthropomorphism? Is the text stating its knowledge as if it were a human, or is it just performing the inescapability of the structures it is casting off? Has de Man's conclusion really eliminated anthropomorphism and reduced it to the trope of personification, or is anthropomorphism inescapable in the notion of mourning? Is this what lyric poetry—so often structured around the relation between loss and rhetoric—must decide? or finesse? The least we can say is that de Man has given the last word in his own text to a personification.

II

That which henceforth is to be "truth" is now fixed; that is to say, a
uniformly valid and binding designation of things is invented and the
legislature of language also gives the first laws of truth: since here, for the
first time, originates the contrast between truth and falsity. The liar uses
the valid designations, the words, in order to make the unreal appear as
real, e.g., he says, "I am rich," whereas the right designation of his state
would be "poor."—Nietzsche, "Truth and Falsity in an Ultramoral Sense"

The case of *Rowland v. California Men's Colony* is based on a provision in the U.S. legal code permitting a "person" to appear in court *in forma pauperis*. The relevant legislation reads in part:

> Any court of the United States may authorize the commencement, prosecution or defense of any suit, action, or proceeding, civil or criminal, or appeal therein, without prepayment of fees and costs or security therefor, by a person who makes affidavit that he is unable to pay such costs or give security therefor. (28 U.S.C. §1915(a) [1966])

In other words, a "person" may go to court without prepayment of fees if the "person" can demonstrate indigence. The question to be decided by the court is whether this provision applies to artificial persons like corporations or councils, or whether it is meant to apply only to individuals. In the case that led to *Rowland*, a council of prisoners in California attempted to bring suit against the correctional officers of the prison for the restoration of the practice of providing free cigarettes for indigent prisoners, which had been discontinued (*Rowland*, 194). They tried to sue in forma pauperis on the ground that the warden forbade the council to hold funds of its own. The district court found that they had not sufficiently proved indigence. They were allowed to appeal in forma pauperis in order to enable the court to decide whether the council, as an artificial legal person, is entitled to sue in forma pauperis. The appeals court decided that they were so entitled,[36] but this conflicted with the ruling by another circuit.[37] The Supreme Court in *Rowland* considered whether the provisions for proceeding in forma pauperis should apply only to natural persons or also to legal persons like associations and councils. The case is therefore about what a person is, and how you can tell the difference between a natural person and an artificial person.

Justice David Souter's majority opinion begins with something that in many ways resembles de Man's stutter of infinite enumeration. In order to find out what the legal meaning of "person" is, Souter turns to what is called the "Dictionary Act." The Dictionary Act gives instructions about how to read acts of Congress; it states: "In determining the meaning of any Act of Congress, unless the context indicates otherwise, the word[s] 'person' . . . include[s] corporations, companies, associations, firms, partnerships, societies, and joint stock companies, as well as individuals" (1 U.S.C. §1 [1985]). Thus, the word *person does* include artificial entities unless the context indicates otherwise. Next Souter asks, but what does *context* mean? He turns to *Webster's New International Dictionary*, in which he notes that it means "the part or parts of a discourse preceding or following a 'text' or passage or a word, or so intimately associated with it as to throw light on its meaning."[38] The context, then, is the surrounding words of the act. Of course, *Webster's* does offer a second meaning for the word *context*: "associated surroundings, whether material or mental"—a reference not to the surrounding text but to the broader reality or intentionality—but Souter dismisses this by saying, "we doubt that the broader sense applies here." Why? Because "if Congress had meant to point further afield, as to legislative history, for example, *it would have been natural* to use a more spacious phrase, like 'evidence of congressional intent,' in place of 'context'" (200, emphasis added).

The word *natural*, which is precisely at issue here—since the court is, after all, trying to find out whether the statute applies only to natural persons—is here applied to an artificial person, Congress, which is personified as having natural intentionality: "If Congress had meant . . ." The court's decision repeatedly relies upon this type of personification; it is as though Souter has to treat Congress as an entity with intentions, even natural intentions, in order to say that Congress could not have meant to include artificial entities in its ruling. There is a personification of an artificial entity, Congress, embedded in the very project of interpreting how far the law will allow for artificial entities to be considered persons.

Turning to the Dictionary Act for *person* and to *Webster's Dictionary* for *context*, Souter also notes that he has to define *indicates*. The difficulty of doing so pushes him into a volley of rhetorical flourishes: "A contrary 'indication' may raise a specter short of inanity, and with something less than syllogistic force" (201).

Indicates, it seems, means more than nonsense but less than logical necessity. In other words, the task of reading becomes an infinite regress of glossing terms that are themselves supposed to be determinants of meaning. De Man's linguistic stutter returns here as the repeated effort to throw language outside itself. We could read a text, this implies, if only we were sure of the meaning of the words *context* and *indicate*. But those are precisely the words that raise the question of meaning in its most general form—they cannot be glossed with any finality because they name the process of glossing itself.

Souter's text, in fact, is most anthropomorphic at those points where the infinite regress of language is most threatening. Congress is endowed with "natural" intentionality in order to sweep away the abyss of reference. Souter's dismissal of the prisoners' association as an "amorphous legal creature" (204) is the counterpart to the need to reinforce the anthropomorphizability of the artificial legal creature, Congress.[39] Congress, then, is perhaps an example of de Man's "proper name."

Souter's opinion proceeds to detail the reasons he thinks the in forma pauperis ruling should apply only to natural persons. He wonders: if an affidavit alleging poverty is required for a person to proceed in forma pauperis, then can an artificial entity plead poverty? Souter again turns to *Webster's Dictionary* to find that poverty is a human condition, defined as "wanting in material riches or goods; lacking in the comforts of life; needy" (203). Souter also refers to a previous ruling, which holds that poverty involves being unable to provide for the "necessities of life."[40] It is as though only natural persons can have "life," and that life is defined as the capacity to lack necessities and comforts. "Artificial entities may be insolvent," writes Souter, "but they are not well spoken of as 'poor'" (*Rowland*, 203). An artificial entity cannot lack the necessities and comforts of life. Only life can lack. The experience of lack differentiates natural persons from artificial persons. To lack is to be human. In a sense, we have returned to de Man's question about mourning. Is lack human, or just a structure? Whatever the case, the court holds that associations cannot be considered persons for the purpose of the in forma pauperis procedure.

The majority opinion garnered only four votes, however (194). A dissenting opinion, written by Justice Clarence Thomas, argues that there is no reason to restrict the broad definition of "person" to natural persons in this case (213). Thomas quotes the court's view of "poverty" as an exclusively "human condition" and comments:

> I am not so sure. "Poverty" may well be a human condition in its "primary sense," but I doubt that using the word in connection with an artificial entity departs in any significant way from settled principles of English usage. . . . Congress itself has used the word "poor" to describe entities other than natural persons, referring in at least two provisions of the United States Code to the world's "poorest countries"—a term that is used as a synonym for the least developed of the so-called "developing countries." (218–19)

Souter has glossed the word *poor* as though speakers of English could use it only literally. Thomas responds by including the figurative use of *poor* as included within normal usage. The boundaries between natural persons and artificial persons cannot be determined by usage because those boundaries have always already been blurred. In treating Congress as an entity with natural intentions, indeed, Souter has already shown how "natural" the artificial can be.

At another point, Thomas takes issue with Souter's discussion of a case in which an association or corporation *is* considered a person despite strong contextual indicators to the contrary. In the case of *Wilson v. Omaha Indian Tribe*,[41] it was decided that "white person" could include corporations because the "larger context" and "purpose" of the law was to protect Native Americans against non–Native American squatters, and that purpose would be frustrated if a "white person" could simply incorporate in order to escape the provision of the law.[42] Souter admits that "because a wholly legal creature has no color, and belongs to no race, the use of the adjective 'white' to describe a 'person' is one of the strongest contextual indicators imaginable that 'person' covers only individuals" (*Rowland*, 209). Thomas argues that if the court "was correct in holding that the statutory term 'white person' includes a corporation (because the 'context' does not 'indicate otherwise')—the conclusion that an association is a 'person' for *in forma pauperis* purposes is inescapable" (214 n1). Perhaps another inescapable conclusion is that despite its apparent reference to the physical body, the phrase "white person" is the name, not of a natural, but of a corporate person.

Thomas refutes the reasons Souter has given for finding that artificial entities are excluded from the in forma pauperis provision, noting that there may be sound policy reasons for wanting to exclude them, but that the law as written cannot be construed to have done so (215–16). The court's job, he writes, is not to make policy but to interpret a statute. "Congress has created a rule of statutory construction (an association is a 'person') and an exception to that rule (an association is not a 'person' if the 'context indicates otherwise'), but the Court has permitted the exception to devour the rule [a nice personification]" (222). Thomas thus argues that the court treats the rule as if artificial entities were excluded rather than included unless the context indicates otherwise. "Whatever 'unless the context indicates otherwise' means," writes Thomas, "it cannot mean 'unless there are sound policy reasons for concluding otherwise'" (214).

> Permitting artificial entities to proceed *in forma pauperis* may be unwise, and it may be an inefficient use of the Government's limited resources, but I see nothing in the text of the *in forma pauperis* statute indicating that Congress has chosen to exclude such entities from the benefits of that law. (215–16)

Thus Thomas's two conservative instincts are at war with each other: he would like the government not to spend its money, but he would also like to stick to the letter of the law.

The question of what counts as a juridical person has, in fact, been modified over time in the legal code. It was in 1871 (significantly, perhaps, at the beginning of the end of post–Civil War Reconstruction) that Congress first passed the so-called Dictionary Act, in which it stated that the word *person* "may extend and be applied to bodies politic and corporate."[43] More recently, the question of fetal personhood has been debated, not only in the *Roe v. Wade* decision, in which it was decided that a fetus was not a legal person,[44] but also in *Weaks v. Mounter*, in which it was decided that a fetus *was* a person who could sue for intrauterine injuries, but only after birth.[45] Recently, the question of granting patents for forms of life like oil slick–eating bacteria or genetically altered mice has raised the question of whether a hybrid between humans and close animal relatives can be patented.[46] And more recently, of course, the question of the ethics and legality of cloning humans has been raised.[47] The law has reached another crisis about the definition of "person." In an article on constitutional personhood, Michael Rivard writes:

> Current law allows patents for genetically-engineered animals but not for human beings. Humans are not patentable subject matter because patents are property rights, and the Thirteenth Amendment forbids any grant of property rights in a human being. Nevertheless, this exclusion for humans will prove impossible to maintain: within ten to thirty years, or perhaps sooner, advances in genetic engineering technology should allow scientists to intermingle the genetic material of humans and animals to produce human-animal hybrids. . . . It may soon be possible to patent—and to enslave—human-animal hybrids who think and feel like humans, but who lack constitutional protection under the Thirteenth Amendment.[48]

Recall that the Thirteenth Amendment is the amendment that abolishes slavery. The constitutional protection against slavery operates as a constraint on the patent office, but it does so in a paradoxical way. The fear of reinstituting something like slavery, or property in humans, is a reaction to, but also a sign of, what must be an ongoing research goal to come as close as possible to creating the ownable, enslavable human.[49]

Constitutional personhood has in fact often been defined in proximity to slavery. In the most notorious example, the *Dred Scott* case of 1857,[50] we find many of the same issues of legal standing, personhood, and interpretation that were present in *Rowland*. This case, too, is about who has the right to sue. In *Dred Scott* the operative word is *citizen* rather than *person*, but as Justice Roger Taney put it in his prefatory remarks, "The words 'people of the United States' and 'citizens' are synonymous terms, and mean the same thing" (*Dred*

Scott, 404). Many of the same issues of legal rights and protections, as well as legal interpretation, arise. Dred Scott, whose original legal status was that of a slave, was taken by his master to free territory. Upon his return to Missouri, he sued for his freedom, arguing that his stay in free territory made him free. Taney ruled not only that Scott was not free, but that he was not a citizen with the right to sue, and indeed that persons of African descent had no rights that the white man was bound to respect. Taney derives this opinion from the words of the Constitution and of the Declaration of Independence. He quotes the words of the Declaration:

> We hold these truths to be self-evident: that all men are created equal; that they are endowed by their Creator with certain inalienable rights; that among them is life, liberty, and the pursuit of happiness; that to secure these rights, governments are instituted, deriving their just powers from the consent of the governed. (410)

Then Taney goes on to say, "The general words above quoted would seem to embrace the whole human family, and if they were used in a similar instrument at this day would be so understood" (410). In other words, he sees as his task only to interpret the meaning of the law, not to bring it up to date, which would, in a sense, be a policy decision. He goes on to explain why the Declaration of Independence could not have meant what it says:

> It is too clear for dispute that the enslaved African race were not intended to be included and formed no part of the people who framed and adopted this Declaration; for if the language, as understood in that day, would embrace them, the conduct of the distinguished men who framed the Declaration of Independence would have been utterly and flagrantly inconsistent with the principles they asserted. . . . Yet the men who framed this Declaration were great men—high in literary acquirements, high in their sense of honor and incapable of asserting principles inconsistent with those on which they were acting. (410)

Thus, enslaved African Americans could not have been included among the people, because the framers were great men and could not have been inconsistent. Notice how literature is brought in to confirm their greatness: they were high in literary attainments; they did not use words lightly. The greatness of white men requires that they not be inconsistent. In order for the founding fathers to maintain their greatness, the African American has to have no rights. If the United States has reached a crisis over the rights of

Africans, it is more important to maintain the consistency of the founding fathers than to enact the literality of their words. The phrase "all men," like the word *man*, introduces a crisis or a stutter if it is opened as anything other than a given.

This split between the framers and their words—this advance of the words over their understood meaning—is also pointed out by Don Fehrenbacher in his book *Slavery, Law, and Politics*.[51] He (along with many others) notes that the Constitution never uses the word *slavery* even in the three clauses that apply to that institution, as if the framers obscurely knew that the institution would disappear. The most subtle sign of that nudging into disappearance is a revision of the Fugitive Slave Clause (Article IV, section 2, clause 3). Fehrenbacher writes:

> Perhaps most revealing of all was a last-minute revision of the fugitive slave clause. As it came from the committee of style, the clause began: "No person legally held to service or labour in one state, escaping into another, shall . . . be discharged from service. . . ." The revised version read: "No person held to service or labour in one state, under the laws thereof." Because of its contextual ambiguity, the word "legally" would have permitted the inference that the Constitution explicitly affirmed the legality of slavery. The framers, in shifting to the phrase "under the laws thereof," lent strong support to those anti-slavery spokesmen of a later day who would insist that slavery was without national existence and strictly the creature of local law.[52]

It is amazing what a difference such a small change can introduce, by shifting an implicit endorsement of the legality of slavery to a mere description of its legality in some states. Fehrenbacher ends his discussion by saying, "it is as though the framers were half-consciously trying to frame two constitutions, one for their own time and the other for the ages, with slavery viewed bifocally—that is, plainly visible at their feet, but disappearing when they lifted their eyes."[53] A written text of law can thus contain a double intention, the trace of a compromise between differing opinions. No wonder interpreting the law's intention is so complicated. That intention can always already be multiple. The distinction Thomas made between interpreting the law and making policy cannot hold if the law's ambiguity allows for the possibility that the policy it governs will change.

III

The "inhuman" is not some kind of mystery, or some kind of secret; the inhuman is: linguistic structures, the play of linguistic tensions, linguistic events that occur, possibilities which are inherent in language— independently of any intent or any drive or any wish or any desire we might have. . . . If one speaks of the inhuman, the fundamental non-human character of language, one also speaks of the fundamental non-definition of the human as such.
—Paul de Man, *Conclusions on Walter Benjamin's "The Task of the Translator"*

Only smoking distinguishes humans from the rest of the animals.
—Anonymous (quoted in Richard Klein, *Cigarettes Are Sublime*)

The case of *Rowland v. California Men's Colony* was ostensibly about whether a council of inmates could sue prison officials in forma pauperis to get their cigarettes back. The details of the case seemed irrelevant to the question of whether an artificial person has the right to sue in forma pauperis. Yet perhaps some of those details deserve note. Is it relevant that the suit to decide this question was brought by a council of inmates? The phenomenon of the inmate civil suit has grown to the point where the case law may very well be transformed by it. In a 1995 study of inmate suits in California, it was reported that "for the last fourteen years at least, the federal courts have faced a growing caseload and workload challenge posed by inmate cases. . . . By 1992, these filings numbered nearly 30,000, and constituted 13% of the courts' total civil case filings nationwide."[54] The majority of these suits are filed in forma pauperis.[55] The Supreme Court's decision may well have been affected by what Thomas calls "policy considerations" (*Rowland*, 217).

If prisoners are affecting the nature of civil proceedings, they are also, at least figuratively, affecting theoretical discussions about the nature of rational choice and the evolution of cooperation. The celebrated "Prisoner's dilemma" has been central to questions of self-interest and social goods since it was introduced by Albert Tucker in 1950.[56] Max Black has even entitled his discussion of these issues "The 'Prisoner's Dilemma' and the Limits of Rationality."[57] Why is it that the theoretical study of rational choice has recourse to "man" conceived as a prisoner? Does this have anything to do with the poets' tendency to see the sonnet form as a prison?

And is it by chance that *Rowland* is about cigarettes? On the one hand, it seems paradoxical that the council has to demonstrate its indigence in order to pursue its suit against the prison directors for depriving them of cigarettes;

in prisons, cigarettes function as a form of currency. On the other hand, it seems fitting that the personhood of the association is the counterpart to the humanity of the inmates, which, as common wisdom (quoted above, second epigraph) would have it, is demonstrated by the act of smoking. The prisoners would thus, in a very attenuated way, be suing for their humanity. As Richard Klein has wittily shown, smoking serves no function other than to enact a structure of desire—of human desire for self-transcendence, for repetition, for bodily experience corresponding to something other than the "necessities of life" required for existence alone: in short, desire for the sublime.[58]

The sublimity of cigarettes has become increasingly imperceptible in the United States, with the rise of smoking bans and health warnings, but Klein makes it clear that cigarettes were always good because they were bad. "Cigarettes are bad. That is why they are good—not good, not beautiful, but sublime."[59] They were not, in fact, always the un-American objects they appear to be today: "Whenever the society needed more soldiers . . . smoking cigarettes changed its value and became not only laudatory but patriotic."[60] In addition, cigarettes occupy a strange niche with respect to the U.S. government. Recent debates about whether or not nicotine is a drug that should be regulated by the Food and Drug Administration (FDA) have been conducted on the assumption that the FDA, an agency of the executive branch of government, is the appropriate body to deal with this vexed question. But in fact, as John Jevicky has argued, Congress has repeatedly reserved for itself the right to regulate tobacco products, except insofar as they are labeled for a medicinal purpose.[61]

Both a drug and not a drug, both legal and banned, a soldier's comfort and a veteran's cancer, the relation between cigarettes and "natural persons" raises the question of what "natural" means. But cigarettes have raised the question of the rights of "corporate persons" in interesting ways, too, through recent wrongful death suits against tobacco companies. In attempting to keep the records of damaging research about nicotine out of the courts by appealing to attorney–client privilege, the defendant corporations are testing the limits of corporate personhood.[62] In other words, tobacco is located precisely at crisis points in the definition of both natural and artificial persons.

If anthropomorphism relies on the givenness of "man" for its rhetorical effect, tobacco seems well placed both to instate and to undercut what counts as "human." Indeed, in one of Klein's most powerful and sweeping observations, tobacco, a Native American product, is what brought modern Western man into being:

The introduction of tobacco into Europe in the sixteenth century corresponded with the arrival of the Age of Anxiety, the beginning of modern consciousness that accompanied the invention and universalization of printed books, the discovery of the New World, the development of rational, scientific methods, and the concurrent loss of medieval theological assurances. The Age of Anxiety gave itself an incomparable and probably indispensable remedy in the form of tobacco; it was an antidote brought by Columbus from the New World against the anxiety that his discoveries occasioned in the Eurocentered consciousness of Western culture, confronted by the unsuspected countenance of a great unknown world contiguous with its own. The paradoxical experience of smoking tobacco, with its contradictory physical effects, its poisonous taste and unpleasant pleasure, was enthusiastically taken up by modernity as a drug for easing the anxiety arising from the shock of successive assaults on old certainties and the prospect of greater unknowns.[63]

In the article cited above by Michael Rivard, "Toward a General Theory of Constitutional Personhood," the drive to formulate a clear-cut definition of what would count as a constitutional person appears to be operating under the imperative precisely to counter the "assaults on old certainties and greater unknowns" caused by the possibility of transgenic humanoid species. But in its nearly one hundred pages of argument for an ironclad "personhood presumption theory," the fundamental definition of the constitutional person turns out very much to resemble de Man's stutter or Souter's abyss of reference. Rivard quotes Daniel Dennett quoting Harry Frankfurt elucidating the fundamental characteristic of self-awareness:

> Besides wanting and choosing and being moved *to do* this or that, men may also want to have (or not to have) certain desires and motives. They are capable of wanting to be different, in their preferences and purposes, from what they are.[64]

This is paradoxical enough to be true (and reminiscent of Lacan's theory of the mirror stage[65]), but it is hard to see how the capacity for self-difference can be tested and legislated as a basis for constitutional personhood.

In Rivard's view, "corporations would be presumed constitutional *non*persons," especially for liberty-related rights, unless the corporation could rebut its nonperson status by showing specific natural persons "who would be affected if the corporation were denied these rights."[66] This is the opposite of the Dictionary Act, which considers a corporation a person "unless the context indicates otherwise." Rivard is arguing for the rights of new biological species who can pass the "self-awareness test" (wanting to be different from what one is), and he claims that corporations, by their nature, do not pass this test.

But the question of the nature of corporations as persons has never been a simple one, as Rivard admits. Gregory A. Mark has outlined in detail the history of corporate personhood.[67] The relation between corporations and the natural persons who compose them has grown more complicated over time. In most discussions of the matter, it is the "natural" person that functions as the known quantity, and the "artificial" that is either just an "aggregate" of natural persons, or a fiction created by the state, or a mere metaphor, or actually resembles (is *like*, to return to the Baudelairean word) a natural person in that it has a "will" of its own. Such a corporate will is a form of agency separate from that of the natural corporators, who exist behind the "veil" of the corporation.[68]

Much of Mark's article concerns the exact rhetorical valence of this personification:

> American law has always recognized that people's activities could be formally organized and that the resulting organizations could be dealt with as units. Personification, however, is important because it became far more than a quaint device making it possible for the law to deal with organized business entities. In American legal and economic history, personification has been vital because it (1) implies a single and unitary source of control over the collective property of the corporation's members, (2) defines, encourages, and legitimates the corporation as an autonomous, creative, self-directed economic being, and (3) captures rights, ultimately even constitutional rights, for corporations thereby giving corporate property unprecedented protection from the state.[69]

Mark takes seriously the role of language in the evolving history of the corporation. Philosophers and legislators have gone to great lengths to minimize the rhetorical damage, to eliminate personification as far as possible, but he asserts that it is not just a figure of speech to speak of a corporation's "mind," or even its "life." "Practical experience, not just anthropomorphism, fixed the corporate mind in the management hierarchy."[70] The corporation resembles a human being in its capacity to "take resolves in the midst of conflicting motives," to "will change."[71] Yet the analogy is not perfect. The corporation, for example, unlike its corporators, is potentially immortal. The effect of personification appears to derive its rhetorical force from the ways in which the corporation *resembles* a natural person, yet the corporation's immortality in no way diminishes its personification. When Mark says that it is "not just anthropomorphism" that underpins the agency of the corporation,[72] he still implies that we can know what anthropomorphism is. But his final sentence stands this presupposition on its head. Far from claiming that a corporation's characteristics are derived from a knowable human essence, Mark suggests that what have been claimed to be the essential characteristics of man (especially "economic man") have in fact been borrowed from the nature of the corporation:

> Personification with its roots in historic theological disputes and modern business necessity, had proved to be a potent symbol to legitimate the autonomous business corporation and its management. Private property rights had been transferred to associations, associations had themselves become politically legitimate, and the combination had helped foster modern political economy. The corporation, once the derivative tool of the state, had become its rival, and the successes of the autonomous corporate management turned the basis for belief in an individualist conception of property on its head. The protests of modern legists notwithstanding, the business corporation had become the quintessential economic man.[73]

Theories of rationality, naturalness, and the "good," presumed to be grounded in the nature of "man," may in reality be taking their notions of human essence not from "natural man" but from business corporations.

Ambivalence about personification, especially the personification of abstractions, has in fact permeated not only legal but also literary history. Nervousness about the agency of the personified corporation echoes the nervousness Enlightenment writers felt about the personifications dreamed up by the poets. As Steven Knapp puts it in his book *Personification and the Sublime*:

> Allegorical personification—the endowing of metaphors with the agency of literal persons—was only the most obvious and extravagant instance of what Enlightenment writers perceived, with a mixture of admiration and uneasiness, as the unique ability of poetic genius to give the force of literal reality to figurative "inventions." More important than the incongruous presence of such agents was their contagious effect on the ostensibly literal agents with which they interacted.[74]

The uncanniness of the personification, then, was derived from its way of putting in question what the "natural" or the "literal" might be.

What the personification of the corporation ends up revealing, paradoxically enough, is that there is nothing "natural" about the natural person often taken as its model. The natural person, far from being a "given," is always the product of a theory of what the given is. This point may be made more clearly through an extreme version of corporate personhood. In a study of corporate rights, Meir Dan-Cohen goes so far as to create the notion of a "personless corporation," a corporate "person" entirely controlled by computers, which would nevertheless still possess a "will" and a "personhood" of its own.[75] Similarly, we might now ask how it has come to seem "natural" that the "natural person" with which the corporate person is compared is somehow always a "genderless person"; that *un*natural genderless person who serves to ground both anthropomorphism and rational choice.

We have finally come back to the question of whether there is a difference between anthropomorphism and personification, which arose at the end of the discussion of the essay by Paul de Man. It can now be seen that everything hangs on this question. Anthropomorphism, unlike personification, depends on the givenness of the essence of the human; the mingling of personifications on the same footing as "real" agents threatens to make the uncertainty about what humanness is come to consciousness. Perhaps the loss of unconsciousness about the lack of humanness is what de Man was calling "true 'mourning.'"[76] Perhaps the "fallacious lyrical reading of the unintelligible" is exactly what legislators count on lyric poetry to provide: the assumption that the human *has been* or *can be* defined. The human can then be presupposed without the question of its definition being raised as a question—legal or otherwise. Thus the poets truly would be, as Shelley claimed, the "unacknowledged legislators of the world,"[77] not because they covertly determine policy, but because it is somehow necessary and useful that there *be* a powerful, presupposable, unacknowledgment. But the very rhetorical sleight of hand that would instate such an unacknowledgment is indistinguishable from the rhetorical structure that would empty it. Lyric and law are two of the most powerful discourses that exist along the fault line of this structure.

NOTES

"Anthropomorphism in Lyric and Law." Reprinted by permission of the *Yale Journal of Law & the Humanities* 10, no. 2 (2013): 549–74.

1. See, for example, Richard A. Posner, *Law and Literature: A Misunderstood Relation* (Cambridge, MA: Harvard University Press, 1988); Richard H.

Weisberg, *The Failure of the Word: The Protagonist as Lawyer in Modern Fiction* (New Haven, CT: Yale University Press, 1984); Peter Brooks, "Storytelling without Fear? Confession in Law and Literature," *Yale Journal of Law and the Humanities* 8, no. 1 (1996): 1–29; Robert Weisberg, "The Law-Literature Enterprise," *Yale Journal of Law and the Humanities* 1, no. 1 (1988): 1–68; Robin West, "Authority, Autonomy, and Choice: The Role of Consent in the Moral and Political Vision of Franz Kafka and Richard Posner," *Harvard Law Review* 99, no. 2 (1985): 384–428. But see Thomas Grey, "Steel against Intimation: The Motive for Metaphor of Wallace Stevens, Esq.," *Yale Journal of Law and the Humanities* 2, no. 2 (1990): 231–52, and Margaret Jane Radin, "After the Final No There Comes a Yes: A Law Teacher's Report," *Yale Journal of Law and the Humanities* 2, no. 2 (1990): 253–66, for an interesting discussion of Wallace Stevens, as well as the more extended treatment of Wallace Stevens in Thomas Grey, *The Wallace Stevens Case: Law and the Practice of Poetry* (Cambridge, MA: Harvard University Press, 1991).

2. William Wordsworth's sonnet "Nuns Fret Not at Their Convent's Narrow Room," contains the lines, "In truth the prison, unto which we doom / Ourselves, no prison is: and hence to me, / In sundry moods, 'twas pastime to be bound / Within the Sonnet's scanty plot of ground." William Wordsworth, "Nuns Fret Not at Their Convent's Narrow Room," in *Wordsworth Selected Poetry and Prose*, ed. Geoffrey H. Hartman (New York: NAL, 1970), 169.

3. John Keats's sonnet on the sonnet begins, "If by dull rhymes our English must be chained, / And, like Andromeda, the sonnet sweet / Fettered." John Keats, "On the Sonnet," in *The Selected Poetry of John Keats*, ed. Paul de Man (New York: NAL, 1966), 264.

4. One of several poems by Baudelaire entitled "Spleen" describes a mood produced by or analogized to a rainy day: "Quand la pluie étalant ses immenses traînées / D'unc vaste prison imite les barreaux." Charles Baudelaire, "Spleen," in *Oeuvres complètes*, ed. Claude Pichois (Paris: Gallimard, 1975), 1:75.

5. For a suggestive discussion of what it means for a text to obey the law of genre, see Jacques Derrida, "The Law of Genre," in *Acts of Literature*, ed. Derek Attridge (New York: Routledge, 1991), 220.

6. Paul de Man, "Anthropomorphism and Trope in the Lyric," in *The Rhetoric of Romanticism* (New York: Columbia University Press, 1984), 239–62.

7. De Man, "Anthropomorphism and Trope in the Lyric," 262.

8. John Keats, "Ode on a Grecian Urn," in *Selected Poetry*, 252, 253. This allusion to Keats's "Ode on a Grecian Urn" stands in for the premise of the compatibility of literary aesthetics with linguistic structures, and of linguistic structures with perceptual or intuitive knowledge, that de Man is often at pains to contest. See his remarks on the pedagogical model of the *trivium* in Paul de Man, "The Resistance to Theory," in *The Resistance to Theory* (Minneapolis: University of Minnesota Press, 1986), 3–20.

9. De Man, "Anthropomorphism and Trope in the Lyric," 239.

10. Friedrich Nietzsche, "Truth and Falsity in an Ultramoral Sense," in *Critical Theory since Plato*, ed. Hazard Adams (Fort Worth: Harcourt Brace Jovanovich, 1992), 634–39. If the Keats poem asserts that aesthetic and epistemological structures are compatible, Nietzsche's text, for de Man, is a parody of that claim.

11. Nietzsche, Truth and Falsity in an Ultramoral Sense," 636.

12. De Man, "Anthropomorphism and Trope in the Lyric," 240.

13. De Man, "Anthropomorphism and Trope in the Lyric," 241.

14. De Man, "Anthropomorphism and Trope in the Lyric," 241.

15. The translations are mine, made for the purpose of bringing out those aspects of the poems that are relevant to my discussion.

16. Baudelaire, "Correspondances," in *Oeuvres complètes*, 1:11.

17. Baudelaire, "Obsession," in *Oeuvres complètes*, 1:75–76.

18. De Man, "Anthropomorphism and Trope in the Lyric," 249.

19. De Man, "Anthropomorphism and Trope in the Lyric," 249.

20. De Man, "Anthropomorphism and Trope in the Lyric," 261.

21. See Paul de Man, "Allegory and Irony in Baudelaire," in *Romanticism and Contemporary Criticism*, ed. E. S. Burt et al. (Baltimore: Johns Hopkins University Press, 1993), 101–19. This essay is part of the Gauss Seminar given by de Man in 1967.

22. Lacan writes, "What I have called paranoic [paranoid] knowledge is shown, therefore, to correspond in its more or less archaic forms to certain critical moments that mark the history of man's mental genesis, each representing a stage in objectifying identification." Jacques Lacan, "Aggressivity in Psychoanalysis," in *Ecrits*, trans. Alan Sheridan (New York: W. W. Norton, 1977), 17.

23. De Man, "Anthropomorphism and Trope in the Lyric," 261.

24. De Man, "Anthropomorphism and Trope in the Lyric," 259.

25. Lacan, "Aggressivity in Psychoanalysis," 9.

26. Lacan, "Aggressivity in Psychoanalysis," 9.

27. See Sigmund Freud, "Beyond the Pleasure Principle," in *The Standard Edition of the Complete Psychological Works of Sigmund Freud*, ed. and trans. James Strachey (New York: W. W. Norton, 1953), 18:3–64.

28. See Jacques Derrida, "To Speculate—on 'Freud,'" in *The Post Card*, trans. Alan Bass (Chicago: University of Chicago Press, 1987), 257–409.

29. De Man, "Anthropomorphism and Trope in the Lyric," 262.

30. De Man, "Anthropomorphism and Trope in the Lyric," 262.

31. De Man, "Anthropomorphism and Trope in the Lyric," 262.

32. De Man, "Anthropomorphism and Trope in the Lyric," 242.

33. De Man, "The Resistance to Theory," 10.

34. De Man, "Anthropomorphism and Trope in the Lyric," 262.

35. De Man, "Anthropomorphism and Trope in the Lyric," 262.

36. See *California Men's Colony v. Rowland*, 939 F.2d 854 (9th Cir. 1991), rev., 506 U.S. 194 (1993).
37. See *FDM Mfg. Co. v. Scottsdale Ins. Co.*, 855 F.2d 213 (5th Cir. 1988).
38. *Webster's New International College Dictionary*, 2nd ed. (Springfield, MA: Merriam-Webster, 1942), 576, quoted in *Rowland*, 199.
39. In a response to the present essay when it was delivered at the Yale Law School, Shoshana Felman made the brilliant suggestion that Souter would have wanted to rewrite Baudelaire's "Correspondances" as: "Le Congres est un temple où de vivants pilliers laissent parfois sortir de confuses paroles . . ." The neoclassical, Parnassian architecture of official Washington, DC, and the common metaphorical expression "pillars of the community" add piquancy to this suggestion.
40. *Adkins v. E.I. Dupont de Nemours & Co.*, 335 U.S. 331, 339 (1948).
41. *Wilson v. Omaha Indian Tribe*, 442 U.S. 653 (1979). Both Souter and Thomas discuss *Wilson* in their *Rowland* opinions. See *Rowland*, 209 and 214 n.1.
42. *Rowland*, 214 n.1 (discussing *Wilson*, 725).
43. Act of Feb. 25, 1871, ch. 71, §2, 16 Stat. 431.
44. See *Roe v. Wade*, 410 U.S. 113 (1973).
45. See *Weaks v. Mounter*, 493 P.2d 1307 (Nev. 1972).
46. In *Diamond v. Chakrabarty*, 447 U.S. 303 (1980), the Supreme Court ruled that a "live, human-made micro-organism is patentable subject matter." In 1989, Harvard University received a patent for a genetically altered mouse or "oncomouse." See Sheldon Krimsky, *Biotechnics and Society: The Rise of Industrial Genetics* (Westport, CT: Praeger, 1991), 44–45; Ned Hettinger, "Patenting Life: Biotechnology, Intellectual Property, and Environmental Ethics," *Boston College Environmental Affairs Law Review* 22, no. 2 (1995): 267–305.
47. See Gina Kolata, "Scientist Clones Human Embryos and Creates an Ethical Challenge," *New York Times*, October 24, 1993, A1.
48. Michael D. Rivard, "Toward a General Theory of Constitutional Personhood: A Theory of Constitutional Personhood for Transgenic Humanoid Species," UCLA *Law Review* 39, no. 5 (1992): 1428–29.
49. See A. Leon Higginbotham Jr. and Barbara Kopytoff, "Property First, Humanity Second: The Recognition of the Slave's Human Nature in Virginia Civil Law," *Ohio State Law Journal* 50, no. 3 (1989): 520 ("The humanity of the slave, requiring that he be treated with the care due other humans and not like other forms of property, became *part* of the owner's property rights.").
50. *Dred Scott v. Sandford*, 60 U.S. (19 How.) 393 (1857).
51. Don E. Fehrenbacher, *Slavery, Law, and Politics: The* Dred Scott *Case in Historical Perspective* (New York: Oxford University Press, 1981).
52. Fehrenbacher, *Slavery, Law, and Politics*, 14.
53. Fehrenbacher, *Slavery, Law, and Politics*, 15.

54. Kim Mueller, "Inmates' Civil Rights Cases and the Federal Courts: Insights Derived from a Field Research Project in the Eastern District of California," *Creighton Law Review* 28 (1995): 1258–59. In the Eastern District of California, inmates' civil rights actions constituted nearly 30 percent of the case filings. See Fehrenbacher, *Slavery, Law, and Politics* (California Men's Colony is not in the Eastern District; it is in San Luis Obispo, in the Central District).

55. See Mueller, "Inmates' Civil Rights Cases and the Federal Courts," 1276, 1281.

56. See Ronald J. Gilson and Robert H. Mnookin, "Disputing through Agents: Cooperation and Conflict between Lawyers in Litigation," *Columbia Law Review* 94 (1994): 514, n15 (discussing how Tucker created the original version of the game).

57. Max Black, "The 'Prisoner's Dilemma' and the Limits of Rationality," in *Perplexities: Rational Choice, the Prisoner's Dilemma, Metaphor, Poetic Ambiguity, and Other Puzzles* (Ithaca, NY: Cornell University Press, 1990); see also Robert Axelrod, *The Evolution of Cooperation* (New York: Basic Books, 1984).

58. See Richard Klein, *Cigarettes Are Sublime* (Durham, NC: Duke University Press, 1993). Klein notes (8), incidentally, that Baudelaire is one of the first French writers to use the word *cigarette* in print (in his *Salons de 1848*).

59. Klein, *Cigarettes Are Sublime*, 2.

60. Klein, *Cigarettes Are Sublime*, 4.

61. See John E. Jevicky, "FDA's Regulation of Tobacco Products: A Flagrant Disregard of Congressional Intent," *North Kentucky University Law Review* 24 (1997): 535–51. Jevicky explains: "In 1906, Congress's enactment of the Pure Food and Drugs Act gave no authority over tobacco products to FDA's predecessor, the Bureau of Chemistry. In 1914, the Bureau of Chemistry decided that, even though smoking was already widespread, tobacco not labeled for a medicinal purpose did not fall within the jurisdiction of the Pure Food & Drugs Act" (537). The analogy with recent discussions of the legality of marijuana is striking.

62. See Clay Calvert, "Smoking Out Big Tobacco," *Pepperdine Law Review* 24 (1997): 391–453; Christine Hatfield, "The Privilege Doctrines—Are They Just Another Discovery Tool Utilized by the Tobacco Industry to Conceal Damaging Information?," *Pace Law Review* 16 (1996): 525.

63. Klein, *Cigarettes Are Sublime*, 27.

64. Rivard, "Toward a General Theory," 1486, quoting Daniel Dennett, *Brainstorms: Philosophical Essays on Mind and Psychology* (Cambridge, MA: MIT Press, 1981), 281, quoting Harry Frankfurt, "Freedom of the Will and the Concept of a Person," in *What Is a Person?*, ed. M. Goodman (Clifton, NJ: Humana Press, 1988), 127.

65. See Lacan, "The Mirror Stage as Formative of the Function of the I as Revealed in Psychoanalytic Experience," in *Écrits*, 1.

66. Rivard, "Toward a General Theory," 1501–2.

67. See Gregory A. Mark, "The Personification of the Business Corporation in American Law," *University of Chicago Law Review* 54 (1987): 1441.

68. The history of theories of corporate personhood is summarized in Mark, "The Personification of the Business Corporation in American Law," 1441–83, and in Rivard, "Toward a General Theory," 1450–65. The term *veil* used to refer to the personified appearance of the corporation has long been used in rhetorical treatises to describe the nature of allegorical representation. See, for example, Pierre Fontanier, *Les Figures du Discours* (Paris: Flammarion, 1968). Allegory "consists of a proposition with a double meaning, literal and spiritual at once, through which one presents a thought under the image of another thought, capable of rendering it more striking or more perceptive than if it had been presented *without any sort of veil.*" Fontanier, *Les Figures du Discours*, 144 (translation mine; emphasis added). In *Rowland*, Souter speaks of "piercing the veil" of the association in order to see the individuals who compose it. See *Rowland*, 194, 195, 207. A veil, then, is a sign in both legal and literary language that a figurative dimension must be taken into consideration.

69. Mark, "The Personification of the Business Corporation," 1443.

70. Mark, "The Personification of the Business Corporation," 1475.

71. Mark, "The Personification of the Business Corporation," 1476.

72. Mark, "The Personification of the Business Corporation," 1475.

73. Mark, "The Personification of the Business Corporation," 1482–83.

74. Steven Knapp, *Personification and the Sublime: Milton to Coleridge* (Cambridge, MA: Harvard University Press, 1985), 2.

75. Meir Dan-Cohen, *Rights, Persons, and Organizations: A Legal Theory for Bureaucratic Society* (Berkeley: University of California Press, 1986), 46–51.

76. De Man, "Anthropomorphism and Trope in the Lyric," 262.

77. Percy Bysshe Shelley, "A Defense of Poetry," in *Critical Theory Since Plato*, ed. Hazard Adams (Fort Worth: Harcourt Brace Jovanovich, 1992), 529.

CHAPTER 18

Using People
Kant with Winnicott

Using people, transforming others into a means for obtaining an end for oneself, is generally considered the very antithesis of ethical behavior. And with good reason. Faced with the violence of colonial, sexual, and even episte-mological appropriation, ethical theorists have sought to replace domination with respect, knowledge with responsibility. But it often seems as though a thought that begins in intersubjectivity or mutuality ends up sounding like a mere defense of the Other against the potential violence of the Subject. All *too* often, such theorists conclude, as does the following translator of Emman-uel Levinas: "Ontology becomes indebtedness to what is, a quiet listening vigilant against its own interference, cautious of its own interventions, careful not to disturb."[1] But if ethics is defined in relation to the potentially violent excesses of the subject's power, then that power is in reality being presup-posed and reinforced in the very attempt to undercut it. What is being denied from the outset is the subject's *lack* of power, its vulnerability and dependence. Respect and distance are certainly better than violence and appropriation, but is ethics only a form of restraint? In this chapter I take for granted the necessity of critiques of the imperial subject, but I would nevertheless like to question the model of intactness on which such critiques usually rely. Might there not, at least on the psychological level, be another way to use people?

The classic formulation of the stricture against using people is given in Kant's Second Critique: "It follows of itself that, in the order of ends, man (and every rational being) is an end-in-himself, i.e., he is never to be used merely as a means for someone (even for God) without at the same time being himself an end. . . . This moral law is founded on the autonomy of his will as a free will, which by its universal laws must necessarily be able to agree with that to which it subjects itself."[2] Kant, of course, warns against treating people as a means *without* also treating them as an end, which is not the same as excluding using people altogether. But using people has nevertheless acquired an entirely negative connotation ("I feel so *used!*").

Using people can be understood simply as exploitation, as when a person with power or resources makes use of the undercompensated labor of others to increase his or her power or resources. Or, interpersonally, using people is commonly associated with a scenario in which one person professes to be interested in another person in order to obtain something for him- or herself. Less instrumentally but just as commonly, people can also use other people in the service of their own narcissistic consolidation, as when, in Heinz Kohut's words, "the expected control over the narcissistically cathected object . . . is closer to the concept which a grownup has of himself and of the control which he expects over his own body and mind than to the grownup's experience of others and of his control over them (which generally leads to the result that the object of such narcissistic 'love' feels oppressed and enslaved by the subject's expectations and demands)."[3] The literary elaboration of this narcissistic enslavement takes the form of idealization and thingification, from Pygmalion's beloved ivory girl to the female bodies turned to milk, cherries, pearls, and gold through the magic of poetry. One of the founding insights of feminist criticism has been to point out that the idealized, beloved woman is often described as an object, a thing, rather than a subject. But perhaps the problem with being used arises from an inequality of power rather than from something inherently unhealthy about *willingly* playing the role of thing. Indeed, what if the capacity to become a subject were something that could best be *learned* from an object? Not an idealized object but rather, say, a smelly blanket with a frayed edge?

That smelly blanket has played a starring role in the theory of transitional objects worked out by D. W. Winnicott. The objectness of the object is fundamental to its function, yet Winnicott is careful to caution against simply equating the transitional object with the blanket, thumb, or teddy bear that may take on this role. Transitional objects, he explains, are the first "not-me" possessions, objects that are neither "internal" to the baby (that is, hallucinatory, like, at first, the mother's breast) nor "external," like reality, of which at first the baby has no knowledge, but something in between. The transitional object is not a narcissistic object—it does not offer an image of body whole-ness like the image in Lacan's mirror. It is not an image but a thing.[4] The most valuable property of the transitional object is probably its lack of perfection, its irrelevance to the question of perfection.

As its name implies, the transitional object is a "between." It is often associated with the blanket or teddy bear to which the child grows attached, but Winnicott tries to keep opening a different space between—between, for example, the thumb and the teddy bear. Winnicott's task is to put some-thing into words that is hard to put into words. In the introduction to *Playing and Reality*, he explains that what he is trying to keep hold of is not an object but a paradox:

> It is now generally recognized, I believe, that what I am referring to in this part of my work is not the cloth or the teddy bear that the baby uses—not so much the object used as the use of the object. I am draw-ing attention to the paradox involved in the use by the infant of what I have called the transitional object. My contribution is to ask for a par-adox to be accepted and tolerated and respected, and for it not to be resolved. By flight to split-off intellectual functioning it is possible to resolve the paradox, but the price of this is the loss of the value of the paradox itself. This paradox, once accepted and tolerated, has value for every human individual who is not only alive and living in this world but who is also capable of being infinitely enriched by exploitation of the cultural link with the past and with the future.[5]

This is a typical move in Winnicott's text: going within a sentence or two from establishing the finest possible distinction to making the broadest pos-sible cultural claims. This is indeed a huge claim, that accepting and tolerat-ing the still-not-really-explained paradox opens the way for all of cultural life. The paradox of the transitional object functions like the transitional object itself, as a domain of play and illusion that allows an interpreter, like an infant, to accept and tolerate frustration and reality. To intellectualize too soon is here to think of the transitional object as an object rather than a paradox.

Winnicott's theory of transitional phenomena is itself a transitional phe-nomenon in theory. He describes development as having a beginning, a middle, and an end, and says that theorists have not said enough about the middle. Much of his writing involves making the right space for itself ("prepare the ground for my own positive contribution")—situating exactly what he is saying between two things he is not saying. This expanded middle is where Winnicott's unparalleled subtlety is located, between two crudenesses—the crudeness of the way in which he describes the mother's task of being perfectly available and then optimally frustrating as a task that is only seen from the infant's point of view, and the way he privileges heterosexual reproductivity as a sign of adult health (the blightedness, for example, of those whom he pronounces "not married"). Winnicott's beginning and end shed no new analytical light on normative stereotypes of the good mother and the healthy adult (happily married with children). But in his own domain—somewhere between where the good mother becomes the good enough mother and where the healthy adult can play—he rises to the occasion to "put into words" something that ordinary language has to stretch to render.

"I hope it will be understood that I am not referring exactly to the little child's teddy bear or to the infant's first use of the fist (thumb, fingers). I am not specifically studying the first object of object-relationships. I am concerned with the first possession, and with the intermediate area between the subjective and that which is objectively perceived" (3). Winnicott says he is "reluctant to give examples." The naming and exemplifying functions of language are the ones to hold in abeyance, to make room for something not-to-be-formulated. "Of the transitional object it can be said that it is a matter of agreement between us and the baby that we will never ask the question: 'Did you conceive of this or was it presented to you from without?' The important point is that no decision on this point is expected. The question is not to be formulated" (12). This, then, is the paradox, which he explains in a later essay in similar terms: "The baby creates the object, but the object was there waiting to be created and to become a cathected object" (89). Winnicott explicitly envisions the transitional object as a kind of navel of the arts: he includes not only objects but also words, patterns, tunes, and mannerisms in his lists of things that can function as transitional objects.

This paradox of unlocatability is also, in fact, similar to the paradox of the moral law in Kant, as stated in a note to the *Foundation of the Metaphysics of Morals*: "The only object of respect is the law, and indeed only the law which we impose on ourselves and yet recognize as necessary in itself."[6] This is not to say that the moral law *is* the transitional object, but only to suggest that it manifests the same kind of paradox.

The function of the transitional object in Winnicott, then, is to open a space for experience: the transitional object is that through which the baby gains experience of a state between the illusion of the mother's total adaptation to needs and reality's total indifference to them. The object helps the baby learn to tolerate frustration, loss of omnipotence, separation.

The transitional object is not only something that cannot be understood in terms of a dichotomy between subject and object, since it helps bring that dichotomy into being, but is also something about which there is agreement as to what will not be asked. A space is made for the object within language. The transitional object is part of a contract of nonformulation. The apparent one-on-one relation between baby and thing is set in a social, almost legal, dimension agreed to by adults. In one of Winnicott's many lists, this one called a "Summary of Special Qualities in the Relationship," the first special quality is a question of rights: "The infant assumes rights over the object." I'd like to look closely at this list of qualities. Listen for the grammatical roles of the infant, the object, and "us," and for the relations between active and passive verbs.[7]

1. *The infant assumes rights over the object, and we agree to this assumption. Nevertheless, some abrogation of omnipotence is a feature from the start.*

   In this first point, the infant is the subject, and the object an object. The word *assumption* plays a complicated role here: do we agree to the infant's assumption of rights, or do we agree to the assumption that the infant has rights? Are we agreeing to the rights, or to the idea? In the second sentence, "infant," "object," and "us" have all grammatically dropped out. Instead, we find a description of a feature: abrogation of omnipotence. Who is abrogating omnipotence? The infant whose rights are not absolute? Or "us," whose agreement is not entirely the law here. An obvious reading would have it that although the infant is allowed power over the object, the nature of this power is from the start a falling away from the kind of power an infant experiences over an internal object. Nevertheless, the sentence describes the abrogation of omnipotence as if it had a separate existence, as if it were functioning as a transitional object in its own right.

2. *The object is affectionately cuddled as well as excitedly loved and mutilated.*

   In this second point, and in all five remaining points, the object is the subject of the sentence. Here, the infant is the implicit agent of verbs in the passive voice. Why is the infant not mentioned? It is as though the sentence has to be written from the point of view of the object, as though the actions of cuddling, loving, and mutilating had to be experienced by the object rather than enacted by the infant. As though the infant cannot be allowed to have so much agency without violating the nature of the transitional phenomenon.

3. *It must never change, unless changed by the infant.*

This is a law, but whose? Is it a warning to the parents not to wash the blanket? Is it a condition of the object's being considered a transitional object by the infant? Is it a rule the object must obey, or the adults? Or an apprenticeship in agency that must be practiced by the infant?

4. *It must survive instinctual loving, and also hating and, if it be a feature, pure aggression.*

Is this a law or a test? The difference between this point and the second one is this emphasis on survival, about which we will say more in a moment.

5. *Yet it must seem to the infant to give warmth, or to move, or to have texture, or to do something that seems to show it has vitality or reality of its own.*

Why does this "it must" begin with "yet"? This feature has a logical relation of contrast to the preceding one, but what is the contrast? It must survive . . . yet it must seem to live. Is survival not an appearance of life? Perhaps the object's survival in point four is a sign of its inanimateness; its thingliness resists destruction as a living thing could not. And yet it does have vitality to the extent that it has reality.

6. *It comes from without from our point of view, but not so from the point of view of the baby. Neither does it come from within; it is not a hallucination.*

This point in many ways returns to the first point. Baby and adult points of view are both mentioned, this time with more contrast. It is a question of inside and outside in two ways: where is the object (inside or outside the baby); where is the point of view (inside or outside the baby). The second sentence is a return to the abrogation of omnipotence: the object is not a hallucination. Thus the baby's point of view is not described: only what it is not (the object comes neither from without nor from within—this was the question not to be formulated, and it is still, in a sense, not formulated here).

The seventh feature begins like the others, but the voice of the theorist soon takes over, with a celebration of culture that reads like an epitaph to the object:

7. *Its fate is to be gradually allowed to be decathected, so that in the course of years it becomes not so much forgotten as relegated to limbo. By this I mean that in health the transitional object does not "go inside" nor does the feeling about it necessarily undergo repression. It is not forgotten and it is not mourned. It loses meaning, and this is because the transitional phenomena have become diffused, have become spread out over the whole intermediate territory between "inner psychic reality" and "the external world as perceived by two persons in common," that is to say, over the whole cultural field.*

"Its fate is to be gradually allowed to be decathected." What is the point of view of this sentence? It begins from the point of view of the object, facing its fate. Winnicott's capacity to capture the pathos of the object as it loses meaning, and to do so without overt personification, is somehow very moving. Yet the sentence is not entirely from the object's point of view: its fate is to be *gradually allowed to be* decathected. Temporality belongs to the infant, not to the object. Unless of course the object always wanted to be deca-thected, and is gradually freed from the infant's interest. The infant's role in the object's experience of fate is to let the object go. But Winnicott does not say: "The infant gradually outgrows the object." The change in the infant is experienced as a change in the object, yet it is experienced only *by* the object, since it is a change that involves losing the object's capacity to have a point of view.

After these seven points, Winnicott concludes, "At this point my subject widens out into that of play, and of artistic creativity and appreciation, and of religious feeling, and of dreaming, and also of fetishism, lying and steal-ing, the origin and loss of affectionate feeling, drug addiction, the talisman of obsessional rituals, etc." (5). Winnicott, in his description of these mani-festations of play, does not play so freely as to fail to distinguish, by adding the word *also*, between good play and bad play.

But what about the question of using people? Doesn't "using people" still sound like something unethical? Let us return to Winnicott, this time to an essay entitled "The Use of an Object and Relating through Identifications" (86–94). In this essay, Winnicott distinguishes between object relating and object use. Some patients, it seems, are unable to "use" the analyst. Instead, they "relate to" the analyst by constructing a false self capable of finishing the analysis and expressing gratitude. But the real work has not been done. What is that real work? In comparing the analyst to the transitional object,

Winnicott suggests that the subject's problem is an inability to "use people." This, then, is the notion of "using people" that we wish to explore through Winnicott.

Winnicott's analysis shows that, in some patients, the inability to use people leaves them trapped in a narcissistic lock in which nothing but approval and validation, or disapproval and invalidation, can be experienced. The whole scenario of destruction and excited love, which the transitional object must survive, cannot happen. The properly used object is one that survives destruction. The survival of the object demonstrates that the baby is not omnipotent, that the object is not destroyed by destruction, that the object will not retaliate in kind if the baby attacks, that the object will not leave if the baby leaves. Separation is possible only if the baby believes the object will still be there to come back to. The baby cannot *use* the object for growth if the baby cannot separate from it for fear of destroying it or losing it—object relating is contrasted with object use in that object use involves trust that separation can occur without damage, while object relating means that attention to the object must be constantly maintained and damage repaired, otherwise the object will be destroyed or will leave. At stake is the place of reality: "If all goes well; the infant can actually come to gain from the experience of frustration, since incomplete adaptation to need makes objects real, that is to say, hated as well as loved" (11)—that is, ambivalence is a sign that the object is real.

Analytic patients who are unable to "use" the analyst are stuck in a fantasy of omnipotence (the analyst will not survive my rage), which is based on a denied dependency (I cannot survive if the analyst does not survive). Thus, the relation implies a power inequality that is both exaggerated and denied. Such people think the analyst cannot survive use, which might involve "excitedly loving and mutilating." But if the patient does learn to use people, Winnicott writes, "In psychoanalytic practice the positive changes that come about in this area can be profound. They do not depend on interpretive work. They depend on the analyst's survival of the attacks, which involves and includes the idea of the absence of a quality change to retaliation. These attacks may be very difficult for the analyst to stand" (92). At this point, Winnicott drops in a note: "When the analyst knows that the patient carries a revolver, then, it seems to me, this work cannot be done." The patient must experience the infantile magnitude of his destructiveness without making it real. Which means that the analyst must remain in the power position—but not truly in danger—in order to exercise therapeutic inertness. Using the analyst means experiencing all the infantile feelings of omnipotence and dependency so as to learn to tolerate and integrate them rather than shut them out through a false system of premature respect and concern. The ethical position of the analyst is to refrain from retaliating *and* to refrain from interpreting. In this, the analyst is in the classic ethical position of the powerful one exercising restraint. It is in the less powerful position that, paradoxically, restraint has become the problem. By allowing the patient the space and the time to try out both the feelings—of omnipotence and powerlessness—and their meanings, the patient comes into a more realistic and creative relation to his true strengths and limits. The object becomes real because it survives, because it is outside the subject's area of omnipotent control. The narcissistic lock of reparation and retaliation is opened to let in the world.

As is usual with Winnicott, something other than a mere description of these psychic processes happens in his text *in language*. Let me quote an extended passage from the middle of the essay. "This change (from relating to usage) means that the subject destroys the object. From here it could be argued by an armchair philosopher that there is therefore no such thing in practice as the use of an object: if the object is external, then the object is destroyed by the subject" (90). The armchair philosopher is here playing the role of the intellectualizer away of the paradox: the object is either inside or outside, destroyed or not destroyed. But look at what happens to the armchair philosopher in the next sentence: "Should the philosopher come out of his chair and sit on the floor with his patient, however, he will find that there is an intermediate position." The dead metaphor of the chair comes alive in order to propel the philosopher onto the floor, where what he will find is an intermediate position. Something about that intermediate position is enacted by this passage from metaphor to literality. The intermediate position is not in space but in what it is possible to say. "In other words, he will find that after 'subject relates to object' comes 'subject destroys object' (as it becomes external); and then may come '*object survives* destruction by the subject.'" The intermediate position is the between as beyond. "But there may or may not be survival." The realness of the object requires that the possibility exists for it to really be destroyed.

> A new feature thus arrives in the theory of object-relating. The subject says to the object: "I destroyed you," and the object is there to receive the communication. From now on the subject says: "Hullo object!" "I destroyed you." "I love you." "You have value for me because of your survival of my destruction of you." "While I am loving you I am all the time destroying you in (unconscious) *fantasy*." (90)

The object is there to receive the communication. The structure of address animates the object as a "you," a destroyed "you," a loved because destroyed "you." The object's survival of destruction is what makes it real. The reality of others depends on their survival, yes, but also on their destruction (in fantasy).

Winnicott's dramatized direct address to the object seems excessive with respect to what is required by the description. That is, the language of address adds something. What does it add?

As a way of approaching this question, let me return for a moment to Kant. This point in Winnicott recalls a strange moment in Kant's *Critique of Practical Reason*, in which he suddenly, and without warning, directly addresses duty in one long sentence:

> Duty! Thou sublime and mighty name that dost embrace nothing charming or insinuating but requirest submission and yet seekest not to move the will by threatening aught that would arouse natural aversion or terror, but only holdest forth a law which of itself finds entrance into the mind and yet gains reluctant reverence (though not always obedience)—a law before which all inclinations are dumb even though they secretly work against it: what origin is there worthy of thee, and where is to be found the root of thy noble descent which proudly rejects all kinship with the inclinations and from which to be descended is the indispensable condition of the only worth which men can give themselves?[8]

Isn't this a version of the question not to be formulated about the transitional object—did you create that or did you find it? Could there be a relation between duty and the teddy bear, not because the teddy bear teaches concern for others but because in neither case is it possible to say whether the object is inside or outside the subject? And does direct address to an abstract or inanimate object somehow act out the paradox that must be tolerated if there is to be a full range of cultural life?

The ludic side of Kant is usually quite well concealed. Yet here, in the middle of a discussion of "the incentives of pure practical reason," after scornful comments about fanaticism and sentimentalism, Kant suddenly feels an impulse to play. In a long-drawn single breath, he utters an apostrophe, playing at animating Duty, sublime and mighty name. In the midst of describing duty as that which "elevates man above himself as a part of the world of sense," that which gives "personality, i.e., the freedom and independence from the mechanism of nature," Kant's language suddenly generates a personality beyond the world of reference, a personification to receive the communication.[9]

In Winnicott, as we have seen, the subtle animation of the object, or at least the object's point of view, is a constant feature. That Winnicott's language is often out in a space of play ahead of him, or encrypted in a space within him, is something of which he himself occasionally takes note. Beginning an essay entitled "The Location of Cultural Experience" with an epigraph from Tagore, he writes, "The quotation from Tagore has always intrigued me. In my adolescence I had no idea what it could mean, but it found a place in me, and its imprint has not faded" (95). His ability to describe language as having a place rather than a meaning is already a structure of object use. In another essay, Winnicott finds himself quoting a Shakespeare sonnet, and lets it lead him where he wasn't necessarily planning to go:

> The object is repudiated, re-accepted, and perceived objectively. This process is highly dependent on there being a mother or mother figure prepared to participate and to give back what is handed out.
>
> This means that the mother (or part of mother) is in a "to and fro" between being that which the baby has a capacity to find and (alternatively) being herself waiting to be found.
>
> If the mother can play this part over a length of time without *admitting impediment* (*so to speak*) then the baby has some experience of magical control. . . .
>
> In the state of confidence that grows up when a mother can do this difficult thing well (not if she is unable to do it), the baby begins to enjoy experiences based on a "*marriage*" of the omnipotence of intrapsychic processes with the baby's controlling of the actual. (47, emphasis added)

Marriage follows upon not admitting impediments, not because all roads in Winnicott should lead to marriage (although they do) but because Winnicott is capable of *using* language in just the way he speaks of *using* objects—using language to play fort-da with, and letting language play him. His actual interpretations often draw his material back into a frustratingly familiar ideology, but his descriptions of language acting in him or on him somehow escape that closure. (Even his anti–birth control essay, "The Pill and the Moon," involves his involuntary composition of a poem.)[10]

Winnicott ends the paragraph of dialogue between infant and object, and by implication between patient and therapist, by concluding, "In these ways the object develops its own autonomy and life, and (if it survives) contributes-in to the subject, according to its own properties" (90). The object's own properties operate like a third in the relation between baby and object—a third that makes it possible to experience the world, a third composed of the interaction itself. Winnicott ends his article on the use of an object by saying: "Study of this problem involves a statement of the positive value of destructiveness. The destructiveness, plus the object's survival of the destruction, places the object outside the area of objects set up by the subject's projective mental mechanisms. In this way a world of shared reality is created which the subject can use and which can feed back other-than-me substance into the subject" (94).

Perhaps a synonym for "using people" would be, paradoxically, "trusting people," creating a space of play and risk that does not depend on maintaining intactness and separation. It is not that destructiveness is always or in itself good—far from it. The unleashed destructiveness of exaggerated vulnerability or of grandiosity without empathy is amply documented. But *excessive* empathy is simply counterphobic. What goes unrecognized is a danger arising not just from infantile destructiveness but from the infantile *terror* of destructiveness—its exaggerated and paralyzing repression. Winnicott describes the process of learning to overcome *that* terror, which allows one to trust, to play, and to experience the reality of both the other *and* the self. And this, it seems to me, suggests the ethical importance of "using people."

NOTES

"Using People: Kant with Winnicott." From *The Turn to Ethics*, Marjorie Garber, Beatrice Hanssen, and Rebecca Walkowitz, eds. (New York: Routledge, 2000). Reproduced with permission of Taylor & Francis Group LLC. Permissions conveyed through Copyright Clearance Center.

1. See Emmanuel Levinas, *Ethics and Infinity*, trans. Richard A. Cohen (Pittsburgh, PA: Duquesne University Press, 1985). Levinas himself avoids thus grounding ethics in *restraint* by defining the subject not in isolation but always in relation to the Other, for whom and to whom the subject is responsible, without any prior intactness or guarantee. My quarrel here is more with a sort of "Levinas effect" than with any particular writing, whether by Levinas or others.

2. Immanuel Kant, *Critique of Practical Reason*, trans. Lewis White Beck (London: Macmillan, 1956), 136.

3. Heinz Kohut, *The Analysis of the Self* (New York: International Universities Press, 1971), 33.

4. To give you an idea of the horror of a transitional object that *would* be a mirror double, I refer you to My Twinn, a company that makes dolls "individually

crafted to look like your daughter," available online. The proud parent is invited to choose among skin tones, eye colors, hair color and style, and to diagram birthmarks, moles, and freckles. Renaissance blazons that dismembered the female body were nothing compared to this parental dissection and commodification of the living child. Suppose the girl gets one for her birthday, and the dog eats it? Wouldn't the doll require a kind of protection that is the very model for enslavement to the ideal *I*? As if the daughter does not have enough trouble with the mirror stage, she must be haunted by this Dorian Gray–like perfect unchanging object as she herself grows up, gets pimples, falls into puberty.

5. D. W. Winnicott, *Playing and Reality* (London: Tavistock, 1971), xi–xii. Page numbers in parentheses refer to this volume.

6. Immanuel Kant, *Foundation of the Metaphysics of Morals*, section 1, note.

7. "Summary of Special Qualities in the Relationship," in Winnicott, *Playing and Reality*, 5.

8. Kant, *Critique of Practical Reason*, 89.

9. Kant, *Critique of Practical Reason*, 89.

10. For an excellent feminist critique of Winnicott's image of motherhood, see Carolyn Dever, *Death and the Mother from Dickens to Freud* (Cambridge: Cambridge University Press, 1998), chap. 2, "Psychoanalytic Cannibalism."

CHAPTER 19

Ego Sum Game

One of the obvious assumptions we make is that the human "self" is a person, not a thing. But might this assumption be more problematic than it appears? We have seen how necessary transitional objects are to the development of a person. But is "knowing oneself" as deadly for every human being as it proved to be for Narcissus?

Narcissus, it will be recalled, was born to the water nymph Leiriope, who asked the blind seer, Tiresias, whether her son would have a long life. "If he ne'er know himself," was the seer's reply according to Ovid, who tells the story in his *Metamorphoses*. Tiresias had been blinded by an irate Juno for having said that women enjoy sex more than men do. Juno and Jove had submitted their sexual query ("Who has more pleasure—men or women?") to Tiresias, who was the only mortal who had lived as both a woman and a man. Jove, who lamented Tiresias's blinding but could not undo it, gave him the gift of prophecy as compensation.

The problem would seem to arise when the "self" becomes known—known as an object of knowledge. But if the "self" becomes an object of knowledge, it can *only* be known as an object among other objects, and not as a subject. "The self then, quite analogous to representations of objects," writes Heinz Kohut—one of the most important practitioners of American self-psychology, speaking against a common assumption about studying the "self"—the self, then, "is a content of the mental apparatus but is not one of its constituents, i.e., not one of the agencies of the mind."[1] Kohut calls *self-objects* other people who are treated as if they were parts or extensions of the self. The difference between self and other becomes very murky if one comes to know oneself only when what appears to be another is revealed to be the self. This is what Narcissus comes to recognize, much to his rue. It is no accident that the patients Kohut studies are those who have difficulty telling self from other—patients he has dubbed "narcissistic personalities."

Rather than inflicting their perfection and self-admiration on others, Kohut's narcissistic personalities are far more likely to use other people to shore up their own defects or to possess talents that they do not have. The tyranny of such people comes from their fear of others' freedom and their investment in others' capacity to compensate for what they believe they lack, not from some sense of their own superiority. But one would never guess this from the story Ovid tells of Narcissus, a youth who withheld himself from everyone who was smitten by his unusual beauty, men and women alike, until the day he fell passionately in love with his own image.

The narrative voice that tells the tale seems to know about Narcissus's delusion before Narcissus does. At the height of Narcissus's passion, the narrator steps forward and addresses his character thus: "O fondly foolish boy, why vainly seek to clasp but a fleeting image? What you seek is nowhere; but turn yourself away, and the object of your love will be no more. That which you behold is but the shadow of a reflected form and has no substance of its own."[2] The dramatic irony of the situation seems to be too much for the narrator, but, apparently not hearing this sagacious warning, Narcissus persists in his delusion, addressing the image as an unresponsive youth, and then shouting out, "Oh, I am he!"—"*iste ego sum*"—in recognition as he expires. It is at the moment of apostrophizing the figure he comes to know as an inanimate object that Narcissus starts to die. In other words, Narcissus now recognizes that the *other* is himself, and that love is impossible between them not because they cannot come together but because they cannot get far enough apart: "What I desire," laments Narcissus, "I have; the very abundance of my riches beggars me. Oh, that I might be parted from my own body! And, strange prayer for a lover, I would that what I love were absent from me!" Note that Narcissus says nothing about delusions or insubstantialities. What he regrets is not being able to merge with what he already is.

The narrator, however, is from the beginning as good an empiricist as the young chimpanzee will later be for Jacques Lacan. He makes a point of not being taken in for a minute by Narcissus's delusion and knows all the time where reality is. No matter what emotional event is taking place, he always pays attention to what is going on behind the curtain of fantasy. Desire and delusion, shadow and substance, must be distinguished at all costs. In order not to be duped by desire, it is good to be securely grounded in the real.

Here, for instance, is how the narrator-witness describes Narcissus's first encounter with his image, the youth having lain down to quench his thirst in a beautiful hidden pool while hunting: "While he seeks to slake his thirst another thirst springs up, and while he drinks he is smitten by the sight of the beautiful form he sees. He loves an unsubstantial hope and thinks that substance which is only shadow." Note how the narrator hastens to tell us the real truth of the case, to make sure we know right away that Narcissus is suffering from a delusion. There is almost a taboo against sharing in that delusion, remaining in the space of desire, taking a shadow for a substance. Falling in love with a beautiful form, however, suggests more than emptiness: it suggests a realm of aesthetics. Could it be that the aesthetic and the fantasmatic are related, or at least equally indifferent to the empirical difference between "real" and "not real"?

It is not just that Narcissus recognizes that the other is the self; he also recognizes that the self is another: "iste *ego sum*," "je *est un autre*." In other words, Narcissus, in his climactic recognition scene, shouts not "the other is *here*" but "I am *there*." *Iste* is a there-word, not a here-word: "*Iste*, ista, istud, istius (pronoun). That of yours; (*law*) your client, the plaintiff, the defendant; (*contemptuous*) the fellow; that, such." *Iste*, says the dictionary, is thus a distancing, almost dismissive word, and the self recognized "over there" is a self that has become an object. By becoming an object, though, it lends itself to the confusions from which Narcissus suffers. A self-image can suffer all the distortions to which any *image* is susceptible, but it can be known only as an object, not a subject. A subject can only cry out, "I am that!"—which does not at all imply that the subject can *be* that.

The claim that the subject has *being* seems to be taken for granted as springing from Descartes. In his discovery scene in the second meditation, he details the process of radical doubt, and then realizes that even if he is deceived in everything, he cannot doubt the fact that he doubts. "*Cogito ergo sum*" is what we all learn he says at that moment (although he says it nowhere in that form): "I think, therefore I am." The content of thought—its truth or falsity—is not relevant; what gives the subject being is the fact that, while thinking about this problem, he exists. It is interesting to note that in Latin, the language the *Meditations* were first published in, and in 1647 still the language of serious scholarship, the pronouns are not necessarily included because they are redundant if one can tell who is speaking from the conjugation of the verb. In translating Freud into English, in contrast, Alex Strachey and his team *added* Latin pronouns—*ego*, *id*, and *superego*—where Freud had merely used the nominalization of the German pronouns—*das Ich*, *das Es*, and so on. The ego, id, and superego seem to be either excessive or lacking—and not just in a figurative sense but in every context where their nature is discussed.

The ego, the id, and the superego, in spite of their differences from anything experienced, says Kohut, are agencies of the mind, whereas the "self," more synthetic, more directly similar to what is experienced, is a mere "content" of the mental apparatus. Ego, id, and superego constantly struggle for control over the subject, whereas the "self" is something the subject treats as an object, constantly fine-tuning its perceived nature. "Ego, id, and superego are the constituents of a specific, high-level, i.e., experience-distant, abstraction in psychoanalysis: the psychic apparatus. . . . The self, however, emerges in the psychoanalytic situation and is conceptualized, in the mode of a comparatively low-level, i.e., comparatively experience-near, psychoanalytic abstraction, as a content of the mental apparatus."

Can the subject, then, have a descriptive qualifier of any kind and remain a subject? Does a predicate transform the subject into an object? Does a subject have to be unqualified to remain subject? On the one hand, to describe is to view from a distance; on the other, an agent can tell certain things about himself. He certainly does not see himself as being "without qualities." But can a subject articulate its own predicate, or is that one of those things that ground a subject but cannot be articulated by the "I" who speaks, without endangering the status of subject? Are these questions that can be answered on the empirical or simply the rhetorical level? In other words, does it matter what is *known* about a subject, or only what is *said*?

To complicate things still further, one can ask, Is *being* a predicate? Is *being* something a subject can *have* and remain a subject? Let us return to Descartes for a moment. Is he saying more in formulating "I think, therefore I am" than simply using "I" properly: "I think, therefore 'I' is"? Does the sentence mean "I think, therefore I have being," or "I think, therefore I know the rules of grammar"?

Evidence that Descartes was profoundly worried about such things comes up when he has barely introduced his discovery: "I am, I exist, is necessarily true every time I pronounce it or conceive it in my mind. What then have I previously believed myself to be? Clearly, I believed myself to be a man. But what is a man?"[3] It is at this point that Descartes distinguishes between the evidence of the senses (which can always deceive me) and the evidence of reason (which, even if mistaken, *is*), and relies on the mind/body distinction to make his claim for the irrefutability of the existence of the thinking subject. Yet the question of what a man is continues to haunt him. Later in the essay, he writes, "Words impede me, and I am nearly deceived by ordinary language. . . . So I may by chance look out of a window and notice some men passing in the street, at the sight of whom I do not fail to say that I see men. . . . [A]nd nevertheless, what do I see from this window but hats and cloaks which might cover ghosts or automatons which move only by springs?"[4] A century later, a watchmaker in Neuchâtel, Switzerland, made an exquisite mechanical scribe capable of writing "I think, therefore I am" on a piece of paper spread out on his writing table. Nothing Descartes writes proves that the being whose existence he had demonstrated was human: he discovered certainty only in the subject ("I am"), and not in any predicate ("I am X"). The mechanism hiding beneath those hats and cloaks might only be the mechanics of language.

Over time, however, the psychology that has developed from Descartes's formula has tended to conflate the ego with the self, the "content" of the mental apparatus, to take the subject for a substance. American "ego psychology"—which combines the English translation of Freud with the ideology of the self-made man—works on reshaping the "ego" as if it were both mental *content* and mental *agency*, and as if it were the "self" who speaks about itself during a psychoanalytic session. The problem of any discordance between subject and self is not addressed, and the therapy has as its job to reshape the entity it is addressed by.

It is from American ego psychology that Jacques Lacan is most invested in distinguishing his own theories. He often uses Descartes as a clear example of the conflation of ego, self, and subject that is the delusion of which he would most like to rid psychoanalysis. For him, Freud's great discovery was the *non*-coincidence between consciousness and being, the split between the thinking subject and his unconscious. To make that distinction clear, he comes more and more to situate his theory of the human subject as a subject in language and to study the exact function of language in the split between subject and unconscious. An early text like "Le stade du miroir" (1949) tries to isolate the moment when desire splits from reality; when the libidinal role of the non-coincidence between "I think" and "I am" is fixed. The text begins:

La conception du stade du miroir . . . ne m'a pas paru indigne d'être rappelée à votre attention: aujourd'hui spécialement quant aux lumières qu'elle apporte sur la fonction du *je* dans l'expérience que nous en donne la psychanalyse. Expérience dont il faut dire qu'elle nous oppose à toute philosophic issue directement du *cogito*.[5]

The conception of the mirror stage ... has since become more or less established in the practice of the French group. However, I think it worthwhile to bring it again to your attention, especially today, for the light it sheds on the formation of the *I* as we experience it in psychoanalysis. It is an experience that leads us to oppose any philosophy directly issuing from the *Cogito*.[6]

Later, in a 1957 lecture given, precisely, in the "amphithéâtre Descartes" at the Sorbonne, Lacan, being struck by the way in which Saussure-derived work in linguistics illuminated Freud and provided a clarification that was not available to Freud himself, expresses his distance from the *Cogito* in the following terms:

Je pense, donc je suis (cogito ergo sum) ...

La place que j'occupe comme sujet du signifiant est-elle, par rapport à celle que j'occupe comme sujet du signifié, concentrique ou excentrique? Voilà la question.

Il ne s'agit pas de savoir si je parle de moi de façon conforme à ce que je suis, mais si, quand j'en parle, je suis le même que celui dont je parle. ...

C'est-à-dire que c'est peu de ces mots dont j'ai pu interloquer un instant mes auditeurs: je pense où je nc suis pas, donc je suis où je ne pense pas. ...

Ce qu'il faut dire, c'est: je ne suis pas, là où je suis le jouet de ma pensée; je pense à ce que je suis, là où je ne pense pas penser. (516)

I think, therefore I am (cogito ergo sum) ...

Is the place that I occupy as the subject of a signifier concentric or excentric, in relation to the place I occupy as subject of the signified?— that is the question.

It is not a question of knowing whether I speak of myself in a way that conforms to what I am, but rather of knowing whether I am the same as that of which I speak.

That is to say, what is needed is more than these words with which, for a brief moment I disconcerted my audience: I think where I am not, therefore I am where I do not think.

What one ought to say is: I am not wherever I am the plaything of my thought; I think of what I am where I do not think to think. (165–66)

But according to the Lacan who wrote the account of "the mirror stage" in 1949 (after having introduced the term in 1936), the breakthrough occurred not as a commentary on a philosophical text but through a fact of comparative psychology:

> Le petit d'homme à un âge où il est pour un temps court, mais encore pour un temps, dépassé en intelligence instrumentale par le chimpanzé, reconnaît pourtant déjà son image dans le miroir comme telle. . . .
>
> Cet acte, en effet, loin de s'épuiser comme chez le singe dans le contrôle une fois acquis de l'inanité de l'image, rebondit aussitôt chez l'enfant en une série de gestes où il éprouve ludiquement la relation des mouvements assumés de l'image à son environnement reflété, et de ce complexe virtuel à la réalité qu'il redouble, soit à son propre corps et aux personnes, voire aux objets, qui se tiennent à ses côtés. (93)

> The child, at an age when he is for a time, however short, outdone by the chimpanzee in instrumental intelligence, can nevertheless already recognize as such his own image in a mirror. . . .
>
> This act, far from exhausting itself, as in the case of the monkey, once the image has been mastered and found empty, immediately rebounds in the case of the child in a series of gestures in which he experiences in play the relation between the movements assumed in the image and the reflected environment, and between this virtual complex and the reality it reduplicates—the child's own body, and the persons and things, around him. (1)

Lacan pursued his studies in psychiatry during the great age of behaviorism: experimenters with animals demonstrated how higher animals acquired conditioned reflexes that involved nothing mental at all. The experiments with dogs, cats, and rats presupposed an analogy between human beings and the species in question. The experiments were designed to demonstrate learned or developmental stages in all animals (including humans) that needed no psychic input: what looked like desire or intention could be explained by the pure mechanics of the body. Every form of salivation was Pavlovian. Freud had exaggerated the role of the psyche in human behavior along with the difference between human beings and other animals. Behaviorism was a welcome and demystifying corrective. Lacan's expression "le petit d'homme" is a sign of this mentality: it refers to a comparison between the "young" of two different animals; it is treating "man" as a species.

The little ape at first takes his image as another, and, when he recognizes that there is no other there, he loses interest. Dogs often bark at the dog in the mirror, while cats look for the other cat behind it. But the human baby's interest *increases* when he realizes that the other is himself; his fascination at seeing the "him" that others see leads him to test his movements against those of the image. In other words, it is not that his image is "merely" redundant as it is for other animals; it is the human image that now has reality in the world. Narcissus, therefore, made the mistake of the ape: he fell in love with his image *as if* it were another, and his tragedy was that his love was impossible if it were not. Narcissus, too, has no interest in his own image, and fades away as soon as he realizes that he loves himself. In a way, therefore, Narcissus is no narcissist: he gets no farther than the chimpanzee. His story is about the inability to become human. Normally, the human baby adopts as his "self" an image that shows him more unified and powerful than he is:

> Cet événement peut se produire, on le sait depuis Baldwin, depuis l'âge de six mois, et sa répétition a souvent arrêté notre méditation devant le spectacle saisissant d'un nourisson devant le miroir, qui n'a pas encore la maîtrise de la marche, voire de la station debout, mais qui, tout embrassé qu'il est par quelque soutien humain ou artificiel (ce que nous appelons en France un trotte-bébé), surmonte en un affairement jubilatoire les entraves de cet appui, pour suspendre son attitude en une position plus ou moins penchée, et ramener, pour le fixer, un aspect instantané de l'image. (93–94)

> This event can take place, as we have known since Baldwin, from the age of six months, and its repetition has often made me reflect upon the startling spectacle of the infant in front of the mirror. Unable as yet to walk, or even to stand up, and held tightly as he is by some support, human or artificial (what in France, we call a *trotte-bébé*), he nevertheless overcomes, in a flutter of jubilant activity, the obstructions of his support and, fixing his attitude in a slightly leaning-forward position, in order to hold it in his gaze, brings back an instantaneous aspect of the image. (1–2)

Lacan's attitude is markedly ambivalent about comparative biology. On the one hand, Lacan underlines what *differentiates* man from other species (this will only expand as Lacan explores the role of human language): whereas the chimpanzee loses interest when he realizes that the image is not "real," the human being comes to "know himself" through it. On the other hand, species that illustrate the developmental role of the double—pigeons or migratory locusts, for example—show that the mimeticism that seems at work uniquely in man exists elsewhere in nature. What is specific about humans can't be studied through other species, but if something that seems unnatural can be found in nature, that strengthens the argument for it.

What matters in the mirror stage, then, is not whether the image in the mirror is self or other, but how the subject recognizes that what the mirror promises to do is to give it a predicate. The subject jubilates because the image (which is now recognized to be the self) is *superior* to the little human who does the looking. The image seems to stand erect and to exemplify a wholeness that the little human, feeling weak and fragmentary, does not experience. Part of the image's perfection, indeed, inheres in the fact that *it does not feel*. Here is how Lacan describes that developmental moment:

> Il y suffit de comprendre le stade du miroir *comme une identification* au sens plein que l'analyse donne à ce terme: à savoir la transformation produite chez le sujet, quand il assume une image,—dont la prédestination à cet effet de phase est suffisament indiquée par l'usage, dans la théorie, du terme antique d'*imago.*
>
> L'assomption jubilacoire de son image spéculaire par l'être encore plongé dans l'impuissance motrice et la dépendance du nourrissage qu'est le petit homme à ce stade *infans,* nous paraîtra dès lors manifester en une situation exemplaire la matrice symbolique où le *je* se précipite en une forme primordiale. . . .
>
> Cette forme serait plutôt au reste à désigner comme *je-idéal.* . . . Mais le point important est que cette forme situe l'instance du *moi,* dès avant sa détermination sociale, dans une lignée de fiction, à jamais irréductible pour le seul individu,—ou plutôt, qui ne rejoindra qu'asymptotiquement le devenir du sujet, quel que soit le succès des synthèses dialectiques par quoi il doit résoundre en tant que *je* sa discordance d'avec sa propre réalité.
>
> C'est que la forme totale du corps par quoi le sujet devance dans un mirage la maturation de sa puissance, ne lui est donnée que comme *Gestalt,* c'est-à-dire dans une extériorité où certes cette forme est-elle plus constituante que constituée. (94–95)

We have only to understand the mirror stage *as an identification,* in the full sense that analysis gives to the term: namely the transformation that takes place in the subject when he assumes an image—whose predestination to this phase-effect is sufficiently indicated by the use, in analytic theory, of the ancient term *imago*.

This jubilant assumption of his specular image by the child at the *infans* stage, still sunk in his motor incapacity and nursling dependence, would seem to exhibit in an exemplary situation the symbolic matrix in which the *I* is precipitated in a primordial form. . . .

This form would have to be called the Ideal-I, if we wished to incorporate it into our usual register, in the sense that it will also be the source of secondary identifications, under which term I would place the functions of libidinal normalization. But the important point is that this form situates the agency of the ego, before its social determination, in a fictional direction, which will always remain irreducible for the individual alone, or rather, which will only rejoin the coming-into-being (*le devenir*) of the subject asymptotically, whatever the success of the dialectical syntheses by which he must resolve as *I* his discordance with his own reality.

The fact is that the total form of the body by which the subject anticipates in a mirage the maturation of his power is given to him only as *Gestalt*, that is say, in an exteriority in which this form is certainly more constituent than constituted. (2)

The subject, according to Lacan, identifies here with a form—not with *being*—a form that interests the subject precisely because it *anticipates* stages of his development where he will be superior to what he is now. The subject, in other words, assumes an identity derived from the *discrepancy* between a present and an ideal self—and *that* is what is recognized with such jubilation. Henceforth the real self for the subject is the one in the mirror: the total form of a body standing erect and transcending all support. An idealization. A fiction. An object.

The unchanging and unfeeling image of this idealization will haunt the subject his whole life. No matter what he does, he can neither catch up to it nor equal it. He is not pursuing a "fair youth" like Narcissus; he is pursuing himself. The impossible coincidence from which Narcissus suffered, however, exists at the heart of the subject. The subject *is* this noncoincidence, this split between an "armor of alienating identity" from the mirror image and a "corps morcelé" that is "animated" by a trembling reality ("en opposition à la turbulence de mouvements dont il s'éprouve l'animer").

In other words, like Narcissus, the subject, too, has fallen in love with a form. The word *form* is used so often by Lacan to describe this moment that one cannot help thinking that the founding moment for the subject is its shift to an aesthetic—or fantasmatic—world where images, not substances, shape human beings. It does not matter to the subject whether the mirror image is "real"; what matters is the image it conveys of the self. In its fixity and persistence, it resembles a statue, and indeed Lacan refers to the "statue in which man projects himself," while Narcissus sits fascinated by his image "like a statue carved from Parian marble." For Lacan, the possibility of becoming a statue is not something that may or may not happen to a subject. It *must* happen if the little man is to become human. A baby cannot become a little human being without identifying with a statue. Michael Borsch-Jakobson, in his book *Lacan: The Absolute Master*, and particularly in the chapter "The Statue Man," accuses Lacan of treating the human infant as a thing and preferring form to affect; but Lacan's emphasis on the role of form and shape does not deny feeling: he studies, rather, what is distinctive in the human species. It is precisely the unreal that can seem not to foster the best use of feelings. Feelings are something that man shares with animals. What makes him human is something counterintuitive, something contrary to life.

This dimension of loving a form is what differentiates, for Lacan, humans from other species. The world man creates ends up being populated by "automates," says Lacan. Descartes was right to wonder what was under those hats and coats. While all other animals measure information by its empirical usefulness, man alone does not have to connect a "substance" with a "form." Later, when it comes to formulating the difference between the "language of bees" and human language, Lacan will say that although bees have a very sophisticated set of signals to tell other bees where the honey is, they cannot say where it was yesterday, or tell the other bees a lie. It is the capacity *not* to tell the truth, to separate forms without substance from the tyranny of the referential, that characterizes the human. The human being differs from other animals because he submits to the judgment of those that measure him against an ideal image, not a reality.

In his earliest writings, indeed, Lacan was seeking to formulate the nature of this difference. When differentiating the human concept of family from that of other species, he called the human family "an institution," while for other species it was a biological group. Where animals have instincts, humans have complexes. At that time he attributed those differences to a difference between nature and culture. Later he would say that the human being learns desire at the same moment as prohibition, so that a "complex" is an image of the forbidden as desirable, the desirable as forbidden, a contradictory psychology which can only be imprinted through language.[7]

The identification with a beautiful form is an identification of life itself as imperfection. Only the inanimate has the fixity, the lack of feeling, the lack of need that corresponds to the unchanging ideal. While in love with an image that never had needs, Narcissus himself disregarded his own, and died behaving like the non-living thing he loved. In the poem that ends her volume of complete works, Sylvia Plath, too, seems to find that perfection in death:

The woman is perfected.
Her dead

Body wears the smile of accomplishment. . . .[8]

Death, however, is not the only way to achieve the stillness of the ideal. What happens in the mirror stage is the self's identification with a still image, which then becomes the version of superiority that the living self will try to equal. In its fixity, it contrasts with the experience of weakness and fragmentation that is retrospectively established as the subject's present and actual reality. The image offers a fiction of wholeness that the subject will strive to resemble. In other words, the subject comes into being in the gap of inferiority between a flawed viewer and the anticipated wholeness of an armor of fiction, an armor of inanimateness. What happens in the mirror stage is the conflating of libidinal investments with beautiful forms: the fantasmatic and the aesthetic are henceforth the "reality" of the self. And the definition of "person" would then be: the repeated experience of *failing to become a thing*.

That the mirror stage sets up the attractions and dangers of the aesthetic, fantasmatic domain is indicated in a surprising way by a medieval romance: Guillaume de Lorris's *roman de la rose*, one of the earliest treatises of "courtly love" and the allegorical mechanics of desire. As the lover enters more deeply into the garden that will contain his beloved, he drinks from a fountain engraved warningly with the epitaph of Narcissus. Here died Narcissus, says the fountain, and (implicitly) here will die all those who suffer from the same delusion. The dreamer, however, has already caught sight of his beloved, on a rosebush—reflected in the water—on which the beautiful bud is growing. The object of desire is thus first perceived as an image reflected in what the text will call the "mireors périlleus."[9] The subject must drink from the waters of reflection in order to tie together libidinal and aesthetic fascination—in order to desire an image.

In *Le roman de la rose* the text is narrated by a subject who tells his dream. The dream-narrative is a common allegorical device, and although the sleeper could not be telling us his dream while he is asleep, the presence of not two but *three* consciousnesses is not as marked as, say, in Ovid's tale of Narcissus, where the narrator warns, distances himself, and laments. In Lacan's account of the mirror stage, too, the narrator is a third—an observer who comments on the story he is telling. It is Lacan himself, trained observer that he is, who says:

> Cet événement pent se produire, on le sait depuis Baldwin, depuis l'âge de six mois, et sa répétition a souvent arrêté *notre méditation* devant le spectacle saisissant d'un nourisson devant le miroir . . . tout embrassé qu'il est par quelque soutien humain ou artificiel (ce que *nous* appelons en France un trotte-bébé). (93; emphasis added)

> This event can take place, as we have known since Baldwin, from the age of six months, and its repetition has often made me reflect upon the startling spectacle of the infant in front of the mirror . . . held tightly as he is by some support, human or artificial (what in France, we call a *trotte-bébé*). (1)

Conscious of giving this talk in Zurich, and thus of presenting himself as a scientific researcher knowledgeable about French terms of art like *trotte-bébé*, Lacan presents the baby's joy as observed during his own astute "meditation," scientific and familial.

Thus the role of the "third" in these scenes is either identificatory (as in Ovid) or scientific (as in Lacan), but in both cases the libidinal investment is described as inhering wholly in what happens in the relation between the other person and his mirror image. In a short narrative by Heinrich von Kleist, however, the role of the "third" is hardly objective:

> "About three years ago," I related, "I was swimming with a young man over whose physical form a marvelous grace seemed to shine. He must have been just sixteen or so, and only the first signs of vanity, induced by the favors of women, could be seen, as it were, in the farthest distance. It so happened that shortly before, in Paris, we had seen the famous statue called the Spinario, the youth removing a thorn from his foot—copies of it are familiar and can be found in most German collections. A glance in a large mirror recalled it to him at a moment when, in drying himself, he happened to raise his foot to a stool—he smiled and mentioned the discovery he had made. I indeed had noticed it too in the very same instant, but either to test the self-assurance of the grace with which he was endowed, or to challenge his vanity in a salutary way, I laughed and said he was seeing phantoms. He blushed

and raised his foot a second time to prove it to me, but the attempt, as might easily have been foreseen, did not succeed. Confused, he raised his foot a third and fourth time; he must have raised it ten times more: in vain! He was unable to produce the same movement again. And the movements that he did produce had so comical an effect that I could barely suppress my laughter."[10]

NOTES

"Ego Sum Game," reprinted by permission of the publisher from Barbara Johnson, *Persons and Things*, 47–60 (Cambridge, MA: Harvard University Press). © 2003 by the President and Fellows of Harvard College.

1. Heinz Kohut, *The Analysis of the Self* (New York: International Universities Press, 1983), xv.
2. Ovid, *Metamorphoses*, trans. Frank Justus Miller, Loeb Classical Library (Cambridge, MA: Harvard University Press, 1971), 154–55.
3. René Descartes, "Second Meditation," in Descartes, *Philosophical Essays* (Indianapolis: Bobbs Merrill, 1964), 82.
4. Descartes, "Second Meditation," 89.
5. Jacques Lacan, "Le stade du miroir comme formateur de la function du *Je* telle qu'elle nous est révélée dans l'expérience psychanalytique," in Lacan, *Ecrits* (Paris: Editions du Seuil, 1966), 93.
6. Jacques Lacan, "The Mirror Stage as Formative of the Function of the *I* as Revealed in Psychoanalytic Experience," in Lacan, *Ecrits: A Selection*, trans. Alan Sheridan (New York: W. W. Norton, 1977), 1.
7. In Jacques Lacan, *L'éthique de la psychanalyse, 1959–1960*, ed. Jacques-Alain Miller (Paris: Editions du Seuil, 1986); *The Ethics of Psychoanalysis*, trans. with notes by Dennis Porter (New York: W. W. Norton, 1992).
8. Sylvia Plath, "Edge," in Plath, *The Collected Poems* (New York: Harper and Row, 1981).
9. *Le roman de la rose*, 112, line 1568.
10. Heinrich von Kleist, *An Abyss Deep Enough: Letters of Heinrich von Kleist, with a Selection of Essays and Anecdotes*, ed., trans., and introduction by Phillip B. Miller (New York: Dutton, 1982), 214–15.

CHAPTER 20

Melville's Fist

The Execution of *Billy Budd*

I. The Sense of an Ending

Truth uncompromisingly told will always have its ragged edges;
hence the conclusion of such a narration is apt to be less finished
than an architectural finial.—Herman Melville, *Billy Budd*

The plot of Melville's *Billy Budd* is well known, and, like its title character, appears entirely straightforward and simple. It is a tale of three men in a boat: the innocent, ignorant foretopman, handsome Billy Budd; the devious, urbane master-at-arms, John Claggart; and the respectable, bookish commanding officer, Captain the Honorable Edward Fairfax ("Starry") Vere. Falsely accused by Claggart of plotting mutiny aboard the British man-of-war *Bellipotent*, Billy Budd, his speech impeded by a stutter, strikes his accuser dead in front of the Captain, and is condemned, after a summary trial, to hang.

In spite of the apparent straightforwardness of the facts of the case, however, there exists in the critical literature on *Billy Budd* a notable range of disagreement over the ultimate meaning of the tale. For some, the story constitutes Melville's "testament of acceptance,"[1] his "everlasting yea,"[2] his "acceptance of tragedy,"[3] or at least his "recognition of necessity."[4] For others, Melville's "final stage" is, on the contrary, "irony"[5]: *Billy Budd* is considered a "testament of resistance,"[6] "ironic social criticism,"[7] or the last vituperation in Melville's "quarrel with God."[8] More recently, critical attention has de-voted itself to the fact of ambiguity itself in the story, sometimes deploring it,[9] sometimes reveling in it,[10] and sometimes simply listing it.[11] The ambigu-ity is attributed to various causes: the unfinished state of the manuscript, Melville's change of heart toward Vere, Melville's unreconciled ambivalence toward authority or his guilt about paternity, or the incompatibility between the "plot" and the "story."[12] But however great the disagreement over the *mean-ing* of this posthumously published novel, all critics seem to agree in con-sidering it as Melville's "last word." "With the mere fact of the long silence in our minds," writes J. M. Murry, "we could not help regarding 'Billy Budd' as the last will and spiritual testament of a man of genius."[13]

To regard a story as its author's last will and testament is clearly to grant it a privileged, determining position in the body of that author's work. As the word implies, the "will" is taken to represent the author's final "intentions": in writing his "will," the author is presumed to have summed up and evaluated his entire literary output, and directed it—as proof against "dissemination"—toward some determinable destination. The "ending" thus somehow acquires the metalin-guistic authority to confer finality and intelligibility upon all that precedes it.

Now, since this sense of Melville's ending is so central to *Billy Budd* criti-cism, it might be useful to take a look at the nature of the ending of the story itself. Curiously enough, we find that *Billy Budd* ends not once, but no less than four times. As Melville himself describes it, the story continues far beyond its "proper" end: "How it fared with the Handsome Sailor during the year of the Great Mutiny has been faithfully given. But though *properly* the story ends with his life, something in the way of sequel will not be amiss" (405). This "sequel" consists of "three brief chapters": (1) the story of the death of Captain Vere after an encounter with the French ship, the *Athée*; (2) a transcription of the Budd–Claggart affair published in an "authorized" naval publication, in which the characters of the two men are reversed, with Budd represented as the depraved villain and Claggart as the heroic victim; and (3) a description of the posthumous mythification of Billy Budd by his fellow sailors and a transcription of the ballad written by one of them, which presents itself as a monologue spoken by Billy on the eve of his execution. Billy Budd's last words, like Melville's own, are thus spoken posthumously—indeed, the final line of the story is uttered from the bottom of the sea.

The question of the sense of Melville's ending is thus raised not only *by* the story but also *in* the story. But far from tying up the loose ends of a con-fusing literary life, Melville's last words are an affirmation of the necessity of "ragged edges":

The symmetry of form attainable in pure fiction cannot so readily be achieved in a narration essentially having less to do with fable than with fact. Truth uncompromisingly told will always have its ragged edges; hence the conclusion of such a narration is apt to be less finished than an architectural finial. (405)

The story ends by fearlessly fraying its own symmetry, thrice transgressing its own "proper" end: there is something inherently improper about this testamentary disposition of Melville's literary property. Indeed, far from totalizing itself into intentional finality, the story in fact begins to repeat itself—retelling itself first in reverse, and then in verse. The ending not only has no special authority: it problematizes the very *idea* of authority by placing its own reversal in the pages of an "authorized" naval chronicle. To end is to repeat, and to repeat is to be ungovernably open to revision, displacement, and reversal.[14] The sense of Melville's ending is to empty the ending of any privileged control over sense.

II. The Plot against the Characters

For Tragedy is an imitation, not of men, but of action and of life, and life consists in action, and its end is a mode of action, not a quality. Now character determines men's qualities, but it is by their actions that they are happy or the reverse.—Aristotle, *Poetics*

In beginning our study of *Billy Budd* with its ending, we, too, seem to have reversed the "proper" order of things. Most studies of the story tend to begin, after a few general remarks about the nature of good and evil, with a delineation of the three main characters: Billy, Claggart, and Vere. As Charles Weir puts it, "The purely physical action of the story is clear enough, and about its significant details there is never any doubt. . . . It is, therefore, with some consideration of the characters of the three principal actors that any analysis must begin."[15] "Structurally," writes F. B. Freeman, "the three characters *are* the novel" (73).

Melville goes to great lengths to describe both the physical and the moral characteristics of his protagonists. Billy Budd, a twenty-one-year-old "novice in the complexities of factitious life" is remarkable for his "significant personal beauty," his "reposeful good nature," his "straightforward simplicity," and his "unconventional rectitude." But Billy's intelligence ("such as it was," says Melville) is as primitive as his virtues are pristine. He is illiterate, he cannot understand ambiguity, and he stutters.

Claggart, on the other hand, is presented as the very image of urbane, intellectualized, articulate evil. Although "of no ill figure upon the whole," something in Claggart's pallid face consistently inspires uneasiness and mistrust. He is a man, writes Melville, "in whom was the mania of an evil nature, not engendered by vicious training or corrupting books or licentious living, but born with him and innate, in short, 'a depravity according to nature'" (354). The mere sight of Billy Budd's rosy beauty and rollicking innocence does not fail to provoke in such a character "an antipathy spontaneous and profound."

The third man in the drama, the one who has inspired the greatest critical dissent, is presented in less vivid but curiously more contradictory terms. The *Bellipotent*'s captain is described as both unaffected and pedantic, dreamy and resolute, irascible and undemonstrative, "mindful of the welfare of his men, but never tolerating an infraction of discipline," "intrepid to the verge of temerity, though never injudiciously so" (338). While Billy and Claggart are said to owe their characters to "nature," Captain Vere is shaped mainly by his fondness for books:

> He loved books, never going to sea without a newly replenished library, compact but of the best. . . . With nothing of that literary taste which less heeds the thing conveyed than the vehicle, his bias was toward those books to which every serious mind of superior order occupying any active post of authority in the world naturally inclines: books treating of actual men and events no matter of what era—history, biography, and unconventional writers like Montaigne, who, free from cant and convention, honestly and in the spirit of common sense philosophize upon realities. (340)

Vere, then, is an honest, serious reader, seemingly well suited for the role of judge and witness that in the course of the story he will come to play.

No consideration of the nature of character in *Billy Budd*, however, can fail to take into account the fact that the fate of each of the characters is the direct reverse of what one is led to expect from his "nature." Billy is sweet, innocent, and harmless, yet he kills. Claggart is evil, perverted, and mendacious, yet he dies a victim. Vere is sagacious and responsible, yet he allows a man whom he feels to be blameless to hang. It is this discrepancy between character and action that gives rise to the critical disagreement over the story: readers tend either to save the plot and condemn Billy ("acceptance," "tragedy," or "necessity"), or to save Billy and condemn the plot ("irony," "injustice," or "social criticism").

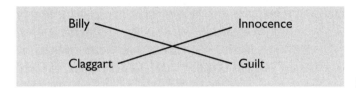

FIG. 20.1

In an effort to make sense of this troubling incompatibility between character and plot, many readers are tempted to say of Billy and Claggart, as does W. Y. Tindall, that "each is more important for what he is than what he does. . . . Good and bad, they occupy the region of good and evil."[16] This reading effectively preserves the allegorical values suggested by Melville's opening chapters, but it does so only by denying the importance of the plot. It ends where the plot begins: with the identification of the moral natures of the characters. One may therefore ask whether the allegorical interpretation (good versus evil) depends as such on this sort of preference for "being" over "doing," and, if so, what effect the incompatibility between character and action may have on the allegorical functioning of *Billy Budd*.

Interestingly enough, Melville himself both invites an allegorical reading and subverts the very terms of its consistency when he writes of the murder: "Innocence and guilt personified in Claggart and Budd in effect changed places" (380). Allowing for the existence of personification but reversing the relation between personifier and personified, positioning an opposition between good and evil only to make each term take on the properties of its opposite, Melville thus sets up his plot in the form of a chiasmus (see figure 20.1).

This story, which is often read as a retelling of the story of Christ, is thus literally a cruci-fiction—a fiction structured in the shape of a cross. At the moment of the reversal, an instant before his fist shoots out, Billy's face seems to mark out the point of crossing, bearing "an expression which was as a crucifixion to behold" (376). Innocence and guilt, criminal and victim, change places through the mute expressiveness of Billy's inability to speak.

If *Billy Budd* is indeed an allegory, it is thus an allegory of the questioning of the traditional conditions of allegorical stability. The fact that Melville's plot requires that the good act out the evil designs of the bad while the bad suffer the unwarranted fate of the good indicates that the real opposition with which Melville is preoccupied here is less the static opposition between evil and good than the dynamic opposition between a man's "nature" and his acts, or, in Tindall's terms, the relation between human "being" and human "doing."

Curiously enough, it is precisely this question of "being" versus "doing" that is brought up by the only sentence we ever see Claggart directly address to Billy Budd. When Billy accidentally spills his soup across the path of the master-at-arms, Claggart playfully replies, "Handsomely done, my lad! And handsome *is* as handsome *did* it, too!" (350; emphasis mine). The proverbial expression "handsome *is* as handsome *does*," from which this exclamation springs, posits the possibility of a continuous, predictable, transparent relationship between "being" and "doing." It supposes that the inner goodness of Billy Budd is in harmonious accord with his fair appearance, that, as Melville writes of the stereotypical "Handsome Sailor" in the opening pages of the story, "the moral nature" is not "out of keeping with the physical make" (322). But it is precisely this continuity between the physical and the moral, between appearance and action, or between "being" and "doing," that Claggart questions in Billy Budd. He warns Captain Vere not to be taken in by Billy's physical beauty: "You have but noted his fair cheek. A mantrap may be under the ruddy-tipped daisies" (372). Claggart, indeed, soon finds his suspicions confirmed with a vengeance: when he repeats his accusation in front of Billy, he is struck down dead. It would thus seem that to question the continuity between character and action cannot be done with impunity, that fundamental questions of life and death are always surreptitiously involved.

In an effort to examine what it is that is at stake in Claggart's accusation, it might be helpful to view the opposition between Billy and Claggart as an opposition not between innocence and guilt but between two conceptions of language, or between two types of reading. Billy seemingly represents the perfectly *motivated* sign; that is, his inner self (the signified) is considered transparently readable from the beauty of his outer self (the signifier). His "straightforward simplicity" is the very opposite of the "moral obliquities" or "crookedness of heart" that characterizes "citified" or rhetorically sophisticated man. "To deal in double meanings and insinuations of any sort," writes Melville, "was quite foreign to his nature" (327). In accordance with this "nature," Billy reads everything at face value, never questioning the meaning of appearances. He is dumbfounded at the Dansker's suggestion, "incomprehensible to a novice," that Claggart's very pleasantness can be interpreted as its opposite, as a sign that he is "down on" Billy Budd. To Billy, "the occasional frank air and pleasant word *went for what they purported to be*, the young sailor never having heard as yet of the 'too fair-spoken man'" (365–66; emphasis mine). As a reader, then, Billy is symbolically as well as factually illiterate. His literal-mindedness is represented by his illiteracy because, in assuming that language can be taken at face value, he excludes the very functioning of *difference* that makes the act of reading both indispensable and undecidable.

Claggart, on the other hand, is the very image of difference and duplicity, both in his appearance and in his character. His face is not ugly, but it hints of something defective or abnormal. He has no vices, yet he incarnates evil. He is an intellectual, but uses reason as "an ambidexter implement for effecting the irrational" (354). Billy inspires in him both "profound antipathy" and a "soft yearning." In the incompatibility of his attributes, Claggart is thus a personification of ambiguity and ambivalence, of the distance between signifier and signified, of the separation between being and doing: "apprehending the good, but powerless to be it, a nature like Claggart's, . . . what recourse is left to it but to recoil upon itself" (356). As a reader, Claggart has learned to "exercise a distrust keen in proportion to the fairness of the appearance" (364). He is properly an ironic reader, who, assuming the sign to be arbitrary and unmotivated, reverses the value signs of appearances and takes a daisy for a mantrap and an unmotivated accidental spilling of soup for an intentional sly escape of antipathy. Claggart meets his downfall, however, when he attempts to master the arbitrariness of the sign for his own ends, precisely by falsely (that is, arbitrarily) accusing Billy of harboring arbitrariness, of hiding a mutineer beneath the appearance of a baby.

Such a formulation of the Budd–Claggart relationship enables one to take a new look not only at the story itself but at the criticism as well. For, curiously enough, it is precisely this opposition between the literal reader (Billy) and the ironic reader (Claggart) that is reenacted in the critical readings of *Billy Budd* in the opposition between the "acceptance" school and the "irony" school. Those who see the story as a "testament of acceptance" tend to take Billy's final benediction of Vere at face value: as Lewis Mumford puts it, "As Melville's own end approached, he cried out with Billy Budd: God Bless Captain Vere! In this final affirmation Herman Melville died."[17] In contrast, those who read the tale ironically tend to take Billy's sweet farewell as Melville's bitter curse. Joseph Schiffman writes: "At heart a kind man, Vere, strange to say, makes possible the depraved Claggart's wish—the destruction of Billy. 'God bless Captain Vere!' Is this not piercing irony? As innocent Billy utters these words, does not the reader gag?" (133). But since the acceptance/irony dichotomy is already contained within the story, since it is obviously one of the things the story is *about*, it is not enough to try to decide which of the readings is correct. What the reader of *Billy Budd* must do is to analyze what is at stake in the very opposition between literality and irony. This question, crucial for an understanding of *Billy Budd* not only as a literary but also as a critical phenomenon, will be taken up again in the final pages of the present study, but first let us examine further the linguistic implications of the murder itself.

III. The Fiend that Lies Like Truth

Outwardly regarded, our craft is a lie; for all that is outwardly seen of it
is the clean-swept deck, and oft-painted planks comprised above the
water-line; whereas, the vast mass of our fabric, with all its store-rooms of
secrets, forever slides along far under the surface.—Melville, *White Jacket*

If Claggart's accusation that Billy is secretly plotting mutiny is essentially an affirmation of the possibility of a discontinuity between being and doing, of an arbitrary, nonmotivated relation between signifier and signified, then Billy's blow must be read as an attempt violently to deny that discontinuity or arbitrariness. The blow, as a denial, functions as a substitute for speech, as Billy, during his trial, explains: "I did not mean to kill him. Could I have used my tongue I would not have struck him. But he foully lied to my face, and in presence of my captain, and I had to say something, and I could only say it with a blow" (383). But in striking a blow in defense of the sign's motivation, Billy, paradoxically enough, actually personifies the very *absence* of motivation.

"I did not mean. . . ." His blow is involuntary, accidental, properly unmotivated. He is a sign that does not mean to mean. Billy, who cannot understand ambiguity, who takes pleasant words at face value and then obliterates Claggart for suggesting that one could do otherwise, whose sudden blow is a violent denial of any discrepancy between his being and his doing, thus ends up radically illustrating the very discrepancy he denies.

The story thus takes place between the postulate of continuity between signifier and signified ("handsome is as handsome does") and the postulate of their discontinuity ("a mantrap may be under the ruddy-tipped daisies"). Claggart, whose accusations of incipient mutiny are apparently false and therefore illustrate the very double-facedness which they attribute to Billy, is negated for proclaiming the very lie about Billy which Billy's act of negation paradoxically proves to be the truth.

This paradox can also be stated in another way, in terms of the opposition between the performative and the constative functions of language. Constative language is language used as an instrument of cognition—it describes, reports, speaks *about* something other than itself. Performative language is language which itself functions as an act, not as a report of one. Promising, betting, swearing, marrying, and declaring war, for example, are not descriptions of acts but acts in their own right. The proverb "handsome is as handsome does" can thus also be read as a statement of the compatibility between the constative ("being") and the performative ("doing") dimensions of language. But what Billy's act dramatizes is precisely their radical *incompatibility*— Billy performs the truth of Claggart's report to Vere only by means of his absolute and blind denial of its cognitive validity. If Billy had understood the truth, he would not have performed it. Handsome cannot both be and do its own undoing. The knowledge that being and doing are incompatible cannot know the ultimate performance of its own confirmation.

Melville's chiasmus thus creates a reversal not only between the places of guilt and innocence but between the postulate of continuity and the postulate of discontinuity between doing and being, performance and cognition. When Billy's fist strikes Claggart's forehead, it is no longer possible for knowing and doing to meet. Melville's story not only reports the occurrence of a particularly deadly performative utterance; it itself *performs* the radical incompatibility between knowledge and acts.

All this, we recall, is triggered by a stutter, a linguistic defect. No analysis of the story's dramatization of linguistic categories can be complete without careful attention to this glaring infelicity. Billy's "vocal defect" is presented and explained in the story in the following terms:

> There was just one thing amiss in him . . . , an occasional liability to a vocal defect. Though in the hour of elemental uproar or peril he was everything that a sailor should be, yet under sudden provocation of strong heart-feeling his voice, otherwise singularly musical, as if expressive of the harmony within, was apt to develop an organic hesitancy, in fact more or less of a stutter or even worse. In this particular Billy was a striking instance that the arch interferer, the envious marplot of Eden, still has more or less to do with every human consignment to this planet of Earth. In every case, one way or another he is sure to slip in his little card, as much as to remind us—I too have a hand here. (331–32)

It is doubtless this Satanic "hand" that shoots out when Billy's speech fails him. Billy is all too literally a "*striking* instance" of the workings of the "envious marplot."

Melville's choice of the word *marplot* to characterize the originator of Billy's stutter deserves special note. It seems logical to understand that the stutter "mars" the plot in that it triggers the reversal of roles between Billy and Claggart. Yet in another sense this reversal does not *mar* the plot, it *constitutes* it. Here, as in the story of Eden, what the envious marplot mars is not the plot but the state of plotlessness that exists "in the beginning." What both the Book of Genesis and *Billy Budd* narrate is thus not the story of a fall, but a fall into story.

In this connection, it is not irrelevant to recall what it is that Claggart falsely accuses Billy of: precisely of instigating a *plot*, of stirring up mutiny against the naval authorities. What Claggart is in a sense doing by positing this fictitious plot, then, is trying desperately to scare up a plot for the story. And it is Billy's very act of denial of his involvement in any plot that finally brings him *into* the plot. Billy's involuntary blow is an act of mutiny not only against the authority of his naval superiors but also against the authority of his own conscious intentions. Perhaps it is not by chance that the word *plot* can mean both "intrigue" and "story": if all plots somehow tell the story of their own marring, then perhaps it could be said that all plots are plots against authority, that authority is precisely that which creates the scene of its own destruction, that all stories necessarily recount by their very existence the subversion of the father, of the gods, of consciousness, of order, of expectations, or of meaning.

But is Billy truly as "plotless" as he appears? Does his "simplicity" hide no division, no ambiguity? As many critics have remarked, Billy's character seems to result mainly from his exclusion of the negative. When informed that he is being arbitrarily impressed for service on a man-of-war, Billy "makes no demur" (323). When invited to a clandestine meeting by a mysterious stranger, Billy acquiesces through his "incapacity of plumply saying *no*" (359). But it is interesting to note that although Billy thus seems to be "just a boy who cain't say no," almost all the words used to describe him are negative in form: innocent, un-conventional, il-literate, un-sophisticated, un-adulterate, and so on. And although he denies any discrepancy between what is said and what is meant, he does not prove to be totally incapable of lying. When asked about the shady visit of the afterguardsman, he distorts his account in order to edit out anything that indicates any incompatibility with the absolute maintenance of authority. He neglects to report the questionable proposition even though "it was his duty as a loyal bluejacket" (362) to do so. In thus shrinking from "the dirty work of a telltale" (362), Billy maintains his "plotlessness" not spontaneously but through a complex act of filtering. Far from being simply and naturally pure, he is obsessed with maintaining his own irreproachability in the eyes of authority. After witnessing a flogging, he is so horrified that he resolves "that never through remissness would he make himself liable to such a visitation or do or omit aught that might merit even verbal reproof" (346). Billy does not simply exclude the negative: he represses it. His reaction to questionable behavior of any sort (Red Whiskers, the after-guardsman, Claggart) is to obliterate it. He retains his "*blank ignorance*" (363) only by a vigorous act of erasing. As Melville says of Billy's reaction to Claggart's petty provocations, "the ineffectual speculations into which he was led were so disturbingly alien to him that *he did his best to smother them*" (362; emphasis mine).

> In his *disgustful recoil* from an overture which, though he but ill comprehended, he *instinctively knew* must involve evil of some sort, Billy Budd was like a young horse fresh from the pasture suddenly inhaling a vile whiff from some chemical factory, and by repeated snortings trying to *get it out* of his nostrils and lungs. This frame of mind *barred all desire* of holding further parley with the fellow, even were it but for the purpose of gaining some enlightenment as to his design in approaching him. (361; emphases mine)

Billy maintains his purity only through constant, though unconscious, censorship. "Innocence," writes Melville, "was his blinder" (366).

It is interesting to note that while the majority of readers see Billy as a personification of goodness and Claggart as a personification of evil, those who do not tend to read from a psychoanalytical point of view. Much has been made of Claggart's latent homosexuality, which Melville clearly suggests. Claggart, like the hypothetical "X—," "is a nut not to be cracked by the tap of a lady's fan" (352). The "unobserved glance" he sometimes casts upon Billy contains "a touch of soft yearning, as if Claggart could even have loved Billy but for fate and ban" (365). The spilling of the soup and Claggart's reaction to it are often read symbolically as a sexual exchange, the import of which, of course, is lost on Billy, who cannot read.

According to this perspective, Claggart's so-called evil is thus really a repressed form of love. But it is perhaps even more interesting to examine the way in which the psychoanalytical view treats Billy's so-called goodness as being in reality a repressed form of hate:

> The persistent feminine imagery . . . indicate[s] that Billy has identified himself with the mother at a pre-Oedipean level and has adopted the attitude of harmlessness and placation toward the father in order to

avoid the hard struggle of the Oedipus conflict. . . . That all Billy's rage and hostility against the father are unconscious is symbolized by the fact that whenever aroused it cannot find expression in spoken language. . . . This is a mechanism for keeping himself from admitting his own guilt and his own destructiveness.[18]

All of Billy's conscious acts are toward passivity. . . . In symbolic language, Billy Budd is seeking his own castration—seeking to yield up his vitality to an authoritative but kindly father, whom he finds in Captain Vere.[19]

Quite often a patient begins to stutter when he is particularly eager to prove a point. Behind his apparent zeal he has concealed a hostile or sadistic tendency to destroy his opponent by means of words, and the stuttering is both a blocking of and a punishment for this tendency. Still more often stuttering is exacerbated by the presence of prominent or authoritative persons, that is, of paternal figures against whom the unconscious hostility is most intense.[20]

Although *Billy Budd, Sailor* is placed in historical time, . . . the warfare is not between nations for supremacy on the seas but between father and son in the eternal warfare to determine succession.[21]

When Vere becomes the father, Claggart and Billy are no longer sailors but sons in rivalry for his favor and blessing. Claggart manifestly is charging mutiny but latently is accusing the younger son or brother of plotting the father's overthrow. . . . When Billy strikes Claggart with a furious blow to the forehead, he puts out the "evil eye" of his enemy-rival, but at the same time the blow is displaced, since Billy is prohibited from striking the father. After Claggart is struck and lies on the deck "a dead snake," Vere covers his face in silent recognition of the displaced blow.[22]

Billy's type of innocence is . . . *pseudoinnocence*. . . . Capitalizing on naiveté, it consists of a childhood that is never outgrown, a kind of fixation on the past. . . . When we face questions too big and too horrendous to contemplate, . . . we tend to shrink into this kind of innocence and make a virtue of powerlessness, weakness, and helplessness. . . . It is this innocence that cannot come to terms with the destructiveness in one's self or others; and hence, as with Billy Budd, it actually becomes self-destructive.[23]

The psychoanalytical reading is thus a demystification of the notion of innocence portrayed in *Billy Budd*. In the psychoanalytical view, what underlies the metaphysical lament that in this world "goodness is impotent" is the idea that it is impotence that is good, that harmlessness is innocent, that naiveté is lovable, that "giving no cause of offense to anybody" and resolving never "to do or omit aught that might merit . . . reproof" (346) are the highest ideals in human conduct. While most readers react to Billy as do his fellow crew members ("they all love him," 325), the psychoanalysts share Claggart's distrust ("for all his youth and good looks, a deep one," 371) and even disdain ("to be nothing more than innocent!," 356).

In this connection it is curious to note that while the psychoanalysts have implicitly chosen to adopt the attitude of Claggart, Melville, in the crucial confrontation scene, comes close to presenting Claggart precisely as a psychoanalyst:

> With the measured step and calm collected air of an asylum physician approaching in the public hall some patient beginning to show indications of a coming paroxysm, Claggart deliberately advanced within short range of Billy and, mesmerically looking him in the eye, briefly recapitulated the accusation. (375)

It is as though Claggart as analyst, in attempting to bring Billy's unconscious hostility to consciousness, unintentionally unleashes the destructive acting-out of transferential rage. The fatal blow, far from being an unmotivated accident, is the gigantic return of the power of negation that Billy has been repressing all his life. And in his blind destructiveness, Billy lashes out not only against the "father" but also against the very process of analysis itself.

The difference between the psychoanalytical and the traditional "metaphysical" reading of *Billy Budd* lies mainly in the status accorded to the fatal blow. If Billy represents pure goodness, then his act is unintentional but symbolically righteous, since it results in the destruction of the "evil" Claggart. If Billy is a case of neurotic repression, then his act is determined by his unconscious desires and reveals the destructiveness of the attempt to repress one's own destructiveness. In the first case, the murder is accidental; in the second, it is the fulfillment of a wish. Strangely enough, this question of accident versus motivation is brought up again at the end of the story, in the curious fact of the lack of spontaneous ejaculation in Billy's corpse. Whether the lack of spasm is as mechanical as its presence would have been, or whether it results from what the purser calls "will power" or "euthanasia," the incident stands as a negative analogue of the murder scene. In the former, it is the absence; in the latter, the presence, of physical violence that offers a challenge to interpretation. The burlesque discussion of the "prodigy of repose" by the purser and the surgeon, interrupting as it does the solemnity of Billy's "ascension," can have no other purpose than that of dramatizing the central importance for the story of the question of arbitrary accident versus determinable motivation. If the psychoanalytical and the metaphysical readings, however incompatible, are both equally supported by textual evidence, then perhaps Melville, rather than asking us to choose between them, is presenting us with a context in which to examine what is at stake in the very oppositions between psychoanalysis and metaphysics, chance and determination, the willed and the accidental, the unconscious and the moral.

IV. The Deadly Space Between

And thus do we of wisdom and of reach,
With windlasses and with assays of bias,
By indirections find directions out.
—*Hamlet* II.i

While Billy thus stands as a performative riddle (are his actions motivated or accidental?), John Claggart is presented as an enigma for cognition, a man "who for reasons of his own was keeping *incog*" (343; emphasis mine). Repeatedly referred to as a "mystery," Claggart, it seems, is difficult, even perilous, to describe:

> For the adequate comprehending of Claggart by a normal nature these hints are insufficient. To pass from a normal nature to him one must cross "the deadly space between." And this is best done by indirection. (352)

Between Claggart and a "normal nature," there exists a gaping cognitive chasm. In a literal sense, this image of crossing a "deadly space" in order to reach Claggart can be seen almost as an ironic prefiguration of the murder. Billy does indeed "cross" the "space" between himself and Claggart by means of a "deadly" blow. The phrase "space between" recurs, in fact, just after the murder, to refer to the physical separation between the dead Claggart and the condemned Billy:

> Aft, and on either side, was a small stateroom, the one now temporarily a jail and the other a dead-house, and a yet smaller compartment, leaving a *space between* expanding forward. (382; emphasis mine)

It is by means of a deadly chiasmus that the spatial chasm is crossed.

But physical separation is obviously not the only kind of "deadly space" involved here. The expression "deadly space between" refers primarily to a gap in cognition, a boundary beyond which ordinary understanding does not normally go. This sort of space, which stands as a limit to comprehension, seems to be an inherent feature of the attempt to describe John Claggart. From the very beginning, Melville admits: "His portrait I essay, but shall never hit it" (342). What Melville says he will *not* do here is precisely what Billy Budd *does* do: hit John Claggart. It would seem that speaking and killing are thus mutually exclusive: Billy Budd kills because he cannot speak, while Melville, through the very act of speaking, does not kill. Billy's fist crosses the "deadly space" *directly*; Melville's crossing, "done by indirection," leaves its target intact.

This state of affairs, reassuring as it sounds on a moral level, is, however, rather unsettling if one examines what it implies about Melville's writing. For how reliable can a description be if it does not hit its object? What do we come to know of John Claggart if what we learn is that his portrait is askew? If to describe perfectly, to refer adequately, would be to "hit" the referent and thus annihilate it; if to know completely would be to obliterate the very object known; if the perfect fulfillment of the constative, referential function of language would consist in the total obliteration of the object of that function; then language can retain its "innocence" only by giving up its referential validity. Melville can avoid murder only by grounding his discourse in ineradicable error. If to cross a space by indirection—that is, by rhetorical displacement—is to escape deadliness, that crossing can succeed only on the condition of radically losing its way.

It can thus be said that the "deadly space" that runs through *Billy Budd* is located between cognition and performance, knowing and doing, error and murder. But even this formulation is insufficient if it is taken to imply that doing is deadly, while speaking is not, or that directness is murderous while avoidance is innocent. Melville does not simply recommend the replacement of doing by speaking or of direct by indirect language. He continues to treat obliquity and deviation as evils, and speaks of digression as a "literary sin":

> In this matter of writing, resolve as one may to keep to the main road, some bypaths have an enticement not readily to be withstood. I am going to err into such a bypath. If the reader will keep me company I shall be glad. At the least, we can promise ourselves that pleasure which

is wickedly said to be in sinning, for a literary sin the divergence will be. (334)

Directness and indirectness are equally suspect, and equally innocent. Further complications of the moral status of rhetoric will be examined later in this study, but first let us pursue the notion of the "deady space."

If the space at work in *Billy Budd* cannot be located simply and unequivocally *between* language and action or between directness and indirection, where is it located and how does it function? Why is it the space itself that is called "deadly"? And how, more particularly, does Melville go about *not* hitting John Claggart?

Melville takes up the question of Claggart's "nature" many times. Each time, the description is proffered as a necessary key to the understanding of the story. And yet, each time, what we learn about the master-at-arms is that we cannot learn anything:

> Nothing was known of his former life. (343)

> About as much was really known to the *Bellipotent*'s tars of the master-at-arms' career before entering the service as an astronomer knows about a comet's travels prior to its first observable appearance in the sky. (345)

> What can more partake of the mysterious than an antipathy spontaneous and profound . . . ? (351)

> Dark sayings are these, some will say. But why? Is it because they somewhat savor of Holy Writ in its phrase "mystery of iniquity"? (354)

And, after informing us that the crossing of the "deadly space" between Claggart and a "normal nature" is "best done by indirection," Melville's narrator takes himself at his word: he digresses into a long fictitious dialogue between himself as a youth and an older "honest scholar" concerning a mysterious Mr. "X—" whose "labyrinth" cannot be penetrated by "knowledge of the world," a dialogue so full of periphrases that the youthful participant himself "did not quite see" its "drift" (353). The very phrase "the deadly space between" is, according to editors Hayford and Sealts, a quotation of unknown origin: the source of the expression used to designate what is not known is thus itself unknown. Even the seemingly satisfactory Platonic definition of Claggart's evil—"Natural Depravity: a depravity according to nature"—is in fact, as F. B. Freeman points out, nothing but a tautology. Syntactically, the definition fulfills its function, but it is empty of any cognitive information.

The *place* of explanation and definition is repeatedly filled, but its *content* is always lacking. What the progress of Melville's description describes is an infinite regress of knowledge. The "deadly space" is situated not between Claggart and his fellow men, but within Melville's very attempts to account for him.

It would seem that rather than simply separating language from action, the space in question is also at work within language itself. In the tautology of Claggart's evil, it marks an empty articulation between the expression and its definition. Other linguistic spaces abound. What, indeed, is Billy's fateful stutter, if not a deadly gap in his ability to speak? The space opened up by the stutter is the pivot on which the entire story turns. And the last words of the dying Captain Vere, which stand in the place of ultimate commentary upon the drama, are simply "Billy Budd, Billy Budd," the empty repetition of a name. At all the crucial moments in the drama—in the origin of evil, in the trigger of the act, in the final assessment—the language of *Billy Budd* stutters. At those moments, the constative or referential content is eclipsed; language conveys only its own empty, mechanical functioning. But it is precisely these very gaps in understanding that Melville is asking us to understand.

The cognitive spaces marked out by these eclipses of meaning are important not because they mark the limits of interpretation but because they function as its *cause*. The gaps in understanding are never directly perceived as such by the characters in the novel; those gaps are themselves taken as interpretable signs and triggers for interpretation. The lack of knowledge of Claggart's past, for example, is seen as a sign that he has something to hide:

> Nothing was known of his former life. . . . Among certain grizzled sea gossips of the gun decks and forecastle went a rumor perdue that the master-at-arms was a *chevalier* [Melville's emphasis] who had volunteered into the King's navy by way of compounding for some mysterious swindle whereof he had been arraigned at the King's Bench. *The fact that nobody could substantiate this report was, of course, nothing against its secret currency*. . . . Indeed a man of Claggart's accomplishments, without prior nautical experience entering the navy at mature life, as he did, and necessarily allotted at the start to the lowest grade in it; a man too who never made allusion to his previous life ashore; these were circumstances which *in the dearth of exact knowledge* as to his true antecedents opened to the invidious *a vague field for unfavorable surmise*. (343)

In other words, it is precisely the absence of knowledge that here leads to the propagation of tales. The fact that nothing is known of Claggart's origins is not a simple, contingent, theoretically remediable lack of information: it is the very *origin* of his "evil nature." Interestingly, in Billy's case, an equal lack of knowledge leads some readers to see his origin as divine. Asked who his father is, Billy replies, "God knows." The divine and the satanic can thus be seen as metaphysical interpretations of discontinuities in knowledge. In *Billy Budd*, a stutter and a tautology serve to mark the spot from which evil springs.

Evil, then, is essentially the misreading of discontinuity through the attribution of meaning to a space or division in language. But the fact that stories of Claggart's evil arise out of a seemingly meaningless gap in knowledge is hardly a meaningless or innocent fact in itself, either in its causes or in its consequences. Claggart's function is that of a policeman "charged among other matters with the duty of preserving order on the populous lower gun decks" (342). As Melville points out, "no man holding his office in a man-of-war can ever hope to be popular with the crew" (345). The inevitable climate of resentment surrounding the master-at-arms might itself be sufficient to turn the hypothesis of depravity into a self-fulfilling prophecy. As Melville puts it, "The point of the present story *turn[s] on the hidden nature* of the master-at-arms" (354). The entire plot of *Billy Budd* could conceivably be seen as a consequence not of what Claggart *does*, but of what he *does not say*.

It is thus by means of the misreading of gaps in knowledge and of discontinuities in action that the plot of *Billy Budd* takes shape. But because Melville describes both the spaces and the readings they engender, his concentration on the vagaries of interpretive error open up within the text the possibility of substantiating quite a number of "inside narratives" different from the one with which we are explicitly presented. What Melville's tale tells is the snowballing of tale-telling. It is possible, indeed, to retell the story from a point of view that fully justifies Claggart's suspicions, merely by putting together a series of indications already available in the narrative:

1. As Billy is being taken from the merchant ship to the warship, he shouts in farewell, "And good-bye to you too, old *Rights-of-Man*." Lt. Ratcliffe, who later recounts the incident to Claggart (as is shown by the latter's referring to it in making his accusation to Vere), interprets this as "a sly slur at impressment in general, and

that of himself in especial" (327). The first information Claggart is likely to have gleaned on Billy Budd has thus passed through the filter of the Lieutenant's interpretation that the handsome recruit's apparent gaiety conceals resentment.

2. When Billy resolves, after seeing the flogging of another novice, "never to merit reproof," his "punctiliousness in duty" (346) is laughed at by his topmates. Billy tries desperately to make his actions coincide with his desire for perfect irreproachability, but he nevertheless finds himself "getting into petty trouble" (346). Billy's "unconcealed anxiety" is considered "comical" by his fellows (347). It is thus Billy's obsessive concern with his own perfection that starts a second snowball rolling, since Claggart undertakes a subtle campaign of petty persecutions "to try the temper of the man" (358). The instrument used by Claggart to set "little traps for the worriment of the foretopman" is a corporal called "Squeak," who, "having naturally enough concluded that his master could have no love for the sailor, made it his business, faithful understrapper that he was, to foment the ill blood by perverting to his chief certain innocent frolics of the good-natured foretopman, besides inventing for his mouth sundry contumelious epithets he claimed to have overheard him let fall" (357). Again, Claggart perceives Billy only through the distortion of an unfavorable interpretation.

3. With this impression of Billy already in his mind, Claggart proceeds to take Billy's spilling of the soup across his path "not for the mere accident it assuredly was, but for the sly escape of a spontaneous feeling on Billy's part more or less answering to the antipathy on his own" (356). If this is an over-reading, it is important to note that the critical tendency to see sexual or religious symbolism in the soup scene operates on exactly the same assumption as that made by Claggart: that what appears to be an accident is actually motivated and meaningful. Claggart's spontaneous interpretation, hidden behind his playful words ("Handsomely done . . ."), is not only legitimate enough on its own terms, but receives unexpected confirmation in Billy's naïve outburst: "There now, who says that Jemmy Legs is down on me!" This evidence of a preexisting context in which Claggart, referred to by his disrespectful nickname, has been discussed by Billy with others—apparently a number of others, although in fact it is only one person—provides

all the support Claggart needs to substantiate his suspicions. And still, he is willing to try another test.

4. Claggart sends an afterguardsman to Billy at night with a proposition to join a mutinous conspiracy of impressed men. Although Billy rejects the invitation, he does not report it as loyalty demands. He is thus protecting the conspirators. Claggart's last test has been completed: Billy is a danger to the ship. In his function as chief of police, it is Claggart's duty to report the danger. . . .

This "reversed" reading is no more—but certainly no less—legitimate than the ordinary "good versus evil" interpretation. But its very possibility—evoked not only by these behind-the-scenes hints and nuances but also by the "garbled" newspaper report—can be taken as a sign of the centrality of the *question of reading* posed not only *by* but also *in* the text of *Billy Budd*. Far from recounting an unequivocal "clash of opposites,"[24] the confrontation between Billy and Claggart is built by a series of minute gradations and subtle insinuations. The opposites that clash here are not two *characters* but two *readings*.

V. Three Readings of Reading

It is no doubt significant that the character around whom the greatest critical dissent has revolved is neither the good one nor the evil one but the one who is explicitly presented as a *reader*, Captain Vere. On some level, readers of *Billy Budd* have always testified to the fact that it is reading, as much as killing, that is at the heart of Melville's story. But how is the act of reading being manifested? And what, precisely, are its relations with the deadliness of the spaces it attempts to comprehend?

As we have noted, critical readings of *Billy Budd* have generally divided themselves into two opposing groups, the "testament of acceptance" school on the one hand and the "testament of resistance" or "irony" school on the other. The first is characterized by its tendency to take at face value the narrator's professed admiration of Vere's sagacity and the final benediction of Vere uttered by Billy. The second group is characterized by its tendency to distance the reader's point of view from that of any of the characters, including the narrator, so that the injustice of Billy's execution becomes perceptible through a process of reversal of certain explicit pronouncements within the tale. This opposition between "acceptance" and "irony" quite strikingly mirrors, as we mentioned earlier, the opposition within the story between Billy's naiveté and Claggart's paranoia. We will therefore begin our analysis of Melville's study of the nature of reading with an examination of the way in which the act of reading is manifested in the confrontation between these two characters.

It seems evident that Billy's reading method consists in taking everything at face value, while Claggart's consists in seeing a mantrap under every daisy. Yet in practice, neither of these methods is rigorously upheld. The naïve reader is not naïve enough to forget to edit out information too troubling to report. The instability of the space between sign and referent, normally denied by the naïve reader, is called upon as an *instrument* whenever that same instability threatens to disturb the *content* of meaning itself. Billy takes every sign as transparently readable as long as what he reads is consistent with transparent peace, order, and authority. When this is not so, his reading clouds accordingly. And Claggart, for whom every sign can be read as its opposite, neglects to doubt the transparency of any sign that tends to confirm his own doubts: "the master-at-arms *never suspected the veracity*" (357) of Squeak's reports. The naïve believer thus refuses to believe any evidence that subverts the transparency of his beliefs, while the ironic doubter forgets to suspect the reliability of anything confirming his own suspicions.

Naiveté and irony thus stand as symmetrical opposites blinded by their very incapacity to see anything but symmetry. Claggart, in his antipathy, "can really form no conception of an *unreciprocated* malice" (358). And Billy, conscious of his own blamelessness, can see nothing but pleasantness in Claggart's pleasant words: "Had the foretopman been conscious of having done or said anything to provoke the ill-will of the official, it would have been different with him, and his sight might have been purged if not sharpened. As it was, innocence was his blinder" (366). Each character sees the other only through the mirror of his own reflection. Claggart, looking at Billy, mistakes his own twisted face for the face of an enemy, while Billy, recognizing in Claggart the negativity he smothers in himself, strikes out.

The naïve and the ironic readers are thus equally destructive, both of themselves and of each other. It is significant that both Billy and Claggart should die. Both readings do violence to the plays of ambiguity and belief by forcing upon the text the applicability of a universal and absolute law. The one, obsessively intent on preserving peace and eliminating equivocation, murders the text; the other, seeing nothing but universal war, becomes the spot on which aberrant premonitions of negativity become truth.

But what of the third reader in the drama, Captain Vere? What can be said of a reading whose task is precisely to read the *relation* between naiveté and paranoia, acceptance and irony, murder and error?

For many readers, the function of Captain Vere has been to provide "complexity" and "reality" in an otherwise "oversimplified" allegorical confrontation:

> Billy and Claggart, who represent almost pure good and pure evil, are too simple and too extreme to satisfy the demands of realism; for character demands admixture. Their all but allegorical blackness and whiteness, however, are functional in the service of Vere's problem, and Vere, goodness knows, is real enough.[25]

> *Billy Budd* seems different from much of the later work, less "mysterious," even didactic. . . . Its issues seem somewhat simplified, and, though the opposition of Christly Billy and Satanic Claggart is surely diagrammatic, it appears almost melodramatic in its reduction of values. Only Captain Vere seems to give the story complexity, his deliberations acting like a balance wheel in a watch, preventing a rapid, obvious resolution of the action. . . . It is Vere's decision, and the debatable rationale for it, which introduces the complexity of intimation, the ambiguity.[26]

As the locus of complexity, Captain Vere then becomes the "balance wheel" not only in the clash between good and evil but also in the clash between "accepting" and "ironic" interpretations of the story. Critical opinion has pronounced the Captain "vicious"[27] and "virtuous,"[28] "self-mythifying"[29] and "self-sacrificing,"[30] "capable"[31] and "cowardly,"[32] "responsible"[33] and "criminal,"[34] "moral"[35] and "perverted,"[36] "intellectual"[37] and "stupid,"[38] "moderate"[39] and "authoritarian."[40] But how does the same character provoke such diametrically opposed responses? Why is it the *judge* that is so passionately judged?

In order to analyze what is at stake in Melville's portrait of Vere, let us first examine the ways in which Vere's reading differs from those of Billy Budd and John Claggart:

1. While the naïve/ironic dichotomy was based on a symmetry between *individuals,* Captain Vere's reading takes place within a social *structure*: the rigidly hierarchical structure of a British warship. While the naïve reader (Billy) destroys the other in order to defend the self, and while the ironic reader (Claggart) destroys the self by projecting aggression onto the other, the third

reader (Vere) subordinates both self and other, and ultimately sacrifices both self and other, for the preservation of a political order.

2. The apparent purpose of both Billy's and Claggart's readings was to determine *character*: to preserve innocence or to prove guilt. Vere, on the other hand, subordinates character to action, being to doing: "A martial court," he tells his officers, "must needs in the present case confine its attention to the *blow's consequence*, which consequence justly is to be deemed not otherwise than as the *striker's deed*" (384).

3. In the opposition between the metaphysical and the psychoanalytical readings of Billy's deed, the deciding question was whether the blow should be considered accidental or (unconsciously) motivated. But in Vere's courtroom reading, both these alternatives are irrelevant: "Budd's intent or non-intent is nothing to the purpose" (389). What matters is not the cause but the consequences of the blow.

4. The naïve or literal reader takes language at face value and treats signs as *motivated*; the ironic reader assumes that the relation between sign and meaning can be *arbitrary* and that appearances are made to be reversed. For Vere, the functions and meanings of signs are neither transparent nor reversible but fixed by socially determined *convention*. Vere's very character is determined not by a relation between his outward appearance and his inner being but by the "buttons" that signify his position in society. While both Billy and Claggart are said to owe their character to "Nature," Vere sees his actions and being as meaningful only within the context of a contractual allegiance:

> Do these buttons that we wear attest that our allegiance is to Nature? No, to the King. Though the ocean, which is inviolate Nature primeval, though this be the element where we move and have our being as sailors, yet as the King's officers lies our duty in a sphere correspondingly natural? So little is that true, that in receiving our commissions we in the most important regards ceased to be natural free agents. When war is declared are we the commissioned fighters previously consulted? We fight at command. If our judgments approve the war, that is but coincidence. (387)

Judgment is thus for Vere a function neither of individual conscience nor of absolute justice but of "the rigor of martial law" (387) operating *through* him.

5. While Billy and Claggart read spontaneously and directly, Vere's reading often makes use of precedent (historical facts, childhood memories), allusions (to the Bible, to various ancient and modern authors), and analogies (Billy is like Adam, Claggart is like Ananias). Just as both Billy and Claggart have no known past, they read without memory; just as their lives end with their reading, they read without foresight. Vere, on the other hand, interrogates both past and future for interpretative guidance.

6. While Budd and Claggart thus oppose each other directly, without regard for circumstance or consequence, Vere reads solely in function of the attending historical situation: the Nore and Spithead mutinies have created an atmosphere "critical to naval authority" (380), and, since an engagement with the enemy fleet is possible at any moment, the *Bellipotent* cannot afford internal unrest.

The fundamental factor that underlies the opposition between the metaphysical Budd/Claggart conflict on the one hand and the reading of Captain Vere on the other can be summed up in a single word: *history*. While the naïve and the ironic readers attempt to impose upon language the functioning of an absolute, timeless, universal law (the sign as *either* motivated *or* arbitrary), the question of *martial* law arises within the story precisely to reveal the law as a *historical* phenomenon, to underscore the element of contextual mutability in the conditions of any act of reading. Arbitrariness and motivation, irony and literality, are parameters between which language constantly fluctuates, but only historical context determines which proportion of each is perceptible to each reader. Melville indeed shows history to be a story not only of events but also of fluctuations in the very functioning of irony and belief:

The event *converted into irony for a time* those spirited strains of Dibdin. . . . (333)

Everything is *for a term venerated* in navies. (408)

The opposing critical judgments of Vere's decision to hang Billy are divided, in the final analysis, according to the place they attribute to history in the process of justification. For the ironists, Vere is misusing history for his own self-preservation or for the preservation of a world safe for aristocracy. For those who accept Vere's verdict as tragic but necessary, it is Melville who has stacked the historical cards in Vere's favor. In both cases, the conception of history as an interpretive instrument remains the same: it is its *use* that is being judged. And the very fact that Billy Budd criticism itself historically moves from acceptance to irony is no doubt itself interpretable in the same historical terms.

Evidence can in fact be found in the text for both pro-Vere and anti-Vere judgments:

> Full of disquietude and misgiving, the surgeon left the cabin. Was Captain Vere suddenly affected in his mind? (378)

> Whether Captain Vere, as the surgeon professionally and privately surmised, was really the sudden victim of any degree of aberration, every one must determine for himself by such light as this narrative may afford. (379–80)

> That the unhappy event which has been narrated could not have happened at a worse juncture was but too true. For it was close on the heel of the suppressed insurrections, an aftertime very critical to naval authority, demanding from every English sea commander two qualities not readily interfusable—prudence and rigor. (380)

> Small wonder then that the *Bellipotent*'s captain . . . felt that circumspection not less than promptitude was necessary. . . . Here he may or may not have erred. (380)

The effect of these explicit oscillations of judgment within the text is to underline the *importance* of the act of judging while rendering its outcome undecidable. Judgment, however difficult, is clearly the central preoccupation of Melville's text, whether it be the judgment pronounced *by* Vere or *upon* him.

There is still another reason for the uncertainty over Vere's final status, however: the unfinished state of the manuscript at Melville's death. According to editors Hayford and Sealts,[41] it is the "late pencil revisions" that cast the greatest doubt upon Vere; Melville was evidently still fine-tuning the text's attitude toward its third reader when he died. The ultimate irony in the tale is thus that our final judgment of the very reader who takes history into consideration is made problematic precisely by the intervention of history: by the historical accident of the author's death. History here affects interpretation not only within the content of the narration but also within the very production of the narrative. And what remains suspended by this historical accident is nothing less than the exact signifying value of history itself. Clearly, the meaning of "history" as a feature distinguishing Vere's reading from those of Claggart and Budd can in no way be taken for granted.

VI. Judgment as Political Performance

When a poet takes his seat on the tripod of the Muse, he cannot control his thoughts. . . . When he represents men with contrasting characters he is often obliged to contradict himself, and he doesn't know which of the opposing speeches contains the truth. But for the legislator, this is impossible: he must not let his laws say two different things on the same subject.—Plato, *The Laws*

In the final analysis, the question is not: what did Melville really think of Captain Vere? but rather: what is at stake in his way of presenting him? What can we learn from him about the act of judging? Melville seems to be presenting us less with an *object* for judgment than with an *example* of judgment. And the very vehemence with which the critics tend to praise or condemn the justice of Vere's decision indicates that it is judging, not murdering, that Melville is asking us to judge.

And yet Vere's judgment *is* an act of murder. Captain Vere is a reader who kills, not, like Billy, *instead of* speaking, but rather, precisely *by means of* speaking. While Billy kills through verbal impotence, Vere kills through the very potency and sophistication of rhetoric. Judging, in Vere's case, is nothing less than the wielding of the power of life and death through language. In thus occupying the point at which murder and language meet, Captain Vere positions himself precisely astride the "deadly space between." While Billy's performative force occupies the vanishing point of utterance and cognition, and while the validity of Claggart's cognitive perception is realized only through the annihilation of the perceiver, Captain Vere's reading mobilizes both power and knowledge, performance and cognition, error and murder. Judgment is precisely cognition functioning as an act. It is this combination of performance and cognition that defines Vere's reading not merely as historical but as *political*. If politics is defined as the attempt to reconcile action with understanding, then Melville's story offers an exemplary context in which to analyze the interpretive and performative structures that make politics so problematic.

That the alliance between knowledge and action is by no means an easy one is amply demonstrated in Melville's story. Vere, indeed, has often been seen as the character in the tale who experiences the greatest suffering: his understanding of Billy's character and his military duty are totally at odds. On the one hand, cognitive exactitude requires that "history" be taken into consideration. Yet what constitutes "knowledge of history"? How are "circumstances" to be defined? What sort of causality does "precedent" imply? And what is to be done with overlapping but incompatible "contexts"? Before deciding upon innocence and guilt, Vere must define and limit the frame of reference within which his decision is to be possible. He does so by choosing the "legal" context over the "essential" context:

> In a *legal view* the apparent victim of the tragedy was he who had sought to victimize a man blameless; and the indisputable deed of the latter, *navally regarded*, constituted the most heinous of military crimes. Yet more. The *essential right and wrong* involved in the matter, the clearer that might be, so much the worse for the responsibility of a loyal sea commander, inasmuch as he was not authorized to determine the matter on that *primitive* basis. (380)

Yet it is precisely this determination of the proper frame of reference that dictates the outcome of the decision: once Vere has defined his context, he has also in fact reached his verdict. The very choice of the *conditions* of judgment itself constitutes a judgment. But what are the conditions of choosing the conditions of judgment?

The alternative, it seems, is between the "naval" and the "primitive," between "Nature" and "the King," between the martial court and what Vere calls the "Last Assizes" (388). But the question arises of exactly what the concept of "Nature" entails in such an opposition. In what way, and with what changes, would it have been possible for Vere's allegiance to be to "Nature"? How can a legal judgment exemplify "primitive" justice?

In spite of his allegiance to martial law and conventional authority, Vere clearly finds the "absolute" criteria equally applicable to Billy's deed, for he responds to each new development with the following exclamations:

"It is the divine judgment of Ananias!" (378)
"Struck dead by an angel of God! Yet the angel must hang!" (378)

> "Before a court less arbitrary and more merciful than a martial one, that
> plea would largely extenuate. At the Last Assizes it shall acquit." (388)
> "Ay, there is a mystery; but, to use a scriptural phrase, it is a 'mystery
> of iniquity,' a matter for psychological theologians to discuss." (385)

This last expression, which refers to the source of Claggart's antipathy, has already been mentioned by Melville's narrator and dismissed as being "tinctured with the biblical element":

> If that lexicon which is based on Holy Writ were any longer popular, one might with less difficulty define and denominate certain phenomenal men. As it is, one must turn to some authority not liable to the charge of being tinctured with the biblical element. (353)

Vere turns to the Bible to designate Claggart's "nature"; Melville turns to a Platonic tautology. But in both cases, the question arises: what does it mean to seal an explanation with a quotation? And what, in Vere's case, does it mean to refer a legal mystery to a religious text?

If Vere names the Absolute—as opposed to the martial—by means of quotations and allusions, does this not suggest that the two alternative frames of reference within which judgment is possible are not Nature and the King but rather two types of textual authority: the Bible and the Mutiny Act? This is not to say that Vere is "innocently" choosing one text over another, but that the nature of "Nature" in a legal context cannot be taken for granted. Even Thomas Paine, who is referred to by Melville in his function as proponent of "natural" human rights, cannot avoid grounding his concept of nature in biblical myth. In the very act of rejecting the authority of antiquity, he writes:

> The fact is, that portions of antiquity, by proving every thing, establish nothing. It is authority against authority all the way, till we come to the divine origin of the rights of man, at the Creation. Here our inquiries find a resting-place, and our reason a home.[42]

The final frame of reference is neither the heart nor the gun, neither Nature nor the King, but the authority of a Sacred Text. Authority seems to be nothing other than the vanishing point of textuality. And Nature is authority whose textual origins have been forgotten. Even behind the martial order of the world of the man-of-war, there lies a religious referent: the *Bellipotent*'s last battle is with a French ship called the *Athée*.

Judgment, then, would seem to ground itself in a suspension of the opposition between textuality and referentiality, just as politics can be seen as that which makes it impossible to draw the line between "language" and "life." Vere, indeed, is presented precisely as a reader who does not recognize the "frontier" between "remote allusions" and current events:

> In illustrating of any point touching the stirring personages and events of the time he would be as apt to cite some historic character or incident of antiquity as he would be to cite from the moderns. He seemed unmindful of the circumstance that to his bluff company such remote allusions, however pertinent they might really be, were altogether alien to men whose reading was mainly confined to the journals. But considerateness in such matters is not easy to natures constituted like Captain Vere's. Their honesty prescribes to them directness, sometimes far-reaching like that of a migratory fowl that in its flight never heeds when it crosses a frontier. (341)

Yet it is precisely by inviting Billy Budd and John Claggart to "cross" the "frontier" between their proper territory and their superior's cabin, between the private and the political realms, that Vere unwittingly sets up the conditions for the narrative chiasmus he must judge.

As was noted earlier, Captain Vere's function, according to many critics, is to insert "ambiguity" into the story's "oversimplified" allegorical opposition. Yet at the same time, it is precisely Captain Vere who inspires the most vehement critical oppositions. Captain Vere, in other words, seems to mobilize simultaneously the seemingly contradictory forces of ambiguity and polarity.

In his median position between the Budd/Claggart opposition and the acceptance/irony opposition, Captain Vere functions as a focus for the *conversion* of polarity into ambiguity and back again. Interestingly, he plays exactly the same role in the progress of the plot. It is Vere who brings together the "Innocent" Billy and the "guilty" Claggart in order to test the validity of Claggart's accusations, but he does so in such a way as to effect not a clarification but a reversal of places between guilt and innocence. Vere's fatherly words to Billy are precisely what triggers the ambiguous deed upon which Vere must pronounce a verdict of "condemn *or* let go." Just as Melville's readers, faced with the ambiguity they themselves recognize as being provided by Vere, are quick to pronounce the Captain vicious *or* virtuous, evil *or* just; so, too, Vere, who clearly perceives the "mystery" in the "moral dilemma" confronting him, must nevertheless reduce the situation to a binary opposition.

It would seem, then, that the function of judgment is to convert an ambiguous situation into a decidable one. But it does so by converting a difference *within* (Billy as divided between conscious submissiveness and unconscious hostility, Vere as divided between understanding father and military authority) into a difference *between* (between Claggart and Billy, between Nature and the King, between authority and criminality). A difference *between* opposing forces presupposes that the entities in conflict be knowable. A difference *within* one of the entities in question is precisely what problematizes the very *idea* of an entity in the first place, rendering the "legal point of view" inapplicable. In studying the plays of both ambiguity and binarity, Melville's story situates *its* critical difference neither within nor between, but precisely in the very question of the *relation between the two* as the fundamental question of all human politics. The political context in *Billy Budd* is such that on all levels the differences *within* (mutiny on the warship, the French revolution as a threat to "lasting institutions," Billy's unconscious hostility) are subordinated to differences *between* (the *Bellipotent* versus the *Athée*, England versus France, murderer versus victim). This is why Melville's choice of historical setting is so significant: the war between France and England at the time of the French Revolution is as striking an example of the simultaneous functioning of differences within and between as is the confrontation between Billy and Claggart in relation to their own internal divisions. War, indeed, is the absolute transformation of *all* differences into *binary* differences.

It would seem, then, that the maintenance of political authority requires that the law function as a set of rules for the regular, predictable misreading of the "difference within" as a "difference between." Yet if, as our epigraph from Plato suggests, law is thus defined in terms of its repression of ambiguity, then it is itself an overwhelming example of an entity based on a "difference within." Like Billy, the law, in attempting to eliminate its own "deadly space," can only inscribe itself in a space of deadliness.

In seeking to regulate the violent effects of difference, the political work of cognition is thus an attempt to *situate* that which must be eliminated. Yet in the absence of the possibility of knowing the locus and origin of violence, cognition itself becomes an act of violence. In terms of pure understanding, the drawing of a line *between* opposing entities does violence to the irreducible ambiguities that subvert the very possibility of determining the limits of what an "entity" is:

> Who in the rainbow can draw the line where the violet tint ends and the orange tint begins? Distinctly we see the difference of the colors, but where exactly does the one first blendingly enter into the other? So with sanity and insanity. In pronounced cases there is no question about them. But in some supposed cases, in various degrees supposedly less

pronounced, to draw the exact line of demarcation few will undertake, though for a fee becoming considerate some professional experts will. There is nothing nameable but that some men will, or undertake to, do it for pay. (379)

As an act, the drawing of a line is not only inexact and violent: it is also that which problematizes the very possibility of situating the "difference between" the judge and what is judged, between the interests of the "expert" and the truth of his expertise. What every act of judgment manifests is not the value of the object but the position of the judge within a structure of exchange. There is, in other words, no position from which to judge that would be outside the lines of force involved in the object judged.

But if judging is always a *partial* reading (in both senses of the word), is there a place for reading beyond politics? Are we, as Melville's readers, outside the arena in which power and fees are exchanged? If law is the forcible transformation of ambiguity into decidability, is it possible to read ambiguity *as such*, without that reading functioning as a political act?

Even about this, Melville has something to say. For there is a fourth reader in *Billy Budd*, one who "never interferes in aught and never gives advice" (363): the old Dansker. A man of "few words, many wrinkles," and "the complexion of an antique parchment" (347), the Dansker is the very picture of one who understands and emits ambiguous utterances. When asked by Billy for an explanation of his petty troubles, the Dansker says only, "Jemmy Legs [Claggart] is down on you" (349). This interpretation, entirely accurate as a reading of Claggart's ambiguous behavior, is handed down to Billy without further explanation:

Something less unpleasantly oracular he tried to extract; but the old sea Chiron, thinking perhaps that for the nonce he had sufficiently instructed his young Achilles, pursed his lips, gathered all his wrinkles together, and would commit himself to nothing further. (349)

As a reader who understands ambiguity yet refuses to "commit himself," the Dansker thus dramatizes a reading that attempts to be as cognitively accurate and as performatively neutral as possible. Yet however neutral he tries to remain, the Dansker's reading does not take place outside the political realm: it is his very refusal to participate in it, whether by further instruction or by direct intervention, that leads to Billy's exclamation in the soup episode ("There now, who says Jemmy Legs is down on me?"). The transference of knowledge is not any more innocent than the transference of power. For it is precisely through the impossibility of finding a spot from which knowledge could be all-encompassing that the plays of political power proceed.

Just as the attempt to "know" without "doing" can itself function as a deed, the fact that judgment is always explicitly an act adds a further insoluble problem to its cognitive predicament. Since, as Vere points out, no judgment can take place in the Last Assizes, no judge can ever pronounce a Last Judgment. In order to reach a verdict, Vere must determine the consequences not only of the fatal blow, but also precisely of his own verdict. Judgment is an act not only because it kills, but because it is in turn open to judgment:

> "Can we not convict and yet mitigate the penalty?" asked the sailing master. . . .
>
> "Gentlemen, were that clearly lawful for us under the circumstances, consider the consequences of such clemency. . . . To the people the foretopman's deed, however it be worded in the announcement, will be plain homicide committed in a flagrant act of mutiny. What penalty for that should follow, they know. But it does not follow. *Why?* They will ruminate. You know what sailors are. Will they not revert to the recent outbreak at the Nore?" (389)

The danger is not only one of repeating the Nore mutiny, however. It is also one of forcing Billy, for all his innocence, to repeat his crime. Billy is a politically charged object from the moment he strikes his superior. He is no longer, and can never again be, plotless. If he were set free, he himself would be unable to explain why. As a focus for the questions and intrigues of the crew, he would be even less capable of defending himself than before, and would surely strike again. The political reading, as cognition, attempts to understand the past; as performance, it attempts to eliminate from the future any necessity for its own recurrence.

What this means is that every judge is in the impossible position of having to include the effects of his own act of judging within the cognitive context of his decision. The question of the nature of the type of historical causality that would govern such effects can neither be decided nor ignored. Because of his official position, Vere cannot choose to read in such a way that his reading would not be an act of political authority. But what Melville shows in *Billy Budd* is that authority consists precisely in the impossibility of containing the effects of its own application.

As a political allegory, Melville's *Billy Budd* is thus much more than a study of good and evil, justice and injustice. It is a dramatization of the twisted relations between knowing and doing, speaking and killing, reading and judging, which make political understanding and action so problematic. In the subtle creation of Claggart's "evil" out of a series of spaces in knowledge, Melville shows that gaps in cognition, far from being mere absences, take on the performative power of true acts. The *force* of what is not known is all the more effective for not being perceived as such. The crew, which does not understand that it does not know, is no less performative a reader than the Captain, who clearly perceives and represses the presence of "mystery." The legal order, which attempts to submit "brute force" to. "forms, measured forms," can only eliminate violence by transforming violence into the final authority. And cognition, which perhaps begins as a power play against the play of power, can only increase, through its own elaboration, the range of what it tries to dominate. The "deadly space" or "difference" that runs through *Billy Budd* is not located *between* knowledge and action, performance and cognition: it is that which, within cognition, functions as an act: it is that which, within action, prevents us from ever knowing whether what we hit coincides with what we understand. And this is what makes the meaning of Melville's last work so . . . *striking.*

NOTES

"Melville's Fist: The Execution of *Billy Budd.*" *Studies in Romanticism* 18, no. 4 (1979): 567–99. Reprinted with permission.

Epigraph from Herman Melville, *Billy Budd*, in *"Billy Budd, Sailor," and Other Stories*, ed. H. Beaver (New York: Penguin Books, 1967), 405. Unless otherwise indicated, all references to *Billy Budd* are to this edition, which reprints the Hayford and Sealts Reading Text.

1. E. L. Grant Watson, "Melville's Testament of Acceptance," *New England Quarterly* 6 (1933): 319–27.
2. The expression appears in both J. Freeman, *Herman Melville* (New York: Macmillan, 1926), 136, and R. M. Weaver, *The Shorter Novels of Herman Melville* (New York: Liveright Publishing, 1928), li.
3. W. E. Sedgwick, *Herman Melville: The Tragedy of Mind* (Cambridge, MA: Harvard University Press, 1944), 231–49.
4. F. B. Freeman, *Melville's Billy Budd* (Cambridge, MA: Harvard University Press, 1948), 115–24.
5. J. Schiffman, "Melville's Final Stage: Irony," *American Literature* 22 (1950): 128–36.
6. P. Withim, *"Billy Budd*: Testament of Resistance," *Modern Language Quarterly* 20 (1959): 115–27.
7. K. E. Zink, "Herman Melville and the Forms—Irony and Social Criticism in *Billy Budd,*" *Accent* 12 (1952): 131–39.

8. L. Thompson, *Melville's Quarrel with God* (Princeton, NJ: Princeton University Press, 1952).

9. K. Ledbetter, "The Ambiguity of *Billy Budd*," *Texas Studies in Literature and Language* 4 (1962): 130–34.

10. S. E. Hyman, quoted in R. H. Fogle, "*Billy Budd*—Acceptance or Irony," *Tulane Studies in English* 8 (1958): 107.

11. E. M. Cifelli, "*Billy Budd*: Boggy Ground to Build On," *Studies in Short Fiction* 8 (1976): 463–69.

12. L. T. Lemon, "*Billy Budd*: The Plot against the Story," *Studies in Short Fiction* 2 (1964): 32–43.

13. J. M. Murry, "Herman Melville's Silence," *Times Literary Supplement*, July 10, 1924, 433.

14. Interestingly enough, reversibility seems to constitute not only *Billy Budd*'s ending but also its origin: the *Somers* mutiny case, which commentators have seen as a major source for the story, had been brought back to Melville's attention at the time he was writing *Billy Budd* by two opposing articles that reopened and retold the *Somers* case, forty-six years after the fact, in precisely antithetical terms.

15. Charles Weir Jr., "Malice Reconciled," in *Critics on Melville*, ed. Theodore Rountree (Coral Gables, FL: University of Miami Press, 1972), 121.

16. W. Y. Tindall, "The Ceremony of Innocence," in *Great Moral Dilemmas in Literature, Past and Present*, ed. R. M. McIver (New York: Harper and Row, 1956), 75.

17. *Herman Melville* (New York: Harcourt, Brace and World, 1929), 357.

18. From Richard Chase, *Herman Melville: A Critical Study* (New York: Macmillan, 1949), 269–70.

19. Chase, *Herman Melville*, 269.

20. O. Fenichel, *The Psychoanalytic Theory of Neuroses*, quoted in Stafford, *Billy Budd and the Critics* (Belmont, CA: Wadsworth, 1969), 176.

21. Edwin Haviland Miller, *Melville* (New York: Persea Books, 1975), 358.

22. Miller, *Melville*, 362.

23. Rollo May, *Power and Innocence* (New York: W. W. Norton, 1972), 49–50.

24. Murry, "Herman Melville's Silence," 433.

25. Tindall, "The Ceremony of Innocence," 74.

26. John Seelye, *Melville: The Ironic Diagram* (Evanston, IL: Northwestern University Press, 1970), 162.

27. K. Widmer, *The Ways of Nihilism* (Los Angeles: California State Colleges Publication, 1970), 21.

28. H. Arendt, *On Revolution* (New York: Viking, 1963), 77–83.

29. Widmer, *Ways of Nihilism*, 33.

30. M. Stern, *The Fine Hammered Steel of Herman Melville* (Urbana: University of Illinois Press, 1957), 206–50.

31. Weir, "Malice Reconciled," 121.

32. Withim, "*Billy Budd*: Testament of Resistance," 126.

33. Weir, "Malice Reconciled," 121.

34. Thompson, *Melville's Quarrel with God*, 386.

35. Weir, "Malice Reconciled," 124.

36. L. Casper, "The Case against Captain Vere," *Perspective* 5 (1952): 151.

37. Weir, "Malice Reconciled," 121.

38. Thompson, *Melville's Quarrel with God*, 386.

39. J. E. Miller, "*Billy Budd*: The Catastrophe of Innocence," MLN 73 (1958): 174.

40. Widmer, *Ways of Nihilism*, 29.

41. Editors' Introduction, *Billy Budd, Sailor* (Chicago: University of Chicago Press, 1962); see esp. 34–35.

42. Thomas Paine, *The Rights of Man* (Garden City, NY: Anchor Press, 1973), 303.

PART IV

Pedagogy and Translation

CHAPTER 21

Nothing Fails Like Success

As soon as any radically innovative thought becomes an *ism*, its specific ground-breaking force diminishes, its historical notoriety increases, and its disciples tend to become more simplistic, more dogmatic, and ultimately more conservative, at which time its power becomes institutional rather than analytical. The fact that what is loosely called deconstructionism is now being widely institutionalized in the United States seems to me both intriguing and paradoxical, but also a bit unsettling, although not for the reasons advanced by most of its opponents. The questions I shall ask are the following: How can the deconstructive impulse retain its *critical* energy in the face of its own success? What can a reader who has felt the surprise of intellectual discovery in a work by Jacques Derrida or Paul de Man do to remain in touch not so much with the content of the discovery as with the intellectual upheaval of the surprise? How can that surprise be put to *work* in new ways?

I would like to begin by examining briefly two types of accusations commonly directed *against* deconstruction: the literarily conservative, which accuses deconstruction of going too far, and the politically radical, which accuses deconstruction of not going far enough. The first type comes from well-established men of letters who attempt to defend their belief in the basic communicability of meanings and values against what is said to be the deconstructionists' relativism, nihilism, or self-indulgent love of meaninglessness. What I shall try to determine is not whether misunderstanding is a mere accident or the inevitable fate of reading, but rather what the relation is between deconstruction and the type of logic on which these opponents' accusations of relativism and solipsism are based. Consider the following sentences taken from well-known critiques of deconstruction:

> In revisionist criticism the first consequence of calling discourse itself into question is the proposition that all criticism amounts to misreading, and thus one reading is as legitimate as another.

> But if all interpretation is misinterpretation, and if all criticism (like all history) of texts can engage only with a critic's own misconstruction, why bother to carry on the activities of interpretation and criticism?

> In the absence of any appeal to such a coercive reality to which the plurality of subjectivities can be referred, all perspectives become equally valid.

> Certainty and piety of all kinds are systematically undermined in favor of a universal relativism of values and judgment. Just as the revisionists are led to reduce the act of criticism to a given critic's subjective preference, so do professors relegate judgment of all sorts to the students' subjective preferences.

> What Deconstruction urges is not a new system of thought but skepticism toward all the old ways, which are construed as really only one way.[1]

The logic behind such utterances is the logic of binary opposition, the principle of noncontradiction, often thought of as the very essence of Logic as such. The arguments can be reduced to the following logical formulas:

1. If all readings are misreadings, then all readings are equally valid.
2. If there is no such thing as an objective reading, then all readings are based on subjective preferences.
3. If there is no absolute truth, then everything is relative.
4. To criticize is to be skeptical; to put in question is to dismiss.

In other words, if not absolute, then relative; if not objective, then subjective; if you are not for something, you are against it. Now, my understanding of what is most radical in deconstruction is precisely that it questions this basic logic of binary opposition, but not in a simple, binary, antagonistic way. Consider the following passage from Derrida's *Dissemination*:

> It is thus not simply false to say that Mallarmé is a Platonist or a Hegelian. But it is above all not true. And vice versa.[2]

Instead of a simple "either/or" structure, deconstruction attempts to elaborate a discourse that says *neither* "either/or," *nor* "both/and" nor even "neither/nor," while at the same time not totally abandoning these logics either. The very word *deconstruction* is meant to undermine the either/or logic of the opposition "construction/destruction." Deconstruction is both, it is neither, and it reveals the way in which both construction and destruction are themselves not what they appear to be. Deconstruction both opposes and redefines; it both reverses an opposition and reworks the terms of that opposition so that what was formerly understood by them is no longer tenable. In the case of the much-publicized opposition between speech and writing, deconstruction *both* appears to grant to writing the priority traditionally assigned to speech *and* redefines "writing" as *différance* (difference/deferment) so that it can no longer simply mean "marks on a page" but can very well also refer to those aspects of spoken speech (nonimmediacy, the non-transparency of meaning, the gap between signifier and signified) that are normally occulted by traditional notions of what speech is. In the case of the opposition between objectivity and subjectivity, deconstruction *seems* to locate the moment of meaning-making in the nonobjectivity of the act of reading rather than in the inherent givens of a text, but then the text seems already to anticipate the reading it engenders, and at the same time the reader's "subjectivity" is discovered to function something like a text, that is, something whose conscious awareness of meaning and desire is only one aspect of a complex unconscious signifying system which determines consciousness as one of its several effects. To imply that subjectivity is structured like a machine, as Paul de Man does in his essay "The Purloined Ribbon,"[3] is both to subvert the opposition between subject and object (since a machine is considered to be an object) and to displace the traditional notion of what a subject is. If the original opposition between subject and object corresponds, as Gerald Graff would have it, to the opposition between the pleasure principle and the reality principle,[4] what deconstruction shows is that there is *something else involved* that puts in question the very separability of the pleasure principle and the reality principle, something that continuously generates effects that can be explained by neither. Freud called this something the death instinct, but this death instinct is to be understood as what ceaselessly escapes the mastery of understanding and the logic of binary opposition by exhibiting some "other" logic one can neither totally comprehend nor exclude. It is the attempt to *write with* this "other" logic that produces the appearance of obscurity in many deconstructive texts. Any statement that *affirms* while using a logic different from the logic of binary opposition will necessarily not conform to binary notions of "clarity."

Hence, if deconstruction focuses on the act of reading rather than on the objective meaning of a text, this in no way entails any greater degree of self-indulgence than the belief in conventional values does: on the contrary, at its best it undoes the very comforts of mastery and consensus that underlie the illusion that objectivity is situated somewhere outside the self. Thus, the incompatibility between deconstruction and its conservative detractors is an incompatibility of logics. While traditionalists say that a thing cannot be both A and not-A, deconstructors open up ways in which A is necessarily but unpredictably already different from A.

Now we come to the second type of critique of deconstruction, which accuses it of not living up to its own claims of radicality, of working with too limited a notion of textuality, and of applying its critical energy only within an institutional structure that it does not question and therefore confirms.[5] This charge, which judges deconstruction against its own claims to an unflagging critical stance, is one which deconstruction must in fact continuously make against itself. Any discourse that is based on the questioning of boundary lines must never stop questioning its own. To reserve the deconstructive stance solely for literary criticism without analyzing its institutional underpinnings and economic and social relations with the world is to decide where the boundaries of the very critique of boundaries lie. To read a text apart from the historical and biographical conditions and writings that participate in its textual network is to limit a priori the kinds of questions that can be asked. Why, therefore, do some deconstructors tend to avoid going beyond the limits of the literary text?

There are, I think, three reasons for this unwarranted restriction. The first is entailed by the current institutionalization of deconstruction: the more it becomes entrenched as the self-definition of some literary critics in their opposition to other literary critics, the more it will resist problematizing the institutional conditions of literary criticism as such. The other two reasons spring out of an oversimplified understanding of certain aspects of deconstructive theory. To say, as Derrida has said, that there is nothing outside the text is not to say that the reader should read only one piece of literature in isolation from history, biography, and so on. It is to say that *nothing* can be said to be *not* a text, subject to the différance, the nonimmediacy, of presence or meaning. Even the statement that there is nothing outside the text cannot be taken to be the absolute certainty it appears to be, since it has to include itself in its own consequences. If there is nothing outside the text, then how can *any* locus of research or action be considered a priori as illegitimate?

The final reason for the conservatism of some forms of deconstruction is more pervasive: in questioning the nature of knowledge and causality, deconstruction has often given nothing but negative help in the attempt to read literature or philosophy *with* history and biography. In saying that history is a fiction, a text subject to ideological skewings and mystifications, and that it cannot be relied upon as a source of objective knowledge, deconstructive theory sometimes seems to block all access to the possibility of reading explicitly "referential" documents in conjunction with literary or speculative texts. Yet in practice, we find Derrida drawing upon Freud's life and letters in his analysis of *Beyond the Pleasure Principle* (in *La Carte Postale*), and de Man often beginning an article with a historical account that in some way doubles the rhetorical problem he is about to discuss. The question, then, is how to use history and biography *deconstructively*, how to seek in them not answers, causes, explanations, or origins, but new questions and new ways in which the literary and nonliterary texts alike can be made to read and rework each other.

I would now like to outline a few general remarks about how to avoid becoming too comfortable in the abyss. To go back to the original objection that "if all readings are misreadings, then all readings are equally valid," how is it possible to maintain that some readings are better than others in a way that cannot be entirely reduced to a binary opposition? Since it is obvious that no deconstructor actually thinks all readings are equally valid, what kind of evaluation does deconstruction permit?

The sentence "all readings are misreadings" does not *simply* deny the notion of truth. Truth is preserved in vestigial form in the notion of error. This does not mean that there is, somewhere out there, forever unattainable, the one true reading against which all others will be tried and found wanting. Rather, it implies (1) that the reasons a reading might consider itself *right* are motivated and undercut by its own interests, blindnesses, desires, and fatigue, and (2) that the *role* of truth cannot be so simply eliminated. Even if truth is but a fantasy of the will to power, *something* still marks the point from which the imperatives of the not-self make themselves felt. To reject objective truth is to make it harder to avoid setting oneself up as an arbitrary arbiter. Therefore, the one imperative a reading must obey is that it follow, with rigor, what puts in question the kind of reading it thought it was going to be. A reading is strong, I would therefore submit, to the extent that it encounters and propagates the surprise of otherness. The impossible but necessary task of the reader is to set herself up to be surprised.

No methodology can be relied on to generate surprise. On the contrary, it is usually surprise that engenders methodology. Derrida brings to his reader the surprise of a nonbinary, undecidable logic. Yet comfortable undecidability needs to be surprised by its own conservatism. My emphasis on the word *surprise* is designed to counter the idea that a good deconstructor must constantly put his own enterprise into question. This is true, but it is not enough. It can lead to a kind of infinite regress of demystification, in which ever more sophisticated subtleties are elaborated within an unchanging field of questions.

How, then, can one set oneself up to be surprised by otherness? Obviously, in a sense, one cannot. Yet one can begin by transgressing one's own usual practices, by indulging in some judicious time-wasting with what one does not know how to use, or what has fallen into disrepute. What the surprise encounter with otherness should do is lay bare some hint of an ignorance one never knew one had. Much has been made of the fact that "knowledge" cannot be taken for granted. But perhaps rather than simply questioning the nature of knowledge, we should today reevaluate the static, inert concept we have always had of ignorance. Ignorance, far more than knowledge, is what can never be taken for granted. If I perceive my ignorance as a gap in knowledge instead of an imperative that changes the very nature of what I think I know, then I do not truly experience my ignorance. The surprise of otherness is that moment when a new form of ignorance is suddenly activated as an imperative. If the deconstructive impulse is to retain its vital, subversive power, we must therefore become ignorant of it again and again. It is only by forgetting what we know how to do, by setting aside the thoughts that have most changed us, that those thoughts and that knowledge can go on making accessible to us the surprise of an otherness we can only encounter in the moment of suddenly discovering we are ignorant of it.

NOTES

"Nothing Fails Like Success." sce *Reports* 8 (fall 1980). Reprinted with permission of the University of Houston-Victoria.

This chapter was originally written for a session at the 1980 MLA Convention organized by the Society for Critical Exchange on the topic "The Future of Deconstruction." While I would want to argue some of the points a bit differently now (and perhaps with different examples), the basic thrust of the essay seems to me to be, if anything, even more relevant today. In the years since this essay was written, many more critiques of deconstruction have appeared, both from the left and from the right, but I leave the references as they were in 1980. Some of the later material will present itself in this book in dialogue with other chapters.

1. Peter Shaw, "Degenerate Criticism," *Harper's* (October 1979): 97; M. H. Abrams, "The Deconstructive Angel," *Critical Inquiry* (spring 1977): 434; Gerald Graff, *Literature against Itself* (Chicago: University of Chicago Press, 1979), 39; Shaw, "Degenerate Criticism," 93; and Denis Donoghue, "Deconstructing Deconstruction," *New York Review of Books*, June 12, 1980, 37.

2. Jacques Derrida, *Dissemination*, trans. Barbara Johnson (Chicago: University of Chicago Press, 1981), 207.

3. Paul de Man, "The Purloined Ribbon," in *Glyph 1: Johns Hopkins Textual Studies* (Baltimore: Johns Hopkins University Press, 1977). Reprinted as "Excuses" in *Allegories of Reading* (New Haven, CT: Yale University Press, 1979).

4. Graff, *Literature against Itself*, 65.

5. See, for example, Jeffrey Mehlman, "Teaching Reading," *Diacritics* (winter 1976); Gayatri Chakravorti Spivak and Michael Ryan, "Anarchism Revisited," *Diacritics* (summer 1978); John Brenkman, "Deconstruction and the Social Text," *Social Text* 1 (winter 1979); and Edward Said, "Reflections on Recent American 'Left' Literary Criticism," *boundary 2* 8, no. 1 (1979), reprinted in *The World, the Text, and the Critic* (Cambridge, MA: Harvard University Press, 1983).

CHAPTER 22

Bad Writing

Le Mal—une forme aigüe du Mal—dont elle [la littérature] est
l'expression, a pour nous, je crois, la valeur souveraine.

[Evil—an accute form of Evil—of which literature is the expression,
has for us, I think, the highest value.]
—Georges Bataille, *La Littérature et le Mal*

In 1963 Anne Sexton composed an elegy for Sylvia Plath called "Sylvia's Death,"
in which she wrote, "and I know at the news of your death, / a terrible taste
for it, like salt."[1] This elegy is unusual in that it expresses not loss but sexual
jealousy. Sylvia's death has awakened an overwhelming appetite and envy, a
terrible taste.

Critics have often accused Anne Sexton of terrible taste, putting unseemly
parts of the female body on display and lusting after death self-indulgently,
even to the point of feeling robbed personally when someone else commits
suicide. But lyric poetry has always been obsessed with death, and I would
argue that in seeing Sexton as all symptom and all body, readers have missed
her inventive exploration of more technical questions of lyric voice. For when
she calls Sylvia's death "an old belonging," something one's mouth opens onto,
she is talking about the way in which death's terrible taste has filled poets'
mouths for a long time, like salt.

The fact that the history of lyric poetry is so bound up with the nature of
elegy has created the impression that the lyric was invented to overcome
death, not desire it. Poetry, in this view, acts as a consolation, a monument,

a promise of immortality beyond the grave. Yet even the most traditional elegy contains the guilty secret that desire is not all for life, that poetry offers something other than life as object of desire. From Narcissus, in love with an image, and Apollo or Petrarch, consoling themselves with a laurel branch, to Keats's "half in love with easeful death," Milton's *Lycidas*, or Wordsworth's "Lucy" poems, the mourned person provides an occasion for poetic performance, not just loss. From there to Sexton's "Wanting to Die," the distance is not as great as some would have it.

But the conflation of the desire for writing with the desire for death does not perfectly flow from the fact that both are desires for something other than biological life. It is true that Narcissus dies from loving an image, but the critical theory of the "Death of the Author" was not about literal death but about interpretation and authorial intention. Indeed, it is precisely in the case of an author who has committed suicide that readers who normally restrict their interest to features internal to a text develop a terrible taste for biography as a tool for understanding poetry. Readers are unable to resist asking the poems to tell us why the poet killed herself. The dead author returns to life with a vengeance as the site of an intention to die.

There are two profound taboos threatened when the poet is a woman. There is something monstrous by definition when a woman chooses death over life because she has so often been the guardian of the life forces, associated with reproduction, comfort, other-directedness, and maternal care. When a woman writes about bodies that matter and yet can be accused in any way of being a "bad mother" or even of being something other than a counterpart to a man, she is violating the very conditions of her visibility and is much more likely to be seen as a "bad writer" than to participate in the culturally valued badness that poetry's job is to hold up to the laws of the marketplace—or of reproduction.

The cultural prestige of *Le Mal* probably reached its height with Baudelaire's 1857 publication of *Les Fleurs du Mal*. *Le Mal* is notoriously hard to translate into English. Is it "evil"? "Badness"? "Sickness" ["à Théophile Gautier, je dédie ces fleurs maladives"]? "Suffering"? "Melancholy" [spleen]? "romanticism" [*Mal du siècle*]? But sardonic delight in thumbing one's nose at bourgeois "virtue" was de rigueur for postrevolutionary French poetry. Rimbaud's mother, for example, forbade her son to read the unseemly writings of "M. Hugot [*sic*],"[2] and parents threatened to withdraw their children from their English class when it was learned that the mild-mannered M. Mallarmé had published poetry.[3] It is perhaps surprising that the Second Empire courts took literally Baudelaire's poetic celebrations of evil and prosecuted him for them. But it is even more surprising how surprised he seemed by this. The rise of the bourgeoisie in France was particularly gender divided: women stood for virtue, men for badness of every sort—so much so that Baudelaire could exemplify his badness through lesbianism but could disqualify women completely as readers of his book.

Something of Baudelaire's "badness" is lost, I think, when it is translated by Mallarmé into obscurity alone. Baudelaire explained in an unfinished draft of a preface that "famous poets had long divided up the most flowery realms of poetry. I thought it would be pleasant, and enjoyable precisely to the extent that the task was difficult, to extract *beauty* from *le Mal*."[4] This is a defense of difficulty, too, but not in the same sense as Mallarmé's "I say: a flower! and . . . musically arises . . . that which is absent in all bouquets."[5] Contemporary defenses of difficult writing have gone in the direction of Mallarmé's obscurity rather than Baudelaire's evil. The "death of the author," in fact, is prefigured in Mallarmé's famous statement, "The pure work implies the speaking disappearance of the poet, who yields initiative to words."[6] But this is a death without a corpse, without decay, without worms, without *vers*. Mallarmé makes of death a principle of structure so far-reaching that it took the whole twentieth century to understand it. Nevertheless, while making death infiltrate every aspect of signification, Mallarmé is also in some way repressing it, and repressing the badness that no principle can eliminate.

That badness returns, paradoxically, not in the defenses but in the attacks on "bad writing" that have often accompanied obscurity. A sense of such contests at the end of the nineteenth century can be gleaned from Mallarmé's testy defense in his essay "Mystery in Letters":

> De pures prérogatives seraient, cette fois, à la merci des bas farceurs.
>
> Tout écrit, extérieurement à son trésor, doit, par égard envers ceux dont il emprunte, après tout, pour un objet autre, le langage, présenter, avec les mots, un sens même indifférent: on gagne de détourner l'oisif, charmé que rien ne l'y concerne, à première vue.
>
> Salut, exact, de part et d'autre—
>
> Si, tout de même, n'inquiétait je ne sais quel miroitement, en dessous, peu séparable de la surface concédée à la rétine—il attire le soupçon: les malins, entre le public, réclamant de couper court, opinent, avec sérieux, que, juste, la teneur est inintelligible.
>
> Malheur ridiculement à qui tombe sous le coup, il est enveloppé dans une plaisanterie immense et médiocre: ainsi toujours—pas tant, peut-être, que ne sévit avec ensemble et excès, maintenant, le fléau.

Il doit y avoir quelque chose d'occulte au fond de tous, je crois déci-
dément à quelque chose d'abscons, signifiant fermé et caché, qui habite
le commun: car, sitôt cette masse jetée vers quelque trace que c'est une
réalité, existant, par exemple, sur une feuille de papier, dans tel écrit—
pas en soi—cela qui est obscur: elle s'agite, ouragan jaloux d'attribuer les
ténèbres à quoi que ce soit, profusément, flagramment.

Sa crédulité vis-à-vis de plusieurs qui la soulagent, en faisant affaire,
bondit à l'excès: et le suppôt d'Ombre, d'eux désigné, ne placera un mot,
dorénavant, qu'avec un secouement que ç'ait été elle, l'énigme, elle
ne tranche, par un coup d'éventail de ses jupes: "Comprends pas!"—
l'innocent annonçât-il se moucher.[7]

I have permitted myself this extensive quotation because I think it touches
on most of the things that come up when one tries to defend obscurity: the
division between the crowd and the writer, the crowd's refusal to think there
could be obscurity inside everyone, the scapegoating of anyone who suggests otherwise and the paranoid vigilance about it, the accusation that incomprehensible writing is the cause of incomprehension. But the real mystery is
why "I don't understand it" should condemn the *author* rather than the *reader*
or, at least, as Mallarmé goes on to say, should not amount to a suspension
of judgment:

Je sais, de fait, qu'ils se poussent en scène et assument, à la parade, eux,
la posture humiliante; puisque arguer d'obscurité—ou, nul ne saisira
s'ils ne saisissent et ils ne saisissent pas—implique un renoncement
antérieur à juger.[8]

It has become commonplace to allow difficult or transgressive writing to
authors but not to *critics*. Poetic badness and critical obscurity seem very
different, but the condemnation of any writer for obscurity is itself colored
with moral indignation. "Don't understand!" becomes an accusation. When
what was initially condemned enters into the canon, we can smile with superiority at Rimbaud's mother or Baudelaire's and be amazed at their blindness
to poetic genius. Yet in the very act of inventing obscure poetry Mallarmé
invented the "poème critique." In other words, it was when he realized that
the writer and the reader could no longer be disentangled that Mallarmé
became Mallarmé.

The taint of moral unseemliness does not last forever, but literature nevertheless keeps enough of that initial *frisson* to give literary studies a somewhat bad conscience. As Peter Brooks put it: "We teachers of literature have

little hard information to impart, we're not even sure what we teach, and we have something of a bad conscience about the whole business."⁹ Brooks's remarks come in the context of a defense of studying literature as a specific object. It was written for a fascinating compilation of reports and responses published in 1995 as *Comparative Literature in the Age of Multiculturalism*, in which it is suggested that literature be considered "one discursive practice among many others."¹⁰ Comparative literature, it seems, threatens to dissolve into "cultural studies," seen as the triumph of, as Baudelaire would put it, "bonnes actions" over "beau langage." In fact, none of these slippery slopes are unavoidable, but the best way to make sure that literature doesn't dissolve is precisely to keep that "bad conscience."

Comparative literature as a field seems to need to defend itself against the Scylla of "theory" and the Charybdis of "translation." Although many writers recognize the necessary and irreversible changes each has contributed to the field, they lament the day when comparative literature meant reading several languages and literary traditions in the original. Yet their guilt about "elitism" or "Eurocentrism" leads them to overlook some obvious defenses that no one calls up. They mount, with increasing feebleness, what might be called a "Protestant" defense of multiple languages: it is hard to learn a language; therefore, students who learn more than one have to make more effort and be more talented. Here is how Harry Levin, author of the first report in 1965, put it: "If we profess to cover more ground than our sister departments we should honestly acknowledge that we must work harder, nor should we incur their suspicion by offering short-cuts."¹¹ This is true only to the extent that languages can only be learned in school. The decline of language teaching therefore makes this way of learning languages even harder. But instead of merely failing to teach languages, the public school system actually *discourages* the use of any language other than English. Education consists, then, of *unlearning* languages, not learning them. Before becoming an elite capable of mastering several languages, children must first pass into the elite of people who speak only English. The number of languages spoken in American homes is everything a dream of multiculturalism could ask for: it is not an idea; it is a reality. If comparative literature could tap into *that* multiculturalism, however, it would tap into the true obscurities and insolubilities of a world that cannot be studied as an object. Every comparatist would already be a part of it.

The "good" object, multiculturalism, would present all the dilemmas of the modern world that its idealization—the "It's a small world after all" refrain—represses. But the "bad" objects, theory and translation, are actually two versions of the same unrepression. It is not just that theory involved a mad impetus to translation but that the theory that transformed literary studies utterly transformed the practice of translation. Translating Derrida or Lacan became an art in itself, and respect for specific effects sometimes became so great that more and more words were left in the original and glossed. Thus, more and more French, Greek, or German words began to have currency in theoretical discourse, which, in turn, increased the anger of beginning readers frustrated at what felt like unnecessary impotence to the point that they felt like slamming down the book, snarling something like, "Take your *Nachträglichkeit* and shove it!"

In 1959 it was still possible to write, as did a translator of Hegel's *Encyclopedia*:

> To translate the world's worst stylist literally, sentence by sentence, is possible—it has been done—but it is perfectly pointless; the translation, then, is every bit as unintelligible as the original. But the world's worst stylist is, alas, also one of the world's greatest thinkers, certainly the most important for us in this twentieth century. In the whole history of philosophy there is no other single work that can hold a candle to his *Logic*; a work incomparable in its range, depth, clarity of thought, and beauty of composition—but it must be decoded.
>
> The attempt must be risked, therefore, to rescue its grandeur from its abstruse linguistic chaos. . . . This is like detective work: what Hegel means, but hides under a dead heap of abstractions, must be guessed at and ferreted out. I have dared to translate—not the ponderous Hegelian jargon, which is as little German as it would be English—but the thought. My "translation," then, is a critical presentation or rendition; it is not a book about Hegel because it faithfully follows the order and sequence of his paragraphs.[12]

After the theory revolution it is no longer possible so serenely to separate style from thinking, idea from language, thought from jargon. The understanding that thought is not separable from its expression—and in that way sometimes escapes the control of the author himself—is what deconstruction found within the structuralism that claimed a panoptic view of meaning making. "As little German as it would be English" indicates that the original is worth translating precisely because it is foreign to its *own* language. When Mallarmé contributed a series of his "poèmes critiques" without translation to W. H. Henley's journal the *National Observer*, a letter from a reader protested that he was ready to accept the anomaly in order to brush up on his

French but that Mallarmé was writing in a language that was "as little French as it would have been English."[13] Poetry, for Mallarmé, was that which "de plusieurs vocables refait un mot total, neuf, *étranger à la langue*."[14] For Walter Benjamin, too, translation was "only a somewhat provisional way of coming to grips with the foreignness of languages."[15] Only through translation does the work's foreignness to *its own* language become apparent.

If deconstruction is what is often meant by "theory," whether for good or ill, no one could insist more on going back to the original language than Jacques Derrida. His essay on Plato discovers in the word *pharmakon* an undecidability that all translators—and therefore all Platonisms—have assumed was a decidability. The divide between *poison* and *remedy* happens *in translation*. It is not, however, that such inadequate translations could be avoided if one stayed with the original. It is that an actual history, shaped by a decision that the translators could not choose not to make, makes the original perceptible as resisting it. As Derrida tells his Japanese translator, "The question of deconstruction is also through and through *the* question of translation."[16]

The worry about translation is, of course, always a worry about *bad* translation ("the inaccurate transmission of an inessential content," as Benjamin puts it).[17] But the suspicion is that what is essential about a literary work is precisely what is *always* lost in translation, which is why so many poets have been so intent on *finding* it. That is perhaps why both Baudelaire and Mallarmé wanted to translate the quintessential bad poet of American literature, Edgar Allan Poe. And this takes us back to the badness of literature.

Some time ago, when I came across a reference to one of my colleagues in the *Boston Globe* as a professor of "comparable literature" (October 20, 2000, B4), I realized that the field itself is oddly named. Why *isn't* it called "comparable literature" in fact? Doesn't the classic version of the field assume that you can take, say, romanticism, and compare its French, German, and English versions, which are presumed to be comparable? What does "comparative literature" really mean? That what is studied is comparatively (but not absolutely) literary? Perhaps—but could this have been the original intent? The field that depends on comparison for its very definition somehow at the same time opposes some sort of resistance to comparability. Just enough to echo the irony in the story of Elena Levin explaining to someone why her husband, Harry, author of the 1965 report, was busy working: "The Professors are here to compare the literatures." It is as if the field defined by comparison unconsciously upholds the adage, "*Comparaison n'est pas raison*," or agrees with William Blake when, in his poem "Jerusalem," he has his hero, Los, howl:

"I must Create a System, or be enslav'd by another Mans; / I will not Reason & Compare: my business is to Create."[18]

In order to explore this odd resistance to comparison, I turn to three more texts that each embody some form of "bad writing": popular culture, philosophy, and teaching manuals. My three texts are the 1995 film *Clueless*, H. Vaihinger's book *The Philosophy of "As If"* (first published in German in 1911), and Andrew Boyd's *Life's Little Deconstruction Book* (billed by the publisher as "Po-Mo to Go").

In the film *Clueless*,[19] the exclamation "As if!" is used by the protagonist, fifteen-year-old Beverly Hills high school student Cher Horowitz, to project the frame of reference of other persons into pure fantasy—theirs—and to expel it from herself. For example, when an unprepossessing high school boy approaches Cher in an interested manner, she says, "Ew! Get away from me! *As if*!" In other words, "*As if* I would go out with you!" "In your dreams!" "You wish!" When another boy, Elton, reveals that he is interested in *her*, not in the new girl, Tai, with whom she has been trying to fix him up (this is one of the few places where Jane Austen's *Emma* is recognizable as a source), Cher exclaims "Me? *As if*! Don't you mean Tai?" In other words, "*As if* I had been flirting with you for myself!" "*As if* I had been the object rather than the subject!" Another example: when Cher reports that her teacher has said that her arguments are unresearched, unstructured, and unconvincing, she exclaims, "*As if*!"—which I guess means, "Who is *he* to say such a thing?"

The Beverly Hills high school dialect in the film thus makes use of the expression *as if* in an interpersonal sense. It is always an exclamation and always casts desire or doubt away from the speaker and onto the addressee. I don't have time to do a reading of the film as a rhetorical treatise, but as a study of substitution, transformation (the makeover), and the narcissism of small differences, it would lend itself very well to such treatment.

For Hans Vaihinger *as if* is an essential mental function enabling people to use fictions "as if" they were true: religions, philosophies, even mathematical constructs. As he writes in the preface to the English edition, "An idea whose theoretical untruth or incorrectness, and therewith its falsity, is admitted, is not for that reason practically valueless and useless; for such an idea, in spite of its theoretical nullity, may have great practical importance."[20] Kant's *Ding an sich*, for example, which can't be proven, is a necessary part of his philosophical system, just as imaginary numbers operate as a necessary part of a system of calculations, even though, in the end, they don't exist.

Life's Little Deconstruction Book is organized as a series of maxims.[21] There are 365 of them—one for every day of the year (I'm not sure what the reader is supposed to do during a leap year). Maxim 33 reads: "Be as if." I guess that must mean something like, "Ontology is performance" or "Whatever you seem to have in your mind *is* your mind." Or, as Pascal might have put it, "Act *as if* you believe, and belief will follow, or at least, you will have gained everything that you would have gained by believing."

Teaching theory, I come up again and again unexpectedly against the problem of belief. In literature I can suspend disbelief, but in theory I feel as if my location with respect to other writers and thinkers is somehow the stuff of the course. Because the writers I am teaching have designs on the most fundamental assumptions I make while I read, I cannot teach them as if they were a subject matter. At the same time, my own relation to the writers has changed over time, and it has changed with respect to that of my students. What is different about teaching theory for me now is the sense of my own historicity. Yet if I look at the theory I teach exclusively from the outside, I am not teaching theory but history. There would certainly be usefulness in teaching the history of theory, but it would not give access to the "Aha!" that ignites an interest in theory in the first place. When Frantz Fanon says about his reaction to Sartre's reading of Aimé Césaire's poetics of Negritude, "I needed *not* to think I was just a minor term in a dialectic," he is saying, in effect, I needed to read *as if* I believed in the Negritude I now take a distance from, in order to get to the next stage in my thinking. *As if* is something that cannot happen right if it happens in the mode of *as if*.

I have found that the way in which students dismiss or take distance from the texts we read in a theory course follows patterns that are quite different from critiques. And that perhaps was true of my own dismissals of their predecessors. But my task is to make sure the students actually *read* whatever is on the syllabus—which may now include some of those predecessors I am reading for the first time. "Bracketing the referent" or "preferring *langue* to *parole*" are important ways of seeing the limitations of Saussure, but they help only in understanding what Saussure *didn't* do, not what he *did* do—not what those limits *enabled* but only what they prevented. Understanding the conceptual breakthrough involved in saying, "In language there are only differences," depends on pausing there long enough (recall Cher's reaction to stop signs—"I totally paused") to see *what Saussure was critiquing himself.* Thought as a *break* is different from thought as a *chain*.

The same is true for elements of a theory—say, female sexuality in Freud— from which one knows one has taken a critical distance, or elements in a theory—say, ethnocentrism in Lévi-Strauss—where one may be critical of a framework of which one is nevertheless still a part. What has been called "political correctness" is something I would prefer to call "double consciousness"—the knowledge that one is viewed, not just viewing. W. E. B. Du Bois defined double consciousness, famously, as "the sense of always looking at one's self through the eyes of others, of measuring one's soul by the tape of a world."[22] The strength of those "others" produces double consciousness. But how can white double consciousness or male double consciousness or Eurocentric double consciousness be anything but reactive and defensive, if the power of those "others" is itself what consciousness was defined against? Double consciousness would feel a lot like paranoia. No wonder people might attempt to eradicate it. But in this case, as they say, even paranoids have real enemies. Or perhaps we should say, denying paranoia doesn't make those "real others" go away. What does the necessity of double consciousness have to do with the question of teaching *as if* one believed?

The dangers of representativeness and tokenism are precisely the dangers of losing the "foreignness" of texts to their *own* languages. But to fear such a danger is to forget that what should happen in literature courses is *reading*. Yes, the changes might reflect an unquestioned notion of individualism. And yes, the students will not see that from which a syllabus is departing. But surely the students have imbibed cultural assumptions that will be defamiliarized by some of the texts. Perhaps the use of tokens or of islands of knowledge in a sea of ignorance can homogenize all differences into various versions of the same. But even when something like colonialism attempted to reproduce itself in, say, the Caribbean, it became something quite different from what it started out to be. At the same time, how could a syllabus mark radical change within a culture—and an educational system—that changes much more slowly? If the remedy mirrors the system being questioned rather than the questioning, at least the cognitive dissonance that these contradictory energies embody may correspond to a real conflict in the world rather than the wishful thinking that would seek a more effective critique.

Actually taking seriously the works being read has to become transformative eventually because what is secondary revision for one generation may become primary process for the next. The very transferential process that tends to absolutize the authority of a text (as if it had always been on the syllabus) will deabsolutize the assumptions that are still operative in the teachers who have put those books on the syllabus. On the one hand, if the map isn't being changed in the primary process of thinking, changing it in a secondary revision is not really *thought*. But on the other hand, acting *as if* the map were changing might actually make it so, in the long run.

How does the structure of the *as if* function, then, to allow for a heuristic transference and for a transformative double consciousness at once, even though these two processes draw on the contradictory energies of belief, critique, and defense? Let me end with a quotation from Joan Copjec's book *Read My Desire*, in which a structure she actually designates as "as if" is understood through, and clarifies, the Lacanian notion of *suture*:

> Suture, in brief, supplies the logic of a paradoxical function whereby a supplementary element is *added* to the series of signifiers in order to mark the *lack* of a signifier that could close the set. The endless slide of signifiers (hence deferral of sense) is brought to a halt and allowed to function "as if" it were a closed set through the inclusion of an element that acknowledges the impossibility of closure. The very designation of the limit is constitutive of the group, the reality the signifiers come to represent, though the group, or the reality, can no longer be thought to be entirely representable.[23]

What I want to claim here is that the role of academic literary criticism—which is academic precisely because it acknowledges the existence of multiple languages—is always to risk a certain "badness" and to be this suture. It is the field whose only definition is to be the acknowledgment of the impossibility of the field, to be the "as if" of literary closure. Criticism, in other words, is what is *added* to the series of literary signifiers in order to mark the *lack* of a signifier that could close the set. It marks not the *future* of literary studies but the *suture* of literary studies. That is the best way we have of relying on the badness of strangers.

NOTES

"Bad Writing." From Jonathan Culler and Kevin Lamb, *Just Being Difficult? Academic Writing in the Public Arena.* © 2003 by the Board of Trustees of the Leland Stanford Jr. University. All rights reserved. Used with permission of Stanford University Press, www.sup.org.

My epigraph and much of the framework for this essay are taken from the brilliant article by Deborah Jenson, "Gender and the Aesthetic of 'le Mal': Louise Ackermann's Poésies philosophiques, 1871," *Nineteenth-Century French Studies* 23 (1994–95): 175–93.

1. Anne Sexton, *The Complete Poems* (Boston: Houghton Mifflin, 1981), 126.
2. Arthur Rimbaud, *Oeuvres* (Paris: Garnier, 1960), 357.
3. Gordon Millan, *Mallarmé: A Throw of the Dice* (London: Secker and Warburg, 1994), 144.

4. Charles Baudelaire, *Oeuvres completes*, ed. Claude Pichois, vol. 1 (Paris: Gallimard, 1975), 181.

5. Stéphane Mallarmé, *Oeuvres complètes* (Paris: Gallimard, 1945), 368.

6. Mallarmé, *Oeuvres complètes*, 366.

7. Mallarmé, *Oeuvres complètes*, 382–83. [Pure prerogatives would be, this time, at the mercy of low jokers. Every piece of writing, outside of its treasure, must, toward those from whom it borrows, after all, for a different object, language, present, with words, a sense even indifferent: one gains by not attracting the idler, charmed that nothing there concerns him, at first sight. Each side gets exactly what it wants—If, nevertheless, anxiety is stirred by I don't know what shadowy reflection hardly separable from the surface available to the retina—it attracts suspicion: the pundits among the public, averring that this has to be stopped, opine, with due *gravitas*, that, truly, the tenor is unintelligible. Ridiculously cursed is he who is caught up in this, enveloped by an immense and mediocre joke: it was ever thus—but perhaps not with the intensity with which the plague now extends its ravages. There must be something occult deep inside everyone, decidedly I believe in something opaque, a signifier sealed and hidden, that inhabits common man: for, as soon as the masses throw themselves toward some trace that has its reality, for example, on a piece of paper, it's in the writing—not in oneself—that there is something obscure: they stir crazily like a hurricane, jealous to attribute darkness to anything, profusely, flagrantly. Their credulity, fostered by those who reassure it and market it, is suddenly startled: and the agent of darkness, singled out by them, can't say a single word thenceforth, without, a shrug indicating that it's just that enigma again, being cut off, with a flourish of skirts: "Don't understand!"—the poor author innocently announcing, perhaps, that he needed to blow his nose.]

8. Mallarmé, *Oeuvres complètes*, 383. [I know, in fact, that they crowd the stage and expose themselves, actually, in a humiliating posture; since to argue that something is obscure—or, no one will get it if they don't, and they don't—implies a prior suspension of judgment.]

9. Peter Brooks, "Must We Apologize?," in *Comparative Literature in the Age of Multiculturalism*, ed. Charles Bernheimer (Baltimore: Johns Hopkins University Press, 1995), 105.

10. Bernheimer Report, 1993; reprinted in Bernheimer, *Comparative Literature*, 42.

11. Levin Report, 1965; reprinted in Bernheimer, *Comparative Literature*, 25.

12. *Hegel's Encyclopedia of Philosophy*, trans. and annot. Gustav Emil Mueller (New York: Philosophical Library, 1959), 1.

13. One letter to the editor read as follows: "SIR,—I will not, like your 'Constant Subscriber' of last week, protest against all foreign languages. I can read some of them myself, and have relations who can read others. But I shall take it very kindly if the next time M. Stéphane Mallarmé occupies your columns, you kindly append a French translation of his article, or what in Decadish might be

called 'une française traduction.' I am, yours resignedly, ONE WHO USED TO THINK HE COULD READ FRENCH" (*National Observer*, April 9, 1892, 540).

14. Mallarmé, "Crise de vers," in *Oeuvres complètes*, 368 (emphasis mine).

15. Walter Benjamin, *Selected Writings*, ed. Marcus Bullock and Michael W. Jennings, vol. 1 (Cambridge, MA: Belknap Press, 1996), 257.

16. Jacques Derrida, "Letter to a Japanese Friend," in *A Derrida Reader: Between the Blinds*, ed. Peggy Kamuf (New York: Columbia University Press, 1991), 270.

17. Benjamin, *Selected Writings*, 253.

18. William Blake, *The Poetry and Prose of William Blake*, ed. David V. Erdman (New York: Doubleday, 1965), 151.

19. Writ. and dir. Amy Heckerling, prod. and dist. Paramount Pictures, starring Alicia Silverstone as Cher Horowitz.

20. Hans Vaihinger, *The Philosophy of "As If,"* trans. C. K. Cohen (London: Routledge and Kegan Paul, 1924), viii.

21. Andrew Boyd, *Life's Little Deconstruction Book* (New York: W. W. Norton, 1999).

22. W. E. B. Du Bois, *The Souls of Black Folk* (New York: Penguin, 1989), 5.

23. Joan Copjec, *Read My Desire* (Cambridge, MA: MIT Press, 1994), 174–75.

CHAPTER 23

Teaching Deconstructively

Teaching literature is teaching how to read. How to notice things in a text that a speed-reading culture is trained to disregard, overcome, edit out, or explain away; how to read what the language is doing, not guess what the author was thinking; how to take in evidence from a page, not seek a reality to substitute for it.[1] This is the only teaching that can properly be called literary; anything else is history of ideas, biography, psychology, ethics, or bad philosophy. Anything else does not measure up to the rigorous perversity and seductiveness of literary language.

Deconstruction has sometimes been seen as a terroristic belief in meaninglessness. It is commonly opposed to humanism, which is then an imperialistic belief in meaningfulness. Another way to distinguish between the two is to say that deconstruction is a reading strategy that carefully follows both the meanings and the suspensions and displacements of meaning in a text, while humanism is a strategy to stop reading when the text stops saying what it ought to have said. Deconstruction, then, has a lot to teach teachers of literature to the extent that they see themselves as teachers of reading.

What, then, is a deconstructive reading, and how can its strategies be translated into classroom procedures? Deconstruction is not a form of textual vandalism or generalized skepticism designed to prove that meaning is impossible. Nor is it an a priori assumption that every text is self-reflexive, that every text consists only in a play of signifiers, or that every text is about the relation between speech and writing. Rather, it is a careful teasing out of the conflicting forces of signification that are at work within the text itself. If anything is destroyed in a deconstructive reading, it is not meaning per se but the claim to unequivocal domination of one mode of signifying over another. This implies that a text signifies in more than one way, that it can signify something more, something less, or something other than it claims to, or that it signifies to different degrees of explicitness, effectiveness, or coherence. A deconstructive reading makes evident the ways in which a text works out its complex disagreements with itself. As Paul de Man puts it: "The deconstruction is not something we have added to the text but it constituted the text in the first place. A literary text simultaneously asserts and denies the authority of its own rhetorical mode, and by reading the text as we did we were only trying to come closer to being as rigorous a reader as the author had to be in order to write the [text] in the first place."[2] Because deconstruction is first and foremost a way of paying attention to what a text is doing—*how* it means, not just *what* it means—it can lend itself very easily to an open-discussion format in a literature seminar. And because it enables students to respond to what is there before them on the page, it can teach them how to work out the logic of a reading on their own rather than passively deferring to the authority of superior learning.

What kinds of signifying conflict, then, are articulated in, and constitutive of, the literary text? And what sorts of reading do they demand? I will begin by listing quickly a number of examples and then go on to develop three readings more fully, though by no means completely. These cases are designed to stand as examples of the type of challenge to reading that a text might provide—and that deconstructive attention might further—in a classroom.

1. *Ambiguous words.* Derrida's readings often focus on a double-
   edged word as a condensed articulation of conflicting levels of
   assertion in a text. In Plato's *Phaedrus*, for example, the word
   pharmakon can mean both "remedy" and "poison."[3] In referring to
   writing itself as a *pharmakon*, Plato is therefore not making a
   simple value judgment. Yet translators, by choosing to render the
   word sometimes by "remedy" and sometimes by "poison," have
   consistently decided what in Plato remains undecidable, and thus
   have influenced the course of the history of readings of Plato.
   When one recalls the means of Socrates's death, one can see that
   the undecidability between poison and remedy is not a trivial
   matter. Far from posing confined, local interpretive problems,
   ambiguities can stand as the hinge of an entire discourse.

2. *Undecidable syntax.* One of the most condensed examples of syntax as the locus of a suspension of the text's claim structures between two often incompatible possibilities is the rhetorical question. As Paul de Man suggests,[4] a reading of Yeats's poem "Among School Children" is drastically changed if one admits the possibility that its terminal question—"How can we know the dancer from the dance?"—is *not* rhetorical. Or the question with which Baudelaire ends his celebration of a woman's hair in "La Chevelure"—"Are you not the gourd from which I drink the wine of memory?"—suspends the energy of the poem not only between self and other but between the success and the failure of the attempt to rewrite the other as a container for the self.

3. *Incompatibilities between what a text says and what it does.* An obvious example would be the figure known as *praeteritio*, in which a text elaborates itself by detailing at length what it says it will *not* speak about. Variants upon this structure pervade all literature, as when an author devotes much more space to what he wants to eliminate than to what he wants to instate, or when a text in one way or another protests too much. Another rather simple example of the discrepancy between saying and doing occurs in the last line of Archibald MacLeish's "Ars Poetica": "A poem should not mean but be." The line itself does not obey its own prescription: it means—*intends* being—rather than simply being, thus revealing that it is more complicated than it first appears to be for a poem to assert what the relations between meaning and being are.

4. *Incompatibilities between the literal and the figurative.* In Lamartine's poem "L'Isolement," the speaker, who is lamenting the death of his beloved, cries, "There is nothing in common between the earth and me." He then goes on: "I am like the withered leaf." In a poem that is entirely devoted to the question of the mode of aliveness of one whose heart is in another world, this suspended stance between earthliness and unearthliness reveals that the problem of mourning has something to do with the opposition between the figural and the literal, and vice versa.

5. *Incompatibilities between explicitly foregrounded assertions and illustrative examples or less explicitly asserted supporting material.* Derrida points this out in the discrepancy between Saussure's explicit assertion that linguistics should study speech, not writing, and his repeated recourse to linguistic properties that are derivable from writing, not speech. A more literary example can be found in

Wordsworth's "Intimations Ode." The poem begins by asserting the fact of loss:

> There was a time when meadow, grove, and stream,
> The earth, and every common sight,
>> To me did seem
>> Apparelled in celestial light,
> The glory and the freshness of a dream.
> It is not now as it hath been of yore;—
>> Turn wheresoe'er I may,
>>> By night or day,
> The things which I have seen I now can see no more.

This sense of loss expands mythically, phylogenetically, and ontogenetically to include the common experience of all mankind:

> Our birth is but a sleep and a forgetting;
> The soul that rises with us, our life's star,
>> Hath had elsewhere its setting,
>>> And cometh from afar:
>> Not in entire forgetfulness,
>>> And not in utter nakedness,
> But trailing clouds of glory do we come
>> From God, who is our home:
> Heaven lies about us in our infancy!
> Shades of the prison-house begin to close
>> Upon the growing boy,
> But he beholds the light, and whence it flows,
>> He sees it in his joy;
> The youth, who daily farther from the east
>> Must travel, still is Nature's priest,
>>> And by the vision splendid
>>> Is on his way attended;
> At length the man perceives it die away,
> And fade into the light of common day.

But in the supporting invocation to the little child, Wordsworth cuts the ground out from under this narrative of loss:

> Thou, whose exterior semblance doth belie
>> Thy soul's immensity;

Thou best philosopher, who yet dost keep
Thy heritage, thou eye among the blind,
That, deaf and silent, readst the eternal deep,
Haunted for ever by the eternal mind,—
    Mighty prophet! Seer blest!
    On whom those truths do rest,
Which we are toiling all our lives to find,
In darkness lost, the darkness of the grave;
Thou, over whom thy immortality
Broods like the day, a master o'er a slave,
A presence which is not to be put by;
Thou little child, yet glorious in the might
Of heaven-born freedom on thy being's height,
Why with such earnest pains dost thou provoke
The years to bring the inevitable yoke,
Thus blindly with thy blessedness at strife?

The little child, the seer of the light, here turns out to be blind to his very ability to see. The experience of blessed sight, the loss of which Wordsworth began by lamenting, seems never to have existed in the first place as a lived experience. The loss of *something* is a story retrospectively told in order to explain the *sense* of loss. What we have lost by the end of the poem is precisely loss itself.

6. *Obscurity.* A student's first encounter with the work of a poet such as Mallarmé can be profoundly disconcerting. If one attempts to smooth over the difficulties and make the poem add up to a meaning, the student might well ask, "Ce n'est donc que ça?—Why couldn't he have said it in plain, comprehensible language?" One would have to answer that "it" isn't something his language is *saying* but something his language is *doing*.

A look at the sonnet "La chevelure vol d'une flamme à l'extrême occident de désirs" reveals that although one can't make sense of it, it contains an interesting collection of highly charged images and concepts: man and woman, life and death, doubt and joy, truth and mockery, tenderness and defamation, nakedness and jewelry, outward exploits and inner fires, weather, geography, and education. The entire complexity of the world seems to be condensed down to a microchip. This is what Mallarmé called "simplifying the world." But the text itself is far from simple.

What does one do? One starts to ask questions. Does the word *vol* mean "theft" or "flight"? Is the word *or* a noun or a conjunction? Is *continue* a verb, transitive or intransitive, or an adjective? Why is the *I* in parentheses? Discussion of these questions and the attempt to follow out the consequences of each possibility *and* the consequences of their simultaneousness can go on for a long time, but something inevitably gets worked out in this process of asking what each element is doing with respect to other elements in the poem, rather than asking point blank what it *means*. What happens in reading Mallarmé is that one talks one's way into the poem by describing the specificity of one's difficulties. Rather than remain stuck before an obstacle or paralyzed before a forking path, the reader must say: "My reading is blocked here because I can't tell whether this is theft or flight, literal or figurative, noun or verb, statement or question, masculine or feminine, and so forth. But that uncertainty may be precisely what the poem is talking about." The reader can then track down each thread of all possibilities and ask the significance of their coexistence. Eventually, the narrating of one's frustrations and difficulties begins to fill in for, and to partake of, the missing thematic coherence in the poem. The poem is not *about* something *separate* from the activity required to decipher it. Simplification, doubt, distance, and desire—all are acted out by the reading process as well as stated in the poem.

With Mallarmé, in other words, the student can learn to see the *search* for meaning as being illuminating and meaningful in itself. One's struggles with ambiguity and obscurity cease to be obstacles to reading: they become the very *experience* of reading. Meaning is not something "out there" or "in there," to be run after or dug up. It inhabits the very activity of the search. And what better training for "living as and where we live" (as Stevens puts it) than to learn to direct our attention to what we experience *now* rather than to those answers that lie somewhere up the road; to take indecision, frustration, and ambivalence, not as mere obstacles and incapacities, but as the very richness and instructiveness of the reading process? This is what Mallarmé's poetry has to teach, not by *telling* us this, but by making us go through it, interminably, for ourselves.

7. *Fictional self-interpretation.* Sometimes the challenge posed by a
text is not excessive obscurity but, rather, some form of excessive
clarity. Many literary texts appear to comment upon themselves,
to solve the enigmas they set up. A common student response to
texts in which such self-interpretations are explicit is to protest
that the author has taken all the fun away by doing the work the
reader ought to do. Deconstruction, with its insistence on
interpretation itself as a fiction-making activity, enables one to
read such metalinguistic moments as allegories of reading, as
comments on the interpretive process itself, in a sort of inside-
out version of the involvement the student engages in with
Mallarmé.

I would like to conclude with a somewhat more extended version of what
can come out of a discussion of textual self-interpretation. For this, I will comment on two inversely symmetrical thematizations of textuality itself: Hawthorne's "The Minister's Black Veil," in which a character named Reverend
Hooper mysteriously and without warning dons a piece of black crepe, which
he refuses to remove even on his deathbed, and Hans Christian Andersen's
"The Emperor's New Clothes," in which two imposters weave nonexistent
clothes for the emperor, telling him that their cloth has the property of being
invisible to those who are either simpletons or unfit for their offices. The two
stories are thus both woven around a textile: in "The Minister's Black Veil" the
textile is opaque and obscure; in "The Emperor's New Clothes" it is self-
evidently transparent. In foregrounding the textuality of a text, both stories
also situate the activities of writing and reading, and in both cases an explicit
reading is offered as definitive. Both stories indeed end with that reading as a
sort of punch line. In "The Minister's Black Veil" the meaning of the enigmatic
symbol is given by its "author" as follows:

"Why do you tremble at me alone?" cried he, turning his veiled face
round the circle of pale spectators. "Tremble also at each other! Have
men avoided me, and women shown no pity, and children screamed
and fled, only for my black veil? What, but the mystery which it obscurely typifies, has made this piece of crape so awful? When the friend
shows his inmost heart to his friend; the lover to his best beloved; when
man does not vainly shrink from the eye of his Creator, loathsomely
treasuring up the secret of his sin; then deem me a monster, for the
symbol beneath which I have lived, and die! I look around me, and, lo!
on every visage a Black Veil!"[5]

And at the end of the "Emperor's New Clothes," the child in the crowd exclaims, "But the Emperor has nothing at all on!" and the crowd repeats the exclamation as the truth.

In "Minister," then, the definitive reading involves an exposure of universally denied concealment. In "Emperor," it involves the exposure of universally denied exposure. In the first case, the figure of the veil reveals the non-literality of meaning, the darkness that prevents any encounter from being literally face to face. In the second case, the nakedness of the emperor reveals literality *as* meaning. In the first case, the final reader is the veiled author. In the second, the reader is a child. The truth propounded by the first is the inescapability of the figural. The truth propounded by the second is the inescapability of the literal. Yet in both cases, the solving of the obvious textual enigma only serves to resituate the real mystery elsewhere. For in both cases, what remains to be explained is how the apparently inescapable is so apparently escaped. Both texts consist in the putting in question of their own, apparently definitive self-interpretations.

The first thing one notices about each text is that the major part of its energy is devoted to the description of acts of reading. The minister's congregation is obsessed with the question, "What does the veil mean?" By ending the tale with an apparent answer to that question, Hawthorne seems to be usurping the interpretive activity that the reader may feel is rightly hers. But this is so only as long as the reader believes that the *veil* is the text's enigma. By presenting a solution to that enigma, Hawthorne is substituting interpretation itself as a new enigma, as the object of *his* reader's interpretive activity. By putting *en abyme* the question, "What does the veil mean?" Hawthorne substitutes a new question: "What does it mean to ask what the veil means? What do people actually do when they try to determine meaning?" The first thing they do, in both "Minister" and "Emperor," is to deny literality. The minister's parishioners cannot believe that the veil is simply a piece of black crepe. The barrier to communication cannot be seen as meaningless. If this is so, then meaningfulness would seem to inhere in what blocks or veils communication. Yet in "Emperor" it is the very lack of such a blockage that needs to be interpreted. Again, literality cannot be seen as such.

The denial of literality takes place, in both stories, in an intersubjective context in which meaning is tied to a figure of authority. The minister and the emperor are, for their subjects, the guarantors of a meaningful social world. Participation in that world entails the acceptance of official ways of denying literality. Hence the child's literal reading is an asocial reading, a reading that, though correct, is outside the system in which social meanings are agreed upon. The minister's veil and the emperor's clothes are tests of their readers' suitability for membership in the society of which they are a part. The reading activity thus consists of a nervousness of self-examination. Faced with the text, the reader's search for meaning is an examination of *his own* credentials. The emperor's ministers deny simple literality in order to deny the possibility that they themselves are simple. The minister's hidden face forces the parishioners to confront their own hiddenness. In their desire to deny their own hiddenness, they read hiddenness in the other as a sign that he is hiding whatever they are hiding. In revealing on his deathbed that the veil concealed nothing but, rather, that it revealed the fact of concealment, the minister situates the meaning of his symbol, not within it or within his own intentions, but within the readers' blindness to their own misreading— their blindness to their own blindness. Yet the minister cannot face his own veiled image in the mirror, for if his veil's message is the revelation of the universality of concealment, how can the meaning of the veil escape the self-blindness that it says is universal? In living a life that stands as a figure for misreading, the minister, in his triumphant attempt to proclaim obscurity clearly, ends up being the only person who has not read his own figure *correctly.*

The emperor's subjects thus veil from themselves the literality of the invisibility of what they see, while members of the minister's congregation, projecting their own concealments behind the veil, are blind to the possibility that nothing is being concealed—or that concealment is what is being revealed. Both stories dramatize the intrusion—indeed, the inescapability—of allegorical structures in the conduct of "real" life. Socialization is training in allegorical interpretation. But an allegory that reveals that the act of reading consists in a blindness both to literality and to the fact that one is allegorically denying literality puts *us* in a difficult position. If the blindness of the emperor's subjects and of the minister's parishioners is a forgetting of literality through the act of reading *themselves* into the text, then aren't we, by reading the texts as allegories of reading, suffering from the same blindness to the second degree? Yet could we have chosen to read literally? Or is the act of reading always, in a sense, an act of resistance to the letter?

At the beginning of this essay I defined deconstruction as a reading strategy that carefully follows both the meanings and the suspensions and displacements of meaning in a text, while humanism was a strategy to stop reading when the text stops saying what it ought to have said. What the deconstructive reading of Hawthorne and Andersen has shown, however, is that no matter how rigorously a deconstructor might follow the letter of the text, the text will end up showing the reading process as a *resistance* to the letter. The deconstructor thus comes face to face with her own humanism. This is small comfort, of course, since the text has shown humanism to consist in the blindness of self-projection. But then, in the final analysis, it is perhaps precisely as an apprenticeship in the repeated and inescapable oscillation between humanism and deconstruction that literature works its most rigorous and inexhaustible seductions.

NOTES

"Teaching Deconstructively." From *Writing and Reading Differently: Deconstruction and the Teaching of Composition and Literature*, G. Douglas Atkins and Michael L. Johnson, eds. (1985), 140–48. Reprinted with permission of the University Press of Kansas.

1. This is not meant to imply that nothing should be read outside the text at hand, or that a text is unconnected to any discourse outside itself. The "inside" of the text is no more a "given" than the "outside," and what is inside the text is not necessarily accessible to the reader without philological, historical, biographical, etc., research. But it does imply that history, philology, biography, the "spirit of the age," and the "material conditions of production" are not less problematic—or less textual and interpretively constructed—than the literary text they would come to explain. Training in reading must also be training in evaluating the relevance and authority of external resources as well as internal ones.
2. Paul de Man, *Allegories of Reading* (New Haven, CT: Yale University Press, 1979), 17.
3. See Jacques Derrida, "Plato's Pharmacy," in *Dissemination* (Chicago: University of Chicago Press, 1981).
4. In the opening essay of *Allegories of Reading*.
5. Nathaniel Hawthorne, "The Minister's Black Veil," in *The Celestial Railroad and Other Stories* (New York: Signet, 1963), 114.

CHAPTER 24

Poison or Remedy? Paul de Man as Pharmakon

Merciless and Consequent

This *pharmakon*, this "medicine," this philter, which acts as both remedy and poison, already introduces itself into the body of discourse with all its ambivalence. This charm, this spellbinding virtue, this power of fascination, can be—alternately or simultaneously—beneficent or maleficent. If the *pharmakon* is "ambivalent," it is because it constitutes the medium in which opposites are opposed, the movement and the play that links them among themselves, reverses them or makes one side cross over into the other. . . .

It is [. . .] the prior medium in which differentiation in general is produced. [. . .] Writing is no more valuable, says Plato, as a remedy than as a poison. There is no such thing as a harmless remedy. The *pharmakon* can never be simply beneficial.
—Jacques Derrida, "Plato's Pharmacy"

It is hardly surprising that the discovery of Paul de Man's collaborationist writings should have polarized critics into postures of attack and defense. Despite frequent dismissals of the affair as a "teapot tempest," something important seems to be at stake in the "glee" of denunciation or the tortured and tortuous rhetoric of extenuation. The very asymmetry between the ease of attack and the discomfort of defense deserves comment. Deconstructors have often characterized humanist resistance to deconstruction as an intolerance for paradox, ambiguity, or undecidability. Yet in our current inability either to excuse or to take leave of de Man, we are now getting a taste of our own *pharmakon*.

Polarization around de Man can hardly be said to have originated with the current scandal, however. More than any other literary theorist, I think, he has always provoked a vehemently split response. For deconstructors, he was a model of rigor, lucidity, and integrity; for humanists, he was a radical nihilist; for materialist critics, a closet conservative. All three evaluations center on his privileging of language. For many, de Man's work emitted a highly demanding imperative not to shirk the responsibilities of reading or, as it is sometimes put, not to take the impossibility of reading too lightly. For others, his focus on the unreliability and randomness of language undermined the foundations of Western values. And for still others, his characterization of wars and revolutions as by-products of linguistic predicaments was a denial of history and a refusal of politics.

In some ways, all of the above are accurate. If one does not question the nature of Western values or the definitions of history and politics, then one would have to assign de Man to the "poison" position in each, *not* in his early writings, in which he was himself an upholder of Western values welcoming a revolutionary New Order, but in his later writings. But what if the poison in this case were precisely not the opposite of the remedy, but an attempt to get at the poison-remedy split at its root?

The journalists and polemicists are not wrong in locating the specificity of de Man's theory in his focus on language. Their mistake, however, lies in reassigning the certainties they say he takes away. If language is no longer guaranteed to be reliable or truthful, then it must "always" be unreliable, false, or biased. If not necessary, then arbitrary; if not meaningful, then indeterminate; if not true, then false. But de Man's analyses do not perform such certainty reassignments. Rather, they question the very structure and functioning of such either/or logic. To question certainty is not the same as to affirm uncertainty:

> In a genuine semiology as well as in other linguistically oriented theories, the referential function of language is not being denied—far from it; what is in question is its authority as a model for natural or phenomenal cognition. Literature is fiction not because it somehow refuses to acknowledge "reality," but because *it is not a priori certain* that language functions according to principles which are those, or which are like those, of the phenomenal world.[1]

> It is by no means an established fact that aesthetic values and linguistic values are *in*compatible. What is established is that their compatibility, or lack of it, has to remain an open question.[2]

What complicates the picture even further is the fact that, while we might be able to tell the difference between linguistic and purely phenomenal or aesthetic structures ("no one in his right mind will try to grow grapes by the luminosity of the word 'day'"), the distinction is not at all clear in the case of ideology or politics, because "what we call ideology is precisely the confusion of linguistic with natural reality, or reference with phenomenalism." From this de Man goes on to assert:

> It follows that, more than any other mode of inquiry, including economics, the linguistics of literariness ["literature as the place where this negative knowledge about the reliability of linguistic utterance is made available"] is a powerful and indispensable tool in the unmasking of ideological aberrations, as well as a determining factor in accounting for their occurrence. (*RT*, 11)

In the years just prior to his death, de Man seems indeed to have been moving toward establishing a more explicit link between his own theoretical stance and a critique of the ideological foundation of Nazism. Christopher Norris has pointed to that link by entitling his study of de Man *Deconstruction and the Critique of Aesthetic Ideology*. As Walter Benjamin was one of the first to point out, fascism can be understood as an *aestheticization* of politics. In several late essays, de Man locates a crucial articulation in the construction of a protofascist "aesthetic ideology" in Schiller's misreading of Kant's *Critique of Judgment*. Schiller's misreading of the aesthetic in Kant involves a denial of (its own) violence. Schiller's vision of "the ideal of a beautiful society" as "a well executed English dance" has exerted a seductive appeal upon subsequent political visions. In his essay entitled "Aesthetic Formalization,"[3] de Man juxtaposes to this notion from Schiller a short text by Kleist, *Über das Marionettentheater*, in which the grace of such a dance is shown to be produced by substituting the mechanical (a puppet or a prosthesis) for the human body. Schiller's "aesthetic state" is thus an ideal that can only be produced by mutilation and mechanization. The dance-like harmony of a state can only arise through the repression of differences within. In one of the last lectures de Man delivered before his death, he makes the political ramifications of this aesthetic state even clearer:

> As such, the aesthetic belongs to the masses [. . .] and it justifies the state, as in the following quotation, which is not by Schiller:
>
>> "Art is an expression of feelings. The artist is distinguished from the non-artist by the fact that he has the power to give expression to what

he feels. In some form or another: the one in images, a second in clay, a third in words, a fourth in marble—or even in historical forms. The statesman is an artist too. The leader and the led ('Führer und Masse') presents no more problem than, say, painter and colour. Politics are the plastic art of colour. This is why politics without the people, or even against the people, is sheer nonsense. To shape a People out of the masses, and a State out of the People, this has always been the deepest intention of politics in the true sense" (*Michael. Ein deutsches Schicksal in Tagebuchblättern* [1929]).

It is not entirely irrelevant, not entirely indifferent, that the author of this passage is from a novel of Joseph Goebbels. Mary Wilkinson, who quotes the passage, is certainly right in pointing out that it is a grievous misreading of Schiller's aesthetic state. But the principle of this misreading does not essentially differ from the misreading which Schiller inflicted on his own predecessor, namely Kant.[4]

De Man's insistence on violence—disfiguration, death, mutilation—is not a personal predilection for horror, but rather a deep suspicion of false images of harmony and enlightenment. Hidden within the aesthetic appeals of the political images by which he himself was once seduced were forms of violence unprecedented in human history. It seems undeniable that if "the linguistics of literariness is a powerful and indispensable tool in the unmasking of ideological aberrations, as well as a determining factor in accounting for their occurrence," the ideological aberrations he is unmasking were once his own.

It could be objected that his relation to such "aberrations" remains purely cognitive, that "accounting for" occurrences may not be the only possible response to history, and that the ideology de Man "unmasks" remains, in fact, masked. The political implications of his *cognition* remain at odds with the political implications of his *performance*. His refusal to tell his own story, which can be seen both as self-protection and as self-renunciation, was also a silencing of the question of the origins or consequences of his acts of cognition *in the world*. His unmasking of aberrant ideologies maintains a metaphorical, rather than a metonymical, relation to history. Yet those acts of cognition, however insufficient they may seem now, are not to be discarded because of this refusal to go further. In the absence of any guarantee as to Paul de Man's moral character or political vision, his writings remain indispensable in their insistence that the too-easy leap from linguistic to aesthetic, ethical, or political structures has been made before, with catastrophic results.

Yet that insistence is never made unironically, in such a way as to imply that the errors are ultimately avoidable. A typical concluding sentence takes the form of a double negative:

> With the critical cat now so far out of the bag that one can no longer ignore its existence, those who refuse the crime of theoretical ruthlessness can no longer hope to gain a good conscience. Neither, of course, can the theorists—but, then, they never laid claim to it in the first place.[5]

The fact that the theorists never laid claim to a good conscience is by no means reassuring, especially in light of recent developments. Nor does it erase the impression of moral self-satisfaction this sentence conveys. In this typical pharmakon-like ending, de Man makes it difficult to tell which of the possible remedies is more poisonous. All the more so since in the original publication of this essay in the *Times Literary Supplement*, the final sentence had read "neither, of course, can the terrorists."

The Inhuman and the Impersonal

Things happen in the world which cannot be accounted for in terms of
the human conception of language. [. . .] Understand by nihilism a
certain kind of critical awareness which will not allow you to make
certain affirmative statements when those affirmative statements go
against the way things are.
—Paul de Man, "Walter Benjamin's *The Task of the Translator*"

The pleasure with which de Man manipulates terms like *ruthlessness* is unsettling, however much one wishes to believe he is only "warning against unwarranted hopeful solutions." Something of what is at stake may be gleaned from an exchange published in *The Resistance to Theory* between de Man and Meyer Abrams. The exchange occurred during the discussion of de Man's lecture on Walter Benjamin's "The Task of the Translator." Elaborating on the statement that "Benjamin says, from the beginning, that it is not at all certain that language is in any sense human," de Man explains:

> The "inhuman," however, is not some kind of mystery, or some kind of secret; the inhuman is: linguistic structures, the play of linguistic tensions, linguistic events that occur, possibilities which are inherent in language—independently of any intent or any drive or any wish or any desire we might have.

Abrams: I want to go back to the question [...] about language being somehow opposed to the human. I want [...] to provide a different perspective, just so we can settle the matter in a different way. And that perspective won't surprise you because you've heard it before and expect it from me.

de Man: That's very human.

Abrams: Suppose I should say, as many people have said before me, that instead of being the nonhuman, language is the most human of all the things we find in the world, in that language is entirely the product of human beings. [...] Now, suppose that, alternatively to looking at the play of grammar, syntax, trope, somehow opposed to meaning, I should say—and I'm not alone in saying this—that language, through all these aspects, doesn't get between itself and the meaning, but instead that language, when used by people, makes its meaning. [...] What can be more human than the language which distinguishes human beings from all other living things? [...] All I want to do is present the humanistic perspective, as an alternative, an optional alternative, which appeals to me. Instinctively, it appeals to me.

de Man: Well, it appeals to me, also, greatly; and there is no question of its appeal, and its desirability. The humanistic perspective is obviously there [...] [But] a certain kind of critical examination [...] *has to* take place, it has to take place not out of some perversity, not out of some hubris of critical thought or anything of the sort, it has to take place because it addresses the question of what actually happens. Things happen in the world which cannot be accounted for in terms of the human conception of language. And they always happen in linguistic terms. [...] And good or bad things, not only catastrophes, but felicities also. [...] One could say, with all kinds of precautions, and in the right company, and with all kinds of reservations—and I think it's a very small company—that Benjamin's concept of history is nihilistic. Which would have to be understood as a very positive statement about it. [...] Understand by nihilism a certain kind of critical awareness which will not allow you to make certain affirmative statements when those affirmative statements go against the way things are.[6]

Earlier in the discussion, de Man situated the crux of the difference between himself and Abrams as follows: "If one speaks of the inhuman, the fundamental nonhuman character of language, one also speaks of the fundamental non-definition of the human as such." The problem is not one of deciding whether language is or is not human, but rather of knowing exactly what the word *human* means. Language becomes the pharmakon within which it is both impossible and "desirable"—indeed, urgent—to separate the human from the inhuman. But from what standpoint is such a statement being said?

The question of the humanness or inhumanness of language is very much tied to the question of a *lieu d'énonciation*. In an early and fundamental essay on Mallarmé, entitled "Poetic Nothingness," de Man quotes a famous letter written by Mallarmé at a turning point in his poetic career:

> This last year has been a terrrifying one. My thought has worked through to a Divine Conception. [. . .] I write to inform you that I am impersonal now, and no longer the Stéphane you once knew—but an aptitude the spiritual universe has for seeing itself and for developing, through what once was me.[7]

As de Man demonstrates in his discussion of Benjamin, from the Divine to the inhuman *il n'y a qu'un pas*. De Man follows very much in this tradition of impersonality, which was to lead Mallarmé to the theory of the "elocutionary disappearance of the poet, who leaves the initiative to words." As Hillis Miller points out, "the first person pronoun is used rarely and sparingly by de Man. [. . .] This goes along with an austere rigor that makes his essays sometimes sound as if they were written by some impersonal intelligence, or by language itself."[8] This eclipse of the self by language is both the content and the rhetorical mode of de Man's writing. I have analyzed elsewhere both the grammatical errors and the personifications that mark this apparent eclipse.[9] Here I would like to return to de Man's gloss on Benjamin's suggestion that language might not be in any sense human. The example discussed is strange. Inhumanness seems to inhere in the lack of correspondence between the German word *Brot* and the French word *pain*.

> The translation will reveal a fundamental discrepancy between the intent to name *Brot* and the word *Brot* itself in its materiality, as a device of meaning. If you hear *Brot* in this context of Hölderlin, who is so often mentioned in this text, I hear *Brot und Wein* necessarily, which is the great Hölderlin text that is very much present in this—which in French becomes *Pain et vin*. "Pain et vin" is what you get for free in a restaurant, in a cheap restaurant where it is still included, so *pain et vin* has very different connotations from *Brot und Wein*. It brings to mind the *pain français, baguette, ficelle, bâtard*, all those things—I now hear in *Brot*

"bastard." This upsets the stability of the quotidian. I was very happy with the word *Brot*, which I hear as a native because my native language is Flemish and you say *brood*, just like in German, but if I have to think that *Brod* [*brood*] and *pain* are the same thing, I get very upset. It is all right in English because *bread* is close enough to *Brot* [*brood*], despite the idiom "bread" for money, which has its problems. But the stability of the quotidian, of my daily bread, the reassuring quotidian aspects of the word "bread," daily bread, is upset by the French word *pain*. What I mean is upset by the way in which I mean—the way in which it is *pain*, the phoneme, the term *pain*, which has its set of connotations which take you in a completely different direction.[10]

Later, in his response to Abrams, de Man equates the inhuman with loss of control. That "there is a nonhuman aspect of language is a perennial awareness from which we cannot escape, because language does things which are so radically out of our control that they cannot be assimilated to the human at all, against which one fights constantly" (*RT*, 101). At another point, however, when questioned by Neil Hertz about how a word like *inhuman* can be derived from the connotations of *Brot*, de Man responds by treating the example *itself* as a loss of control:

Well, you're quite right. I was indulging myself, you know, it was long and I was very aware of potential boredom, felt the need for an anecdote, for some relief, and Benjamin gives the example of *pain* and *Brot*, and perhaps shouldn't . . . whenever you give an example you, as you know, lose what you want to say; and Benjamin, by giving the example of *pain* and *Brot*—which comes from him—and which I've banalized, for the sake of a cheap laugh . . . (*RT*, 95–96; ellipses in original)

In its ellipses, its anacoluthons, its denials, this passage comes very close to total incoherence. De Man dismisses the example as a cheap laugh, but his nervousness suggests that he sees it as a slip. What has the slip let show, and what does it have to do with the inhuman? It seems to me that what the slip reveals is not the inhuman but rather the *human* as a loss of control—the de Man that suddenly says "I get very upset," "my native language is Flemish," later feels this small outbreak of exhibitionism as the intrusion of something over which he has lost control. What de Man's categories of human and inhuman seem to lack is a concept of the unconscious. Though he may have reasons to feel it with particular acuity, he is not alone in experiencing the approach to the mother tongue—or perhaps to the mother as such—as the threat of a loss of control. Indeed, even without assigning an unconscious meaning to the example (seeing in it de Man's relation to his mother, or to Belgium), one would have to say that de Man's riff on *pain* and *Brot* sounds suspiciously like a process of free association, a rather exuberant glide along what Lacan would call the signifying chain.

De Man's desire to replace the unconscious with the randomness of language is made explicit in his analysis of Rousseau's slip—Rousseau's blurting out of the name "Marion" as the stealer of a ribbon. De Man writes:

> Because Rousseau desires Marion, she haunts his mind and her name is pronounced almost unconsciously, as if it were a slip, a segment of the discourse of the other. But the use of a vocabulary of contingeny ("le premier objet qui s'offrit") within an argument of causality is arresting and disruptive, for the sentence is phrased in such a way as to allow for a complete disjunction between Rousseau's desires and interests and the selection of this particular name. Marion just happened to be the first thing that came to mind; any other name, any other word, any other sound or noise could have done just as well and Marion's entry into the discourse is a mere effect of chance.[11]

In a way, the entire debate between Lacan and Derrida concerning the purloined letter is summarized here in this discussion of a purloined ribbon. That such was de Man's own understanding of it can be seen not only in the Lacanian phrase "the discourse of the other" but also in the fact that the original title of "Excuses" was "The Purloined Ribbon."

De Man's refusal of psychoanalysis, his desire for chance rather than desire to have the last word, is of a piece with his adoption of a stance of impersonality. But just as his desire to erase the self leaves residues in the grammar of his essays, so too does his self-effacement leave psychoanalytically readable traces in the domain of pedagogy. For the remainder of this essay, I would like to analyze de Man as a pedagogical, rather than merely as an intellectual, figure. I think that it is impossible to understand the intensity of the current debates about de Man without taking the pedagogical arena into consideration. De Man himself characterized his work as "more pedagogical than philosophical; it has always started from the pedagogical or the didactic assignment of reading specific texts rather than, as is the case in Derrida, from the pressure of general philosophical issues."[12] And the editors of the special issue of *Yale French Studies* entitled "The Lesson of Paul de Man" go so far as to say "He was never not teaching."[13]

What Is a Teacher?

A giving which gives only its gift, but in the giving holds itself back and withdraws, such a giving we call *sending*.
—Martin Heidegger, *On Time and Being* (quoted by Alan Bass in his introduction to Derrida's *The Post Card*; Bass's emphasis)

What haunts are not the dead, but the gaps left within us by the secrets of others.—Nicolas Abraham, "Notes on the Phantom"

The title of this section is an allusion to Michel Foucault's influential essay, "What Is an Author?" In that essay, Foucault is at pains to distinguish between a biographical "author" and a textual "author function." In the same way, Paul de Man seemed to want to distinguish between the person of the teacher and the intellectual process in which he or she is engaged:

> Overfacile opinion notwithstanding, teaching is not primarily an inter-subjective relationship between people but a cognitive process in which self and other are only tangentially and contiguously involved. The only teaching worthy of the name is scholarly, not personal; analogies between teaching and various aspects of show business or guidance counseling are more often than not excuses for having abdicated the task.[14]

In her memorial tribute to de Man, Ellen Burt describes eloquently the extent to which de Man succeeded in existentializing this view of the teacher, by conveying "as complete a detachment from the claims of subjectivity or individual personality as was possible."[15] A different kind of example of his pedagogical self-effacement occurs in his introduction to a special issue of *Studies in Romanticism* which presents the work of six of his students. While eventually speaking about "my generation" and "their generation," he nevertheless totally avoids the first-person pronoun in the long opening paragraph in which he refers to their participation in "a [rather than 'my'] year-long seminar sponsored by the National Endowment for the Humanities" or "various graduate seminars." "It would be an injustice to see in them only the product of a single 'school' or orthodoxy, thus reducing their challenge to mere anecdote." Rather, he asserts, "the essays collected in this volume come as close as one can come, in this country, to the format of what is referred to, in Germany, as an *Arbeitsgruppe*, an ongoing seminar oriented towards open research rather than directed by a single, authoritative voice."[16] Yet no one is fooled by these denials of authority. They serve only to increase the impression of authority he conveyed. Again and again both admirers and critics testify to his authority as paradoxical. The memorial tributes are eloquent on the subject:

> I want to speak not about de Man's power as a teacher and as a writer, but about the extraordinary intellectual authority he exerted on his friends and colleagues, at least on me. Paul de Man much disliked words like "power," "force," or "authority," especially when applied to the academic world. He would have smiled ironically again and more than a little scornfully at the idea that he had what those words name, though obviously he did. (J. Hillis Miller)

> His jokes would always be in some sophisticated manner joking at his own expense, pedagogically disclaiming, in a Nietzschean manner, his own authority. [. . .] Paul disclaimed his own authority, yet none had more authority than him. (Shoshana Felman)

> The last thing he probably would have wanted to be was a moral and pedagogical—rather than merely intellectual—example for generations of students and colleagues, yet it was precisely his way of not seeking those roles that made him so irreplaceably an exception, and such an inspiration. (Barbara Johnson)

It has recently been remarked that the unearthing of de Man's early writings has induced deconstructors to abandon their anti-biographical stance and to search for intentions, mitigating circumstances, and contextual elements that might help to understand the man. What this reveals, however, is not that the person of the author has suddenly been brought back from exile, but that that person was always already there, idealized as impersonal. In other words, it was not *despite* but rather *because* of his self-effacement that students and colleagues were led to substantialize and idealize him, as if the teacher as person could simply be deduced from the teacher-function. They took him as a metaphor, not a metonymy, of his persona. Just as in a psychoanalytic situation the analyst's silence allows the analysand to construe him or her as a subject-presumed-to-know, de Man's silence about himself (including—but not restricted to—his past) created a blank on which admirers could project their idealizations. This fascination clearly had its dangers—but where did we get the idea that powerful teaching could ever be purely beneficent? Western philosophy indeed originated with a text that saw the teacher as *pharmakon*, perched between enlightenment and corruption.

De Man's blank was in fact itself already constructed out of transferential idealization. As de Man told Stefano Rosso, "I have a tendency to put upon texts an inherent authority. [...] I assume, as a working hypothesis, (as a working hypothesis because I know better than that), that the text *knows* in an absolute way what it's doing."[17] In a passage in which de Man describes his discovery through Reuben Brower of pedagogy as a subversive activity, he explains teaching as an induction into this type of heuristic transference onto a text as a site of (perhaps inhuman) knowledge:

> Students, as they began to write on the writings of others, were not to say anything that was not derived from the text they were considering. They were not to make statements that they could not support by a specific use of language that actually occurred in the text. They were asked, in other words, to begin by reading texts closely as texts and not to move at once into the general context of human experience or history. Much more humbly or modestly, they were to start out from the bafflement that such singular turns of tone, phrase, and figure were bound to produce in readers attentive enough to notice them and honest enough not to hide their non-understanding behind the screen of received ideas that often passes, in literary instruction, for humanistic knowledge. [...] Mere reading, it turns out, prior to any theory, is able to transform critical discourse in a manner that would appear deeply subversive to those who think of the teaching of literature as a substitute for the teaching of theology, ethics, psychology, or intellectual history. Close reading accomplishes this often in spite of itself because it cannot fail to respond to structures of language which it is the more or less secret aim of literary teaching to keep hidden.[18]

If this type of teaching is subversive—and it is certainly subversive in the ways de Man describes—it is because it is *materialist*—it takes language not only on the level of meaning but on the level of meaning-production and -disruption. But in another way, this teaching is also deeply conservative, not in its content but in the frame it draws around that content. The instructions to the students are phrased in the grammar of an absolute but hidden authority: "students were not to . . . they were to . . ." Listen to the description Richard Ohmann gives of a not-so-different set of instructions to the student taking the Advanced Placement English course:

> Another thing a student is supposed to be is objective. The Acorn Book says that his Advanced Placement English course will teach him how to read *and respond* to works of literature, but if the descriptive material and the examinations are any indication, the Advanced Placement Pro-

gram actually teaches the student not to respond to literature, not with his feelings. His concern must be with "organization of the elements of the poem," with "particular uses of language" that express a contrast, with the function of minor characters, with the way structure, imagery, and sound contribute to the whole meaning of a poem—"your feeling about the poem is important," he is implicitly told, "only as the outcome of careful reading." His role is that of the neutral instrument, recording and correlating the facts and drawing conclusions. If any need or interest other than the formalistic drove him to read the work, or indeed, if something within turns him *against* the work, he will quickly learn to suppress these unwelcome responses. They are not among the competencies that will move him a step up the ladder. To his reading of a poem he is supposed to bring the techniques he has mastered, and only those. He is, in other words, alienated in very nearly the Marxian sense, and, of course, the ideal student is of the middle class. Docility, care, tidiness, professional ambition, the wish for objectivity, these are all qualities valued particularly by the middle class and encouraged in its young.[19]

By thus drawing a frame around the text as a *sujet supposé savoir*, the teacher can teach the student not to ask certain questions about the literary canon or about the teacher. It is no accident that few students ever asked de Man what he had done during the war. De Man's subversive teaching certainly unsettled many of the assumptions that have accompanied the humanist understanding of the canon, but he did nothing to unseat the traditional white male author from his hiding place behind the impersonality of the universal subject, the subject supposed to be without gender, race, or history. He created a slightly idiosyncratic canon of his own (in part through throw-away lines like "in the profession you are nobody unless you have said something about this text"), but he did not suggest that there were multiple literary histories, or readers with completely different senses of what was urgent. Perhaps it was not his place to do so. His pedagogy was a pedagogy of self-difference and self-resistance within a traditional understanding of canonical texts and questions. It is up to us to open the subversiveness of teaching further—*without* losing the materialist conception of language that remains de Man's truly radical contribution.

NOTES

"Poison or Remedy? Paul de Man as Pharmakon." *Colloquium Helveticum* 11/12 (1990): 7–20. Reprinted by permission of *Colloquium Helveticum*.

1. Paul de Man, "The Resistance to Theory," in *The Resistance to Theory* (Minneapolis, University of Minnesota Press, 1986), 11; emphasis mine (hereafter, *RT*).
2. Paul de Man, "The Return to Philology," in *RT*, 25; emphasis mine.
3. "Aesthetic Formalization: Kleist's *Über das Marionettentheater*," in *The Rhetoric of Romanticism* (New York: Columbia University Press, 1984) (hereafter *RR*).
4. Paul de Man, "Kant and Schiller," in *Aesthetic Ideology* (Minneapolis: University of Minnesota Press, 1996), 154–55.
5. "The Return to Philology," 26.
6. "Conclusions: Walter Benjamin's *The Task of the Translator*,'" in *RT*, 96–104.
7. Quoted in Paul de Man, "Poetic Nothingness," in *Critical Writings 1953–1978* (Minneapolis: University of Minnesota Press, 1989), 25.
8. J. Hillis Miller, "'Reading' Part of a Paragraph in *Allegories of Reading*," in *Reading de Man Reading*, ed. Lindsay Waters and Wlad Godzich (Minneapolis: University of Minnesota Press, 1989), 165.
9. See my essay entitled "Rigorous Unreliability" in *A World of Difference* (Baltimore: Johns Hopkins University Press, 1987).
10. "The Task of the Translator," 87.
11. Paul de Man, "Excuses," in *Allegories of Reading* (New Haven, CT: Yale University Press, 1979), 288.
12. "An Interview," in *RT*, 117.
13. Foreword to *The Lesson of Paul de Man*, Yale French Studies no. 69, ed. Peter Brooks, Shoshana Felman, and J. Hillis Miller (New Haven, CT: Yale University Press, 1985).
14. "The Resistance to Theory," 4.
15. "In Memoriam," in *The Lesson of Paul de Man*, 11.
16. *Studies in Romanticism* 18 (winter 1979): 495.
17. "An Interview," 118.
18. "The Return to Philology," 23, 24.
19. Richard Ohmann, *English in America* (New York, Oxford University Press, 1976), 57.

CHAPTER 25

Taking Fidelity Philosophically

While the value of the notion of fidelity is at an all-time high in the audio-visual media, its stocks are considerably lower in the domains of marital mores and theories of translation. It almost seems as though the stereo, the Betamax, and the Xerox have taken over the duty of faithfulness in reproduction, leaving the texts and the sexes with nothing to do but disseminate. This is perhaps the inevitable result of the intersection between contemporary psychoanalytical, Marxist, and philosophical critiques of consciousness, on the one hand, and modern technology, on the other. When computers, automated assembly lines, and photocopiers advantageously replace human memories and hands, and when language, ideology, and the unconscious are aptly compared to machines of which we are the puppets, it is difficult to know what to do with that defensive excrescence called consciousness. From that point of view, the crisis in marriage and the crisis in translation are identical. For while both translators and spouses were once bound by contracts to love, honor, and obey, and while both inevitably betray, the current questioning of the possibility and desirability of conscious mastery makes that contract seem deluded and exploitative from the start. But what are the alternatives? Is it possible simply to renounce the meaning of promises or the promise of meaning?

Fortunately, I must address translation, not matrimony. Yet the analogy between the two is extremely far-reaching. It might, however, seem that the translator ought, despite or perhaps because of his or her oath of fidelity, to be considered not as a duteous spouse but as a faithful bigamist, with loyalties split between a native language and a foreign tongue. Each must accommodate the requirements of the other without their ever having the opportunity to meet. The bigamist is thus necessarily doubly unfaithful, but in such a way that he or she must push to its utmost limit the very capacity for faithfulness. Yet in the realm of translation, it is precisely today that, paradoxically enough, at the moment when the strictures of this double alliance are being made rigorously explicit, the notion of fidelity itself is being put in question. Both these movements come to a large extent from the work of Jacques Derrida, about whose relation to translation I would like now to make a few brief remarks.

It seems, in retrospect, as though literary criticism in the United States had long been on the lookout for someone to be unfaithful with. All signs seem to indicate that, in some strata, it has chosen Derrida, perhaps because he is such a good letter writer. Yet paradoxically enough, what seems to be happening to the seductive foreignness of Derrida's thought in this country is that it begins, as Rodolphe Gasché has recently pointed out,[1] to bear an uncanny resemblance to our own home-grown New Criticism. It is as though, through our excursion into the exotic, we had suddenly come to remember what it was that appealed to us in what we were being unfaithful to. This transferential bigamy or double infidelity thus indicates that it is not bigamy but rather incest that is at stake in the enterprise of translation. Through the foreign language we renew our love-hate intimacy with our mother tongue. We tear at her syntactic joints and semantic flesh and resent her for not providing all the words we need. In translation, the everyday frustrations of writing assume an explicit, externally projected form. If we are impotent, it is because Mother is inadequate. In the process of translation from one language to another, the scene of linguistic castration—which is nothing other than a scene of impossible but unavoidable translation and normally takes place out of sight, behind the conscious stage—is played on center stage, evoking fear and pity and the illusion that all would perhaps have been well if we could simply have stayed at home.

But it is the impossibility of staying home with the mother tongue that is precisely at the core of the philosophy of Jacques Derrida. For Derrida's work, in fact, has always already been (about) translation. His first book was a translation of Husserl's "Origin of Geometry." Derrida's theory and practice of *écriture*, indeed, occupy the very point at which philosophy and translation meet. To gauge the extent of Derrida's subversive intervention in the history of philosophy, let us first quote from a translator's note that typifies the classical attitude toward the relations between philosophy and translation. The note introduces an English edition of Hegel's *Ency-clopedia*:

> To translate the world's worst stylist literally, sentence by sentence, is possible—it has been done—but it is perfectly pointless; the translation, then, is every bit as unintelligible as the original. But the world's worst stylist is, alas, also one of the world's greatest thinkers, certainly the most important for us in this twentieth century. In the whole history of philosophy there is no other single work which could hold a candle to his *Logic*; a work incomparable in its range, depth, clarity of thought, and beauty of composition—but it must be decoded.
>
> The attempt must be risked, therefore, to rescue its grandeur from its abstruse linguistic chaos. . . . This is like detective work: what Hegel means, but hides under a dead heap of abstractions, must be guessed at and ferreted out. I have dared to translate—not the ponderous Hegelian jargon, which is as little German as it would be English—but the thought. My "translation," then, is a critical presentation or rendition; it is not a book about Hegel because it faithfully follows the order and sequence of his paragraphs.[2]

Presiding over classical notions of philosophy and translation are thus the separability of style and thought and the priority of the signified over the signifier, whose only legitimate role is to create order and sequence. Faithfulness to the text has meant faithfulness to the semantic tenor with as little interference as possible from the constraints of the vehicle. Translation, in other words, has always been the translation of *meaning*.

Derrida's rearticulation of philosophy and translation is obviously not designed to evacuate meaning entirely. But his concept of textuality displaces the very notion of *how* a text means. What goes on in every text far exceeds what can be reduced to so-and-so's "thought." Derrida's own ingenious translations, such as that of Hegel's *Aufhebung* by *la relève*, are attempts to render all the often contradictory meanings of a term in such a way that crucial logical complexities are not oversimplified. It is quite often by finding the pressure points previously lost in translation that Derrida rearticulates philosophy with itself. The most striking example is the Platonic word *Pharmakon*, which can mean both "poison" and "remedy" and thus makes problematic any statement in which it occurs. Previous translators had chosen to render one side or the other of its ambivalence at a time, thus deciding what in Plato remains undecidable. I quote from my own translation of Derrida's remarks in *La Dissémination*:

In our discussion of this text we have been using an authoritative French translation of Plato, the one published by Guillaume Budé. In the case of the *Phaedrus*, the translation is by Léon Robin. We will continue to refer to it, inserting the Greek text in parentheses, however, whenever it seems opportune or pertinent to our point. Hence, for example, the word *pharmakon*. In this way we hope to display in the most striking manner the regular, ordered polysemy that has, through skewing, indetermination, or overdetermination, but without mistranslation, permitted the rendering of the same word by "remedy," "recipe," "poison," "drug," "philter," etc. It will also be seen to what extent the malleable unity of this concept, or rather its rules and the strange logic that links it with its signifier, has been dispersed, masked, obliterated, and rendered almost unreadable not only by the imprudence or empiricism of the translators, but first and foremost by the redoubtable, irreducible difficulty of translation. It is a difficulty inherent in its very principle, situated less in the passage from one language to another, from one philosophical language to another, than already, as we shall see, in the tradition between Greek and Greek; a violent difficulty in the transference of a non-philosopheme into a philosopheme. With this problem of translation we will thus be dealing with nothing less than the problem of the very passage into philosophy.[3]

It is thus precisely the way in which the original text is always already an impossible translation that renders translation impossible. Interestingly, the passage I have just quoted, in making explicit the problem of translation, presents an insoluble dilemma to the English translator. Since its point hangs on a French translation to which the English no longer directly refers, the translator must either transpose the point onto English translations—which, incidentally, bear it out equally well—thus fictively usurping the status of original author, or retain the reference to French, thus fictively returning to the original language. This difficulty, indeed, perfectly illustrates the point it conveys: the more a text is worked through by the problem of translation, the more untranslatable it becomes.

Derrida's entire philosophic enterprise, indeed, can be seen as an analysis of the translation process at work in every text. In studying the *différance* of signification, Derrida follows the misfires, losses, and infelicities that prevent any given language from being *one*. Language, in fact, can only exist in the space of its own foreignness to itself. But all of Western philosophy has had as its aim to repress that foreignness, to take a text that is "as little German as it would be English" and to make it into the transparent expression of a great philosophic thought. Not only, however, is this self-*différance* the *object* of Derrida's attention: it is an integral part of the functioning of his own écriture. The challenges to translation presented by Derrida's writing have continually multiplied over the years. From the early, well-bred neologisms to a syntax that increasingly frustrates the desire for unified meaning, Derrida has even, in *Living On*[4]—first published in English—gone so far as to write *to* the translator *about* the difficulties he is in the act of creating for him, thus figuratively sticking out his tongue—his mother tongue—at the borderline between the translated text and the original.

It is thus a greatly overdetermined paradox that the translation of Derrida's writings should have become such a thriving industry in the United States today. The translator faces the impossibility and the necessity of translation on four fronts: within the text Derrida is reading; within what Derrida says about it; within the way Derrida says it; and within the very notion of translation that all of these areas imply. Indeed, the radicality of the revolution in the relations between signifiers and signifieds makes the project of separating these four fronts impossible. Yet the violence implied by classical faithfulness to the spirit at the expense of the letter cannot be avoided by simple faithfulness to the letter of any text. For it is necessary to be faithful to the violent love-hate relation *between* letter and spirit, which is already a problem of translation within the *original* text. If the original text is already a translatory battle in which what is being translated is ultimately the very impossibility of translation, then peacemaking gestures such as scrupulous adherence to the signifier are just as unfaithful to the energy of the conflict as the tyranny of the swell-footed signified. The translator must fight just as hard against the desire to be innocent as against what we today consider the guilty desire to master the text's message. It is, indeed, at the moment of translation that the textual battle comes into its own. Translation is a bridge that creates out of itself the two fields of battle it separates. Heidegger could have been talking about translation when he wrote of the bridge:

> It does not just connect banks that are already there. The banks emerge as banks only as the bridge crosses the stream. The bridge designedly causes them to lie across from each other. One side is set off against the other by the bridge. Nor do the banks stretch along the stream as indifferent border strips of dry land. With the banks, the bridge brings to the stream the one and the other expanse of the landscape lying behind them. It brings stream and bank and land into each other's neighborhood.[5]

The bridge of translation, which paradoxically releases within each text the subversive forces of its own foreignness, thus re-inscribes those forces in the tensile strength of a new neighborhood of otherness. Yet all travelers on that bridge are answering a summons that repulses them at every step, a summons reminiscent of the sign Lautréamont sets up in front of Maldoror, containing a warning that is received just a moment too late to be heeded: "Vous, qui passez sur ce pont, n'y allez pas." "You who are crossing over this bridge, don't get to the other side."

NOTES

Reprinted from "Taking Fidelity Philosophically," from *Difference in Translation*, Joseph F. Graham, ed. © 1985 by Cornell University. Used by permission of the publisher, Cornell University Press.

1. Rodolphe Gasché, "Deconstruction as Criticism," *Glyph* 6 (1979): 177–215.
2. *Hegel's Encyclopedia of Philosophy*, trans. and annot. Gustav Emil Mueller (New York: Philosophical Library, 1959), 1.
3. Jacques Derrida, *Dissemination*, trans. Barbara Johnson (Chicago: University of Chicago Press, 1981), 71–72.
4. Jacques Derrida, "Living On," in *Deconstruction and Criticism* (New York: Seabury Press, 1979).
5. Martin Heidegger, "Building Dwelling Thinking," in *Poetry, Language, Thought*, trans. Albert Hofstadter (New York: Harper and Row, 1971), 152.

CHAPTER 26

The Task of the Translator

For if the sentence is the wall before the language of the
original, literalness is the arcade.
—Walter Benjamin, "The Task of the Translator"

I. "Tableaux Parisiens"

Why did Walter Benjamin translate Charles Baudelaire? And why did Benjamin begin with just the "Tableaux Parisiens," the section Baudelaire added to *Les Fleurs du Mal* after the courts forced him to remove six poems out of the original hundred? Baudelaire's post-trial (post-traumatic?) poems fit Benjamin's later preoccupation with Paris and with modernity, but they had not at the time begun to inspire the thoughts to which Benjamin would later return. And why has Benjamin's prefatory essay, "The Task of the Translator," become so famous without any discussion—either by Benjamin or by his readers—of the poet to whose work this essay served as an introduction? It seems as though Baudelaire were only a pretext for Benjamin to indulge in—and speculate about—translation itself.

Baudelaire is first mentioned in Benjamin's correspondence in early 1915, between the time of his friend Fritz Heinle's suicide and Benjamin's break with the mentor of his youth, Gustav Wyneken. Both events were occasioned by the First World War, which put an abrupt end to Benjamin's childhood idealism—as well as to the illusions of a whole generation of Europeans. Wanting to establish a relation to literature that would decisively break with the attachments of the past, Benjamin turned his back on the conception of literature most congenial to him, which was identifiably propagated by the circle around Stefan George. For them, the poet was a seer, an aristocrat of the spirit, a voice crying out against the evils of the marketplace and the degradations of modern life. Benjamin seemed to need to renounce the self-satisfactions of such an elite and visionary company in order to grapple *literarily* with what was actually happening.

For Baudelaire, though, translation had come early: about a year after his own suicide attempt and before the revolution of 1848 (and almost ten years before the publication of *Les Fleurs du Mal*), he discovered Edgar Allan Poe with "a strange sort of shock."[1] Baudelaire's Poe translations were the most lucrative of his publications, thus at once calming (a bit) his excruciating debt anxiety, opening up the world of a misunderstood *semblable*, and, perhaps, revealing something that only translation could teach. Stéphane Mallarmé, powerfully affected by Baudelaire, went so far as to learn English in order to read Poe and ended up enslaved to the profession of high school English teacher for the rest of his life. Along the way, he translated the poems that Baudelaire had not touched. Benjamin, too, when he approached translating Baudelaire, had just broken with his parents and needed to earn a living. The relation between translation and the marketplace deserves further study, especially when the marketplace is being resisted or failed at by modes of writing that remain—intentionally or not—unsalable in their mother tongue.

The most aesthetically successful translation—one of many—of Baudelaire's *Flowers of Evil* into German was already in its sixth edition by the time Benjamin published his "Tableaux Parisiens" in 1922. It was written—of course—by Stefan George. Benjamin had owned George's *Die Blumen des Bösen* since 1918. It seems likely, therefore, that Benjamin first turned to Baudelaire in order to make his break with George on George's own turf. What Benjamin didn't know then was how many times Baudelaire would also occasion his breaks with *himself*. But why was *translation* the ground on which the early battle was fought?[2] Could it have been otherwise?

In a note on Baudelaire written in 1921 or 1922—and thus contemporaneous with his translations—Benjamin differentiates himself from his illustrious precursor:

> *Spleen et idéal.* Because of the abundance of connotations in this title, it is not translatable. Each of the two words on its own contains a double meaning. Both *spleen* and *idéal* are not just spiritual essences but also an intended effect upon them, as is expressed in [Stefan] George's trans-

lation *Trübsinn und Vergeistigung* [Melancholy and Spiritualization].
But they do not express only that intended effect; in particular, the sense
of a radiant and triumphant spirituality—such as is evoked in the sonnet
"L'Aube spirituelle," among many others—is not rendered adequately
by *Vergeistigung*. *Spleen*, too, even when understood merely as intended
effect, not as archetypal image, is more than *Trübsinn*. Or rather, it is
Trübsinn only in the final analysis: first and foremost, it is that fatally
foundering, doomed flight toward the ideal, which ultimately—with
the despairing cry of Icarus—comes crashing down into the ocean of
its own melancholy. In both the oldest and the most recent foreign word
in his language, Baudelaire indicates the share of time and eternity in
these two extreme realms of the spirit. And doesn't this ambiguous title
also imply that archetypal image and intended effect are mysteriously
intertwined? Doesn't the title mean that it is the melancholic above all
whose gaze is fixed on the ideal, and that it is the images of melancholy
that kindle the spiritual most brightly?[3]

Spleen et idéal is the name of the opening section of *Les Fleurs du Mal*, a
section that Benjamin did *not* translate. Later, however, he did translate the
introductory poem to the volume "Au lecteur," which George had pointedly
excluded from it. Arguing that Baudelaire's fascination with disgusting
things was no longer shared by those who took his work seriously, George
explained in the foreword to his translation that

> es bedarf heute wohl kaum noch eines hinweises dass nicht die ab-
> schreckenden und widrigen bilder die den Meister eine zeit lang ver-
> lochten ihm die grosse verehrung des ganzen jüngeren geschlechtes
> eingetragen haben sondern der eifer mit dem er der dichtung neue ge-
> biete eroberte und die glühende geistigkeit mit der er auch die sprödesten
> stoffe durchdrang. so ist dem sinne nach "SEGEN" das einleitungsgedicht
> der BLUMEN DES BÖSEN und nicht das fälschlich "VORREDE" genannte.
> mit diesem verehrungsbeweis möge weniger eine getreue nachbil-
> dung als ein deutsches denkmal geschaffen sein.[4]

"Bénédiction" was a far more appropriate poem to begin the volume than
any prefatory poem would be. The elimination of "Au lecteur" and the opening provided by "Bénédiction" place the center of gravity of the volume for
George in the realm of transcendental otherworldly poetic justice rather than
in a relation to the things of this world. Baudelaire's originality—the appeal
of the things that disgust us the most—becomes for George an indictment

of the world from which the poet longs to escape, not an indictment of the perversity of the will of the poet. This is why George has no use for images that evoke the specificity of the modern world. Contrasting Benjamin's translation of "Paysage" with George's, Momme Brodersen writes:

> The city, which is the focal point of the "Tableaux Parisiens" cycle, does not appear in George's translations, or is not recognizable as such. He archaizes "Les tuyaux, les clochers, ces mâts de la cité" to become "Den rauchfang den turm und die wolken weit" [The chimney, the tower, and the clouds afar]: the city is simply avoided, so that its specific profile melts into the physiognomy of a rural centre in this German version. How differently this reads in Benjamin's "Auf Turm und Schlot, die Masten von Paris" [To the tower and smokestack, the masts of Paris]![5]

George "translates" into "poetic language" what in Baudelaire breaks out of it. All the things the "poetic" avoids—industry, social unrest, technology—become materials for Baudelaire not *in spite of* their unpoeticness but *because of it*.

But in the act of crisping the edges of Baudelaire's city, Benjamin also solidifies the beings in it. George's soft focus, on the other hand, is sensitive to fleeting images and to the quality of subjective perception per se, not simply to what is perceived. A comparison of the translations of "A une passante" is instructive. This is a poem that will later become so central to Benjamin's reading of Baudelaire that, in the Baudelaire book, he quotes it in its entirety—not once but twice. It is even arguable that the title *Passagen Werk* is a reminiscence of that poem. The word *pas* in French, from which all these words are derived, means "step"—but it also means "not." There is thus a floating negation over "passing" that may or may not have an effect. The description of "love at last sight"[6] in "A une passante" exemplifies for Benjamin Baudelaire's intense but circumscribed capacity for loving and looking. It is somewhat surprising, then, that here Benjamin translates the title as "Einer Dame" (To a Lady), thus missing all the nuances that would later form his theory of modernity. George, in contrast, translates it as "Einer Vorübergehenden" (To a Passing Woman), which preserves the structure of substantivizing a feminine noun out of an adjective of fleetingness. The grammatical crystallization duplicates the sudden appearance of the woman in the crowd. She precipitates out from the supersaturated solution of the poet's expectations.

Even a quick glance at George's translation of Baudelaire reveals how anomalous his German is. Instead of the usual punctuation, he scans the poems with floating dots that seem to function like breaths. He does not capitalize nouns the way German usually does; in fact he doesn't capitalize the first word of a sentence, which is not always a sentence. He reserves capitals only for the beginnings of lines of poetry and for special meanings: the word *Master* in his preface or, in "Bénédiction," the words *Gott* (God), *Enterbte* (Disinherited One), *Kräfte* (Strengths), *Mächte* (Powers), *Thronen* (Thrones), *Schmerz* (Pain), *Palmyren* (Palmyra), and *Strahlenherd* (Hearth of Rays). Most of these words—*but not all*—had been capitalized by Baudelaire. *Strahlenherd*, in particular, capitalized and modified by *heiligen* (holy), heightens the sacredness of the poet's consecration. Baudelaire says that the rays are "Puisée au foyer saint des rayons primitifs" (Drawn from the sacred hearth of primal rays). This is precisely the halo that the prose writer Baudelaire will drop in the mud and then *not* go to look for in the lost and found. At the end of "Some Motifs in Baudelaire," Benjamin quotes almost the whole of the prose poem "Perte d'auréole" to mark how far from his transcendental origins Baudelaire had come.

Benjamin did not at all follow George's lead in idiosyncratic German, but that is far from implying that capitalization was not an issue for him. Because capitalization in French is a traditional sign of allegory, Benjamin was very attentive to Baudelaire's use of capital letters. "One must make one's way through *Les Fleurs du Mal* with a sense for how things are raised to allegory," he writes in his *Arcades Project*. "The use of uppercase lettering should be followed carefully."[7] This is what normally becomes impossible in German: by capitalizing all nouns, German loses the capacity to distinguish between the allegorical and the nonallegorical. It was perhaps an over-sensitivity to such loss that led George to experiment with capitalization. In the poem "Le cygne," where Baudelaire says, "tout pour moi devient allégorie" (everything for me becomes allegory), the word Baudelaire capitalizes is *Travail* (Work). This is not just any word. Emblazoned on the gates of concentration camps ("Arbeit macht frei"), it was a perversion of the central concept of Marxism ("Workers of the world, unite!"); that is, the most material and least figurative of human activities. The capital letter thus, in a sense, allegorizes the unallegorizable. If Work is awakening ("le Travail s'éveille"), this also has everything to do with the "travaux" of modern Paris—including the construction work that totally transformed the city under the direction of Baron Georges Eugène Haussmann. Haussmann himself, it seems, made liberal use of capitalization. Benjamin quotes from an article of 1882 about Haussmann's *Mémoires*:

He [Haussmann] demolished some *quartiers*—one might say, entire towns. There were cries that he would bring on the plague; he tolerated such outcries and gave us instead—through his well-considered architectural breakthroughs—air, health, and life. Sometimes it was a Street that he created, sometimes an Avenue or Boulevard; sometimes it was a Square, a Public Garden, a Promenade. He established Hospitals, Schools, Campuses. He gave us a whole river. He dug magnificent sewers. (*Mémoire du Baron Haussmann*, volume 2 [Paris, 1890], pp. x, xi. Extracts from an article by Jules Simon in *Le Gaulois*, May 1882.)

And Benjamin goes on to note: "The numerous capital letters appear to be a characteristic orthographic intervention by Haussmann."[8]

The title Benjamin envisaged for his work on Baudelaire appears to fluctuate between *Charles Baudelaire: A Lyric Poet in the Era of High Capitalism* and *Paris: The Capital of the Nineteenth Century*. Is this double sense of the word *capital* a mere coincidence? Are the two senses of the word related thematically as well as verbally? Are they similar to the two senses of the word *revolution* in the titles of the two leading surrealist journals (*The Surrealist Revolution* and *Surrealism in the Service of the Revolution*)? In other words, can these two seemingly unrelated senses of *capital* tell us something about connections we might not otherwise look for?

These two senses of *capital*—the economic basis of capitalism and the main city of a state—are both etymologically related to the Latin word for "head": *caput*. With the French Revolution, the head of the old regime was literally decapitated, but the two senses of *capital* rushed in to fill the void. The city and the market were the seats of power in the modern world. But exactly what does the "head" have to do with it? In some way, Benjamin treated as a genuine unknown the question of where the "head" is in modernity. This is partly a question of where power, control, and centrality are located, but it is also related to the unsettling place of the head in general. A head cannot appear in Benjamin without quickly turning into a skull. The death's head does not result from the event of death alone: mortality grins out in the midst of the liveliest images. In his *Origin of German Tragic Drama*, Benjamin famously sums up the relation between death and meaning:

Whereas in the symbol destruction is idealized and the transfigured face of nature is fleetingly revealed in the light of redemption, in allegory the observer is confronted with the *facies hippocratica* of history as a petrified, primordial landscape. Everything about history that, from the very beginning, has been untimely, sorrowful, unsuccessful, is expressed in a face—or rather in a death's head. And although such a thing lacks all "symbolic" freedom of expression, all classical proportion, all humanity—nevertheless, this is the form in which man's subjection to nature is most obvious and it significantly gives rise not only to the enigmatic question of the nature of human existence as such, but also of the biographical historicity of the individual. This is the heart of the allegorical way of seeing, of the baroque, secular explanation of history as the Passion of the world; its importance resides solely in the stations of its decline. The greater the significance, the greater the subjection to death, because death digs most deeply the jagged line of demarcation between physical nature and significance.[9]

But what does death have to do with economics and topography? The corpse seems to come from a completely different universe from the workman or the citizen. Perhaps Benjamin's study of Baudelaire was an attempt to link the two. Baudelaire is, after all, the author of "Une charogne."

II. Let There Be Light

God said: Let there be light! And there was light. God saw the light: that it was good. God separated the light from the darkness. God called the light: Day! and the darkness he called: Night!
—Genesis 1:3–5, The Schocken Bible

It is perhaps time to turn to "The Task of the Translator" in order to shed some light—or perhaps some darkness—upon these questions. The only marked French presence in the preface—which, as we noted, does not mention Baudelaire—is an untranslated sentence by Mallarmé. The fact that the French sentence remains untranslated in a German edition presumably meant for people who don't read French is itself bizarre. In the German edition of the *Collected Works*, there is no footnote. In English, the sentence is translated (in a footnote) as follows:

The imperfection of languages consists in their plurality; the supreme language is lacking: thinking is writing without accessories or even whispering, the immortal word still remains silent; the diversity of idioms on earth prevents anyone from uttering the words which otherwise, at a single stroke, would materialize as truth.[10]

Benjamin cuts the quotation off here, leaving the reader to desire the supreme, but lacking, language that would be the material truth. The counterfactual conditional—if the diversity of languages didn't prevent it, the supreme language *would be* the truth—establishes the image of a language just out of reach, but therefore *almost grasped*. Mallarmé, however, continues with two important qualifications to this true language: first, if it existed there would be no need for poetry; second, the *lack* of correspondence between sound and sense is what makes us believe in the possibility of their harmony.

> Les langues imparfaites en cela que plusieurs, manque la suprême: penser étant écrire sans accessoires, ni chuchotement mais tacite encore l'immortelle parole, la diversité, sur terre, des idiomes empêche personne de proférer les mots qui, sinon se trouverait, par une frappe unique, elle-même matériellement la vérité. Cette prohibition sévit expresse, dans la nature (on s'y bute avec un sourire) que ne vaille de raison pour se considérer Dieu; mais, sur l'heure, tourné à de l'esthétique, mon sens regrette que le discours défaille à exprimer les objets par des touches y répondant en coloris ou en allure, lesquelles existent dans l'instrument de la voix, parmi les langages et quelquefois chez un. A côté d'*ombre*, opaque, *ténèbres* se fonce peu; quelle déception, devant la perversité conférant à *jour* comme à *nuit*, contradictoirement, des timbres obscur ici, là clair. Le souhait d'un terme de splendeur brillant, ou qu'il s'éteigne, inverse; quant à des alternatives lumineuses simples—*Seulement, sachons n'existerait pas le vers*: lui, philosophiquement rémunère le défaut des langues, complément supérieur.[11]

[Languages imperfect insofar as they are many, the supreme one is lacking: thought considered as writing without accessories, not even whispers, still *stills* immortal speech; the diversity, on earth, of idioms prevents anyone from proffering words that would otherwise be, struck uniquely, the material truth. This prohibition is explicitly devastating, in nature (one bumps up against it with a smile) where nothing leads one to take oneself for God; but, at times, turned to aesthetics, my own sense regrets that discourse fails to express objects by touches corresponding to them in shading or bearing, since they do exist among the many languages and sometimes in one. Beside *ombre* |shade|, which is opaque, *ténèbres* |shadows| is not very dark; what a disappointment, in front of the perversity that makes *jour* |day| and *nuit* |night|, contradictorily, sound dark in the former and light in the latter. Hope for a resplendent word glowing, or being snuffed, inversely; so far as simple luminous alternatives are concerned—*Only*, be aware that *verse would not exist:* ||it, philosophically makes up for languages' deficiencies, as a superior supplement.] (translation mine)

Mallarmé explicitly equates the missing language with the language of God; or rather, he reminds us that here, on Earth, nature gives us no reason to take ourselves for the Creator. What stands in the way is a prohibition, not just an impossibility. An angel blocks the way back. This implies that the original language—both Genesis and John begin with "In the beginning . . ."— *was* the material truth. God's language disappeared with the multiplicity of languages. The story we tell about that fall into diversity is the story of the Tower of Babel. Diversity itself is a sign of sin. Before the fall, there was unity. Adam named the animals in such a God-language. The animals got names before languages became plural. This implies that the original language was perfectly referential. God was perfect reference. In fact, God created by naming: "Let there be . . ." and "He called." Then he gave the power to name to his creature, Adam, who filled in the rest of the world. Adam named, but he did not create. He brought the animals into language, not into being. But if he brought the animals into language, they must have first existed outside it. The referential world outside of language stilled the creative word—the word that was itself material. The unity of "the word was God" becomes "the word was *with* God." The word could no longer have *been* God if it was *with* God. One only says "with" about two separate things.

In the beginning, therefore, there was no outside to language. God brought the world out of the void in the act of speaking. But for Adam, already, the world and language were two separate things. For him, in fact, naming the animals brought into being *that separation*. What concept of unity, then, would account for the pre-Babelian but noncreative word?

The question we have just asked appears directly related to the "pure language" that translation enables one to glimpse according to "The Task of the Translator." "All suprahistorical kinship between languages consists in this: in every one of them as a whole, one and the same thing is meant. Yet this one thing is achievable not by any single language but only by the totality of their intentions supplementing one another: the pure language" (*Selected Writings*, 1:257). Where I have somewhat tendentiously translated Mallarmé's "complément" as "supplement," the English translator has Benjamin actually say "supplement" for "ergänzend," about which the dictionary says: "*pr. p. & adj.*, supplementary; complementary." Is *supplement* a synonym for *complement* then? If so, all of Jacques Derrida's work on the difference be-tween them is collapsed into nothing, and Jacques Lacan would be wrong to claim of *jouissance féminine*:

> It none the less remains that if she is excluded by the nature of things, it is precisely that in being not all, she has, in relation to what the phal-lic function designates of *jouissance*, a supplementary *jouissance*.
>
> Note that I said *supplementary*. Had I said *complementary*, where would we be! We'd fall right back into the all.[12]

It is thus the status of that "all" that is at stake. *Ergänzend* is a present parti-ciple containing the root *ganz*, "whole." The process of completing a whole would seem to dictate the translation of "complement" for both Benjamin and Mallarmé. But there are at least two reasons not to settle for the "all" too soon: if poetry "makes up for the deficiency of languages that is caused by their plurality," then although poetry is an *attempt* to make up for such deficiency once and for all, poetry's very ongoing existence requires that it always fail. And if "the process of trying to make a whole" is a translation of *ergänzend*, then it names not a successfully completed state but a process that stops being ongoing if it succeeds. Thus, what is lacking as a *result* de-pends on believing that success is just around the corner, but as a process whose ongoingness depends on its failure, the "whole" must never be achieved in *fact*. And that failure to achieve a whole has something to do with sexual difference.

Neither Mallarmé nor Benjamin comes anywhere near asking the ques-tion of sexual difference. And yet their ambivalence about the nature of wholeness—ardently desired but somehow taboo if one is to continue to exist—could be connected to it. After all, it is sexual difference that guaran-tees that every life that exists (at least until cloning) have two parents. Or rather, a sperm cell and an egg cell—not necessarily a father and a mother. Life is thus defined as having a double origin—unlike creation itself, which all comes from God, or Adam and Eve, who are not two separate beings; Eve was produced by budding, like yeast. She is simply made out of Adam.

But what is Adam made out of? Dust, says the Bible. The same dust that the serpent is condemned to eat; the same dust to which mortals who die must return. The book of Genesis itself has two origins: in the first account of creation, God says: "Let us make humankind, in our image, according to our likeness! Let them have dominion over the fish of the sea, the fowl of the heavens, animals, all the earth, and all the crawling things that crawl upon the earth! God created humankind in his image, in the image of God did he create it, male and female did he create them" (Genesis 1:26–27).[13] In the second story, not only did God not create them male and female but also there is no mention of images or likenesses. It is because God is trying to make a companion for Adam that He makes all the other creatures that Adam names. It is because God's creations still haven't given Adam a proper companion ("no helper corresponding to him") that God puts Adam to sleep and performs His rib surgery. Adam's use of language thus occurs at the moment that God is trying and failing to make him a *semblable*. It happens in the place of a sexual difference that, even after the creation of Eve, still has not occurred. In the first story, too, the double origin is in doubt: how can both male and female be in the "image" of God? There are, of course, answers, but they all assume that difference has not really been created, that male and female are really the same.

In an early, unpublished essay entitled "On Language as Such and on the Language of Man," Benjamin, too, considers that, whether or not one believes in it, the creation story in the Bible must "evolve the fundamental linguistic facts":

> The second version of the story of the Creation, which tells of the breathing of God's breath into man, also reports that man was made from earth. This is, in the whole story of the Creation, the only reference to the material in which the Creator expresses his will, which is doubtless otherwise thought of as creation without mediation. In this second story of the Creation, the making of man did not take place through the word: God spoke—and there was. But this man, who is not created from the word, is now invested with the *gift* of language and is elevated above nature. (*Selected Writings*, 1:67–68)

The "material" out of which God shaped Adam is the earth, not language. Adam *has* language precisely to the extent that he is not *made* by it. In the creative word, the thing *was* the word; in Adam's language, the material thing *is in need* of the word. Adam provides a name to a thing that exists apart from it. "Making something out of material" means that form and content are different.

The problem with our myths of the origin of language is that they don't deal with this crucial difference between creative and uncreative referentiality. We tend to imagine the original language as if it were Adam's language, but Adam's language is not the same as God's. The lost language is considered the language of perfect naming (the sign as perfectly "motivated," to use Saussure's vocabulary), while God's destruction of the Tower of Babel consists precisely in propagating a new diversity of names (the arbitrariness of the sign). In Eden, the "tree" of knowledge was not supposed to be "arb(itrai)re." But how can we imagine a language that is itself materially the truth if it is not creative? Of what "material" could the truth be if it does not immediately *bring into being* what it names? How might a language unmediatedly refer if reference itself is mediation?

The problem, I think, is that we tend to think of Adam's language as *similar* to God's. But God's speech is creative to the extent that it is *not* based on similarity. Not, at least, until the creation of man. A God that tries to make a being similar to himself is already a God that takes himself as an object, a God who is well on his way to the sin of self-consciousness. When Adam names the animals, nothing is said about similarity. In fact, proper names are "proper" because they have no semantic content. To play with the semantic content of a name ("That thou art Peter [Petrus], and upon this rock [petra] I will build my church"; "Pierre qui roule n'amasse pas mousse") is usually disparaged as accidental (and such wordplay, as "the lowest form of humor"), and not seen as a trace of the original language. Yet somehow we retain this image of the one originary language involving a perfect coincidence of sound and sense. Why do we have this fantasy? Why can't we give it up?

It is perhaps not that motivated signs are what we have fallen away from but, rather, what we are trying to climb up to. As Mallarmé puts it, poetry makes up for the imperfections of language caused by its plurality (if there are multiple languages, if they "supplement" each other, no one of them can be "elle-même la vérité"; their very differences reveal that the sign is arbitrary). What makes us long for a perfect correspondence between words and meanings is our perception of its contingent lack in any existing language; that is, of its possibility in general. With a little tweaking, we think, we should surely be able to seize what seems so close! "Mon sens regrette que le discours défaille à exprimer les objets par des touches y répondant en coloris ou en allure, lesquelles existent dans l'instrument de la voix, parmi les langages et parfois chez un. A côté d'*ombre*, opaque, *ténèbres* se fonce peu; quelle déception, devant la perversité conférent à *jour* comme à *nuit*, contradictoirement, des timbres obscur ici, là clair." The closeness that is perceived but somehow "perversely" unaccomplished is not only not achieved in language but, it seems, sometimes willfully contradicted. "Day" and "night" (in French) sound like they mean the opposite of what they do mean. This *jour* and *nuit* are not just examples of language's perversity, however. They happen to be the first two words spoken by God during the creation. If *jour* and *nuit* sound like the opposite of what they mean, then we have fallen very far from the creative word. The arbitrariness of language *is* its perversity. Human language in no way resembles the creative word.

This "light" seems destined to show up again and again to debunk the belief that meaning and reality coincide. When Benjamin, in the same essay, says, "That which in a mental entity is communicable *is* its language," he uses the example of a lamp. "The language of this lamp, for example, communicates not the lamp (for the mental being of the lamp, insofar as it is *communicable*, is by no means the lamp itself) but the language-lamp, the lamp in communication, the lamp in expression." In other words, what is communicated is a certain mode of communicability—the significance of a thing *for* someone and *for* that mode of communicability. By concentrating on "mental being," Benjamin establishes the problem of language in the context of life. "Mental being" can exist only *for* someone. But by including God among such possible beings, Benjamin establishes a structure of addressedness that doesn't presuppose a contingent addressee.

We will shortly turn to Paul de Man's essay on Benjamin's "Task of the Translator," but here I would like to point out that he, too, uses that "light" to demystify the same illusion. "No one in his right mind will try to grow grapes by the luminosity of the word 'day,'" he writes in *The Resistance to Theory*, "but it is very difficult not to conceive the pattern of one's past and future existence as in accordance with spatial and temporal schemes that belong to fictional narratives and not to the world."[14]

Even the "coloris ou . . . allure" of the speaker himself enters into the swirl of floating signifiers for Mallarmé once the possibility of taking oneself for God (that is, for colorless) is eliminated. The patterns of black and white in Mallarmé's work owe much to the "perversity" of their liberation. But he would never have foreseen the use that Aimé Césaire would make of that same passage. In an interview in which Césaire was asked why he continued to write in French and not in the more "authentic" Creole, he replied:

Ah! je ne suis pas prisonnier de la langue française! Seulement, j'essaie, j'ai toujours voulu *infléchir* le français. Ainsi, si j'ai beaucoup lu Mallarmé, c'est parce qu'il m'a montré, parce que j'ai compris à travers lui, que la langue, au fond, est arbitraire. Ce n'est pas un phénomène naturel. Cette phrase prodigieuse que Mallarmé a écrite: "*Mon sens regrette que le discours défaille . . . Seulement*, sachons *n'existerait pas le vers*: lui, philosophiquement rémunère le défaut des langues." Mallarmé a toujours été étonné et frappé de la malencontreuse idée qu'on a eu d'appeler *le jour*: le jour et *la nuit*: la nuit, alors que les sonorités porteraient au contraire. Il serait plus naturel d'appeler la nuit: *le jour*, avec cette voyelle longue, cette chose qui *vous tombe dessus*; c'est cela, la nuit! Tandis que le mot *nuit*, avec cet *i* coloré, conviendrait beaucoup mieux à la clarté du jour.[15]

[Ah! I am *not* a prisoner of the French language! Nevertheless, I try, I've always wanted to *inflect* French. Thus, if I've read a lot of Mallarmé, it is because he showed me, because I understood through him, that language, finally, is arbitrary. It's not a natural phenomenon. That prodigious sentence that Mallarmé wrote: "*My own sense regrets that discourse fails . . . Only*, be aware that *verse would not exist*: |1 |it, philosophically makes up for languages' deficiencies." Mallarmé was always surprised and struck by the infelicitous idea that you could call *day*: day, and *night*: night, whereas the sonorities would rather suggest that it should be the other way around. It would be more natural to call night: *day* |jour|, with that long vowel, that thing that *falls*: that's what night is! While the word *night* |nuit| with that colorful *i*, would correspond much more closely to the clarity of day.]

In the hands of the foremost poet of Negritude, it is the bright *i* that is "colored." Day and night, light and dark, the first things created, are not fixed: it depends on who is viewing them. The "gift" of language must be "inflected," but it carries the inertia of ideology (is no longer ex nihilo) and therefore cannot be created entirely anew.

III. Pain

And as they were eating, Jesus took bread, and blessed it, and brake it,
and gave it to his disciples, and said, Take, eat; this is my body.
—Matthew 26:26, King James Bible

Among the moments in Benjamin's "Task of the Translator" that Paul de Man lingers upon in his own analysis of Benjamin's essay, none is more significant than Benjamin's example of the difficulty of translating both the denotation and the network of associations called up by every sign. Benjamin writes:

In the words *Brot* and *pain*, what is meant is the same, but the way of meaning it is not. This difference in the way of meaning permits the word *Brot* to mean something other to a German than what the word *pain* means to a Frenchman, so that these words are not interchangeable for them; in fact, they strive to exclude each other. (*Selected Writings*, 1:257)

"What is meant is the same." Does this mean, "What is named is the same thing"?[16] Is the sameness something outside of language or inside it? If what is meant is the same *object*, then that sameness exists to the extent that "what is meant" is equivalent to "what is referred to": the sameness *in the world*. The role of all languages would be to point noisily toward the same "thing," the thing that would silence them, the thing whose reality doesn't depend in any way on language. Translation would thus liberate the "thing" from language altogether, and one would approach a form of communication that would be "matériellement la vérité."

But if the "thing" *is* liberated from language altogether, then we no longer have to do with translation. Translation is a relation between two languages, not a relation between words and things. What is the sameness that all languages share if it isn't the language of things? What is the sameness that French and German share if it is something entirely *within* language? What do French and German share if their referential meanings are *mutually exclusive*? The object remains the same and the words compete for the same space, yet they are not interchangeable because *one is French and the other German*. The sameness they share is their linguisticness itself, and they necessarily imply the rest of a language, the rest of a world that is specifically German or French. "Language communicates the linguistic being of things," writes Benjamin in "On Language as Such and on the Language of Man" (*Selected Writings*, 1:63). "Translation attains its full meaning in the realization that every evolved language (with the exception of the word of God) can be considered a translation of all the others" (69–70). "The German language, for example, is by no means the expression of everything we could— theoretically—express *through* it, but is the direct expression of that which communicates *itself* in it" (63). These are not national characteristics of *persons* but linguistic characteristics of the *language*.

After mentioning that *Brot* and *pain* strive to exclude each other, Benjamin goes on:

As to what is meant, however, the two words signify the very same thing. Even though the way of meaning in these two words is in such conflict, it supplements itself in each of the two languages from which the words are derived; to be more specific, the way of meaning in them in relation to what is meant. In the individual, unsupplemented languages, what is meant is never found in relative independence, as in individual words of sentences; rather, it is in a constant state of flux—until it is able to emerge as the pure language from the harmony of all the various ways of meaning. (257)

Until there is more than one language, then—until there is translation—language is absolute in relation to things. The language of an original is compared only to the world. But the moment a comparison is set up that requires one language to be seen in terms of another, both languages are seen in their systematicity, their linguisticness. "Language communicates the linguistic being of things" (63). This, however, is not exactly the same as "mental being": "Mental being is identical to linguistic being only insofar as it is capable of communication" (63). This means that there is such a thing as mental being that is not capable of being communicated. Translation, confronting the difference between what is linguistic and what is untranslatable, makes possible a glimpse of the mental being of mankind that is not linguistic. But in that it is not linguistic, it is incapable of being communicated. "No poem is intended for the reader, no picture for the beholder, no symphony for the audience" (253). In the original is glimpsed that incommunicable mental being that no translation can capture, yet until what *is* communicable has been collected, the incommunicable is not glimpsed as such. It is at the moment of translation that the original gives off fleetingly its glow of incommunicability. It is a "love at last sight" seen at the moment it disappears, like Baudelaire's "Passante": "Ô toi que j'eusse aimée! ô toi qui le savais!" (O you I would have loved! O you who knew it!). Its temporality is the imperfect subjunctive. "Just as a tangent touches a circle lightly and at but one point—establishing, with this touch rather than with the point, the law according to which it is to continue on its straight path to infinity—a translation touches the original lightly and only at the infinitely small point of the sense, thereupon pursuing its own course according to the laws of fidelity in the freedom of linguistic flux" (261). The German word here translated (twice) as "lightly" is *flüchtig*, "fleeting(ly)." Transitoriness, not imperceptibleness, is what is emphasized. The fact that "light" is the first thing God created must be an accident, mustn't it? We have no way of talking about these creations ex nihilo of translation.

If the creative word was "elle-même matériellement la vérité," then the miracle of transubstantiation is an attempt to return to it: "Take, eat; this *is* my body." In the *Brot* and *pain* example, Benjamin may well have consciously or unconsciously brought up a figure that refers to the Eucharist—to the separation between Judaism and Christianity, as well as to that between Catholics and Protestants (a rift created, after all, *by translation*), over its nature. Does the bread *become* Christ's body or *represent* it? For whom? The gap between God's language and Adam's is replayed as soon as translation is admitted. And the question of whether the Messianic wait can end in *this* world or not is an argument that Benjamin will never renounce. But in fact it is not Benjamin but rather Paul de Man who turns Benjamin's "bread" into Hölderlin's "bread and wine":

> If you hear *Brot* in this context of Hölderlin, who is so often mentioned in this text, I hear *Brot und Wein* necessarily, which is the great Hölderlin text that is very much present in this—which in French becomes *pain et vin*. "Pain et vin" is what you get for free in a restaurant, in a cheap restaurant where it is still included, so *pain et vin* has very different connotations from *Brot und Wein*.[17]

As we move from German to French, we move from a great poem to a cheap restaurant. We also move from transubstantiation to digestion. The "presence" of Hölderlin behind all this is asserted with a lot of authority, but the phrase "so often mentioned in this text" indicates that such a "presence" needs some justification as an association. In other words, this "necessary" association is far from automatic, even if the excess of assertiveness is meant to silence any doubts. "Hölderlin" and "Brot und Wein" may well be "present," but it is that fluctuating subject (sometimes "you" and sometimes "I") who "hears" the association. If there is any doubt about who is free-associating and what is necessarily present, de Man goes on to make clear just how arbitrary and individual some associations can be:

> *Pain et vin* has very different connotations from *Brot und Wein*. It brings to mind *pain français, baguette, ficelle, bâtard*, all those things—I now hear in *Brot* "bastard." This upsets the stability of the quotidian. I was very happy with the word *Brot*, which I hear as a native because my native language is Flemish and you say *brood*, just like in German, but if I have to think that *Brot* [*brood*][18] and *pain* are the same thing, I get very upset. It is all right in English because "bread" is close enough to *Brot* [*brood*], despite the idiom "bread" for money, which has its problems. But the stability of my quotidian, of my daily bread, the reassuring quotidian aspects of the word "bread," daily bread, is upset by the French word *pain*. What I mean is upset by the way in which I mean—the way in which it is *pain*, the phoneme, the term *pain*, which has its set of connotations which take you in a completely different direction. (87)

In this set of associations, de Man seems to offer some very revealing things: "bastards," mother tongues, daily bread, and being upset. These seem all the more revealing in that later, in the question period following his lecture, de Man seems to feel guilty about them and to disavow their importance:

> Well, you're quite right. I was indulging myself, you know, it was long, and I was very aware of potential boredom, felt the need for an anecdote, for some relief, and Benjamin gives the example of *pain* and *Brot*, and perhaps shouldn't . . . whenever you give an example you, as you know, lose what you want to say; and Benjamin, by giving the example of *pain* and *Brot*—which comes from him—and which I've banalized, for the sake of a cheap laugh . . . (95–96)

This set of associations could at first be read as an unusual admission of personal pain and autobiographical precision. To demonstrate the power of the signifier, de Man speaks about his native language, illegitimacy, perhaps his mother. His attempts to take the whole thing back later serve only to reinforce the impression that something has slipped out. The comment is similar to what Freud says while analyzing the Irma dream: peering down a woman's throat, he cuts off his analysis by saying, "Frankly, I had no desire to penetrate more deeply at this point."[19] The sexual desire and repression seem so obvious that the comment is read as a simple denial of Freud's wish. And both in de Man's case and in Freud's, the moment *may* be truly revealing. Whatever psychoanalytic paydirt one would hit, however, the very intense interest of the revelation would obscure the theoretical point. By treating the play of a signifier or the text of a dream as signifying only something about individual psychology, the two texts are distracted away from making a general point. Whatever is true of the individuals Paul de Man and Sigmund Freud, the point is that *everyone* has a set of associations for every signifier, and everyone dreams. The writers are trying to talk about *that*. In both cases it is the power and communicativeness of something unconscious and unmeant that is in question. Individual psychology is an effect, not a cause, of something that happens independently of any intention. The very fact that the two men unwillingly say revealing things is the only way to make their point, but it is at their own expense.

De Man's analysis of Benjamin's essay on translation begins with the somewhat banal but often overlooked problems that arise when the essay itself is translated:

> If I say stay close to the text, since it is a text on translation, I will need— and that is why I have all these books—translations of this text, because

if you have a text which says it is impossible to translate, it is very nice to see what happens when that text gets translated. And the translations confirm, brilliantly, beyond any expectations which I may have had, that it is impossible to translate, as you will see in a moment. (74)

He goes on to show that "translatable" and "untranslatable," "human" and "inhuman," which seem diametrically opposed, are in fact close enough to have induced the translators into French (Gandillac) and English (Zohn) to mistake them for each other. The expression he singles out for particular comment is "Wehen," which both the English and the French translator have rendered "birth pangs." The scenario of suffering designed to lead to new life is everywhere suggested by Benjamin's text, but here he says merely "die Wehen des eigenen"—"the suffering of the self-identical." Thus, de Man notes, the proper translation of "Wehen" would be neither "birth pangs" nor "death pangs" but, rather, "pains." But Ah! says the alert reader, welcoming a presence that has been lingering on the edge of consciousness for an English speaker all this time. "Pain" is the English pronunciation of that *pain* whose Frenchness was so emphasized before. What was untranslatable—but nevertheless a gold mine of associations—in the French *pain* becomes, in English, the correct translation of the German original, but by a path that is completely "illegitimate": the word the translators have missed here is not a translation but the mispronunciation of a word that shows up elsewhere. Trying not to hear it is itself part of the process for an English speaker.

The task of the translator suddenly becomes even more complicated if he has to edit out a swarm of associations that are not functional in order to stick to "what is meant." Clearly those associations form no part of "what is meant," and their presence is purely irrelevant. Yet the linguistic "noise" of the act of translating, in *not* being meant or intended, comes close to the pure linguisticness of language itself. The very obstacles to translation, then, may point toward the "pure language" that translation enables one to glimpse.

IV. The Breaking of the Vessel

Fragments of a vessel that are to be glued together must match one another in the smallest details, although they need not be like one another. In the same way a translation, instead of imitating the sense of the original, must lovingly and in detail incorporate the original's way of meaning, thus making both the original and the translation recognizable as fragments of a greater language, just as fragments are part of a vessel.
—Benjamin, "The Task of the Translator"

When Benjamin compares translation to archeology, he refers to two entirely different notions of the wholeness that has to be pieced together. The wholeness of the original is an illusion that can be maintained only so long as the original is not translated. "Whereas content and language form a certain unity in the original, like a fruit and its skin, the language of the translation envelops its content like a royal robe with ample folds" (*Selected Writings*, 1:258). Wholeness itself is an illusion; the vessel seems whole in the original language only because the skin and the fruit have been produced together. Any translation immediately has to separate them. The appearance of wholeness is fragmented the moment the signifier and the signified are linked by the "folds" of a different system of differences. Blinded by the mirage of wholeness in the original language, the translator nevertheless has no choice but to fragment the vessel. The original reveals its illusion of wholeness to have already drawn on resources that were, at bottom, arbitrary. The work of art has simply found a way to make that arbitrariness work *for* it. The precarious appearance of unity was achieved by using the fortuitousness of the original language, but in any other language, such luck falls apart. In the process, though, the *two* languages are "recognized" as fragments of a larger vessel. Behind the diversity of languages shimmers a "pure" vessel whose unity no one will ever piece together. And yet, only translation can make it visible at all. Humpty Dumpty's great fall creates the desire to put an egg back together again. But the wholeness translation reveals is not a restoration. The completion it points to is still—and perhaps forever, in human time—deferred.

Even if one resists believing that there is a divine creator at the beginning and the end, the structure of what comes in between is shaped by the notions of the Fall and the Telos. An unreachable something and an unreachable nothing are less different than any assertion of the nature of that something—or of that nothing. Thus, even if I don't believe that the ultimate wholeness really exists, the piecing together of the fragments made visible by translation is structured as if it could. Benjamin's "Messianism" needs to be understood as asserting nothing more than that. Whenever the shape of what exists can only be accounted for by positing a God, Benjamin defines God as that which would explain it. Thus, *by definition*, God exceeds any presence or knowledge one could have without Him. He exists in the shape of what is lacking. The image of a missing piece would occur to almost anyone here *except* Benjamin—God would exist as something that would make the world coherent. But Benjamin insists that God can take the shape of something lacking *without* positing the coherence of the world. The wholeness of the vessel can be a different fantasy each time any two pieces happen to fit together. But the fantasy of wholeness can have a structural effect even if it has no validity. Even the assertion that wholeness is *always* a fantasy testifies to the ubiquity of such a fantasy.

At this point in my argument it was clear to me that I needed to know something about Kabbalah, the scholarly specialty of Gershom Scholem, who was Benjamin's close friend and correspondent for all of Benjamin's life. Always deferring a move to Palestine that he kept describing to Scholem (who had moved there in 1923) as imminent, Benjamin showed great interest in what Scholem was investigating, requesting copies of Scholem's research on Kabbalah while sending to Jerusalem copies of everything he (Benjamin) was writing. What Scholem says about the image of "the breaking of the vessels" is, however, less unambiguous than I had expected. Loaded with scholarly meticulousness and nowhere asserted as true, Scholem writes:

> Isaac Luria's main preoccupation, it would appear, was to trace the further development of the vessels that received the light of emanation which shone into primordial space after the act of *zimzum* ["contraction"].[20]

The moment of creation is slowed down, therefore, into successive moments: into primordial space shone the light of the emanation of a God whose existence was attested by that very light. But "in the beginning was a contraction"? Surely it's only in English that the allusion to the end of pregnancy is readable! Following the progress of that ray, Scholem goes on:

> In the actual emergence of these vessels a part was played both by the lights that were located in the *tehiru* [primordial space] after the *zimzum* and by the new lights that entered with the ray. The purpose of this process was the elimination (*berur*) of the forces of *Din* [judgment] that had collected, a catharsis that could have been attained either by eliminating these forces from the system entirely or else by integrating them within it by first "softening" and purifying them—two conflicting approaches which we frequently encounter side by side. (136)

Encountering conflicting forces side by side seems to be the *aim* and not the infelicity of Luria's creation story. What needs to be explained is not unity but plurality. Thus, there are two ways primordial space can be filled:

> Practically speaking, a point can expand evenly in one of two ways, circularly or linearly, and herein is expressed a basic duality that runs through the process of creation. (136)

We recognize here, whether the connection was present to his mind or not, Benjamin's tangent:

> Just as a tangent touches a circle lightly and at but one point, . . . a translation touches the original lightly and only at the infinitely small point of the sense, thereupon pursuing its own course according to the laws of fidelity in the freedom of linguistic flux. (*Selected Writings*, 1:261)

Translation, then, combines the contradictory resources of these two forces. But what of the kabbalistic "breaking of the vessels"? After describing the disagreements over the nature and sources of the primordial rays, Scholem writes:

> At this point, however, there occurred what is known in Lurianic Kabbalah as "the breaking of the vessels" or "the death of the kings." The vessels assigned to the upper three *Sefirot* managed to contain the light that flowed into them, but the light struck the six *Sefirot* from *Hesed* to *Yesod* all at once and was too strong to be held by the individual vessels; one after another they broke, the pieces scattering and falling. (138)

From this quotation, one begins to understand Benjamin's unusual tolerance for elaborate stories whose surface absurdity is no obstacle to his taking them seriously. (Blanqui's *L'Eternité des astres* comes immediately to mind.) The story of the contraction does not at all point toward a mysterious, mystic unity, but rather *away from it*. Introducing Lurianic doctrine, Scholem writes:

> The main originality of this Lurianic doctrine lay in the notion that the first act of the *Ein-Sof* [the infinite, literally "without end"] was not one of revelation and emanation, but, on the contrary, was one of concealment and limitation. (129)

The vessel exists, one might say, only in order to break. Unity may well have existed in the beginning, but it is not a unity we are progressing *toward*. In fact, every effort to patch the vessel together only breaks it further. And *that* ends up being the thankless but necessary task of the translator.

NOTES

"The Task of the Translator," reprinted by permission of the publisher from Barbara Johnson, *Mother Tongues: Sexuality, Trials, Motherhood*, 40–64 (Cambridge, MA: Harvard University Press), © 2003 by the President and Fellows of Harvard College.

1. Claude Pichois and Jean Zeigler, *Baudelaire*, trans. Graham Robb (London: Vintage, 1989), 145.

2. Momme Brodersen, in his biography of Benjamin, puts his finger squarely on this point: "In addition, Benjamin's Baudelaire translations are primarily the aesthetic evocation and revocation of a man whom, for the whole of his life, he not only considered a great poet and translator, but in addition to whom he remained highly indebted for a long time on numerous accounts: in questions of literary taste and aesthetic judgement, indeed in his entire bearing as a writer. As such, these translations were a move to free himself from a man whose influence on his thought and creative output cannot be overestimated." Momme Brodersen, *Walter Benjamin*, trans. M. R. Green and I. Ligers (London: Verso, 1996), 111.

3. Walter Benjamin, *Selected Writings*, ed. Marcus Bullock and Michael W. Jennings (Cambridge, MA: Harvard University Press, 1996), 1:362; brackets are the editors'.

4. Stefan George, *Die Blumen des Bösen* (Berlin: Georg Bondi, 1918), 5; punctuation and capitalization are George's.

5. Brodersen, *Walter Benjamin*, 111–12.

6. Walter Benjamin, *Charles Baudelaire: A Lyric Poet in the Era of High Capitalism*, trans. Harry Zohn (London: NLB, 1955), 125 ("The delight of the urban poet is love—not at first sight, but at last sight").

7. Walter Benjamin, *The Arcades Project*, trans. Howard Eiland and Kevin McLaughlin (Cambridge, MA: Harvard University Press, 1999), 205.

8. Benjamin, *The Arcades Project*, 127.

9. Walter Benjamin, *The Origin of German Tragic Drama* (London: NLB, 1977), 166.

10. Benjamin, *Selected Writings*, 1:263.

11. Stéphane Mallarmé, *Oeuvres complètes* (Paris: Gallimard, 1945), 363–64.

12. Jacques Lacan, *Feminine Sexuality: Jacques Lacan and the École Freudienne*, ed. Juliet Mitchell and Jacqueline Rose, trans. Jacqueline Rose (New York: W. W. Norton, 1982), 144.

13. The Schocken Bible, trans. Everett Fox (New York: Schocken, 1995), 15.

14. Paul de Man, *The Resistance to Theory* (Minneapolis: University of Minnesota Press, 1986), 11.

15. Jacqueline Leiner, *Imaginaire, langage, identité culturelle, négritude* (Paris: Jean-Michel Place, 1980), 144.

16. See Carol Jacobs's remarks about Harry Zohn's translation of *Illuminations*: "His translation results in phrases such as 'the same thing,' 'the same object,' where the German speaks neither of things nor objects." Carol Jacobs, *In the Language of Walter Benjamin* (Baltimore: Johns Hopkins University Press, 1999), 81.

17. De Man, *Resistance*, 87.

18. Because this is the transcription of a lecture, it is impossible to say whether *Brot* or *brood* is the correct term, especially since de Man has just stated that they sound alike. The written hesitation cannot mirror the oral conflation.
19. Sigmund Freud, *The Interpretation of Dreams* (New York: Avon, 1965), 146.
20. Gershom Scholem, *Kabbalah* (New York: Meridian, 1974), 136.

CHAPTER 27

Teaching Ignorance
L'Ecole des femmes

The teaching of ignorance is probably not what the majority of pedagogues have in mind. It may, indeed, be a structurally impossible task. For how can a teacher teach a student not to know, without at the same time informing her of what it is she is supposed to be ignorant of? This, at any rate, is the problem faced by the would-be professor, Arnolphe, in Molière's play *L'Ecole des femmes*.

Negative Pedagogy

In the opening lines of the play, Arnolphe is explaining to his friend Chrys-alde his pedagogical method for turning an innocent young girl into a faithful wife. He has picked out a docile four-year-old, paid off her mother, and kept her locked up and ignorant ever since.

> I'm rich enough, I think, to have felt free
> To have my wife owe everything to me.
> From her dependency has come submission;
> She cannot flaunt her wealth or her position. . . .
> In a small convent, undisturbed by man,
> I had her raised according to my plan,
> Which was to have them try as best they could

To keep her ignorant and therefore good.
Thank God, the outcome answered my intent,
And now she has grown up so innocent
That I bless Heaven for having been so kind
As to give me just the wife I had in mind.[1]

Young Agnes, in other words, has sprung fully disarmed from the brow of Arnolphe. But the middle-aged protector's belief that his charge's total ignorance of the world will ensure her fidelity to him is soon undercut by the arrival on the scene of young Horace, the son of an old friend of Arnolphe's. Horace gaily recounts to the older man the tale of his encounter with a young girl whom he has spotted on the balcony of a house in which some jealous old tyrant has tried to imprison her. Not realizing that his confidant is his foe, Horace keeps Arnolphe informed of the progress of his love, and for the rest of the play Arnolphe is condemned to hear from the mouth of his young rival the detailed account of the failure of his own desperate attempts to forestall the completion of his ward's education. In the seemingly gratuitous ending, the long-absent fathers of the two young people return to the city with the intention of joining their children in marriage, only to learn, much to their satisfaction, that this is the very plan their children have already conceived. Arnolphe, his dreams of domestic bliss thus dashed, leaves the stage in speechless frustration.

This *School for Wives* could thus be aptly renamed "the portrait of an antiteacher." Not only does Arnolphe intend that this student learn nothing, but even in this negative pedagogy, he fails. His methods are unsound, his lessons backfire, and his classroom is, at the end of the play, silent and empty. The pedagogical model presented to us by the play is apparently designed to be roundly disavowed. Indeed, perhaps the delight with which we literature teachers view the play arises out of the ease with which we can dissociate ourselves from Professor Arnolphe. Yet our delight is perhaps not without discomfort: this image of the ridiculousness of age, power, and authority is painted upon a figure whose role is after all similar to our own. For Molière, too, it seems that Arnolphe was mainly designed as an object of disavowal— precisely because the middle-aged suitor was also, secretly, an object of repressed identification. In 1662, at the age of forty, Molière himself had married the charming but spoiled twenty-year-old sister or daughter of his life-long companion or mistress, having doted on the girl since birth. In the context of what would seem to be a hyperbolic representation of denial, our concentration on the ridiculousness of the desire to possess and repress may therefore perhaps be blinding us to the ways in which Arnolphe's aims and strategies may not be so different from our own.

What, then, are Arnolphe's pedagogical imperatives? In the first scene of the play, Arnolphe is presented to us not as a teacher but as a critic. The object of his criticism is the rampant spread of cuckoldry in the city. It is when his friend Chrysalde warns him that the very outspokenness of his widely published criticism may turn against him that Arnolphe details the pedagogical strategies he has designed to keep his forehead free of decoration.

> *Chrysalde*: My fear for you springs from your mocking scorn,
>   Which countless hapless husbands now have borne;
>   No lord or rustic past his honeymoon
>   Has to your criticism been immune; And everywhere you go, your chief delight
>   Is in the secrets that you bring to light.
>
> *Arnolphe*: In sum, when all around lies comedy
>   May I not laugh, as spectator, at what I see?
>   When fools . . .
>
> *Chrysalde*: But he who laughs as loud as you
>   Must fear that he'll in turn be laughed at, too.
>
> *Arnolphe*: Lord, my friend, please don't be so upset:
>   The one who catches *me* is not born yet.
>   I know each cunning trick that women use
>   Upon their docile men, each subtle ruse,
>   And how they exercise their sleight-of-hand.
>   And so against this mishap I have planned.
>   My plighted wife will, through her innocence,
>   Preserve my brow from noisome influence. (1.1; TM)

Universal cuckoldry, in pedagogical terms, can be seen as the tendency of students to seek to learn from more than one teacher. The anxiety of influence Arnolphe expresses here involves the fear that *his* will not be the only school his future wife will attend. In Arnolphe's view of education, then, the sole measure of pedagogical success is to be the only teacher the student listens to.

At the same time, as critic, Arnolphe can maintain his smug spectator status only so long as he *is* his pupil's only teacher. As soon as she begins taking lessons from someone else, Arnolphe's critical detachment from the spectacle of cuckoldry will collapse. It would seem, then, that as soon as there is more than one effective source of authority in a pedagogical system, it is impossible for the teacher-critic to remain masterful, objective, and external to the object of his criticism.

The question of criticism and its exteriority to spectacle is in fact an extremely complex one in the context of Molière's *School for Wives*, not only because the play casts Arnolphe in the role of critic of cuckolds that make a spectacle of themselves but also because the play itself was the object of criticism in no fewer than nine subsequent theatrical productions, two of them by Molière himself. Hardly had the play proven itself to be a success when rival troupes and roving journalists began to attack it both in print and on the stage. Through the existence of these critical comedies, we begin to suspect that not only can *teaching* serve as a source of humor, but there appears to be something funny about criticism as well.

An Obscene Article

The first of Molière's comic defenses of *L'Ecole des femmes*, entitled *Critique de l'Ecole des femmes*, is a mocking representation of his critics. It opens, as do many of today's critical polemics, with a discussion of the fashionable tendency to resort to obscure jargon and far-fetched puns. It soon turns out that among these pretentious neologisms is the strange word *obscénité*, which is used by the *précieuse* Climène to denounce the scandalous suggestiveness of some of Agnes's seemingly innocent remarks. The example chosen by Climène takes place in the course of an oral examination administered by Arnolphe to Agnes on the subject of the unauthorized visit of young Horace, about which Arnolphe has just learned.

> *Arnolphe*: Now, besides all this talk, these tendernesses,
>   Didn't he also give you some caresses?
>
> *Agnes*: Indeed he did! He took my hands and arms
>   And kissed and kissed them with unending charms.
>
> *Arnolphe*: Agnes, was there anything else he took?
>   (*Seeing her taken aback*)
>   Ouf!
>
> *Agnes*: Well, he . . .

Arnolphe: What?

Agnes: Took . . .

Arnolphe: Augh!

Agnes: My . . . [2]

Arnolphe: Well?

Agnes: Now look.
  I'm sure you will be angry. I don't dare.

Arnolphe: No.

Agnes: Yes.

Arnolphe: Good lord, no.

Agnes: Promise me, then, swear.

Arnolphe: I swear.

Agnes: He took . . . You'll be mad, I know you.

Arnolphe: No.

Agnes: Yes.

Arnolphe: No, no. Damn it, what an ado!
  What did he take?

Agnes: He . . .

Arnolphe (aside): I'm in agony.

Agnes: He took my ribbon that you'd given me.
  I couldn't help it, he insisted so.

Arnolphe (sigh of relief): All right, the ribbon. But I want to know
  If kiss your arms is all he ever did.

Agnes: What? Are there other things? (2.5; TM)

The teacher, here, is testing his pupil to make sure that she has not learned anything in his absence. The hesitations of the pupil all seem to the examiner to be signs that she has learned what he does not want her to know. While she only knows *that* she is being censured, he interprets her embarrassment to mean that she knows *what* she is being censured *for*. The farther the examination proceeds, the closer the examiner comes to telling her what he does not want her to know—telling her, at least, that there are things he is not telling her.

In the discussion of this passage in the *Critique*, Climène views the ellipses after "he took my . . ." (*il m'a pris le . . .*) as a scandalous allusion, while Uranie defends its innocent literality.

> *Climène*: What! isn't modesty obviously wounded by what Agnes says in the passage we are speaking of?

> *Uranie*: Not at all. She doesn't pronounce a single word that is not in itself perfectly decent; and, if you want to hear something else behind it, it's you who are making things dirty, not Agnes; since all she's talking about is a ribbon taken from her.

> *Climène*: Oh! ribbon all you want! but that *le* on which she pauses wasn't put there for peanuts. Strange thoughts attach themselves to that *le*. That *le* is a furious scandal, and whatever you may say, the insolence of that *le* is indefensible. (Scene 3; TM)

The discussants are thus divided between those with the apparent naiveté of an Agnes and those with the overactive imagination of an Arnolphe. While there is something comical about the desire to censor something that is perceived only by those who wish to censor it, the Agnesian reading is clearly just as inadequate as the Arnolphian. Because the play presents us not only with the suspended *le* but with Arnolphe's alarmed reaction to it, it is not possible for us not to know that strange thoughts can attach themselves to that *le*. Yet what is it of Agnes's, in fact, that Arnolphe is afraid Horace might have seized? No one obvious word offers itself to complete the thought in Arnolphe's horrified mind as he hears "Il m'a pris le . . ." He took my *what*? Perhaps the truly scandalous effect of this ellipsis lies neither in what it says nor in what it conceals but in the fact that while searching for something with which to fill the blank, the reader or spectator is forced to run mentally up and down the entire female anatomy. Represented both as an absence, a blank, and as a succession of dots, a plurality of small discrete points, female sexuality is both expressed and repressed through this impossibility of summing it up under a single article.

Arnolphe is here up against the problem faced by every parent: it is always either too soon or too late to teach children about sexuality. When the play begins, Arnolphe has been handling Agnes's sex education simply by attempting to insure that no learning will take place. Agnes is seen as a *tabula rasa*—

a blank on which nothing is written unless some outside agency comes to write upon it. With the unexpected arrival of a more active tutor, Arnolphe is forced to change his pedagogical strategy. He now attempts to manipulate Agnes's dawning awareness of her own ignorance in such a way as to play up his superior knowledge and to cast doubt on his rival's good faith and on the value of what she has learned.

> *Arnolphe*: All this, Agnes, comes of your *innocence.*
> What's done is done. I've spoken. No offense.
> I *know* your lover wants but to deceive, To win your favor and then laugh and leave.

> *Agnes*: Oh, no! He told me twenty times and more.

> *Arnolphe*: *You do not know* what empty oaths he swore.
> But *learn this*: to accept caskets—or candies—
> And listen to the sweet talk of these dandies,
> Languidly acquiesce in their demands, And let them stir your heart and kiss your hands,
> This is a mortal sin, one of the worst.

> *Agnes*: It's all, alas, so pleasant and so sweet!
> I marvel at the joy that all this brings
> And *I had never known* about such things.

> *Arnolphe*: Yes, there's great pleasure in this tenderness,
> In each nice word and in each sweet caress;
> But these have need of honor's discipline,
> And only marriage can remove the sin. (2.5; emphasis mine)

Arnolphe's challenge here is to give Agnes the impression that for every new thing she learns there is a danger of which she is still ignorant and from which his superior wisdom must save her. Yet it is impossible for Arnolphe to cast doubt on the meaning of Horace's pleasurable lessons without at the same time instructing Agnes in the possibility of deception and the manipulation of appearances. Agnes indeed soon proves herself to be a gifted student of the techniques of duplicity.

The Institutionalization of Ignorance

Satisfied that he has convinced Agnes that he has saved her from the road to perdition, Arnolphe decides to give his bride-to-be a full-fledged lesson in the virtue of wifely ignorance. And at this point where the paradoxes of teaching ignorance become most explicit, the tyrannical schoolmaster has recourse to the *book* as a pedagogical aid.

The book Arnolphe assigns to Agnes is entitled *The Maxims of Marriage; or, The Duties of the Married Woman.* In typical teacherly fashion, he asks the student to read the book through carefully and promises to explain it to her when she has finished. The book contains a list not of duties but of interdictions: a wife belongs to no one but her husband; she should dress up only for him, receive no visitors but his, accept presents from no man, and never seek to do any writing, to join any feminine social circles, to visit the gambling table, or to go on walks or picnics. In short, the book for the first time replaces the absence of teaching with the active teaching of the content of ignorance. In place of her former lack of knowledge, the pupil now possesses a knowledge of what she is not supposed to know.

It might perhaps be interesting to ask whether the pedagogical function of the book *in* the play is in any way parallel to the functioning of the play *as* book in its pedagogically oriented editions. For *The School for Wives*, like the rest of Molière's plays, is published in France in pocket editions copiously annotated for use in the high school classroom. Molière, indeed, is one of the central devices used by the French school system to teach children to become French. Through these schoolbook editions of French classics, the student absorbs along with the text a certain conception of what his cultural heritage is and what the study of classical texts involves. According to the Bordas edition of *L'Ecole de femmes*, however, this play is a relatively recent addition to the high school curriculum. The first two paragraphs of the discussion of the play are entitled, respectively, "Une pièce ignorée dans nos classes" (A play that is unknown in our classrooms) and "Un chef d'oeuvre pourtant" (A masterpiece nevertheless). The editors explain the play's ostracism as follows: "The very theme of this comedy (the fear of cuckoldry), the boldness of the opinions and problems it raises, the salty Gallic vocabulary that comes up in the conversations between Arnolphe and Chrysalde, were all cause for alarm. But isn't this a form of narrow-mindedness that no longer corresponds to our time?"[3] The liberated attitudes of modern editors have thus made it possible to remedy French schoolchildren's ignorance of a play about teaching ignorance. But have all forms of ignorance been thereby dispelled?

What is striking about this particular play is precisely the fact that the female pupil in the play is of the same age as her high school readers. That this is a play about adult authority and adolescent sexuality seems to be completely glossed over by the editors. It is interesting to follow the techniques of avoidance manifested by the footnotes and commentaries that run the length of the play, sometimes taking up more room on the page than the play itself. Faced with that suggestive little *le* in "il m'a pris le . . . ," for example, the editor of the Larousse edition (whose professional title, I note, is "Censeur au lycée de Strasbourg") writes: "A slightly off-color double-entendre, which many contemporaries reproached Molière for, and which he made the mistake of denying in *The Critique of the School for Wives*."[4] The editor of the Bordas edition, on the other hand, doesn't see what all the fuss is about. "Much ink has been shed over these lines. They have been called scandalous. But all this is just a farcical device. Agnes's words are but a theatrical necessity designed to make us laugh at Arnolphe's stupidity. It is he who, through his questions and frowns, terrifies Agnes, prevents her from answering, and prolongs the suspense. Arnolphe is the one responsible for the ambiguity, which is well suited to his character. The whole scene, about which no one today would think of taking offense, is simply and openly funny, and the whole audience thinks of nothing but laughing" (Bordas, 71). Thus, either the ellipsis "il m'a pris le . . ." is an obscenity, or it is a mere joke, a "theatrical necessity." The idea that laughter and obscenity can go together is scrupulously avoided by those who are serving the text up to high school minds.

Yet behind the controversy of Agnes's *le* lies the whole question of female sexuality, which the controversy is in fact designed to occult. The editors' more direct reactions to Agnes's dawning sexuality are of two kinds: they drown it with erudition or they surround it with danger signs. When Agnes first describes her awakening desire, she says to Arnolphe:

> He swore he loved me with a matchless passion
> And said to me, in the most charming fashion,
> Things which I found incomparably sweet
> And every time I hear his voice repeat
> Those things, I tingle deep inside me and I feel
> I don't know what it is from head to heel. (2.5; TM)

The last two lines render the French "Là-dedans remue / Certain je ne sais quoi dont je suis toute émue." In the Bordas edition, we find the following note on "je ne sais quoi": "Concerning the frequent use of 'je ne sais quoi' in the language of classicism, there is a very interesting study by Pierre-Henri Simon in his book, *The Garden and the Town*, 1962. This indeterminate expression expresses the irrational and mysterious sides of love, and this is why, according to Mr. Simon, it is the poets and novelists who deal with love that use the expression most frequently" (Bordas, 67). What this note does is to use knowledge provided by Mr. Simon to say "je ne sais quoi" about Agnes's "je ne sais quoi." The sexual component of Agnes's *non-savoir* is being occulted and defused through the asexual notions of irrationality and mystery.

But it is toward Agnes's so-called pleasure principle that the editors are most severe. When Agnes asks Arnolphe, "How can one chase away what gives such pleasure?" the editors ask, "Is this purely instinctive morality without its dangers?" (Bordas, 111). "Can Agnes understand that something pleasant might be morally forbidden?" (Larousse, 62). Both editors express relief that Agnes has not fallen into the hands of a lover whose intentions are less honorable than Horace's. "Judge Agnes's imprudence," exhorts the Larousse editor. "Show that Molière is also pointing out—for the benefit of the spectator— the danger Agnes would have been in if Horace had not been an honest man" (104). Clearly, an honest man is required to protect unsuspecting girls against the dangers of their own liberation. In warning the young readers against learning too well the sexual lessons that Agnes seems to have learned, the editors of the school editions of *The School for Wives* thus unwittingly but inevitably find themselves playing a role similar to that of Arnolphe with respect to their students' sexual education. In repressing the nature of the lesson learned in the play, they, too, are in the business of teaching ignorance.

This similarity between the teachers *of* the text and the teacher *in* the text should give us pause. Could it be that the pedagogical enterprise as such is always constitutively a project of teaching ignorance? Are our ways of teaching students to ask *some* questions always correlative with our ways of teaching them *not to ask*—indeed, to be unconscious of—others? Does the educational system exist in order to promulgate knowledge, or is its main function rather to universalize a society's tacit agreement about what it has decided it does not and cannot know? And is there some fundamental correlation between the teaching of ignorance and the question of femininity?

Molière's "Feminism"

The question of education and the question of femininity are surprisingly interconnected in the seventeenth century. The burning feminist issue was not yet voting or working, but getting an education equal to a man's. Treatises explaining at length the futility and even the danger of educating women were long the order of the day. As Fénelon wrote in his treatise on the education of women:

Let us now take a look at what a woman needs to know. What are her jobs? She is in charge of her children's upbringing—the boys' up to a certain age and the girls' until they either marry or enter a convent. She must also oversee the conduct, morals, and service of the servants, see to the household expenditures, and make sure all is done economically and honorably. . . .

Women's knowledge, like men's, should be limited to what is useful for their functions; the difference in their tasks should lead to the difference in their studies. It is therefore necessary to restrict women's education to the things we have just mentioned.[5]

Because a woman was always under the protection of her father, her husband, or the church, her education was confined to preparing her for tasks in harmony with these forms of dependency.

Similarly, the governing purpose behind Arnolphe's pedagogical enterprise was the fear that a learned wife would make him a cuckold. Ignorance, it seemed, was the only way to ensure fidelity. What this implies, paradoxically enough, is that education is an apprenticeship in unfaithfulness. The fear of giving women an education equal to that of men is clearly a fear that educated women will no longer remain faithful to the needs of patriarchal society. Citing the case of Agrippa d'Aubigné, Gustave Fagnier writes in his study of women in the early seventeenth century:

> Even though he admired the women who in his time had achieved a scholarly reputation, Agrippa d'Aubigné declared to his daughters, who had consulted him on the question, that a more than ordinary education was, for middle-class girls like themselves, more of a disadvantage than an advantage: the duties of married life and motherhood would take away its profit, for, as he graciously put it, "when the nightingale has her young, she sings no longer"; then, too, education makes one vain, makes one neglect the household and disdain one's husband, blush at one's poverty, and it introduces discord into the home.[6]

The purpose of all education, then, was to foster the harmony of the patriarchal home.

So strong are the mechanisms for preserving the existing hierarchies of sex roles and social classes that the serious struggles of seventeenth-century women to cross the barriers of class and rank and achieve greater power and independence have come down to us through the distorting mirrors of the ridiculousness of *préciosité*. Yet behind the prudes, the coquettes, and the learned ladies, one can discern an attempt to avoid the bonds of the patriarchal marriage system, to free female sexuality from the constraints of annual childbirth and the double standard, to seek a female identity not exclusively defined in terms of men, and, in a gesture that seems almost post-Saussurian, to free language from its slavishly referential relation to a reality that might somehow thereby itself be escaped. The very extent to which these precious ladies are today not so much forgotten as they are *remembered as ridiculous* is a proof both of their power and of their impotence.[7] While Molière, in other plays, chooses to mock the *Précieuses* for their linguistic excesses and their self-delusions, this play in which no *précieuse* actually appears puts its finger on a much more serious cause for concern. It is precisely when Agnes argues with Arnolphe—clearly and without periphrasis—as *a subject who knows what she wants* that Arnolphe compares her to a *Précieuse*: "Just hear how this bitch argues and replies. Damn it! Would a *précieuse* say any more?" (5.4; TM).

It is interesting to note that in the updated Larousse edition of *L'Ecole des femmes*, one of the questions proposed as a discussion topic to the students is "Was Molière a feminist?" (142). It is even more interesting to note that the answer is already tucked away in the presentational material that precedes the play: "We should recognize that Molière, who, in this play, shows himself to be a feminist, has sided for the education of women and for the liberalization of morals and religion" (18). The assertion of Molière's feminism has indeed become almost a commonplace of academic criticism. As one of the pillars of seventeenth-century studies, Georges Mongrédien, puts it, "It is clear that *L'Ecole des femmes* is a feminist play—as indeed is *Les Précieuses ridicules* in a certain way—that [Molière] is militating for a girl's freedom to choose on the basis of love (Brunetière called it 'nature')."[8]

These notions of freedom of choice, love, and nature are all, of course, names for the granting of greater happiness to women without their acquiring greater power or independence and without any changes being made in the structure of society. By saying that Molière has written a feminist play, the schoolbook editors are not only saving him from the charge of misogyny; they are also offering their students a nonsubversive conception of what feminism is: something designed to make women happier with society as it is.

It can easily be seen that although Molière in *L'Ecole des femmes* is taking women's side in advocating their right to marry the man of their choice, he is not really suggesting that anything in the social *structure* be changed. Agnes's newly discovered sense of her own desire is quickly reintegrated into structures that are in no way disturbed by it. When Agnes takes the independent step of fleeing from Arnolphe to Horace, Horace can think of nothing better to do with her than to entrust her to the father-surrogate Arnolphe, unaware that he is the very rival from whom she has just escaped. Agnes's final liberation from Arnolphe, indeed, occurs only through the fortuitous fact that her long-lost father has arranged with Horace's father that the two young people should marry. The happy ending is decreed by the same kind of paternal authority as that represented by Arnolphe. The liberation of the woman here occurs merely as a change of fathers. Agnes will "belong" to Horace no less surely, although more willingly, than she would have "belonged" to Arnolphe. What has been seen as Molière's feminism is actually a form of benevolent paternalism and not in any sense a plea for the reorganization of the relations between the sexes. Like all forms of liberalism, it is an attempt to change attitudes rather than structures.

And yet surely a play that so lucidly personifies and ridicules the excesses of patriarchal power cannot simply be located within phallocentric discourse. Molière's irony would seem to baffle any clear-cut inside/outside categorization. The play consistently undercuts the ideology to which it nevertheless still adheres. Can literature somehow escape or transform power structures by simultaneously espousing and subverting them? The question must be asked of all great literary demystifications: to what structure of authority does the critique of authority belong? This is perhaps *the* feminist question par excellence. For some help in dealing with it, we will now return to the more specifically pedagogical level of our inquiry.

How Agnes Learns

What, then, does Agnes learn in this School for Wives, and what do we learn from her about teaching? Of all the things that Arnolphe wants Agnes *not* to learn, it seems that writing is the object of his most violent suspicions. Not only is writing included in the book of don'ts for the married woman, but from the very beginning it is clear that in Arnolphe's mind feminine writing constitutes the husband's royal road to cuckoldry. "A woman who's a writer knows too much," he tells Chrysalde; "I mean that mine shall not be so sublime, and shall not even know what's meant by rhyme" (1.1). In the game of "corbillon," in which each contestant must answer the question "Qu'y met-on?" (What goes into it?) with something that rhymes with *on*, Arnolphe hopes his wife will answer "une tarte à la crème." Her virginal innocence thus depends on her having absolutely no sense of an ending that rhymes with *on*. What Arnolphe wishes to exclude from Agnes's knowledge is play—here, the play of language for its own sake, the possibility that language could function otherwise than in strict obedience to the authority of proper meaning. Agnes indeed demonstrates her ignorance of wordplay when she answers the go-between's report that she has wounded the heart of young Horace by saying, "Did I drop something on him?" Yet when Arnolphe attempts to stop all commerce between the two young people, Agnes is able to come up with the idea of attaching a secret love letter to the stone she has been instructed by Arnolphe to toss at Horace. How has this naive literal reader so quickly learned the art of sending a double message? What teacher has made her into so skilled a wielder of ambiguity?

According to Horace, fatuously enough, that teacher is "love."

> Love is a great teacher, you must agree,
> Making us what we never thought to be
> And in a moment, under his direction,
> Our character can change its whole complexion.
> He breaks down even natural obstacles
> And seems to manage sudden miracles. . . .
> He makes the dullest soul agile and fit
> And gives the most naive its share of wit.
> That miracle has happened to Agnes. (3.4)

As an explanation of Agnes's ingenuity in hitting upon the paper and stone device, Horace personifies love as a master teacher. Yet it is not love alone that has made Agnes clever. It is the necessity of complying with the contradictory demands of *two* ardent teachers. As long as the first teacher's power remained absolute and unquestioned, Agnes remained ignorant and unimaginative. Her first acquaintance with her second teacher was not very promising, either. As Agnes describes it:

> Out on the balcony to get the air
> I saw, under those trees right over there
> A most attractive young man passing by
> Who bowed most humbly when he caught my eye.
> And I, not wishing to be impolite,
> Returned a deep bow, as was only right.
> Promptly he makes another bow, and then,
> I naturally bow to him again;
> And since he then goes on to number three,
> Without delay he gets a third from me.

He passes by, comes back . . . well, anyhow,
Each time he does he makes another bow,
And I, observing this most carefully,
Returned him every bow he made to me.
The fact is, if the light had not grown dim,
I would have gone on trading bows with him
Because I did not want to yield, and be
Inferior to him in courtesy. (2.5)

If Arnolphe is a teacher of the "do as I say" school, Horace clearly belongs to the school of "do as I do." This opposition between the didactic and the mimetic is in fact the classical polarity into which teaching methods can be divided. From the moment there are two teachers at work, however, they both resort to the method of telling Agnes that she is somehow in the wrong. From Horace she learns of the wound her eyes have inflicted, which she must cure by applying more of the evil as its own remedy. From Arnolphe she learns that she must cleanse the sin of Horace's caresses by marrying. When Arnolphe clarifies the point by indicating that *he* is the one she must marry, she suddenly, for the first time, learns to turn to rhetoric, to find a linguistic substitute, however minimal, for the thought she realizes she must not say.

Agnes: How happy I will be with him!

Arnolphe: With whom?

Agnes: With . . . h'm.

Arnolphe: H'm? h'm is not my taste.
In choosing a husband you're showing undue haste. (2.5; TM)

At the end of the scene, Agnes is still protesting the necessity of renouncing such a good-looking man, and Arnolphe, to end the discussion, says, "Enough, I am master. I speak, you obey." This, in its simplest terms, is Arnolphe's conception of teaching. His pedagogical aim is to apply and guarantee his own mastery: mastery over language, over knowledge and ignorance, and over the types of outside influence he will or will not permit. In Arnolphe's system, everything is divided between mastery and cuckoldry, between univocal instructions and treacherous ambiguity.

While Arnolphe says "I am your master," Horace says "I am your victim." The position of pseudo-weakness seems to work better than the position of absolute power, but it nevertheless takes the powerful pull of two contradictory systems of demands to shape Agnes into a fully intelligent subject—a writing subject. In learning to manipulate both writing and ambiguity, Agnes marks the destruction of *any* position of absolute mastery. Indeed, when Arnolphe learns of Agnes's letter, he exclaims: "Her writing has just about killed me" (3.5; TM). Let us now look at that letter in order to analyze the way it manifests its discovery of intelligence at the intersection of contradictory lessons.

> I want to write you, and I am at a loss how to set about it. I have thoughts that I would like you to know [J'ai des pensées que je désirerais que vous sussiez]; but I don't know how to go about telling them to you, and I mistrust my own words. As I am beginning to realize that I have always been kept in ignorance, I am afraid of putting down something that may not be right and saying more than I ought. Truly, I don't know what you've done to me; but I feel that I am mortally unhappy over what they're making me do to you, that it will be terribly hard for me to get along without you, and that I would be very glad to be yours. Perhaps it's a bad thing to say that; but anyway I can't help saying it, and I wish it could be done without its being wrong [Peut-être qu'il y a du mal à dire cela; mais enfin je ne puis m'empêcher de le dire, et je voudrais que cela se pût faire sans qu'il y en eût]. They keep telling me that all young men are deceivers, that I mustn't listen to them, and that everything you say to me is only to take advantage of me; but I assure you that I have not yet been able to imagine that of you, and I am so touched by your words that I cannot possibly believe they are lies. Tell me frankly what the truth is in all this; for after all, since there is no malice in me, you would be doing a terrible wrong if you deceive me, and I think I would die of sorrow. (3.4)

In many ways, this letter shows the simultaneity of liberation and repression. It is the only passage in the play written in prose. This stylistic change is felt as a liberation from the artifice of verse, but at the same time the letter is not given any line numbers, thus making it impossible to refer to the letter as one refers to the rest of the play. Editorial tradition treats the letter as if it does not count, while by that very exclusion giving the letter a special privilege. The letter is primarily an expression of Agnes's fear of being somehow in the wrong. The desire not to transgress any rule, even a grammatical one, leads to acrobatics of subordination on every level. Agnes's crucial discovery that she might not know what she is still ignorant of is accompanied by a generalized distrust of saying what she means. This love letter is less an expression of love than an inquiry into the conditions under which an expression of love might be possible.

Yet time and again this heavily self-censored letter has been viewed as the very voice of innocent nature. Horace rhapsodizes:

All that was in her heart, her hand has penned,
But that in touching terms of kindliness,
Of simple innocence and tenderness.
In short, just the way I'm speaking of,
Nature expresses the first pangs of love. (3.4)

And the editor of the Larousse edition instructs his students to "analyze the freshness and spontaneity of the feelings expressed in this letter" (80). This tendency to view Agnes's self-censorship as spontaneous and natural would indicate that, for Horace and for the censor from Strasbourg, the desire not to displease is an innate component of women's nature.

Contradiction; or, The Subject of Teaching

We have thus come to a paradoxical set of conclusions about the nature of the pedagogical process. Learning seems to take place most rapidly when the student must respond to the contradiction between *two* teachers. And what the student learns in the process is both the power of ambiguity and the non-innocence of ignorance. It could be objected, however, that while the efficacy of contradiction-as-teacher may be demonstrable in the burlesque world of tyrannical cuckolds and ingenious ingenues, not every pedagogue is as repressive as an Arnolphe. What if the schema were reversed, for example, and the teacher, instead of saying "I am master," should choose to say "I am ignorant"?

If, as Neil Hertz would have it, the allusion to Socrates is characteristic of "the earnest moment in teachers' imaginings of themselves,"[9] it would seem that we have now begun speaking in earnest. It is therefore all the more astonishing to discover the very same conjunction of love, writing, and pedagogical rivalry as the mainspring of the Socratic dialogue itself, as we find it exemplified in Plato's *Phaedrus*, which can indeed be read as one of the most fundamental of Western treatises on teaching.

The dialogue begins on a street in Athens, where Socrates runs into the handsome Phaedrus, fresh from a lesson with his master, Lysias. It seems that Lysias has written a speech demonstrating that one should yield rather to a nonlover than to a lover (isn't this precisely what Arnolphe is trying to convince Agnes of?), and that Phaedrus is now heading for the fields in order to practice reciting it. Socrates, contrary to his usual habits, is lured out of the city by the promise of hearing the words of this rival teacher. Inspired by the subject and by the fair interlocutor, Socrates, after hearing Lysias's discourse, launches into two contradictory speeches of his own on love, then goes on to try to teach Phaedrus what effective teaching ought to be. A crux of the Socratic view of teaching is his apparent preference for direct speech over writing. The man who has real knowledge to impart

> will not, when he's in earnest, resort to a written form . . . , using words which are unable either to argue in their own defense when attacked or to fulfill the role of a teacher in presenting the truth. . . . Far more noble and splendid is the serious pursuit of the dialectician, who finds a congenial soul and then proceeds with true knowledge to plant and sow in it words which are able to help themselves and help him who planted them; words which will not be unproductive, for they can transmit their seed to other natures and cause the growth of fresh words in them.[10]

What is odd about this law of living dialectical teaching is that Socrates refuses to abide by it in the opening lines of the dialogue. When Phaedrus offers to recite Lysias's speech from memory, Socrates replies, "Good, good, dear boy, if you will start out by showing me what you have under your cloak in your left hand. As a matter of fact, I'd guess that you're clutching the very speech. If that's the case, please realize that though I'm very fond of you, *when we have Lysias right here*, I have no intention of lending you my ears to practice on" (5; emphasis mine). While Socrates is profiting from the fact that Lysias's written words cannot defend themselves aloud, he nevertheless grants them greater authority than he does to Lysias's supposedly more legitimate seed-carrier, Phaedrus himself. The proponent of spoken dialectic has thus been prompted to deny the power of the written word only after he has first been seduced out of himself precisely by the power of the written word. The devaluation of writing that has, according to Jacques Derrida, structured the whole of Western thought can thus be seen as a mere tactical move in a game of pedagogical rivalry.

Before Socrates and Lysias come to look too much like Horace and Arnolphe, it might be well to analyze the two texts with respect to the project—expressly undertaken by both Arnolphe and Socrates—of teaching nothing but ignorance. Up to now we have been viewing the teaching of ignorance in a purely negative light, as a repressive method of instructing the student *not to know*. What Socrates seeks, on the other hand, is to teach the student *that he does not know*. To teach ignorance is, for Socrates, to teach to *unknow*, to become conscious of the fact that what one thinks is knowledge is really an array of received ideas, prejudices, and opinions—a way of *not* knowing that one does not know. "Most people are unaware that they do not know" (16). "I am not teaching . . . anything, but all I do is question."[11] "I know only that I am ignorant."

Plato's challenge as a writer and a student was to cast an ignoramus in the role of *sujet supposé savoir*. The philosophical debate over "how far Socrates was serious about his ignorance," as Kierkegaard puts it,[12] arises out of the contradiction between Plato's transferential fantasy of the teacher as subject presumed to know and the content and method of that teacher's teaching, namely, the constant profession of ignorance. Because we see Socrates only through the eyes of Plato's transference, we will never really know whether or not he was "serious" about his ignorance. But the dynamism of the Socratic dialogue in a sense makes the question irrelevant. For if the ideal pedagogical climate, in the *Phaedrus* as well as in the *School for Wives*, is one in which the conflicts and contradictions *between* teachers serve as the springboard for learning, then learning does not result from a personifiable cause. Whether the teacher professes to be in possession of knowledge or of ignorance, the student in effect learns from what the teacher is not in possession of.

To retain the plurality of forces and desires within a structure that would displace the One-ness of individual mastery could perhaps be labeled a feminization of authority. For just as Agnes's *le* cannot designate any single organ as the graspable center of female sexuality, and just as the existence of more than one sex problematizes the universality of any human subject of knowledge, so contradiction suspends and questions the centering of Western pedagogical paradigms around the single authoritative teacher. In this sense, paradoxically enough, it could be said that Plato's belief in Socrates's pedagogical mastery is an attempt to repress the inherent "feminism" of Socrates's ignorance. And it is out of this repression of Socrates's feminism that Western pedagogy springs. The question of education, in both Molière and Plato, is the question not of how to transmit but of how to *suspend* knowledge. That question can be understood in both a positive and a negative sense. In a negative sense, not knowing results from repression, whether conscious or unconscious. Such negative ignorance may be the necessary by-product— or even the precondition—of any education whatsoever. But positive ignorance, the pursuit of what is forever in the act of escaping, the inhabiting of that space where knowledge becomes the obstacle to knowing—*that* is the pedagogical imperative we can neither fulfill nor disobey.

NOTES

"Teaching Ignorance." *Yale French Studies* 63 (1982): 165–82. Reprinted by permission of *Yale French Studies*.

1. *The School for Wives*, 1.1. In quoting from *L'Ecole des femmes* and the *Critique de l'Ecole des femmes* in English, I have generally followed the Donald Frame translation (*Tartuffe and Other Plays by Molière* [New York: NAL, 1967]); passages in which I have modified the translation will be marked "TM" (translation modified). All translations of other French texts are my own.
2. In French: "Il m'a . . . pris . . . le . . ."
3. *L'Ecole des femmes*, ed. Pierre Cabanis (Paris: Bordas, 1963), 14. Henceforth referred to as "Bordas."
4. *L'Ecole des femmes*, ed. Gérard Sablayrolles (Paris: Larousse, 1965), 58. Henceforth referred to as "Larousse."
5. Fénelon, *De l'education des filles* (1687), ch. 11.
6. Gustave Fagnier, *La Femme et la société française dans la première moitié du XVIIᵉ siècle* (Paris: J. Gamber, 1929), 11–12.
7. For valuable analyses of *préciosité* and feminism, see Dorothy Anne Liot Backer, *Precious Women* (New York: Basic Books, 1974); Carolyn C. Lougee, *Le Paradis des femmes* (Princeton, NJ: Princeton University Press, 1976); and Ian Maclean, *Woman Triumphant* (Oxford: Clarendon, 1977).
8. Georges Mongredien, *La Querelle de "L'Ecole des femmes"* (Paris: Librarie Marcel Didier, 1971), xxviii.
9. Neil Hertz, "Two Extravagant Teachings," *Yale French Studies* 63 (1982): 59.
10. Plato, *Phaedrus*, trans. W. C. Helmbold and W. G. Rabinowitz (Indianapolis: Library of Liberal Arts, 1956), 70–71.
11. Plato, *Meno*, trans. G. M. A. Grube (Indianapolis: Hackett, 1976), 15.
12. Søren Kierkegaard, *The Concept of Irony*, trans. Lee M. Capel (Bloomington: Indiana University Press, 1965), 285.

Afterword
Barbara's Signature

Shoshana Felman

It is unusual for a person to write her own memorial. However, this is what Barbara Johnson did in June 2009, when she communicated to her mother, two months before her death, her plan for her memorial: which music she would like to have played and which literary quotes she wanted to include in her posthumous commemoration.[1] She was not sentimental. She was practical. The grief, the heartbreak, the surprise were ours. As always, Barbara was ahead of us. She simply told us how she wished to be remembered. The meaning of her choices, right then in June, remained obscure to me. All I could see was the tragic heroism, the existential pathos of this last creative act.

Only later—when she was no longer with us—did I start to ponder and reflect on the meaning of these quotes with which she wished to sign her life, to read this message she was sending us ahead of time, across her own mortality, in the immortal literary words of others, into which she secretly injected her own voice: her understated, yet semantically authoritative signature. In what follows, I share my testimonial (factual and imaginative) reading of this final signifying gesture.

In the last year of her life, Barbara was rereading Proust—and writing (on his model) her own autobiography. Proust was inspiring because he, too, was writing from his sickbed. Like Proust, Barbara was resuscitating and recording her early childhood reminiscences. But in June 2009 she knew she was running out of time, and thus she interrupted the writing of her memoirs to plan her own memorial. So she left us (as I later understood)—in the music she wished played and in literary quotes she wished recited in her memory—her own self-epitaph, her riddling epitaphic discourse, in lieu of her autobiography.

The epitaph—part literature, part music—expresses Barbara in combining three joint cultural traditions, linking the French music of the haunting "Organ Symphony" of Camille Saint-Saëns[2] that Barbara—like Proust—admired,[3] to the English lyric poetry of William Blake[4] to the American autobiographical memoir of Henry David Thoreau.[5]

Massachusetts-born, Harvard-educated Thoreau is the only one of these on whom Barbara had written in the past, in her book *A World of Difference*.[6] Why *Walden*?, I asked myself. Why then, in 1987? And why now again, in this memorial? Can I presume that Thoreau's memoir could be an allegory of Barbara's own cutoff autobiography? On Barbara's example as a reader, I read *around* the paragraphs that she selected to recite to us.[7]

From its first pages, what is most striking about *Walden* is that it is an autobiography of loneliness. "When I wrote the following pages, I lived alone, in the woods, on the shores of Walden Pond, in . . . Massachusetts," Thoreau writes. "Some have asked . . . if I did not feel lonesome; if I was not afraid; . . . I undertake to answer" (5). "At night there was never a traveler passed my house, or knocked on my door" (91). "There too, . . . I sometimes expected the visitor who never came" (182).

To this loneliness was added, in Barbara's case, the deprivation caused by the disease. I imagine that the restricted view Thoreau describes from the window of his house became for Barbara a metaphor for her own restricted view—her confined space. "From this point," Thoreau writes, "I could not see over and beyond the woods which surrounded me" (62). But *Walden* at the same time is empowering, in giving hope that isolation and confinement can be transcended through one's own creative inner life. "Although the view from my door was still more contracted," Thoreau affirms and Barbara would concur, "I did not feel crowded or confined in the least. There was pasture enough for my imagination" (63).

Barbara preserved her greatness despite her illness, because she had the power to sustain her life by "pasturing"—precisely—in what she always loved: reading and writing. "My residence [Thoreau notes] was more favorable . . . to serious reading, than a university." Like Thoreau, Barbara believed that "To read well . . . is a noble exercise . . . It requires a training such as athletes underwent, the steady intention of almost the whole life to this object" (72). As the athletic reader that she was—always tackling in priority the most challenging of texts—Barbara was in natural agreement with her Massachusetts compatriot: "Yet this only is reading, in a high sense, not that which lulls us as a luxury . . . but *what we have to stand on tip-toe to read*, and devote our most alert and wakeful hours to" (56).[8]

"*Walden's* great achievement," Barbara wrote, "is to wake us up to our own losses, to make us participate in the trans-individual movement of loss in its infinite particularity, urging us passionately to follow the track of—we know not quite what, as if we had lost it, or were in danger of losing it, our-selves" (*World*, 53).

Barbara makes the point that the meaning of the loss can never be reduced to intelligibility. And so will Barbara's epitaph—her loss, our loss of her—remain obscure. "*Walden* is obscure, therefore," Barbara writes, "to the extent that Thoreau has literally crossed over into the very parable he is writing . . . and where, he tells us, [here Barbara quotes Thoreau again]: "if you stand right *fronting* and *face to face with a fact*, you will see the sun glimmer on both its surfaces, as if it were a cimeter, and feel its sweet edge dividing you through the heart and marrow" (*Walden*, 70; *World*, 56).

Barbara teaches us to "front a fact"—the fact of death—even while the "fronting" "divides us through the heart and marrow." She was not afraid to "front" her own forthcoming death. But what she wanted above all was to "front" life.

"I went to the woods" (she tells us in Thoreau's words), "because I wished to live deliberately, *to front* only the essential facts of life. . . . I did not wish to live what was not life, living is so dear; nor did I wish to practice resignation, until it was quite necessary" (65).

In June 2009, two months before her death, Barbara must have turned back to her own writing. "*Walden's* great achievement," she possibly recalled her words, "is to wake us up to our own losses, in making us participate in the trans-individual movement of loss." What strikes me as characteristic—and utterly remarkable—in Barbara's treatment of Thoreau is this paradoxical reversal: in 1987, when she was young, radiant, and glamorous, Barbara was writing on Thoreau's rhetoric of loss, obscurity, and secret unintelligible grief. But in June 2009, facing her own death, she chose to address us with Thoreau's passionate emphasis on life.

Barbara does not just reclaim Thoreau, in other words, as her bond with her own writing, as well as with her childhood and her native Massachusetts legacy. She rearticulates this legacy with a pathbreakingly creative listening sensitivity and with the new inflection of a stunningly original American, *female-gendered* voice.

That is, she has inscribed Thoreau's text with her signature and has returned it to us with "the surprise of otherness." "A reading is strong"—she often theorized—"when it encounters and propagates the surprise of otherness,"— a shift of ground or a shift in understanding that suddenly reveals an old text in a totally surprising new light.[9] The advent of such "surprise" is the brilliant signature of Barbara's style as reader and as a theorist of reading.

Such a surprise was reserved in her 1987 reading of Thoreau's "obscurity" and the rhetoric of loss in *Walden*. And it is yet a different, a surprisingly other Thoreau that, following her rules of reading, she reveals to us again at her memorial. The lonely pond—a metaphor for the lone self—becomes a multilayered ciphered signifier, through which *Walden* speechlessly inscribes a subtext of Barbara's own singular autobiography.

Barbara's family had a cabin on the shores of a New Hampshire pond, in which she spent many happy summers of her childhood. There, she and her siblings shared their readings of Thoreau. For Barbara, therefore, the pond connotes both the benevolence of Nature[10] and a Proustian recollection of her childhood, to which she is returning now, in including *Walden* in her self-commemoration.[11] It is on these Proustian shores of memory, on the path leading to that pond, that Barbara asked her family to spread her ashes.

"The indescribable innocence and beneficence of Nature—of sun and wind and rain, of summer and winter—[Thoreau wrote]—such health, such cheer, they afford forever! And such sympathy have they ever with our race . . . Shall I not have intelligence with the earth? Am I not partly leaves and vegetable mould myself?" (96).[12]

The symbolic meanings of Thoreau for Barbara thus change kaleidoscopically, according to the different periods of her life. In June 2009, when she envisions her memorial, Thoreau stands both for the beginning and for the ending of her life, both for her origin and for her destination.

Through *Walden*, Barbara therefore tells us not just what it means to be alone and to stand alone but what it means to be a reader, what it means to write with her own life, and more fundamentally, what it means to live—and die, and—like Thoreau—to speak, to teach, and be an educator from within the intersection and the bond *between* death and life. "Will you be a reader, a student merely, or a seer?," Thoreau writes: "Read your fate, see what is before you, and walk into futurity" (79). In June, Barbara walked into futurity.

"I believe that men are generally still a little afraid of the dark," Thoreau conceded, and Barbara would second: "Yet I experienced sometimes that the most sweet and tender, the most innocent and encouraging society may be found in any natural object . . . I was suddenly sensible of such sweet and beneficent society in Nature, in the very patterning of the drops, and in every sound and sight around my house, an infinite and unaccountable friendliness all at once like an atmosphere sustaining me" (91–92).

In her last years, Barbara used to say to me, very like Thoreau: "I find it wholesome to be alone the greater part of the time. To be in company, even with the best, is soon wearisome . . . I love to be alone." Thoreau continues, famously: "I never found the companion that was so companionable as solitude. . . . A [wo]man thinking or working is always alone" (94–95).

Barbara shared with her compatriot the paradox of this unusual courage of aloneness, remarkably combined with its opposite: an other-oriented sense of educational service and commitment to his own community.[13] She also shared his taste for laughter and satire, his funny outlook on society's absurdities, and his extraordinarily perceptive, lucid, witty, mordant sense of humor.

I can picture Barbara saying laughingly in Thoreau's words, of her tiny Harvard residence: "I had three chairs in my house; one for solitude, two for friendship, three for society. When visitors came in larger and unexpected numbers there was but the third chair for them all, but they generally economized the room by standing up" (97).[14]

In June 2009, when writing her own requiem, Barbara turned to Thoreau for the last time, as both a secret sharer in her solitude and a companion, a secret ally in the sublime effort to transcend. No longer a mere advocate of Nature (as in her childhood); no longer a mere chronicler of grief and loss (as in *A World of Difference*), Thoreau becomes a strength-dispensing teacher of survival. Barbara repeats to us this lesson of survival—to console us, to empower us, to teach us. In signing her memorial, what she has bequeathed to us is an imperative of life—and an exceptional autobiography of self-reliance, even in disease.

ON HER FRENCH SIDE, which her memorable self-epitaph expresses in the bursting organ music of Saint-Saëns and in the overriding Proustian inspiration,[15] Barbara loved to quote an enigmatic declaration by Mallarmé, on whose poetry she wrote her first book[16] and whose poetic prose she lovingly translated in her last years.[17] "Does something like Letters exist?" Mallarmé asked when visiting Oxford (*Divagations*, 185). "I reply," he then declared, "with an exaggeration, and warning you against it: Yes, Literature exists and, if you will, alone, in exception to everything" (186).

In her self-epitaph,[18] Barbara has given us again this absolute poetical reply, as a living allegory of her life and work and as the living signature of her own genius: "Yes, Literature exists." "And if you will, alone." "In exception to everything."

So Barbara's delicate and daring genius, from which we have still everything to learn, henceforth "takes refuge in the future."[19]

NOTES

Copyright © 2014 Shoshana Felman.

1. This plan envisioned by Barbara in June 2009 was later followed on two distinct occasions: first at the Johnson family celebration of her life, a memorial that took place two days after her passing, in the church of her native town Westwood (Boston), on August 30, 2009; and later, at the (national and international) memorial tribute to Barbara hosted by her home institution, with her Harvard colleagues and invited speakers from other universities, a ceremony that took place at the Sackler Auditorium of Harvard University on March 26, 2010.

2. This was the musical "postlude" (a name Barbara gave it) following the literary recitations: Camille Saint-Saëns, Symphony No. 3 in C Minor, Op. 78, "Organ Symphony." "I have given all I had to give," Saint-Saëns said on finishing this unique symphony, his greatest, and the last symphony he wrote. He dedicated it to Franz Liszt, his admired composer-mentor and model virtuoso performer, when Liszt was dying (the "Organ Symphony" premiered in London in 1886, some two and a half months before Liszt's death, with its composer as conductor). Barbara loved the whole symphony, and for her memorial chose (in the interest of time) merely the conclusion: "Maestoso—Allegro." It was played at Harvard in Barbara's preferred performance, with conductor Charles Munch and the Boston Symphony.

3. Proust admired Saint-Saëns's work as a summit of French music and as the epitome of the work of art, that alone can recapture "lost time." Saint-Saëns could be one of the models for the musician Vinteuil and for the leitmotif of "the Vinteuil Sonata," in *A la recherche du temps perdu*.

4. At Barbara's request, "Jerusalem" by William Blake (from the preface of *Milton*) was both recited, and sung, at the Harvard memorial.

> "Jerusalem"
> And did those feet in ancient time
> Walk upon England's mountains green?
> And was the holy Lamb of God,
> In England's pleasant pastures seen?
>
> And did the Countenance Divine,
> Shine forth upon our clouded hills?

And was Jerusalem builded here,
Among these dark Satanic Mills?

Bring me my Bow of burning gold!
Bring me my Arrows of desire:
Bring me my Spear: O clouds unfold!
Bring me my Chariot of fire!

I will not cease from Mental Fight,
Nor shall my Sword sleep in my hand:
Till we have built Jerusalem
In England's green & pleasant Land.

The Selected Poems of William Blake (London: Wordsworth Poetry Library,
1994), 319–20

This poem—Blake's most famous lyric (written in 1800–1804, engraved
1809–10)—is an homage to his mentor, Milton, who remained a visionary
genius despite his onset of physical blindness.

Blake's poem was set to music by Sir Hubert Parry in 1916. At Barbara's
request, the singer of the song at the memorial was Karen Swann, Barbara's
childhood neighbor and family friend. The two women—in their maturity both
accomplished university literature professors—used to sing together as children
in the Westwood church choir. It was as if the beautiful soprano voice of Karen
Swann substituted for the voice of Barbara herself, in absentia singing the song.

No poetic words could describe better Barbara's "Arrows of desire," her
"Chariot of fire," her passionate commitment to a higher justice, her gift of
herself to the community, and her constant "Mental Fight" to "rebuild
Jerusalem" at Harvard.

5. Henry David Thoreau, *Walden* (first published as *Walden, or Life in the Woods*);
in Thoreau, *Walden, Civil Disobedience, and Other Writings*, 3rd ed., ed. William
Rossi (New York: W. W. Norton, 2008) (page numbers will refer to this edition).
Barbara selected three paragraphs from *Walden* for her memorial: they were
read aloud in both memorials by her brother, Bruce Pollack-Johnson. The
selected excerpts—in the following order specified by Barbara—were as follows:

> [From chapter 2] *I went to the woods because I wished to live deliberately, to
> front only the essential facts of life, and see if I could not learn what it had to
> teach, and not, when I came to die, discover that I had not lived. I did not wish
> to live what was not life, living is so dear; nor did I wish to practise resignation,
> unless it was quite necessary. I wanted to live deep and suck out all the marrow
> of life, to live so sturdily and Spartan-like as to put to rout all that was not life,
> to cut a broad swath and shave close, to drive life into a corner, and reduce it to
> its lowest terms, and, if it proved to be mean, why then to get the whole and*

genuine meanness of it, and publish its meanness to the world; or if it were sublime, to know it by experience, and be able to give a true account of it in my next excursion. For most men, it appears to me, are in a strange uncertainty about it, whether it is of the devil or of God, and have somewhat hastily concluded that it is the chief end of man here to "glorify God and enjoy him forever. (65, Thoreau's emphasis)

[From chapter 1] *If I knew for a certainty that a man was coming to my house with the conscious design of doing me good, I should run for my life, as from that dry and parching wind of the African deserts called the simoom, which fills the mouth and nose and ears and eyes with dust till you are suffocated, for fear that I should get some of his good done to me—some of its virus mingled with my blood. No, in this case I would rather suffer evil the natural way. A man is not a good man to me because he will feed me if I should be starving, or warm me if I should be freezing, or pull me out of a ditch if I should ever fall into one. I can find you a Newfoundland dog that will do as much. Philanthropy is not love for one's fellow-man in the broadest sense.* (54, Thoreau's emphasis)

[From chapter 18] *Why should we be in such desperate haste to succeed and in such desperate enterprises? If a man does not keep pace with his companions, perhaps it is because he hears a different drummer. Let him step to the music which he hears, however measured or far away.* (219)

6. Barbara Johnson, "A Hound, a Bay Horse, and a Turtle Dove: Obscurity in *Walden*," in Barbara Johnson, *A World of Difference* (Baltimore: Johns Hopkins University Press, 1987); hereafter abbreviated *World*. Page numbers refer to this edition.

7. See Johnson in her essay on Thoreau: "Before going back to attempt a different kind of analysis of this passage, I would like first to quote . . . the paragraph that immediately precedes the hound-horse-dove passage in the text. . . . There appears at first sight to be no relation between these two paragraphs. Yet the very abruptness of the transition, the very discrepancy of rhetorical modes, may perhaps indicate that the first paragraph consists in a set of instructions about how to read the second." *World*, 52.

8. Emphasis mine. In the cited texts, emphasis is mine unless otherwise indicated.

9. "The impossible but necessary task of the reader is to set herself up to be surprised," Barbara writes. "Yet this cannot become a simple doxa, a facile formula for slogan-imitation," she warns us. "No methodology can be relied on to generate surprise. It is usually surprise that engenders methodology." "It is only by forgetting what we know how to do, by setting aside the thoughts that have most changed us, that those thoughts and that knowledge can go on making accessible to us the surprise of an otherness we can only encounter in

the moment of suddenly discovering that we are ignorant of it." Barbara Johnson, "Nothing Fails Like Success," in *A World of Difference*, 15–16.

10. See Thoreau on "the beneficence of Nature," 96.

11. Barbara discussed with me many writers whom she loved, but never once mentioned Thoreau. My retrospective intuition of the autobiographical impulse embodied in her posthumous quotations of Thoreau was born only after much reflection, not on first reading but only after her death, out of my attempt to re-read this final message and attempt to decipher her epitaphic self-commemoration. As it happened, following the Harvard memorial (at the end of March 2010), I found an unexpected outside confirmation of this intuition, among the newspaper clips preserved by Barbara's mother related her daughter's youth, journal fragments I became aware of—and could read for the first time—when her mother shared these clips with me after the memorial. Among those clips, describing Barbara's distinction since her very early youth, there was the following astonishing mention of Thoreau by the seventeen-year-old Barbara, interviewed by a journalist of the local Westwood newspaper, in her capacity as the most outstanding Westwood High School student. I cannot resist quoting directly from this article (1964), titled "Versatile Johnson." "Barbie Johnson is an outstanding student, there is no doubt about that," the article reads. "A National Merit Finalist, National Honor Society Member, she has received these and numerous other scholastic awards in her years at Westwood High School. Barbie, who has the fortune to understand most everything she tackles, has been accepted at Oberlin College in Ohio, where she plans to major in English . . . 'But,' she added a little shyly, 'my real ambition is to be a hermit for a few years and live on a moor in England and write like Thoreau.' I assured her we'd be checking the best-seller list in a few years. She said. 'Well, I'm going to write anyway—don't know if they'll ever get published.'" At about the same period or shortly before, in her junior high school year (1964), Barbara wrote and typed the following self-portrait (today among the papers archived by her mother), a fragment of youthful autobiographic record that, from a distance of time, could complement (explain some layers of) the final autobiographic record embodied in her epitaph: "Many forces have helped sculpture my life," Barbara writes at age seventeen.

> "I am the product of their chipping, but I think that, like Michelangelo's David, the basic shape of my raw marble has dictated an underlying structure to the sculptors. With care they have sought out my softness and my hardness until they begin to uncover what was perhaps already in the rock.
>
> Travel has always been an enriching experience for me. In 1963, I went to France, where I not only visited magnificent cathedrals, chateaux and palaces, but also—far more important to me—found a home in the hearts of

the French family with whom I spent the four most wonderful weeks of my life. Their friendship and understanding increased immeasurably my knowledge both of French and of human nature. In addition to France, I have toured the United States, this time with my own family. For us, the family communion inside the car was just as meaningful as the scenery outside the car, and some of the memories I cherish most are of simple happiness which could just as well have occurred in our own living room.

The most important sculptors of my life are teachers. Three, a music teacher and her husband, a piano genius, and an English teacher, have probably carved me deeper than any other people outside of my home. Because of the inspiration and affection of the music teacher and her husband, a brilliant young pianist, I eked out every speck of talent in me with hours of practice over my old piano. I had just begun to see into the depths of music when the husband was killed in an automobile accident. Stunned, I shied way from music for many months. Although gradually I returned to my piano, I still felt a great emptiness. At last the emptiness was filled with a new love of writing, reading, and thinking, a new awareness of all that is in the world, because of my English teacher. Her enthusiasm and understanding awakened a spark which had long lain dormant within me. I looked with new eyes, wrote with a new hand, thought with a new mind. Now, after three years, her inspiration is still strong within me, and I, too, want to teach English.

Perhaps I should mention that although people are a vital part of my life, I find it necessary to be alone often with myself. In the summer I find refuge beside a quiet New Hampshire lake; in the winter, in the woods behind our house. A quiet walk almost anywhere will soothe the frustrations of my too much ordered life and leave me eager to rejoin the bursting stream of humanity.

I rest on a solid base of family affection and approval, without which the rest of me might easily crumble. However, as my form emerges from the marble and I begin to tingle with new twinges of individuality, I look forward to the day when some of the props which hold me to the base will be chipped away, and I can stand secure, but free."

12. "I had not lived there a week before my feet wore *a path from my door to the pond-side* [Thoreau had written]; and though it is five or six years since I trod it, it is still quite distinct. It is true . . . that others may have fallen into it, and so helped to keep it open. The surface of the earth is soft and impressible by the feet of men; and so with the paths which the mind travels" (217).

"To follow the trail of what is lost," Barbara had written in her *Walden* essay, "is possible only . . . if the loss is maintained in a state of transference from traveler to traveler, so that each takes up the pursuit as if the loss were his own.

Loss, then, ultimately belongs to an other; the losses we treat as our own are perhaps losses of which we never had conscious knowledge ourselves . . . *Walden*'s great achievement is to wake us up to our own losses, to make us participate in the trans-individual movement of loss in its infinite particularity" (*World*, 52).

13. "We belong to the community," Thoreau writes, and Barbara would concur.

14. Barbara could have equally echoed Thoreau's paradox: "I had more visitors while I lived in the woods than at any other period of my life" (100).

15. As the reader will recall, Proust and Barbara share their admiration of Saint-Saëns, of whom Proust speaks in *A la recherche du temps perdu*. Barbara's acoustic epitaph also bears the trace of Mallarmé, even though the epitaph does not mention him explicitly. The haunting link between "Music and Letters" that structures her epitaph is a link that Mallarmé (her most beloved poet) emphasized and famously conceptualized by him as constitutive of poetry as such—constitutive of the poetic utterance's interplay between sound and silence, obscurity and clarity. "I pose, at my own risk," Mallarmé wrote, "that Music and Letters are two sides of the same coin; here extending into obscurity; there dazzling with clarity . . . One of the modes inclining to the other, disappearing there" (Stéphane Mallarmé, "Music and Letters," in *Divagations*, trans. Barbara Johnson [Cambridge, MA: Belknap Press of Harvard University Press, 2007], 189; hereafter abbreviated *Divagations*). All citations from Mallarmé refer to this edition. There is also a singular autobiographic depth to the relation between music and letters (as well as to the relation between life and death) in Barbara's memory of her young life (see note 11).

Structured as an exchange and an acoustic interaction between music and letters, Barbara's epitaph retains, indeed, its Mallarméen musical obscurity, even while it proclaims its semantic and discursive, literary clarity.

16. Barbara started her career by publishing her first book—remarkably—in France, in French, about Mallarmé's poetry. See Barbara Johnson, *Défigurations du langage poétique: La Seconde révolution baudelairenne* (Paris: Flammarion, 1979). Amazingly, this book (which at its origin was her dissertation) is still in print today: it has become a classic of French literary criticism. Since her days at Yale, Barbara was an unconditional admirer of Mallarmé, and a gifted scholar and disciple of his poetically dazzling style of thought and expression. Barbara and Mallarmé are both essentially poetic thinkers, as well as border-crossers between languages and cultures. Both derived their greatness from their original transactions between the foreign and the native. Mallarmé—like Barbara (although inversely)—shuttled between French and English, in his quest for the poetic. In his profession, he taught English. In his vocation as a poet, he learned English—so he later said—merely to translate the poetry of Edgar Allan Poe into his native French. (See "Autobiography," *Divagations*, 2–3.) Both saw a mission in translating the "surprise of

otherness"—the genius, and the shocking strangeness—of the poets they loved. Like Barbara, Mallarmé loved "the surprise of otherness," and she loved him for the thinking pathos—and the existential poignancy—of his linguistic powers of surprise.

17. In the last years of her life, coping with disease, Barbara clung to poetry and beauty: returning to her first French love, she set out to translate the very beauty of the untranslatable (the strange poetic French genius of Mallarmé) into her native tongue. And she accomplished the impossible in giving us an exquisite Mallarmé—in English. See Stéphane Mallarmé and Barbara Johnson, *Divagations*.

18. In her memorial, written with her voice from life.

19. Mallarmé's expression, in *Divagations*, Barbara's translation, 63.

Bibliography

BOOKS

Moses and Multiculturalism. 2010. Berkeley: University of California Press.
Persons and Things. 2008. Cambridge, MA: Harvard University Press.
Mother Tongues. 2003. Cambridge, MA: Harvard University Press.
The Feminist Difference: Literature, Psychoanalysis, Race, and Gender. 1998.
   Cambridge, MA: Harvard University Press.
The Wake of Deconstruction. 1994. Oxford: Blackwell.
A World of Difference. 1987. Baltimore: Johns Hopkins University Press.
The Critical Difference: Essays in the Contemporary Rhetoric of Reading. 1980.
   Baltimore: Johns Hopkins University Press.
Défigurations du langage poétique: la seconde révolution baudelairienne. 1979. Paris:
   Flammarion.

TRANSLATIONS

Divagations, by Stéphane Mallarmé (translation, introduction, and notes). 2007.
   Cambridge, MA: Belknap Press of Harvard University Press.
"Poetry without Verse," by Tzvetan Todorov. 1983. In *The Prose Poem in France:
   Theory and Practice*, ed. Mary Ann Caws and Hermine Riffaterre, 60–78. New
   York: Columbia University Press.
"Endurance and the Profession," by Jean-Francois Lyotard (with Christophe
   Gallier and Steven Ungar). 1982. *Yale French Studies* 63: 72–77.
Dissemination, by Jacques Derrida (translation, introduction and notes). 1981.
   Chicago: University of Chicago Press.
"Freud's Hand," by Philippe Sollers. 1979. *Yale French Studies* 55/56: 329–37.
"Fors: The Anglish Words of Nicolas Abraham and Maria Torok," by Jacques
   Derrida. 1977. *Georgia Review* 31: 64–116.

EDITED VOLUMES

Freedom and Interpretation: Oxford Amnesty Lectures of 1992. 1993. New York: Basic Books.

Consequences of Theory (with Jonathan Arac). 1990. Baltimore: Johns Hopkins University Press.

The Pedagogical Imperative: Teaching as a Literary Genre. 1982. *Yale French Studies* 63.

EDITORIAL PROJECTS

The Norton Anthology of Criticism and Theory (principal ed. Vincent B. Leitch). 2001. New York: W. W. Norton.

A New History of French Literature (principal ed. Denis Hollier). 1989. Cambridge, MA: Harvard University Press.

ARTICLES AND CHAPTERS

"Headnotes." 2003. *College English* 66, no. 2 (November): 177–85.

"Allegory and Psychoanalysis." 2003. *Journal of African American History* 88, no. 1 (winter): 66–70.

"Bad Writing." 2003. In *Just Being Difficult?*, ed. Jonathan Culler and Kevin Lamb, 157–68. Palo Alto: Stanford University Press.

"Art for Something's Sake." 2002. *Journal of Aesthetic Education* 36, no. 3 (fall): 28–30.

"Bringing Out D. A. Miller." 2002. *Narrative* 10, no. 1 (January): 3–8.

"Doing Time: Re-Reading Paul de Man's 'Literary History and Literary Modernity.'" 2002. In *Time and the Literary*, ed. Karen Newman, Jay Clayton, and Marianne Hirsch, 169–80. London: Routledge.

"Using People: Kant with Winnicott." 2000. In *The Turn to Ethics*, ed. Marjorie Garber, Beatrice Hanssen, and Rebecca Walkowitz, 47–63. New York: Routledge.

"Anthropomorphism in Lyric and Law." 1998. *Yale Journal of Law and the Humanities* 10, no. 2 (summer): 549–74.

"Moses and Intertextuality: Sigmund Freud, Zora Neale Hurston, and the Bible." 1997. In *Poetics of the Americas*, ed. Bainard Cowan and Jefferson Humphries, 15–29. Baton Rouge: Louisiana State University Press.

"The Alchemy of Style and Law." 1996. In *The Rhetoric of Law*, ed. Austin Sarat and Thomas R. Kearns, 261–74. Ann Arbor: University of Michigan Press.

"Mallarmé Gets a Life." 1996. In *London Review of Books: An Anthology*, ed. Jane Hindle, 168–72. London: Verso.

"Ode on a Public Thing." 1996. In *Field Work*, ed. Marjorie Garber, Paul Franklin, and Rebecca Walkowitz, 137–41. New York: Routledge.

"Whose Life Is It, Anyway?" 1996. In *The Seductions of Biography*, ed. Mary Rhiel and David Suchoff, 119–22. New York: Routledge.

"Muteness Envy." 1995. In *Human, All Too Human*, ed. Diana Fuss, 131–48. New York: Routledge.

"'Aesthetic' and 'Rapport' in Toni Morrison's *Sula*." 1993. *Textual Practice* 7, no. 2 (summer): 165–72.

"Lesbian Spectacles: Reading *Sula, Passing, Thelma and Louise*, and *The Accused*." 1993. In *Media Spectacles*, ed. Marjorie Garber, Jann Matlock, and Rebecca Walkowitz, 160–66. New York: Routledge.

"Discard or Masterpiece? Mallarmé's *Le Livre*." 1992. In *The Marks in the Fields: Essays on the Uses of Manuscripts*, ed. Rodney Dennis and Elizabeth Falsey. Cambridge, MA: Harvard University Press.

"The Postmodern in Feminism: A Response to Mary Joe Frug." 1992. *Harvard Law Review* 105, no. 5: 1076–83.

"The Quicksands of the Self: Nella Larsen and Heinz Kohut." 1992. In *Telling Facts: History and Narration in Psychoanalysis*, ed. Joseph H. Smith and Humphrey Morris, 184–99. Baltimore: Johns Hopkins University Press.

"A Note on the Wartime Writings of Paul de Man." 1990. In *Literary Theory Today*, ed. Peter Collier and Helga Ryan. Ithaca, NY: Cornell University Press.

"Gender and Poetry: Charles Baudelaire and Marceline Desbordes-Valmore." 1991. In *Displacements: Women, Tradition, Literatures in French*, ed. Joan de Jean and Nancy K. Miller, 163–81. Baltimore: Johns Hopkins University Press.

"Euphemism, Understatement, and the Passive Voice: A Genealogy of Afro-American Poetry." 1990. In *Reading Black, Reading Feminist*, ed. Henry Louis Gates Jr., 145–54. New York: Meridian.

"Philology: What Is at Stake?" 1990. *Comparative Literature Studies* 27, no. 1: 26–30.

"Poison or Remedy? Paul de Man as Pharmakon." 1990. *Colloquium Helveticum* 11/12: 7–20.

"Writing." 1990. In *Critical Terms for Literary Study*, ed. Frank Lentricchia and Thomas McLaughlin, 39–49. Chicago: University of Chicago Press.

"Interview with Hulk Hogan." 1989. *Blast Unlimited* 1.

"Is Female to Male as Ground Is to Figure?" 1989. In *Feminism and Psychoanalysis*, ed. Richard Feldstein and Judith Roof, 255–68. Ithaca, NY: Cornell University Press.

"The Lady in the Lake," "The Dream of Stone," and "The Liberation of Verse." 1989. In *A New History of French Literature*, ed. Denis Hollier. Cambridge, MA: Harvard University Press.

"Response to Henry Louis Gates, Jr." 1989. In *Afro-American Literary Study in the 1990s*, ed. Houston A. Baker Jr. and Patricia Redmond, 39–43. Chicago: University of Chicago Press.

"The Re(a)d and the Black: Richard Wright's Blueprint." 1990. 1988. In *Modern Critical Interpretations of Richard Wright's* Native Son, ed. Harold Bloom, 115–23. New York: Chelsea House.

"Response to Michael Riffaterre." 1988. *Yale Journal of Criticism* 1, no. 2: 177.

Interview. 1987. In *Criticism in Society*, by Imre Salusinzky, 150–75. New York: Routledge.

"Secret Sharing: Reading Conrad Psychoanalytically" (in collaboration with Marjorie Garber). 1987. *College English* 49, no. 6 (October): 628–40.

"Apostrophe, Animation, and Abortion." 1986. *Diacritics* 16, no. 1 (spring): 29–47.

"In Memoriam: Paul de Man." 1985. *Yale French Studies* 69: 9–10.

"Taking Fidelity Philosophically." 1985. In *Difference in Translation*, ed. Joseph Graham, 142–48. Ithaca, NY: Cornell University Press.

"Teaching Deconstructively." 1985. In *Writing and Reading Differently: Deconstruction and the Teaching of Composition and Literature*, ed. G. Douglas Atkins and Michael L. Johnson, 140–48. Lawrence: University Press of Kansas.

"Thresholds of Difference: Structures of Address in Zora Neale Hurston." 1985. *Critical Inquiry* 12, no. 1 (autumn): 278–89.

"Gender Theory and the Yale School." 1984. *Genre* 17, no. 1/2.

"Mallarmé as Mother." 1984. *Denver Quarterly* 18, no. 4 (winter): 77–83.

"Metaphor, Metonymy, and Voice in Zora Neale Hurston's *Their Eyes Were Watching God*." 1984. In *Black Literature and Literary Theory*, ed. Henry Louis Gates Jr., 205–19. New York: Methuen.

"Rigorous Unreliability." 1984. *Critical Inquiry* 11, no. 2: 278–85.

"Disfiguring Poetic Language." 1983. In *The Prose Poem in France: Theory and Practice*, ed. Mary Ann Caws and Hermine Riffaterre, 79–97. New York: Columbia University Press.

"My Monster/My Self." 1982. *Diacritics* 12, no. 2 (summer): 2–10.

"Teaching Ignorance: *L'école des femmes*." 1982. *Yale French Studies* 63: 165–82.

"Le dernier homme." 1981. In *Les Fins de l'homme: Actes du colloque de Cérisy sur Derrida*. Paris: Galilée. Translated by Bruce Robbins as "The Last Man," in *The Other Mary Shelley*, ed. Esther Schor, Audrey Fisch, and Anne Mellor, 258–66. Oxford: Oxford University Press, 1993.

"Les Fleurs du Mal Armé." 1981. *Michigan Romance Studies* 2. Translated and extended in *Lyric Poetry: Beyond New Criticism*, ed. Patricia Parker and Chaviva Hosek, 264–80. Ithaca, NY: Cornell University Press, 1985.

"Nothing Fails Like Success." 1980. *SCE Reports* 8 (fall).

"Melville's Fist: The Execution of *Billy Budd*." 1979. *Studies in Romanticism* 18, no. 4: 567–99.

"The Critical Difference: BartheS/BalZac." 1978. *Diacritics* 8, no. 2: 2–9.

"The Frame of Reference: Poe, Lacan, Derrida." 1977. *Yale French Studies* 55/56 ("Literature and Psychoanalysis"): 457–505.

"Poetry and Performative Language." 1977. *Yale French Studies* 54 (*"Mallarmé"*): 140–58.

"Quelques conséquences de la différence anatomique des textes." 1976. *Poétique* 28 (December): 450–65.

"Défigurations." 1975. *Littérature* 18 (May): 100–110.

"La vérité tue: une lecture de *Conte*." 1973. *Littérature* 11 (October): 68–77.

Index

Dinnerstein, Dorothy, 179–80, 183–85

discourse, 16, 32, 87, 88, 95, 97n9, 103, 117, 124, 136, 138, 141, 152, 167, 174, 196, 235, 256, 303, 328–30, 413

disfiguration, 360. *See also* figure

displacement, 29, 79, 87–88, 136, 195, 210, 215n4, 232, 291, 303, 347, 355; of the letter, 87–88

dissemination, 64, 70–73, 81, 94–96, 290

Dissemination (Derrida), 14–25, 328, 373–74

double, xxx, 20–21, 23, 47, 64, 68–70, 80, 82, 119, 139, 153, 170, 184, 250, 261n68, 283, 294, 296, 348, 361, 372, 378, 382, 386–87, 411, 413; double bind, 49, 139, 153, 184; double consciousness, 119, 342–43

Dred Scott v. Sandford, 248–49

DuBois, Page, 159, 164

DuBois, W. E. B., 119, 343

Dust Tracks on a Road (Hurston), 132–34

ear, xiv

L'Ecole des femmes (Molière), 401–19

ego, xxi, 194–95, 198, 200, 278–79, 284; superego, 227, 278

Eliot, George, 55n3

Eliot, T. S., 205

ellipsis, 60, 80, 103, 227, 236, 364, 405, 406, 409

Emerson, Ralph Waldo, 37, 38, 41

epistemology, 31, 236–38, 258n10

erotic, 142–45, 159, 160, 171, 188. *See also* autoeroticism; female eroticism; heteroeroticism

Essais de linguistique générale (Jakobson), 108

ethics, xii, xxi, 224, 248, 262–73, 347, 360, 368

euphemism, 12, 101, 103–5

exploitation, 197, 263–64, 371

Fagnier, Gustave, 411

Fanon, Frantz, 176, 342

fashion, 10, 45, 108, 148, 404

father, 68, 70, 82–83, 97n13, 126, 130–32, 137, 170–71, 182, 185, 188, 206, 208–9, 212, 230–31, 298–99, 301, 306, 318, 386, 402, 411–12; Captain Vere as, 300, 317; primal, 136. *See also* founding fathers; law of the father

female body, 7, 83–86, 202, 210, 274n4, 334. *See also* body

female-female eroticism, 142. *See also* erotic; homosexuality; lesbian

feminine, 8, 11, 103, 174, 182, 188–90, 202–3, 299, 352, 407, 413. *See also* femininity; *jouissance*

femininity, 11, 83, 152, 159, 187, 189, 410. *See also* feminine

feminism, xxx, 120, 211, 213–14, 215, 410, 412, 419, 420n7

Fénelon, François, 410

Fictions of Sappho (de Jean), 162

figuration, xxiii. *See also* disfiguration

figurative language, xiv, xvii–xviii, xxi–xxiii, xxv, 21, 34, 36–37, 39–43, 47–48, 50, 52–55, 71, 85, 87, 108, 112–16, 130, 133, 147, 167–68, 170, 187, 217–18, 220, 231–33, 237, 246, 251, 254–55, 278, 349, 353–54, 368, 375, 381

Fish, Stanley, xxix–xxx

Fitts, Dudley, 165

Flaubert, Gustave, 118, 152, 155–57, 160, 166

Fleurs du Mal, Les (Baudelaire), xxviii, 155, 161–64, 168, 230, 335, 377–79, 381

Forché, Carolyn, xiv

foreignness: of Derrida's thought in the United States, 372; of languages, 14, 168, 340, 343, 374, 376

form: aesthetic, 359; beautiful, 277, 286; versus content, 60, 158, 201; domain of, 197; human, xix, xxii–xxiv, 218,

Hood, Thomas, 208
hooks, bell, 120–21, 212
human, xviii–xxv, 41, 47, 53, 101, 105–6, 136, 138–39, 193–98, 201, 218–19, 222–26, 229, 242–43, 246, 252–56, 275, 279, 281–85, 293, 359–64, 383, 389, 395; anthropomorphism and, 235, 237; cloning and, 248; dehumanizing, 224, 229; de Man and, 362–63; monster and, 180. *See also* anthropomorphism; inhuman; nonhuman; person; personhood
humanism, 182, 197–98, 347, 355–56, 357–58, 368–69
human rights, xiv, xxx, 193–99, 316. *See also* rights
Hunter, Holly, 206, 210, 213
Hurston, Zora Neale, xxix, 108–25, 126–40
Husserl, Edmund, 14, 195, 372
hymen, 23, 25, 78

idealization, 71, 87, 141, 201, 203, 205, 213, 263, 284, 338, 367
identity, 67, 72, 112, 116–17, 141, 152, 165, 180, 195, 197, 225, 284; difference and, xxviii, 4–5, 15, 25, 67, 88, 117, 134, 136, 195; female, 411; race and, 131, 134; sexual, 183. *See also* identity politics
identity politics, xiv, xxx
ideology of totality, 7–9
ignorance, xi, xiii, 7, 9, 299, 332, 343, 401–19
imaginary, xviii, 11, 19, 73, 85, 194, 341; Lacan and, xxi, 67–68, 70
impersonal, impersonality, 41, 197, 361, 363, 365, 367, 369
In a Different Voice (Gilligan), 224
inanimate, xxi, 174, 218, 222, 224–25, 229, 235, 267, 271, 276, 286. *See also* animation
incest, 19, 68, 70, 83, 206, 216n10, 372

infant, 139n3, 179, 185, 264, 265–68, 269, 273, 272, 285, 282, 287
In forma pauperis, 244, 246–47, 251
inhuman, xxv, 184, 243, 251, 361–65, 368, 395. *See also* human; nonhuman
innocence, 43, 206, 292–94, 297, 299–300, 303, 309, 311, 315, 317, 320, 403, 407, 416, 417, 424
intention, xii, xxxi, 20, 28, 52, 53, 92–93, 80, 167, 193, 201, 335, 355, 360, 367, 385, 394; in *Billy Budd*, 290, 291, 295, 298, 301; legal, 245, 250
intersubjectivity, 62, 63, 76, 262, 354
intertextuality, 58, 126–40
Irigaray, Luce, 203
irony, 130, 156, 276, 289, 292, 295–96, 308–13, 317, 340, 413

Jakobson, Roman, 108–10, 116–17, 220; "Two Aspects of Language and Two Types of Aphasic Disturbances," 108–10
Johnson, James Weldon, 101, 119
Jonson, Ben, 231
Joplin, Patricia, 204
Jowett, Benjamin, 156
Judaism, 127, 392
judgment, xxiii, 48, 92, 124, 156, 164, 166, 167, 183, 285, 328, 337, 348; in *Billy Budd*, 311; *jouissance*, 203, 386

Kabbalah, 397–98
Kafka, Franz, 167
Kant, Immanuel, xviii, xxi, 164, 195, 262–74, 341, 359, 360
Kaplan, Jonathan, 143
Kazin, Alfred, 38
Keats, John, xiii, 200–205, 208, 215n4, 229, 235, 236, 257n3, 257n8, 258n10, 335; "Ode on a Grecian Urn," 200–205, 208, 215n4
Kierkegaard, Søren, 418

Kleist, Heinrich von, 287, 359
knot, 78, 91
Kohut, Heinz, xvii, xx, 263, 275, 276, 278

Lacan, Jacques, xvii, xx–xxi, xxiv, xxvii, xxix, 15, 24, 29–30, 57–98, 130, 139, 174, 195, 202–5, 231–32, 241–42, 276, 339, 344, 365; *jouissance* and, 202–3, 386; "The Mirror Stage" ["Le stade du miroir"], 195, 253, 264, 279–87; Saussure and, 174. *See also* suture
LaCapra, Dominick, 157
lack, xix, 9–11, 15, 18–20, 24, 58, 64, 70, 72, 76, 81, 88–89, 94, 149, 203, 225, 228, 246, 256, 262, 264, 276, 278, 286, 301, 305–6, 344, 354, 363, 383–84, 386, 388, 396, 408
Lakoff, George, 112
Lamartine, Alphonse de: "L'Isolement," 349
Larsen, Nella, 141–43
law, xxiii, xxix, xxxi, 29, 82, 88, 94, 130, 176, 198, 235–61, 277, 309, 312–15, 318–20; of the father, 68–73; moral, 263, 265; Moses and, 126, 128, 130, 134; of the phallus, 72; of the signifier, 73. *See also* trials
lesbian, lesbianism, xxx, 141–45, 158, 162–65, 336. *See also* homosexuality
Levinas, Emmanuel, 262, 273n1
Levin, Harry, 338, 340
Lévi-Strauss, Claude, 342
literalization, xxiii, 10–11, 144, 222, 230
literality, xx, 8–9, 12, 40–43, 87, 163, 250, 256, 270, 296, 312, 335, 354–55, 377, 405, 413; *Billy Budd* and, 293–97; "The Emperor's New Clothes" and, 354–55. *See also* figurative language
literary criticism, 3–4, 13, 58, 64, 117, 330, 344, 372

literary history, 179, 236, 240–42, 255, 334. *See also* history
Locke, Alain, 128
Locke, John, 194
logic, 15, 19–20, 23–25, 42, 64, 76–78, 80–84, 86, 102, 134, 136, 221, 224, 227, 230, 327–30, 332, 344, 348, 358; of binary opposition, 328–30; of censorship, 162; female, 224; parergonal, 76–77, 81
logocentrism, 11, 15–17, 21, 23, 71, 72, 75, 85, 97n9
logos, 11, 15, 24, 90, 170
Longfellow, Henry Wadsworth, 45
Lorris, Guillaume de, 286
loss, xxii–xxiii, 18, 33, 38, 40–41, 53, 54, 72, 117, 142, 152, 159, 183, 204, 215, 219–21, 224, 228, 231, 233n13, 243, 266, 334–35, 350–51, 374, 423–25; of control, 364–65
love, 10–11, 19, 51, 89–90, 113, 123, 170, 180, 214, 263, 276, 282, 286, 299, 380, 409, 412, 414, 416–17
Lowell, James Russell, 37
Luker, Kristen, 226
lyric, xxiii–xxv, xxviii, xxix, 41, 103, 159, 218, 222–23, 232, 233n2, 235–61, 334, 382. *See also* poetry

Macbeth (Shakespeare), 83, 87
MacKinnon, Catharine, 145, 156, 226
Madame Bovary (Flaubert), 118, 152, 155
MacLeish, Archibald: "Ars Poetica," 201, 349
Mallarmé, Stéphane, xxviii, 23, 26–35, 96, 151, 201, 202, 230, 328, 335–40, 351–53, 363, 378, 383–90, 425, 431n15, 431n16; "La Chevelure vol d'une flame," 351; "Don du poème," 230; "The Mystery in Letters," 26–28
Mamelles de Tirésias, Les (Apollinaire), 230

Narcissus, xx–xxi, 149, 237, 275–77, 282–87, 335

nature, 15, 18, 21, 41–42, 47, 170, 221, 237–38, 240–41, 271, 283, 285, 292–94, 304, 306, 311, 315–16, 318, 359, 382–85, 387, 389–90, 412, 416, 424–25

Negritude, 342, 390

neutrality, 57, 75, 94, 151–53, 157

New Testament, 41

Nietzsche, Friedrich, 4, 15, 149, 194, 195, 236–38, 243, 367

new historicism, 148

nonhuman, xxi, 52, 362, 364. *See also* human; inhuman

Norris, Christopher, 359

object, xix, xxiv, 9, 19, 40–41, 68–70, 77, 86, 94, 194–95, 200–215, 263–73, 273n4, 275–78, 284, 286, 319, 329, 338, 341, 388, 391; partial, 72, 85. *See also* objects; transitional objects

objectivity, 78, 94, 265, 272, 287, 328–31, 368–69, 403

objects, xviii–xx, 86, 87, 89, 94, 218, 222–24, 263, 265, 272–73, 275–76. *See also* object; transitional objects

obscurity, xiii, 6, 26–29, 37–43, 329, 336–38, 351–55, 423–24

Oedipal structure, 67–70, 76, 83–85, 131, 299–300

Oedipus, 70, 83, 149, 185

Ohmann, Richard, 368–69

On Liberty (Mill), 198

oneness, 116–17. *See also* unity

oppression, 120–21, 197–98

origin, origination, xviii, 48–50, 81–82, 95, 130, 134, 136, 138, 151–52, 165–75, 185, 306, 316, 318, 331, 339–40, 360, 374–75, 385–88, 392, 395–96; of writing, 166

Otherness, xi–xv, xviii, xx, 10–12, 19, 22, 40, 67, 71, 81, 86, 89–90, 95–96, 119, 122, 139, 141, 149, 159, 198, 208, 218, 222–23, 228, 231–32, 234n19, 262, 273, 273n1, 276–77, 282, 283, 332, 341, 343, 365–66, 376, 424

Ovid, 237, 275–76, 287

ownership, 72, 207

Oxford Amnesty Lectures, xxx, 193–94, 196

paradox, 77–81, 156, 264–65, 270–71, 296, 357, 375, 407, 425, 431

paraphrase, 58–60

parenthood, 179–80. *See also* motherhood

parergonal logic, 76–77, 80–81

particularity, 40, 138–39, 141, 423

Pascal, Blaise, 342

passing, 142, 149

Passing (Larsen), 141–43

passive voice, 101–3, 266

paternity, 137, 290

patriarchal power, 212, 215, 413

patriarchy, 143, 145, 158, 171, 205, 226, 411

patricide, 82, 130, 136

Patterson, Charles, 202

Peairs, Edith, 38

pedagogy, xiv–xv, xvii, xxxi–xxxii, 27, 241, 365, 368, 369, 401–2, 419

performance, xv, 96, 303, 314, 320–21, 335, 341, 360

performative, 93, 238, 296–97, 302, 314–15, 319, 321

person, xvii–xviii, xx–xxv, 52, 55n4, 56n6, 149, 151–53, 218, 220, 222, 224, 226, 227, 229, 231, 236, 238, 241, 244–56, 263, 275, 281, 286, 363, 366–67. *See also* human; personhood; thing

personhood, xiv, xxii–xxiii, 226, 229, 248, 252–54, 256. *See also* human; person personification, xviii–xxv, 11, 47–48, 50, 52, 55–56, 231, 243, 245, 247, 254–56, 268, 272, 293, 295–96, 299, 363, 413–14, 419. *See also* anthropomorphism

Petrarch, Francesco, 214–15, 335

Phaedo (Plato), 156

Phaedrus (Plato), 136, 158, 164, 166, 348, 374, 417–19

phallic mother, 145

phallogocentrism, 72, 85. *See also* logocentrism

phallus, 70–73, 84–90, 94, 203. *See also* castration

philosophy, xvii, 4, 14–15, 24, 149, 151, 159, 166–67, 170, 195, 226, 280, 331, 339, 341, 347, 367, 372–75

Pharmakon, 23, 24, 166–67, 340, 348, 357, 361, 363, 367, 373–74

Piaget, Jean, 32

Piano, The (Campion), 206–15

Pichois, Claude, 161–62

Pinard, Ernest, 160–63

pivot, pivoting, 26, 28, 29, 33

Plath, Sylvia, xvii, 286, 334

Plato, 15, 24, 136, 149, 155–56, 158–59, 161, 164, 166–67, 195, 304, 316, 318, 328, 340, 348, 356, 357, 373–74, 417–19

Playing and Reality (Winnicott), 264–73

Pleasure Principle, 45, 242, 329, 331, 409

Poe, Edgar Allan, xxix, 44–55, 57–96, 97n13, 340, 378, 431n16; "Philosophy of Composition," 44–55; "The Purloined Letter," xxix, 57–96; "The Raven," 45, 50, 52–55

poetry, xxiv, xxviii, 26–34, 44–55, 101–7, 110, 111, 155–56, 159, 161–65, 200–205, 208, 214, 217–34, 235, 241–43, 256, 263, 334–39, 349, 352, 363, 379–80, 384, 386, 388. *See also* lyric

political correctness, xxx, 145, 213, 342

politics, xxi, xxiii, xxv, xxvii, xxx, 78, 110, 120, 138–39, 141, 145, 156–58, 175, 194, 213, 217, 226–28, 232, 250, 255, 311, 314–21, 327, 358–60

Pommier, Jean, 159

Ponge, Francis, 201

Pope, Alexander, 45

poststructuralism, xii, xxvii, 151

Praeteritio, 349

pregnancy, 185, 223, 226, 230, 232, 397

property, 94, 113, 138, 171, 176, 194, 197, 248, 254–55, 264, 291

Proust, Marcel, 151, 421–25, 426n3

psychoanalysis, xix, xxx, 14, 15, 30, 67–96, 97n9, 127–30, 136, 185, 206, 232, 241, 264–73, 278–88, 299–302, 311, 365, 367, 371, 394

Ptolemy, Ptolemaic, 22, 29, 34

Pygmalion, 7–8, 263

race and racism, xiv, 101–40, 197–98, 247, 249, 369

rape, 143–44, 203–4, 209–11, 214–15

reader, 3, 6–7, 9, 17, 27, 34, 36–39, 42, 46–48, 53–54, 57–58, 63, 66, 74, 81, 86, 90–91, 93–96, 107, 120, 151–53, 156, 161–64, 174, 183–86, 221–23, 229, 292–95, 308–14, 317, 319, 321, 329–30, 332, 334–37, 352, 354–56, 368–69, 392, 410, 413, 424

readerly, 6–12. *See also* writerly

reading, 33–34, 53, 57–96, 194, 245, 289–321, 327–31, 343, 347–56, 358–69; Barthes and, 6–9, 12; deconstructive, 5, 17–23, 57–96, 166–67, 195, 198; as a lesbian, 141–45; psychoanalytical, 57–96, 301–2; rereading and, 3–4, 198

realism, 157, 163–64, 310

repetition, 4, 45, 49–50, 52–55, 63–65, 67, 69, 82, 91, 96–98, 145, 242, 252, 305 representation, xxxi, 6, 16, 17, 76, 80, 85, 90–91, 112, 156–57, 159, 161, 170, 172

repression, xxviii, 7, 14, 16, 23, 52, 60, 72, 95, 97n9, 104, 130, 138, 142, 156, 159, 162, 164, 175, 180, 182, 189, 195, 198, 205, 268, 273, 299, 301, 318, 321, 336, 338, 359, 374, 394, 402, 406, 410, 419

reproduction, 159, 170–71, 174–75, 197, 265, 335

Republic, The (Plato), 155–56, 159

Resistance to Theory, The (de Man), 257n8, 358–59, 361, 389

rewriting, 30, 126, 131, 135, 139, 184, 222, 229

rhetoric, xviii, xxv, 12, 17, 22, 41–43, 44, 48, 87, 94–95, 103–4, 108, 112, 158, 214, 217–18, 220–21, 224–25, 232, 236–38, 254–56, 304, 331, 348–49; of universality, 136, 176

rhetorical figure, xviii, xxi–xxii, 41–43, 115, 217–20, 232. *See also* figurative language

rights, xiv, xxiii, xxx, 176, 193–98, 224, 226, 236, 241, 248–56, 266, 316; civil, 197

Rimbaud, Arthur, 335, 337

Roe v. Wade, 226, 236, 248

Roiphe, Katie, 213–14

Roman de la Rose, Le (Guillaume de Lorris), 286

Ronsard, Pierre de: "Mignonne, allons voir si la rose," 110

Rousseau, Jean-Jacques, 4, 17–21, 74, 81, 189, 195, 365

Rowland v. California Men's Colony, 236, 244, 246–48, 251, 261n68

S/Z (Barthes), 3–12, 150

Sappho, 159, 162, 164–65, 168

Sarrasine (Balzac), 7–12, 150–51

Saussure, Ferdinand de, xxix, xxxi, 4, 16, 174, 280, 342, 349, 411

Schiller, Friedrich, 359–60

Scholem, Gershom, 397–98

Second Amendment, 197, 248

Second Empire, 156, 161, 335

seduction, 7–8, 150, 155, 206

seductiveness: of literary language, 347; of literature, 356; of metaphor, 112; of unity, 241; of a universal language, 123

Sedgwick, Eve, 171

self, selfhood, xviii–xxi, 5, 15–19, 23, 29–30, 49, 57, 115–17, 119, 179–90, 193–96, 198, 221–23, 268, 273, 275–88, 294, 300, 310–11, 330–31, 343, 349, 363–67, 424; self-difference, self-division, 117, 119, 122–24, 134–38, 253, 369, 375; self-image, 107, 115, 277; self-presence, 15–16, 72. *See also* subject

Seneca, 58, 75

Sexton, Anne, xiii, 227–28, 334–35; "The Abortion," 227; "Menstruation at Forty," 228; "Wanting to Die," 335

sexual abuse, 205–6, 214. *See also* rape; sexual violence

sexual difference, 5, 70, 89, 91, 138, 151–52, 158–59, 169–71, 174–76, 178n28, 180, 202–3, 386–87

sexuality, xiv, 12, 18, 89–91, 113, 151–53, 205, 210, 342, 406–11, 419. *See also* bisexuality; heterosexuality; homosexuality; sexual difference

sexual politics, 120, 226

sexual violence, 143–45, 204–6, 209–15. *See also* rape; sexual abuse

Shakespeare, William, 83, 87, 171–73, 205, 230, 272, 302

Shelley, Mary, 179–90

Shelley, Percy Bysshe, 179, 186–89; "Ode to the West Wind," xxii, 218, 220–22

Sidney, Sir Philip, 230

unity, xxx, 8–9, 12, 15, 67–70, 73, 77, 117–18, 167, 171–72, 195, 240–41, 385, 396–98

universality, universalizing, universalism, xiv, 22, 47, 113, 117–18, 122–24, 136–41, 153, 172, 175–76, 197, 355, 369, 410, 419

U.S. Constitution, 197, 226, 248–50, 253, 254

Vaihinger, Hans, 341

vehicle, 39, 42, 52, 82, 115, 201, 292, 373. *See also* tenor

Venus, 202

victim, victimhood, 65, 135, 187, 211–15. *See also* sexual abuse; sexual violence

voice, 7, 11, 24, 71–72, 101–25, 141, 153, 206–11, 218–27, 231–32, 242

Walden (Thoreau), 36–43, 223, 422–24, 427n5

Watkins, Gloria (bell hooks), 120, 212

Western philosophy, 14–15, 24–25, 166–67, 195, 367, 374. *See also* philosophy

Wheatley, Phillis, 101, 103–7; "On Being Brought from Africa to America," 105; "To the Right Honourable William, Earl of Dartmouth," 103, 105–6

whiteness, 111, 120, 202, 310; white liberalism, 107

Wilde, Oscar, 213

Winnicott, D. W., xvii–xx, xxiv, 262–74; "The Location of Cultural Experience," 272; "The Use of an Object and Relating through Identifications," 268

Wollstonecraft, Mary, 179, 188

women, xxx, 118, 137, 142–44, 158–61, 170–72, 175–76, 179, 185, 189, 197, 202–3, 205, 209–15, 226, 410–12, 417; black, 119–24, 131–33, 142, 176, 228; poetry and, 52, 159, 161, 202–5; poets, 103, 159, 230–31, 335–36

Wordsworth, William, 44–56, 200, 222, 235, 335; "Ode: Intimations of Immortality," 350–51; preface to *Lyrical Ballads*, 44–55; "Strange Fits of Passion," 46–47, 50–52

Wright, Richard, 101, 103, 119–20

writerly, 6–9, 12. *See also* readerly

writing, 19, 21, 81–82, 136, 152–53; "the scene of writing," 64, 79; speech and, 15–20, 23–24, 60, 329, 347, 349, 417; "the trial of writing," 166–67

Yeats, William Butler: "Among School Children," 349